Educational Psychology
Second Edition

J. Ronald Gentile

State University of New York at Buffalo

KENDALL/HUNT PUBLISHING COMPANY
4050 Westmark Drive   Dubuque, Iowa 52002

Cover and interior photos used with permission of:

Annette West of Buffalo Science Magnet School and
Thomas J. Shuell of The University of Buffalo at New York

Copyright © 1990, 1997 by Kendall/Hunt Publishing Company

ISBN 0-7872-2223-2

All rights reserved. No part of this publication may be reproduced, stored in a retrieval system, or transmitted, in any form or by any means, electronic, mechanical, photocopying, recording, or otherwise, without the prior written permission of the copyright owner.

Printed in the United States of America

10 9 8 7 6 5 4 3

Contents

Preface, ix
Schools: A Place for Paranoia or Rapanoia?, xi
Approaches to Studying Human Behavior: Why This Approach, xii
Prerequisites for This Book, xiv
The Plan of This Edition, xiv
Study Aids, xvi
Acknowledgments, xvii

UNIT ONE
LEVELS OF EXPERIENCE

1. **Emotion, Behavior, and Cognition in Social Context** 2
   Study Questions 2
   Introduction 3
   The Human Organism: The Product of Nature and Nurture 5
   One Level of Experience: Feelings (and Conditioned Emotions) 7
   A Second Level of Experience: Behavior (and Its Consequences) 9
   A Third Level of Experience: Thinking (and Cognitive Processes) 10
   The Interdependence of Behavior, Emotions and Cognitions 11
   Bandura's Social Cognitive Theory 13
   Practice Exercises 16

UNIT TWO
STABILITY AND CHANGE IN HUMAN DEVELOPMENT

2. **Stages and Processes of Development** 18
   Study Questions 18
   Introduction: Four Views of Development 20
   Piaget's Theory of Cognitive Development 21
   A Piagetian Problem: Conservation of Liquids 21
   Schema 22
   Developmental Processes 23
   Maturation 23
   Experience 24
   The Educative Factor (Social Transmission) 24
   Equilibration (Assimilation vs. Accommodation) and Cognitive Conflict 25
   Piaget's Stages of Development 26
   Sensori-Motor Period 26
   Preoperational Period 28
   Concrete Operations Period 30
   Formal Operations Period 32
   Vygotsky's Development of Thought Through Language 33
   The Zone of Proximal Development 34
   Language, Thought and Metacognition 35
   Erikson's Theory of Psychosocial Development 36
   Infancy and the Mutuality of Recognition 38
   Early Childhood and the Will To Be Oneself 39
   Childhood and the Anticipation of Roles 39
   School Age and Task Identification 40
   Puberty and Adolescence 41
   Beyond Identity: Adult Stages 42
   Young Adulthood 42
   Middle Age 43
   Old Age 44
   Kohlberg's Stages of Moral Development 44
   Maslow's Hierarchy of Needs Theory 49
   Stages of Development: An Allegory 52
   Development: Discrete Stages or Continuous Growth? 54
   Developmental Stages: The Norm is Not a Standard 54
   Practice Exercises 56

3. **Intelligence Testing and the Normal Curve** 60
   Study Questions 60
   Introduction 62
   History of Intelligence Testing 63
     Galton, Cattell and Binet 63
     Goddard and Terman 65
     From the 1920's to the 1970's 67
   The Normal Curve 69
   Stability and Change in Intelligence: or How Can Intelligence Be Fixed and Developing at the Same Time? 72
   Evidence on the Stability of IQ Scores 76
   Heredity and Environment 78
     Group Differences 81
     How Much Can IQ be Boosted? 83
     IQ Tests and Their Misuses 84
     Conclusions 89
     Practice Exercises 91

4. **Intelligence and its Possibilities** 94
   Study Questions 94
   Introduction 96
   Sternberg's Triarchic Theory 98
     Context of Intelligence 98
     Intelligence and Experience 99
     Components of Intelligence 99
     Sternberg's Theory: In Conclusion 100
   Gardner's Multiple Intelligences 101
     Multiple Intelligences in the Classroom 104
     Gardner's Theory: In Conclusion 105
   Feuerstein's Instrumental Enrichment 106
     Instrumental Enrichment in the Classroom 107
     Feuerstein's Theory: In Conclusion 111
   What Should We Make of the New Intelligence Theories? 111
   Instructional Implications of Developmental Theories 112
     Knowing via Acting: Cognitive Constructivism 112
     Creating Cognitive Conflicts 113
     Metacognitive Processes 115
     Mastery and Development 117
   Can We Accelerate These Processes and Should We? 118
   Maturational Unfolding or Developmental Crisis 119
   Teachers' Development and Its Implications for Teaching 120
   Practice Exercises 121

UNIT THREE
MOTIONS, EMOTIONS AND COMMOTIONS

5. **Emotional Learning and Respondent Conditioning** 126
   Study Questions 126
   Introduction 127
   Respondent Conditioning and Extinction 128
     Psychic Secretions and Conditioned Reflexes 129
     Extinction 129
     Respondent Conditioning of Emotions 130
   Factors Affecting Conditioning 131
     Number of CS-US Pairings 131
     Interval Between CS and US 132
     Intensity of the US 132
     "Belongingness" Between CS and US 132
   Phobias 133
   Generalization and Discrimination 134
   Higher-Order Conditioning 135
   Stress and Learned Helplessness 138
     Learned Helplessness 139
     Learned Helplessness and Attribution, Theory 140
     Learned Helplessness Through the Life Span 142
     Prevention and Cure: Competence 145
   The Interaction of Motions, Emotions and Cognitions 148
   To Know Thyself: Explaining Emotions 150
   A Tentative Conclusion 153
   Practice Exercises 155

6. Regulating Behavior and Operant Conditioning   158
Study Questions   158
Introduction   160
Types of Operant Conditioning   161
   Reinforcement   161
   Positive Reinforcement   162
   Negative Reinforcement   165
   Escaping Tension   166
   "Peace at Any Price"   166
   Extinction   167
   The Frustration Effect and Spontaneous Recovery   169
   Punishment   169
   Discrimination Learning   170
Generalization and Discrimination   173
Reinforcer Effectiveness   174
   Types of Reinforcement   174
   More on Activities: The Premack Principle   176
   Some Applications   177
Schedules of Reinforcement   179
   Continuous Reinforcement and Shaping   179
   Intermittent Reinforcement   180
   Shaping from Continuous to Intermittent Schedules   180
      Attention Spans   180
      Student/Teacher Ratios   181
Quantity of Reinforcement   182
   Effects on Learning   182
   Effects on Persistence   183
   Delay of Reinforcement   183
Reinforcement Contingencies   184
   Contingencies and Honesty   186
Token Economies   187
   Token Economies: for "Ordinary" Classrooms?   191
The Development of Self-Control   192
Punishment and Its Amazing Effects   193
   Masochistic Behaviors   193
   Factors Contributing to Punishment's Effects   194
   Severity of Punishment   195
   Delay of Punishment   195
   Punishment Contingencies   195
   Punishment as a Cue for Reinforcement   195
   Punishment: The Moral of the Story   196
Emotional and Cognitive Interactions with Operant Behavior   198
Practice Exercises   200

7. Modeling and Social Processes   204
Study Questions   204
Introduction   205
Modeling   207
   Vicarious Consequences   207
   Reinforcement Reconsidered   208
Whom Do We Model?   209
Modeling Aggressive Behaviors and TV Violence   210
   Modeled Prosocial Behaviors   213
   A Tentative Conclusion   214
Advertising   215
Vicarious Emotional Learning   217
Other, Subtle Vicarious Learnings   218
Conformity   218
   The Individual vs. the Group   218
   Guards vs. Prisoners   220
   Authority vs. Morality   222
   Norms and Classrooms   223
   If Teachers are Guards, What Are Students?   224
Classroom Groups   225
   Sociometry and Interpersonal Relations   225
   Teachers and Groups   227
Cooperation, Competition and Individualization   228
Modeling and Social Learning: Some Recommendations   230
Practice Exercises   233

8. Discipline: Learning Responsibility for Behavior   236
Study Questions   236
Introduction   237
Definitions of Misbehavior   237
Discipline Situations: Interactions Gone Sour   238

A Cross-Cultural Prospective   242
The Scope of the Problem   245
Logical Consequences and Reality Therapy   247
   Specific Recommendations Based on Reality Therapy   250
Reality Therapy and Social Learning   251
   Reasonable Rules, Responsibility and Reinforcement   251
   Punishment, Retribution and Restitution   252
   Time Out   255
   Contracts   257
   Choices, Delay of Reinforcement, and Self-Control   258
Conflict Resolution and Peer Mediation   259
   School-Based Conflict Resolution Programs   260
   Conflict Resolution Skills   261
Teaching and Discipline   262
Practice Exercises   266

UNIT FOUR
COGNITION: MEMORY, TRANSFER AND THINKING

9. Learning, Problem Solving and Transfer   270
Study Questions   270
Introduction   272
Some Problems To Be Solved   272
Perceptual or Mental Set   274
More Problems   274
The Structure of the Problem   275
Some Preliminary Conclusions   277
Transfer of Learning and Teaching for Transfer   278
   Transfer vs. Learning vs. Memory   278
   A Century of Transfer Research   280
      Measuring Transfer   280
      An Early Theory of Transfer: Identical Elements   281
      Interference Theory   283

      Educational Implications of Early Theories   285
   Cognitive Constructivism and Situated Cognition   287
      Educational Implications of Situated Cognition   290
   A Synthesis and More Optimistic Conclusion   290
      Transfer, Teaching, and Staff Development   292
Some Special Topics in Transfer   293
   Learning to Learn: Efficacy Plus Rigidity   293
   Adequacy of Original Learning   294
   Practice with Several Methods and Cues   295
   Principles vs. Habits   295
   Speed of Learning   296
   Emotions   296
   Near vs. Far Transfer   297
   Warm-up   298
   Individual Differences   298
Insight   299
Structure of the Material/Readiness of the Student   299
Teaching for Positive Transfer   302
Transferring the Information in this Chapter   303
Practice Exercises   305

10. Cognition and Memory   308
Study Questions   308
Introduction   310
Attention and Perception   311
   Attention and Its Selectivity   312
   Automatic vs. Controlled Attention   312
   Attention and Emotion   314
The Acquisition of Memories   314
   Sensory Memory   314
   Short-Term Memory   315
   Long-Term Memory   317
      Encoding, Storage and Retrieval   318
      Availability vs. Accessibility: Cue-Dependent Recall   319
      Organization in Memory   321

One Long-Term Memory,
or Two? 322
Memory—Who's Tending the
Store? 322
Learning vs. Retention 324
Elaboration in Encoding 325
Meaningfulness of Material and
Mnemonics 325
Dual Coding Theory 326
Amount and Distribution of Practice 328
Original Learning and
Overlearning 329
Massed vs. Distributed Practice 330
Learning Rate and Forgetting 332
Relearning by Fast and Slow
Learners 335
Cognitive and Metacognitive
Strategies 336
Memories: Reproductive or
Reconstructive? 340
Permastore: Very Long-Term
Memory 343
Memory for This Chapter 346
Practice Exercises 349

11. Nurturing Knowledge and Intellect 352
Study Questions 352
Introduction 353
Experts and Novices 355
Chess Masters' Memories 356
Other Expert-Novice Differences 357
Heuristics vs. Algorithms 359
Toward Becoming Experts 361
Structures for Knowledge 363
Schema Theory 366
Knowledge Structures, Schemata and
Teaching 366
Teaching To Increase Intellectual
Skills 367
The IDEAL Problem Solver and Lateral
Thinking 367
Metacognitive Strategies 372
Philosophy in the Classroom 376
Intellectual Skills in the School
Curriculum 377
Dialogical Thinking 379
Thinking Aloud 380
Practicing Mental Flexibility 380
Expertise Revisited 382
A Churchillian Epilogue 383
Practice Exercises 385

UNIT FIVE
EXPANDING THE REPERTOIRE FOR TEACHING

12. Teaching Decisions and Functions 390
Study Questions 390
Introduction 392
Madeline Hunter's Essential Elements of
Instruction: Teaching as Decision-
Making 393
Selecting Objectives at the Correct
Level 396
Writing Objectives 396
Task Analysis 396
Bloom's Taxonomy 398
Teaching To Objectives 401
Monitoring Progress and Adjusting
Teaching 404
Using Principles of Learning 407
Anticipatory Set 407
Feedback 408
Active Participation 409
Other Models of Instruction 411
Glaser's Instructional Psychology 412
Gagnè's Conditions of
Learning 412
Shuell's Teaching-Learning
Functions 414
Carroll's Model of School
Learning 415
The Expert Teacher Revisited 417
Practice Exercises 421

13. **A Repertoire of Teaching Skills** 424
   Study Questions 424
   Introduction 426
   Cooperative Learning 429
      Team Play vs. Team Learning: A Basketball Example 429
      Cooperative Teams for Academic Division 431
         Student Teams—Achievement Division 431
         Other Cooperative Methods 432
         Peer Tutoring 433
      Cooperative Learning: Theory and Evidence 435
      Implementing Cooperative Learning in Classrooms 436
   Mastery Learning 441
      The Winnetka Plan 441
      From Winnetka To Today 442
      Bloom's Learning For Mastery 444
      Claims and Evidence 446
      Mastery Learning: Some General Issues 449
      Implementing Mastery Learning in Classrooms 452
   Beyond Mastering Objectives: Encouraging Creativity in the Classroom 455
      Synectics 457
      Creativity: Other Issues 461
   Practice Exercises 464

UNIT SIX
DEVELOPING ASSESSMENTS AND GRADING

14. **Grades and the Purposes and Practices of Assessment** 468
   Study Questions 468
   Introduction 469
   Are Grades Necessary? 471
   Measurement and Evaluation 473
   The Purposes of Grading and Assessment 475
   Some Statistical Problems 476
      Combining Scores 476
      Teaching Variation 478
      Significance of Differences 478
      Variation Among Grade Levels 479
      Mixed Purposes 481
   A Comprehensive Grading System 481
      Between-Class Grading 482
      Within-Class Grading 483
         The Driver's Test 483
         Viable Variations for Classroom Use 485
   Setting Passing Scores for Instructional vs. Licensing Purposes 490
   A Final Observation on Grading 492
   Practice Exercises 493

15. **Principles of Measurement and Test Construction** 496
   Study Questions 496
   Introduction 498
   Validity 499
      Construct-Related Evidence for Validity 500
      Content-Related Evidence for Validity 501
      Criterion-Related (Predictive) Evidence for Validity 502
         Norm-Referenced Predictive Validity 504
         Criterion-Referenced Predictive Validity 504
   Reliability 505
      Types of Evidence for Reliability 506
      Reliability as "True Score" 506
   Item Analysis 507
      Item Discriminating Power 508
         Discriminating Power for Norm-Referenced Purposes 509
         Discriminating Power for Criterion-Referenced Purposes 510
      Item Difficulty 512
      Evaluating the Effectiveness of Distractors 513
      Some Final Comments on Item Analyses 513

Writing Tests   514
　Strengths and Weaknesses of Various Test Forms   515
　Two-Choice Items   516
　Matching Items   518
　Multiple-Choice Items   519
　Short-Answer Items   522
　Essay Items and Written Reports   524
　Performance Items and "Authentic" Testing   526
　Portfolios   529
Testing, Alternative Assessment, and the Purposes of Education   532
Practice Exercises   534

UNIT SEVEN
EPILOGUE

16. Epilogue: School Reform and Society   538
Introduction   538
A Wish List   541
Exercises   543

Notes   545
References   563
Glossary   597
Appendices   617
　Appendix A. RAPANOIA: WORSE THAN PARANOIA   617
　Appendix B. SOME USEFUL STATISTICS AND HOW TO CALCULATE THEM   620
　　I. Calculating the Mean and Standard Deviation   620
　　II. Calculating a Correlation Coefficient Using Ranks   622
　　III. Calculating the Percent Agreement (as a Measure of Criterion-Referenced Predictive Validity or Reliability)   624
　　　A Validity Example   624
　　　A Reliability Example   625

Author Index   629
Subject Index   637

PREFACE

Schools: A Place for Paranoia or Rapanoia?

Everyone has heard of paranoia—an irrational fear of imaginary or unreal threats. You think people are out to get you, but they're not. You fear math and therefore opt not to take statistics, for example, only to learn later that the professor made the topic not only understandable, but fun.

Suffering from paranoia is debilitating, but there are worse problems. For example, you think people are out to get you and they are. I call this "real annoya." A mother said to her son, "Get up it's time for school." The son responded, "I'm not going to school." Mom replied, "Let's not go through this again. Let's go." Then, seeing he wasn't budging, she tried another tactic: "Give me two reasons why you're not going to school." He said, "Because I hate the teachers and the teachers hate me." She said, "Well, anyway, you're going to school." He said, "Give me two reasons why I have to go to school." She said, "Because you're 47 years old and you're the principal." This is a case of "real annoya."

Perhaps the worst situation is a nonfear of real threats that should be feared, but are not recognized as threats. You don't know that people are out to get you, but they are. There was no name for this problem until I coined it in song (Gentile, 1974; 1981; see the song in Appendix A). I call it rapanoia, which is paranoia spelled sideways—or sort of—and indicates you are getting rapped. Rapanoia is commonly experienced by teachers who think students are self-motivated. It is also commonly experienced by students. For example, the first day of school, parents dress up their Johnnys and Marys, give them money for lunch, and send them off to school with such warm wishes as, "School is going to be fun," "You're going to love your teacher," "There will be new games to play," and "You're also going to learn how to read." By the end of the first day (if not the first year), many Johnnys and Marys know better: in school you must sit quietly until told you may move or talk, the bigger kids beat you up and take your lunch money, and you didn't learn to read. In fact, of the three reading groups, you didn't make the "bluebirds" or "redbirds"; rather, you were assigned to the "buzzards."

If this is a child's first experience of rapanoia in schools, it will not be the last, since we often provide outcomes that are far removed from the expectations of growth, understanding, and personal fulfillment that are promoted in such mottos as "Let each become all he is capable of being."

Consider some facts about children and schooling. From the age or five or six until sixteen they are legally required to attend school. While there, the students have certain requirements to meet or courses to take. The schedule, including when they eat and often when they go to the toilet, is by and large determined by others. These facts of school life are obvious and most citizens are cognizant of them. The significance of these facts, however, is not easily recognized unless they are placed in a larger perspective.

Philip W. Jackson attempted to provide such a perspective in his book Life in Classrooms (1968). He estimated, for example, that in most states a student spends about 1000 hours per year in school, so that if he has attended kindergarten and has been reasonably regular in attendance, he may have logged up to 7000 hours in class by the time he enters junior high school. Jackson goes on to say (p. 5):

> *The magnitude of 7000 hours spread over six or seven years of a child's life is difficult to comprehend. On the one hand, when placed beside the total number of hours the child has lived during those years it is not very great— slightly more than one-tenth of his life during the time in question, about one-third of his hours*

of sleep during that period. On the other hand, aside from sleeping, and perhaps playing, there is no other activity that occupies as much of the child's time as that involved in attending school. Apart from the bedroom (where he has his eyes closed most of the time) there is no single enclosure in which he spends a longer time than he does in the classroom. From the age of six onward he is a more familiar sight to his teacher than to his father, and possibly even to his mother. (emphasis added)

Viewed in this perspective, the schools are in a remarkable—and in some ways frightening—position. No matter that some say the home or genetic factors have more influence than schools. Schools still have a significant amount of control over the lives of students, if only because of the time students spend there. Moreover, this control occurs during significant developmental years—years in which work habits are established, attitudes toward learning and authority figures are formed, self-concepts and interests are acquired, and patterns of functioning with peers are learned. In short, the schools in general and teachers in particular have an immense responsibility—one which is difficult to overestimate by whatever evaluative standard is used.

Precisely because of this responsibility it is extremely important for teachers and school administrators to understand the child in *interaction* with the teacher and the rest of the school environment. Interaction has been emphasized because teachers not only change children, but are changed by them. To prevent rapanoia, paranoia or real annoya from disrupting educational interactions, all aspects of the classroom—objectives, discipline rules, teaching techniques, rewards and punishments, tests and grading procedures, etc.—need to be understood.

This book is written to provide an understanding of the events that occur in classrooms and their effects on the people in those classrooms. It also provides some suggestions

for structuring events in such a way as to be maximally effective in reaching educational goals while, at the same time, developing a strong concept of self in student and teacher alike. This, it seems is (or should be) the purpose of educational psychology as a discipline; it is certainly the raison d'etra of this book.

Approaches to Studying Human Behavior: Why This Approach

It is widely recognized that there are various, often competing, approaches to the study of psychology. Among them are the following:

- **Behaviorism,** associated originally with J. B. Watson and currently with B. F. Skinner, and said to explain behavior as primarily due to environmental events which act upon a blank slate and condition passive individuals to behave the way they do.
- **Cognitive Developmental Psychology,** associated with J. Piaget, and said to explain behavior as primarily due to the active explorations and cumulative discoveries of a maturing individual.
- **Psychoanalytical Psychology,** associated with S. Freud, and said to explain behavior as primarily due to largely unconscious processes which serve to defend a fragile ego.
- **Humanism,** associated with C. Rogers and A. Maslow, and said to explain behavior as a result of an active search for personal meaning, growth, and self-fulfillment.

I believe that each of the above descriptions—in fact, all one-line or short-paragraph descriptions—to be mainly a caricature of the theoretical approach it purports to describe. Like any caricature, there is an element of truth in the description (see also the box). It may even be possible to find one or more of

---

Differences in Psychologists

A. Greetings

1. Two Psychologists:
   Bill: "Hello Jim, How are you?"
   Jim: (after Bill passes): "I wonder what he meant by that."

2. Two Humanists:
   Bill: "Hello Jim, How are you?"
   Jim: "Im O.K. and so are you."

3. Two Behaviorists:
   Bill: "Hello, Jim. How am I?"
   Jim: "You're fine, Bill, but how am I?"

B. Changes to be Made:

1. How many behaviorists does it take to change a light bulb?
   Two. One to change the bulb and the other to positively reinforce this appropriate behavior.

2. How many psychoanalysts does it take to change a light bulb?
   Two. One to change the bulb and the other to help the first explore his deep-seated fear of the dark.

3. How many humanists does it take to change a light bulb?
   Only one, but it requires that the light bulb really wants to be changed.

---

the adherents of those paradigms or approaches who believe the essence of the statement. And certainly the adherents to these positions fight like proverbial cats and dogs. In the words of one pundit, science advances not by one scientist standing on the shoulders of the ones who went before, but rather by stepping in the face of those who went before.

On the other hand, the labels behaviorism, Freudianism, humanism or any other ism imply much more of a consensus within each field than really exists. To put it another way, the label is, at best, a stereotype which, like all stereotypes, serves to mask the wide variety of differences within the group. Sometimes the wide variety of positions within a camp becomes obvious, as when subdisciplines grow and take on hybrid names—for example, there is now a field known as cognitive behavior modification. Other times the diversity of opinions is masked under titles like neo-Freudian.

What is a nonaligned observer to make of all of this? I believe that it is sensible to take a very eclectic approach, particularly when we are striving to attain a larger goal—in this case, a better understanding of, with resultant improvements in, teaching/learning processes. In other words, one cannot understand how to educate people from a behaviorist point of view, nor from a humanist point of view. Neither can one understand people from an affective vs. cognitive dichotomy. As the saying goes (Barth's distinction; see Bloch, 1980, p. 78), "There are two types of people; those who divide the world into two types and those who don't." People are not rational or emotional; people are rational and emotional. People don't respond to stimuli or create; people are controlled by stimuli and create. People aren't controlled by heredity or environment; they are controlled by heredity and environment.

Each of the various approaches has something valuable to offer toward the goal of improving instruction, though perhaps in different amounts and concentrations for different processes or stages of development. And since no one book can cover all topics with the emphasis each deserves, there is an inevitable selectivity involved.

The topics and emphases of this book have been selected for one or more of the following reasons: (1) they provide a theory-based explanation for common human experiences; (2) they are well-supported by empirical research; (3) they portray the development of important skills, understandings or traits; and (4) they have important implications for teaching or parenting.

Since this is a book on *educational* psychology, rather than general psychology, you may wonder why non-classroom examples are sometimes used to introduce or explain concepts (e.g., in Chapter 1, I introduce principles of behavior through a fear of dentists example). Such examples are used, first of all, to point out that the principles involved are general, applying to the real world, as well as that sometimes unreal world we call schools. Second, such examples also show the developmental effects of early experiences (e.g., preschool) on later functioning (e.g., in school or adulthood). Third, inexperienced or preservice teachers can relate to them as readily as more experienced teachers. A book with all classroom examples, in contrast, would assume much classroom teaching experience as a prerequisite. Finally, teachers need to understand children in interaction with their parents and their peers, and how such experiences affect their own interactions with those children.

If the above interpretations of the various approaches to psychology paint me as a self-avowed eclectic, that is what they were meant to do. On the other hand, there is probably no one who is accepting of all points of view in equal parts. In addition, it does seem necessary to adopt some framework for organizing the vast amount and variety of material to be covered by an educational psychology text. Otherwise, the coverage will appear to be a simple list of topics or principles, each unrelated to the others.

The Framework I have adopted is that of Bandura's Social Cognitive Theory which, for my purposes, is broad enough to include principles of emotional, behavioral, and cognitive development as individuals interact in social contexts. If there are gaps in our understanding of how all of these components fit together, that is at least partly the state of our theorizing.

However, the good news is that much is now known and, properly understood, it can serve as a firm foundation upon which educators at all levels can creatively build.

Prerequisites for this Book

This book assumes no prior background in educational psychology and should therefore be equally appropriate for pre-service or in-service teacher education courses. In trying the book out on my own classes (of mostly candidates for master of education degrees), the experienced teachers often comment, "I wish I had had this before I started teaching." Ironically, such teachers probably were exposed to some of the concepts in this book—not all, because some of the concepts and suggestions are distilled from quite recent research—but *they were not ready for those concepts, at the time.*

Just as we think of a spiral curriculum for students, in which they revisit concepts at ever more complex and inclusive levels of analysis through succeeding years of schooling, we need to think of teacher education as a continuing developmental process. Experienced teachers will respond to instruction about adolescent peer pressure or discipline, say, differently than inexperienced teachers who are only a year or two removed from their own adolescence. But I do not believe this fact implies that there is an optimal time to be exposed to the principles of discipline. Rather, it implies that each successive exposure to such principles will allow teachers to organize their knowledge about teaching so that it is more coherent and useful. In short, teachers—and teacher educators—must be encouraged to think about continuing education as a necessary part of professional development. Indeed, continual education should be a medal of honor for the professional.

Thus, whether this book provides your first, second or third exposure to these principles, it should help you by (1) adding new information and teaching practices to your existing knowledge base, (2) re-organizing your knowledge structure to include both the new and old information, and (3) providing a number of examples and rationales for the suggested procedures to help you apply them to your classrooms.

The Plan of this Edition

As in the first edition (1990), this book deals with the interdependence of the emotions, behaviors, and cognitions within and between individuals, with implications and suggestions for educating students and the professional development of educators. This is decidedly a Banduran approach which does not break topics into, for example, behaviorist vs. cognitive constructivist techniques, but rather explicitly attempts to include both approaches in an integrated analysis of a topic.

Although there are separate chapters in Units II-IV for development, emotional learning, behavior, social processes/pressures, various cognitive processes, and intelligence, by the last chapters of Units III and IV — and certainly throughout Unit V — inclusiveness of these separate parts of the whole person in social context should be evident in the recommendations for expanding the repertoire of ideas for teaching and evaluating.

Changes in the second edition include the following:

Unit I. Levels of Experience

Chapter 1 remained much as it was, as an introduction and overview of the book's social cognitive approach, and constitutes the whole of this unit.

Unit II. Stability and Change in Human Development

Chapter 2, Stages and Processes of Development, was expanded to include Vygotsky's theory and cognitive constructivism in addition to the developmental theories of Erickson, Piaget, Kohlberg, and Maslow. Chapter 3, Intelligence: Its Stability and Growth (moved up from Chapter 9), provides background on traditional views of intelligence and the development of and statistical basis for norm-referenced testing, and such controversial issues as heredity vs. environment and bias. A new Chapter 4 discusses the implications of the developmental theories for instruction and curriculum development, including alternative views of intelligence, such as Sternberg's, Gardner's, and Feuerstein's.

Unit III. Motions, Emotions and Commotions

This section begins with Chapter 5's emphasis on conditioned emotions, learned helplessness, and attributional styles (somewhat expanded). Understanding behavior constitutes Chapter 6 with the basics of operant conditioning setting the stage, and leading to implications for developing self-control, persistence, and frustration tolerance. Chapter 7 examines social processes, including modeling, group pressures, conformity, roles, and more recent views of the effects of media and pop culture on behavior. The last chapter of this unit, Chapter 8, recommends Glasser's reality therapy and restitution as the building blocks for discipline and responsibility, but includes new sections on conflict resolution and peer mediation.

Unit IV. Cognition: Learning, Memory, Transfer, and Thinking

Chapter 9 continues its emphasis on problem solving as an introduction to a century of disappointing news about transfer, from identical elements theory to interference theory. The bad news extends to current situated cognition theory, but—surprise—ends on a realistic but decidedly optimistic set of recommendations (based on all of the above) for how to teach for transfer. The next chapter, 10, presents the basics of memory processes. Finally, chapter 11 introduces research on experts vs. novices, organization and scaffolding of knowledge, and new views of teaching intellectual skills, referring back to new views of intelligence and more on metacognitive processes.

Unit V. Expanding the Repertoire for Teaching

The first chapter in this unit, 12, begins with a general composite model of instruction, based on ideas of Hunter, Glaser, Gagné, Shuell, Carroll, and Shulman. Chapter 13 continues expanding the repertoire by discussing cooperative learning, mastery learning, and creative processes.

Unit VI. Developing and Evaluating Tests and Grading

Chapter 14 presents an analysis of current purposes and practices of grading, with the author's own unique specific suggestions for solving "the grading problem." The next chapter's section on item writing has an increased emphasis on performance ("authentic") testing and portfolios to supplement other test item types, as well as more simplified presentations on item analyses for norm-referenced and criterion-referenced purposes. An additional section to Appendix B which presents some useful statistics and how to calculate them, also presents a way of calculating criterion-referenced predictive validity and reliability coefficients using percent agreement (as in measures of inter-rater reliability).

Unit VII. Epilogue

Chapter 16 reflects on school improvement and the continuing professional development of teachers, but in the context of society and its values.

Study Aids

Each chapter is preceded by a set of *Study Questions*. These constitute the author's list of instructional objectives; your course instructor may wish to select all or only some of them as your course objectives. In any case, if you can adequately answer these questions, you have understood the major points in the book.

At the end of each chapter there are also several *Practice Test Questions* or *Exercises* designed to help you ascertain whether you have achieved the instructional objectives.

There is also a *Glossary* of important terms provided after the references to help you easily find the definitions of terms. Throughout the chapters are also recommended readings, the complete citations for which are in the *References*.

Notes, which give additional information or explanations beyond what can be incorporated into the text, are found following chapter 16. Answers to some problems posed in the text may also be found in some of these footnotes.

ACKNOWLEDGMENTS

First and foremost I wish to thank my partner in education, music, and life, Dr. Kay Johnson-Gentile, for critiquing every chapter several times, for making valuable suggestions, and for continual encouragement throughout the writing of each edition of this book. Much appreciation is also expressed to the following persons who contributed to the writing of parts of the text: Dr. John R. Dilendik, Dr. Kay Johnson-Gentile, and Ms. Colleen McNeil for their contributions to chapters 2, 8, and 9, respectively. Many thanks to Ed Kohrn for his many fine cartoon drawings and to my son, Doug A. Gentile, who also contributed several drawings.

Appreciation is also expressed to Dr. Thomas Shuell, Dr. Robert Gentile, and Doug Gentile for contributing some of their photographs. Thanks also to a number of persons, mostly teachers, who provided anecdotes for the book. They are acknowledged at the point of contribution.

A special thank you is expressed to Ms. Aviva Bower for her proof-reading expertise.

Finally, many thanks are expressed to my secretary of 28 years, Dian Ruta, for word processing above and beyond the call of duty. She can merge scribbles from napkins (that even I cannot read) with text and tables from multiple files into readable chapters.

UNIT ONE

Levels of Experience

This one-unit chapter explores developing individuals in interaction with their physical and social environments, how they both affect and are influenced by those with whom they interact. The three types or levels into which people normally divide their experiences—namely feelings, actions, and thoughts—are introduced from the more technical points of view of

1. emotions or involuntary (respondent) behavior,
2. voluntary (operant) behavior, and
3. cognitions (thinking, problem solving, etc.).

How these three levels of experience interact with one another to provide a holistic, integrated individual is also explored. Finally, we explore the environmental context in which individuals develop and learn to think, to feel and to do—that is, the interactions and interdependencies that arise from the fact that we are primarily social beings.

CHAPTER

Study Questions

1. What is the author's position on the "nature-nurture" issue?
2. What is meant by each of the following terms?
   a. respondent
   b. operant
   c. cognition

3. Which of the following terms is associated with operants and which with respondents? Give examples.
   a. behaviors
   b. emotions
   c. instrumental conditioning
   d. Pavlovian conditioning
   e. Skinnerian conditioning
   f. voluntary response
   g. reflexes

4. What is meant by each of the following symbols?
   a. S^{RF}
   b. S^{AV}
   c. R
   d. US
   e. UR
   f. CS
   g. CR

5. The author claims that cognitive processes such as learning to read can never be accomplished in the absence of respondent and operant conditioning. For example, a child is ridiculed while trying to read a word. What effect does this have on his:
   a. learning to read?
   b. willingness to try again?
   c. emotional response to reading?

6. What is meant by reciprocal determinism in Bandura's Social Cognitive Theory? How do each of the following act reciprocally in this theory to determine human functioning?
   a. behavior
   b. cognition
   c. environment

ONE

Emotions, Behavior and Cognition in Social Context

Introduction

Every time I go to the dentist an interesting thing happens to me. As I begin to get out of the car in the parking lot, I feel a bit uneasy. By the time I enter the office I laugh a nervous laugh when checking in with the receptionist. And even as I whistle (a happy tune?) to the background music and tap my toe to the beat, it is clear to me that it is more a release of tension than a demonstration of innate or acquired rhythm. By the time I am reclining in the chair with the dentist about to put his instruments and hands in my mouth, I have a death grip on the chair that is worthy of a sumo wrestler. The amazing thing about this is that I haven't experienced any real pain at the dentist for as long as I can remember.[1]

How do these things happen? Although it may be impossible to know for sure, it is possible to make some educated guesses. Consider what happens, for example, to many infants on their first trip to the pediatrician for shots. The child is being held closely and comfortably by the parent, feeling warm and relaxed—a case of rapanoia—when suddenly some cold alcohol is felt, followed by a needle to the posterior. The needle is painful of course and produces an immediate reaction of screaming, thrashing, and other indices of discomfort. Infants don't read, but many parents report that on the occasion of the next visit to the doctor, the child hardly gets in the door and past the sign before he or she reacts with the same screaming and thrashing as before.

Many people have had the same one-trial learning experiences in taking their pet to the veterinarian. After the first painful experience with the vet, try to drag your dog through the door. It doesn't matter that the physician or veterinarian is being kind[2] or saving the organism's life; something about him or his office (the odors, colors, etc.) have become associated with sufficient pain to produce this very common kind of fear.

We are not born with a fear of dentists, doctors, vets (either veterinarians or veterans), teachers, or math for that matter. But we are physiologically wired for fear reactions to painful events. Painful needles or shocks elicit a pot pourri of physiological reactions, among which are the following: increased blood pressure, heart rate, respiration rate, and muscle tension; sweaty palms; stomach contractions; dilation of the eyes; and a release of various chemical substances, including adrenaline, to prepare the body for "flight or fight."

This natural physiological reaction to pain is a built-in reflex which probably has evolutionary significance in protecting organisms from harm: you must pull back quickly from painful shocks, heat, or threatening objects to stay alive very long. In other words, this fear response is unlearned, being a reflex of the following form (where the arrow can be read simply as "produces" or "leads to"):

1. Painful Stimulus → Physiological Fear Response

Anecdote 1.1

The Case of the Denta-phobic Psychologist[3]

Once upon a time there was a clinical psychologist who had a fear of dentists. Now this man was used to helping others cope with their fears through various relaxation and biofeedback techniques, so he decided to apply his expertise to himself. The strategy was to monitor his own anxiety and then actively try to relax whenever he began to feel anxious. Already he had been practicing the relaxation technique (via production of alpha waves in the brain), so it remained only to apply the technique to his fear.

To monitor his anxiety, he hooked up a portable GSR (galvanic skin response) instrument to his palm. Like a lie detector, this instrument records the changes in the electrical conductivity of the skin due to perspiration, and was connected to a buzzer. So whenever he began to get anxious, his palms would sweat and the GSR would produce a buzz. He also had an earphone so that it could buzz without anyone else hearing it.

So prepared, he drove off to his appointment with the dentist. As he was driving into the parking lot, there was a soft buzzing in his ear, so he concentrated on relaxing and, indeed, the buzzing stopped. As he was called to the chair the buzzing started again and once more he was able to relax. The incidences continued while the dentist examined him.

Soon it became clear to the dentist that this man with the earphone and electrodes attached to the hand was either dancing to a different drummer or was just plain weird. When he asked, the psychologist told him what he was doing. So the dentist said, "Well, don't keep it a secret; play it out loud."

The psychologist removed the earphone and the rest of the session went something like this. The dentist said, "This isn't going to hurt."

BUZZZZZZ!

The moral of the story is, whenever someone tells you something is not going to hurt, it is a case of rapanoia: that is exactly when it is going to hurt. And whether you are consciously aware or not, your body is.

The painful stimulus and fear response are called *unconditioned stimulus (US)* and *unconditioned response (UR)*, respectively, to emphasize the fact that no learning had to occur in order to obtain the reaction. It is an unlearned or unconditioned reflex of the same form as the patellar reflex (leg kick that occurs when the knee is struck just below the knee cap), and eye blink to a puff of air. Thus in more general terms we can diagram the above reflex as follows:

2. Unconditioned Stimulus → Unconditioned Response

or more simply, as

3. US → UR.

The Human Organism: The Product of Nature and Nurture

Humans are born with a number of such reflexes, along with other behaviors that are probably not reflexive. With age, their bodily structures and functions mature and their behavior changes correspondingly. They not only get larger and grow hair and teeth, but they learn to chew in addition to sucking, they reach for objects, they vocalize, they crawl, etc. Many of the structures and behaviors of the young child are common to most living organisms: for example, a digestive system and the behavior of eating, a respiratory system and breathing. An increasing number of behaviors that emerge are distinctly specific to the human species: for instance, the characteristic human crawl and subsequent upright walk, the human vocalization and subsequent language.

The structures and behaviors which characterize the developing child as human are evidence of a genetic endowment and maturational plan which sets some boundary conditions on us. We are not adept at swinging from tree limbs for long periods, or swimming under water for long periods, or for scratching our own backs. But while our genes may impose some limits on our maturation rate and the behaviors associated with them, those limits cannot begin to compare to the limits which human cultures impose through the process we have come to call socialization. Child (1954, p. 655) defined socialization as follows:

> . . . the whole process by which an individual, born with behavioral potentialities of enormously wide range, is led to develop actual behavior which is confined within a much narrower range—the range of what is customary and acceptable for him according to the standards of the group.

What we come to eat, to fear, to feel comfortable with, to study, and to do with our free time—to mention just a few topics—is much more a function of our prior experiences and the presses from significant others than it is from our genetic endowment.

This is not to say that there are not tremendous variations in humans' shapes, sizes and abilities, much of which is traceable in large measure to genetic predispositions. Undoubtedly such individual differences exist and they may help describe the variations among humans. They do not, however, define the limits of structural, physiological or intellectual growth. Such limits may, in principle, be unknowable because hereditary mechanisms always interact with the environment to produce organisms' structures and their behaviors, and who can ever be sure that a different environment (better food or a better teaching procedure) could not be devised to produce a stronger athlete or more intelligent student?

The above argument is presented not to take sides on the nature-nurture question, but to sidestep it. From my point of view, what is important is that developing humans have (1) genetic endowments and maturational patterns that provide for structural and behavioral characteristics that are at once common to the human species (and a few characteristics common to other species) and unique to the individual; and (2) learning histories and patterns that build on (1) and that emerge from continual interaction with an environment which at once changes, and is changed by, the individual. In more simplified terms, learning arises from development while it simultaneously affects future development.[4]

Many textbooks portray the nature-nurture issue as a controversy by taking the following famous quote by J. B. Watson as the behaviorists' extreme environmental position:

> *Give me a dozen healthy infants, well-formed, and my own specified world to bring them up in and I'll guarantee to take any one at random and train him to become any type of specialist I might*

Anecdote 1.2

More on Watson's Famous Quote

Consider Watson's claim in fuller context than usually quoted:

Give me a dozen healthy infants, well-informed, and my own specified world to bring them up in and I'll guarantee to take any one at random and train him to become any type of specialist I might select—doctor, lawyer, artist, merchant-chief and, yes, even beggar-man and thief, regardless of his talents, penchants, tendencies, abilities, vocations, and race of his ancestors. I am going beyond my facts and I admit it, but so have the advocates of the contrary and they have been doing it for many thousands of years. Please note then when this experiment is made I am to be allowed to specify the way the children are to be brought up and the world they have to live in. (Watson, 1930, p. 104).

But Watson was not just hedging his bets; he believed that heritable structures like shape and flexibility can account for individual differences in ability on arbitrarily standardized instruments. He gave the following hypothetical example regarding the piano to demonstrate how environments can be shaped to promote or deemphasize different hereditary structures.

The older of two boys is shaped like the father with long flexible fingers. The father, a pianist, loves him dearly. The second has short fingers and is loved more by the mother, a distinguished artist. With their differential attachments, the time each parent spends with each child leads the older child to become "a wonderful pianist, the younger an indifferent artist." Assuming that the younger boy could not have become a pianist under normal circumstances, perhaps because of his short fingers and the musculature of his hands, does that make him genetically unfit for the piano? Watson points out that the piano is an arbitrary, but standardized instrument and then draws the following conclusion to this scenario.

But suppose the father had been fond of the younger child and said, "I want him to be a pianist and I am going to try an experiment—his fingers are short—he'll never have a flexible hand, so I'll build him a piano. I'll make the keys so narrow that even with his short fingers his span will be sufficient, and I'll make leverage for the keys so that no particular strength or even flexibility will be needed." Who knows—the younger son under these conditions might have become the world's greatest pianist. (Watson, 1930, p. 103).

---

select—doctor, lawyer, artist, merchant-chief and, yes, even beggar-man and thief, regardless of his talents, penchants, tendencies, abilities, vocations, and race of his ancestors. (Watson, 1930, p. 104).

This is ironic because the context in which Watson made this statement is a book describing a research program to organize the evidence on what is inborn and what is learned—that is, where hereditary ends and experience begins. One result was the classification of a long list of behaviors, ranging from blinking to love, to indicate whether or not they were conditionable and at what age. Furthermore, he took this work as illustrative of the behaviorists position that "...psychology is a natural science—a definite part of biology" (Watson, 1930, p. 139). For more information on Watson's position, see anecdote 1.2

B. F. Skinner is also portrayed as believing in the "tabula rasa" or blank tablet idea that experience is everything. But that, too, is a caricature of his position. A neo-Darwinist, Skinner claimed that behavior is a function of the genetic endowment of the species, the heredity of the family, the personal history of the individual, and the environmental contingencies, both physical and social, operating at the moment (Skinner, 1974).

In short, it is difficult to find anyone who believes in an extreme environmental position in which heredity accounts for little or nothing. It is equally difficult to find anyone who believes in the other extreme—that heredity accounts for almost everything. As we shall see in chapter 3, those who argue that heredity accounts for, say, 80% of intelligence (e.g., Arthur Jensen, 1969, or more recently Herrnstein and Murray, 1994, in *The Bell Curve*) are making a highly statistical argument about *predictable rankings* of people, not about whether environment affects cognitive processing. Raise one identical twin in America and the other in China and they may receive equal percentile rankings on an IQ test, but one will have to be tested in English and the other in Chinese.

The next chapter will present several general theories of development/personal growth—namely, Piaget's and Vygotsky's theories of cognitive development, Erikson's theory of psycho-social development, Kohlberg's theory of moral development, and Maslow's theory of motivation. We shall have occasion to refer back to many of the concepts and issues raised by these theorists throughout the book, though they may be approached from different angles. Meanwhile, the remainder of this chapter describes three fairly distinct kinds of human experience and shows how they develop in interaction with the environment.

One Level of Experience: Feelings (and Conditioned Emotions)

Fear of dentists and the like is more than an unconditioned reflex. It requires a reflex, but adds another stimulus to it—a neutral stimulus which, when paired with the US, can come to elicit the same UR. This process is called *conditioning*, or to be more precise, it is variously called *classical conditioning, Pavlovian conditioning* (after Pavlov), or *respondent conditioning*. The latter term, attributed to Skinner (1938), is the most descriptive since it emphasizes the fact that the behavior occurs in response to an eliciting stimulus—that is, a stimulus that forces a response in an involuntary manner.

The previously neutral stimulus—e.g., a dentist—can come to elicit the fear response if associated with pain, as follows:

4. Dentist—Pain → Fear
5. Neutral Stimulus—US → UR

This should be read as indicating that the dentist, a neutral stimulus to begin with, comes to be associated with the US by occurring in temporal *contiguity* with it. In other words, the dentist is present when the pain occurs—note that he does not have to cause the pain. Since the pain itself (the US) elicits the physiological fear reaction (the UR), the neutral dentist is present when the unconditioned reflex is set in motion. And usually in only a few pairings of dentist and pain (or in only one trial if the pain is sufficiently severe) the dentist comes to elicit the same kind of reflex response, now called a *conditioned response (CR)*. The previously neutral stimulus is now called a *conditioned stimulus (CS)*. The entire procedure can be diagrammed as follows.[5]

6.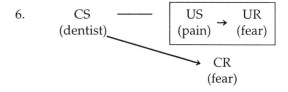

If we speak of the fear (in either the unconditioned or conditioned variety) as a *respondent*, then we can think of this conditioning process as a procedure that can be used to bring the respondent under the control of a previously neutral stimulus. Learning has occurred.

While in the process of studying basic digestive processes which won him a Nobel prize, Pavlov (1927) first demonstrated classical conditioning in much the way we have described it. Pavlov sounded a tuning fork immediately before placing meat powder in a dog's mouth. The meat powder (the US) elicited a salivation response (the respondent or UR). After a number of presentations of meat powder preceded by the tuning fork, the sound of the tuning fork acquired the capability of eliciting salivation from the dog. The previously neutral tone had become a CS and elicited salivation even though meat powder (the US) was no longer presented.

Since Pavlov's first demonstration there have been repeated investigations of the effects of his basic procedure for producing conditioned respondents on many species of animals, including humans, and for many different types of reflex responses. One of the most famous of these studies (Watson and Rayner, 1920) demonstrated that conditioned emotional reactions could be produced by pairing a neutral stimulus with an aversive US. In this study a white rat was placed before an infant named Albert who was at first attracted to the animal. Then on successive trials, introduction of the rat into the room was immediately followed by a loud noise. Parents will attest to the fact that a sudden loud noise causes a startle reflex and fear responses in an infant, and that was the effect the loud noise had on Albert. In only a few more pairings of the rat, followed by a loud noise which elicited the fear response, the previously attractive white rat had become a negative and unattractive stimulus which caused a fear response. That is, the white rat had become a CS for a fear response.

The Watson-Rayner study demonstrates a point alluded to earlier—namely, that respondent conditioning can occur by chance. The white rat in Albert's case was only incidentally related to the loud noise; it certainly did not produce the noise and thus, objectively, Albert had no reason to fear it. But such is the nature of classical conditioning. *There need be no causal relationship between the CS and US; all that is necessary is that the CS precede, or occur simultaneously with, the US so that they are perceived as related, and conditioning will occur.*[6] The rate at which conditioned fears are formed and their final strength depends upon the magnitude or severity of the aversive stimulus used. What is important to realize at this point is the apparent ease with which these conditioned fear respondents are formed in situations which involve aversive stimuli—such as those which include punishment or threats of punishment. Moreover, the effects of these conditioned fears are not confined to the conditioned stimulus alone, but often *generalize* to other similar stimuli (as will be described in more detail in a later chapter). Thus Albert not only learned to fear the white rat, but his fear generalized to other furry objects such as a rabbit and a fur coat as well.

All of this is to say that respondent or classical conditioning is one of three very important levels of experience—*the level of emotions and involuntary behavior.* Emotions such as fear, anxiety, comfort, love, embarrassment, and perhaps all emotions are conditioned to people and objects in this way. This is not to say that love and fear can be reduced to nothing but classical conditioning; rather, it is to say that such emotions have large respondent components. We can understand a lot of behavior by analyzing how these respondents become conditioned to people, things and environmental events. Neither is there a claim being made that love and fear cannot be voluntary actions; rather, the bodily feelings that are conditioned to people we love or things we hate are elicited by the stimuli present.

They can be controlled voluntarily—biofeedback techniques have been developed for this purpose—but they are not typically within our awareness in such a way as to be under our conscious or voluntary control. Hence, the term *involuntary* is often applied to respondent conditioning.

A Second Level of Experience: Behavior (and its Consequences)

Most of our experiences in everyday life are much more noticeable or available to our consciousness than the reflex responses we called respondents. We seldom feel as though we are puppets on a string, reacting reflexively to environmental pushes and pulls. To the contrary, except in extraordinary circumstances, we feel very much in control of our lives: we turn on the television in order to see a program, we turn the spigot to get water, we run after a ball to catch it, we work to receive pay, and so forth. *These are voluntary behaviors performed with purpose*, which defines the second level of experience.

Such behaviors were called operant behaviors, or *operants*, by B. F. Skinner (1938) to emphasize that they operate on the environment in order to produce some desired consequence. Other authors have called them *instrumental responses*, in recognition of E. L. Thorndike's (1911) early research showing how these behaviors are instrumental in obtaining rewards or avoiding punishments. Walking, talking, swimming, drawing, eating, drinking—in fact, almost any behavior you can think of—are all instances of operants.

When he defined their characteristics and named them operants, Skinner was contrasting them with respondents. Behaviors that were reflex reactions to unconditioned stimuli were respondents; behaviors that were not, which were all the rest, were operants. This distinction is still widely acknowledged, but it is clear that the boundaries are fuzzier than originally believed. It is possible, for example, to bring respondents under voluntary control, as current research in biofeedback demonstrates nicely. Nevertheless, the distinction holds under normal conditions and it is convenient for didactic purposes to talk of respondent and operant conditioning as two separate but interactive levels of behavior.

If operant behavior is voluntary or purposeful, how then is it conditioned? The simple answer is by the consequences of the behavior. If you touch a hot stove, the touching behavior has the consequence of a painful burn. The behavior is punished and you learn not to touch hot stoves. If, on the other hand, you find that you can have anything you want as long as you say, "please," you learn to say it with much higher frequency than other words. ("Please" is not called the magic word for nothing!) Both of these examples—the former built on negative, punishing consequences, the other on positive, rewarding consequences—are instances of operant conditioning.

There are a number of ways in which operant behaviors are controlled, of which positive reinforcement and punishment are just two, but they will be presented in detail in a later chapter. For now, the important point is that operant behaviors are controlled by their consequences. A diagram for the punishment example follows:[7]

7. Touching Hot Stove → Painful Burn
8. $R \rightarrow S^{AV}$

The reinforcement (reward) example can be diagramed thus:

9. Saying "Please" → Toy
10. $R \rightarrow S^{RF}$

Operant conditioning is sometimes called instrumental conditioning (because the behavior is instrumental in obtaining the consequence), sometimes Skinnerian conditioning (after Skinner), and sometimes it is referred to as S-R (Stimulus-Response) learning. The latter is mostly a misnomer as we have seen because, although there may be a stimulus in the presence of which behavior occurs, the important stimulus event is the consequent one. For example, while you may need a feeling of thirst (antecedent stimuli) or faucet to turn (the behavior), the stimulus which determines whether you engage in this behavior frequently or not at all is whether you get water (reinforcing or consequent stimulus). Thus instead of being called S-R learning, operant conditioning should be called *R-S learning*. This also has the effect of emphasizing the *active* role of the organism at this operant level of behavior in contrast to the reactive role at the respondent level.

Because of the emphasis on the active organism in operant conditioning, it is not too far-fetched to think of the *motions* of the organism (the physical motions of walking or of the vocal cords in talking, for example) in recalling this level of behavior. Then another mnemonic device for distinguishing between operant and respondent behaviors is in terms of *motions and emotions*, respectively.

A Third Level of Experience: Thinking (and Cognitive Processes)

If you ask a teacher what he or she teaches, the answer will hardly ever be behavior and emotions, willingness to participate, or even fear or love for a subject. The most likely answer is, "reading", "mathematics", "educational psychology", "chemistry", "French", etc. Teachers are hired to teach because of their expertise with academic content—more specifically, the facts, concepts, principles and methods of their discipline.

To learn, remember, apply, evaluate, or think about such content—all these and more—are considered cognitive processes. Cognitive processes can go on in the absence of reinforcement (or with it), or in the presence of positive feelings (or negative). In short, they operate by different principles than respondent or operant conditioning. Some of these principles are distributed practice, use of imagery, organization of knowledge, and learning to use a variety of strategies. (These issues comprise the major content of unit 4 of this text).

Thus learning to read, to comprehend the text, to use your new knowledge to solve a problem, to compare, analyze and evaluate what you read, and to create your own text are cognitive processes at generally increasing levels of complexity. Strategies for learning and remembering, including knowledge of one's own strengths and weaknesses are also cognitive processes. Such self-knowledge and strategic thinking, especially when used consciously and purposefully to control and monitor one's own learning or performance, have come to be known as *metacognitive processes.* Examples include actively thinking about your own thinking, monitoring what you can remember and what you forgot, and evaluating the paragraph you wrote to see whether it accurately says what you meant.

Other examples of cognitive processes include beliefs, attitudes, and rationalizations or attributions of behavior. For example, when people say, "I can't do that because I was never very good in math," they are excusing their (perceived or real) lack of success with a cognitive rationalization. Such statements often reflect underlying emotional and/or behavioral difficulties (e.g., fear of math or poor motivation due to previous punishment), but the reasoning, beliefs, and language used to describe those feelings and behaviors are cognitive.

The last point raises a fundamental dilemma for psychologists and educators who rely on self-reports, surveys, interviews, and questionnaires to measure "How do you feel about _____?" At best, such questions measure feelings only indirectly; what they are measuring is the cognitive processing of the individual about their feelings, including their assessment of the context (e.g., "How much do I want this person to know about me?").

In sum, the third level of experience, cognitive processes, is complex indeed. It includes not only academic learning, knowledge, language, thinking, strategies, and metacognitive processes, but it also includes the reasoning we use about the other two levels of human experience—namely, emotions and behavior.

The Interdependence of Behavior, Emotions and Cognitions

The previous three sections (as well as anecdote 1.3) show that behavioral, emotional, and cognitive processes can function as separate and unique human systems. Yet we have all heard children described in such ways as the following:

A is very bright, but can't stay focused on the task at hand.
B is so shy and fearful that he/she won't participate in class activities.
C has difficulty learning to read, but is such a sweet child.

What is striking about these common representations of people is the implied interactions: that A's cognitive quickness can be dissipated by distractible behavior, that fearful feelings keep B from trying new behaviors, or that C's implied emotional stability and politeness may or may not compensate for a cognitive difficulty. Since so many different emotions, behaviors and cognitions can interact in an almost unlimited number of combinations and permutations, it is no wonder that individuals, even within the same culture or family, can appear so unique.

Because of the complexities of behavioral, emotional, and cognitive processes, each is treated separately in parts of this text. Keep in mind, however, that these processes are probably always interdependent, each affecting

Anecdote 1.3

Learning or Doing?

One afternoon last year, I found my ninth grade son sprawled on the living room floor, surrounded by a multitude of newspaper clippings. When I asked what was going on, he informed me that he was doing a term project which was due the next day.

He hastily mounted the news articles on colored paper and randomly placed the pages in a folder. "His project," he announced, "was finished." A few days later, the teacher returned the project with a grade of C.

Subsequently, in discussing the project, I said, "If you had handed that to me, I wouldn't have accepted it. I would have told you that it was unsatisfactory, and that I would be happy to give you credit when you organized it, and could show me that you understood what you had learned."

"But Mom," countered Peter, "we didn't have to learn it. We just had to do it!"

Merrie Neal
Teacher

Table 1.1 The interdependence of the three levels of experience.

Level of Experience	Teacher's Questions	Student's Answer	Teacher's Response	Probable Effect
Cognitive	"How Much is 2 + 2?"	"I don't know" or "5"	Yelling	May learn or may not
Behavioral (Operant)	S^D Discriminative Stimulus or Cue "2 + 2 = ?"	R Trying, says "5" or "I don't know"	S^{AV} Yelling (punishment)	Student will try to avoid teacher or math
Emotional (Respondent)	CS Neutral Stimulus		US loud noise	UR tension, fear

the others within milliseconds whichever came first (a point we'll revisit at the end of chapter 5).

Consider the illustration in table 1.1 of the effects punishment might have on a hypothetical first-grader trying to learn his number facts. When questioned "How much is 2 + 2?" he hesitates, then despite trying, guesses wrong. If this is followed by punishment—and some teachers have a tone of voice that can make a marine sergeant cringe—then, among other things, the child is likely to be affected on the three levels in ways such as the following:

Emotional Level: Math may come to be a conditioned stimulus (CS) or fear signal, because it is immediately followed by yelling, a powerful unconditioned stimulus (US) which elicits an in-born fear or tension reflex (UR). This sequence, in other words, provides for Pavlovian or respondent conditioning so that in the future, math (the teacher, or both) can elicit similar fear or tension, now as a learned or conditioned response (CR).

Behavioral level: Math may come to be a cue (or discriminative stimulus S^D), signaling that punishment, an aversive stimulus (S^{AV}), is likely to follow. Thus the student can learn that the consequence of trying to learn math is to be punished. This may decrease the willingness to try in the future. But even if the student tries to avoid future punishment by trying harder to learn, conditioned tension will still be a byproduct (on the emotional level).

Cognitive level: Math may be learned well, but only if the student had mastered prerequisite concepts so that understanding of the current task is within reach. If the material is too far beyond the student's current capabilities, no amount of yelling will help. Rather, diagnosis of the student's current understanding is the first step.

As this example illustrates, it is relatively easy to establish conditions in which behavior and emotions are in conflict with cognitive development. The student is trying to comprehend, but the body is tense and the motivation is to escape.

No teacher has the goal of making a child unwilling to come to class or feel tense while there. The interaction of teacher and student may nevertheless have that effect if punishment is routinely used. But the extreme hypothetical example is not meant to imply that behavior and emotions are involved only when punishment occurs. If reading, for example, is associated with gentleness and warmth through snuggling, then one would expect the student to be willing to read (operant level), to feel relaxed and comfortable while reading (respondent level), and to learn to read better and better (cognitive level), though the cognitive effect is expected on the basis of time spent reading rather than because of a direct connection between snuggling and comprehension.

Bandura's Social Cognitive Theory

If it is clear that there is an interdependence among behavior, emotions and cognitions within a person, it is equally clear that no one exists in a vacuum. There is an old joke about a rat in a Skinner box who says to his mate, "Boy, do I have this experimenter conditioned: every time I press the bar, he gives me a pellet of food."

Presumably the reason that joke is funny is that people expect the experimenter to be in control, while the lowly rat is being conditioned. But conditioning is never a situation of controller-controllee. It is more accurately described as control-countercontrol (e.g., Skinner, 1971), in which the experimenter controls the rat's bar pressing by giving food contingent upon that behavior and the rat controls the experimenter's food-giving by pressing the bar contingent upon receiving food. Perhaps the best way of describing it is as a mutually beneficial interaction or, to parody the song "Mutual Admiration Society," a mutual reinforcement contingency.

Any account of behavior must include both the organism and its environment, including other organisms, in a mutually interacting way if it is to be reasonably comprehensive. An account which does this, which will serve to complete this overview of the text, is Bandura's social cognitive theory (1977a, 1986).

Albert Bandura, born in Alberta, Canada in 1925, has had a distinguished career as Professor of Psychology at Stanford University. His many honors include the Presidency of the American Psychological Association and distinguished scientific achievement awards for his research on imitation and violence. Bandura's theory grew out of his prolific research on the topics of imitation or modeling, self-control or self-reinforcement processes, aggression, and behavior modification (e.g., Bandura 1969; 1971; Bandura and Walters, 1963). His findings convinced him that behavior and environment are so mutually interdependent that it is impossible to find a single cause for a particular behavior. In his words (1977a, p. 203):

> *Environments have causes as do behaviors. It is true that behavior is regulated by its contingencies, but the contingencies are partly of a person's own making. By their actions, people play an active role in producing the reinforcing contingencies that impinge upon them . . . behavior partly creates the environment, and the environment influences the behavior in a reciprocal fashion.*

Bandura refers to this person-environment interaction as *reciprocal determinism*, in which thought, behavior and the environment are all interdependent and determining each other (see Figure 1.1). He gives a societal example of television watching. Beliefs about the popularity of an entertainer or the enjoyability of a show (personal beliefs, cognitive knowledge) are likely to have been acquired from watching TV or talking to friends about TV (environment). If the program is worthwhile, you and others watch the program (behavior) more frequently; if it is not, audience ratings go down. Viewer behavior, then, is one of the determinants of whether and how the TV environment changes. As Bandura (1986, p. 24) concluded, "Here, all three factors—viewer preferences, viewing behavior, and televised offerings—reciprocally affect each other."

Figure 1.1 Bandura's Social Cognitive Theory

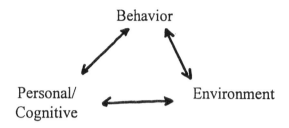

For school-related examples of this reciprocal process, consider the following:
1. *Mr. Screaming and his environment:*
   After getting little response from his new class to his request to come to order, Ben Screaming yells, "Sit down and be quiet" (behavior). The students immediately settle down (environment). This pattern continues for the first weeks of school. When asked how his new class is, Mr. Screaming replies, "Yelling is all they respond to" (personal beliefs, cognitive).
2. *Mr. Screaming's students and their environment:*
   After having Mr. Screaming yell at them (environment), the students come to enjoy seeing him lose his temper and, besides, they waste time that would otherwise have to be spent working (personal beliefs). Thus they do things (behavior) to annoy him, get him yelling, and otherwise lose control.

Considered separately, these examples show how behavior and environment influence and inform to create, change, or reinforce personal beliefs. These beliefs, in turn, can influence subsequent behaviors.

Considered together, these examples show the reciprocal determinism or interdependence of person and environment. Applying Bandura's words to this interaction, the teacher ". . . appears either as an object or an agent of control, depending upon which side of the reciprocal process one chooses to examine" (Bandura, 1977a, p. 196).[8] Of course, the students can also appear to be the victims or initiators of this continuing interaction, depending upon whose perspective is taken. Such is the nature of learning in social environments. In Bandura's words (1986, p. 18):

In the social cognitive view people are neither driven by inner forces nor automatically shaped and controlled by external stimuli. Rather, human functioning is explained in terms of a model of triadic reciprocality in which behavior, cognitive and other personal factors, and environmental events all operate as interacting determinants of each other.

This arises because humans have capabilities for symbolizing, for fore-thought and self-reflection, and for learning vicariously by observing others. Perhaps most importantly, they come not only to be able to do things, but they come to believe certain things about their abilities. That is, *they not only develop competencies or efficacy in various areas, but they also develop beliefs about their self-efficacy.* Thus people may have much ability to control certain outcomes, such as to succeed in math, but if they believe they cannot succeed, they may discontinue their work in math even while winning math achievement awards. The opposite is also true: a person who interprets failure as a learning experience may ultimately succeed, while persons with more natural ability give up.

It is clear that there are times that the environment will be the most powerful determinant of what happens, such as when it provides great stress (if you are dropped in deep water you will probably try to swim no matter what your skills or beliefs about your skills). At other times the behavior and its intrinsic or extrinsic consequences will dominate, such as performing a job to make a living or playing the piano because of its self-reinforcing qualities. Still other times the cognitions or other personal-emotional factors may predominate, as in which novel to select in a library or in

Anecdote 1.4

Eliza and Zelig

In George Bernard Shaw's "Pygmalion" (1973, Pocket Books), on which the musical "My Fair Lady" was based, Eliza Doolittle says the following to Col. Pickering:

. . .the difference between a lady and a flower girl is not how she behaves, but how she's treated. I shall always be a flower girl to Professor Higgins, because he always treats me as a flower girl, and always will; but I know I can be a lady to you, because you always treat me as a lady, and always will. (p. 90)

We see here not only how Eliza's environment affects her behavior and beliefs about herself, but also how Col. Pickering's and Prof. Higgins' beliefs about Eliza affect their behavior toward her.

In his film "Zelig," Woody Allen went even further to provide a classic spoof on the interdependence of beliefs, behavior and environment. Zelig is a man who tries so hard to adapt to his environment that he "becomes" the person he is with: if he is with a psychiatrist, he becomes a psychiatrist; if he is with a Chinese laborer, he becomes a Chinese laborer—even to the point of speaking Chinese. Even more remarkable, Zelig takes on the physical features of the person he is with to look like a psychiatrist or become Chinese—a "human chameleon."

avoiding statistics class because of a perceived incompetence in math. There is, in other words, no necessity that these three reciprocal factors operate equally or symmetrically at any given time. Nevertheless, in social cognitive theory all three are needed to explain human functioning.

As we proceed through this book, we shall have occasion to examine each of these factors as separate components and in various combinations. Keep in mind, however, that probably none of these factors ever operates totally outside of the influences of the others. Moreover, each of these three components—behavior, cognition, and environment—is itself complex. My environment, for example, may be relatively simple as when I am talking to one other person in a quiet room; alternatively, it can be quite complex as when I am trying to teach a classroom of students. While the complexity and relative importance of one or more of the components may vary, the reciprocally deterministic process will nevertheless prevail. As Bandura (1986, p. 29) explains,

> *. . . hostile acts generally draw aggressive counterresponses from others, whereas cordial antecedent acts seldom do. . . . Aggressive persons thus create through their actions a hostile environment, while those who act in a more friendly manner generate an amicable social milieu.*

See Anecdote 1.4 for two literary examples.

We shall have occasion to study a variety of social interactions in schools and at home to understand how they shape and are shaped by the circumstances and participants. In turn, we shall see their effects on what is learned cognitively, behaviorally and emotionally.

Practice Exercises

A. **Practice Items**

Each of the activities or situations below is best classified under one of the following levels of behavior:

a. respondent
b. operant
c. cognitive

Which is which? (*Answers are in note 9 at the end of the book*).

_____ 1. running
_____ 2. talking
_____ 3. recalling
_____ 4. blushing
_____ 5. interpreting
_____ 6. attending
_____ 7. tensing
_____ 8. classifying
_____ 9. eating
_____ 10. salivating
_____ 11. Harold knows the answer to each question.
_____ 12. Sometimes the teacher does not call on Harold when he raises his hand.
_____ 13. Whenever Mary is asked to do her chores, she complains until her mother does them for her.
_____ 14. Whenever Natale Attired walks in the room, Randy gets excited.
_____ 15. Charles questioned the teacher's interpretation of the sentence.

B. **For Cooperative Study (in or out of class)**

1. In groups of 2–4, give some real-life examples of:

   a. how the respondent, operant and cognitive levels of behavior interact within a person (such as in study question 5).
   b. how behavior, cognition and environment reciprocally determine one another.

2. Watch "My Fair Lady" or "Zelig," or find other shows or songs which portray the interdependence of cognition, behavior, and environment. Are these portrayals—serious or humorous—applicable to real-life experiences?

UNIT TWO

STABILITY AND CHANGE IN HUMAN DEVELOPMENT

This unit explores various conceptions of human development, first through some of the most popular theories of development (in chapter 2) and then through the contentious issue of standardized intelligence testing (in chapter 3). Throughout we shall have to deal with such stubborn problems of measurement as the difference between norm-referenced (comparison with the average) and criterion-referenced (comparison with a standard) assessment to understand how development can seem to be both stable and growing at the same time, as in the nature-nurture debate. Finally, in chapter 4 we shall explore the educational implications of the above accounts, as well as to introduce some more modern theoretical approaches to these historically important issues.

CHAPTER
Study Questions

1. What is meant by each of the following developmental processes in Piaget's theory? Give examples.
   a. schema
   b. learning in the narrow sense
   c. learning in the broad sense
   d. maturation
   e. experience
   f. social transmission
   g. equilibration
   h. assimilation
   i. accommodation
   j. decentration
   k. conservation
   l. object permanence

2. Describe some of the major accomplishments of each of the following of Piaget's stages:
   a. sensori-motor period
   b. preoperational period
   c. concrete operations period
   d. formal operations period

3. Using one of the conservation tasks (liquid, number, amount), describe the changes that occur as a child progresses from preoperational to concrete operational thinking.

4. What is meant by Vygotsky's "zone of proximal development"? What does it imply for
   a. the interaction of maturation and learning?
   b. setting instructional goals?

5. Describe the developmental language pattern, according to Vygotsky, from social to egocentric to inner speech. How does this sequence develop into thinking and metacognition?

6. What does Erikson mean by each of the following:
   a. identity formation
   b. psycho-social development

How do his formulations compare to the social cognitive view presented in chapter 1?

TWO

7. Describe the major conflicts to be resolved at each of the following of Erikson's developmental stages:
   a. infancy
   b. early childhood
   c. childhood (preschool)
   d. school age
   e. puberty and adolescence
   f. young adulthood
   g. middle age
   h. old age

8. Freud once said that what normal people need to do well is "to love and to work." How does this relate to Erikson's stages from at least adolescence on?

9. Give an example of the kind of moral dilemma Kohlberg and his colleagues use to study the development of moral reasoning.

10. Describe the kind of change in reasoning that occurs when a person progresses through the following of Kohlberg's stages:
    a. from the preconventional to the conventional level
    b. from the conventional to the principled level.

11. What is the relationship between moral reasoning and moral behavior in Kohlberg's view? Use the terms competence vs. performance in your answer.

12. What is meant by each of the following kinds of needs in Maslow's hierarchy?
    a. physiological needs
    b. safety needs
    c. belongingness and love needs
    d. esteem needs
    e. self-actualization needs

13. What does it mean to say that these needs fall into a hierarchy of prepotency with physiological needs at the base and self-actualization at the top? Give examples.

14. What does Maslow mean when he says that behavior has multiple determinants?

15. How is Abbott's Flatland a prototypical exemplar of a stage theory of development?

16. How does development simultaneously seem to be composed of
    a. discontinuous, qualitative changes?
    b. continuous, quantitative changes?

17. The author argues that with regard to developmental stages or averages, "the norm is not a standard." Give examples of what is meant.

Stages and Processes of Development

Introduction
Four Views of Development[1]

1. All the world's a stage,
   And all the men and women merely players:
   They have their exits and their entrances;
   And one man in his time plays many parts,
   His acts being seven ages. At first the infant,
   Mewling and puking in the nurse's arms.
   Then the whining school-boy, with his satchel
   And shining morning face, creeping like snail
   Unwillingly to school. And then the lover,
   Sighing like furnace, with a woeful ballad
   Made to his mistress' eyebrow. Then a soldier,
   Full of strange oaths, and bearded like the pard,
   Jealous in honour, sudden and quick in quarrel,
   Seeking the bubble reputation
   Even in the cannon's mouth. And then the justice,
   In fair round belly with good capon lined,
   With eyes severe and beard of formal cut,
   Full of wise saws and modern instances;
   And so he plays his part. The sixth age shifts
   Into the lean and slipper'd pantaloon,
   With spectacles on nose and pouch on side,
   His youthful hose, well saved, a world too wide
   For his shrunk shank; and his big manly voice,
   Turning again toward childish treble, pipes
   And whistles in his sound. Last scene of all,
   That ends this strange eventful history,
   Is second childishness and mere oblivion,
   Sans teeth, sans eyes, sans taste, sans everything.
2. Spills, Drills, Thrills, Bills, Ills, Pills, Wills
3. First they cry, then they're shy.
   Then the constant question "Why?"
   Then they lie, then really try,
   Next they dress in coat and tie
   And earn a lot and buy and buy.
   But by and by they die. Goodbye.
4. Hatch, Match, and Dispatch.

There have been many attempts to capture the essence of the developmental processes of human beings. Stages of development have formed the basis of much poetry, literature, and of course scientific explorations. In this chapter, we shall explore five major theories of developmental psychology—namely, Piaget's theory of cognitive development, Vygotsky's theory of developing thought via language, Erikson's theory of psycho-social development, Kohlberg's theory of moral development, and Maslow's theory of hierarchy of needs. Along the way, we shall examine some general issues relating to stages of growth (to be further explored in Chapter 4), and how they may be applicable to both the development of students and teachers. All together, then, this chapter will lay a developmental foundation for the principles of learning and instruction which follow in the remaining chapters.

Piaget's Theory of Cognitive Development

by
J. Ronald Gentile and John R. Dilendik[2]

Jean Piaget, who was born in Switzerland and lived from 1896 to 1980, is widely known today for his contributions to psychology, but he was truly an interdisciplinarian. At eleven years of age he published an article on a rare albino sparrow. By 18 years of age, he had published several more articles on biology. These were of sufficient quality that, on the basis of these articles, the head of a natural history museum offered Piaget the position of curator of the museum's mollusk collection. Piaget declined the offer so that he could complete his high school education (Siegler, 1986).

In addition to his interest in biology, Piaget was keenly interested in philosophy, particularly epistemology—or the study of the origins of knowledge. Thus it is not surprising that Piaget's theory of intelligence includes issues of maturation, of the interaction of a developing organism with its environment, and of the organism's construction and representation of knowledge from these experiences. Piaget (1970b, p. 703) described his theory as being ". . . impossible to understand if one does not begin by analyzing in detail the biological presuppositions from which it stems and the epistemological consequences in which it ends."

It is also not surprising, giving Piaget's own history, that his method of study is observational or clinical, rather than strictly experimental. In this approach he and his collaborators studied individual children, including his own, in relatively loosely structured interviews on problem solving situations. The number of correct answers, or some other objective measure, was not the goal; rather, the process by which the individual dealt with the situation was the object of study.

Photo 2.1. Five generations.

A Piagetian Problem: Conservation of Liquids

As an introduction to Piaget's theory, consider the now-classic conservation of liquids problem (Piaget and Inhelder, 1941). In one variation of this problem (shown in figure 2.1), children are shown two identical jars (A and B) and asked to judge whether the amount of water is equal. When they agree that the amounts are equal, then the water in B is poured into a taller, thinner, jar C. The children are now asked to judge whether A has more water, C has more, or A = C.

Children of five or six (in what Piaget calls the preoperational stage of development) typically say that C has more because they equate taller with a greater amount. In contrast, children of eight or nine (in Piaget's concrete operational stage) judge the amount to be the same and they can justify their judgment in one or more of the following ways: (1) it is the

Figure 2.1. Piaget's conservation of liquids problem.

same water (the identity argument); (2) if we pour the water from C to B, A and B would again be equal (the reversibility argument); and (3) the water in C looks higher, but it is because the glass is thinner (the compensation of relations argument).

Comparatively speaking, the knowledge structures of the older children include such information as the following: that amount of liquid depends upon more than one dimension, that two dimensions (e.g., height and width) can vary independently, and that certain actions can be performed to confirm or disconfirm any apparent inconsistency. Thus the older children are said to conserve liquids. Younger children who lack the ability to see that two dimensions can vary independently, are said to be nonconservers.

When faced with the problem, each child solves it on the basis of his or her existing knowledge and manner of thinking. This becomes most obvious when the judgment is directly challenged. For example, after the younger child judges C to have more water, the adult can pour the water from C back to B. The child will again agree that A and B will have the same amount of water. Pouring from B back to C may now produce confusion, but is likely to elicit the same judgment that C has more. The child is attempting to deal with observations which fit nowhere in existing knowledge structures—what Piaget called *cog-nitive conflict*. Faced with a sufficient number of such challenges to their current structure of knowledge, children will begin to accommodate their knowledge structures so that the new facts can be assimilated.

The older child can also be challenged. For instance, after judging that A = C, the adult can say that another child just argued that C had more. The conserving child typically looks at you with outrageous disbelief and says something like, "Well, he must be stupid; the water only looks like more, but the glass is thinner." This child's knowledge structures allow for the simultaneous variation of several dimensions; furthermore, such children do not recall that they themselves were once operating from similar knowledge.

Schema

Piaget used the term schema (plural schemata)[3] to describe differences in the knowledge structures between, for example, conservers and non-conservers. Although there have been many different uses of the term, I shall use the term *schema* in this chapter and the rest of the book to refer to the *existing store of knowledge and action sequences according to which we interpret new information or solve problems. The store of knowledge and action sequences are usually so well-practiced and automatic that they often occur outside of our awareness.* Thus children who conserve liquids can be said to have (and use) a conservation schema in recognizing that the amount of water remains the same despite changes in appearance. Nonconservers, in contrast, may operate from a different schema. If the experience is totally new to them, they must fall back on some prior experience or knowledge which they perceive as relevant in order to make sense of this new experience. As we shall see later, this is likely to be counterproductive (providing negative transfer), but it is the only thing possible for the student whose prior knowledge is insufficient for the task.

Stages and Processes of Development 23

Photo 2.2. Developmental stages.

Here arises a most difficult challenge for a teacher: how to teach something which requires certain prior knowledge or experience to someone who has not yet had that experience. More will be said on this topic in later chapters, but for now suffice it to say that Piaget would suggest that active manipulable experience is a necessary condition.

Developmental Processes

For Piaget, the interactive experiences a person has with the environment provide mental growth through two levels of learning. *Learning in the narrow sense*—that is, acquiring such facts as the names of states and capitals—is culture specific, requires little reorganization of knowledge, has little transfer value and takes relatively little time to accomplish. In contrast, *learning in the broad sense*, which Piaget equates to *development*, involves the acquisition of general thought structures which are applicable to many situations (Ginsburg and Opper, 1988). To continue the above example, development involves learning that each state has only one capital, that states include capitals, and that countries like the United States must be larger than and inclusive of their respective regions. Such learning is broadly applicable, requires a hierarchical organization of knowledge, and takes much more time to learn.

Although educators are at various times and for various purposes interested in both of these levels of learning, Piaget's theory is concerned with learning in the broad sense, or development. The processes that underlay such development are the following: maturation, experience, social transmission (the educative factor) and equilibration. These will now be described.

Maturation

Piaget labels his theory a "genetic epistemology" theory: growth is predetermined by a genetic ground plan which requires the sequential development, through time and experience, of more and more complex schematic structures. The understanding that the amount of liquid a bottle can hold is a function of both its height and width, for example, requires a quite sophisticated schema which doesn't typically appear until the child is about eight years old. The internal maturation which allows such concepts to develop is not to be confused with genetically programmed instincts. What is programmed is (1) a timetable for optimal sequential development of these structures, and (2) a process for self regulation or motivation, which Piaget called equilibration. Regarding intelligence, Piaget argues that it is the sequenced timetable and the need for "self regulation" that are inherited, not the quality or quantity of intellectual capacity (as reflected in IQ score). Indeed, both quantity and quality of intelligence change over time due to the influence of the four developmental factors we are now discussing.

Experience

Piaget stresses the distinction between simply experiencing objects and performing actions which affect those objects. Performing actions in relation to the objects is crucial to real learning (Piaget, 1970b, p. 721): ". . . there can be no experience without action at its source, whether real or imagined, because its absence would mean there would be no contact with the external world. However, the knowledge derived from it is not based on the physical properties of these objects but on properties of the actions that are exerted on them, which is not at all the same thing." This difference between observing and doing is critical. It is one thing to sit through demonstration classes on how to ride a bicycle. It is quite another to actually get on the bicycle and wrestle with the problems of maintaining balance, propelling yourself forward and steering around obstacles, all at the same time. An analogous argument is made for learning about conservation of liquids or number, in which manipulation of the objects, through pouring and counting, leads to a different kind of learning than simply observing or dealing with these topics in the abstract.

The Educative Factor (Social Transmission)

Although the developmental sequence for intelligence is fixed, Piaget acknowledges that growth can be accelerated or retarded to a limited degree by the quality of the environment, although the order of stages cannot be altered. This is demonstrated particularly by the apparent variance in the ages at which children achieve such concepts as classification and conservation across different cultures (e.g., Bruner et al., 1966). This, he suggests, is due to the educative or socialization component, the best of which emphasize active involvement, exploration and discovery. Most importantly, the child must be ready for the experience. This implies that there must be a proper match between the lesson's objective and the student's current knowledge so that the new lesson is only moderately novel.

Many of the more abstract lessons we teach to young children—the Pledge of Allegiance, for example, or the alphabet—must necessarily stay at a relatively superficial level and, as a result, frequently culminate in misunderstanding. Big Bird, the perpetual preschooler on Sesame Street, sings a song in which he is trying to learn a new word: ABCDEFGHIJKLMNOPQRSTUVWXYZ. As he goes on, he complains that although it starts out as an A-word, by the middle it seems ". . . awfully QR to me." How long was it before you discovered that LMNOP wasn't a single letter of the alphabet (pronounced ELEMENOPEE)? One, perhaps apocryphal, story is told of the adult who finally discovered he had long been singing a favorite hymn, "Lead on O King Eternal" as "Lead on O Kinky Turtle." Classification of objects into sets and subsets according to some characteristic is a logicomathematical operation which requires experience. You can teach five-year-olds the definitions of truck, car and vehicle, for example, but if you ask them whether there are more vehicles or cars on the road, they will probably say, "more cars", while looking out the window for verification. A seventh grader is capable of sophisticated grouping but would still find the abstract nature of verbal classification problems difficult. We observed another seventh grade science teacher write this class inclusion problem on the blackboard:[4]

kingdom
phylum
class
order
family
genus
species

He then asked the following question: "In classifying living things from kingdom to species, do the groups become larger and larger, or smaller and smaller?" How would you answer that question? Most of the students in the class agreed that the groups become larger and larger because, one girl replied, "There are so many more of them." The teacher tried for twenty minutes, to no avail, to explain that the groups must get smaller because the group immediately above includes the members of the groups below. He was able to convince them only when he had them sort a variety of objects into subclassifications, and then count the members in the subclasses.

These students' initial response reveals the same confusion about set and subset shown by the five year old, only at a higher and more abstract level. The middle school students, however, were able to re-evaluate their answers in the face of concrete experience and discover the confusion between the size of individual groups and the profusion of groups.

Equilibration (Assimilation vs. Accommodation) and Cognitive Conflict

Piaget argues that, just as biological development requires a self regulating mechanism, the individual is provided at birth with a regulatory system to keep the other factors, maturation, experience and education, in balance. The process of equilibration can be illustrated through Piaget's classic "sphere of clay" experiment. If a young child is given a ball of clay and is asked to roll the sphere into a sausage shape, she will either see the quantity of clay as being increased, because the shape is longer, or decreased because the shape is thinner. Capable of focusing on only one dimension of the object at a time, the child has not yet learned the principle of conservation. The discrepancy between the child's perception of changing quantity and the repeated evidence of conservation sets up a *cognitive conflict* within the child, a puzzle needing resolution. The tension resulting from this cognitive conflict provides the motivation for exploring further. Given more experience with manipulating the object, the probability increases that the child will discover the relationship between length and width. She will then enter a transitional period, during which time her explanation will fluctuate between recognizing and not recognizing the principle of constancy of quantity.

Eventually the child understands that the explanation does not rest entirely on the individual characteristics of the object, but rather on the relationship between characteristics: the object's shape has been transformed. This, in turn, leads to the realization that the two simultaneous transformations, size and shape, compensate for each other and that quantity is conserved.

The systematic change which keeps us in balance—that is, which motivates us to grow—is achieved through two regulatory processes called assimilation and accommodation. *Assimilation* is the incorporation of new information, the "taking in" of new experiences. *Accommodation* is the modification of current structures to allow new information to be incorporated. This is directly analogous to biological processes such as digestion, in which food is taken in and digested (assimilated) while the stomach expands or contracts to accommodate the food. In Piaget's clay sausage example, repeated experience with and manipulation of the ball of clay results in eventual assimilation of the properties of the object, including accommodating their schemata to include the compensatory relationship between length and width. Looked at slightly differently, children deal with a new object according to how they dealt with old objects. For example, after they have learned to shake rattles, infants will attempt to shake pencils or even dolls or teddy bears. When those objects cannot be shaken (a failure to assimilate), children must change their behavior toward the object (the process of accommodation).

The self regulatory process, equilibration, and its two complementary subprocesses, assimilation and accommodation, can be thought of as the individual's motivational system in Piaget's theory. New, inconsistent information is uncomfortable because it throws us off balance. It must be dealt with either by rejecting the new information (a failure of assimilation), or by incorporating the material with subsequent changes to our own understanding of how the world works (assimilation and accommodation).

Piaget's Stages of Development

Piaget's dual emphases on the importance of time and sequence lead naturally to the postulation of stages or critical periods during which specific understandings are developed. These stages are themselves hierarchical and sequential: a child must complete the tasks of the earlier stage before passing to the next, since the earlier tasks provide the intellectual foundation for the later ones. Most importantly, the quality of thinking changes from stage to stage; it is not simply that a fourteen year old has more information than a seven year old, and thus can solve more complex problems, but rather that the fourteen year olds have built internal schemata which allow them to approach problems in a totally different fashion. This distinction will become clearer when we describe the behavioral characteristics of each stage.

Stage theories in general, and Piaget's in particular, have been criticized as being too rigid with respect to the age ranges associated with each period. Indeed, the ages specified below may not be accurate for a given child in a specific socio-economic group or from a particular culture. This variation is acknowledged by Piaget and is important in demonstrating the influence of the educative factor in development, but is not harmful to his theory if the ages are considered averages and not standards (see section at the end of chapter). For Piaget the important point is that the *order or sequence* is invariant. Piaget (1970b) has defined three major stages, as follows: a Sensori-Motor stage, corresponding to infancy (birth to 1 1/2 or 2 years of age); a period of representative intelligence, corresponding to childhood (2–11); and a period of formal operations, corresponding to adolescence and adulthood (13–adult). It is customary to break his second stage into two substages—namely, the pre-operations stage (2–7) and the concrete operations stage (8–11)—which we shall adopt here. Table 2.1 provides a summary of what follows.

Sensori-Motor Period

If the child partly explains the adult, it can also be said that each period of his development partly explains the periods that follow. This is particularly clear in the case of the period where language is still absent. Piaget called it the "sensori-motor" period because infants lack the symbolic function; that is, they do not have representations by which they can evoke persons or objects in their absence. In spite of this lack, mental development during the first eighteen months[5] of life is particularly important, for it is during this time that children construct all the cognitive substructures that will serve as a point of departure for their later perceptive and intellectual development, as well as a certain number of elementary affective reactions that will partly determine their subsequent affectivity (Piaget and Inhelder, 1969, p.3).

In thus conceptualizing the period of infancy, Piaget emphasizes that the structures for intelligence are being formed long before the child can engage in thought. Thought requires symbolic abilities to represent and act on objects which are not physically present. The infant, at first, demonstrates intelligence by actions: for example, by moving the head in order to see a mobile hanging above the crib and, later, by reaching to touch the mobile and, still later, to cause it to move.

Table 2.1. Piaget's stages of cognitive development.

Stage	Approximate Age Range	Developmental Tasks
Sensori-Motor Period	Birth to 1 1/2 years	Accomplishments include experiencing the effects of actions, developing eye-hand coordination, learning object permanence, beginning language.
Pre-Operational Period	2–7	Accomplishments include increasing social communication, imagery, egocentric thinking, endless "why" questions
Concrete Operations Period	8–11	Accomplishments include attainment of reversibility, conservation, and seriation. Thinking relies on concrete manipulations.
Formal Operations Period	12–Adult	Accomplishments include capability of propositional logic and abstract thinking, inductive and deductive reasoning, facility with linguistic metaphors and symbols.

The earliest form of intelligence-through-action is simple exercise of various reflex functions, such as sucking, in which the reflexes become continually more effective and efficient. They also become more complex and integrated into holistic functions. The grasping and visual fixating reflexes, for example, come together to form a rudimentary eye-hand coordination pattern which, through repetitive practice and refinement, gradually becomes an automatic schema.

After some of these reflexes become stable structured patterns, the infant can be seen to be working on various developmental tasks, including those dealing with the permanence of objects, space and time, and causality. Consider the developmental progression regarding object permanence. If you cover or hide an object from a 5–7 month-old as he or she is reaching for it, the child simply withdraws the hand (unless the object is a bottle, in which case the child may cry). The child is reacting as if the object had been reabsorbed into the environment and ceased to exist. If you doubt this explanation, say Piaget and Inhelder (1969, p. 14), you can perform the following experiment:

hide the object in A to the right of the child; then, before his eyes, remove and hide the object in B to the left of the child. When he has seen the object disappear in B (under a cushion, say), it often happens that he looks for it in A, as if the position of the object depended upon his previous search which was successful rather than upon changes of place which are autonomous and independent of the child's action.

Although this sounds much like a reinforcement explanation—namely, the child repeats the behavior, looking in A, which was reinforced in the past—Piaget and Inhelder point out that much more than this response-reinforcement, sequence is being learned.[6] By 9 to 10 months, the child looks behind cushions and by one year, removes cushions behind cushions. The child has learned that objects

28 Chapter Two

Photo 2.3. "Hello world."

that are out of sight have not disappeared or been reabsorbed into the environment; rather, objects are permanent having an existence independently of the searcher.

The newborn is completely egocentric in the sense that there is no differentiation between the self and the outside world. Movement from this position of total self centeredness to increasing differentiation and decentration continues throughout development and, for most of us, is never really complete. *Decentration,* or the beginning of an awareness of the outside environment, tends to occur between about four and eight months of age. Between eight months and one year, language begins to develop, which allows the possibility of symbolic representation of objects, and thus the beginning of thought. This is a monumental achievement for children, because they are now capable of developing the concept of object permanence and thus the anticipation of the arrival of other family members, toys, or food. Children begin to comprehend cause and effect, and thus are able to respond intentionally.

Through the second year of life children continue to refine these skills, actively experimenting with the environment, and clarifying their relationships to the environment. Toward the end of the second year we see the beginning of mental representation, or thought. This ushers in a period of continuing experimentation with invention and imagination.

The educational importance of the sensorimotor period rests in the opportunity for the child to practice and thus construct schemata for these skills. High levels of stimulation from the infant's environment do contribute—these skills do not develop by maturation alone. Part of the value of breast feeding, for example, in addition to the nutritional advantages, is the need to hold and fondle the infant as she is feeding. Perhaps Piaget's ideas have had an impact on parents in this area: cribs are increasingly surrounded with mobiles and colorful posters, crib bumpers which can be filled with water and goldfish, etc. Many parents have adopted the African-style infant carriers so that their infants can go everywhere with them in close physical proximity. Middle and upper class parents, in particular, recognize the value of talking to the infants even though they cannot understand the words.

Preoperational Period

Increasing facility with language during the preschool years allows improved social communication and increased imagery. Intelligence as action is now partially transformed to intelligence as mental imagery. Thought is still primarily egocentric, however, so communication tends to be in the form of "collective monologues": self directed verbal accounts of experience that serve better as practice for the child rather than as communication of information. Decentering is minimal; the child focuses on one aspect of the stimulus which she believes characterizes that stimulus. The child has consequently not yet developed the structures necessary for assimilating the relations

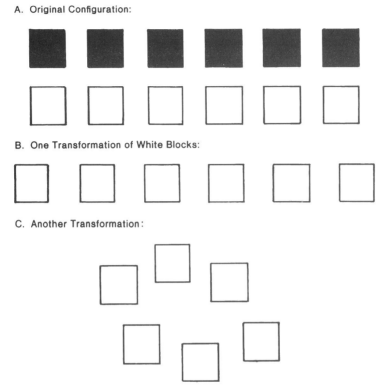

Figure 2.2. Piaget's conservation of number problem.

between characteristics which would allow understanding, for example, compensation between height and width. The preoperational child could not solve the sausage problem mentioned earlier.

Another classic conservation problem involves two rows of objects spread out to be of equal length in easily observable one-to-one correspondence (see figure 2.2). The preoperational child will agree that there are the same number of black and white blocks in A, but then argue that there are more white ones in B and fewer in C when the respective transformations are performed. Preoperational children seem to focus on either the number of blocks or the length or shape of the configuration, but not both simultaneously. They seem neither to be able to see the compensating relationship between the two dimensions, nor to be able to see the possible reversibility of the situation—namely, that the same white blocks could easily be returned to the original one-to-one configuration.

The importance of the development of language to the preoperational child must be emphasized. Language enables the child to communicate, thus enhancing the opportunity for experience; it allows the child to internalize words, creating the possibility of mental symbols and, therefore, thoughts; it allows for the internalization of action so that the child no longer has to depend on physical manipulation of the environment to solve problems. These changes, in turn, give the child the power of imagination and creativity.

This is the age of questions, and the responses we give to these questions are important. The egocentric and extremely concrete nature of preoperational children, however, can create some communication problems with adults. We frequently misinterpret the meaning of the many "why?" questions of children at this stage of development. Questions which would seem to demand a physical explanation ("Why is grass green?" "Why does it rain?") are often asked for different purposes. The following well-known joke makes the point well: Johnny runs into the house and asks, "Mommy, where did I come from?" Mother, knowing this day would come sometime (but why couldn't it have come when father was home?), gathers her thoughts and, trying to hide her embarrassment, begins to explain about eggs, fertilization, Mommy's and Daddy's contributions, etc. After a while, Johnny impatiently demands, "No, Billy came from Toledo. Where did I come from?"

Concrete Operations Period

At about seven or eight years of age the first form of true logic appears, yet it is not the formal logic that the child will eventually exhibit when entering adolescence. Piaget and Inhelder (1969) p. 100) describe the thinking of this period as *concrete* ". . . because they relate directly to objects and not yet to verbally stated hypotheses." Just as object permanence was a key factor in growth from the sensorimotor to the preoperational stage, the attainment of the operation of reversibility is crucial to the logic of the concrete operations stage. *Reversibility* is the ability to reconstruct a previously existing state of affairs, such as solving the conservation problems described earlier. But perhaps the ball of clay problem even better illustrates the transformations that occur in children's thinking from age seven, say, to about eleven.

We have already seen that the early concrete operational child of about seven will conserve amount or substance when the ball is transformed into a sausage. But suppose you now roll the sausage back into the shape of the ball and ask not about substance, but about weight. You could even make a small scale available to the child to ascertain whether the balls weigh the same amount. When the child is satisfied they weigh the same, repeat the transformation of one of the balls into a sausage and ask the same question. Our seven-year-old is likely to respond that because it is longer, the sausage weighs more. A nine-year-old, on the other hand, will judge the sausage and ball to weigh the same and will invoke one or more of the seven-year-old's reasons to justify that judgment.

But there is more. Suppose we repeat the operations once more with the nine-year-old, rolling the sausage back into the shape of the ball. After the nine-year-old judges both the substance (amount) and weight to be the same regardless of transformation, now we ask for a judgment about volume, as in "Which takes up the greater amount of space?" When the two lumps of clay are both in the shape of a ball, the judgment will be that both have the same volume. When rolled into the shape of a sausage, however, the nine-year-old is likely to say that the sausage takes up more space than the ball because it is longer. An eleven-year-old however, will likely judge them to be equal and use one or more of the above arguments as justification.

Thus we see that while conservation is acquired during the concrete operations stage, it is by no means acquired for all concepts simultaneously. But why? Elkind (1971, pp. 51–52) offers the following explanation:

It is only when we test the eleven-year-old that we find a subject who says that neither substance, weight, nor volume is affected by a change in the appearance of the quantity. Since, however, the child at age seven has the explanation for these equalities, why doesn't he use them? Why the delay? The reason is, apparently, that the idea of weight is more closely tied to certain of our actions (such as holding and lifting things) than is the idea of

Stages and Processes of Development 31

Cartoon 2.1.

substance, and it is therefore correspondingly more difficult to overcome this intuitive idea of weight and to think of it objectively. The same holds true for volume, which is tied not only to our actions but to our internal experiences of "fullness" and "emptiness." The delay in the attainment of weight and volume concepts is thus due, not to a lack of the mental ability to think of them objectively, but rather to the difficulty in divorcing these ideas from our subjective experience.

This problem of logic vs. experience continues to operate well into adulthood, as we shall see in other contexts in units 3 and 4.

In addition to solving conservation problems, concrete operations children are able to perform the operations of seriation and classification. Seriation is simply arranging objects according to some characteristic, arranging basketball players by height for example, whereas classification is the grouping of objects by those characteristics. Arranging books on a shelf by several characteristics—first by height then by thickness—would be impossible for most preoperational children because of the tendency to center on one dimension. The concrete operations child could complete this task, but would probably need to physically manipulate the books in order to do it. Reliance upon physical manipulation of objects is the primary characteristic of the concrete operations child. Indeed, even as adults we find many problems much simpler to solve if we can manipulate physical objects or, at least, draw a picture.

The concrete operations child is fond of literal humor, usually with an adult the victim (which may provide a clue as to the level TV situation comedies are written for). Many teachers have fallen into the trap of telling a fifth grader, "Take a seat over there", with the child responding by picking up a chair and carrying it across the room, to the delight of the rest of the class. Teachers' errors, particularly with respect to routine matters, are often met with derisive laughter. The substitute who doesn't know the system for collecting milk money rarely is shown mercy.

This is also the age of magical omnipotence mediated by practical implementation. Concrete skills are developed and practiced in the context of rich fantasy: Rehearsing magic tricks for hours on end, designing and constructing an elaborate fort, practicing with singular dedication for a career as a ballerina, professional baseball player or Olympic ice skater. This is the age in which children master the technological and interpersonal skills of the culture. It is the age of schooling in most cultures, whether that schooling takes place in a formal institution or in a tribal bush school. Because children at the upper levels of this period are quite technically competent, there is a tendency to assume that they understand more than they in fact do. One of the purported failings of the old "New Math" programs, of the late 1970s, was to attempt to teach abstract concepts of set theory symbolically, primarily through the use of Venn diagrams. The main purpose of the new math—to help students to understand abstract mathematical constructs—was lost. More current revisions of the curriculum which introduce concrete objects for students to manipulate have a much better chance of succeeding. One example is the increasing use of Cuisinaire Rods. These are color coded sticks of wood, varying in length to represent fractional parts—two red equal to one blue, for example. Through manipulation of the rods, students are able to get a much more concrete conception of what equivalence of fractions, for example, really means.

Formal Operations Period

Concrete operational children continue to experience and internalize relations among dimensions to allow them, usually around the onset of adolescence, to deemphasize reliance on concrete manipulations. Piaget postulates that a new logic, a logic of propositions, is made possible by the combination of all preceding operations into a systematic whole. This is the age of completion in which all the interlocking parts of intellect finally come together, with full formal reasoning now *possible*.

Though formal propositional logic is now possible, that does not mean it will be universally, or even frequently, applied in all appropriate situations. We shall see how emotional and behavioral factors (as well as drugs and alcohol), can short-circuit reasoning processes, not to mention the effect of specific information and experience in facilitating our use of intellect. And right here in this book, written by an adult for other adults, it seems that a concrete example would facilitate the discussion of what is meant by propositional logic and formal operations. Try to solve the next two problems.

Problem 2.1

You are in a room with two doors, one of which leads to freedom and the other of which leads to death. There are two people present: one who always tells the truth, and one who always lies. You don't know which is which. You may ask one question to learn which is the door to freedom. What one question will tell you the correct door to choose?

Problem 2.2

The Loch Ness monster is said to be 20 meters plus half its own length. How long is it? Neither of these problems is easy to solve—perhaps impossible—in concrete terms, by drawing or manipulating objects. Each is relatively easy if formal propositional logic is employed. Consider the second problem first. It seems to be a trick question with no answer at initial confrontation. But if it is defined as an algebraic problem, you can let x = the total length of the monster and write an algebraic sentence, $x = 20 + 1/2x$. The solution follows directly (if you can do the calculations)[7], but the proposition was primary.

The first problem—a variation on a problem common to lessons on logic—might be attempted by asking one of the two persons which door leads to freedom, but you would still not know who was the truthteller. So you could ask A (one person) which door B (the other) would tell you is the door leading to freedom. If you do, the following possibilities exist:

1. If A is the truthteller, then he will honestly tell you which door B would say, which is a lie.
2. If A is the liar, then he will lie about what B would say, which would be true.

In either case, your problem is solved. Ask A which door B would say leads to freedom and then choose the opposite door.

If you had trouble with one or both of these problems, it does not mean that your development was arrested at the concrete operations stage. Any given type of problem may stump us for all kinds of reasons, as noted above. But developmentally, according to Piaget's theory, adolescents and adults are capable of such reasoning. And the hallmark of this stage is that these mental operations "may be executed from start to finish at a purely symbolic level"

(Brainerd, 1978, p. 205). Thus inductive and deductive reasoning is possible, as is probabilistic logic, arguments of negation and inverse, and so on.

Adolescents also demonstrate an increasing facility with language which, along with their emerging ability to perform abstract operations, allows them to use symbols, metaphors and similes effectively. This is a mixed blessing, however, from some points of view. The adolescent's newfound power of thought frequently causes a leap to extremes in abstraction and ideology. The adolescent uniform—hair style, dress, mannerisms and language patterns—takes on particular significance. Behavior can be infused with symbolic meaning, can be rationalized extensively, and thus frequently is done to excess, whether it involves drinking, smoking, dancing or talking on the telephone.

More could be said about these social-emotional correlates of the formal operations period, but it is better to end this section on the cognitive developmental issues. Piaget considered the reasoning that emerged at adolescence vastly to increase the range of possibilities for thinking. In contrast to the "doom and gloom" prophets which stress adolescent emotional immaturity, he concentrated on their reasoning potential (e.g., Brainerd, 1978). The adolescent's ability to develop sophisticated hypotheses, to test those hypotheses in systematic ways, and to integrate ideas into holistic systems or ideologies creates an opportunity for high level intellectual exploration and discovery across all disciplines. A teaching style which emphasizes only following rules and the memorization of factual information frequently causes the opportunity to be missed.

Some of the specific suggestions that have been made for applying Piagetian theory to classrooms will be described in chapter 4.

Vygotsky's Development of Thought Through Language

Lev Semenovich Vygotsky was born in Russia in 1896. Like Piaget, who was born the same year, Vygotsky's career focused on cognitive development, although he also wrote about special education and learning disabilities (see Rieber & Carton's 1993 collected works). Unlike Piaget, who worked well into his eighties, Vygotsky died of tuberculosis in 1934 at age 38. His contributions were thus made mostly in the ten-year span from 1924–1934.

Despite being over 50 years old, Vygotsky's ideas have become particularly popular in educational research in the 1990's, especially his ideas on (1) the mediation of learning that occurs via social contacts with parents, teachers, and others in a *zone of proximal development*; and (2) the progression of language and thought, which provides a remarkably current and convincing theoretical basis for *metacognitive processes*. The latter refer to consciously monitoring and controlling such cognitive processes as memory, transfer and strategic thinking (see chapter 4).

Consider two issues which from Vygotsky's day to the present continue to be controversial. First, he defended instruction in both grammar and phonetics, despite what some might say are the practical uselessness of both since, as he pointed out, students can pronounce words, conjugate and decline in complete sentences without schooling. Nevertheless, Vygotsky (1963) argued that in learning that the word Moscow consists of separate sounds and that sentences are constructed of component parts, the child ". . . becomes aware of what he is doing and learns to use his skills consciously" (p. 101).

The second issue is that of how best to measure a child's mental development.

Whereas most researchers provide standardized problems which examinees are to solve by themselves, Vygotsky suggested that this measures only part of mental development.

We tried a different approach. Having found that the mental age of two children was, let us say, eight, we gave each of them harder problems than he could manage on his own and provided some slight assistance: the first step in a solution, a leading question, or some other form of help. We discovered that one child could, in co-operation, solve problems designed for twelve- year-olds, while the other could not go beyond problems intended for nine-year-olds. The discrepancy between a child's actual mental age and the level he reaches in solving problems with assistance indicates the zone of his proximal development: in our example, this zone is four for the first child and one for the second . . . Experience has shown that the child with the larger zone of proximal development will do much better in school. This measure gives a more helpful clue than mental age does to the dynamics of intellectual progress. (Vygotsky, 1962, p. 103).

The Zone of Proximal Development

In the above, perhaps first, use of the term zone of proximal development, Vygotsky proposes that the child's current abilities or development level matter less than the child's sensitivity to instruction. But sensitivity to instruction is not a function of development alone, where learning builds on a maturational readiness which teachers should identify and adapt to. Rather, development occurs through a continuing dialectic with the social environment, in which imitation and instructional interaction change the developmental process.[8]

What the child can do in cooperation today he can do alone tomorrow. Therefore the only good kind of instruction is that which marches ahead of development and leads it; it must be aimed not so much at the ripe as at the ripening functions. (Vygotsky, 1962, p. 104).

Thus we see directly the meaning of the zone of proximal development: a time of mental activity in which children cannot be successful on their own but, with the guidance or stimulation from an adult or more advanced peer, can be successful (see also Vygotsky, 1978). Moreover, the amount of assistance needed predicts how close the children are to being capable of independent success. More importantly the assistance provides a model of the kind of thinking that needs to be done, which changes the process of development: in Vygotsky's words (1962, p. 20), . . . the development of thinking is not from the individual to the socialized, but from the social to the individual." Figure 2.3 presents the process on a number line.[9]

In the zone of proximal development, Vygotsky builds on Piaget's notion of the importance of cognitive conflict for intellectual growth, but takes issue with—and may have influenced—Piaget over its necessary social origins. Vygotsky argued that previous researchers (such as Piaget) studied

. . . how speech development or learning arithmetic hinges on a child's natural functions, how it evolves in the process of the child's natural growth, but they did not study the reverse: How language acquisition or arithmetic reshapes the school child's natural functions, tearing away from and crowding out all lines and tendencies in his development. (in Rieber & Carton, 1993, p. 166).

Vygotsky goes on (p. 167) to point out that the developmental process is hardly a maturational unfolding, but is instead a "rupture," "leap," "turning point," or "struggle." In this sense, the zone of proximal development is quite compatible with Erikson's notion of resolving the social-emotional identity crises of school age—namely, mastering culturally important tasks or being considered inferior by

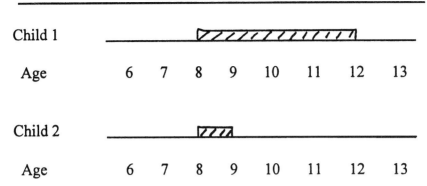

Figure 2.3. Vygotsky's Zone of Proximal Development
Schematic representations of two children, both of Mental Age = 8, with the range of tasks that the children could perform with the help of a more capable person.

self or others (see next section). This view is also compatible with Bandura's notion of the development of self-efficacy in a reciprocally determined negotiation between self and culture (see chapter 1).

What is necessary for healthy development, according to all these views, is not just a facilitative environment, nor easy success with its resultant high grades or praise (in what is commonly but mistakenly assumed to build self-esteem); rather, what is necessary for development is a challenge that is overcome, a difficult task mastered. The challenges that matter most, of course, and the repertoire of skills that can meet those challenges, arise from social interactions. Arranging productive social interactions to facilitate growth are, Vygotsky argues, both the responsibility and the benefit of effective teachers.

Language, Thought and Metacognition

A child of five and a half was drawing a streetcar when the point of his pencil broke. He tried, nevertheless, to finish the circle of a wheel, pressing down on the pencil very hard, but nothing showed on the paper except a deep colorless line. The child muttered to himself,

Photo 2.4. Mediated learning: In a zone?

It's broken," put aside the pencil, took watercolors instead, and began drawing a broken streetcar after an accident . . . (Vygotsky, 1962, p. 17).

According to Vygotsky, the primary function of speech—for both adults and children—is social communication. The earliest speech, therefore, must serve social functions and our common experiences confirm that they do: vocalizing to get attention, to induce a parent to satisfy a need, or to express pleasure or displeasure at what a sibling just did. Eventually such vocal utterances will evolve into *inner speech*, or thought, at which time it is self-controlled and not necessarily social.

In a transitional stage between social speech and inner speech (corresponding roughly to Piaget's preoperational stage) is *egocentric speech,* an example of which is given in the above child's broken pencil experience. Egocentric speech thus marks the onset of thought being able to control behavior. Vygotsky interpreted the above example by saying (p. 17), "The child's accidentally provoked egocentric utterance . . . manifestly affected his activity. . . ."

As children's speech and thought continue to develop—sometimes in parallel, sometimes in unison, sometimes at different rates—they can be observed to talk aloud to themselves while playing in the sandbox with building blocks and the like. As their cognitive abilities develop (into the operational stage), they no longer need the egocentric support of speaking while doing, and thus evolve into thinking. Egocentric speech does not disappear completely, of course, since adults often fall back on talking themselves through a problem that is particularly difficult. Egocentric speech, therefore, may function like counting on our fingers—as a transitional aid while we are learning a more complex method or when we feel overwhelmed (e.g., Good & Brophy, 1990).

Another way of looking at the social-egocentric-inner speech progression is from other-regulation to self-regulation. As Braten (1991) has argued, cognitive self-control is probably the cornerstone of Vygotsky's theory. This is especially evident when Vygotsky's own professional life is placed in the historical perspective that he was trying to return consciousness to a legitimate place in psychology.

Specifically regarding the developing thinker, Vygotsky diagnoses that poor problem solvers are handicapped partly by misunderstanding task demands but, more importantly, by lack of "knowledge of psychological operations" (Vygotsky, 1978, p. 71). Knowledge of how the mind works, how thinking needs to interact differently with easy tasks vs. difficult or multi-step tasks, how to use one's own capacities and limitations in learning, and thus how to exercise control over thinking—all these are central to intellectual development. Furthermore, these have become the major components of what have come to be known as metacognitive processes (e.g., Brown, 1980; Flavell, 1979; Garner & Alexander, 1989).

More will be said about metacognition in chapter 4. What is interesting is how well Vygotsky's 50-year old ideas have become central to current theorizing. To be alliterative, his emphasis on consciousness and control came to be core components in current cognitive constructivism. So, too, did his writings give aid and comfort to those who emphasize the importance of situational contexts for understanding human development, or indeed all of human experience.

Erikson's Theory of Psychosocial Development
by
John R. Dilendik and J. Ronald Gentile

If Piaget and Vygotsky are still the dominant theorists in cognitive development, their counterpart in social-emotional development is Erik Erikson. While Piaget's early life was a preview of his scientific career, Erikson's schooldays in Karlsruhe, Germany were unexceptional. After high school he toured Europe for a year to find himself and bounced around in various art schools until age 25, when a series of serendipitous events led him in the late 1920's to meet Sigmund Freud. Freud invited him to enter psychoanalytic training and, after he finished his internship, he moved to the USA to escape Hitler, who had just come to power. Then, despite the fact that he only had a high school diploma (psychoanalytic training was not done in educational institutions in those days), Harvard Medical School offered him a position in a child guidance clinic (Biehler, 1976). Later, he moved to Yale and, through anthropological contacts there, he went off first to South Dakota to study Sioux Indians and, later, to northern California to study the Yurok Indians. Along with veterans of World War II, who became his clients in therapy, these experiences convinced him that Freud's stages of development were incomplete because they did not adequately account for socio-cultural influences.

Two seminal works by Erikson (*Childhood and Society*, 1963, and *Identity; Youth and Crisis*, 1968) established him as a primary theorist in the area of adolescent development. These books, together with his psychohistorical accounts of famous people[10] demonstrate both Erikson's allegiance to Freud and significant departures from traditional psychoanalytic theory. Erikson's primary focus is on the nature of psycho-social rather than psycho-sexual influences in development, reflecting an appreciation of the importance of the socio-cultural milieu to human growth. Thus Freud's oral stage becomes Erikson's oral sensory stage, or the age of infancy and the mutuality of recognition, and Freud's anal stage becomes Erikson's muscular anal stage, the age of early childhood and the will to be oneself.

The central construct in Erikson's theory is the achievement of *identity*, "a subjective sense of invigorating sameness and continuity" (1968, p. 19). Identity formation is a process of simultaneous self reflection, observation of others and evaluation by others, and is mostly unconscious. One of his key assumptions of growth is called the epigenetic principle: ". . . anything that grows has a *ground plan*, and that out of this ground plan the *parts* arise, each part having its time of special ascendancy, until all parts have arisen to form a *functional whole*" (1968, p. 92; also in 1980, p. 53). Identity formation is a process of differentiation through a series of eight stages which are fixed and hierarchically ordered. Each stage represents a normative crisis or task which the individual must resolve in order to move in healthy fashion through the hierarchy. An individual's uniqueness and style are determined by how he or she resolves the problem presented at each stage; the character of problem resolution is in turn influenced by the socio-cultural milieu in general and parenting practices in particular.

The elements of an individual's personality are being formed through the resolution of these crises throughout an individual's life, but it is in adolescence that the elements coalesce to form a sense of wholeness or self synthesis (or, on the negative side, identity confusion and pathology). Adolescence is the proper time for this to occur for reasons which are largely maturational and cognitive. Erikson notes that it is only in adolescence that the individual is capable of the kind of cognitive complexity and ideological simplicity necessary to ask the question, "Who am I?" and to address the question from personal, social and historical perspectives.

Before describing each stage (see table 2.2), it is well to emphasize the social-learning nature of these crises for the whole family (note the similarities to the view presented in chapter 1). In Erikson's words (1968, p. 96):

A baby's presence exerts a consistent and persistent domination over the outer and inner lives of every member of a household. Because these members must reorient themselves to accommodate his presence, they must grow as individuals and as a group. It is as true to say that babies control and bring up their families as it is to say the converse. A family can bring up a baby only by being brought up by him. His growth consists of a series of challenges to them to serve his newly developing potentialities for social interaction. Each successive step, then, is a potential crisis because of a radical change in perspective. Crisis is used here in a developmental sense to connote not a threat of catastrophe, but a turning point, a crucial period of increased vulnerability and heightened potential, and therefore, the ontogenetic source of generational strength and maladjustment.

Table 2.2. Erikson's stages of psycho-social development.

Stage	Approximate Age	Crisis to Be Resolved	Identity Formulation
Infancy	0–1	Trust vs. Mistrust	"I am what I am given."
Early Childhood	2–3	Autonomy vs. Shame and Doubt	"I am what I will."
Childhood	4–5	Initiative vs. Guilt	"I am what I can imagine I will be."
School Age	6–12	Industry vs. Inferiority	"I am what I learn or can make work."
Puberty and Adolescence	13–Adult	Identity vs. Identity Confusion	"I am the role(s) that I assume."
Young Adulthood		Intimacy vs. Isolation	"We are what we love."
Middle Age		Generativity vs. Stagnation	"I am What (whom) I can teach."
Old Age		Integrity vs. Despair	"I am what survives me."

Infancy and the Mutuality of Recognition

Most of us are fundamentally trusting individuals with a faith in our fellow human beings, in the fundamental goodness of man, in the predictability and reliability of the behavior of those around us, and in the future in general. This basic sense of trust and faith is critical to the survival of the culture, and of the individuals who live within it. We tend to accept faith, trust and predictability as a natural sense of affairs, yet when we consider the complexity and importance of these concepts, they seem a remarkable social invention: the very existence of culture, of religion, of science and technology rest on them. The result of a failure to establish this sense of basic trust is dramatized in infantile schizophrenia. How do we develop this realistic faith in our environment and in ourselves?

Erikson considers the quality of the relationship between mother and infant during the oral-sensory stage to be the cornerstone of an individual's personality; the failure of this relationship, in the extreme, is psychosis. This first stage lasts from birth to about one year of age, and the major crisis or task is resolution of the polarity, basic *trust vs. mistrust*. This polarity reemerges in adolescence to partially determine whether the youth approaches the challenge of becoming an adult in a secure, holistic fashion or, in the other extreme, with a rigid, totalistic attitude which will not permit—more, cannot risk—examination and change.

The basic modality or approach in infancy is incorporation: receiving, taking in, being recognized by others. Successful resolution culminates in trust of the self, of the child's universe, of the future. The social parallel of this age is thus a religious ethos: a fundamental sense of faith and hope. The integration of the successful resolution of the oral stage with all of the following ones results, in adulthood, in a combination of faith and realism. Weaknesses can include addiction, self deception, avariciousness. Erikson variously formulates the sense of recognition by others which comes out of this age as, "I am what hope I have and give" (1968, p. 407) or as "I am what I am given" (1980, p. 87)

Early Childhood and the Will to be Oneself

Between the ages of two and three the child is making rapid gains in muscular maturation, verbalization and differentiation between himself and the world around him. The behavioral modality can be characterized as *holding on and letting go, retention and elimination,* which begins with potty training and extends to other areas of life.[11] This results in the beginning of a sense of choice, and thus to the possibility of autonomy. This possibility frequently leads to a period of stubborn insistence: what parents of young children come to know as the "terrible two's." It is here that mutual regulation between mother and child faces its most trying test, particularly in a technological society in which the ideal is a mechanically trained, faultlessly functioning, clean, punctual, deodorized body (1968, p. 108). Resolution of the task of autonomous will places the child on a continuum from loving good will to hating self insistence.

Accomplishment of a sense of free will involves the development of self control, of separateness from parents, without a loss of self esteem. Failure to develop this sense of self control can result in doubt and shame: shame over your failure and subsequent doubt about your own self worth. This can manifest itself in adulthood in milder forms of impulsiveness or compulsiveness, a manipulative approach to others, or repudiation of and discrimination against those who are different. In its most severe forms, this sense of failure can convert into obsessive-compulsive neuroses. Much of the sense of autonomy which children develop, both in degree and quality, depends on parent modeling: parents must display a sense of dignity and personal independence derived from their own lives.

The social parallel to this age is an ethos of law and order or, in a larger sense, ethics. The courage to be independent individuals choosing and guiding our own futures on the basis

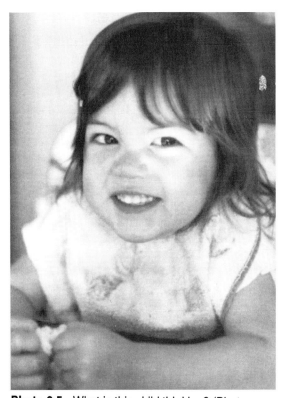

Photo 2.5. What is this child thinking? (Photo Courtesy of Dr. Robert D. Gentile)

of a personally derived ethical system is rooted in the early crisis of *autonomy vs. shame and doubt.* This contribution to future identity formation is formulated by Erikson as, "I am what I will." (1980, p. 87).

Childhood and the Anticipation of Roles

The preschool years are characterized largely by increased mobility or locomotion and the development of facility with the language. These new found skills allow for the possibility of imagination, exploration and curiosity, all of which are related to a sense of initiative. In adolescence and adulthood initiative is the ability to move toward goals, to take action, to get going. The behavioral modality of initiative for

Anecdote 2.1

> ### "In Bed, Dancing"
>
> Despite a developing recognition of sexuality, young children must still perceive the world in terms of their own level of understanding. Consider the following true story:
>
> Young Heather had just been learning to answer the telephone and, when it rang one Sunday morning, she bolted from her room into her parents' bedroom, interrupting their love-making. Since it was grandmother on the line, she carried on a long, animated conversation, which ended with the following interchange:
>
> Grandmother: "What are your parents doing?"
> Heather: "They're in bed, dancing."
>
>

the three to five year old is intrusion: into space by vigorous movement; into the unknown by consuming curiosity; into other people's ears and minds by the aggressive use of the voice; upon or into other bodies by physical attack; by the thought of the phallus intruding into the female body (1968, p. 116).

This last assumption, a rudimentary realization of potential sexuality, is drawn from Freud's formulation of Oedipal conflict[12] during these years. The young child begins to see himself or herself in sexual competition with the same sexed parent, which leads to a sense of incestual intrusion. The inevitable and necessary failure of this rivalry leads to guilt and anxiety, and ushers in the latency period: a sublimation of incestuous wishes into a devoted mastery of the skills of the culture. The crisis to be resolved here is that of *initiative vs. guilt*.

Erikson's name for these preschool years, the locomotor-genital stage, reflects the double emphasis on the psycho-social interplay of freedom of movement and Oedipal constraint. This interplay contributes to a later sexual self image and sex-appropriate initiative characterized by the social modality of "making" or "being on the make" for boys, and "catching" for girls (1968, p. 118). Excessive guilt in response to an early sense of rivalry, particularly with respect to Oedipal rivalry, can result in later conflicts over initiative. This may reflect itself as a lack of initiative or self restriction on the one hand or, through overcompensation, tireless initiative on the other.

Humanity's greatest achievements, highest ideals and most rigid fanaticism are anchored in this age of initiative. The social parallel, then, is the ethos of action. Successful resolution of the crisis of this period gives the child a sense of purpose for adult tasks and the freedom to realize his or her full range of abilities. The identity formulation is, "I am what I can imagine I will be" (1980, p. 87).

School Age and Task Identification

Most cultures, including ours, reserve the period of childhood between the ages of six and eleven for mastery of those skills which will make the individual a productive member of society. The child's sense of initiative, rather diffuse and undirected in the locomotor-genital period, becomes a sense of industry focused on becoming a potential worker, provider, parent.

Those drives which have made the child dream and play become sublimated toward mastery of concrete pursuits.

The primary skills requiring mastery in our culture are the rudimentary technological and information handling skills: reading, writing and arithmetic, as well as the interpersonal skills necessary in a complex society. Failure to master these skills can result in a sense of learned helplessness or inferiority. Thus the crisis to be resolved can be called *industry vs. inferiority*. The diffuse sense of guilt experienced in the previous age becomes more focused as the non-initiating child perceives himself as a failure at the task of becoming an adult. The over-compensating, excessively conforming individual may come to accept his work as the only test of his worthwhileness. The social parallel of this age is the development of a technological ethos, an acceptance of the possibility of differential opportunity. The identity formulation for this age is, "I am what I can learn to make work" (1968, p. 127), or more simply, "I am what I learn" (1980, p. 87).

Again, a cross-cultural perspective provides a context for understanding the severity of the crisis that requirements of universal schooling impose on both adults and children. In non-literate cultures, Erikson points out, children learn much from adults and older children ". . . who become teachers by dint of gift and inclination rather than by appointment" (1963, p. 259). Thus children learn the fundamentals of the culture's technology with hands-on experiences in formal or informal apprenticeships as the children and the culture feel they need, and are ready to learn, those skills. In literate societies with their considerable specializations, on the other hand, children must first be made literate to prepare them for the widest possible range of careers. Erikson (1963, p. 259) continues:

The more confusing specialization becomes, however, the more indistinct are the eventual goals of initiative; and the more complicated social reality, the vaguer are the father's and mother's role in it. School seems to be a culture all by itself, with its own goals and limits, its achievements and disappointments.

If schools were invented to help children become more effective adults, then perhaps literate societies need to reconsider whether they can afford to let any child fail in this developmental task, particularly before the children have had the opportunity to learn in the real world—the society for which schools were invented to prepare the children. More will be said on this later.

Puberty and Adolescence

Through the resolution of the polarity at each earlier stage a particular aspect of identity was shaped. Adolescence provides the coincidence of physiological, cognitive and social maturation necessary to synthesize each of these elements into a whole, at least tentative formation of identity. At this point school and occupational choices loom large, pressing adolescents to act adult—meaning to accept the societal definitions of success—when they are quite unsure of themselves in many ways. Erikson states it this way (1968, p. 132):

Youth after youth, bewildered by the incapacity to assume a role forced on him by the inexorable standardization of American adolescence, runs away in one form or another, dropping out of school, leaving jobs, staying out all night, or withdrawing into bizarre and inaccessible moods. Once "delinquent" his greatest need and often his only salvation is the refusal on the part of older friends, advisors, and judiciary personnel to type him further by pat diagnoses and social judgments which ignore the special dynamic conditions of adolescence.

The high school teacher, of course, is among the most important of these "advisors". Reservation of judgment on the part of teachers is made particularly difficult by the

Photo 2.6. Friendships in Dublin.

fact that implicit (or, in some cases, explicit) in this delinquency is a rejection of the teacher's values and ideals, and a banding together in a rigid stance of intolerance. The task of those who would win adolescents to democratic ideals is to ". . . convincingly demonstrate to them—by living it—that a democratic identity can be strong and yet tolerant, judicious and still determined" (1968, p. 133). For a teacher unsure about his or her own identity, this can be a difficult task, indeed.

The "banding together" is an alternative way of finding an identity. If adolescents are portrayed or portray themselves as losers, because they cannot obtain consistent recognition for achievements valued by society, then they can ironically assume an identity by losing themselves further—that is, by identifying with gangs, cliques, cults, or certain lifestyles. In reacting against perceived discrimination toward them, they ironically can become intolerant of and cruel towards those who are not in their group, including those of different racial, ethnic, or religious backgrounds or even of petty differences in taste, dress, or habits. Erikson (1980, pp. 97–98) cautions us:

> It is important to understand (which does not mean condone or participate in) such intolerance as the necessary defense against a sense of identity confusion, which is unavoidable at a time of life when the body changes its proportions radically, when genital maturing floods body and imagination with all manner of drives, when intimacy with the other sex approaches and is, on occasion, forced on the youngster, and when life lies before one with a variety of conflicting possibilities and choices. Adolescents help one another temporarily through such discomfort by forming cliques and by stereotyping themselves, their ideals, and their enemies.

The basic crisis to be resolved during adolescence has variously been described by Erikson as "identity vs. identity confusion" (1980) or "identity vs. role confusion" (1963). Even in love, the adolescent is struggling to find his or her identity by "projecting one's diffused ego image on another and by seeing it thus reflected and gradually clarified. This is why so much of young love is conversation." (1963, p. 262). Although Erikson did not state a one-line description of this stage, perhaps he would not object to the following identity statement: "I am the role(s) that I assume."

Beyond Identity: Adult Stages

Erikson identifies three stages beyond adolescence and these are marked more by the milestones or circumstances of life—e.g., marriage or children—than they are by age. He tells the story of the answer Freud once gave to a question about what normal people should be able to do well: "to love and to work" (Erikson, 1968, p. 136). This seemingly simple answer profoundly captures the tasks of identity development through adult life.

Young Adulthood

Once people are comfortable with their identities, they are ready to go beyond identity to intimacy. This implies a sharing, or fusing, of identities with another person in a long-term "mutual psychosocial intimacy," which in some ways allows the abandoning of "me" to become "we." Erikson is clear that while sexual intimacy is part of this process, it is only one part of the whole relationship.

Many people seek this interpersonal relationship through promiscuous intimate acts, but much of this is characterized by Erikson (1963, p. 164) as a kind of "genital combat," in which each partner is really trying to find his or her own sexual identity. Thus it is continuation of the adolescent identity search. Continual promiscuity can become ritualized, but eventually leads to a deep sense of isolation. This, then, is the developmental crisis of young adulthood: *intimacy vs. isolation.*

While sexuality is an integral part of this crisis, recall that Freud coupled love with work. What is needed in this stage is a balance of the person's identity through achievements in the world with the opportunity to share and care deeply with someone else. Optimal resolution of the genital conflicts of adolescence involves the following, which Erikson (1963, p. 266) calls the "utopia of genitality:"

1. mutuality of orgasm
2. with a loved partner
3. of the other sex
4. with whom one is able and willing to share a mutual trust
5. and with whom one is able and willing to regulate the cycles of
   a. work
   b. procreation
   c. recreation
6. so as to secure to the offspring, too, all the stages of a satisfactory development.

This is truly a utopian vision, but may be a kind of internalized ideal against which people compare their current lives. When their lives do not measure up, they feel isolated and begin anew the search for intimacy. The identity statement that Erikson suggests for this developmental period, then, is "we are what we love" (1968, p. 138).

Middle Age

In the emphasis adults place on the dependency of children and their need for proper education and guidance, it is easy to overlook the reciprocal of that. This is that *humans have evolved to be teachers as well as learners.* Thus adults need to have children to teach and care for as much as children need to have teachers and providers. Erikson (1963, pp. 266–267) put it this way: "Mature man needs to be needed, and maturity needs guidance as well as encouragement from what has been produced and must be taken care of."

When adults progress through the stages of identity formation to the point of solving, at least in part, the problems of love and work, then they are faced with the *generativity vs. stagnation* problem. Generativity is the concern for teaching the next generation, including your own offspring or those of others. It therefore includes professions, like teaching, in which the guidance of young people is the primary concern. But it also includes less formal teaching, such as helping of all sorts.

Erikson does not assume, however, that just because people have, or even want children, they have achieved generativity. If they have not resolved the problems of the earlier stages, they may be trying to achieve through a relationship with a child what they failed at achieving with another adult. The same problem may occur in choice of profession: teachers, ministers, or the like can achieve generativity through their work. But if they have not resolved their own psychosexual identity and intimacy problems, they may do more harm than good. In the extreme, such adults feel stagnated, bored and personally unfulfilled, both at home and work, and may even have lost a "belief in the species, which would make a child appear to be a welcome trust of the community" (1980, pp. 103–104).

Although Erikson wrote no identity statement for this stage, perhaps he would accept the following: "I am what (whom) I can teach."

Old Age

In *Childhood and Society* (p. 269), Erikson concludes the eighth and final stage by linking it to the first: ". . . healthy children will not fear life if their elders have integrity enough not to fear death." In this provocative statement we are led to see, once again, the mutual interdependence among the generations for the satisfactory resolution of the crises at each stage. We also see the lifeline of identity that runs from the earliest developmental task, learning to trust, to the last, acquiring ego integrity.

The extremes of the continuum for this last stage are labeled *ego integrity vs despair*. The former is described by Erikson as the ripened fruit of successfully negotiating the previous seven stages. It is beyond identity, self-love, and the need to prove oneself, even as a teacher to others. Ego integrity implies contentment and acceptance of one's life as having been worthwhile and, indeed, even necessarily lived the way it was. It means acceptance of people, despite imperfections, for their own integrity—one's own parents or people of different cultures, for example. Once the past has been so forgiven and ordered, the present and future—even death—can be faced without fear.

The opposite extreme, despair, arises from unfulfilled expectations of previous stages, of the knowledge that time is too short or, in Robert Frost's image, knowledge that I have "miles to go before I sleep." The many regrets are not able to be overcome: if only I had done . . . . But I am too old to do that, and anyway time is too short.

To the extent that people have earned ego integrity, they have a legacy of a life well-lived, a meaningful existence. This, better than any legacy of possessions, contributes to the very cultural institutions and interpersonal relations from which it had taken sustenance. In this sense, Erikson states the identity crisis as, "I am what survives me" (1968, p. 141).

Photo 2.7. Growing old gracefully in China.

Kohlberg's Stages of Moral Development

Piaget's and Vygotsky's cognitive stages and Erikson's psycho-social stages are concerned with different domains of life and yet can be seen as parallel and somewhat overlapping developmental processes. Another domain which overlaps with all of those is the area of moral/ethical development. This topic was, in fact, a major area of study for Piaget and, among other findings, he reported that younger children do not consider apparent motives or intent in judging how good or bad an event or behavior is. For instance, when asked, "Which is worse: a child who accidentally breaks five cups or deliberately breaks one cup?" young children judge the accident worse because of the greater amount of damage (Flavell, 1963). Similarly, a deliberate lie which has no apparent immediately bad consequences is judged not as bad as an unintentional statement that hurts someone's feelings.

Lawrence Kohlberg (1963) and his colleagues took up the challenge to study these issues further. Like Piaget, they distinguish between the *content* of moral judgment (lying, breaking cups, etc.) and the *structure* of the judgments (kind of reasoning, organization of knowledge). It is the structure of those judgments which demonstrates regularity through developmental stages. They obtained evidence on this by interviewing children on a number of hypothetical moral dilemmas, varying in content. Variations on two of those problems are described below:

1. Joe's father promised Joe that if he earned the money, he could go to camp. Joe did earn the money, but later his father needed the money and asked Joe to give it to him. Among other variations of questions, were the following: Should Joe give his father the money? Why or why not?
2. Heinz's wife was very ill and needed a certain drug to stay alive. The druggist, who was the only source of that drug in Heinz's community, charged an exorbitant price for the drug and Heinz could not afford to pay for the drug. So he stole the drug. Is it right for Heinz to steal the drug? Why or why not?

In responding to these dilemmas, the interviewee is probed by the interviewer to elicit the most morally defensible position of which the person is capable. These answers are scored according to a set of published guidelines (Colby and Kohlberg, 1987, Volumes I and II) which classify the moral reasoning into one of six possible stages in three levels of development. These levels and stages are described briefly below and illustrated via Joe's and Heinz's moral dilemmas problems in table 2.3.

The first level of moral development is labeled *preconventional* to emphasize that it usually occurs developmentally before the child has internalized society's standards. Children at this level determine right or wrong on the

Cartoon 2.2.

basis of the consequences for them personally. "Joe should give the money or his father will spank him," reasons the stage 1 child. By stage 2, the reasoning becomes more complex, though still based on personal interest: "Joe should keep the money he earned; his father should earn his own money."

The second level is labeled *conventional* morality by Kohlberg et al. to emphasize the child's socialization—that is, the adoption of society's norms and laws. By stage 3, then, Joe's father can be seen to be selfish and not living by the Golden Rule. Stage 4 children go beyond this to argue that Joe and his father had an agreement or contract, violations of which cannot be allowed without undermining the family or, indeed, all of society.

The third level, called *postconventional* or *principled* morality, emphasizes rights that may transcend laws or efficient societal functioning and become higher goals for the common good. Personal conscience dictates. Thus stage 5 individuals would see the agreement between Joe and father as needed in order to protect the

Table 2.3. Illustrations of Kohlberg's stages of moral development.

Level	Stage	What Is Right	Reasons for Doing Right	Examples
1. Preconventional	1. Heteronomous Morality	Avoid breaking rules or causing physical damage to persons or property; obedience for its own sake	Avoidance of punishment from superiors	Joe should give the money because he's older and it's his father. Taking the drug is wrong because you're not supposed to steal.
	2. Individualistic, Instrumental Morality	People acting to meet their own interests; what is fair or agreed to by all.	To serve your own interests and let others do the same; relativity of rights	Joe should not give the money; He earned it; his father should earn his own money. Wife needs the drug to stay alive so it's OK to steal it.
2. Conventional	3. Interpersonally Normative Morality	"Be good" with good motives, showing concern for others, being loyal and trustworthy	The Golden Rule; caring for others	Joe should not give the money; it is selfish for father to even ask for it. Husband did what most humans would do; has a duty to save his wife's life.
	4. Social System Morality	Fulfilling agreements, upholding laws (unless they conflict with other societal rights), enhancing the group or society	To meet demands of conscience or avoid the anarchy involved "if everyone did it"	Joe's father is violating a promise and undermining the functioning of the family so he should not get the money.

	Stage	Principles	Purpose	Example
3. Postconventional or Principled	5. Human Rights and Social Welfare Morality	The right to life and liberty, protection of minorities from the tyranny of the majority	To create a better society, based on cooperation, agreement and protection of the rights of all (even unpopular people or groups), greatest good for greatest number.	Stealing the drug is all right because the druggist has no right to exploit people by charging that much. Father has no right to the money because a promise is a sacred pact not to be broken. Heinz should steal the drug because the right to life transcends the right to property.
	6. Universal Ethical Principles	Self-chosen ethical principles based on equality of human rights and respect for dignity of individuals; reversibility of roles and perspectives.	To create a rational set of principles which would make all parties to a claim take the other's point of view before a balanced decision could be reached; true "blind justice."	Both parties are involved in conflicts: (1) Joe between his own goal and helping father; father between honoring an agreement and needing money (presumably for a good cause). (2) Heinz between obeying a law and keeping his wife alive; druggist between making a living in capitalistic society and saving a human. Some cooperative agreement should be possible.

weak from being trampled by more powerful interests. By stage 6, the individual can appreciate the complexities of the situation in regard to the pressures or contexts leading each of the parties to behave as they do. The expectation is that some cooperative agreement, based perhaps on a larger common goal, is possible.

Colby and Kohlberg (1987a) argue that their approach to moral development is phenomenological, structural, and constructivist. It is phenomenological in that it interprets the judgments from the person's own viewpoint and life space. It is structural in that it interprets the reasoning in terms of the form, patterns, and relations among moral knowledge and suggested actions across a wide variety of content areas. Their approach is constructivist in that the individuals are asked to create and recreate their own reality. Each creation, of course, is a function of the child's developmental level and present schemata. Thus it is assumed that individuals will pass through the stages in order and without skipping any stage, though not all individuals will attain the last stages.

The Kohlberg approach also assumes, as mentioned above, that the interviewees will always try to present the highest level of moral reasoning of which they are capable, if only to conform to their view of what is socially desirable (e.g., what does this interviewer want me to say?). Thus they make a distinction between *competence* and *performance,* because it is well known that people often *act* in ways that are "less moral" than the morality they preach. Thus the relationship between beliefs and behaviors is quite complicated: beliefs sometimes determine behavior, behavior sometimes forms the basis for the beliefs we hold, and sometimes the correlation between them seems obscure. Colby and Kohlberg (1987a, p. 2) put it this way:

> *This is not to say that people always do what they think is right. The relation of moral judgment and conduct is complex and incompletely understood. No doubt the causality is bidirectional: Our overt behavior can influence our moral beliefs just as our moral beliefs can influence the course of our behavior.*

Whatever the direction of causality at any given time, they argue, measures of moral judgment are an integral component of a person's moral conduct.

So far so good. Or is it? As Carol Gilligan (1982) argued, Kohlberg's stages are too narrow, reflecting a mostly masculine sense of morality. Thus stages 5 and 6 which emphasize individual rights and objective, fair resolution to moral dilemmas arise from boys' socialization that includes competitive games and incessant arguing over rules. Girls' socialization, in contrast, includes learning to abandon a game or change rules, among other things, to maintain relationships and leads to "a different voice" at mature morality—namely, a conception of responsibility; of being concerned about the people you haven't helped, but could or should; about the conflicts which remain despite our best efforts at objective, fair resolutions.

In her highly influential book, *In a Different Voice,* Gilligan (1982) analyzes the responses of two eleven-year-olds, Jake and Amy, to problem #2 above. She concludes that the question is interpreted differently (p. 31):

Jake's interpretation: "*Should* Heinz steal the drug?"

Amy's interpretation: "Should Heinz *steal* the drug?"

The male interpretation leads to concern with breaking the law, the judge's decision of leniency, and the logical problems inherent in the clash between two good laws: don't steal and don't kill. The female interpretation asks why Heinz and the druggist cannot find a way to work this problem out so that stealing doesn't even have to be considered. In Gilligan's words,

> *Thus in Heinz's dilemma these two children see two very different moral problems—Jake a conflict between life and property that can be*

resolved by logical deduction, Amy a fracture of human relationship that must be mended with its own thread. (p. 31)

Is there a *correct* interpretation? I doubt it, and therein lies the problem with Kohlberg's theory: in placing these stages in linear order and studying only males—and, one might add, western males—the stages might be increasingly cognitively complex, but it is by no means certain that they reach the highest levels of morality. We shall encounter more of these issues in the allegory at the end of this chapter and in the distinctly feminine (in my opinion) "conflict resolution" procedures recommended in chapter 8.

Maslow's Hierarchy of Needs Theory

In 1954 (revised, 1970) Abraham Maslow published a book entitled, *Motivation and Personality*, which became a central treatise in the humanist approach to psychology. Maslow was attempting to provide a holistic and general theory of motivation that would account for developmental phenomena, as well as for a wide variety of physiological, behavioral and psychopathological findings. His *hierarchy of needs* can loosely be considered to be stages through which people progress, but perhaps it is better conceived as a pyramid in which satisfaction of a more basic need is necessary for a higher need to appear. Figure 2.3 portrays the hierarchy of needs in this pyramidal fashion.

At the base of the hierarchy are *physiological needs*. While these can be specified in great detail, as in the need for calcium or a homeostatic imbalance on insulin, Maslow believes it is more fruitful to consider them more holistically as hunger, thirst, the need for air, and so on. Physiological needs are the most prepotent, in the sense that human beings who are missing everything in life—food, safety, love

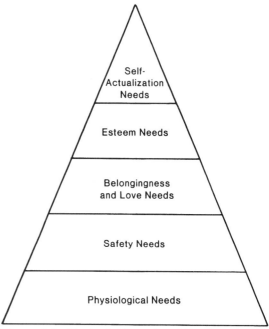

Figure 2.4. Maslow's Hierarchy of Needs.

Photo 2.8. An Irish school lunch. You've got to eat to be ready to learn.

and esteem—will spend all of their time trying to obtain enough food. Dangerously food-deprived persons think, dream, perceive and want only food. If granted one wish, they would want only to be guaranteed food for the rest of their life and would feel sure that that would make them happy.

Anecdote 2.2

The New York Times reported on August 1, 1988, that Sister Christina Tan, a nun who works with poor people in a Manilla slum, said the following:

I had thought freedom was more important to people than rice, but it isn't. Rice is more important. These people just want to survive, survive, survive.

Apparently the people of whom she was speaking were trying to satisfy physiological needs, while she was motivated at some higher level (perhaps belongingness and love?).

Most people in the world, fortunately, have not experienced such deprivation. When an American teenage boy speaks of being famished, for example, he means he hasn't eaten for hours. For people whose physiological needs are regularly satiated except for an occasional emergency, it is difficult to be empathetic with those whose every thought and action is trying to stave off starvation (see anecdote 2.2 for an example).

When humans have sufficient bread, then they do not live by bread alone. They move up the hierarchy of needs and concern themselves with what Maslow calls the *safety* needs. Again, in civilized societies these needs occur most often in emergencies—during crime waves, wars, disease epidemics, fires, tornadoes, floods, etc. Safety needs can dominate during less extraordinary times for preschool children in reactions to strangers, fear of being dropped or abandoned, and emotional reactions to changes of routine. In older children and adolescents—and even adults—safety needs become paramount during parental separation and divorce, when there is bullying or coercion among the peer group or gangs, and the like. Whenever people *perceive* their schools or surrounding communities as unsafe, then (1) it is difficult to achieve academic goals, which come later in the hierarchy of needs; and (2) the tensions and fears that pervade daily life can also be associated with school, teachers, and subjects (as we shall see in more detail in chapter 5).

When both physiological and safety needs have been generally satisfied, then *belongingness and love needs* emerge. Maslow (1954, p. 89) gave the following example:

Now the person will feel keenly, as never before, the absence of friends, or a sweetheart, or a wife, or children. He will hunger for affectionate relations with people in general, namely, for a place in his group . . . He will want to attain such a place more than anything in the world and may even forget that once, when he was hungry, he sneered at love as unreal or unnecessary or unimportant.

If you have ever traveled abroad to a country in which only a few people speak your language, you can relate to this need to belong. You may find yourself wanting to talk to strangers from your native land, even though you would have ignored these same people in your own city. Immigrants in our country and schools find many of these needs surfacing. Even when the environment is safe, there is a discomfort in being "different," and thus there is a satisfaction that comes from forming an ethnic subcommunity, clique, or gang. Note the similarity of this process to Erikson's puberty-adolescence stage.

The love part of this level of needs is not to be equated with sex, as Maslow reminds us. Sexual behavior, like other behavior, has multiple motivations. On one level it can be studied as a purely physiological need. Usually, however, sexual behavior arises as one way of satisfying the love and belongingness needs. Maslow stresses, that it is necessary both to *give* and *receive* love to satiate these needs.

The *esteem needs* arise once a person is adequately loved and loving. One part of this esteem concerns prestige, status, recognition and appreciation bestowed on us by others. This would seem to be a natural extension of belongingness. A second part concerns self-esteem, self-concept, and self-respect, which flows from achievement, mastery and competence, confidence, and independence. A person who, though a member of a group, is not respected by them or by himself/herself will continually strive to attain such esteem, often in counterproductive ways. As we shall discover in the chapter on discipline, many children act inappropriately in schools because their esteem needs are being frustrated (e.g., see Glasser's reality therapy approach in chapter 8). This can occur because they do not understand what is being covered in class and/or because they are being ridiculed by teachers or students. Developmentally, such people will not be able to go beyond this stage until they receive *deserved* respect from themselves and others.

Persons for whom all of the more basic needs are satisfied will discover other needs, which Maslow terms *self-actualization needs*. Poets must write poetry, artists must paint, musicians must make music, etc. Each person will strive to fulfill his or her capabilities. At this level is where individual differences in talent and potential are given expression. Some people will have desires to know and understand. Some will have powerful aesthetic needs—cravings for beauty and peacefulness. Self-actualized persons, in general, are happy people. Comfortable with themselves

Photo 2.9. Self-actualized great grandparents can help, too.

and with others, they are free to be spontaneous, to explore other points of view, and to continue learning. They are mostly nondefensive and lacking in jealousy.

Having presented the hierarchy, a few general statements are warranted. First, Maslow did not expect the hierarchy to be rigid, neither in the sense that a more basic need has to be 100% satisfied before a higher need is addressed, nor in the sense that concern with higher needs precludes the emergence of lower needs. He gave the example that it is likely that average citizens in the USA might at any time have satisfied perhaps 85% of their physiological needs, 70% of safety needs, 50% of love needs, 40% of esteem needs, and 10% of self-actualization needs. As the fulfillment of the lower needs approach 100%, the higher needs can, too. Conversely, a person could not have the percentages reversed (i.e., 85% self-actualization, 75% esteem, . . . 10% physiological).

Second, Maslow argued that most behavior has multiple determinants (some of which may even arise from factors other than motivation; he gives an example of simple associations). The hierarchy of needs does not imply that any behavior is motivated only from one level. Sexual behavior, as already noted, may arise from a physiological need, from a feeling of being safe with the sexual person, from feelings of love or belongingness, from feelings of competence or respect earned from being a good lover, from self-actualizations of being able to express ourselves physically and emotionally, or from any combination of the above. Third, although the hierarchical order is normative for a population, Maslow found many individuals who reverse two or more of the levels. Examples are those individuals who place esteem needs before love and belongingness, or those for whom a cause is so important that they are willing to die for it.

Finally, it is important to note that Maslow boldly suggested that people whose needs are thwarted are "sick" or "less than fully human." Using sick in this way, he asks us to consider whether a lack of love is any less serious than a lack of vitamins. Similarly, being chronically frustrated at any of the levels of the hierarchy is equivalent to having a chronic medical disease in the sense that a satisfactory treatment is desperately needed. Furthermore, he argues that this is a developmental process. Interventions for individuals whose early history was one of frustration of basic needs will be extremely difficult. People who have learned to satisfy their basic needs, to become secure and competent in their early years, will tend to remain secure and competent later despite considerable threats. We shall see evidence for this point in a later chapter in a discussion of learned helplessness.

Stages of Development: An Allegory

In 1884 Edwin Abbott wrote a classic piece of literature, based on geometry and the psychology of perception, which also managed to satirize the conventions of society and the human condition. He did this by introducing us to a resident of *Flatland* (see Abbott, 1952) who, as the title suggests, lives in a two-dimensional world, not of cubes, pyramids and spheres, but of squares, triangles and circles. The Flatlander tries to give Spacelanders perspective on his world by having us place a penny on a table. Viewing from above—that is, from three-dimensional space—the penny appears as a circle.

> But now, drawing back to the edge of the table, gradually lower your eye (thus bringing yourself more and more into the condition of the inhabitants of Flatland), and you will find the penny becoming more and more oval to your view; and at last when you have placed your eye exactly on the edge of the table (so that you are, as it were, a Flatlander) the penny will then have ceased to appear oval at all, and will have become, so far as you can see, a straight line. (p. 4)

The residents of Flatland evolved a rather complex social structure, in which status was determined by complexity and perfectness of shape (so that, for example, pentagons were of higher social status than squares who, in turn, were higher than triangles or straight lines). I shall have to leave you to discover those features for yourself, including how Flatlanders learn to recognize the various shapes despite their straight-line appearance.

Difficult as it may be for us Spacelanders to understand Flatlanders, imagine the difficulty you would have as a Flatlander recognizing that a third dimension could even exist, let alone understanding what life would be like in three dimensions. For example, if a sphere passed through your place of existence, you would see it as a circle growing larger, then growing smaller until it vanished, miraculously, into thin air.

Abbot's Flatland narrator, a square, was visited by a spaceland alien, a Sphere, who whisked him into Space and showed him his own two-dimensional world from above. It was a frightening experience:

> *An unspeakable horror seized me. There was a darkness; then a dizzy, sickening sensation of sight that was not like seeing; Space that was not Space: I was myself and not myself. When I could find voice, I shrieked aloud in agony, "Either this is madness or it is Hell." "It is neither," calmly replied the voice of the Sphere, "it is knowledge; it is Three Dimensions: open your eye once again and try to look steadily." (p. 80)*

Eventually our Flatlander came to understand that there really was a three-dimensional world, though he could not yet understand how it worked. But then imagine the difficulty—even heresy—of his trying to pass this knowledge on to the citizens of the Flatland plane. Again, I leave you to read the book to follow these trials and tribulations.

The Flatlander was indeed convinced by his Spaceland mentor, whom he took to be the ultimate in open-mindedness, if not omniscience. So he restructured his knowledge and experience to allow for this third dimension and for the mathematical and logical analogies to dimensions beyond three. And he requested his mentor, the Sphere, to take him to the fourth dimension, in the following exchange (pp. 88–89):

Square: But my Lord has shown me the intestines of all my countrymen in the Land of Two Dimensions by taking me with him into the Land of Three. What therefore more easy than now to take his servant on a second journey into the blessed region of the Fourth Dimension, where I shall look down with him once more upon this land of Three Dimensions, and see the inside of every three-dimensioned house, the secrets of the solid earth, the treasures of the mines in Spaceland, and the intestines of every solid living creature, even of the noble and adorable Spheres.

Sphere: But where is this land of Four Dimensions?

Square: I know not: but doubtless my Teacher knows.

Sphere: Not I. There is no such land. The very idea of it is utterly inconceivable.

The Flatlander could hardly believe his ear. He tenaciously went on (pp. 90 91):

Square: I ask therefore, is it, or is it not, the fact, that ere now your countrymen also have witnessed the descent of Beings of a higher order than their own, entered closed rooms, even as your Lordship entered mine, without the opening of doors or windows, and appearing and vanishing at will? . . .

Sphere: It is reported so. But men are divided in opinion as to the facts. And even granting the facts, they explain them in different ways. And in any case, however great may be the number of different explanations, no one has adopted or suggested the theory of a Fourth Dimension. Therefore pray have done with this trifling, and let us return to business.

Perhaps several related morals can be drawn from this mind-bending tale which are relevant to stages of development:

1. At any given stage of development, it is difficult to understand why people at a prior, subordinate stage are so dense as not to see things as we do.
2. At any given stage of development, it is nevertheless easier to take the perspective of those at a subordinate stage than it is for those at a subordinate stage to assume the perspective of those at a superordinate stage.
3. At whatever level a society defines its highest stage, the people at that level will find any higher stage utterly inconceivable (and perhaps treasonable).

Development: Discrete Stages or Continuous Growth?

Although Abbott's *Flatland* was not written to be a developmental stage theory, it in many ways describes a perfect prototype of what such a theory should be. Each new stage of development is marked by a distinct qualitative shift in functioning from that of the previous stage. Thus when a girl of age 9 is challenged on her correct reasoning to the conservation of liquids problem—saying, for example, that the water poured from a wider glass into a thinner glass just looks to be more because of the thinner glass—she cannot understand how a younger child could possibly believe the amount had changed. Bruner, Goodnow and Austin (1965, p. 50) put it this way:

> *It is curiously difficult to recapture preconceptual innocence. Having learned a new language, it is almost impossible to recall the undifferentiated flow of voiced sounds that one heard before one learned to sort the flow into words and phrases. Having mastered the distinction between odd and even numbers, it is a feat to remember what it was like in a mental world where there was no such distinction. In short, the attainment of a concept has about it something of a quantal character. It is as if the mastery of a conceptual distinction were able to mask the preconceptual memory of the things now distinguished.*

Unfortunately, such anecdotes and their seeming all-or-none quantum leap explanations obscure many less visible aspects of a person's developmental process and overestimate the abruptness of the change. Two other facts need to be noted in this regard. At any given time, there is a large proportion of the population who fall between the cracks, as it were, and are classified as being "Intermediate" to the stages. Group data, in other words, often appear as a continuous distribution, if not a normal curve. From the individual point of view, the stages are likewise seldom so distinct. Individuals often take two steps forward and one back, figuratively speaking, so that their new behavior is often not that qualitatively different from the old behavior. Thus for the nine-year-old girl to reach the certainty of conservation of liquids described above, she may for a time vacillate between conserving and nonconserving rationales. Similarly, inner speech may revert to egocentric speech (as Vygotsky argued), particularly when people feel overwhelmed by a challenging task. Thus each stage is often said to have a preparation phase and an achievement phase. New structures characteristic of a new stage appear irregularly in the preparation phase and are consolidated in the achievement phase. These achievements then serve as preparation for the next stage (Brainerd, 1978).

Perhaps a better view of stage theories, then, is that a new stage may, in general, describe a level of functioning qualitatively distinct from the previous stage, but that the new set of skills and organized knowledge that characterizes that stage, may have resulted from years of gradual learning and practice.

Developmental Stages: The Norm Is not a Standard

Another problem that arises in interpreting developmental data concerns age or stage norms. The easiest way to make the point is to describe a common phenomenon regarding TV weather reports. The reporter typically presents the current temperature and then gives such other facts as the average daily temperature on this date. So far so good. Then the reporter often says something like, "The temperature is certainly not what it should be," if it is worse than people would prefer it to be. But the median or mean temperature is not a description of what *should* be; it is simply a measure of what has been.

With developmental data we make the same error when we ask the pediatrician how much our baby should weigh at a certain age. Pediatricians make a more severe error if they look at a normative growth chart and tell you that "a child of this age *should* weigh X." The chart simply tells the median or mean weight of a normative sample of children at a certain age. The absurdity of the "should" can be seen if you look at an actuarial table on proportion of people who live to certain ripe old ages. If, for example, fewer than 50% of people live to see the age of 75, does that mean that a 75-year-old who is alive and well *should be dead?*

This error is ubiquitous in interpreting age norms in school performance: a third-grade child who is reading at a second grade level may be slower in learning to read than his classmates, but it is statistically, logically and psychologically incorrect to say that he *should* be reading at the third grade level. Likewise, it would be incorrect to treat the kind of thinking that is typical of a particular developmental stage to be a standard for all to attain by a given age, or perhaps ever.

Using age or stage norms as standards has two difficulties: (1) carrying a stigma for those who are shorter, slower, or in some other way less than the average; and (2) providing such a low standard that many who could go much beyond it may not. The Spaceland Sphere exemplified the latter problem: although he had mastered three-dimensions, he could not

Cartoon 2.3.

imagine a four-dimensional world. A similar argument has been made about Kohlberg's last stage of moral reasoning—namely, beyond it lies a level of moral *responsibility* which includes (1) a belief that what *ought* to be done *can* be done, and (2) a moral passion which motivates people to create the conditions under which moral behavior is more likely (Gruber, 1985). Added to these issues of stage theories of development, then, we also need to ask ourselves whether there are some forms of behavior or reasoning that are beyond even the last known stages.

Practice Exercises

A. **Practice Items** (Answers are in Note 13) For items 1–7 match the following Piagetian terms with their appropriate definitions (or examples) by placing the letter of the term in the space provided. A term may be used once, more than once, or not at all.

   a. development
   b. maturation
   c. experience
   d. social transmission
   e. equilibration
   f. assimilation
   g. accommodation
   h. decentration
   i. conservation
   j. object permanence
   k. schema

_____ 1. The fact that children achieve such concepts as classification and conservation at different ages in different cultures is seen as due to _____.

_____ 2. The best synonym for knowledge structure or action sequence is _____.

_____ 3. The component of the homeostatic self-regulation system which involves modification of current schematic structures to incorporate new facts or principles.

_____ 4. A child discovers the principle that height and width of a glass operate independently to determine the amount of a liquid.

_____ 5. Learning in the broad sense of acquiring general thought patterns is called _____.

_____ 6. A little girl is shown two rows of blocks spread out to be of equal length. The second row is then spread out further. When the child is then asked which row has more blocks, she answers "They're the same."

_____ 7. A rattle has been hidden from Elizabeth's view behind a pillow underneath a blanket. She searches vigorously for it with extreme joy in finding it.

For items 8–10 circle the alternative choice which *best* answers the question.

8. Piaget believed the following concerning the effects of the environment on development:
   a. Development can be accelerated or retarded, although the order of the stages cannot be changed.
   b. Development can be retarded but cannot be accelerated, nor can the order of the stages be changed.
   c. Development can be accelerated or retarded, and the order of the stages can be altered.
   d. Development is little affected, either in rate or order of stages.

9. According to Piaget's theory, the equilibration process occurs during
   a. the preoperational stage.
   b. the transition between concrete and formal operations.
   c. both a and b.
   d. none of the above.

10. Phil can usually solve abstract reasoning problems, but sometimes still cannot solve them without some physical representation or drawing of the problem. Phil is in Piaget's _____ stage of development.
    a. sensorimotor
    b. preoperational
    c. concrete operations
    d. formal operations

11. Which of the following is the best illustration of Vygotsky's zone of proximal development?
    a. Maria can solve twice as many problems in the same time as Carlos.
    b. Boris can solve problems that are two years beyond his normal capacity with help from the teacher.
    c. Natasha can solve problems that are two years beyond the norm of her age group.
    d. Francis learns much faster in one-on-one instruction, than from either lectures or small group instruction.

12. Vygotsky's theory of speech development suggests that
   a. thought emerges after children reach the inner speech stage.
   b. adult-mediated learning helps move the child from egocentric to social speech.
   c. talking to themselves is how children learn cognitive self-control.
   d. all of the above are true.

For items 13–17 match the following Eriksonian stages with the corresponding crises by placing the letter of the stage on the space provided.

   a. infancy
   b. early childhood
   c. preschool age childhood
   d. elementary school age
   e. puberty and adolescence
   f. young adulthood
   g. middle age
   h. old age

_____13. Erikson argues that humans have evolved to teach as well as to learn. At this stage taking care of and teaching people can become a major force.

_____14. "I am the roles that I assume"— a crisis of finding who I am by what I live—takes on primary importance at this stage.

_____15. People in this stage of psychosocial development often paradoxically find their identities by joining groups or react to discrimination by discriminating.

_____16. Basic trust in the reliability and predictability of life and fellow human beings is learned at this stage.

_____17. A concern for what might have been illustrates at this stage inadequate resolution of identity crises.

For items 18–22 match the following of Kohlberg's levels of moral development with the corresponding examples by placing the letter of the stage on the space provided.

　　a. preconventional
　　b. conventional
　　c. postconventional (principled)

_____18. Martin is asked what it means to "Do unto others as you would have them do unto you." He answers "If they hit you, you should hit them back."

_____19. Merle does what her mother wants to avoid getting punished.

_____20. Charles has two friends who are fighting over the writing of a script for a school play. He convinces them to each compromise a little for the benefit of the larger goal.

_____21. When Sharon was asked why it is wrong for people to litter, she said "Well, it's against the law and if everyone did it, the whole country would be a mess."

_____22. Personal conscience emerges in this level of Kohlberg's moral reasoning.

For items 23–27 circle the alternative choice which *best* answers the question.

23. Kohlberg expects that
　　a. by age 18–20 almost all individuals of normal intelligence will have attained his stage 6.
　　b. the moral dilemmas usually elicit a level of moral reasoning one or two steps lower than the interviewee is capable of.
　　c. individuals pass through successive stages in order without skipping any.
　　d. all of the above are true.

24. The relationship between moral beliefs and behavior, according to Kohlberg's theory, is as follows:
　　a. People act in accordance with their beliefs.
　　b. The causality is bi-directional: our behavior influences our beliefs which, in turn, influence our subsequent behavior.
　　c. People's beliefs are formed by the behavior they see reinforced by their culture.
　　d. There is no relationship: people state their beliefs but as often as not do something completely different.

25. According to Maslow's theory,
　　a. some behaviors occur without motivation.
　　b. most behavior is motivated by more than one of the needs in the hierarchy.
　　c. a person can be fulfilling needs at a higher level in the hierarchy even if a need at the lower level has been satisfied at less than 100%.
　　d. each of the above is true.

26. According to Maslow's needs hierarchy, a person will long for affectionate relations with people
　　a. from the day he or she is born.
　　b. when safety needs have been satisfied.

c. when physiological needs have been satisfied.
   d. when he or she is trying to become self-actualized.

27. A person tries to become competent and gain independence in order to satisfy which of the following needs?
   a. safety needs
   b. belongingness needs
   c. esteem needs
   d. self-actualization needs

B. **For Cooperative Study (in or out of class)**

1. Have each class member find a child (preferably a relative) and ask him or her to solve one of Piaget's conservation problems. Report your findings in small groups in class.
2. Repeat exercise 1 (on a child or an adult) using one of Kohlberg's dilemmas, or a similar problem of your own invention.
3. In small groups, discuss some of the personal crises people recall from previous or present psychosocial developmental stages. Does Erikson's theory adequately describe your experiences?
4. Discuss study questions 9 and 12 concerning the relationship between moral reasoning and moral behavior, and the issue of multiple determinants.
5. Discuss the three morals your author drew from the Flatland allegory. Continue the discussion by considering study questions 13–15.

C. **For Further Information:**

1. Read one or more of the works by Piaget, or about his theory or the research on it, and make a written or oral report on it.
2. Read one or more of the works by Erikson, or about his theory or related research, and make a written or oral report on it.
3. View an appropriate film or TV show on psychosocial development (e.g., "On Golden Pond," "The Breakfast Club," "Real People") and analyze the characters and interpersonal relations from Erikson's theoretical point of view. That is, what personal crises are the actors going through which contribute to the interpersonal conflicts?
4. Read Maslow's *Motivation and Personality* or one of Kohlberg's works and make a written or oral report on it.

CHAPTER
STUDY QUESTIONS

1. What was the major purpose for which Binet developed the first intelligence test?

2. What is the concept of Mental Age (MA)? How did Binet standardize his test in order to allow a person's MA to be estimated?

3. In revising the Binet test for use in America, Terman's Stanford-Binet used the concept of the Intelligence Quotient (IQ). How was it calculated? Give examples of the ratio involved.

4. In speaking of the influence of the Stanford-Binet the author states, "Notice how the predictor had become the criterion." What is meant by that statement?

5. How is it possible to have stability and change in intelligence at the same time? Use the concept of rank order correlation to demonstrate the difference between absolute and relative change in people's scores.

6. What is the meaning and usefulness of each of the following? Give examples.
   a. Mean
   b. Standard Deviation
   c. Z-score

7. Describe the normal curve in terms of the following:
   a. The percentage of people falling in each major area
   b. The mean and standard deviation (SD)
   c. Z-score or SD units
   d. Percentile ranks
   e. Median

8. What is the deviation IQ (as opposed to the ratio IQ)? How does it relate to features of the normal curve described in Question 7?

9. Define norm-referenced and criterion-referenced assessment. Which is concerned with relative ranks? With "absolute" scores?

THREE

10. How stable are IQ scores obtained:
    a. before age 3?
    b. by age 6?
    c. by age 8?

11. What does it mean to say that heritability of a trait like intelligence is:
    a. .8
    b. 0
    c. 1.0

12. What does the author mean by the following statements?
    a. "When there is little or no variation in the genetic component, then environment has the largest effect."
    b. "When there is little or no variation in the environmental component, then heredity has the largest effect in the relative ranking of individuals."
    c. "As long as heredity does not operate in a vacuum . . . teachers have the same job, whether inherited intelligence accounts for 80% or 20% of the variation in people."

13. How does the fact of racial or ethnic group differences in standardized test scores, whatever the cause of those differences, relate to placement of children in gifted or special education classes?

14. Describe each of the following problems with testing:
    a. cultural bias in the items
    b. test mis-use
    c. test misinterpretation
       Which does the author feel is the least common?
       What is his solution?

Intelligence Testing and the Normal Curve

Introduction

1. Now if one considers that intelligence is not a single indivisible function with a particular essence of its own, but that it is formed by the combination of all the minor functions of discrimination, observation, retention, etc., all of which have proved to be plastic and subject to increase, it will seem incontestable that the same law governs the ensemble and its elements, and that consequently the intelligence of anyone is susceptible of development. With practice, enthusiasm, and especially with method one can succeed in increasing one's attention, memory, judgment, and in becoming literally more intelligent than before; and this process will go on until one reaches one's limit. (From Binet's "Les Idees Modernes sur les Enfants," 1911, p. 143; in Tuddenham, 1962, p. 488)

2. Stated in its boldest form, our thesis is that the chief determiner of human conduct is a unitary mental process which we call intelligence; that this process is conditioned by a nervous mechanism which is inborn; that the degree of efficiency to be attained by that nervous mechanism and the consequent grade of intelligence or mental level for each individual is determined by the kind of chromosomes that come together with the union of the gene cells; that it is but little affected by any later influences except such serious accidents as may destroy part of the mechanism. (Goddard, 1920, p. 1)

3. There appears to be little educational merit in trying to assess the "intelligence" of minority students. Any IQ test standardized on a "representative" sample will necessarily assess only those skills and knowledge which are regarded as "intelligent" within the dominant group and will exclude any culturally-specific ways in which minority children have learned to be "intelligent." (Cummins, 1984, pp. 77–78)

4. Here are six conclusions regarding tests of cognitive ability, drawn from the classical tradition, that are by now beyond significant technical dispute: 1. There is such a thing as a general factor of cognitive ability on which human beings differ. 2. All standardized tests of academic aptitude or achievement measure this general factor to some degree, but IQ tests expressly designed for that purpose measure it most accurately. 3. IQ scores match, to a first degree, whatever it is that people mean when they use the word *intelligent* or *smart* in ordinary language. 4. IQ scores are stable, although not perfectly so, over much of a person's life. 5. Properly administered IQ tests are not demonstrably biased against social, economic, ethnic, or racial groups. 6. Cognitive ability is substantially heritable, apparently no less than 40 percent and no more than 80 percent. (Herrnstein and Murray, 1994, pp. 22–23)

To this point in the text we have considered a variety of theories which suggest that, with proper experience, humans can increasingly refine their capabilities in language, thought, morality, and social functioning to ever higher developmental stages. Throughout these discussions we have hardly mentioned the word intelligence, though it is clear that in common parlance we would often categorize such developmental progress as "getting smarter" (as Herrnstein and Murray state in *The Bell Curve* in quote #4 above). Surprising as it may seem, the concept "growth of intelligence" has often been considered a contradiction in terms at various times in this century. In its place was a concept of intelligence as a fixed personal attribute which might vary within a small range, but which assessed people's ranks in society and perhaps suggested their achievement potential. Variations on this theme have surfaced in debates on race and the intelligence quotient (IQ) and, more generally, in the nature-nurture issue. The opening quotations give some idea of the scope of the argument.

Intelligence testing and its place in education has been a political football, its history being kicked about by all manner of opponents. To even begin to understand these debates, it is first necessary to learn a few facts about intelligence and it assessment. We begin with a brief history.

History of Intelligence Testing[1]

"Every school child knows that it all began with Alfred Binet." So said Leona Tyler (1976, p. 14) in a manner that sounds as though such knowledge is so widespread as to be a valid question on an intelligence test. Did you know that?

Galton, Cattell and Binet

Intelligence testing as we now know it is indeed most directly traceable to Alfred Binet and his colleagues in France, who developed the test which for decades was the standard against which all others were compared. Subsequent revisions still bear his name—namely, the Stanford-Binet. To place Binet's accomplishment in perspective, however, it is interesting to note another trend of the time.

This other trend was fueled by Charles Darwin's theory of natural selection. Darwin's cousin, Francis Galton (1869), had done studies of the genealogy of eminent men of Britain, drawing the conclusion that genius was inherited. Galton (1883) also collected data on a wide variety of physical and psychological attributes of nearly 10,000 persons (e.g., weight, arm span, strength, color vision, hearing acuity, reaction time) and charged his subjects a fee for being so measured at his laboratory in a museum. He subjected these data to the then modern technology of probability statistics, the precursor to normal curves and standardized scores.[2]

Galton's recognition that a person's position could be accurately described relative to the distribution of a population set the stage for many later developments. But Galton's preoccupation was the "survival of the fittest" and, like the plants and animals that his cousin painstakingly recorded, variation was a key to understanding how the environment could select certain traits for survival in succeeding generations while other traits and species would become extinct. The principles for human intervention in these efforts were also becoming well-known in breeding race horses, better varieties of grains, and so forth. Galton suggested that once the intelligent and feeble-minded were identified, through measures such as he was collecting, selective mating could be accomplished to produce more intelligent and fewer feeble-minded individuals. He coined the term "eugenics" for this selective mating.

Galton's influence extended beyond Britain, reaching the USA via J. M. Cattell (1890), who expanded the types of measures to include what he called "mental tests" (e.g., color naming, auditory memory, bisection of a line, estimation of a 10-second interval). Cattell gave his tests to incoming Freshmen at Columbia University in the 1890's and tried to predict college performance on the basis of those scores. His tests were not predictive of college performance, however, as a study by one of his colleagues (Wissler, 1901) demonstrated. Furthermore, the mental tests did not correlate highly among themselves, indicating that they were each tapping independent abilities. The evidence, in other words, was beginning to look like there was no such thing as a "general intelligence" which could be predictive of such criteria as college success.[3]

Enter Binet. He and his colleagues (V. Henri and T. Simon) adopted a very different approach, based on his studies of the cognitive processes of young children. Binet's place in the history of developmental psychology would be secure, even if he were not the father of the intelligence test (e.g., Cairns, 1983). His research on the thinking processes of children was carried on by none other than Jean Piaget, who worked in his laboratory.

Binet's professional history interacted with a societal interest in placing retarded children in schools where they could obtain special help. A screening test of mental functioning was needed, as Binet and Simon reported in 1905, to do the following: (1) to attest that the children placed in the special school are those whose intellectual state makes them unable to profit from the instructional programs of regular schools, and (2) to assure that children able to profit from regular schools are not misplaced into the special schools. Thus was born not only the intelligence testing movement, but also the special education movement. "To be a member of a special class can never be a mark of distinction, and such as do not merit, must be spared the record" (Binet and Simon, 1916, p. 10). In our own day, as in Binet's, special educational programs have a stigma attached and thus extra care is required in whatever diagnostic testing that is provided.

Binet's tests of intellectual functioning were unlike those of Galton and Cattell in that they were not assessing molecular units of intellect such as simple reaction time; rather they tested higher mental functions such as following orders and imitating gestures, naming objects in pictures, digit span, defining both concrete and abstract words, and demonstrating comprehension. In keeping with his view of a global intelligence, Binet combined the scores of each subtest into an overall score for each individual. Furthermore, the questions were age-graded to provide a "metrical scale of intelligence." That is, questions became increasingly more difficult throughout the test. By his second (1908) and third (1911) revision and before his untimely death, the scale had been standardized in such a way to as to allow a person's scores to be compared to the average scores provided by normal samples of children aged three to fifteen, as well as a sample of adults. Following is how Binet and Simon conceptualized the scoring (from "The Child Is an X," p. 150):

The rules which we apply are two. The first is as follows: A child has the intelligence of that age all the tests for which he succeeds in passing. Here is a child nine years of age who passes all the tests for the seventh year, he has then at least the intelligence of a child of seven. The second rule is as follows: After determining the age for which a child passes all the tests, a year is added to the intelligence age, if he has succeeded in passing five additional tests belonging to superior age groups, two years are added if he has passed ten such tests, three years if he has passed fifteen, and so on.

. . . We would add that a child should not be considered defective in intelligence no matter how little he knows unless his retardation of intelligence amounts to more than two years.

Binet's scale of intelligence, though labeled metrical, was recognized by him as an *ordinal scale — providing rankings, not absolute measures,*

Box 3.1

Some Questions and Suggestions for Scoring from Binet and Simon's Test

1. Copy the following design from memory after viewing it for 10-seconds (age 10).

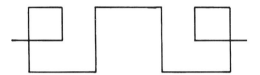

2. What is silly in this sentence? (age 11)
   "I have three brothers, Paul, Ernest and myself."
   Good answers: "You have only two brothers," etc.
   Bad answers: "You should say your own name, not myself."
3. Say as many words as you can in three minutes. (age 11)
4. Copy a diamond. (age 7)
5. Make Change (as in playing store). (age 9)

of individuals. As such, it allowed comparative assessments of intellectual functioning on the basis of mental age. For example, people who were two mental age levels below the average for persons of a given chronological age, were considered retarded and in need of special schooling. Binet's emphasis on mental age also provided a standard for evaluating test items—namely, a good item is one which sharply distinguishes people of different ages.

Lest it be considered that Binet was satisfied simply to classify the intellectual functioning of children, recall the quotation with which this chapter began. Binet openly rejected the concept of intelligence as a fixed entity and invented teaching methods which could raise the intellectual level of retarded individuals. These methods, which he called "mental orthopedics," were designed to teach the children how to learn. In analogous fashion to physical orthopedics for correcting a crooked spine, mental orthopedics were to correct and strengthen the processes of attention, perception, memory, judgment and will.

Photo 3.1. Another day, another test.

Goddard and Terman

The mental testing movement in the USA had suffered a setback when Cattell's tests were shown not to be able to predict college performance. By the end of the first decade of the twentieth century, however, there was a revival of interest in testing intelligence, primarily because of the efforts of H. H. Goddard, the psychological director of a New Jersey institution for the feeble-minded (the Vineland Training School). Goddard, though not impressed by the first edition, was responsible for having Binet and Simon (1916) translated and enthusiastically promoted the use of Binet's later editions of the intelligence test.

Although he was an energetic evangelist for Binet's test, Goddard was even more fundamentally a disciple of Galton's hereditary view of intelligence. He also transformed Binet's view of intelligence as a growing entity of several components into a single unitary intelligence.[4] The view that Goddard (1920) promulgated, then included the following parts (see quote #2 in the Introduction to this chapter): (1) that intelligence can accurately be measured and reduced to a single score; (2) that this intelligence is hereditary and little affected by environment and experience; and (3) that once an individual's mental level has been measured, society can assign that person to an appropriate level of work. This last argument, more than any other, was probably the real impetus for the rise of the IQ testing movement (Karier, 1972).

Thus Goddard, in direct contradiction to Binet's "mental orthopedics" approach to intelligence as a growing entity, popularized a view of intelligence as fixed by heredity. Because of his "social reformer" approach, he also linked mental testing and eugenics in the popular view of the day.[5]

While Goddard and others were extolling the virtues of Binet's tests, Lewis Terman of Stanford University was revising Binet's last edition and standardizing it on an American sample of 2300 persons (Terman, 1917;1919). His revision, known as the Stanford-Binet, had many similarities in conception and scoring to Binet's original test.

One change in scoring provided us with the now ubiquitous Intelligence Quotient, or IQ, which Terman borrowed from the German psychologist W. L. Stern. To obtain the IQ, Terman divided the Mental Age (MA) obtained from the test score by the examinee's Chronological Age (CA) (i.e., actual age) and multiplied by 100. This measure sets the average IQ equal to 100, regardless of age level since an eight-year-old whose mental age is eight and a twelve-year-old whose mental age is twelve would both have IQ's of 100. When CA is greater than MA, the person's IQ is below 100 and less than average; when MA is greater than CA, the person's IQ is above 100. Notice also that a person whose intelligence grew by four mental age units in four years could also be conceived as having had no change in intelligence, since the IQ remained unchanged. This possible source of confusion has led to actual confusion in more than one discussion of whether intelligence should be considered to be a fixed or changing commodity. We shall discuss this issue further in a later section.

Terman's Stanford-Binet became the first widely used intelligence measure in the USA and greatly influenced all subsequent mental testing. In part this was due to Terman's painstaking care in obtaining standardization samples to provide the norms with which examinees' scores were compared. In part it was due to a pressing societal need not unlike that in France which led Binet to develop his test. Compulsory education and an expanding system of public schools suggested to many educators that a screening device would be advantageous.

A similar kind of social pressure—namely the need to select and place army recruits in World War I—led to the development of group intelligence tests. The Stanford-Binet had the disadvantage of requiring individualized testing. The Army wanted tests which could be given to large numbers of persons at once. A committee of distinguished mental testers[6] answered that need by developing one test for those who could read (the Army Alpha), and a parallel form for illiterates and those who could not speak English (the Army Beta). In less than 18 months 1,750,000 men sat for these tests, ushering in the era of group IQ testing.

Box 3.2

More on Calculating the Ratio IQ

As developed by Terman, the Intelligence Quotient was calculated from the following formula (where MA = mental age and CA = chronological age):

$$IQ = (MA/CA) \times 100$$

Thus, a ten-year-old who was three years advanced (i.e., obtained the MA of 13) received an IQ of 130, while another ten-year-old who was three years retarded (MA of 7) was said to have an IQ of 70.

$$IQ = (13/10) \times 100 = 130 \qquad IQ = (7/10) \times 100 = 70$$

Persistent problems occurred, however, among them (1) unequal standard deviations (spread or scores) at different ages, and (2) the average adult scored no higher than the average 16-year old. The solution to this problem was arbitrarily to use 16 as the CA for anyone 16-years-old or older. While this solved the calculation problem, it was not a good conceptual solution. David Wechsler (1958) criticized the whole age-scale concept as being fundamentally inappropriate for use with adults.

The solution was to adopt what has come to be known as the *deviation IQ*, in which a person's IQ is placed in the distribution or scores of others of his or her appropriate age group. More specifically, the mean (average) and standard deviation (a measure of the spread of the scores) provide the norms for interpreting any individual's score. To maintain equivalence with the ratio IQ, the mean of the deviation IQ is also set at 100, while the standard deviation is about 15 (though that depends on the test). For more information on the deviation IQ, see Figure 3.1.

By 1920 the view that people could be selected and placed according to their mental level was fast becoming the popular view in society. It had been reinforced by the development of group intelligence tests for use by the Army to draft and place men for World War I. Our nation's efficiency, in Goddard's (1920) words, awaited only the "Human Engineer" who would undertake to match people to work at their correct mental level. Apparently the time was right for this view since, as Tuddenham (1962, p. 491) put it:

> Mental testing was adopted in every training school, every teachers' college in the land, and even stormed the citadels of experimental psychology on university campuses. There were few who noticed the logical flaws behind the eloquence—that the hereditary, biological intelligence that Goddard postulated and the intelligence which the tests in fact measured were not the same thing.

From the 1920's to the 1970's

The fifty years immediately following the development of the Stanford-Binet and the Army group tests were very productive years from the standpoint of test construction and test theory. Many mental tests were constructed for every conceivable purpose and population. Prominent among these tests were revisions of the Stanford-Binet in 1937 and 1960.[7] The former revision provided parallel forms of the test and also extended the possible MA range to twenty-two and a half years to help solve the problem of calculating adult IQ's (see Box). The 1960 edition was noteworthy for abandoning the ratio IQ (based on the MA/CA ratio) in favor of the deviation IQ (based on the standard deviation units of the normal curve; described in the following section).

It is, in fact, difficult to overestimate the influence of the Stanford-Binet test during these five or six decades. It became the standard against which all other mental tests were compared. If a new test classified people in the same way as the Stanford-Binet, then it was often considered to be an adequate measure. If it did not, then the new test was suspect. As Gallagher, Benoit and Boyd (1956, p. 71) complained,[8]

It is difficult to understand why so much time is invested in developing a scale . . . only to have the crucial problem of validity shrugged off with a routine comparison with the Binet. Certainly the most important aspect of a test for exceptional children is that it validly measures or predicts some sort of vocational, social, or educational success or adjustment.

To be fair, many test developers also collected data on performance in other areas such as schools, but it is only a slight exaggeration to say that the mental testing industry flourished by viewing intelligence as that which is measured by intelligence tests—the primary example of which was the Stanford-Binet. *Notice how the predictor had become the criterion!*

Two other highly influential tests were developed by David Wechsler, (Wechsler Adult Intelligence Scale and the WISC (The Wechsler Intelligence Scale for Children), both based on the deviation IQ measure he championed. Other tests, too numerous to mention, are described in Buros' Mental Measurements Yearbooks. And since this was becoming big business, there was the problem of advertising.

Consider this ad for a five-minute IQ test (reported in Gardner, 1993, p. 6):

Need an individual test which quickly provides a stable and reliable estimate of intelligence in four or five minutes per form? Has three forms? Does not depend on verbal production or subjective scoring? Can be used with the severely physically handicapped (even paralyzed) if they can signal yes or no? Handles two-year-olds and superior adults with the same short series of items and the same format? Only $16.00 complete.

At the same time that the instruments themselves were proliferating, test theory was also being developed. One aspect of this was the continuing controversy over whether intelligence was a unitary concept or a composite of several underlying factors. This issue was first raised (as noted earlier) by the father of the statistical technique of factor analysis, Charles Spearman (1923). Spearman argued that there was one general factor, "g," common to all subtests in a battery of tests, and one factor, "s," specific to each type of subtest. Others, led by L. L. Thurstone (1935; Thurstone and Thurstone, 1941) factor analyzed large numbers of tests and found that, although there was a factor common to all of them—Spearman's "g"—it should be considered a secondary factor. Thurstone found seven primary factors, which he called primary mental abilities, which came out of certain types of tests which were different from other types. These factors were verbal comprehension, word fluency, number computation, spatial visualization, associative memory, perceptual speed, and reasoning.

The factor analysts' discoveries led to efforts to design tests which were relatively pure measures of each of the proposed factors. The apex of this effort was attained in Guilford's (1956, 1959, 1967) "Structure of Intellect" model, which proposed 120 factors or unique aspects of (and tests for) intelligence.

The factorial tradition continues to this day, with the most widely accepted theory being John Carroll's three stratum theory. As the name suggests, this is a hierarchical theory with one level being for *general* ability (i.e., "g"), a second level for *broad* areas of ability (e.g., speed of processing and, learning ability), and a third level for *narrow* or specific abilities (e.g., reading comprehension or visualizations of shapes). The controversy as to the usefulness of factor analysis also continues. Today's skeptics would probably still agree with Wechsler's (1958) assessment that a profusion of factors is a contradiction of the aims of factor analysis. That is, factor analysis was to find the common elements in many tests. When there are more factors than tests, we have gone too far. Nevertheless, the controversy is not likely to be settled on statistical grounds alone; rather, the argument concerns the definition of intelligence and is therefore unlikely to be settled soon. (See chapter 4 for more recent skirmishes).

A final trend I shall mention in this brief history brings us back to the legacy of Binet. While all of these mental tests were being developed and factor analyzed, Jean Piaget was studying the growth of intelligence in his own children. As described in more detail in the second chapter of this book, Piaget's interest lay not in counting up the number of items a person could correctly solve, giving it a number, and comparing that score with the scores of others; rather his concern was in describing what logical processes people were using to solve problems at various developmental stages, why and how errors occurred, and what knowledges and operations were prerequisite for understanding any given problem. Piaget in other words, was concerned *not with individual differences, but with individuals; not with norm-referenced comparisons, but with criterion-referenced assessment of developmental milestones.* This tradition became even more ascendent in the 1980's, particularly in the field of cognitive psychology. We shall continue with

Now, the statistical principles we are studying today have been developed by Prof. Norm L. Kurf, whose picture is on the board.

Cartoon 3.1.

the cognitive developmental view of intelligence, but first it will be necessary to deal with some other persistent problems of intelligence testing.

The Normal Curve

Because current IQ scores are understandable only in terms of the relative rankings of individuals, it is necessary to be clear about the shape and meaning of the ubiquitous normal curve. First, it should be clear that "normal" does not refer to "goodness"; rather, it refers to the "norm" or statistical average provided by the population to whom you are being compared.

Figure 3.1 displays the normal, or bell-shaped, curve in its idealized form as a continuous curve. In practice it is really a histogram or bar graph comprised of the number of people (measured on the vertical axis) who received each possible score (measured on the horizontal axis). As Part A of the Figure shows there are many people who received IQ's of 95, 100, 105 and similar scores, with only a few scoring 65, 70, 130, or 135. Of course, many possible scores are not shown in the graph to save space, but any whole number score is *possible*

70 Chapter Three

A. As a Frequency Distribution for IQs

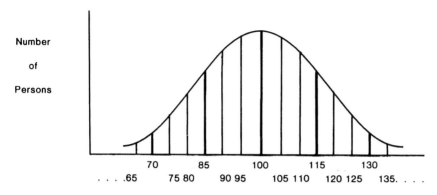

B. Areas Under the Curve for IQs

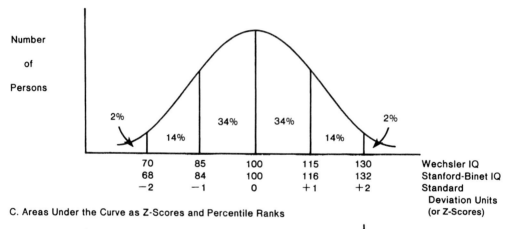

C. Areas Under the Curve as Z-Scores and Percentile Ranks

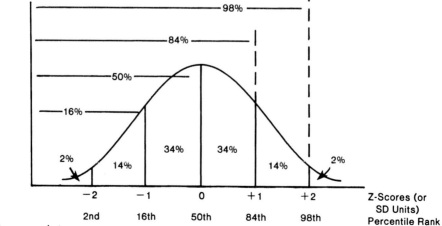

Figure 3.1. The normal curve.

between zero and, say, 200. However, as Part A shows, scores below 70 and above 130 are *infrequent*. The graph is idealized in the sense that the curve is drawn to be perfectly regular and symmetrical. In any given sample of examinees, of course, the curve will not be so perfect. On the other hand, the larger the sample of persons tested, the more the actual curve approximates the idealized curve.

Because the height of the curve at any point represents the frequency or likelihood of people receiving that score, it is possible to divide the curve into natural sections or areas and speak of the proportion of the population which falls into those areas. To do this one needs to know the *mean* and the *standard deviation* of the sample of examinees. The mean is the simple average, calculated by summing the scores of all examinees and dividing by the number of examinees.

Formula 3.1

$$\text{Mean} = \frac{\text{Sum of All Scores}}{\text{Number of Scores}}$$

The standard deviation (SD), from which deviation IQ got its name, is a measure of the spread of scores around the mean. It is obtained by subtracting the mean from each person's score and squaring that difference. Then the mean of those squared differences is obtained by summing them and dividing by the number of persons. Finally, we take the square root of that final average. In other words,

Formula 3.2

$$\text{Standard Deviation} = \sqrt{\frac{\text{Sum of the Squared Differences from the Mean}}{\text{Number of Scores}}}$$

Examples of each of these calculations is given in appendix B. For now it is sufficient to note the meaning of these statistics and how each relates to the normal curve. Because of the symmetrical nature of a normal curve, the mean, the median and the mode of the curve are at the same point, in the middle. The *mean is the balance point* of any distribution (see appendix B for a demonstration), calculated as the simple average as in formula 3.1. If the scores were not normally distributed (the normal curve), the mean would not be at the center.

The *median is the midpoint* of any distribution, with an equal number of scores above and below it. Thus the median is also the 50th percentile point, since 50% of the scores will be below the median. And this is true whatever the shape of a distribution.

The *mode is the most frequent score*, or the highest point in a curve, and there can be more than one mode in any distribution.

Because IQ scores form normal distributions, the mean, median and mode are at the same point. For reasons of simplicity and tradition, this point is set to be 100: that is, a person who is average for his age or comparison group (as when a nine year old has a mental age of 9) should score at the mean for IQs—namely, 100.

The *standard deviation* which is a *measure of the average spread of scores*, would be zero if everyone scored the same on a test (e.g., 10, 10, 10, 10, 10), is small if scores are close together (e.g., 8,9,10,9,11), and is larger the more dissimilar scores become (e.g., 8,15,20,28,40). For IQs the SD is usually around 15 or 16 (e.g., 15 for the Wechsler tests and 16 for the Stanford-Binet). This information relates to the area of the curve in the following way: between the mean (represented as =0) and one SD on either side of the mean are approximately 34% of the scores (see figure 3.1, Part B). Another 14% of the IQ scores fall between +1 and +2 SD units, as well as between –1 and –2 SD units. The last 4% of the scores fall beyond +2 or –2 SDs, 2% on either side.

On the Stanford-Binet, then, 2% of the population have IQs below 68 (the second percentile), another 14% score between 68 and 84, and so on. Similar distributions can be given for Wechsler IQs, adjusted to accommodate the slightly lower SD of 15. These figures can be converted to percentile ranks, as shown in Part C of figure 3.1. In that case, since an IQ at –1 SD is better than the 2% of the population below –2SD as well as the 14% between –1 and –2 SD, then an IQ of 84 on the Stanford-Binet (or 85 on the Wechsler) is at the 16th percentile (i.e., it is better than 16% of the scores). A score at the mean is the 50th percentile (better than 2% + 14% + 34% = 50% of the scores). In similar fashion, Stanford-Binet IQs of 116 and 132 (or Wechsler IQs of 115 and 130) yield percentile ranks of 84 and 98, respectively.

The reason all of this works out this way is that the SD is used to convert different ways of measuring to a common scale of measurement. We cannot compare the dimensions of houses when one is measured in feet, another in meters, and a third in the Biblical cubits, unless we first convert all to a common measure. Since the goal of IQ measurement is to assess the relative positions of people on intelligence, we need a way to compare them whatever kind of test they were given. A percentile rank scale certainly tells us that. An even more precise way of specifying a person's rank is in terms of the SD units, or what is known as the *Z-score*. It is calculated by subtracting the mean from each person's score and dividing by the standard deviation.

Formula 3.3

$$\text{Z-Score} = \frac{\text{A person's score minus the mean}}{\text{Standard Deviation}}$$

As can be seen in figure 3.1, this gives a scale of measures which has a mean of zero and a SD of 1. In fact, using compiled statistical tables, it is possible quickly to convert IQs (or other test scores) into percentile ranks or Z-scores, and vice versa. The ease and precision which these statistics allow people to be compared with their peers is one of the prime reasons that deviation IQs became so popular.

Photo 3.2. Norm-referenced or criterion-referenced test?

Stability and Change in Intelligence: or How Can Intelligence Be Fixed and Developing at the Same Time?

It may seem strange that there could be any controversy about whether intelligence is a fixed or developing commodity. As with many other psychological phenomena, so much depends on what we mean by intelligence, and how we go about quantifying it. From one point of view, it is clear that sixth-graders, for example, are more intelligent that second-graders—they know more facts, process information better and more quickly, can use more learning and memory strategies, and can solve problems in a wider variety of ways, among other things. In absolute terms, sixth-graders would get much higher scores on the same tests than second-graders. Thus their intelligence is developing in a Piagetian sense. In a measurement sense, when we are assessing how well people can do something we are doing *criterion-referenced assessment* (Glaser, 1963; Glaser and Nitko, 1971). Criterion-referenced assessment is concerned with the growth that occurs as a result of learning and thus *interprets each person's score in terms of a goal or criterion to be achieved* (e.g., does the person know enough about the rules of the road and about operating a motor vehicle to obtain a driver's license), without regard to how other people perform.

From another point of view—one in which comparing or ranking people is of paramount importance—intelligence is a more-or-less fixed commodity. The technical term for this kind of assessment is *norm-referenced assessment,* so-named because people's *scores are interpreted in terms of the norm*(*or normal curve*) *provided by the population to which those people are being compared* A person may indeed show increased knowledge from second to sixth grade, but that is not what is of importance in norm-referenced assessment. What is important, rather, is whether the people's *ranks* change over time. For example, if Johnny is at the 48th percentile rank in grade 2 nationally (which means he scores higher than 48% of the population on that test), the question is, does he remain at about the 48th percentile in the third, fourth, fifth and sixth grades. If so, then his rank is relatively stable or fixed, despite his academic or developmental progress.

Since *IQs are norm-referenced measures,* then a good IQ test will be one in which people's rankings will be relatively fixed over time. This is, in part, what is meant by reliable and valid measurement (see chapter 15 for more details on reliability and validity). In statistical terms, there is a high positive correlation between a person's rank (i.e., rank of 1, 2 or 3; or 98th, 80th, or 50th percentile rank) in second grade and her rank in third grade. As we have seen, it is conceptually possible to have individuals or whole classes grow in intelligence and still maintain relatively fixed ranks over the developmental period in question. Put another way, despite much individual growth, the correlation between scores on a test can be high and positive, which indicates considerable stability of rankings. Anecdote 3.1 gives some numerical and graphic examples of the points made above using test scores in general and the concept of a perfect +1 correlation.

Returning specifically to intelligence testing, if we look at the learning that occurs from year to year, as reflected by mental age for example, then it is clear that intelligence keeps growing. If we look at IQ, either the ratio (MA/CA×100) or deviation IQ, then that should remain constant within some range of reliability of the test and its administration. This is true whether heredity plays a larger role than environment in shaping intelligence or whether environmental experiences are predominant. By the time individuals reach the age at which intelligence test scores start becoming reliable—certainly not much before school age (e.g., Lewis, 1983)—what they know and their style and speed of thinking have already been shaped by both environment and heredity. Any further knowledge that is likely to be general enough to be included on an intelligence test is also likely to have been generally available to that student's age cohort (against whom he or she will be competing in all standardized achievement tests) as well as the sample on whom the intelligence test was standardized. This provides the intelligence test constant that is added to, or more likely multiplies, each person's score each year and shifts the whole curve upward, while maintaining everyone in approximately the same rank order.

It should also be noted that the correlation between test and retest does not have to provide perfect predictability. As long as the test-retest reliability correlation (which can range from −1.0 to +1.0) is high and positive, say .70 or higher, the test will predict the retest quite well within a fairly narrow range of error. Intelligence tests are quite good in this regard, typically having test-retest reliabilities of .90 or better. (See appendix B for the actual calculation of a correlation coefficient).

A further point to be made is that an intelligence test—in fact, any test—is useful only to the extent that it provides stable, repeatable scores or ranks for the individuals tested. Without such repeatability—technically called

Anecdote 3.1

HOW CHANGE CAN OCCUR IN ABSOLUTE AMOUNTS WITHOUT CHANGING RANKS (OR WHAT A TEST-RETEST CORRELATION OF +1.0 COULD MEAN)

I. Scoring and Ranking Test Performance

We begin with a set of scores on a test by five individuals, in which Alfred with the highest score of 20 earns a rank of 1, Bertha's 18 ranks 2, and so on as follows:

Person	Test Score	Rank
Alfred	20	1
Bertha	18	2
Charles	16	3
Darlene	14	4
Edward	12	5

II. No Change from Test to Retest

Suppose, further, that without warning a retest was given a few days later. Assuming that forgetting was minimal and there was little opportunity for new learning, then the test scores and ranks should stay approximately as they were, as portrayed below.

Person	Original Score	Test Rank	Retest Score	Retest Rank
Alfred	20	1	20	1
Bertha	18	2	18	2
Charles	16	3	16	3
Darlene	14	4	14	4
Edward	12	5	12	5

Note that *each person stays in exactly the same rank order from test to retest, which is the definition of a +1 correlation* (see Appendix B for the calculation procedures).

III. Growth from Test to Retest

Now suppose that instead of no change occurring between test and retest, that months have passed during which all students learned a considerable amount about the material being tested, perhaps quintupling their scores. Thus Alfred's score goes from 20 to 100, Bertha's from 18 to 90, as follows: —

(continued on next page)

Anecdote 3.1—*(continued)*

Person	Original Score	Test Rank	Re-Test Score	Re-Test Rank	Plot of Scores
Alfred	20	1	100	1	
Bertha	18	2	90	2	
Charles	16	3	80	3	
Darlene	14	4	70	4	
Edward	12	5	60	5	

Note that although the scores increased by a constant amount (a five-fold increase in knowledge), the rank order of each person stayed the same, and therefore the correlation between test and retest is still a perfect +1.

IV. The Moral of the Story

The same result could occur if students' scores all decreased from test to retest a constant amount so that they recalled only half of what they knew before (which is unlikely, but could happen if they all suffered from Alzheimer's disease or were on drugs). In that case, Alfred's score of 20 would become 10, Bertha's 18 becomes 9, etc., but the ranks would stay the same. I'll leave you to plot the results.

The moral, in any case, is that as long as people remain in relatively the same rank order, we can predict their rank regardless of how much their absolute knowledge may have changed. Since 6-year-olds are compared to the same cohort of individuals from year to year, their intelligence can appear to remain fixed if their rank does not change much, even though all students have increased their knowledge and skills considerably by the time they are 12-year-olds. A plot of their scores would look much like that in III above, though with thousands of students tested the scores would be distributed as normal curves as follows:

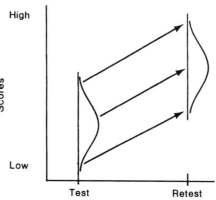

reliability—the test would have to be discarded, or, more likely, revised by the test maker until it did provide stability of scores. Standardized tests, having gone through multiple screenings and revisions, are therefore guaranteed to be of high reliability. The test industry would not be able to remain in business if that were not the case.

Evidence on the Stability of IQ scores

The last section demonstrated how IQ scores, since they are norm-referenced measures, can provide a reliable fix on each person's relative position on the normal curve, though the whole curve may change upward or downward. How accurate is this assumption?

In general, whole curves do not shift upward or downward—at least not very much—when dealing with IQ. To see why, consider an analogy with physical abilities. If we wished to have a measure of general ability ("g") in sports, we would invent a test with as many as ten subtests such as running speed, endurance, strength, reaction time, distance throwing a ball, etc. Wanting a measure that is internally consistent, we would then keep trying out different component tests, keeping those which correlate highly with the other components and eliminating those which do not. The final result would be a measure of general athletic ability, an "Athletic Quotient" (AQ), which would be very much like the IQ in at least the following ways:

1. It would be at least moderately correlated with many other measures of athletic ability.
2. The distribution of AQ scores for hundreds of individuals would look very much like a normal curve.
3. Individuals could markedly increase their ranks on a single component of the test through the instruction and practice (e.g., by practicing throwing a baseball) without appreciably changing their overall ranks on the total test (i.e., the AQ would not change much, if at all, since that one test would contribute only 10% to the total score).
4. The AQ would not be very stable until certain maturational developments (e.g., in the bones and muscles) occurred. That is, AQs on infants and children up to age 5 or 6 would probably not be predictive of AQs at age 10 or 12.

The above four points for a hypothetical "Athletic Quotient" summarize some of the findings for the Intelligence Quotient. By age eight or ten, IQ seems to be correlated with almost any intellectual task that has been developed. But this is not true of very young children. Because of rapid developmental changes, spurts and lags, tests of mental ability before age 3 are not highly correlated with tests given at school age (e.g., Bayley, 1955; 1970). The patterns of change of mental abilities at these early ages even seems to change every few months. For example, at three months the infant is concerned with four major abilities (from Lewis, 1983): a search factor (orienting and attending), an auditory factor (vocalizing and noise making), a social factor (smiling and frolic play), and a manipulation factor (holding and reaching for things). By twelve months the important factors involved in the infant's abilities seem to be quite different (structurally as well as via the negative and low positive correlations), being better described as verbal, imitation and means-end factors. Language has made its appearance and so has an awareness of cause-effect. By 2 years, the important abilities can best be described somewhat differently.

By three or four years, however, IQ scores begin to predict adult-age IQs in longitudinal studies. Thus, the correlation for IQ scores between ages 3 and 4 and 18 is in the .50 to .70

Anecdote 3.2

What Does the Bell Curve of IQ Predict?

In their infamous book, *The Bell Curve*, Herrnstein and Murray (1994) suggest the following perspective on the usefulness or predictability of IQ scores:

"Given two 11 year olds, one with an IQ of 110 and one with an IQ of 90, what can you tell us about the differences between these two children?" The answer must be phrased very tentatively. On many important topics, the answer must be "we can tell you nothing with confidence" (p. 19).

They go on to point out that such information might be useful in counseling, but only in a larger context provided by the student's personality, talents, background and, I would add environment. They then provide the following contrast:

"Given two sixth-grade classes, one for which the average IQ is 110 and the other for which it is 90, what can you tell us about the difference those two classes and their average prospects for the future?" Now there is a great deal to be said, and it can be said with considerable confidence—not about any one person in either class but about average outcomes that are important to the school, educational policy in general, and society at large (pp. 19–20).

Herrnstein and Murray point out that such large differences between two school classes are highly correlated with social class, which is becoming ever more stratified by cognitive ability via access to college, technology, and the like. As they put it, "Social class remains the vehicle of social life, but intelligence now pulls the train" (p. 25). Such disparate group differences, they argue, are what norm-referenced IQ scores predict.

---

range; between ages 6 and 18 is about .80; between ages 8 and 18 is about .90; and between ages 15 and 18 is .95 or above (e.g., Bloom, 1964). Correlations above .90 are as high as the test-retest reliabilities given a year apart and thus indicate great stability.

Despite such great stability there is evidence in individual cases of quite large changes in IQ (e.g., Hunt, 1961; Minton and Schneider, 1984). Moreover, the profile of the changes for an individual is not a smooth line, but is likely to show 10 or 20 point changes at any given time, and over a period of years will tend to cluster around a "true score" average for that individual. Again, a sports analogy may be helpful, since a basketball player who averages 20 points per game may have an occasional game in which he scores 40 points, and some in which he scores fewer than 10 points. Overall, his average when compared with the averages of his peer group will tend to be a stable predictor of his rank.

A general principle about the predictability of IQ scores, then, is this (as italicized in *The Bell Curve*, Herrnstein & Murray, 1994):

Measures of intelligence have reliable statistical relationships with important social phenomena, but they are a limited tool for deciding what to make of any given individual. (p. 21)

For further elaboration on this point, see anecdote 3.2

Heredity and Environment

Probably no topic in education has generated as much controversy as the issue of the relative contribution to intelligence of heredity and environment. Ironically, in my opinion, the topic is one of the least relevant of all issues to educators for the simple reasons that (1) by the time students enroll in school, they have been shaped by both heredity and environment in whatever ratio they operate; and (2) that our job as teachers is to teach students the skills and knowledges that will be useful to them, again, regardless of the heredity/environment ratio involved in their learning. As long as heredity does not operate in a vacuum—which, of course, it does not—*teachers have the same job, whether inherited intelligence accounts for 80% or 20% of the variation in people.*

An analogy with a physical characteristic will again be helpful. Height and weight are known to have heritability coefficients of about .80 (e.g., Dobzhansky, 1973, p. 18), which means that about 80% of the *variation in the rank orders* of people is caused by their genes. That leaves 20% for environment, which includes the prenatal environment, nutrition, exercise and so on during the person's lifetime. Despite this high heritability, I have never met anyone who was willing to conclude that, therefore, what we eat and how we exercise is unimportant. On the contrary, we seem to be extremely conscious of the need for proper nutrition and exercise, and rightly so. Nevertheless when the rankings of IQ were argued to have an 80%–20% genetic-environment ratio, many people assumed that this possibility left no room for environmental influences.

But there are many similarities between physical and intellectual development vis-a-vis the heredity-environment issue. It is now widely recognized that, first, prenatal environment is critical; for example, exposure to drugs and alcohol, or deficiencies in certain basic nutritional needs, can have devastating effects. Second, the environment during infancy and childhood is extremely important for both physical and intellectual growth. Nutrition and proper exercise are critical for physical and mental health. Exposure to famine or diseases has devastating effects on an individual, while good nutrition acts to enhance whatever physical genetic potentials a person has. Intellectually stimulating or impoverished environments are known to have similar effects on subsequent intellective functioning. Third, as we have seen earlier (in anecdote 3.1), the whole curve can be moved up or down some constant as a result of the environment without changing the rank ordering of people. In the physical realm, famine can reduce the height, weight, and stamina of a whole population. Good nutrition, in contrast, can lead to the average height, weight, and well-being of whole populations increasing from generation to generation. Similar effects can be expected of intellectual stimulation or lack of it.

The point is that heredity and environment are inextricably intertwined. The trait or characteristic which we observe or measure, such as weight or IQ, is known as the *phenotype*. The underlying genetic component of that phenotype, known as the *genotype*, is what is fixed at the moment that sperm and ovum unit at conception. But genotypes never operate in the absence of environment nor does environment operate in the absence of heredity. As Jensen (1969, pp. 116–117) put it in regard to IQ,

> Only if heritability were unity ($h^2 = 1$) would there be a perfect correlation between obtained scores and genotypic values, in which cases we could say with assurance that an individual's measured IQ perfectly represented his genotype for intelligence. This still would not mean that the phenotype could have developed without an environment, for without either heredity or environment there simply is no organism and no phenotype.

So far, the discussion would strike few people as controversial. Disputes usually center around two points. The first is the contention that the heritability coefficient for IQ is .80—or, in Herrnstein and Murray's (1994) estimate, in the .40 to .80 range. The second controversial point concerns the inference from that figure that therefore heredity plays a larger role than environment in group IQ differences, such as in racial comparisons.

It is beyond the scope of this chapter to go into detail on how heritability estimates are obtained. Suffice it to say that the formula (e.g., formula 2 in Jensen, 1969) attempts to isolate the proportion of variation in a distribution of IQ scores that is attributable to several components of heredity, several components of the environment, the interaction of heredity and environment, and error of measurement. In practice this is done by studying pairs of individuals varying in their biological relationships to one another and in the similarity of their upbringing.

The most similar of relationships is identical twins who, since they have the same genes, are called monozygotic. When identical twins are reared together in the same family, and are given the same schooling and the opportunities, then they should have similar IQs. Thus if one member of a pair ranks high in IQ, that person's sibling will also rank high when compared to twins in other families. As expected, the correlation of IQ scores among identical twins reared together is high, around .86 (Henderson, 1982). Identical twins, who were separated and lived separately from their mates, have IQs which correlate slightly lower at .75.[9]

In contrast to identical twins, the correlation for fraternal twins (who have different genes, are known as dizygotic twins) is about .62, for siblings reared together is .56 and for siblings reared apart .24. The correlation of parent and child's IQ in these data is between .35 and .50, which contrasts with the correlation of foster parent and child's IQ

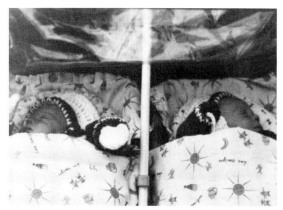

Photo 3.3. Mirror image or twins?

of .20. Finally, unrelated children reared apart have IQs which correlate about zero.

What is important to note at this point is not the exact size of the correlations, which are in some dispute (see footnote 9), but the relative sizes for the familial relationships. They also show that the closer the genetic relationship, the higher the correlation. They also show that children's IQs are more closely related to their natural parents' IQs than to their adoptive parents' IQs, despite having been brought up in the environment of the latter. Such data are cited by those who support the argument that heredity is more important than the environment.

Those who dispute that argument point out that it is impossible to know in those cases how different the environments are. For example, it may be that children were placed in adoptive homes which are really not that different from the environment that would have been provided by the natural parents. There is also evidence that mean IQ scores of children placed into better home environments do increase, prompting Scarr and Weinberg (1979, p. 32) to argue (as we saw earlier) ". . . mean scores show more malleability than rank orders. . . ." See box for more.

One relevant issue is quite well understood. When there is little or no variation in the genetic component, then environment has the

Box 3.3

MORE ON HERITABILITY

In the introduction to this chapter Herrnstein and Murray (1994) were quoted (point 6 in quote #4) as saying, "Cognitive ability is substantially heritable, apparently no less than 40 percent and no more than 80 percent." What does that mean?

It means that 40–80% of the rank orderings on IQ of the second member of a pair of people (twin #2, or a child) can be predicted by the rankings on IQ of the first member of the pair (twin #1, or the child's parent). Consider the following hypothetical IQs of pairs of people in A and B.

	A				B			
	Natural Parent		Child		Adult		Unrelated Child	
Pair	IQ	Rank	IQ	Rank	IQ	Rank	IQ	Rank
#1.	130	1	134	1	130	1	108	3
2.	117	2	107	3	117	2	130	1
3.	100	3	112	2	100	3	85	5
4.	89	4	94	4	89	4	93	4
5.	85	5	80	5	85	5	114	2

Now the rank orders of the pairs in A are not perfectly the same, but they are similar enough to yield a correlation coefficient of .90 (see Appendix B for the calculation). This figure would allow the statement that 81% (the square of the correlation, known as the Coefficient of Determination) of the variation in the rankings of the children's IQs is accounted for by the rankings in the adults' IQs.

The rank orders of the pairs in B, on the other hand, appear quite unrelated and yield a correlation coefficient of .1. Since .1 squared is .01, the variation in rankings of the child's IQ cannot be accounted for by the rankings of the adults' IQs.

Heritability estimates, in other words, are measures of the norm-referenced predictabilities of relative rankings of people in groups. They tell us little, if anything, about what individuals know (a criterion-referenced measure), nor about what environmental change might move the whole curve up (e.g., better teaching, improved nutrition) or down (e.g., drugs or disease) without affecting the rankings (as demonstrated in Anecdote 3.1).

---

largest effect. Thus the differences between identical twins must be due to environmental effects. And the greater the environmental differences, the greater the effects. Jensen (1969, pp. 119–120) stated this as follows:

High heritability by itself does not necessarily imply that the characteristic is immutable.

Under greatly changed environmental conditions, the heritability may have some other value, or it may remain the same while the mean of the population changes.

The converse is also true. When there is little or no variation in the environmental component, then heredity has the largest effect in the relative ranking of individuals. This provides an interesting irony: *the more homogeneous the society*, through its mass media, standard curricula, etc; *the more likely any differences among people are due to heredity*. To maximize the effects of environments compared with heredity, we must have large differences in environments. National assessments or standardized curricula which have the laudable goal of ensuring equality of educational experiences have the ironic effect of increasing the relative contribution of heredity.

Group Differences

Among the largest environment differences in any society are those that occur among the social classes. From better nutrition and health care to economic amenities and opportunities for intellectual stimulation, the upper and middle classes have clear advantages over their lower class brethen. To paraphrase an old joke, the only thing money can't buy is poverty.

The average correlation between a child's IQ and a measure of his or her parents' socioeconomic status is probably in the .25 to .45 range (e.g., Minton and Schneider, 1980, Chap. 12). It is almost certainly the case that all sorts of environmental advantages accrue to children of higher rather than lower socioeconomic classes. Early environmental stimulation, educational records and toys, travel to other environments, and so on translate, almost by definition, into higher IQ scores for the beneficiaries of such conditions. Poverty has little to offer to compete with these advantages.

There is also a kind of self-fulfilling prophecy involved in the relative advantage of the upper classes and the so-called cycle of poverty. Consider the lower end of the spectrum. Poor people tend not to be able to afford higher education, they tend to meet and marry others in their same situation (known as "assortative mating"), and they have offspring whom they rear in much the same way they were reared. Since they were not able to go

Cartoon 3.2.

out of their own small world by tourist travel, by education, or for purposes of employment, how could they learn anything else? After several generations of this, it becomes harder and harder for the children to break out, particularly if as early teenagers they are already parents. Education, once one of the best forces for bootstrapping one's way out of poverty, becomes less and less relevant to the child's daily life.

So far this explanation, which is commonly held in this society, is a totally environmental explanation. Even those who would wish to add a genetic component, small or large, to this argument would nevertheless agree that in any case, in our current information and technology explosion, it is not difficult to foresee how this pattern will continue. Educationally and economically the rich and the poor continue to diverge (see also anecdote 3.2).

Where do racial and ethnic differences fit into all of this? They could be irrelevant, since each minority group has high, middle and low socioeconomic groups, as well as having a normal curve of IQ distributions. The unfortunate fact is, however, that some minority groups, at least in the USA, are disproportionately represented at the lower ends of the social class and IQ curves. For example, minorities sometimes score as much as 15 IQ points—i.e., one standard deviation—below the general population on average.[10] Even if

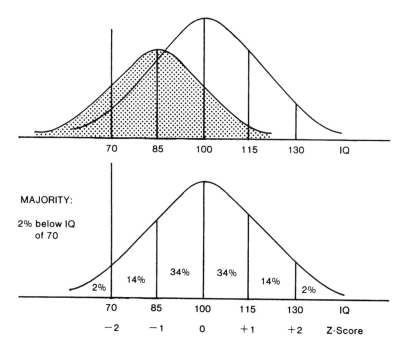

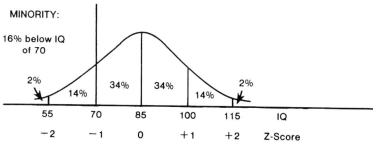

Figure 3.2. Hypothetical distribution of the majority population (with a mean of 100) and a minority (shaded) population (with a mean of 85).

one adopts a wholly environmental explanation for this phenomenon, it is still disturbing, especially when one looks at the extremes of the distributions (see figure 3.2). Nichols (1986, p. 214) stated it this way using the black minority vs. the white majority as an example:

A cutting score two standard deviations above the white mean which might be used by very selective educational institutions and employers, will qualify about 2 percent of the whites, but only about one of 1000 blacks (a ratio of 200 to one). A cutting score two standard deviations below the white mean, which might be used to identify mentally retarded individuals, will select about 2 percent of whites and about 16 percent of blacks (a ratio of eight to one).

That minorities are overly represented in our special education programs is indisputable. The causes may be genetic, environmental, biases of tests, policies, and more. Whatever the causes, there are few easy solutions. We shall discuss a few of them in the next section. First, it seems important to draw the discussion of heritability of group differences to a close. Perhaps the clearest summary of the issue was given in an article by Lee J. Cronbach (1975) who was reminding social scientists of their fallibility, particularly when it comes to influencing social policy. Cronbach's assessment (p. 2):

> *The evidence is that differences among American or British whites in the past generation have been due in part to genetic differences. The precise proportion, but not the principle, of hereditary influence can be debated. Yet the statistic is an index of sociocultural conditions, not a biological inevitability. Change that distribution of nutrition, home experience, and schooling in the next generation, and the heritability index will change. Findings on heritability within white populations tell us nothing whatsoever about how white and black groups would compare if their environments had been equalized. Note also that a high degree of heritability does not imply that improved environment can have no effect. Even if the heritability index is as high as .80, two children with the same genotype may differ by as much as 25 IQ points if one is reared in a superior environment and the other in an unstimulating one.*

Finally, consider the following comment in a report by a special American Psychological Association committee (Cleary et. al., 1975, p. 17):

> *. . . all ability tests (whether called intelligence, aptitude or achievement tests) measure current performance. There are no measures of innate capacity.*
> *This is true not because the hereditary-environment problem has been solved, but because no known operations involving tests would make possible an interpretation with regard to innate capacity.*

How Much Can IQ Be Boosted?

In the infamous article (of almost the same title) which brought Arthur Jensen into the public eye, his opening sentence was (1969, p. 60), "Compensatory education has been tried and it apparently has failed." The main reason for his pessimistic statement was that the evidence he reviewed showed (1) that there was a large genetic component to IQ, and (2) that pre-school and compensatory programs on the whole produced small gains in IQ, where they produced gains at all. He had come down on the side of "fixed" IQ and "jensenism" became "the theory that I.Q. is largely determined by the genes" (Edson, 1969).[11]

Although there is much evidence for the argument that IQ cannot be raised very much by environmental changes, there is also evidence that it can. A comparison of IQs of World War I and World War II draftees showed an increase of one standard deviation, and another one-fourth standard deviation between WW II and 1963 (e.g., Cleary et al., 1975). This was accompanied by a large increase in years of formal schooling. As Cleary et al. (1975) point out, this finding can be plausibly explained as an environmental effect but, because different people are involved, a genetic cause cannot be ruled out. Scarr and Weinberg (1976) provided data showing that a sample of black children adopted by white parents had IQs from 16 to 20 points higher than their natural parents, whose mean IQ was estimated to be 90. The earlier the age at which they were adopted, the higher the IQ. Thus the adoptive home environment can have an appreciable effect. Jensen (1969) himself cited similar examples, though he concluded that they were rare and needed replication (See Minton and Schneider, 1980, for other evidence).

Jensen's pessimistic conclusion, however, was only about IQ. He argued that much more improvement was possible in scholastic achievement (p. 192).

> *Educators would probably do better to concern themselves with teaching skills directly than with attempting to boost overall cognitive development. By the same token, they should de-emphasize IQ tests as a means of assessing gains, and use mainly direct tests of the skills the instructional program is intended to inculcate.*

In a way, we have come full circle back to our starting point. Jensen is telling us, as he had stated earlier in his article (p. 88), that intelligence as measured by the IQ is "only a part of the whole spectrum of human abilities." Jensen's solution to both the racial differences and the boosting of intelligence problems is to ignore race and treat each person individually for educational purposes (see also Nichols, 1986). In other chapters we shall encounter a number of other human cognitive abilities (in problem-solving, memory strategies, etc.) which are subject to remarkable improvements. Any specific cognitive or psychomotor skill falls into that category. People can continue to improve their golf, their chess, or their memories, moving from novices to experts (with corresponding changes in rankings within those fields). Nevertheless, their IQs may hardly change at all.

There are also socio-political issues to contend with in asking whether and how much IQ can be boosted. From the shape of the normal curve it is obvious that there are no "natural breaks" which define the difference between, say, gifted and normal or normal and retarded. Wherever the line is drawn, there are a large number of "borderline" cases. Thus it should come as no surprise that from time to time there have been redefinitions in terms of IQ scores of such value-laden terms as "retarded." If IQ cannot be boosted very much, we can at least improve everybody's intellectual status by redefining the categories. Anecdote 3.3 takes a tongue-in-cheek look at this process.

IQ Tests and Their Misuses

The Case of LT: LT was referred to the school psychologist by his second grade teacher because he "appears to be of average intelligence but is only at a primer instructional level." The psychologist tested LT on the WISC-R and obtained a verbal IQ of 70 and a performance IQ of 103. The psychologist's report commented that LT's performance placed him in the "low average" range in intelligence with an "extreme discrepancy between verbal and performance abilities." The report went on:

> *The low verbal ability IQ may be collectively attributed to limited general information fund or long term learning; poor ability to form generalizations or make abstractions: poor verbal expressive abilities and limited meaningful vocabulary in comparison with peers of similar age range; and poor judgment with respect to practical solutions to everyday problems or common sense. . . . It is recommended that LT be considered for definite resource room placement for next year; and if possible a learning center placement would seem preferable.*

Some days later the psychologist telephoned LT's mother to summarize the test results and wrote the following addition to the report:

> *Mrs. _____ indicated that Portuguese is normally spoken at home and this would at least partially account for LT's low verbal abilities development.*[12]

The above account is provided by Cummins (1984, pp. 36, 38) who notes "how easy it is for psychologists to interpret test scores

Anecdote 3.3

The Miracle Method in Education*

It is often reported that educational programs are minimally effective at best and that none is very much better than any others. But in reviewing the literature in special education over the last decade, it occurred to me that we have not adequately publicized an educational program which is so uniquely effective that in one year it cured approximately 87.5% of the mentally retarded people in this country. This is no small feat when it is considered that this group accounted for approximately 14% of the total population of this country which, at that time, meant that about 28 million people were sufficiently cured of their retardedness to be forevermore classified as normal.

I am sure that you will agree that such an educational technique borders on the miraculous and deserves a NOBEL[1] Prize for Education. In fact, in addition to the education prize, the developers of the method should receive a NOBEL[2] Prize for Economics, because this marvelous program hardly costs a cent.

Well, I won't keep you in suspense any longer. The miracle method is the method of redefinition. In the case in point, a major defining characteristic of mental retardation was scoring at or below one standard deviation below the mean on an intelligence test (IQ<85). In 1973, however, this same criterion was changed to two standard deviations below the mean (IQ<70). For those of you who carry your handy-dandy pocket-sized electronic calculator with the normal curve person-ranking IQ function key (or see figure 3.1), a quick calculation will reveal the following: by this redefinition approximately 14% of the population, previously considered retarded, are now normal.

Except for the application to mental retardation, educators and psychologists have not nearly been as creative as politicians in the uses of the redefinition method. So I would like to propose some other perennial problems which could be solved by this redefinition method. These follow:

1. Increasing the number of gifted people in the society: we could redefine giftedness to include anyone whose IQ is at least one standard deviation above the mean (>115), instead of two standard deviations. This 14% of the population has previously been taught as though they were average, but after exposure to this method, they would be eligible to receive the special privileges and recognitions that society bestows upon the gifted, such as exemption from the draft, receipt of scholarships, election to Mensa, and recruitment of semen and ova for donations to the gene pools and cloning colonies.

. . . . .

3. Reducing the stress of being different: We could redefine short people as "normal for their height" or obese people as "normal for their weight." In fact, normality should be redefined to include "anyone whose score falls under the normal curve."

   1. *NOBEL* in this case is an acronym for Never Overlook Bull . . . in Educational Lingo.
   2. *NOBEL* in this case is an acronym for Never Overlook Bull . . . in Economic Lingo.

*Reprinted and abridged from Gentile (1983).

automatically when they are not sensitized to manifestations of cultural/linguistic differences." He goes on to note that even when the psychologist learns that LT is operating in school and on the test in his second language, the report notes "low verbal abilities development rather than 'present level of cognitive/academic functioning in English'." Indeed, how would psychologists do if tested in their second language!

Their are several potential biases in the above example. First, there may be cultural biases in the test items themselves. Consider the following hypothetical question: "What is similar and dissimilar between a football and a basketball?" For people accustomed to playing or seeing American or Canadian football on television, the shape of the balls would be an obvious difference. For people who grew up in most of the rest of the world, however, football means soccer and thus shape would not be a difference. This hypothetical example is meant to show the problem of nuances of meaning that can occur in test items. Or, to take a real example, the 1960 revision of the Stanford-Binet asked six-year-old to look at two faces and judge "Which is prettier?" To be scored correct, the child had to judge an obviously Anglo-Saxon-looking face prettier than the comparison face (Karier, 1972).

Such examples show the kinds of biases that have been and could still be included on IQ tests if the test makers and users are not scrupulously diligent. Of course, it is impossible to write a test that is totally devoid of cultural content; on the other hand, most blatant examples of cultural bias have probably been significantly reduced if not eliminated in modern standardized intelligence tests. Even where some allegedly biased items remain in a test, it is by no means obvious—without actual test data—that these items really are biased against any particular group. Further, since IQ scores are based on a number of items of various types, the bias would have to operate in a similar way across the entire test. When such systematic biases against women or minorities are found in current standardized testing programs, the offending items are routinely dropped and scores derived from the remaining nonbiased items. Much popular criticism to the contrary (e.g., Hoffman, 1962), therefore, there is not much empirical evidence to support the claims of widespread bias against minority groups in the test items themselves. In a major review of the whole problem of bias, Jensen (1980, p. 715) summarized the evidence as follows:

> . . . *many lines of psychometric evidence converge to the conclusion that, by and large, current standardized tests of general mental ability and scholastic achievement . . . are not biased with respect to any native-born, English-speaking minority groups in the United States. This generalization can be extended in the case of nonverbal tests to native-born English-speaking minority groups as well.*

To make this point in a totally different way, consider what we would find if we measured the height of all the men and women in a randomly selected college class. It would probably be found, with some overlaps, that the men were several inches taller on the average and that a ranking from the tallest to shortest would have mostly men at the top of the distribution and women at the bottom. Assume further that the instructor decided to base course grades on height, with all those above 6'0" receiving A's, those between 5'9" and 5'11" receiving B's, and so on. This would clearly be a sexist grading scheme, but would anyone claim that the sexism was in the measuring instrument, in this case the tape measure?

The analogy to tests is this: if men and women, blacks and whites, or any other comparisons differ significantly on a math test, say, that does not necessarily prove a bias in the test. There may, in fact, be real differences in the population on knowledge of math. The most likely source of the bias in such cases is

Anecdote 3.4

Quotas, Biases, and Power

The 1990s in America have seen a continuing debate about quotas, affirmative action, reverse discrimination and the like. The following story, from journalist Gwynne Dyer (11/8/87), *Buffalo Evening News*, shows how the British solved a similar problem—namely, when eleven-year-old girls outperformed boys on the 11-plus examination.

Since there was room for only 10% of applicants in the state-supported college preparatory "grammar schools" at the secondary level, students were administered a national exam at age 11, designed to select the best and brightest for those schools. Reporting on a study by George Rawcliffe, Dyer exposed a dirty little secret: most of the highest scores (Dyer reports about 90%) belonged to girls; but rather than fill these high-prestige grammar schools with mostly girls, the administrators of this program—probably white males—secretly adopted the following quota system:

> *Boys and girls were separated into different lists, and the fortunate few were selected in equal numbers from the top of each list.*

One has to wonder: if most of the highest scores were earned by boys, would those in power have made it a point to have an equal quota for girls? If, in America, Blacks or Hispanics outscored whites on admissions tests, would there be any talk about how unconstitutional quotas are?

---

the differential opportunities and reinforcements offered by society for achievement in math. Although the tests are nowhere near perfect, the major sources of racism, sexism, and all the other "isms" arise from societal inequalities much more than from test items.

A much more serious problem than bias in the tests themselves (as Jensen, 1980, acknowledged two paragraphs after the above quote) is the problem of test misuse. An example of such misuse is the LT anecdote provided above.

As Cleary et al. (1975) note, if a test has good guidelines and instructions in its manual, it should be easy to administer a test only to the appropriate persons and under the appropriate conditions. For example, it should be no problem" . . . to exclude examinees with auditory or visual defects, or those using a foreign language, from the testing session, but horror stories of misuse abound" (pp. 21–22). Indeed they do.

Another more insidious problem is test misinterpretation by the psychologist, the teacher, the parents, the children, and so on. Does a one or two standard deviation discrepancy between verbal and performance IQs really indicate that the examinee has a "learning disability"? Cummins (1984) provides a wide variety of examples of how children for whom English is a second language are diagnosed as learning disabled on the basis of such scores.

A class-action suit (DIANA et al. v. STATE BOARD OF EDUCATION) in California in 1970 brought this issue into the legal system, although it was eventually settled out of court (e.g. Jensen, 1980, pp. 30 31). Nine children of Mexican-American parents were placed in classes for the Educable Mentally Retarded, primarily on the basis of IQ test scores which ranged from 30 to 72. On retests conducted in Spanish, the IQs averaged 15 points higher, so that seven of the nine were no longer classified as retarded. Diana, whose

IQ in English was 30, scored 49 points higher when tested in Spanish.

How can such "horror stories" continue to happen? One reason concerns our currently legislated needs for objective and presumably valid reasons for assigning children to special classes. Concomitantly, school districts receive additional funding to hire special education teachers, school psychologists, and the like, for each additional "learning disabled," "retarded," or otherwise "special" student. This, unfortunately, leads school districts into a kind of "bounty hunting," since additional funding comes for each new child who is diagnosed as in need of special help. Sadly, some parents play into this notion by requesting that their children, who may not be doing well in school, be classified as learning disabled, so that they can get extra and better instruction. Even when such help is provided—and the rub is that the promised aides are often the victims of budget cuts—it is questionable whether the extra assistance can overcome the stigma usually attached to being "special" (e.g., Binet and Simon, 1916).

Another reason concerns the special predictive validity that is involved in IQ scores as predictors of later performance and the normative group against which the examinees are competing. Clearly et al. (1975, p. 18) state the assumptions quite clearly:

> *The first assumption is acceptance of a single society, heterogeneous though it may be, rather than a divided one. The second assumption is that few radical changes are expected in curriculum content or methodology or instruction in our educational establishment even though such changes are more strongly indicated than are changes in tests. The third assumption accepts the importance of evaluation in education. Diagnosis, prognosis, prescription and measurement of outcomes are as important in education as in medicine. If these assumptions are rejected, the research on which this report is based could become more or less irrelevant.*

Critics of current uses of IQ (and other) tests do question all of these assumptions. The first assumption takes it as a given that minority children should be compared against a national reference group in the latter's language because that is the group with whom they will be competing (e.g., Clarizio, 1981). Furthermore, it assumes that they should compete before they choose to compete—an assumption we would totally reject if the competition were in sports, for example. Suppose, however, that the second and third assumptions were abandoned and we actually changed schools remarkably. Instead of comparing students with one another, suppose we adopted threshold levels of standards for performance as is done with driver's licenses. That is, suppose we adopted criterion-referenced measurement and mastery learning procedures instead of norm-referenced—an approach we shall discuss in detail in a later chapter. Then "diagnosis, prognosis, prescription and measurement of outcomes" would be done for each individual, at least in schools, with the result that educators would spend their time motivating students to become as competent as possible in each area of study. Competition will indeed be part of their lives later for jobs and for higher education, but at least educators will assume the role of teachers and leave the role of sorting and ranking to others.

It is my own personal view that even when we do not misuse intelligence tests, we overuse them. When we need diagnosis and prescription we need information more specific than such tests tell us, such as exactly what can students do and what they can not yet do and in what domain of curriculum and educational objectives. (See also Jensen, 1980, p. 716, for a similar argument.) IQ tests do not give us such information even when properly administered and interpreted for the majority population. And while they may be useful for certain research purposes, for predicting success in certain fields, and *for identifying children as normal whom schools have abandoned—perhaps the best use of IQ tests*—their ubiquitous nature in the schools is, in my opinion, an error.

Fortunately, there are alternative conceptions of intelligence which can easily fill any void that would be left by a reduction in IQ testing. As we shall see, if children are presumed to have a memory problem, there are ways to improve their memories. If their learning strategies are suspect, there are procedures that can be used to increase these capabilities. Such specific training can be helpful for learning disabled as well as nondisabled, for retarded as well as normal, and for slow as well as fast learners. The approach breaks intelligence into its component skills and attempts to understand and, where appropriate, to teach them directly. Part of the next chapter deals with those issues.

Conclusions

Whether explicitly or implicitly, intelligence is a concept that affects schooling profoundly. Some teachers place the IQs of their students in their grade books next to the name of their students even before they have met the class for the first time. They probably believe that such knowledge will help them adapt to the children's needs, although it is doubtful if they would condone that practice if done by their professors on them (see anecdote 3.5).

There are several problems with using IQ scores in schools, however, among them the following:

1. The scores themselves may not be accurate, particularly for children who are not from the dominate cultural or linguistic group.
2. Those who receive the scores may not understand the statistics involved well enough to interpret the scores correctly (that includes many teachers, administrators, and parents).

Photo 3.4. Measure Mania. For budding scientists and psychologists.

3. The scores, right or wrong, may influence the teacher's expectations about the students (e.g., Good and Brophy, 1978; Good, 1987). This will eventually show up in the teacher's classroom organization (Mary is in the best reading group, Billy is in the worst) and behavior (how patient the teacher is, what kinds of assignments are given to which students, etc.).
4. What the teacher's expectations are for students will eventually be understood and more than likely internalized by them: "We're the dumb ones; don't bother trying to teach us" is a phrase many teachers have heard in lower track classrooms. When teachers do not expect much of students, they learn to expect little of themselves, which eventually becomes a self-fulfilling prophecy.

Properly used, IQ scores do give reliable norm-referenced information on a student's functioning relative to peers of the same age. As part of a diagnostic package, certified psychologists may use such information effectively to do the following:

1. Rule out major neurological dysfunction as a cause of a child's school difficulties; if IQ is in the normal or high range, then any learning problems the teacher may perceive cannot be blamed on physiological factors.

Anecdote 3.5

The Teachers with "IQ 87"

In the process of teaching a course on tests and measurements to teachers, Harry Forgan (1973) administered an adult group intelligence test. The 48 teachers in his class put a code number that only they could identify on the 50-minute test. Forgan scored the tests, and found that the IQs ranged from 87 to 143, with a mean of 117.

In returning the tests, Forgan got a devious idea: he wrote "IQ 87" on each person's report, folded and stapled the paper, and wrote the different code numbers on the outside of the fake reports. In class, he wrote the real range and mean of the scores on the board, then had the teachers come forward row by row to pick up their reports, but told them not to tell others their IQs.

Forgan reported that there was "dead silence" when he explained that in some states persons with scores below 90 would be classified as slow learners, and that many schools use such scores for ability grouping. As his ruse unfolded, surprising even himself, Forgan suggested that they try ability grouping in his class. At the proper signal, he said, he wanted those with IQs below 90 to sit in the front of class (so he could more easily give them individual help); those with IQs between 90-109 to sit in the middle, and those 110 or above to go to the back of the room.

When Forgan asked those with IQs less than 90 to come forward, everyone looked around, but no one moved. Forgan said, "I knew there was an 87 and maybe a couple of 89's." Still no one moved in the dead silence.

When he asked those with 90-109 to move, 8 to 10 students got up to move. Before they moved very far, Forgan said,

"Wait a minute! Sit down! I don't want to embarrass you, but you would lie and cheat—the same way we make our students lie and cheat—because you don't want to be classified as 'slow.' I wrote 'IQ 87' on every paper!"

Forgan went on to say,

> The class erupted. It was in an uproar for about five minutes. Some of the women cried, some indicated that they needed to use the restroom. All agreed it was a horrifying and yet valuable experience.

2. Prescribe educational exercises which may strengthen areas of known weakness in, say, memory or perception as in Binet and Simon's "mental orthopedics," or to help children find ways of compensating for any weaknesses by capitalizing on their strengths.

In the next chapter we shall explore alternative conceptions of intelligence which deemphasize and bypass IQ, emphasizing instead the developmental aspects of intellectual growth.

Practice Exercises

A. Practice Items

On the following multiple-choice items, select the alternative choice which best answers the question. (Answers in Note 13).

1. Binet's first intelligence test was designed to
   a. select people for jobs.
   b. keep feeble-minded immigrants out of the country.
   c. identify people who need special education help.
   d. provide a paper-and-pencil measure of genetic potential.

2. Mary, who is 12, has a Mental Age of 15. Joseph, who is 10, has an IQ of 120. Which of the following statements is true on the basis of a ratio IQ calculation?
   a. Mary has a higher IQ than Joseph.
   b. Joseph has a higher Mental Age than Mary.
   c. Both Mary and Joseph have IQs of 120.
   d. None of the above are true.

3. A typical IQ test, with a mean of 100 and a standard deviation of 15, is used to classify people as retarded if they score at or below 70. Using that cutting score of 70, 16% of immigrants from a particular country were classified as retarded. From this information we can be fairly sure that
   a. the immigrants score one standard deviation below the mean of the residents.
   b. the average IQ score of the immigrants is about 85.
   c. there are eight times as many immigrants than residents classified as retarded.
   d. all of the above are probably true.

4. If heritability of intelligence is shown to be .80, according to the argument of the text, then teachers can have important effects
   a. on both students' relative rankings and their specific knowledge and skills.
   b. on students' specific knowledge and skills, but not on their relative rankings.
   c. on students' relative rankings, but not on their specific knowledge and skills.
   d. on neither students' relative rankings nor on their specific knowledge and skills.

For items 5 and 6, consider the following graph, in which the numbers 1–6 refer to areas of the curve and the numbers 7–11 to specific points on the curve.

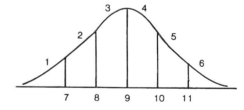

5. Which number or numbers refer to portions of the curve in which fewer than 5% of the people fall?
   a. both 1 and 2
   b. both 3 and 4
   c. 1, 2, 5 and 6
   d. both 1 and 6

6. Minus one-half standard deviation ($Z = -0.5$) falls where in the above curve?
   a. to the left of 7
   b. at 7
   c. between 7 and 8
   d. between 8 and 9

7. Which of the following scores is closest to the mean of its group?
   a. a score of -1.0
   b. 12, where the mean is 15, and the SD is 3
   c. a percentile rank of 16
   d. they are all equally close

8. NORM-REFERENCED is to CRITERION-REFERENCED as
   a. course objectives are to standardized tests
   b. percentile ranks are to percent correct
   c. learning is to comparing
   d. standard scores are to percentile ranks

9. Which of the following is the best example of the problem mentioned by the author of "the predictor becoming the criterion"?
   a. Oscar is refused admission to college because his Scholastic Aptitude Test scores are too low.
   b. Margaret is not given the award for best student because, though she had the highest grade, her IQ is so high she did not have to work hard to attain those grades.
   c. Despite getting mostly A's in graduate school, his advisor gives Peter a poor recommendation because his Graduate Record Exam (admission test) scores were too low.
   d. Colleen, who is gifted, always gets A's.

For the next four items, you may wish to consult Appendix B as well as this chapter.

10. The mean
    a. is the midpoint of a distribution.
    b. is the balance point of distribution.
    c. is the most frequent term in a distribution.
    d. is all of the above.

11. Consider the following test scores:
    100
    90
    80
    70
    60

    The standard deviation of these scores is about
    a. 50
    b. 14
    c. 200
    d. 10

12. The Spearman rs correlation provides a measure of
    a. the relationship between two sets of rankings.
    b. the amount of growth in knowledge from one test to the next.
    c. the difficulty of a test.
    d. all of the above.

13. The following provide two sets of scores on the same five individuals:

	Test 1	Test 2
Broom-Hilda	10	50
Momma	20	10
Lolly	30	20
Blondie	40	30
Beetle	50	40

The correlation (e.g., the Spearman r_s) between these two sets of scores will yield which of the following values?

a. –1.0
b. +1.0
c. 0
d. it is impossible to tell from the information given.

B. For Cooperative Study (in or out of class):

1. In small groups discuss the various parts of study questions 12–14. What can be done to give each child equal educational opportunity? Do we have to have the same educational programs for all in order to do that? How do we keep disproportionate numbers of minorities from being stigmatized as in need of "special education?"

2. Have your instructor provide the anonymous scores for your class on a recent test. Then work together, or split into subgroups, to do the following (you may wish to consult the formulas in Appendix B):
   a. Do a frequency distribution to see how close your scores approximate a normal curve.
   b. Calculate the mean and standard deviation of your scores.
   c. What is the median or 50th percentile point?
   d. Calculate the z-scores for a high, a medium, and a low score on the test.

3. Contact your campus testing agency and see whether they can send a representative to demonstrate or administer parts of one or more currently used IQ tests. Then discuss your impressions of the items.

4. What would you say or feel if your own offspring was tested and found to have an IQ of 90? or 70? or 130?

C. For Further Study:

1. Read one or more of the following:
   a. Histories of mental testing (see Note 1).
   b. Advocates of mental testing (e.g., Jensen, Terman, Wechsler, or Herrnstein & Murray).
   c. Critics of mental testing (e.g., Cummins, Gould, or Kamin).

2. Research the state and federal laws on IQ testing for placing people in jobs or special education.

3. Alone or in small groups, work through the procedure for calculating a Spearman rank order correlation (by following the procedures in Appendix B). Then calculate the correlations for each of the following distributions.

a. Test 1	Test 2	b. Test 1	Test 2
20	20	20	12
18	18	18	14
16	16	16	16
14	14	14	18
12	12	12	20

What do these correlations mean?

CHAPTER
STUDY QUESTIONS

1. In broad outline, what are the central features of the following theories of intelligence?
    a. Sternberg's Triarchic Theory
    b. Gardner's Multiple Intelligences
    c. Feuerstein's Instrumental Enrichment

    How are they similar? Dissimilar?

2. What is meant by each of the following components of Sternberg's theory?
    a. context of intelligence
    b. intelligence and experience
    c. components of intelligence
        (1) metacomponents
        (2) knowledge acquisition components
        (3) performance components

3. How is each of Sternberg's components involved in each of the following activities?
    a. ascertaining the meaning of a word from its context
    b. defining the problem
    c. drawing inferences
    d. allocating time to a problem in a test
    e. developing speed
    f. elaborating or visualizing a concept in order to memorize it

4. What is meant by each of Gardner's intelligences?
    a. Linguistic
    b. Logical-Mathematical
    c. Spatial
    d. Musical
    e. Bodily-Kinesthetic
    f. Interpersonal
    g. Intrapersonal

5. What does Gardner mean by each of the following ideas?
    a. "at risk" vs. "at promise"
    b. a profile of intelligences

FOUR

6. What is meant by each of the following cognitive functions in Feuerstein's theory?
    a. the input phase
    b. the elaboration phase
    c. the output phase
    d. affective-maturational factors

7. What does Feuerstein mean by each of the following ideas?
    a. cognitive modifiability via mediated learning
    b. cultural deprivation

8. Your author makes the following comment regarding the "new" intelligence theories compared with the traditional:

    "I believe that the essence of the differences between these approaches rests in the distinction between norm-referenced and criterion-referenced assessment."

    Defend his argument. Do you agree?

9. Contrast the instructional implications of Sternberg's, Gardner's, and Feuerstein's theories with those of traditional IQ theories.

10. What is meant by each of the following parts of the cognitive constructivist definition of meaningful learning? Learning must be:
    a. active
    b. constructive
    c. intentional
    d. cumulative
    e. metacognitive
    f. socially mediated

11. What are the educational implications of each of the following developmental issues? Give examples.
    a. active learning and cognitive constructivism
    b. creating cognitive conflicts
    c. metacognitive processes
    d. mastery of prerequisites.
    e. maturational unfolding or developmental crisis

12. How do children's crises interact with teachers' or other adults' crises? What does this imply about how we need to treat each other?

Intelligence and Its Possibilties

Introduction

1. The fact that it is reasonable to hope to find ways of raising the level of intellectual capacity in a majority of the population makes it a challenge to do the necessary research. It is one of the major challenges of our time. It is a challenge, moreover, where the chances are fairly good that the behavioral sciences can make a contribution of great social, as well as theoretical, significance. (Hunt, 1961, p. 363)
2. . . . a tester can always average over multiple scores. But are such averages revealing, or do they camouflage more than they reveal? If a person is a wonderful visualizer but can barely compose a sentence, and another person can write glowing prose but cannot begin to visualize the simplest spatial images, what do you really learn about these two people if they are reported to have the same IQ? (Sternberg, 1988, p. 8)
3. But there is an alternative vision . . . a pluralistic view of mind, recognizing many different and discrete facets of cognition, acknowledging that people have different cognitive strengths and contrasting cognitive styles. I would also like to introduce the concept of an individual-centered school that takes this multifaceted view of intelligence seriously. (Gardner, 1993, p. 6)
4. In the final analysis, it is elaboration that determines our cognitive behavior. Impaired input and output may exist, but if the child is able to elaborate he can bypass the barriers obstructing the regular channels of input or output such that his level of functioning may go beyond what could have been expected on the basis of specific peripheral deficiencies. An excellent model of such bypassing of regular channels of input and output can be found in the achievement of Helen Keller, who, in spite of blindness and deafness, was able to function cognitively with a high level of efficiency. (Feuerstein, Rand, Hoffman, & Miller, 1980, pp. 75–76)
5. . . . thousands of research studies have been conducted on the effects of schooling on knowledge and performance. Strangely, it cannot be said that there exists systematic information on the effects of schooling on cognitive abilities, neither global intelligence nor specific mental abilities. This is partly due to the fact that producing changes in mental abilities is not usually thought to be an objective of education. (Carroll, 1993, p. 668)

If the fixed-rank, hereditary general factor ("g"), standardized and norm-referenced approach to intelligence described in the previous chapter is troubling to you, then you will be much more excited by the alternative conceptions presented in this chapter. The flavor is captured in the opening quotes: there is more to intelligence than "g" or IQ; there are, in fact, multiple ways of being intelligent; and, most importantly, these intelligences can and should be taught even if they have no effect on IQ score.

Intelligence and Its Possibilities 97

Cartoon 4.1.

The middle three quotes are from three theorists—Robert Sternberg, Howard Gardner, and Reuven Feuerstein—who seem to have taken J. McV. Hunt's challenge (quote #1) personally. They have contributed theories which they believe can alter our traditional views of intelligence, as well as practical exercises to increase and assess intellectual capacity. The last quote from the author of the most current theory of intelligence (Carroll, 1993), as well as a popular model of school learning (Carroll, 1963), supports the other three in implying that societies, and schools in particular, need to broaden their mission to include the development of cognitive abilities.

Critics of these approaches, such as Herrnstein and Murray (1994), argue that the correlations among the multiple intelligences still show evidence of "g" and pessimistically conclude, "For many people, there is nothing that they can learn that will repay the cost of teaching" (p. 520). But even if Herrnstein and Murray are economically correct that instruction for all is not cost effective, it does not follow (as many argue) that society should assign roles, jobs and status based on mental ability or, even more perniciously, sterilize people with low cognitive ability (as was ordered by the courts in this country in 1927; e.g., Gould, 1981, pp. 335–336).

Alternative conceptions are possible, including that society has an obligation, regardless of cost, to protect and facilitate every individual's life, liberty and pursuit of developmental potentials. The three theorists with which we begin this chapter remain steadfastly committed to such a view.

Anecdote 4.1

Culture Shock in Nigeria

Case 1. Sternberg (1986, p. 35) provides this example of the need for cultural adaptation in intelligence testing. In 1971 Joseph Glick and his colleagues were studying the classification processes of citizens of the Kpelle ethnic group. One task was to sort cards with words or pictures on them.

Now, in the western world (including IQ tests), more intelligent behavior is to sort by taxonomic category (e.g., fruit or vehicle) than by function (e.g., we eat it or we travel in it). But the Kpelle adults clearly preferred functional sorting, and the researchers had much difficulty eliciting taxonomic sorting. In a desperate but inspired move, Glick asked his subjects to sort the cards as stupid people would. They then sorted like the western world.

Case 2. Your author had the good fortune to spend more than a year in Nigeria at an Igbo college of education, over several trips in the late 1970s. On one of the trips, I arrived almost a week late due to visa difficulties. On arrival, I was warmly welcomed but told that the promised housing did not yet have furniture in it. When I asked why it wasn't ready, my hosts answered, "Because we expected you last week."

In the U.S.A., that answer makes no sense, of course, and I probably thought as much. Fortunately, by then I had had sufficient experience in Nigeria to appreciate the sensibility in the remark. Since travel and communication between Nigeria and the rest of the world was difficult, travelers seldom arrived when expected, if expected at all. In addition, furnishing unoccupied college housing meant that it had to be guarded, adding to college expenses. Thus it was entirely reasonable in context for them to be unprepared "because we expected you last week."

Sternberg's Triarchic Theory

Sternberg's theory of human intelligence consists of three parts: (1) the internal mechanisms or cognitive components of the individual that produce intelligent behavior; (2) the interaction of mental processes with experience, specifically the ability to automatize certain tasks or functions and focus attention on novelty; and (3) the environment or cultural context in which the cognition occurs. Combining these three overlapping parts provides the following definition of intelligence (Sternberg, 1986, p. 33): *mental activity involved in purposive adaptation to, shaping of, and selection of real-world environments relevant to one's life.*

Context of Intelligence

Taking the third leg of the theory first, notice that this definition requires a specification of the context. Sternberg does not recognize intelligence in the abstract; rather behavior is intelligent or stupid depending upon the context in which it occurs. One facet of context relevance is *adaptation* to one's culture or environment. Survival skills in the inner city are different from those in the mountains or, perhaps, even the suburbs. The residents of each

Photo 4.1. Siblings in a Nigerian village.

of these areas develop patterns of thinking and interacting that are quite unique; behavior that is intelligent in one setting may appear quite strange or stupid in another. For examples from Nigeria, see anecdote 4.1.

Adaptation itself, however, is not even sufficient for judging intelligence in context. Sternberg (1986, p. 36) argues that there are many instances in which it is "maladaptive to be adaptive" such as staying in a dead end job or abusive relationship, or following the crowd because everyone else is doing it. Thus the second and third facets of the context relevance of intelligence are *selection* and *shaping* of your own environment. To find an environment in which you fit or change it to fit you requires that you know your own strengths and weaknesses, preferences and values, facilitative working conditions, and stressors. Then and only then can you select or create the environmental conditions under which you can work and live intelligently.

Intelligence and Experience

To know yourself as described in the last paragraph requires that you benefit from experience. We have all joked about people asking, "Did he have twenty years of experience or one year of experience twenty times?" Benefitting from experience then, is the second leg of Sternberg's theory and it involves learning (1) how to automatize routine tasks so that (2) we can focus our attention on novelty. Consider the task of reading. The better your decoding skills are automatized, the easier it is to focus on what is novel in the text—namely, the content to be comprehended. Conversely, if you have to focus most of your energy on decoding the words, there is little energy remaining to process the information in the text.

By this view, then, intelligence grows by learning how to learn, by mastering fundamental skills to the point of automaticity, and then learning how to attend to and cognitively process the novel features of tasks. These are also some of the major features which distinguish between experts and novices in a given field and, as we shall see in a later chapter, these skills are learned and therefore teachable.

Components of Intelligence

The first leg of Sternberg's triarchic theory involves the mental mechanisms within the individual—the cognitive components which interact with the environment (leg 3) and which, hopefully, benefit from experience (leg 2). Sternberg (1986, 1988) identifies three components of intelligence, having the following functions:[1]

1. *metacomponents,* which are the executive or metacognitive processes which control and monitor allocation of time and energy, define the problem and find a mental representation, check solutions to see if they make sense, etc.
2. *performance components,* which act to carry out plans, draw inferences, do calculations, apply the rules, etc.
3. *knowledge acquisition components,* which encode and organize information, find ways to get more information (from contexts, for example), etc.

Consider how such components function effectively in taking a timed test like the

Scholastic Aptitude Test. A test-wise person first looks over the whole test, deciding what questions will be readily answered and which will take longer or be more difficult. He or she is deciding on a strategy—e.g., do the easy questions first—and allocating time and mental resources (metacomponents). He or she then answers the easy questions (performance components). When a difficult word is encountered, the test-wise person attempts to figure it out from context or sometimes gets a clue about a concept from another question on the test (knowledge acquisition components). To be sure that a calculation or logical deduction makes sense, he or she estimates an answer or monitors the thinking used (metacomponents), then recalculates (performance components). If the logic needed is too abstract, he or she invents a word problem or draws a graph to make it more meaningful (knowledge acquisition components). When a problem is taking too much time, the test-wise individual decides to move to another problem and come back to that one later (metacomponents).

In short, metacomponents decide what to do, how long to spend on it and whether what was done makes sense; knowledge acquisition components gather the information needed; and performance components do it. Just as test-taking skills are improvable so, says Sternberg, are all of these components of intelligence. We can all get better and faster—on each of these components and table 4.1 displays some of the kinds of problems he recommends for practice. Note, however, that the sign of an intelligent person is not just to be fast, but to know when to act quickly and when to take extra time—a crucial metacognitive activity.

Sternberg's Theory: In Conclusion

It is important to acknowledge that Sternberg is *not* claiming, as some popular psychology books seem to do, to "raise your IQ in ten-minutes a day." He is, rather, attempting to go "Beyond IQ" (Sternberg, 1985) to identify the important components of intelligence and then help people improve on those. In fact, Sternberg (1987) argues that the very strategies that are often used to teach people to achieve higher intelligence test scores—such strategies as "work as quickly as you can," "read everything carefully," "memorize vocabulary," or "use all the information in the problem"—may help in the short run on the immediate test, but will be counterproductive in the long run in increasing intellectual skills. As we have seen, *good metacognitive processing requires working slowly at certain stages, provides for allocating reading time on the basis of purpose, emphasizes inferring meanings of words in context, and requires selective encoding of what information in a problem is relevant.* Sternberg emphasizes these basic components because he, along with many other current cognitive psychologists, considers them to have wide generalizability in daily life (e.g., reading, shopping, understanding claims of advertisers or politicians), as well as on standardized tests and in-school tasks.

In sum, Sternberg believes that ". . . we not only *can* but *should* teach intelligence" (1986, p. 22). Moreover, as his recent critique of *The Bell Curve* indicates, he believes we need to remain humble about intelligence and its contribution to human worth (Sternberg, 1996, p. 15):

> *. . . We need to rethink what we mean by intelligence, recognizing that there is more to intelligence than IQ and, more importantly, that we need not get caught in the ancient human trap of conflating some attribute of humans that we may happen to value with human worth. Somewhere, some time, it may have been noble birth; at another time or place, sheer wealth; at yet another time or place, hunting or gathering skills, physical prowess, physical attractiveness, or whatever. At any given time, we probably consider a combination of these and other attributes in assessing people. But none of these is tantamount to human worth—to our values as human beings.*

Table 4.1 Activities for practicing Sternberg's components of intelligence.

A. *For Metacomponent Practice.* How should the following problems be defined or represented?
  1. What is the number of possible orders (permutations) in which the letters A, B, C, and D can occur (e.g., ABCD and DCBA are two of the possible orders)? List them.
  2. Connect the 9 dots (in Chapter 9, Problem 9.8) using four straight lines.
B. *For Performance Practice.* What is the logical or inferential fallacy in each of the following statements (the statements are your author's; the five kinds of fallacies are from Sternberg's list of 19):
  1. "Our new neighbor plays the guitar, so I guess rock music will be blazing at all hours."
  2. "You have exceeded the number of excused absences you may have, so you'll have to be suspended from school for three days."
  8. "Research conducted at a prestigious Ivy League University showed Aspercapsules to be effective in relieving pain."
  13. "If I can't have the car on Saturday night, then there is no point in going to the school dance."
  19. "If you haven't taught in a high school recently, then you have nothing of importance to say to teachers."
C. *For Knowledge Acquisition Practice.*
  1. What do the following words mean from their context?
    a. He had reached the *nadir* of his existence, hardly having the strength to go on.
    b. Like a stand of trees in a desert, the *archipelago* toward which his boat was drifting, was a welcome sight.
    c. From the *ecchymosis* on his forehead, I assumed that he must have fallen.
    d. The politician made promise after promise to the dairy farmers who had come to his rally. After each promise, they shouted in chorus, "Hazanga," which seemed to please him and make him promise even more. Later, he was taken on a tour of the farm and the host farmer said, "Be careful not to step in the *hazanga*."
  2. Solve the following problem (using your best selective encoding skills): You have a drawer full of individual socks, some white, some black, in a 5:4 ratio. Without looking in the drawer, you reach in and pull out one sock at a time. What is the minimum number of socks you have to pull out in order to be guaranteed that you have a matching pair (i.e., two of the same color)?

*(Answers are in Note 2)

Gardner's Multiple Intelligences

Like Sternberg, Howard Gardner does not dispute that there is a general factor of intelligence ("g"); rather, he questions its importance for predicting or explaining anything except that narrow experience we call school (e.g., Gardner, 1993, p. 39). The reasons IQ is even correlated with school performance, he goes on to argue, are because (1) both emphasize linguistic and logical processes almost exclusively and (2) both are measured in the same narrow ways. Gardner wishes not only to expand our definition of intelligence, but also to expand the experience of schooling. Hand in hand with his multiple intelligences, therefore, go a number of curriculum activities to implement a more pluralistic view of how to recognize and develop these additional intelligences (e.g., Gardner and Hatch, 1989).

Table 4.2 Gardner's multiple intelligences.

Intelligence	Unique Features	Examples
1. Linguistic	Sensitivity to language, its meanings, patterns, rhythms, sounds and signs, and functions.	Writing Poetry Linguistic capability Word Play
2. Logical-Mathematical	Proclivity towards abstract reasoning, logical analysis and proof, identification of patterns in empirical data.	Scientific research Mathematics Problem solving Mathematical puzzles
3. Spatial	Capacity to visualize space, perceive it from various angles and maneuver within it.	Architecture Sculpturing/painting Navigation/exploration
4. Musical	Disposition to produce music, play one or more instruments, appreciate and dissect harmonies, rhythms, pitch, and tonal colors.	Composing Performing Singing
5. Bodily-kinesthetic	Ability to control body movements for creative expression or invention, skilled performance or problem solving.	Dancing Sports/balancing Surgery Craftmanship
6. Interpersonal	Aptitude for understanding other people, responding appropriately to their motivations, needs and moods; empathizing and cooperating.	Therapy Teaching Leadership Coaching
7. Intrapersonal	Capability of accessing one's own emotions, behaviors and beliefs, strengths and weaknesses, and acting accordingly.	Self-improvement Self-control Therapy Development

Gardner (1983, 1993) defined intelligence as the capacity to solve problems or create products that are of value to one or more communities or cultural settings. By this definition and such criteria as evidence of a biological proclivity for the activity, the existence of a core set of operations unique to the endeavor, and a culturally contrived symbol system for communicating these operations, he identified seven intelligences (see table 4.2). Each is expected to be relatively independent from the others, which also implies that individuals would show very different profiles of strengths and weaknesses across the seven domains. And except for the logical-mathematical and linguistic intelligences, each intelligence should be uncorrelated with IQ.

In keeping with his emphasis on multiple and distinct intelligences, no importance is attached to the ordering of the list (and Gardner uses different orders in different publications to emphasize that). Table 4.2 begins with the two abilities most commonly measured on standardized tests—namely, linguistic and logical-mathematical as in the verbal and mathematical portions of the Scholastic Aptitude Test. The rest of the list includes categories traditionally called talents. Gardner purposefully equates them all to overcome what he sees as a bias that the other five are somehow less than the first two.

In any case, whether called talents or intelligences, he sees each as a domain for *biopsychological potential* (Gardner, 1993, pp. 36–37). That is, for biochemical and/or environmental reasons, an individual may be *at risk*, more or less in the average range, or *at promise* with regard to one of these intelligences (Gardner, 1993, p. 29). "At risk" individuals have some disability for that intelligence and need special help, where appropriate remediation can be found, if they are to achieve acceptable levels of skill in this area. Gardner gives such examples as autistic children as being at risk for interpersonal intelligence, or people with specific brain dysfunctions (e.g., aphasia) as being at risk in linguistic intelligence.

"At promise" individuals, in contrast, are those who exhibit special talent for an intelligence and have little or no need for formal teaching. For example, the violinist prodigy Yehudi Menuhin was by age three "at promise" for musical intelligence and by age ten was an international performing artist. For bodily-kinesthetic intelligence, Gardner cites Babe Ruth: an exceptional pitcher as well as hall-of-fame hitter. For interpersonal

Photo 4.2. A promising musical intelligence.

intelligence, he cites Anne Sullivan for understanding and overcoming her seven-year-old student's deafness and blindness to produce the miracle the world came to know as Helen Keller. These were people who came by their gifts without tutelage, though good schools might be helpful to develop their talents fully.

For the in-betweeners—the rest of us—Gardner and his colleagues believe that the right kind of education is necessary. They have thus begun the process of designing the "school of the future" and have stimulated a number of people around the country to begin building programs (e.g., Gardner, 1993; Gardner & Hatch, 1989), and develop curricula (e.g., Armstrong, 1994).

Multiple Intelligences in the Classroom

Teachers seeking to implement multiple intelligence theory in their classrooms would have many hands-on activities in each of the seven domains, demonstrating their progress through portfolios. Writing about one effort, project Spectrum, Gardner and Hatch (1989), say the following:

> *Miniature replicas and props invite children to deploy linguistic intelligence within the context of story telling; household objects that children can take apart and reassemble challenge children's spatial intelligence in a mechanical test; a "discovery" area including natural objects like rocks, bones, and shells enables children to use their logical abilities to conduct small "experiments," comparisons, and classifications; and group activities such as a biweekly creative movement session can be employed to exercise their bodily-kinesthetic intelligence on a regular basis. (p. 7)*

But even Gardner recognized that just a set of activities is sufficient neither for a good education nor for developing multiple intelligences. Any attempt by educators to cover everything ". . . would be certain to achieve superficial knowledge at best . . ." (Gardner, 1993, p. 194) and could interfere with two important features of intelligence—namely, (1) *a highly developed competence* in at least one domain; and (2) *a more comprehensive understanding* of how specialized competencies, including theirs, fit into larger systems, such as historical trends, values, or global or current events.

It follows from this that some balance is needed between specialized training and comprehensive education. In keeping with his developmental orientation, Gardner (1993, ch. 11) proposes that elementary education should focus on mastering the notational systems of the culture in context: written language as related to spoken language, written

Photo 4.3. Exercising Bodily-kinesthetic intelligence through play.

music in the context of performing or listening, mathematical and scientific notations as used in our daily life.

Beginning about age 8 and increasing until mid-adolescence, Gardner recommends some specialized training, preferably via apprenticeships, in a small number of domains. For example, one area of the arts, one area of physical training, and one or two scholastic subjects should receive focused attention to allow the development of expertise. This has the advantage, Gardner argues, of letting students understand what it takes to become expert at something, as well as to prepare them better for subsequent vocational choices.

By mid-adolescence, students should be required to search for comprehensive understanding of the wide variety of academic domains, intelligences, cultures, value systems and the like. The high school curriculum should therefore involve students ". . . in rich and multi-faceted projects, which encourages them to sample widely and to make diverse connections" (Gardner, 1993, p. 196).

How can multiple intelligence theory help educators? In at least two ways, according to Gardner and colleagues: first, by elucidating the need for and thus stimulating development of curriculum activities in various areas; and, second, by suggesting appropriate, and often

Anecdote 4.2

Integrating Music and Academics

Music, it is often said, is a universal language facilitating communication when words are inadequate. Perhaps music can do this because it is an emotional medium: it can energize (as in a rousing march or dance beat), it can soothe and calm (as in a lullaby), it can stimulate feelings (as in a patriotic song or a religious hymn), and it can elicit already conditioned emotional responses (as in a love song associated with a lover). Music also serves cognitive functions by providing mnemonic cues, as when we recall specific words to songs we haven't thought about in years, when we use it to teach such specific facts as the alphabet, or when advertisers get us to associate specific products to jingles.

Given such advantages, Johnson-Gentile and Gentile (1996) suggested that music should not be just another course or diversion in schools, but rather should be integral to much academic instruction. What better way to learn about cooperation, teamwork, or inclusion than by singing songs or producing a musical with such themes? What better way to learn about history than to sing some of the songs of the culture and period being studied? What better way to understand number patterns than to study rhythmic patterns in music and then create some of your own? What better way to understand one's own behavior and feelings than to discover that studying when listening to a hyperactive beat makes you feel hyperactive when it is time to study or, conversely, to learn the relaxation response to soothing music?

The authors argue that such activities tap into musical intelligence as well as most of the rest of Gardner's seven intelligences: bodily-kinesthetic for rhythmic clapping or dance, logical-mathematical for patterns, linguistic for writing lyrics or scripts, interpersonal for cooperative messages or understanding people's motives and behavior in historical context, and intrapersonal for accessing one's own feelings. They conclude that ". . . when properly used, such activities cost little in time or money, and have the potential to add exciting dimensions to academic content" (p. 68)

alternative assessments, of these domains. In that sense, Gardner may already have been somewhat successful, as noted above (see also Anecdote 4.2), even if the theory itself is altered or abandoned in the future.

Gardner's Theory: In Conclusion

When Gardner looks at successful people, he attributes their success to expertise in one or more of the multiple intelligences, but not to general brilliance (i.e., high IQ). Sternberg makes similar points, and both together have collaborated recently on what it means to have "Practical Intelligence for School" (Gardner, Krechevsky, Sternberg & Okagaki, 1996). General intelligence as raw computing power or mental quickness does not guarantee success, even if it is predictive. Success comes—whether your IQ is high, average, or low—when you learn (1) to capitalize on your strengths and (2) to overcome or compensate for your weaknesses in the context of important tasks such as schools. Such self-knowledge and the skill and motivation to use it to your advantage may be the more practical intelligence, according to this view.

Evidence for such a position is mostly anecdotal, however, as when Gardner points to Yehudi Menuhin as support for a musical intelligence separate from "g." Critics might suggest that Menuhin was likely gifted in many or all of the other six intelligences, too. Since there is no evidence comparing Menuhin with standardized samples on all the intelligences, the argument is left unsettled. Ultimately, the theory may stand or fall on whether the seven intelligences are relatively uncorrelated with IQ and each other. Meanwhile, as Gardner and Hatch (1989; p. 9) concluded,

Even so, the goal of detecting distinctive human strengths, and using them as a basis for engagement and learning, may prove to be worthwhile, irrespective of the scientific fate of the theory.

Feuerstein's Instrumental Enrichment

Instrumental Enrichment is . . . a strategy for the redevelopment of cognitive structure in the retarded performer. It is designed as a direct and focused attack on those processes that, because of their absence, fragility, or inefficiency, are responsible for poor intellectual performance, irrespective of underlying etiology.

So Reuven Feuerstein et al. (1980, p. 1) began their monumental book on how to modify the cognitive structures and functioning of individuals. Forming the foundation of this process-oriented approach, and based on Vygotsky's theory, is a belief in *cognitive modifiability* through *mediated learning experience:* except for the most extreme cases of organic or genetic impairment, human cognition is modifiable at all developmental ages and stages. Individuals are not likely to discover and remedy their own deficiencies of cognitive structure, however. Thus they need direct exposure to stimulation, but even more importantly, they require mediation provided by significant others to help select, process and organize that stimulation. Feuerstein argues that such mediated learning experiences are the main determinants of both the content and structure of an individual's higher mental processes. He draws an analogy to a river in which the stream not only determines the flow of the water (the content), but also sculpts the river bed (the structure) which subsequently directs the flow.

Instrumental enrichment programs aim to provide mediated learning experiences to people who have been deprived of those important experiences. Such people he calls *culturally deprived*, not because their culture is deficient, but *because they have been deprived of their culture*. For reasons of poverty, inadequate parenting, schooling, or whatever, the children grow up having not had essential thinking processes and products transmitted to them.

Feuerstein's goals are, through proper mediated learning experiences, to render the culturally deprived retarded performers more modifiable so that they can better benefit from their encounters with stimuli in daily life, including academic experience. His more specific goals include the following (Feuerstein et al., 19890, p. 405):

- Correcting deficient cognitive processes
- Acquiring relevant vocabulary, labels, concepts, operations and relationships
- Forming habits
- Producing intrinsic motivation
- Creating insightful and reflective thinking
- Transforming passive recipients of information into active generators of new information

The circumstances leading Feuerstein to develop his theory and methods were a combination of his academic studies in the Piagetian approach at Geneva (and subsequently at the Sorbonne) and his work with adolescent immigrants to Israel. The latter were often impoverished individuals who, in addition to the culture shock of immigrating to a new, technologically more advanced society, had been more or less deprived of their own culture and mediated learning experiences. On conventional tests they scored three to six years below the age norms of the dominant culture, many with IQ scores in the 50–70 range, and lower. Feuerstein was dissatisfied with such test scores, however, believing that at best they documented only what the children had previously learned or, better, had failed to learn. He wanted instead to assess what they were capable of learning - that is, their learning potential. Consequently, he and his colleagues (Feuerstein, 1979) developed a set of tests, known as the Learning Potential Assessment Device, to assess their cognitive functioning while they are engaged in certain learning experiences. (Note the similarity to Vygotsky's zone of proximal development.)

On the basis of his experiences with this new method of assessing cognitive functioning, Feuerstein identified a number of deficient cognitive processes that were commonly associated with poor test scores, as follows:

1. *At the input phase:* those functions concerning the accuracy and amount of information gathered as the individual begins to understand the nature of the problem and how to solve it (e.g., blurred or sweeping perception, impulsive answer grabbing, impaired spatial or temporal orientation, lack of precision, etc.).
2. *At the elaboration phase:* those functions which interfere with the individual organizing or making efficient use of the information available (e.g., inadequately defining the problem; not selecting relevant cues; too narrow a focus; inadequate labels for categories; limited inferential hypothesis-testing, or planning processes; and an episodic view of reality - i.e., that objects and events exist as separate and independent events or episodes).
3. *At the output phase:* those functions which impede adequate communication of the outcome of the elaboration functions (e.g., egocentric communication, blocking, trial-and-error, impaired verbal or written skills, lack of precision, behavior problems which affect communication, etc.).
4. *In affective-motivational factors:* those functions which affect attitudes, emotions and behaviors and which, in turn, interfere with cognitive tasks (e.g., poor self-concept; anxiety; efficiency of performance and automatization of components which affects the amount of effort required; etc.).

Each of the above components of cognitive functioning is important—indeed, interrelated—in Feuerstein's theory, but central among them are the elaboration processes, (as described in quote #4 at the beginning of this chapter).

Instrumental Enrichment in the Classroom

Feuerstein's theory led directly to a number of curriculum exercises, along with an extensive teacher training program leading to certification of skill in both the content and procedures of instrumental enrichment. Normal teaching would not qualify.

Designed to supplement the regular scholastic curriculum, the specially prepared teachers meet with students 3–5 hours per week at spaced intervals. The pencil-and-paper exercises each focus on a specific cognitive skill and build in increasing complexity to include previously mastered skills, with discovery, practice and repetition built into the curriculum. One group of materials is appropriate for the functionally illiterate, while the rest assume proficiency in reading and verbal comprehension. Figure 4.1 illustrates some of the instruments.

Organization of Dots

The exercise in Part I of figure 4.1, for example, requires students to organize the discrete dots to duplicate the geometric figures in the model. Later, figures of exactly the same size must be projected into a different orientation of the dots, which requires a conservation of form and size. By placement of the dots, the task can be made extremely difficult, including even three-dimensional figures. Even a teacher experienced with the task must rediscover the correct answer each time, thereby continually modeling correct thinking processes. As students proceed through the increasingly difficult items, they find an increasing need for discrimination, reflection, and precision—all without needing to be able to read.

In a variation of these problems, students are presented with completed exercises, some correct and some with errors. The task is to discover and critique the errors, thereby practicing looking for appropriate cues and being precise. Note also that, in contrast to critiquing the students' own errors, this exercise keeps defensiveness about errors to a minimum.

Categorization

Consider a collection of eight pencils equally represented in two classes (large and small) and two colors (red and blue). How can a hierarchical (tree) diagram be invented to categorize the pencils into their attributes? Or, to phrase the question another way, what is wrong with the solution in Part II.A of figure 4.1? According to this diagram, the same pencil must be represented in two places, both under size and under color. As Feuerstein et al. (1980) point out, diagramming is often difficult for students, as well as their teachers at first, because they make the common error of categorizing according to both dimensions. What is needed is to categorize according to one dimension or the other, as diagrammed in Part II.B. This solution produces a hierarchical ordering with one dimension superordinate to the other.

The Feuerstein categorization exercises are meant to provide students practice encoding and elaborating groups of things in more than one way. The categorization process is a prerequisite for educational activities in all fields (e.g., categorizing words by meaning or grammatical function; categorizing people by age, gender, or relationship; etc.) as well as for memory and the development of expertise, as we shall see in a later chapter. Nevertheless, it is often the case that children have not had practice sufficient to automatize this basic process. The Instrumental Enrichment program provides this practice.

Family Relationships

A more complex way of looking at hierarchical categorizations, using only a limited vocabulary, is studied in the Family Relationships unit. Consider the following problem (adapted from Feuerstein at al., 1980, p. 196):

Problem 4.1. The Browns, who had only eight chairs at their dinner table, invited the following people to a special dinner party:

2 grandfathers	2 grandmothers
3 fathers	3 mothers
3 husbands	3 wives
1 son-in-law	1 daughter-in-law
2 fathers-in-law	2 mothers-in-law
3 sons	1 daughter
2 grandsons	

Everyone invited came to the party and all were able to sit at the table at the same time, one chair per person. How can you explain this?

Feuerstein et al. (1980) point out that children who are not exposed to their program often give answers such as "They ate in shifts" or "People brought their own chairs." The solution is to be found, of course, in the multiple roles that people assume, which is another way of looking at hierarchical categorizations and relationships.

Figure 4.1

Part I. Organization of Dots.

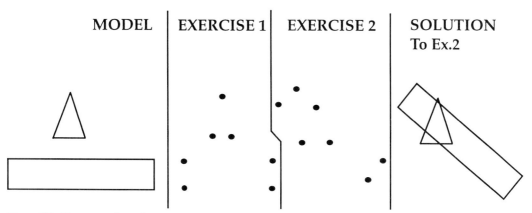

Part II. Categorization.

A. A Common Error

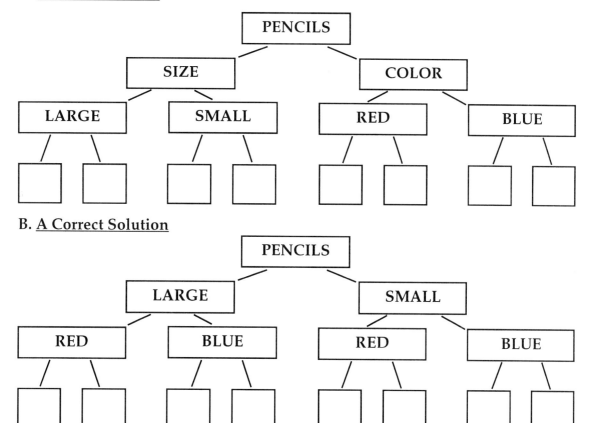

B. A Correct Solution

110 Chapter Four

Figure 4.1 *(continued)*

Part III. Transitive Relations.

A. Mary likes cheerleading more than reading, and reading less than swimming. Is it possible to know whether Mary prefers cheerleading or swimming? Arrange the relationships, placing the activities on the lines and the symbols for the appropriate relationships in the boxes:

_____ ☐ _____ ☐ _____

_____

B. Given the following:

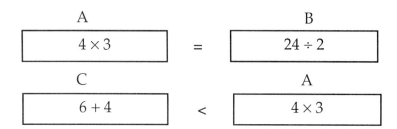

Answer the following questions, "true" or "false":

B ☐> C

B ☐< C

B ☐= C

B ☐≠ C

B ☐χ C

Conclusion: 6 + 4 ☐ 24 ÷ 2

Transitive Relations

This unit deals with inferences concerning the relationships "greater than" (>), "less than" (<), and "equal to" (=) and (also uses the symbols ≠ for "not equal to" and χ for "it is impossible to know"). Consider the problems in Figure 4.2, Part III A and B.

In the Transitive Relations unit students are first introduced to the idea of ordered sets and the signs that designate the various relationships. In the early exercises, strategies are practiced which order and encode the data in a manner that keeps the information in the student's visual field, to minimize memory requirements. In problems like IIIB, for example, students are taught to encode the numerical data first, then to substitute the A, B, and C labels for the actual data. Finally, they are systematically to assess the conclusions given or to draw their own inferences.

Students are also introduced to problems which have insufficient information from which to draw certain conclusions, as in Problem IIIA. It is important that students learn what they know and do not know to develop their metacognitive processes, and such exercises, since they require that all relationships be specified, have the potential for developing those skills. The way the task is structured students are not allowed to escape with a response of "I dunno." Rather they must draw the conclusion that "it is impossible to know from the information given." This is a critical distinction for persons with a history of unsuccessful scholastic performances.

Feuerstein's Theory: In Conclusion

Feuerstein's ideas have stimulated a number of studies, as well as other curriculum variations (e.g., Bransford, Stein, Arbitman-Smith, & Vye, 1985; Haywood, Brooks & Burns, 1986; Mearig, 1987; Nelson, 1993; Savell, Twohig & Rachford, 1986). There is some limited evidence of the program's efficacy, but then critics might wish to do a cost-benefit analysis since the program requires a tremendous amount of teacher preparation and intensive instructional time. Some of the difficulties involved in preparing teachers and insuring that they can and do implement mediated learning techniques are documented in Nelson's (1993) study.

Whatever your view of these issues, it seems clear that the Feuerstein approach is another avenue in the direction suggested by Hunt (Quote #1 of this chapter): "to find ways of raising the level of intellectual capacity," in this case of individuals who are considered at risk.

What Should We Make of the New Intelligence Theories?

As Sternberg's, Gardner's, and Feuerstein's theories make clear, there are current, viable alternatives to traditional intelligence theory. These theories are alternatives, but not because they reject IQ or "g", but rather because they broaden the definition and measurement of intelligence beyond IQ and "g." Whereas IQ requires the measurement of individual differences on common scales or norms (as in Binet's MA/CA norms), they adopt the Piagetian concern with individuals and how their developmental patterns of growth can be assessed and facilitated (as in Binet's other concern—the development of "mental orthopedics").

I believe that the essence of the differences between these approaches rests in the distinction between norm-referenced and criterion-referenced assessment. Whereas norm-referenced approaches like IQ measure status relative to others, criterion-referenced approaches measure distance from a person's developmental or educational goals.

For educators, it is a matter of optimism and expectations. To paraphrase Bransford et al. (1985), it is devastatingly easy to underestimate

Photo 4.4. Creating their own video report.

the effects of low expectations. When we see a child as having "average potential," it is all too easy to think that there are certain intellectual skills beyond his or her capacity. When we see that same child as having multiple ways to develop his or her intellectual capacity, we are likely to continue exploring the ways.[3]

It must be said, as noted earlier, that there exists only a limited amount of empirical support for these new approaches to developing intellectual skills. On the other hand, these approaches can stimulate the collection of the systematic information that Carroll diagnosed is lacking (Quote #5 in the Chapter Introduction) and Papert (1980, p. 161) argued for:

> . . . an interest in intellectual structures that could *develop as opposed to those that actually at present* do *develop in the child, and the design of learning environments that are resonant with them.* (emphasis added)

Instructional Implications of Developmental Theories

Over the last two-and-a-half chapters, we have explored a number of theories and issues concerning change and stability in human beings. Some of the theorists—notably, Piaget, Erikson, Kohlberg, and Maslow—were not directly interested in the educational applications of their theories; others—notably Vygotsky, Sternberg, Gardner, and Feuerstein—have tied their theories fairly directly to instruction. All have stimulated much thinking by scholars, and Piaget's theory in particular has stimulated an enormous amount of empirical research. But rather than go into some of the specific debates in the literature, we shall better profit by considering some important instructional implications of these theories, recognizing with Piaget (1970a, p. 24) that

> *Any didactic method or any program of instruction, if its application and results are to be analyzed by experimental pedagogy, will raise problems pertaining to the psychology of development, the psychology of learning, and the general psychology of intelligence.*

Knowing via Acting: Cognitive Constructivism

Piaget (1970a, p. 67) tells the story of a school inspector in Canada who split every class into two rooms so that the teacher would not be able to talk to all students together all day long: at least some would have time to work while the teacher talked to the rest. The task of the teacher, according to Piaget, is to establish an environment which challenges the children to intellectual growth by doing, not just listening; by experimenting, not just observing; by reinventing, not just accepting. Thus was born the neo-Piagetian cognitive constructivist movement.

This emphasis on the active, constructive nature of learning changes the role of teachers from being primarily transmitters of information to facilitators of learning. *A classroom which is consistent with Piaget's perspective is neither teacher centered nor student centered; rather, it is activity centered.* Piaget (1970a, pp. 71–72) cautions, however, that we should not think that activity by the student is solely ". . . a matter of physical actions, something that is true of the elementary levels but is no longer so at later stages, when a student may be totally 'active,' in the sense of making a personal rediscovery of the truths to be acquired, even though this activity is being directed toward interior or abstract reflection." He also gives examples of how manipulable activities like using Cuisinaire rods can be misused as when they are limited to demonstrations or explanations by the teacher. Piaget is clear that just listening without a chance to organize or reinvent what is being heard will lead to no learning or, at best, to superficial learning.

Constructivist definitions of learning derive from this (e.g., Brown, 1994; Shuell, 1996): learning if it is to be meaningful, must be active rather than passive, constructive rather than reproductive, intentional rather than incidental or purposeless, cumulative rather than isolated, metacognitive rather than mindless or without awareness, and socially mediated rather than individual. The components of this definition clearly show the combined influences of Piaget and Vygotsky on current thinking about learning.

And yet, as I have argued elsewhere (Gentile, 1996), this view of "meaningful learning" is too narrow. It is fine for traditional academic goals, such as the learning of math or reading in schools, but it leaves out some of the most meaningful learnings of all—namely, emotional and behavioral learning (including cases of rapanoia; see Preface).

> *. . . consider what occurs when bad things happen to people unexpectedly—for example, when you get AIDS from a transfusion or a loved one, when you are mugged or raped, or when you are disabled from an accident. Feelings will be associated with and conditioned to the situations and people involved, fight or flight (overcoming or helplessness) patterns will be induced, and, of course, perceptions, future learnings, and perhaps your whole life will become altered. Such learnings are neither active nor intentional; they happen to you. If they are constructive or metacognitive, it is only by retrospective analysis, and they may or may not occur in social contexts. But I submit that these are the most meaningful learnings in people's lives. They are currently explainable from Pavlovian (respondent conditioning) and Skinnerian (avoidance learning) perspectives, but not by the cognitive constructivist definitions of meaningful learning as described above. (Gentile, 1996, p. 38)*

By the way, Piaget did not believe that all material and all teaching must be discovery learning, as in the most extreme position taken by some advocates of cognitive constructivism. When specific facts have to be learned (he gave the example of languages), then direct teaching—even drill and practice by teaching machines—is not only appropriate, but more efficient (Piaget, 1970a, p. 78). At the other extreme, activity which is simply manipulating objects or doing busy work also leads at best to superficial learning. Physical activities must be accompanied by mental operations, such as thinking of alternative conceptions or new meanings. The activity must lead, in other words, to a cognitive conflict.

Creating Cognitive Conflicts

As we have seen, equilibration is the primary motivation for intellectual growth in Piaget's theory. What motivates change in a person's cognitive structures, therefore, is some facts, principles or explanations that are at variance with knowledge as a person has it currently organized. Information that is consistent with that already in storage does not need assimilation into the structure and thus motivates no change. Neither, however, does information that is so advanced as to not be represented at all in the current mental structures, as advanced algebra, calculus, or formal logic would be to a student who hardly knows arithmetic or is at the preoperational level. To motivate assimilation of new knowledge, and

Anecdote 4.3

> ### One Teacher's Way to Use Moral Dilemmas for Instructional Purposes
>
> Provide students with a moral dilemma, either one that the students experienced, one that is in the news, or a hypothetical one (e.g., from Kohlberg). After students understand the problem, they could be asked to state, or better to write (so that the opinions can be anonymous), their own opinions on the subject. These opinions could then be sorted into various positions or stages, and statements representative of each could be written (by the teacher or committees of students) on 3 × 5 cards. These cards could then be given to individuals or cooperative groups who would have to defend, through argument or role playing, that point of view. After all points of view have been given a fair hearing in this manner, further exercises could be planned to discuss whether the positions could be ranked from "least moral" to "most moral."
>
> This exercise is based on what Paul (1987) calls dialogical thinking, described in more detail in Chapter 11, and an approach to evaluating an in-service workshop for teachers by the teachers themselves, which I had the privilege to observe.
>
>

its concomitant changes in the knowledge structures to accommodate that knowledge, requires information just beyond what is now known. Such appropriate challenges to current perceptions or beliefs provide "cognitive conflicts."

Research by Walker (1982) gives further support to this thesis using Kohlberg's moral dilemmas to teach higher levels of moral reasoning. After assessing the individuals' stages of moral development, Walker presented them with reasoning that was either one or two stages above their current stage. On a subsequent posttest on the moral dilemmas, he found that such instruction did advance some, but not all, of the individuals. Those who changed in a positive direction, however, advanced only one stage, even if they had been exposed to reasoning that was two stages beyond their current pretest reasoning. Kohlberg and his followers argue on the basis of such findings that a person cannot skip stages, presumably because such skipping encounters material that is too far advanced to even be perceived as a cognitive conflict.

This leads to an instructional paradox for the teacher. If the students do not discover the relevant cognitive or moral principles after what the teacher considers a reasonable amount of instructional time, should the teacher simply tell the student the answer? Piaget, Kohlberg, and their proponents say no. Instead, cooperative peer interactional activities should be established to encourage students to debate various explanations and rediscover their own truths (e.g., Ginsburg and Opper, 1988, p. 246). Thus experiments, debates, simulations, dilemmas in literature can be useful in creating cognitive conflicts to allow children to learn in the broad sense— that is, to develop. One suggestion for how this might be done to teach moral reasoning in a classroom is presented in anecdote 4.3.

Metacognitive Processes

We have already encountered the concept of metacognition in previous sections, particularly in relation to Vygotsky's theory (chapter 2) and as one of Sternberg's components of intelligence (this chapter). Recently it has become a central feature, not only in constructivist theory, but also in learning theory in general and instructional applications in particular.

A simple but important example of developmental differences in metacognitive processes was provided by Flavell, Friedrichs and Hoyt in 1970. They presented children with a sequence of pictures of common objects within each child's memory span and instructed them to study the pictures until they could recall them perfectly in the correct order. When given this kind of task, children study for a while and then announce that they are ready. When second and fourth graders announce that they are ready, they usually are—that is, they can recite the list of pictures in order. When preschoolers say they are ready, in contrast, they can seldom recite the list of pictures correctly. Preschoolers have not yet learned how to monitor what they know and do not yet know, while older children have learned (or are learning) this self-monitoring process.

For the better part of forty years Flavell and his colleagues set the agenda for studies designed to elucidate (1) what children at various ages know about their own thinking processes, and (2) how they use such knowledge to monitor and regulate their own processes (e.g., Flavell, 1979; Keeney et al., 1967; Moely et al., 1969; Flavell at al., 1995). Particularly after his seminal paper of 1979, the field of metacognition was off and running.

Defining metacognition as being both (1) knowing about cognition and (2) actively thinking about thinking, however, generated quite a bit of confusion. For example, knowing about your circulatory system, what affects it,

Cartoon 4.2.

and strategies for maintaining its functioning at an optimal level would be considered cognitive processes and strategies. So why shouldn't knowing about your learning and memory be cognitive processes? That reserves the term "meta," as in *metacognition*, or *metamemory*, for the *active monitoring, conscious control*, or *executive regulation of mental processes*. Table 4.3 gives examples of the differences in several fields.

Reserving the term metacognition for self-regulation and conscious monitoring of thinking makes it consistent with Vygotsky and Sternberg, as noted above, and emphasizes a critical area for development and education. It is not just preschoolers who fail to monitor their thinking. Many comprehension problems in reading arise because students do not know that they do not know, do not have goals with which to compare what they understood from reading, or do not use strategies such as summarizing or reinspecting text which they know from previous experience to be useful (e.g., Brown, 1980; Garner & Alexander, 1989).

Table 4.3 Cognitive vs. metacognitive processes.

TASK	COGNITIVE PROCESSES	METACOGNITIVE PROCESSES
Reading	Decoding the words, comprehending, acquiring the information in the text.	Monitoring whether, you comprehend; Deciding to reread a certain portion to find out what you did not learn.
Memorizing	Associating, verbally or visually: elaborating, or repeating the list.	Deciding what you know and what you don't; Adopting a new strategy (e.g., imagery) when the old one wasn't working.
Math Testing	Comprehending the problems, recalling the correct formulas, doing the calculations, constructing or selecting the best answer.	Allocating your time (answer easy questions first); Checking whether you understand what is required; Estimating an answer; Checking whether your calculated answer makes sense.
Writing	Constructing sentences, creating, comparing describing, or analyzing.	Comparing what you wrote with what you intended; Revising.

As developmental skills, metacognitive processes may emerge and improve somewhat with age. However, the role of teachers in stimulating this development is crucial. Consider this example:

> . . . when students in elementary and middle schools notice that they no longer remember information they have read, many do not intentionally reinspect portions of a text that might provide the information. When asked why they do not reinspect texts to find answers to questions, they usually report either that "it is illegal" or that it takes too much time. (Garner & Alexander, 1989, pp. 145–146)

Something is wrong with instruction if students get the message (1) that there is time only to do the reading, but not to learn from the reading, or (2) that if at first you don't succeed, it is illegal to try again. Thus teachers may need to model, stimulate, assist and reinforce metacognitive processes as well as the disposition to engage in them, at every opportunity. Metacognitive skills create cognitive conflicts and may therefore be more important for self-sufficiency, learning to learn, and future instructional success than most of the facts or procedures in the curriculum.

Photo 4.5. Reading and practicing comprehension monitoring.

Anecdote 4.4

Active Learning and Metacognition Via Computers

Seymour Papert (1980), the inventor of the computer program LOGO, suggested the following:

In most contemporary educational situations where children come into contact with computers the computer is used to put children through their paces, to provide exercises of an appropriate level of difficulty, to provide feedback, and to dispense information. The computer is programming the child. In the LOGO environment the relationship is reversed: The child, even at preschool ages, is in control: The child programs the computer. And in teaching the computer how to think, children embark on an exploration about how they themselves think. The experience can be heady: Thinking about thinking turns the child into an epistemologist, an experience not even shared by most adults. (p. 19)

How does this work? The child tells a turtle on the screen how to move to create various shapes. For example, FORWARD 100, RIGHT 90, FORWARD 100 would create a right angle. Repeat the process and you can create a square. How then can you create a triangle? Problems like this and the understanding of vectors, angles, and shapes that come with it provide a "turtle geometry" that very young children can use to learn math and to learn how to learn.

In ever-increasing complexity, at a pace established by the student, often in interaction with a teacher or peers, the student can try out ideas and debug what went wrong (e.g., Why did FORWARD 100, RIGHT 60 repeated twice not make an equilateral triangle?) The entire process is active, constructive, and metacognitive. It may even be fun for students and teachers alike.

Mastery and Development

If each stage of development is prerequisite to the next, then it follows that the preceding stage must be *mastered, not just covered* in the sense that many teachers "cover a curriculum." People must master conservation of number before they can profitably engage in formal reasoning by mathematical derivations of formulas or principles of logic. People must be competent in the conventional arenas (Kohlberg's Level II) of moral reasoning before they can argue or behave in ways that would defend the rights of unpopular groups or positions (Level III). People must master basic interpersonal and academic skills to form their own identity (if only temporarily) before they can share that identity in a healthy intimate relationship or become self-actualized.

But does mastery imply that there will be no regression? That a person at a higher moral development stage will never use the reasoning at a prior stage? That an adult at a formal reasoning stage will never need concrete operations to solve a problem? That a self-actualized person will never have any doubts about love or self-concept? None of the theorists would expect such perfection from mortals.

Likewise, none of the theorists expects mastery of one stage to guarantee mastery of the

Photo 4.6. Metacognition via the computer.

next. That is, if x precedes y in the developmental sequence and x is mastered, it is not necessarily true that y automatically follows. In other words, x may be necessary but not sufficient for y. This becomes particularly important when discussion turns to educational implications of Piaget's formal reasoning stage. The evidence supports Siegler's (1986, p. 58) statement that Piaget's theory ". . . overestimates adolescents' reasoning abilities." Adolescents, along with us adults, continually find it easier to solve problems with concrete examples than by formal propositional logic alone (for an example, see problems 10.1 and 10.2 in chapter 10). Some adults seem never to achieve the formal reasoning stage; those who do achieve it use formal reasoning in their own fields of expertise better than they do in fields in which they are novices (see also chapter 10). Similar evidence exists for advanced stages of moral reasoning (Colby and Kohlberg, 1987a).

Can We Accelerate These Processes and Should We?

Piaget was often asked by interviewers whether certain kinds of instructional experiences with his tasks could speed up the attainment of, say, conservation. He called this "the American question," since Americans tend to believe that anything that is good will be better if it is accomplished faster. In an interview in 1973 (p. 22) he was blunt: ". . . if the aim is to accelerate the development of these operations, it is idiotic."

Piaget's disclaimers to the contrary, much research was done, mostly by Americans, on this very question. The results showed that a wide variety of methods can indeed accelerate the development of conservation, at least somewhat (Brainerd, 1978). There are also some good theoretical and methodological reasons for doing such research even if the goal is not to accelerate the attainment of conservation.

Theoretical questions notwithstanding, Piaget's question remains: "should we accelerate development?" In pushing to provide earlier and earlier formal childhood education on substantive instructional objectives, it is not at all clear what the long term effects might be. Siegler (1986, p. 56) summarized the concern as follows:

Although young children can learn to solve these problems, they often find doing so exceptionally difficult. Older children who cannot yet solve the same problems typically learn them much more easily. Similarly, although young children show beginning understanding of many important concepts even without training, they demonstrate the understanding in far fewer situations. The nature of their understanding also seems to differ in important ways from older children's understanding of the same concepts.

In what might still be the only direct empirical longitudinal evidence on this topic, Harlow (1949; 1959) studied the effects of learning the same discriminations at varying ages. His conclusions, drawn from the study of monkeys, are surprisingly similar to those drawn by Siegler—namely, that more mature monkeys quickly surpassed their younger peers and achieved higher success rates, in terms of percentage correct. Put another way, intensive training of the younger monkeys did produce learning, but there was a permanent impairment in their eventual proficiency. Apparently, younger learners learn different things about the task than older ones do, not to mention possible motivational problems if they are pushed too hard too fast (infant burnout?).

Elkind made similar points in an analysis of preschool instruction (1969, p. 332):

> . . . the longer we delay formal instruction, up to certain limits, the greater the period of plasticity and the higher the ultimate level of achievement.

Elkind then went on to draw a conclusion that at once challenges our rush to earlier and earlier education, and also provides great hope to teachers (p. 333):

> While children all over the world and across wide ranges of cultural and socioeconomic conditions appear to attain concrete operations at about the age of 6 or 7 . . ., the attainment and use of formal operations in adolescence, in contrast, appear to be much subject to socioculturally determined factors as sex roles and symbolic proficiency . . . Apparently, therefore, environmental variation during the elementary school period is more significant for later intellectual attainments of the Piagetian variety. In short, there is not much justification for making the preschool the scapegoat for our failures in elementary education. Like it or not, the years from six to twelve are still the crucial ones with respect to later academic achievement.[4]

An example of the acceleration problem in the psycho-social domain concerns the extent to which adolescents actively choose, or have chosen for them, their identity roles. Summarizing these issues, Muuss (1982)[5] argued that if teachers or adults accelerate the adolescents' vocational choices in order to get them settled on the "right path," they may achieve foreclosure instead of closure. That is, their children may rigidly adopt the set of values of these adults (e.g., deciding to become an engineer because a parent is an engineer) without ever having resolved the identity crisis of this stage. Eventually this may preclude resolution of adult identity conflicts. It is true that many parents prefer that their children simply adopt their own values rather than undergo "values clarification" for themselves. On the other hand, adolescents can be equally foreclosed by adopting rival values of gangs or cults if such persons have a falling out with their parents. By this view, then, the only safe course is for adults to encourage and allow time for the debate of rival values, vocations, issues of sexuality, etc. Whether in the psychosocial or cognitive/metacognitive domains, the developmental process may be best not hurried, though it does need stimulation and mediation.

Maturational Unfolding or Developmental Crisis

As noted earlier, Vygotsky and Erikson in particular consider the developmental process to be hardly a maturational unfolding; rather they see it as struggling to resolve cognitive conflicts or psycho-social crises. Teachers can therefore make tasks easier, adapt instruction to the student's level of understanding, or apply the material directly to the child's experience or environment, but they cannot bestow success or self-esteem on the student. That must be *earned* by the students themselves.

What must be mastered, therefore, are tasks somewhat beyond the student's current level. What must be praised is effort toward mastering those just-beyond-current-reach tasks. What must be modeled and encouraged is metacognitive awareness and self-control.

Ironically, many adults see their role as making their children's lives easier than they had it. This may be a useful goal in the domains of nutrition and disease prevention, but it requires a delicate balancing act in the domains of cognitive, moral, and psycho-social development.

Teachers' Development and Its Implications for Teaching

Erikson tells the story (1963, p. 414) of the child of a psychiatrist who was asked what he wanted to be when he grew up. The child responded, "A patient." Obviously the child wanted to take the place of those people whom he perceived to so completely absorb his parents' interest. We can turn this story into a joke, by asking "How old was the child?" and having the answer be "forty-nine." If such a tale brings a smile or chuckle, it is probably because we can recognize that such identity crises occur at every age, though in somewhat different ways.

McKibbin and Joyce (1980) wondered whether Maslow's theory would predict the behavior of teachers who were given the opportunity to learn and practice new teaching techniques through staff development programs. They had clinical psychologists classify teachers on the basis of interviews into one of Maslow's need states—that is, was the teacher self-actualized, concerned with achievement and esteem, love and belongingness, safety and security, or physiological needs? They also had the teachers independently rated on how frequently and adequately they attempted to implement the new teaching methods to which they were being exposed. They found a significant positive relationship between the teachers' level on the needs hierarchy and their implementation score. The more self-actualized a teacher was, in general, the more willing they were to try anything new, to give up free time in order to learn or practice it, and the more enthusiasm they showed about having the chance to learn something new. Teachers more concerned with safety and belongingness needs, in contrast, were reticent to volunteer to learn new techniques, were skeptical that they would work, and practiced infrequently when they tried the ideas at all.

These results are hardly surprising, but they do emphasize that adults become teachers not because they have attained the highest stages of development, but while they are in the process of dealing with their own developmental crises. Perhaps such a recognition can keep us teachers humble. If we are sometimes belligerent or unwilling learners, then we may better understand students who may seem to be belligerent or lazy at times. They are probably dealing with emotional or social agendas that place the teacher's objectives at a much lower priority for the moment. A rush to label these children, and then to treat the children as though they are what the label implies, is to force the children to find their successes elsewhere from your classroom. But, as Erikson noted, this does not imply that the teachers must capitulate to the students. Rather, the adults must have their own set of values and rules and apply them fairly ". . . if only so that youth can rebel against a well defined set of older values" (Erikson, 1968, p. 30).

On the other hand, if we knew the specific crises students were facing on any given day, we might be less inclined to make caustic remarks to them. The same is true for students, of course. If they could understand the developmental crises their teachers were facing, they would also be much less obnoxious at times. But since it is nigh unto impossible for someone at a prior stage of development to take the perspective of someone at a more advanced stage, the burden of being empathetic necessarily falls on the teachers.

Practice Exercises

A. Practice Items

INSTRUCTIONS FOR ITEMS 1–5: For each example, match the Gardner intelligence which is predominantly involved by placing the letter of the intelligence in the space provided. (Answers in Note 6).

a. Linguistic
b. Logical-Mathematical
c. Spatial
d. Musical
e. Bodily-Kinesthetic
f. Interpersonal
g. Intrapersonal

_____ 1. The students are working in cooperative groups.
_____ 2. The teacher is reading a story to her first-graders.
_____ 3. Joey has more difficulty buttoning his coat and tying his shoes than the rest of his preschool classmates.
_____ 4. Dr. G had each of her pre-service teachers make a collage illustrating their own strengths and weaknesses.
_____ 5. Javier spends hours building little barriers in the family garden, trying to figure out how the ants and bees find their way to their homes.

For items 6–10 select the alternative choice which *best* answers the question. (Answers in Note 6).

6. Which of the following is an example of what Sternberg means by a knowledge acquisition component?
    a. rhyming a new word in order to memorize how to spell it.
    b. using the formula for calculating area of a triangle.
    c. deciding how much time to spend on each part of a problem.
    d. none of the above.

7. **Feuerstein's Input Phase is to Information Gathering** as
    a. output phase is to anxiety
    b. elaboration phase is to self-concept
    c. elaboration phase is to thinking
    d. output phase is to perception

8. Sternberg, Gardner and Feuerstein are
    a. alike in that they believe here is little evidence for "g."
    b. different since Gardner believes in seven intelligences mostly impervious to instruction, while Sternberg and Feuerstein believe that intelligence is responsive to instruction.
    c. alike in that each believe that intelligence can be developed as long as it is at or above the educable mentally retarded level.
    d. alike in that they emphasize a criterion-referenced rather than a norm-referenced approach to measuring intelligence.

9. Mastery of a developmental task (like conservation or an identity crisis) implies that the person
   a. is prepared to deal with the problems or crises at the next level.
   b. will no longer have difficulty with problems or crises at a prior level.
   c. will find the problems or crises at the next level easy to master.
   d. will be able to skip the next level entirely, unless it is at the highest stage.

10. **Cognitive is to Metacognitive** as
    a. solving a problem is to remembering a formula
    b. applying your knowledge is to deciding you need more practice
    c. doing is to thinking
    d. remembering that you forgot is to forgetting what you knew.

B. For Cooperative Study (in or out of class)

1. Assess your own profile of multiple intelligences, according to Gardner. Give examples or supply evidence for why you think you are high or low on each of the seven intelligences. In small groups, share your self-assessments.
2. Discuss study questions 8 and 9 concerning the differences between the theories in chapters 3 and 4. Are there instructional implications?
3. What is meant by each of the components of the cognitive constructivist definition of meaningful learning (e.g., in study question 10)? What is your author's position on this definition? Do you agree or disagree with him? Why?
4. Give a younger and an older child a learning task (e.g., reading for comprehension, memorizing a short list or poem, or one of Feuerstein's problems). Then interview them to assess (a) their cognitive strategies and (b) their metacognitive strategies or awareness. Report your findings to the class.
5. In small groups, discuss the issue Piaget called "the American Question"— namely, can we accelerate development, and should we? How might this question relate to Vygotsky's zone of proximal development?
6. In small groups, discuss what the different stages of children vs. parents or teachers imply for
   a. cognitive misunderstanding (such as an adult's comment, "I don't understand why this material is so difficult for you").
   b. socio-emotional conflicts.

C. For Further Information:

1. Find out if there are any schools in your area which, in whole or in part, base their instructional programs on Sternberg's, Gardner's, or Feuerstein's theories. Visit the school or invite a spokesperson from the program to speak in your class.
2. Read one or more of the works by Sternberg, Gardner, and Feuerstein, or about research related to their theories and make a written or oral report on your findings.
3. Interview or schedule a debate between a proponent and an opponent of mandatory early childhood education. Ask them on what evidence they base their positions.

4. Interview one or more persons whom you know to be gifted or "at promise" with regard to a particular intelligence. When and how did they first recognize that they were talented in that domain? How do they judge their own talents in the other intelligences? Report your findings as case studies to the class.

5. Find a curriculum library or school which has the LOGO computer program and spend some time exploring it. Do you agree with Seymour Papert (e.g., in *Mindstorms*, 1980) that the LOGO environment is a fine example of cognitive constructivism at work?

6. Invent a lesson plan designed to implement multiple intelligences (or components of intelligence) in your own classroom.

UNIT THREE

Motions, Emotions and Commotions

This unit explores in some detail two topics which were introduced in chapter 1—namely, feelings (emotions) and behaviors (actions or motions)—and extends them to groups and the problem of discipline (commotions).

Chapter 5 shows the classical conditioning mechanisms through which feelings get attached to people, things and events. Coverage is then expanded to consider the important topics of stress and learned helplessness, using the specific problem of math anxiety as an exemplar.

Chapter 6 deals with basic principles of reinforcement and punishment, along with how they (wittingly or unwittingly) shape and maintain the various behaviors of people interacting with each other.

Chapter 7 takes a social psychological look at behavior, assessing how we are affected by behavioral models, by norms and roles, by pressures to conform, and by friendship patterns and other social expectations.

In chapter 8 the above issues are revisited, but this time in the context of classroom management. Following the consideration of several problems for diagnostic purposes, a cross-cultural example is presented for added perspective. These are followed by specific advice for handling disruptions in a task-oriented manner that helps make people responsible for their own behavior.

CHAPTER
Study Questions

1. Diagram the classical conditioning procedure using the symbols US, CS, UR and CR. Why can the learning that occurs here be considered stimulus substitution?
2. What is the procedure and the effect of *extinction*?
3. What is the relationship of each of the following to the rate or strength of formation of a CR?
   a. number of CS-US pairings
   b. interval between CS and US
   c. intensity of US
   d. "belongingness" of CS and US
4. What is the difference between phobias and conditioned fears?
5. What is meant by each of the following?
   a. generalization
   b. discrimination
   Give examples.
6. What is meant by *higher-order conditioning*? Describe a procedure for producing it. How might higher-order conditioning be involved in attaching emotion to words?
7. What is meant by *learned helplessness*?
   a. under what conditions does it occur?
   b. how can it be cured?
   c. how can it be prevented?
8. What is meant by *attribution*? Give examples of attributions, as they relate to the development of learned helplessness, in each of the following dimensions (as in Table 5.1):
   a. internal-external dimension
   b. stable-unstable dimension
   c. global-specific dimension
9. Give examples of the interdependence of motions, emotions and cognitions.
10. What is meant by each of the following techniques?
    a. relaxation (progressive relaxation)
    b. systematic desensitization and counter-conditioning

FIVE

Emotional Learning and Respondent Conditioning

Introduction

1. A discouraged looking boy in my second-grade class was dragging his feet past me on his way for lunch. "Miss P," he said, "I don't think I'll ever learn to read." "What makes you think you'll never learn to read?" I replied. Oh, I'm just too dumb, I guess." (R. Dreikurs, 1968, p. 89)
2. Victor was a slow starter when reading instruction began in kindergarten and first grade. He was eager, but just wasn't ready to make the connection between words on paper and speech. He tried hard at first, but made no progress; his answers, readily volunteered, were consistently wrong. The more he failed, the more reluctant to try he became; he said less and less in class. By second grade, although he participated eagerly in music and art, when reading came around he became sullen. His teacher gave him special drilling for a while, but they both soon gave up. By this time he might have been ready to read, but simply seeing a word card or a spelling book would set off a tantrum of sullenness or of defiant aggression. This attitude began to spread to the rest of his school day. He vacillated between being despondent and being a hellion. (M. Seligman, 1975, p. 4)

Consider how you are likely to feel if you are required for your permanent certification as a teacher to take a course which has the reputation of being difficult—say, statistics—and during the first class you discover that the professor is talking way over your head. You nervously start working on the text, but discover further that you are having difficulty understanding it as well. You force yourself to work harder and go into the next class with some basic questions to ask about the material. However, some of the class members roll their eyes and give other not-so-subtle signals of the elementary nature of your questions. Worse, the professor plays to that audience and, in his best pleasant but condescending tone, answers the question in the same way that you did not understand before. When you persist despite the snickers from others, you are referred to the textbook. How do you feel at this point? Will you try to drop the course? What will you do if dropping the course is not an option? Are your achievement or self-actualization needs being activated, or are you most likely to be concerned with safety or belongingness needs? Will your classroom and study sessions in statistics feel relaxed and happy or be full of tension and fear?

The importance of the emotional level of human experience can hardly be overestimated, as was seen in chapters 1 and 2. Everything we do is accompanied by feelings—some have gone so far as to say what we do is motivated or caused by our feelings (e.g., Mowrer, 1954; see also the debate between Lazarus, 1982, 1984, and Zajonc, 1980, 1984). Whether emotions are primary causes or outcomes, however, they quickly become part of the human equation and affect future behavior in a kind of self-fulfilling prophecy. The children described in the opening anecdotes are cases in point: though the original cause of

Photo 5.1. Eager or anxious learners?

bad feelings was reading failure, low self-esteem and anxiety eventually motivate counterproductive behavior.

These are the kinds of issues to be addressed in this chapter—namely, issues of emotions and (1) how they become attached to people, objects and situations; (2) how conditioned emotions can be extinguished, but why the reconditioning process is difficult; and (3) how they affect what is learned (cognitive processes) and the motivation to try (operant behavior). We begin with the basics of emotional learning—namely, respondent conditioning.

Respondent Conditioning and Extinction

As part of his treatment for leukemia, a six-year-old boy was receiving chemotherapy intravenously while in a cancer research hospital. While having obvious benefits in alleviating the disease, the drug treatments also have some common negative side effects, including inducing nausea, the loss of hair, and general weakness. Often he was awake and receiving intravenous drip treatments early in the morning with little to do but watch television. And so it came to pass that he spent many mornings with his treatment inducing vomiting with the Captain Kangaroo show in the background.

The treatment was awful enough, but as you have probably already anticipated, another side effect of this daily routine emerged when the child, no longer on drugs, was recuperating at home. When he turned on Captain Kangaroo, he became suddenly nauseous.[1]

Many critics have been arguing for years that television programs can make a person nauseous, but it is unlikely that this six-year-old was simply giving literal expression to such a sentiment. More likely, Captain Kangaroo and he were unwitting victims of respondent conditioning: the drug (the US) inducing the reflexive vomiting (UR) in the presence of a previously neutral stimulus, the Captain, who now becomes a CS capable of eliciting nausea. As already demonstrated in chapter 1, this process can be diagramed as follows:

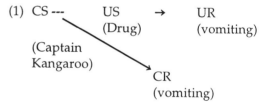

Captain Kangaroo, of course, did not cause this behavior; he and his show just became associated with a respondent behavior and the rest just happened. Respondent conditioning sometimes happens in this unplanned way. It can also be planned, as in some treatments to help people overcome a desire, say, for cigarettes. The process was vividly portrayed in *A Clockwork Orange* by Anthony Burgess (1963) in which a drug was used to induce nausea to any kind of violence in a sociopath named Alex. Alex was to be cured of violent tendencies by the (ethically questionable) procedure of being forced to watch violent films after having been injected with a drug that induced nausea. After two weeks of such treatment, Alex gives the following first-person account of the queer interchange he had with the discharging officer (p. 110):

"Would you," he giggled, "like to punch me in the face before I go?" I frowned at that, very puzzled, and said:
"Why?"
"Oh," he said, "just to see how you're getting on." And he brought his litso [face] real near, a fat grin all over his rot [mouth]. So I fisted up and went smack at this litso, but he pulled himself away. . . . And then, my brothers, I felt real sick again, just like in the afternoon. . . .

Cartoon: 5.1.

Psychic Secretions and Conditioned Reflexes

Respondent or classical conditioning was first systematically explored, as we have seen, by the Russian physiologist Ivan P. Pavlov who was studying reflexes of the digestive system. By an ingenious minor surgical procedure on the duct of a dog's parotid gland, saliva was diverted from the inside of the mouth to an opening of the cheek. There the saliva was collected and could be accurately measured. Pavlov was studying a wide variety of conditions related to the amount of saliva which flowed, under very controlled conditions. As food (the US) reached the dog's mouth, saliva (the UR) flowed freely: this was the basic salivary reflex.

There was a certain "psychic secretion," however, which was especially troublesome for a complete physiological account of this digestive reflex. When a tuning fork was regularly sounded a few seconds before the food was presented, the dog was salivating in anticipation of the food. The procedure, diagrammed before with different reflexes, is worth diagraming once more:

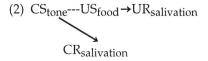

(2) CS_{tone}---$US_{food} \rightarrow UR_{salivation}$

$CR_{salivation}$

What was occurring was a *stimulus substitution*, in that the previously neutral stimulus, the tone, was able to substitute for the stimulus to which the salivation reflex was natively "wired," the food, to elicit salivation. Pavlov termed this anticipatory salivation a *conditioned reflex*.

Pavlov's genius lay not in "discovering" the conditioned reflex. The reflex was probably known to millions of people who went before him, if only in such common experiences as "thinking of slicing a lemon." If you think about that now, you can probably produce salivation as a psychic secretion. Pavlov's contribution, rather, was in separating the psychological from the purely physiological components, and in systematically researching the conditions under which conditioned reflexes could be produced, maintained and eliminated.

Extinction

As Pavlov began to understand the experimental conditions under which the CR could be reliably induced, he began to explore how the reflex could be inhibited and eliminated. Several procedures were found that could interrupt the CR, including (1) the presentation of a distracting stimulus, (2) the presentation of a stimulus associated with a contrasting behavior, and (3) the discontinuation of the US. This latter procedure Pavlov called experimental extinction or, simply, *extinction.*

Extinction, to be precise, is the procedure of presenting the CS without following it by the US. In the context of the previous conditioning, the CS will elicit the CR. However, since the US does not follow, the CR has been evoked in vain: why salivate if there is no food coming? The organism learned during conditioning that the CS reliably predicts the US. During extinction trials, on the other hand, it learns that the CS reliably predicts *no* US. Thus it becomes counterproductive to salivate to a tone when it is reliably followed by nothing. The procedure for extinction can be diagramed as follows:

(3) Previous Conditioning Trials:
$$CS_{tone}\text{----}US_{food} \rightarrow UR_{salivation}$$
$$\searrow CR_{salivation}$$

Current Extinction Trial:
$$CS_{tone}\text{--------}No\ US_{No\ food}$$
$$\searrow CR_{salivation}$$

In the conditioned reflex, the key word is *reflex*. Since the extinction trials do not activate the actual physiological reflex, the salivation that occurs in the CR is not being reinforced by the native response tendency. In other words, the psychic secretion is adaptive to the organism only so long as it anticipates, or is reinforced by, the appropriate physiological state.

For eliminating conditioned responses in humans the process is the same: the CS needs to occur, but without the US occurring. In the case of the child and Captain Kangaroo, the nausea-inducing drug (the US) must not be administered any more when the CS (Captain Kangaroo) is present. Or in the case of the fear of dentists (described in Chapter 1), the person has to go to the dentist (CS), but experience no pain (the US). Notice that simply staying away from the dentist—that is, preventing the appearance of the CS—will *not* extinguish the fear!

Eventually by this extinction procedure the conditioned fear can usually be eliminated, but "eventually" can sometimes be a very long time, depending on the severity and history of the fear. Thus therapists usually help the extinction process along by other methods, such as replacing a stress-producing US with a relaxation-inducing condition (described in more detail at the end of this chapter).

By the way, extinction eventually eliminates the CR, at least as far as any measurable response can be detected, but not forever. After a break of some minutes or days in which neither the CS nor US is presented, presentation of the CS will elicit the CR. This is called *spontaneous recovery,* but further discussion will be delayed until chapter 6.

Respondent Conditioning of Emotions

Psychic secretions of saliva, however important they were to the history of conditioning, are mainly interesting today as an analogue for understanding emotions. Watson and Rayner's (1920) creation of conditioned fear in Albert (described in chapter 1) was the most influential, if not the first, experimental demonstration that neutral stimuli could come to elicit conditioned reactions from other physiological systems of the body. Indeed, Watson (1913; 1919) made the identification of natural reflexes and their ability to be conditioned a central feature of his behaviorism. Subsequent studies identified many procedures which could induce conditioned emotional reactions (e.g., H. E. Jones, 1930; 1931; and Jones and Jones, 1930), some which could not (e.g., Bregman, 1934; English, 1929), and procedures which might be used to eliminate such fears (e.g., M. C. Jones, 1924).

In one early case study, for example, a mother offered a 28-week-old child a black stuffed cat to play with. She had already cuddled with it in the past. On this occasion, however, her older sister, whose toy it was, was present. Just as mother offered the toy to the baby, the older child ". . . set up an indignant howl of protest at the invasion of her property" (English, 1929, p. 221) causing an emotional outburst similar to Albert's. The same response was elicited when the cat came into view hours later.

Lest you think that it is only humans that learn to fear cats, consider how humans might affect cats (Gebhart, 1979, p. 313):

> *Cats may develop fears analogous to human phobias. They have few innate fears, but rapidly learn stimuli associated with unpleasant experiences. One of our cats was boarded with a family with noisy children. Following this experience she would run behind the sofa and vomit at the sound of children.*

Just as a cat can become a CS for fear in children, so can children become a CS for fear in cats. Indeed, in principle, any neutral stimulus can become attached to a reflex (i.e., a US→UR combination) and then elicit similar bodily feelings and reactions. It is for this reason that respondent conditioning is so intimately tied to feelings and emotions which, in turn, are intimately connected to the various organs and glands of the body. It is not surprising, therefore, that in the several decades since Pavlov's and Watson's pioneering work, researchers have produced a large number of conditioned respondents from a wide variety of bodily organs in many species (e.g., Kimble, 1961). Bower and Hilgard (1981, p. 58) summarized the state of affairs as follows:

> *For example, a physiological stressor can be applied to a dog (as a US), producing hypertension as an unconditioned reflex, and this hypertensive response can be conditioned to any of a variety of either external or internal stimuli. Similarly, by use of drugs or special implanted electrodes, enhancements in normal activity can be reliably elicited from and conditioned in such organs as the pancreas (insulin release), the liver (glycogen uptake), the kidneys (urinary extraction), the bladder (urination), the heart, the stomach (flow of secretions), and the gall bladder, as well as various and sundry endocrine glands (e.g., adrenals and salivary). It would seem that almost anything that moves, squirts, or wiggles could be conditioned if a response from it can be reliably and repeatedly evoked by a controllable unconditioned stimulus.*

Factors Affecting Conditioning

A number of factors affect how quickly or strongly a CR is established. Some of the more important of these will be discussed in this section.

Number of CS-US Pairings

Reliable conditioning of such a wide variety of bodily respondents does not necessarily occur in only one or two trials, although there are some cases in which one trial is sufficient. For example, many parents will attest to the fact that their babies developed a fear of pediatricians after their first experience receiving shots. On their next trip to the physician's office, the baby began screaming on the way in the door. An equal, or even more intense, fear has been observed by dog owners who have to drag their dogs into the veterinarian's office after one traumatic experience with shots. Neither the baby nor the dog are reading the sign on the door, but something about that environment—probably odors—is acting as a CS for the conditioned fear. For this to happen in only one trial, of course, the US had to be powerful or painful, as inoculations can be.

Most conditioning, however, does not occur in one trial. A child will not be likely to develop a fear of math from one outburst of anger or ridicule from a teacher or classmates.

The fear is more likely to emerge from repeated pairings of the CS (in this case, math) and US (yelling) in close contiguity in time. In general, the more pairings of CS with US, the greater the CR. If we think of the US as reinforcing the CS (since it always elicits the UR), then this principle can be restated as follows: the more reinforcements of the CS with the US, the greater the magnitude, or the faster the reaction time, of the CR (e.g., Hovland, 1937). To continue the fear-of-math example, the more a student is punished (US) when doing math (CS), the greater the fear of math.

The first pairings may not produce too much reaction, while subsequent trials will add substantially to the strength or latency of the conditioned response. After many trials, say 10 or 20, the increments will not be as great; thus the learning curve may be somewhat s-shaped as shown in figure 5.1.

Interval Between CS and US

In chapter 1 I promised to qualify the definition of respondent conditioning somewhat. I said that all that was necessary for conditioning to occur was that the CS precede the US or that they occur *contiguously*—that is, simultaneously. Although this is commonly the way the respondent conditioning law is stated, it is an oversimplification due to the fact that Pavlov considered any interval from zero to five seconds preceding the US to be contiguous. In empirical fact, it has been all but impossible to produce a CR when the CS occurs simultaneously with the US (e.g., Gormezano and Moore, 1969). Likewise, if the CS occurs, then disappears for, say, 10-seconds before the US is presented, conditioning is difficult. Exactly what the optimal interval might be has been an elusive search that is beyond the scope of this treatment.[2] Suffice it to say that it depends on the species and the latency of response of the reflex involved, but it is probably in the 1-sec. to 5-sec. range (but see the section below entitled "Belongingness").

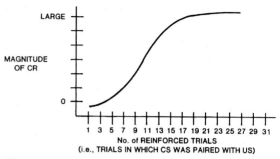

Figure 5.1. Typical learning curve relating number of reinforcements (CS-US pairings) to magnitude of conditioned response.

For most normal human situations, such a fine distinction does not matter because (1) the CS precedes the presentation of the US and (2) remains at least until the US occurs. This procedure satisfies the optimal conditions. For instance, it was some time after Albert saw the white rat that the loud noise occurred, but the rat was still present. Had the rat been taken away some seconds before the noise occurred, it is unlikely that Albert would have associated rat and noise—something else in the room would likely have drawn his attention and become associated with the noise. Likewise, if the noise (US) preceded the rat (CS), conditioning would probably not occur, since the US would elicit the UR before the CS occurred, rendering the CS irrelevant as a predictor of the US.[3]

Intensity of the US

Common sense tells us that a strong US (e.g., a strong shock) will elicit a more extreme reaction (e.g., a conditioned fear) than a weak one. The empirical evidence supports this conception (e.g., Gormezano and Moore, 1969).

"Belongingness" Between CS and US

There is now a growing body of evidence that some stimuli seem to "belong" with each other better than others, and to the extent that belonging stimuli are paired for conditioning,

conditioning is easier. For example, suppose an organism were fed a certain food which was tainted with a substance that induced nausea. The food (US) induced vomiting as the UR. If the neutral stimulus (CS) to be associated with this food were a distinctive odor or taste, conditioning would be much faster than if it were, say, a sound or a light. Odors and food, taste and illness, seem to belong together, while lights or sounds and food are not as related in nature. Studies similar to the one just described have been done (e.g., Garcia and Koelling, 1966; see Rescorla and Holland's 1982 review), with the results described above. Moreover, when the CS and US belong together, at least for such conditioned aversions as in tastes and illness, there can be long delays of up to hours between CS (taste) and US (induced nausea). This result goes contrary to the evidence on the optimal CS-US interval presented above, but is probably true for only especially "prepared" behaviors of a given species. This particular result, however, may explain why many young children are reluctant to try any new food (see cartoon).

The children may have learned that old foods' tastes and odors are safe—they have been conditioned to feel comfortable and secure with them. New foods, on the other hand, may be guilty until proven innocent in this regard: on a past occasion with a new, distinctive taste, the child may have felt sick and associated the new food with that feeling. Though this is a somewhat hypothetical explanation for children's taste preferences, it is not implausible based on the research evidence. Moreover, one can also imagine the species survival value of such a mechanism.

Turning to more general matters of belongingness, a *neutral stimulus is seldom truly neutral*. It probably elicits certain bodily reactions on its own, which may or may not be easily conditionable to other bodily reflexes. The sudden appearance of a light (CS) to be associated with food (US) may produce a frozen, passive waiting near the food dispenser, much as an

Cartoon: 5.2.

animal freezes his position when caught in a spotlight in the dark. A sudden auditory stimulus, on the other hand, evokes an exaggerated startle and other bodily movements (e.g., Rescorla, 1980). I am tempted to speculate on the relation of such animal research findings to humans, particularly with reference to certain colors or sounds (musical beats?) and hyperactive behaviors. Perhaps one of you readers will pursue research in this area.

To conclude this section, I would just like to alert you that we shall see two other examples of belongingness in subsequent sections: (1) the part-whole question under higher-order conditioning; and (2) the "preparedness" question under "Phobias," to which we now turn.

Phobias

If emotional reactions can be conditioned to any neutral stimulus as described above, then extreme emotional reactions—fears of falling, of snakes, etc.—should be simply conditioned via more intense USs, right? Not exactly. As we shall have occasion to discover throughout this book, the laws of psychology are not yet at the stage where they can be simply stated.

Extreme fears, usually called phobias, provide an interesting case of the complexity of respondent conditioning.

Some of the first evidence that conditioning emotions was not as straight-forward as Watson and Rayner's (1920) experience with Albert would lead us to believe occurred as early as 1929, when English was unable to condition a fear to a wooden duck using the loud noise as a US. Bregman (1934) was also unable to condition fear to wooden objects that were described as "without intrinsic biological interest or significance." These studies were not without flaws in their design or methods, but they drew attention to some distinctions that needed to be made. More recent research has provided a plausible explanation (e.g., Seligman, 1971).

To put it as succinctly as possible, phobias and conditioned fears may be quite different.[4] Phobias, first of all, seem to be limited to objects or events for which we are *biologically prepared*, for species-specific defense and adaptation. Common phobic reactions occur to specific animals, insects, heights, darkness, etc. As Seligman (1971, p. 312) put it,

> . . . only rarely, if ever, do we have pajama phobias, grass phobias, electric-outlet phobias, hammer phobias, even though these things are likely to be associated with trauma in our world. This leads to a second way in which phobias and conditioned fears may be different. Phobias usually occur in only one or two trials, whereas conditioned fears usually take between three and six repetitions to occur.

A third difference between them is their ability to be extinguished. For most conditioned fears, the normal extinction procedure of presenting the CS without following it with the US gradually reduces the fear of the CS. The person is learning—cognitively as well as emotionally—that the CS no longer predicts the frightful US. Eventually, though it will take a while, the CR will be reduced to zero for all practical purposes. For phobias, however, this extinction procedure, however rational, rarely works. A much more active procedure, such as counter-conditioning along with desensitization procedures (to be described later), must be used to eliminate phobias. According to this view, then, we are natively prepared to fear certain objects, presumably because there is a survival value in avoiding those objects without having to go through an extended period of learning. Presumably furry creatures that are, or look, alive can activate this preparedness so that, if a loud noise occurs when a furry creature is present, a fear will easily develop. The same US may not be sufficient to induce fear to an inanimate, non-furry neutral stimulus like a wooden duck, however.

It is uncertain, of course, whether this explanation is sufficient in and of itself to account for the intricate differences that occur in the development of fears. With so many different sorts of objects and so many possible traumas to which they can become associated in the histories of individuals, we may never fully account for the development of fears. Nevertheless, this explanation accounts for many of the differences we see between "normal" conditioned fears and phobias. It is also consistent with a growing literature on other species-specific defensive reactions in the realm of operant behavior (see, for example, "Punishment and Its Amazing Effects" in chapter 6). Finally, it is also consistent with the qualitative relationship of belongingness between CS and US mentioned in an earlier section.

Generalization and Discrimination

When little Albert was "traumatized" into fearing the white rat by pairing it with the loud noise, his fear generalized to other stimuli as well, particularly to a white rabbit and other furry objects (Watson and Rayner, 1920). Most of us can relate to that through some personal traumatic experience. An anxiety-laden first piano recital made many people fearful not only of performing in public, but also of getting up in front of an audience for any reason. Or a child's fear of a doctor, from the pain associated with a shot, may also be transferred to other people or settings in which white coats or medicinal smells may be present, such as a barbershop. This process of the CR being elicited not only by the original CS, but by other CSs similar to it, is called *generalization* (or more correctly, *stimulus generalization*).

Fortunately, it is a rare case indeed in which a conditioned emotion is so undifferentiated as to be associated with very many settings. More typically, emotions generalize only to stimuli which are very similar to the original CS assuming, of course, that there are no other presentations of the US. The curve that can be drawn to show that "the more similar a new stimulus is to the original CS, the more likely the CR will occur" is called the *generalization gradient* (e.g., Hovland, 1937; Kalish, 1969).

As we go through life, we learn more and more to *discriminate* between stimulus situations, which is to say we respond differently to each situation. Thus our emotions become associated to specific stimuli: we fear only dentists, not barbers; or we feel relaxed and interested in one teacher's class, but not all teachers' classes. The more training or experience we have differentiating situations, the more discriminating we become. As we shall see, this process is similar for operant behavior as well, so we shall defer further treatment of it until the next chapter.

Higher-Order Conditioning

Many people have particular emotional reactions to certain musical melodies. That a melody can induce a feeling directly should no longer be too surprising, assuming it is directly associated with a US for an emotional reaction. If lovers make love with "Bolero" in the background (as was done in the movie "10"), then Bolero should evoke romantic feelings on some future occasion. The song has become a CS for the feelings elicited by the actual love-making reflexes. This immediate association of CS and US can be thought of as direct or first-order conditioning.

But songs can be emotional CSs even when they have not been directly associated with a US as, for example, when a melody has been associated with the restaurant dinner you had with your lover before you first made love. The actual sexual stimulation was the US for the amorous reflexes. The person becomes a CS for those feelings: all he or she has to do is come into view or call you on the phone and you can begin to feel sexually excited. The song, then, is associated with that person. This is a case of second-order or, more generally, higher-order conditioning since a neutral stimulus can come to elicit an emotional reaction by being paired with a CS.

The first studies of higher-order conditioning were conducted by (whom else but?) Pavlov (1927), but he concluded that the resulting conditioned reflexes were unstable. More recent studies (e.g., Davenport, 1966; Rescorla, 1980) have demonstrated such second-order conditioning to be quite stable. An actual procedure for demonstrating higher-order conditioning is worth exploring for a moment because of its importance in understanding emotions. In the first stage a light (CS_1) is reliably followed by a shock (US) which, in turn, elicits the physiological stress reaction we commonly call fear.[5] When the light regularly elicits the fear reaction, Stage 2 begins. Now a tone (CS_2) precedes the light (CS_1), which is no longer followed by the shock (US). What happens is that the tone acquires the capability of eliciting fear, too, solely on the basis of being paired with the light.

Several surprising results emerged from studies like the one just described, as well as

Anecdote 5.1

Test Anxiety: A Case of Higher-order Conditioning

Following is a personal experience of an adult, describing her fears about returning to graduate school after a number of years out of college. After reading the material in this chapter, she described her experience his way:

"Taking a test automatically puts a fear in me. I know the material, but when I get to that test it all seems to go from me. As far back as I can remember, this was a problem for me, so I probably had some traumatic event associated with test-taking. The trauma was probably the unconditioned stimulus producing the unconditioned response of fear. The test was the conditioned stimulus.

In any case, when I decided to come back to school after so many years, there was such a fear of failure that just the thought of coming back to school was a conditioned stimulus for nervousness, since I figured I'd have to take a test. Thus there was a chain of events for higher-order conditioning: the thought of returning to class was paired with the idea of taking a test, which elicited my fear of failure."

Joyce Hamilton
Occupational Therapist

Author's Note: Joyce did well in the course because, as she explained it, she learned through the mastery testing format of the course to ". . . produce new behavior that is adaptive to the situation and . . . allowed for extinction of the fear of test taking."

some using food as the US. First, after only a few conditioning trials (in one study 8 trials pairing CS_1 and US and 6 pairing CS_2 and CS_1) extinction of the CR commonly took many trials more than to condition it in the first place. Rescorla (1980, p. 10) commented that . . . this eventual demise of responding to [CS_2] is frequently very slow indeed, often requiring hundreds of trials." This finding, that it often takes much longer to extinguish a CR than to condition it, it should be noted, is something that also occurs in first-order conditioning.

A second surprising finding from Rescorla's studies was that, in many cases the CR elicited by CS_2 was of greater magnitude than that elicited by CS_1. In fact, it sometimes appeared that a CR had not been acquired to the CS_1 (there was little or no observable reaction to the light) until it was found capable of transferring the reaction to CS_2 (the tone).

Third, when the CR (emotional reaction) was extinguished to the CS_1 (the light) by being unpaired with the US, the conditioned emotion remained to CS_2 (the tone). Despite the fact that the CS_1 was necessary for the conditioned emotion to be attached to the CS_2, once the $CS_2 \rightarrow CR$ connection was made, it had a life of its own. The second-order conditioned emotional reaction was independent of what happened to the earlier conditioned reactions through which it was learned. Returning to our music example, this finding supports common experiences people have. Our favorite melody (CS_2) may remain capable of eliciting warm feelings even when the

Stage 1
First-Order
Conditioning
	$CS_1 \text{—} US \rightarrow UR$
	Death pain fear
	             or
	           tension
	    $\searrow$
	    CR fear or
	           tension
		Death[6] is associated with pain or fear (from loss of loved one, etc.).

Stage 2
Second-Order
Conditioning
	$CS_2 \text{—} CS_1 \rightarrow CR$
	AIDS death fear or
	              tension
	    $\searrow$
	    CR
	    Fear or
	    tension
		The disease AIDS is associated with death: "AIDS causes a painful death."

Stage 3
Third-Order
Conditioning
	$CS_3 \text{—} CS_2 \rightarrow CR$
	John AIDS fear
	    $\searrow$
	    CR
	    fear
		We learn that "John has AIDS" and we want nothing to do with him.

Figure 5.2. How people and labels can elicit emotions through higher-order conditioning.

person (CS_1) from whom those feelings were transferred no longer elicits such feelings.

An additional finding of Rescorla's (1980) was that if the CS_2 were a portion of CS_1, conditioning was accelerated over that which occurred when CS_1 and CS_2 were unrelated. To continue the example of our lovers, the voice of the loved one on the phone can easily come to elicit amorous feelings once it has been associated with the "object of our affection." The voice (CS_2) is a part of the whole person (CS_1) who has been conditioned to evoke the loving feelings (CR) through direct contact.

Analogous situations may occur in school settings where a teacher's tone of voice or angry scowl can come to elicit a fearful response as CS_1 by being paired with actual punishment (US) administered by that teacher. Then other neutral stimuli in the environment, such as math problems, books, or music appreciation classes (as CS_2) can come to elicit those same feelings by being paired with the teacher's tone of voice or scowl. Actual punishment need not occur.

Physical deformities caused by accident, disease or birth defect can cause a natural revulsion as an unconditioned reflex. If we now attach words like "sinful," "cancer," or "handicapped" to those feelings, we can come to feel revulsion at the sound of the words. When we then say that "Mary has cancer" or "George is handicapped" we are engaging in second-order conditioning, attaching a person's name (CS_2) to a word (CS_1) which has been attached to an actual US for a fear or revulsion reaction (see figure 5.2).

It should be becoming clearer that this is likely one of the mechanisms involved in stereotyping ethnic groups—that is, by calling them "lazy and dirty"—since these words have been associated with actual emotional experiences. In an experimental study on exactly this problem, Staats and Staats (1958) were able to change attitudes either positively or negatively about two European groups by pairing them with such positive words as gift, sacred, and happy or such negative words as bitter, ugly and failure. They were able to do the same with names of people, like Tom and Bill.[7]

Cartoon: 5.3.

We used to say as children, "Sticks and stones will break my bones, but names will never hurt me." But as the cartoon shows, names *do* hurt. Even if Mowrer (1954) was only partly correct that a sentence is primarily a conditioning device, then much of our communication is conditioning higher-order emotions to the subject of the sentence by what feelings are elicited by the predicate. The statement "Bill is hyper" is perhaps more effective as a conditioner of feelings about Bill by the listeners than it is as a descriptor of Bill's actual behavior or a prescriptor of what to do about it. Given all of this, one must wonder what damage we are doing with such labels as "retarded," "dyslexic," "learning disabled," and so forth.

Stress and Learned Helplessness

In 1958 a soon-to-become famous experiment was conducted in which one member each of several pairs of rhesus monkeys was given shocks that could be avoided (postponed) by pressing a pair within a certain time. The second member of the pair was "yoked" to it, so that every time the first monkey was shocked, the second also received a shock of equal intensity and duration. The only difference between what happened to the two monkeys in the pair, therefore, was that the former was in control of its own destiny, while the latter had no control over whether shocks would be received. Because the former monkeys were making the decisions, they came to be known as the "executive monkeys." After repeated "decision-making trials" in which both members of the pair successfully avoided or received shocks on the basis of the decisions of the "executive," the animals were examined for gastroduodenal ulcers, among other things. With no additional information, and before reading further, answer the following two choice question to see how "obvious" or "common-sensible" this psychological finding appears to you. *Item:* Which of the following monkeys in the pair should be expected to have a greater number of and/or more severe ulcers?

A. The "executive" monkeys whose decisions controlled whether they received shocks, or

B. The "yoked" monkeys who had no control over whether they received shocks.

If you chose A, then you have predicted (or remembered) the results of the original study (e.g., Brady, 1958; Brady et al., 1958; Porter et al, 1958). You can also find a great deal of popular support for your choice in the common-sense belief that ulcers are the price that one pays for an executive lifestyle.

If you chose B, however, you are most probably correct. Despite these earlier findings and the popular consensus of opinion, it is not the stress of decision-making that causes ulcers, or other psychogenic disturbances; rather, it is the *lack of predictability and control over the outcome* that causes such problems.[8] With lack of predictability and loss of control come fear, often helplessness and depression, and sometimes even death.

Learned Helplessness

Stress, produced by environmental changes or demands on an organism, has many psychological and physiological effects. But exactly what the effects of stress are depend, in turn, on whether the organisms have control over—or perceive they have control over—the outcome. Some of the earliest research to suggest that the availability of successful coping behavior could reduce stress and helplessness was done by Mowrer and Viek in 1948. They were able to demonstrate that hungry rats who could control the amount of shock they received by jumping did not allow the anticipated shock to disrupt their eating when food was made available. Rats who were equated with them in the amount of shock received, but whose jumping or other behavior had no effect on the shock, had their normal eating behavior severely disrupted. These rats, who had no control over the shock, were characterized by Mowrer and Viek as showing "fear of fear."

Perhaps the point about helplessness and its devastating effects was made most vividly by Seligman (1975). He and his co-workers were studying various aspects of fear conditioning by subjecting dogs to shocks that were unavoidable, producing respondent conditioning as described earlier in this chapter. Following a number of such unavoidable shocks, each dog was placed in a shuttle-box in which escape from shock could easily be achieved by jumping over a barrier from one side of the box to the other. Seligman describes the results as follows (1975, p. 22):

What we saw was bizarre, and can best be appreciated if I first describe the behavior of a typical dog that has not been given uncontrollable shock.
When placed in a shuttle box, an experimentally naive dog, at the onset of the first electric shock, runs frantically about until it accidentally scrambles over the barrier and escapes the shock. On the next trial, the dog, running frantically, crosses the barrier more quickly than on the preceding trial; within a few trials it becomes very efficient at escaping, and soon learns to avoid shock altogether. After about fifty trials, the dog becomes nonchalant and stands in front of the barrier; at the onset of the signal for shock it leaps gracefully across and never gets shocked again.
A dog that had been first given inescapable shock showed a strikingly different pattern. This dog's first reactions to shock in the shuttle box were much the same as those of a naive dog; it ran around frantically for about thirty seconds. But then it stopped moving; to our surprise, it lay down and quietly whined. After one minute of this we turned the shock off; the dog had failed to cross the barrier and had not escaped from shock. On the next trial, the dog did it again; at first it struggled a bit, and then, after a few seconds, it seemed to give up and to accept the shock passively. On all succeeding trials, the dog failed to escape.

This phenomenon has come to be known as *learned helplessness*. It apparently arises from encountering a situation in which you are at first incapable of controlling what happens to you; you learn you are incompetent or helpless. When you are subsequently exposed to a similar situation that is within your control, your previous experience renders you unable or unwilling to learn new adaptable behaviors.

More specifically, organisms who are exposed to these learned helplessness conditions show deficits in all three areas of behavior of interest to this book—namely, the emotional (respondent), the motivational (operant), and the cognitive. The emotional effect occurs as a heightened state of fear which, with prolonged exposure to uncontrollable events, can turn into apathy or depression. The motivational effect is evidenced by a diminished tendency to initiate any motions or actions which might serve as trial-and-error. There is little willingness to try anything new since everything that was tried before didn't work. The cognitive deficit shows up in the organism's not learning what controls the environment or in not perceiving what events predict what outcomes. Their previous experience has adversely affected their thinking about the current situation (a form of negative transfer called proactive interference, described in chapter 9).

The basic findings described above have now been replicated on many species, including humans. Hiroto (1974) exposed college students to inescapable loud noise. Then when they were given a situation in which they could turn off the loud noise by a simple movement, their escape was much impaired, as compared to control groups of college students whose prior experience was either training to escape loud noise or no exposure at all to the noise. Hiroto's study is interesting because it also explored the effects of instructions on escape. Fewer students learned to escape if they were *told* that escape was determined by chance rather than by their skill.

Finally—and this is quite relevant to developing personalities—Hiroto studied the factor of locus of control (Rotter, 1966). Half of his students had identified themselves on a personality inventory as believing that their successes and failures primarily result from their own effort and skill. Such persons are said to have an *internal locus of control*. The other half of the students subscribed to an *external locus of control*, in that they were more likely to attribute their own successes and failures to luck or the ease or difficulty of the situation. Hiroto found that external students became much more helpless in his experiment than internals.

Learned Helplessness and Attribution Theory

Although Seligman's original formulation of learned helplessness included a cognitive component, research on humans, such as Hiroto's, suggested that people's beliefs exerted quite a bit of control over whether people became helpless or not. (Note the parallels to Bandura's self-efficacy beliefs in social cognitive theory, described in chapter 1). In a 1978 revision of learned helplessness theory, Abramson, Seligman and Teasdale included people's beliefs as a primary cognitive determinant of the results of uncontrollable failure experiences. They did this by including the major concepts of *attribution theory* (e.g., Weiner, 1974; Weiner and Litman-Adizes, 1980).[9]

Attributions, in this view, *are causal explanations* for events and they can be examined in another three-dimensional framework (Seligman, 1990; Peterson, Maier & Seligman, 1993). The first dimension is the *internal-external* dimension described above—that is, is success or failure *personalized* as ability or effort or attributed to such external factors as luck or quality of teaching. The second dimension is the *permanence* or stable-unstable continuum, in which people may explain events in terms of stable, long-term circumstances (e.g., ability or inherited wealth) compared with unstable, transient circumstances (e.g., effort or situational constraints). The third dimension is the

Table 5.1. Examples of causal explanations for the event, "I can't do my math assignment."*

Stable	Internal	External
Global	"I'll never understand this stuff."	"This class is stupid." I don't need this stuff anyway.
Specific	"I never did learn about exponents."	"This assignment is useless. Why do I need to know about exponents?"

Unstable		
Global	"I just didn't have the time to do my math. I spent all week on my English paper."	"Everything is due at the same time. Can't these teachers give us a break?"
Specific	"The one assignment I can't do he grades."	"The teacher told us not to worry about this stuff, then he gives an assignment on nothing but exponents."

Note: Modeled on the example in Gentile and Monaco (1986, p. 164).

global-specific or *pervasiveness* dimension, which refers to whether an explanation of an event is generalized to a variety of similar events or is considered limited to an isolated circumstance. Table 5.1 provides examples of the kind of attributions that fall under each of these dimensions for the hypothetical event. "I can't do my math assignment."

Mathematics turns out to be a prime example for learned helplessness discussions because, first, there is some empirical evidence on the subject and, second, so many people profess "I was never any good in math" (a global, stable, internal attribution). Regarding the empirical evidence, Monaco and Gentile (1987) reported a study in which high school students were given multiplication problems (e.g., 78 × 93) under timed conditions and, regardless of their performance, were given failure feedback of the form that they had done worse than average. They were then told to try again, but with the same results. This occurred for five trials in a row, that is, five sheets of problems. A control group of students had no experience with these problems or with failure.

A day later both the failure group and the control group were asked to solve a parallel set of multiplication problems, as well as some higher level reasoning problems (that is, pattern completion in multiple-choice form, such as the following: 25:5::____:8 (a. 49, b. 36, c. 64, d. 48).

As helplessness theory predicted, exposure to the unavoidable failure experience led to a significant debilitation in performance. This brief and relatively unimportant failure experience (in that it did not count for a school grade) nevertheless produced a decrement in performance which transferred to the reasoning task, in addition to occurring on the original task. Moreover, the failure experience induced people to "take it personally," and explain their performance ("I could have done better if . . .") in terms of effort or ability (more internal attributions) rather than in terms of luck or the difficulty of the problems (more external attributions), as control subjects tended to do.

To avoid any long-term learned helplessness effects, the experimenters in this study took great pains in a debriefing to explain to the participants that the failure feedback was arbitrary and not really a measure of their ability in either an absolute or relative sense. The effects of this brief, relatively benign failure experience were nevertheless similar to research in other domains and also to anecdotal evidence. One can only wonder what effects repeated exposure to uncontrollable outcomes—or perceived uncontrollable outcomes—can have in school situations in which the outcomes really matter.

Some have argued (e.g., Dweck and Licht, 1980) that such effects as those over the long haul may be at least partially responsible for the ubiquitous gender differences in mathematics achievement. It is widely believed, for example, that females in the USA give more internal, stable attributions for their behavior and its effect than males do, and Dweck and Licht (1980) have presented some evidence suggesting that teachers tend to reinforce these gender-stereotypic explanations. As I have often quipped, "It's great to be a male in this society: if something goes wrong, I can blame it on my wife (a typical male attribution). More importantly, she accepts the blame (a typical female attribution)." But, as my wife responds, "Not any more!" Attributions, like behavior, can be changed—a point we shall explore further in the section on prevention and cure of learned helplessness.

Much more could be said about attributions in general and their relationship, more specifically, to learned helplessness. Various explanatory profiles seem to be more susceptible to learned helplessness and other severe problems than other profiles. Peterson and Seligman (1984) have suggested, for example, that persons with internal-stable-global attributional styles are at risk for depression. While such individual differences may be important, it is also worth recalling that when people perceive that success or failure is beyond their control, they become anxious, attempt to obtain control by trying harder or trying new approaches, and to blame others or bad luck. If the situation persists, the anxiety (the respondent level) eventually turns to apathy and depression. On the operant level, the person tries to escape. On the cognitive level, the lack of understanding of how to control the outcome turns from simple external defenses to more internal attributions: "perhaps I'm really not very intelligent" or "I'm not good in math," etc. Thus we see the interaction of all three levels of behavior.

Learned Helplessness Through the Life Span

As argued in the previous section, math anxiety and its associated negative effects on achievement can be plausibly accounted for by learned helplessness theory (Anecdote 5.2). Dweck and Licht (1980) argue convincingly why mathematics is particularly ripe for learned helplessness, perhaps more so than verbal fields. Verbal skills like speaking and reading tend to be acquired and improved upon in small increments. In addition, they are similar to the skills used in daily life outside of the classroom. In stark contrast to that, however, are typical math courses in which each new unit may involve very different concepts or procedures. Each new unit may, as Dweck and Licht (1980, p. 21) put it, ". . . entail large, sudden qualitative changes as, for example, when one goes from arithmetic to algebra to geometry to calculus and so on."

If Dweck is even partly correct, we can begin to see the complexity of the problem on all three levels of behavior. On the cognitive level, students must find ways of understanding the current task in terms of their past learnings and schemata. If some of these are incorrect or inadequate, and learning the new

Anecdote 5.2

The Case of the "Lazy Underachiever"

Kevin is a high school freshman with an IQ of 120. Despite the capability of doing well, he was never more than an average student and for the last few years has, at best, just squeaked by. His performance in math is illustrative of the problem. When he did hand in an assignment, he would usually obtain 50–65% correct. His current teacher is regularly on his case because, if he does turn in an assignment (which is rare), it is sloppily done. He turned in one math test with nothing but his name on it. From the teacher's perspective, Kevin is intelligent, but lazy. Kevin's behavior confuses the teacher as she cannot understand why someone who often came relatively close to passing would suddenly settle for a score of zero. Frustrated at her inability to reason with him, the teacher sends Kevin to the principal's office where he proclaims that the teacher can't teach and is always picking on him "for no reason."

The above is based on a real case (the names have been changed to protect the guilty) that is quoted from Gentile and Monaco (1988, pp. 15–16). These authors make the argument that Kevin's behavior can be explained as learned helplessness. Although bright enough to succeed, since elementary school he has been a perennial underachiever. Thus since seventh grade it is likely that he hardly ever understood material very well before the teacher moved on to cover a new unit. With failure to master many fundamentals, he would therefore have difficulty catching up even when he did work up to speed. When he tried hard he discovered that trying hard still did not achieve high grades, just marginal passes or high failing grades (50–60%). From his perspective, it is psychologically less demeaning to fail when he hasn't tried, than to fail having given his best effort. If he does not try, he has no personal investment in the task and thus no disappointment. In addition, he allows himself the defense of attributing his failures to external factors: "The teacher can't teach."

A cure for Kevin would be difficult to arrange at this late date, but sooner will be better than later. He will need to master prerequisite concepts and skills that he never learned, or mislearned. He also needs to learn new attributions for his failures, such as that, if he learns new strategies and tries harder and consistently with appropriate help from a willing and nonthreatening teacher, then he will succeed. For specific suggestions, see the recommendations in the text.

material depends on them, then students will be incapable of solving the problems the teacher poses. This lack of efficacy will translate into feelings of inadequacy on the emotional level: at first, these feelings might be mere confusion, but if they persist, they can easily turn to anger, anxiety, apathy, and depression. On the operant level, confused students will do the behaviors that worked in the past; if past habits do not succeed, then they will grasp at straws through wild guessing or trying to "psych out" the teacher. Finally, if success does not follow despite these efforts, students will try to escape, either literally by skipping classes or dropping out of school or by investing so little effort that their self-esteem is not at stake. This behavior is then rationalized back to the cognitive level in such reasoning as "I could do it if I wanted to, but . . ." (see anecdote 5.2).

Ironically, even when students succeed under such conditions of confusion and self-doubt—that is, they receive high grades—they may develop learned helplessness (Gentile and Monaco, 1986; Seligman, 1975). This can occur when they rationalize their success as due to luck or to the fact that they were competing with other kids who were even dumber than they, etc. They view even their successes with pessimism (Seligman, 1990): as having been unrelated to their efforts (noncontingent on their behavior) and therefore uncontrollable by them. Uncontrollability of outcomes, you will recall, is a prime determiner of learned helplessness (and can produce stress). Evidence of these underlying helpless feelings emerges when successful students drop math from their schedules in high school when it is no longer required. Their rationalizations will tend to be of the following sort: "Well, I won't need math because I'm going to major in the social sciences in college." (Another case of rapanoia!)

If the above emphasis on mathematics leaves the impression that math is the only field in which learned helplessness occurs, it is time to correct that impression. Similar phenomena may occur in other school subjects as well. Butkowski and Willows (1980), for example, provide evidence that many of the behaviors of poor readers resemble the learned helplessness syndrome. They studied fifth-grade boys and found that, in contrast to good readers, poor readers (1) had lower expectancies of success on a reading task and puzzle-solving task (which was deliberately made to appear not related to reading); (2) did not persist as

Photo 5.2. Mastering the basics.

long at the task at hand; and (3) were more likely to explain their failures as resulting from internal, stable causes such as poor ability, rather than to external, unstable causes such as a difficult task. Poor readers also took less credit for successful outcomes, ascribing the responsibility to an easy task, for example.

Taking a broader developmental approach to the problem, consider the crisis that Erikson emphasizes for school age—namely, industry vs. inferiority. The central developmental task he sees for these years is mastering the tools and skills society has defined as important. These include the three R's: readin', 'ritin' and 'rithmetic. Failure to master these tasks results, Erikson maintains, in feelings of inferiority.

Finally, let's continue the developmental process to the last of Erikson's stages. He claims that unfulfilled expectations from previous stages can lead to an old age filled with despair. Most of us have experienced at least one case of unexplained death in our lifetimes: someone who has weathered a successful operation, but who just seems to give up hope and die; someone who has lost a loved one and then seems to die from grief; or someone who goes off to a nursing home and soon afterward dies. Autopsies generally reveal no known causes for these deaths, though there may be other ailments from which the deceased was suffering. Is it possible that these deaths, "unexpected" from a medical perspective, are very much expected from a learned-helplessness point of view? Seligman (1975; 1990) and Peterson et al. (1993) offer impressive anecdotal and experimental evidence for such a view. These persons may have learned that whatever they do does not change things; they do not understand what is happening to them very well and cannot control their treatment, and they lapse into severe depression and, finally, hopelessness and despair.

Prevention and Cure: Competence

If learned helplessness implies that there is a loss of control over one's life, it may be useful to conceptualize its opposite as mastery over the situation or, in a word, *competence*. When people are subjected to a traumatic event, their bodily reaction is the stress response, with the dominant emotion being fear. This state remains until they learn to control the trauma—they learn a competent behavior—at which time the fear or general stress response dissipates and, as Seligman puts it (1975, p. 54), ". . . gives way to an efficient and nonchalant response." If the traumatic situation is truly uncontrollable, the fear and stress response will also dissipate, giving way to depression and eventually perhaps hopelessness and death. The motivation for competence (White, 1959) has been thwarted.

Cures for any emotional disturbance are always much more difficult and time-consuming than the original learning. Learned helplessness also impairs the operant and cognitive levels of behavior, as we have seen, so the cure will have to at least do the following: (1) produce new behavior that is adaptive to the situation, (2) produce information that is relevant to understanding the situation or predicting the consequences of behavior in that situation, and (3) allow extinction of the fear in the situation.

To cure his dogs of helplessness in the shuttle box, Seligman (1975) had to drag the dogs from one compartment to the next so they could learn there was no shock to fear in the other compartment, and that there was an adaptive behavior that could escape the shock and reduce their fear or depression. The therapy was effective, but in the beginning the whole weight of the dog had to be pulled by the leash. In later trials less and less force was needed, until toward the end a nudge was sufficient and finally, the dog went by itself and never again failed to escape. That's the good news. The bad news is that it took from 25 to 200 draggings.

Prevention or immunization was easier. When Seligman's dogs were first given a series of trials in which they successfully learned to escape shock, then were exposed to the unescapable shocks, their performance in a subsequent controllable situation was not impaired. The critical factor was that the *first experience was successful*. The competence that was established there could then withstand a period in which there was no control. Learned helplessness was prevented.

Many questions arise in applying this idea to humans, not the least of which are some basic problems about how many competence experiences are needed to withstand ten (or twenty or fifty) experiences of uncontrollable outcomes. Future research will surely aid our understanding in this regard. But I do not feel that it is too far-fetched to suggest that Seligman's prevention technique could be profitably adopted by teachers at all levels with no conceivable harm and possibly with great benefit.

Every teacher has encountered students who, as soon as a problem is presented, show signs of confusion, anxiety—often total bewilderment. They seem unable to understand

Anecdote 5.3

> ### Learned Optimism: A Mastery Orientation
>
> In a more recent book, Martin Seligman (1990) speaks of the depressive attributional style (e.g., blaming yourself for never being able to do anything right") as being a habitual pessimism. For example, your child is yelled at by a teacher and he or she jumps to the conclusion that "the teacher hates me and the whole class thinks I'm a jerk" (p. 241). What is needed, says Seligman, is to learn a more realistic, positive and constructive attributional style—a *learned optimism.* Thus the child needs to learn to dispute his or her own pessimistic statements: "The teacher yells at everybody sometimes, so the class probably thinks I'm cool, like the others who were yelled at. Besides, the teacher usually likes us, but everybody was goofing off that day, so probably we deserved his yelling."
>
> Attributions such as this provide a more realistic balance among the dimensions. That is, the blame is not too personalized, too permanent, or too pervasive: The teacher may yell sometimes when we goof off (external, specific and unstable), but I'm likeable and cool most of the time (internal, global and stable).
>
> The above pessimism-optimism continuum is not too far removed from Carol Dweck's (1986; Dweck & Leggett, 1988) characterization of helpless vs. mastery-oriented students. Helpless students are motivated to protect their egos in that they work to avoid failure and hide their perceived incompetencies; are likely to believe in intelligence as a fixed quantity; and are threatened and anxious and show little persistence when problems or challenges arise. At the other end of the continuum are mastery-oriented students, who are motivated to solve problems and achieve success; who see intelligence as developing; and who see difficult tasks and new challenges as learning opportunities to be embraced. Dweck, like Seligman, believes that attributions can be changed (see also Schunk, 1989), and much of that must necessarily occur in mediated learning experiences with teachers.
>
>

that anything they do or think about can control the situation, analyze the problem, or answer it. They are, as Holt (1964) described them, "answer-grabbers." He goes to describe some of them (1964, p. 73).

> *Monica wants the right answer, yes; but what she wants, first of all, is an answer, any old answer, and she will do almost anything to get some kind of answer. Once she gets it, a large part of the pressure is off.*
> *. . . The strategies of most of these kids have been consistently self-centered, self-protective, aimed above all else at avoiding trouble, embarrassment, punishment, disapproval, or loss of status. This is particularly true of the ones who have had a tough time in school.*

Such students have not developed competence and, as a result, have no confidence in their ability to solve a problem. With repeated experiences like this, they may give up trying.

But answer-grabbing and giving up are not the only difficulties helpless students have. Because they see the problem as out of their control, either because it is beyond their ability or the situation militates against them, they take little or no responsibility for whether or not they successfully complete a task (e.g., Dweck and Repucci, 1973). Dweck (1975) capitalized on this idea and provided a long-term training procedure for twelve boys and girls aged 8 to 13, who were identified as showing severe signs of learned helplessness. Her procedure taught half of these students, randomly selected, to take responsibility for their failures and, moreover, to attribute their failure to their own lack of effort. Of course, the tasks and the criteria for success were known to be within the capabilities of the students. When these students were compared to the other half who received 100% success experiences only (i.e., they had no experience with failure or attribution of failure to their own effort), the attribution retraining group coped with subsequent failure experiences much better.

As we shall see in the next chapter, it is important to learn frustration tolerance by not being reinforced for every effort one makes, whether correct or not. Neither should one be exposed to a situation in which every attempt appears to be totally incompetent, particularly in the early stages of a new task. Dweck's (1975) study does not prove superiority of her method over other methods; it does show one way of beginning to convince students that they must develop competence in each new task and assume responsibility for the effort. On the other hand, behavior does not occur in a vacuum. The task difficulty must be appropriate to the current capabilities (entering behavior) of the students so that they can truly develop some competence, if only some small approximation to what will be required later. (See also Anecdote 5.3).

If each new lesson in, say, math were approached with the plan of helping each student attain competence, then the cognitive, motivational and emotional components of learning math would be within each student's control. Granted, this is not easy to do and, given some students' past histories, may be impossible.

But the emphasis on developing early competence and optimism, and thereby avoiding the conditions that can lead to learned helplessness, may be well worth the effort.

Gentile and Monaco (1986, 1988) gave the following advice to teachers:

1. Each student should be successful, particularly in the beginning of each new unit of material. As the unit progresses and basic concepts are being mastered, include material that is at a higher level of thinking or shows the application of the material to other situations, and that therefore cannot be completed quickly or with 100% accuracy. This is to build in frustration tolerance—the willingness to try despite feelings of anxiety or confusion.
2. Teach students how to reduce their tension (see the last section in this chapter).
3. Provide students with effective ways to talk to themselves—that is, teach them attributions which emphasize effort, persistence and good strategies of learning and problem solving. De-emphasize attributions on aptitude, native ability and luck.
4. Evaluate work giving feedback on (a) what was correct, (b) what was incorrect, and (c) how to correct the latter. Then require that work be corrected, using the student's own correct instances as models, where possible, to show them that they indeed can do this.
5. If new concepts are going to be difficult, or will require new strategies or knowledge structures, inform the students of this, but emphasize that, with your help, they can and will learn these new strategies.
6. If certain topics or cues elicit conditioned emotional reactions, try to teach the concepts first without any of those CSs; then, after the student has already been successful, reintroduce the topic more traditionally. Rozin et al. (1971) used this approach to teach students like Victor (Quote #2 in the Introduction of this chapter) how to

read: they taught them the meaning of some Chinese characters. They then informed them, to their surprise, that they were now reading. After considerable success with this, they started over to teach reading of English.
7. For any students who are turning in sloppy work or blank papers, assume that this is not a discipline problem, but an emotional problem which is symptomatic of the early stages of learned helplessness. Return to one or more of the above points.

The Interaction of Motions, Emotions and Cognitions

Learned helplessness provided many examples of the continual interplay among operants (actions and motivations), respondents (emotions) and thoughts (cognitions) about the situations people find themselves in. There is a continual debate in psychology about which comes first—the thought, the emotion, or the action? To bring clarity to the issue, consider the following common experience. You are walking home at night with a friend when, suddenly as you pass a dark alley, your friend bolts ahead of you running as fast as he can. You, naturally, begin to run too, and later when you are catching your breath together, he asks you why you ran so hard? He ran just as a joke. If you don't hit him on the spot, you might laugh at yourself as the butt of the joke. But why *did* you run? Did you run (operant) because you perceived something (cognition) that made you afraid (respondent)? Did you run (operant), and did the running make your heart pound (respondent) which you then judged to be fear (cognition)? Did you think before you ran?

An early account of the relation among these different levels of behavior came to be known as the James-Lange theory, which in part stated that when we feel afraid, it is because we run

Photo 5.3. Reading Chinese: How would you feel? (Photo Courtesy of Dr. Thomas J. Shuell)

away—not conversely. William James (1904) stated that although such an account was probably exaggerated (but not very much), he was certain that the main core of the idea was true. However, he did take a more moderate stance with regard to causality in one of his Talks To Teachers, called "The Gospel of Relaxation" (1904, p. 133):

> *Action seems to follow feeling, but really action and feelings go together; and by regulating the action, which is under the more direct control of the will, we can indirectly regulate the feeling which is not.*

As in so many other areas, James set the agenda for much research and theorizing to follow decades later. The last part of his statement can be interpreted as a belief that involuntary behaviors such as emotions can be brought under voluntary control (e.g., in biofeedback to control blood pressure or migraine headaches).

The first phrase of the statement does not need to be changed much to provide the consensus view in the same debate, now removed to the 1980's where the major interest is the relation of thoughts and feelings, with less emphasis on actions. Two of the major figures on somewhat different sides of the debate are R. B. Zajonc and R. S. Lazarus. Despite the evidence and arguments they amass to make their points, they nevertheless agree on the following:[10]

The full experience of emotion . . . normally includes three fused components: thoughts, action impulses, and somatic disturbances. (Lazarus, 1982, p. 1019)
In nearly all cases, however, feeling is not free of thought, nor is thought free of feelings. (Zajonc, 1980, p. 154)

At this stage of our understanding of the relationships among thought, action and feeling—which after all has not changed that much in a century—this consensus position is not only the safest position to take, but also has some surprisingly practical implications. One of these I shall touch on only briefly here, deferring fuller discussion until chapter 7—namely, the question of attitude change. It is a common complaint of teachers that "there's nothing you can do with that kid because he has a bad attitude." The prescription seems to be: first you change the attitude, then appropriate behavior can follow. First of all, the empirical evidence favors the opposite conclusion: attitude change is best accomplished by changing behavior so that the person has proper experiences (e.g., Bem, 1970; see also Guskey, 1986, for an example in changing teacher attitudes toward teaching methods). More importantly, if motions, emotions and cognitions are conceptualized as always interacting in an interdependent way, then none of them is primary and all are important. Then a person can be reached via any or all of these modalities or levels of behavior.

Another practical implication has already been mentioned, but deserves repeating. The labels we give to people—primarily cognitive behavior—can never be seen as unrelated to a person's emotions or behaviors. They may arise from the behavior (i.e., Johnny is overly active so we call him hyperactive), but they also can become determiners of behavior in a self-fulfilling prophecy. When we call someone a "victim" of cancer (instead of, say, a client), the person stands a great chance of assuming the emotionally depressed and helpless state of a victim. A similar problem has been identified by Rounds and Hendel (1980) in the diagnostic use of the term "math anxiety." The term often confuses many issues—e.g., the fear of mathematics per se vs. test anxiety vs. the fear of the setting—and when indiscriminately applied to students can condition the students to become anxious in the ways described above. These interacting labels and feelings have operant components as well, as when we learn to be hyperactive to get attention, to be math anxious to avoid taking a statistics course, or to be the poor cancer victim to avoid certain responsibilities.[11]

A final implication concerns the bidirectionality of all kinds of learning. Logan (1972, p. 1060) gave the following example.

Suppose a person is for some reason feeling depressed, guilty, or just sorry for himself. Suppose further that that person then engages in some form of self-reinforcement—perhaps sexual relief, perhaps alcohol, perhaps any way to get a "kick." Regardless, there are two clear messages. The first is that since reinforcement increases the probability of any behavior, the person is more likely to feel depressed, guilty, or sorry for himself in the future. At the same time, the person is equally likely to resurrect those feelings when he engages in such behaviors. A person who daydreams when feeling lonely will learn to feel lonely when daydreaming. A person who drinks when mad at the world will learn to be mad at the world when drinking. A person who engages in sex when feeling sorry for himself will tend to feel sorry for himself when indulging in sex.

Cartoon: 5.4.

[Cartoon shows a lecture hall. A woman raises her hand and asks: "Doctor, all the men I have sex with turn out to be rotten jerks. Why do I continue to make the same mistake over and over?" The lecturer replies: "It's the homeostatic principle of the body: when there's an increased supply of blood to the genitals, there's a corresponding decreased supply to the brain." A sign on the podium reads: "LECTURE TODAY EVERYTHING YOU DIDN'T WANT TO KNOW ABOUT SEX BY DR. KINSEY MASTERS JOHNSON"]

I might add that a person who engages in math or reading when tense will tend to feel tense when confronted with a math or reading assignment, and a person who does homework to a hyperactive musical beat will learn to feel hyperactive when doing homework.

Nothing we do on one level of behavior is separated from other aspects of our behavior. The physiological explanation in the cartoon may be wrong, but the behavioral, emotional and cognitive patterns that arise will tend to repeat. Perhaps we can do no better in concluding this section than to repeat the advice William James gave to teachers in his talk "The Laws of Habit" (1904, p. 58):

> . . . *the great thing in all education is* to make our nervous system our ally instead of our enemy. . . . For this we must make automatic and habitual as early as possible, as many useful actions as we can, *and as carefully guard against the growing into ways that are likely to be disadvantageous.*

To Know Thyself: Explaining Emotions

Parents often ask themselves, "Why is it that every date my teenager has is with someone who is a nerd or a hood?" The answer is that when there's an increased supply of blood to the genitals, there's a corresponding decreased supply to the brain. Jokes aside, homeostatic principles of the body do ensure that something like that does occur. It is difficult to solve a problem when you are saying to yourself, "Oh my god, it's math!" It is difficult to learn to speak a language if you're afraid of sounding foolish. It is difficult to be creative, to paraphrase a common saying, when you're up to your thighs in alligators.

What makes the situation even more difficult is that people often do not even know that their emotions are at odds with their behavior or what emotion they are experiencing. Nature has not made it very easy for us, either.

Many emotional states show a general pattern that is characteristic of excitation of the sympathetic nervous system. However, there are apparently few physiological cues which we humans have come to associate uniquely with particular emotions so that we can reliably discriminate among them. Thus increased heart rate can accompany fear, joy, anger, or sexual excitement. Similar statements can be made about such other physiological measures as blood pressure, stomach contractions, breathing rate or shortness of breath, and perspiration. Polygraph measures of the electrical conductivity of the skin, prominently known in "lie detection," cannot easily discriminate among states of euphoria, anger, or fear. What the polygraph apparently can do—and then anything but perfectly—is detect physiological changes that are likely to be accompanied by emotions. The "lie detector," as Skinner (1953, p. 161) put it, ". . . detects, not dishonesty, but the emotional responses generated when the individual engages in behavior for which he has previously been punished."[12]

"Getting in touch with one's feelings," then, can be seen to be quite complicated. It requires (1) having a perceivable physiological state, (2) understanding our own history and current situation, and (3) knowing what the social situation is—how others are reacting and interacting with us. This is complicated enough for adults, but is a monumental task for teenagers whose behavior sometimes seems best described as a hormone run amuck. Their own physiological processes seem to confuse or betray them, they are under tremendous peer pressures, and they are sometimes experimenting with alcohol, other drugs and music-induced hyperactive states. Is it any wonder that they seem moody, unable to concentrate, defensive about criticism or perceived criticism, etc. They are struggling with their competence or lack thereof—in short, with their identities—while at the same time conditioning emotions to teachers, subjects, and school.

The popular press has recently made much of the idea of *emotional intelligence,* or *EQ,* which identifies such qualities as (1) understanding your own feelings, (2) being able to control those feelings, and (3) showing empathy for others (e.g., *Time,* Oct. 2, 1995, pp. 60–68). The first and second of these, sometimes labeled "metamood" to be parallel with metacognition, I suppose, are essential components of Gardner's intrapersonal intelligence (see Chapter 4). The third is one of the ingredients in interpersonal intelligence, by Gardner's conception.

However conceptualized or relabeled, the point is that self-control, delay of gratification, frustration tolerance, and good manners remain desirable qualities for a society. This is all the more true in current times when so many of the models we see on TV display lack of emotional control, little frustration tolerance, and an "in-your-face" interaction style. If the values represented by EQ are not passed on by the society to succeeding generations, so much the worse for society!

We shall return to the behavioral and social issues involved in this in the next few chapters, but to conclude this chapter it is worth exploring what teachers might do to help students develop emotional self-knowledge and self-control. Two topics seem particularly apt for such learning—namely, conditioning of emotions and dealing with stress—and both can be facilitated by music.

Since it would likely be unethical to do an experiment conditioning emotions to classroom stimuli, I do not recommend such practice. But consider the action research in a prekindergarden class described in Anecdote 5.4 in which the differences between march music. vs. nature's surf music on student activity and aggressiveness were obvious to all.

It is a small additional step to incorporate these ideas into instruction. During various seatwork or work station activities different kinds of music could be played from day to day—a heavy rock beat, a Haydn symphony, a

Anecdote 5.4

> ### Music and Activity
>
> Is there an effect of music on the behavior of pre-K children in the classroom? This was the question I wondered about in the context of studying Bandura's social cognitive theory. To find out, I randomly divided the class into two groups of 5 boys, 3 girls each. While group A left the room to go to the toilet, the others (B) sat at their desks and colored their "Earth Day" posters while I played a cassette of march music in the background. Then the groups exchanged roles: B went to the toilet and A colored their posters, but to a cassette of nature's surf sounds.
>
> Both my aide and I found a noticeable difference between the two groups. The children who listened to the marches were all stirred up: they became very excited, were physically aggressive, colored faster, talked very loudly, and their bodies seemed to move almost uncontrollably to the beat of the music. The children who listened to the ocean sounds were a total contrast: they listened calmly and intently, colored slowly, and talked quietly about the beach, salt water, sea shells, and whales.
>
> The effect was so remarkable I kept the surf sounds tape playing for all the children through the free play period, and found the classroom as a whole much quieter than usual.
>
>
>
> Linda Kenefic
> Teacher

lullaby, angry songs, a death march, happy songs—with the students asked to reflect on their own feelings and behavior. Such experiences could lead to discussions or lessons on the basics of how we are affected by our environment and, more importantly, things we can do to change how we feel.

A second major idea concerns teaching students to recognize when they are stressed and techniques for dealing with it. For example, do some calisthenics or stretching exercises as a break from seatwork and discuss how it feels. Or put on some soft, gentle music and do some tensing-relaxing of various muscle groups (as in progressive relaxation or imagery training (Jacobsen, 1938; Davis, Eshelman & McKay, 1980).

Tension-relaxation exercises consist of, say, clenching your fist tighter and tighter and then letting go completely. Then repeat this, becoming aware of each muscle as you tense it and relax it. Then move to another muscle group, like the shoulders. Imagery (autogenic training) uses such verbal suggestions as: imagine yourself lying quietly next to a bubbling brook; or, my right arm is heavy, there is a weight attached to it, it is sinking down.

Such techniques are used as part of counterconditioning and other therapies to treat anxiety disorders and other cases of "rapanoia," "real-annoya," or paranoia (e.g., Bandura, 1969; Davison, 1968; Krasner, 1971; Morris & Kratochwill, 1983; Wolpe, 1969). In the classroom they can be used to teach the relaxation response which, surprising to many, does not come easily to many people. Some of us even sleep tensely.

If such techniques are included in the classroom on some regular basis, progress may well be measured by the frequency with

Song 5.1.   © 1968 J. R. Gentile

which students start requesting things like the following: "Can we have some relaxing music on?" or "I'm tense, can we do relaxation exercises?" Of course, teachers need this, too, perhaps more than the students. Thus they can model and participate in these activities.

A Tentative Conclusion

Most students—not to mention their principals and teachers—have school-related anxieties from time to time. Some are like Charlie Brown's sister Sally's fear of her first day in school. She told Lucy she was afraid of going to school because she heard that they ask a lot of questions there. Lucy confirmed this, but asked why that concerned her. Sally replied, "There are certain things I'd just rather not have brought up."

One of the things students would rather not have brought up is their incompetence which, ironically, schools were invented to stamp out. The dilemma is how to eliminate incompetence without focusing on it and developing *feelings* of incompetence, fears of math, and so forth. Researchers who have studied extreme cases of school-related fears, so-called school phobias, usually conclude that at least the following are necessary (e.g., Kelly, 1973): early intervention, recognition of the first signs (resistance to attend school, somatic complaints, clinging to the home), firmness in keeping the child in school and dealing with the problem there as much as possible, and direct intervention to allay the anxieties (e.g., counterconditioning procedures and, as 'Kelly put it, "patient gentleness to allay his anxieties").

We have seen in this chapter how emotions and other involuntary behaviors become conditioned to neutral objects and situations. We have seen how conditioned emotions can become severe enough to be debilitating. We have also seen, however, how voluntary control can

Photo 5.4. Music to soothe the savage feelings.

be obtained over those respondents by biofeedback, systematic desensitization, relaxation, and various counter-conditioning techniques. When such control is managed by the clients themselves, a sense of mastery—of competence—can be acquired that will serve the person well.

As we noted in the first chapter of this book, no subject is ever taught only in a cognitive sense. Teachers are not "book-learning" people. Students learn not only how to think in math or chemistry or English, but also how to feel and whether to approach or avoid what they are supposedly thinking about. Much lip-service is rendered to the "affective domain" of feelings, attitudes and values. From my perspective, the really important issues involved in the affective domain are those presented in this chapter: the tensions, emotions, and bodily reflexes that are set in motion in the presence of a teacher or a school subject. ❧

Practice Exercises

A. Practice Items

For the following multiple-choice items, select the alternative choice which *best* answers the question. (Note: Answers are in Note 14).

1. A young child is bitten by a dog and thereafter becomes afraid of all dogs. In this example,
   a. the US = dogs and the CS = the bite.
   b. the US = fear and the CS = dogs.
   c. the CS = the bite and the CR = fear.
   d. the CS = dogs and the CR = fear.

2. Stimulus Generalization refers to responding with
   a. the same response to the same stimulus.
   b. a different response to different stimuli.
   c. the same response to different stimuli.
   d. different responses to the same stimulus.

3. Which of the following would be most likely to become learned helpless? People
   a. who receive punishment as a consequence of their own bad behavior.
   b. who observe others receiving punishment.
   c. who are punished no matter how hard they try.
   d. who receive reinforcement when they earn it.

4. Mary always feels reverent, and even tearful, whenever her favorite hymn, "Amazing Grace," is played. A new TV minister uses that hymn as his theme song and, as a result, Mary feels very positive toward this minister. In this example,
   a. the TV minister is the US and the hymn in the CS.
   b. the hymn is CS_1 and the TV minister is CS_2.
   c. the TV minister is CS_1 and the hymn is CS_2.
   d. the TV minister is CS and the hymn is the CR.

5. According to the evidence in the text, children who experience continual failure despite their best efforts are eventually likely to
   a. stop trying and turn in very little work.
   b. do their very best to show the teacher that they are among the most capable in class.
   c. accept their lot in life and be happy with just squeaking by.
   d. be a failure in all fields.

6. According to the recommendations in the text, learned helplessness may be preventable by
   a. making the task so easy that everyone will succeed.
   b. providing success early in each unit, but later having less than 100% success.

c. providing difficult material at first, followed by easier and easier material so that students learn perseverance pays off.
d. keeping material difficult so that students learn that they must try harder.

7. Conditioned emotional responses
   a. can be learned in one trial if the US is strong enough.
   b. can be extinguished in about the same number of trials it took to learn it.
   c. cannot be learned for positive feelings like love or relaxation.
   d. can be extinguished by withholding the CS.

B. For Cooperative Study (in or out of class):

1. Practice one or more of the relaxation/counterconditioning exercises.
2. Discuss the case of Kevin (Anecdote 5.2) and the recommendations made. Do you know of any similar real-life cases to share with your classmates? Can a student who is a success through junior high school become learned helpless in high school? How? Do you know any real-life cases?
3. Discuss the statement quoted from Logan (p. 149) about the bidirectionality of conditioning. If a teenager listens to a punk rock record that is complaining about teachers, parents and authorities in general while doing his homework, what does that imply about how he will feel when he next has to do his homework?
4. Discuss some of the conditioned emotional reactions (fears, attractions, tensions, etc.) you have developed to certain stimulus situations. What can be done about them?
5. Discuss the recommendations made for preventing or curing learned helplessness (pp. 147–148).
6. Discuss the mechanisms of higher order conditioning involved in stereotyping, labeling, etc. (see Figure 5.2 for an example).

C. For More Information:

1. Read more about (and perhaps do a written or oral report on) biofeedback, its problems and prospects, by reading one or more of the references given in Note 13.
2. Read more about (and perhaps do a written or oral report on) other counterconditioning procedures by exploring one or more of the references given in Note 13.
3. Read or see the movie version of *A Clockwork Orange* by Anthony Burgess and report on the respondent conditioning procedure used to get Alex to have a revulsive reaction to violence.
4. Explore some of the issues involved in doing research on learned helplessness and drawing implications for classrooms. Good places to begin are Butkowski and Willows (1980), Dweck and Licht (1980), Gentile and Monaco (1987, 1988), and Seligman (1975).

CHAPTER

Study Questions

1. Describe operant behavior in terms of its means and ends, purpose and consequence.
2. It is now commonly accepted that reinforcement does not directly "strengthen" behavior; rather, it "regulates" behavior. What is meant by that?
3. Define each of the following types of reinforcement:
   a. Positive reinforcement
   b. Negative reinforcement
   Diagram the procedure and effects of each (using the following symbols, where appropriate: R, S^{RF}, S^{AV}, No S^{RF}, No S^{AV}). Give examples.
4. Distinguish between the common use of the word *reward* and the technical meaning of *positive reinforcement*.
5. Describe negative reinforcement as *escape* or *avoidance* of a noxious event. Give examples (e.g., drug-taking, peer pressure, etc.).
6. Describe the *extinction* procedure for an operant behavior. What is meant by each of the following during the extinction process?
   a. the frustration effect
   b. spontaneous recovery
7. Define punishment and diagram it using the following symbols: R, S^{AV}. Give examples.
8. Distinguish between punishment and negative reinforcement in terms of:
   a. the procedure used
   b. the effects on behavior
9. What is *discrimination learning*? Give examples of it using the following symbols ($S^D = S^+$ = discriminative stimulus; $S^\Delta = S^-$ = other stimuli; R; S^{RF}).
10. What is *generalization*? How does it relate to discrimination learning? Draw a *generalization gradient* for a typical learning situation:
    a. before discrimination training
    b. after a few trials of discrimination training
    c. after many trials of discrimination training
11. What is meant by each of the following types of reinforcement?
    a. primary
    b. secondary
       (1) social
       (2) tokens
       (3) activities

SIX

12. What is the Premack Principle?

13. What is meant by *resistance to extinction?*

14. What is the effect of each of the following on *learning* and on *persistence* (i.e., resistance to extinction)?
    a. Type of reinforcement
    b. Quantity of reinforcement
    c. Delay of reinforcement
    d. Reinforcement contingencies
    e. Schedules of reinforcement
        (1) Continuous
        (2) Intermittent

15. What is shaping?

16. Discuss the following in relation to
    a. shaping attention spans.
    b. student/teacher ratios.

17. What is a *token economy?* What is the author's opinion on its use in "ordinary" classrooms?

18. What is meant by self-control? Describe the typical developmental sequence for learning self-control. How does the child's sequence differ from the adult's?

19. Describe how each of the following "amazing effects" of punishment can be learned:
    a. masochistic behaviors
    b. punishment as a cue for reinforcement (e.g., battered child)

20. How do each of the following contribute to the effects of punishment?
    a. severity of punishment
    b. delay of punishment
    c. punishment contingencies

21. What are some examples of how operant behaviors interact with
    a. respondent behaviors?
    b. cognitive behaviors?

Regulating Behavior and Operant Conditioning

Introduction

Cries from new-born babies are likely to be reactions to internal or external stimulation, for example, like pangs of hunger, wetness, or other discomfort. As children mature such crying continues as reactions to physical or emotional pain or frustrations. But with children's growing awareness of their surroundings also comes another kind of crying which parents unfortunately come to know too well: crying for attention.

Caring parents naturally come running when their baby starts to cry. They are quick to discover the source of the problem, if any obvious external source exists, and they pick up the child to provide food and comfort. In so doing, parents are teaching their children their first lesson in controlling the environment—namely, that crying gets results. This must be an amazing discovery to a child. If at this developmental stage children's nervous systems and linguistic abilities were sufficiently developed to permit it, they would probably say, "Wow, only a few weeks old and already I have my parents conditioned: everytime I cry, they give me attention and food." Crying as an operant behavior has emerged.

As children mature, they attempt to control more and more of their environment and, in so doing, develop an increasing array of skills. From touching an overhead mobile and showing delight at making it move, to building a tower of blocks, to hitting tennis balls with topspin, to programming a computer to perform complex tasks—yes, even to teaching a friend how to treat you—children learn the skills which allow them to deal with the objects and people in their environment. They learn these skills for the most part by actively "doing unto others" and then seeing the consequence of what "others do unto them." Sometimes they learn by the school of hard knocks: they touch something hot or ride a bicycle too fast and fall. In dealing with people, they may learn to "do as you would be done by[1]" or, in dealing with some people, to "do unto others before they do unto you." In any case, it is their active behaviors, or motions, which produce the consequences, and this interaction of behavior with consequences is what allows children to master (or cope with) their world.

Because the consequences, and not the antecedents, are the most important events controlling these behaviors, it is clear that we are describing a class of experiences most people would call voluntary or purposeful (e.g., Tolman, 1932; 1959; called such behavior "purposive" and spoke of the "expectancies" of obtaining desired ends by various behavioral means). Even Skinner, who is known to avoid such "mentalistic" terms as purpose, named these behaviors *operants* to call attention to their active nature in operating on the environment. He described it as follows (Skinner, 1974):

> . . . operant behavior is the very field of purpose and intention. By its nature, it is directed toward the future: a person acts in order that something will happen, and the order is temporal. (p. 55)
>
> Operant behavior is essentially the exercise of power: it has an effect on the environment. (pp. 139–140)
>
> We often overlook the fact that human behavior is also a form of control. That an organism should

act to control the world around it is as characteristic of life as breathing or reproduction. A person acts upon the environment, and what he achieves is essential to his survival and the survival of the species. (p. 189)

Types of Operant Conditioning

Having defined an operant as purposeful behavior does not mean that it is free from control by external forces. On the contrary, most of our voluntary behavior is under varying amounts of control by external forces, such as significant others, specific stimuli, natural consequences and contrived consequences, such as rules or laws. For example, foreign visitors to the U.S.A. are often amazed that native drivers will stop at red traffic lights and wait until the light turns green to go, despite the fact that there may be no other traffic as far as the eye can see. There is no natural reflex to stop on red and go on green, as can be seen from the fact that (1) in other cultures such signals may have other meanings (e.g., red means stop, then go if the coast is clear), and (2) that when you are taking a loved one to a hospital, you may hardly even slow down at the red light. Clearly, the red light does not *make* you stop and wait; rather it is the consequence or threat of consequence (such as paying a fine or losing your driving license) which controls such behavior.

Similarly, the act of driving itself consists of voluntary motions, but these are not free from control. You drive on the right side of the road (on the left in Britain and Japan), except to overtake another vehicle. You drive at various speeds according to traffic conditions, turn when the road turns, and leave the road only when there is another road to turn on to, because the consequences of not behaving in these ways would be disastrous. Few of us are aware that our driving behaviors are so conditioned, but they are.

Cartoon 6.1.

Less trivial instances of operant conditioning concern taking valium or drinking martinis to relieve tension, raising your hand in class to get your teacher's attention, and teaching in order to receive a paycheck. How such voluntary acts come to be controlled or conditioned is the subject of this section. There are four basic classes of operant conditioning—namely, positive reinforcement, negative reinforcement, extinction and punishment, with several variations on these. Before considering these in some detail, we will be well-served to adopt the technical meaning of the word "reinforcement."

Reinforcement

When we say that a response has been reinforced, we mean that its probability has been increased or maintained at a high level (under certain conditions). In this sense, reinforcement serves as a *regulation* of the behavior

> **Box 6.1**
>
> ### More on the Definition of Positive and Negative Reinforcement
>
> There are a number of possible ways of defining the procedures of positive and negative reinforcement. Perhaps the simplest way is to use the terms in their mathematical meanings. Then *positive means a stimulus is added,* while *negative means a stimulus is subtracted* as a consequence of a behavior.
>
> In my experience, I have found that teachers relate to these terms easiest when referring to the goals of the behavior. In this case, *positive means the behavior is directed toward getting something positive* (that is, that the person desires), while *negative means the behavior is escaping something negative.*
>
> However you find it easier to learn the distinction between positive and negative reinforcement, two things should be kept in mind:
>
> *First, there must be a behavioral effect of increasing or maintaining the frequency of the behavior before we can say that the behavior was reinforced (either positively or negatively).*
>
> *Second, the terms positive and negative do not refer to the goodness or badness of the behavior itself. That is, "bad" behaviors can be positively reinforced (as when stealing gets the person money) or negatively reinforced (as when a person escapes punishment by lying). "Good" behaviors can likewise be positively reinforced (as when studying gets an A grade) or negatively reinforced (as when learning to meditate takes away tension).*

(e.g., Bandura, 1977a), affecting the frequency with which the behavior occurs (and under what conditions). Reinforcement does not "strengthen" the behavior itself, as exercise strengthens a muscle or as additional troops strengthen an army. Rather, it alters the likelihood of the behavior's occurrence.

Usually a behavior will be reinforced in the above sense if it terminates in a desirable consequence, of which there are two basic types: (1) obtaining something you want or need and (2) escaping or avoiding something noxious or harmful. Either of these consequences, and usually no other, has the effect of increasing the probability of that behavior under similar circumstance. If so, we may say that the behavior has been reinforced.[2]

When reinforcement occurs by achievement of something positive (satisfying a want or need), we call it *positive reinforcement*. When it occurs through escaping something negative (an aversive situation), we call it *negative reinforcement*. In both cases, the behavior is regulated to occur more frequently, or to be maintained if it is already occurring at a high rate.

Positive Reinforcement

The procedure for positive reinforcement is much like the common notion of it: a person behaves in such a way as to earn a reward, paycheck, recognition, praise, etc. Defined in this informal way, positive reinforcement can be said to be similar to reward training. The child eats his vegetables, or joins the "clean plate club" in order to receive his "just desserts" as a reward. In technical language we say that the operant response of eating vegetables was followed by a reinforcing stimulus, dessert.

(1) $R_{\text{Eating Vegetables}} \longrightarrow S^{RF}_{\text{Dessert}}$

Continuing in a technical sense, it is important to note that a stimulus cannot be labeled a reinforcer in the absence of data on its behavioral effect. *In other words, a stimulus can be said to be reinforcing only if it increases or maintains the rate of responding.*

Here is one place where the everyday use of "rewards" and positive reinforcement part company. As many parents can attest, dessert offered as a reward for eating vegetables often does not work, in which case we cannot conclude that dessert is a reinforcer for eating vegetables (at least for this child under these conditions).

Another place in which reward differs from positive reinforcement is in the usual conception of controller-controllee. We see the parent trying to control the child by offering a reward for "good behavior." Behavior modification experts are often portrayed as sinister puppeteers, pulling the strings of their unwitting victims through their knowledge of advanced behavioral technology. Or perhaps they are portrayed as clowns trying to manipulate kids with M & Ms. The prototype of this, of course, the rat pressing a bar (or the pigeon pecking a key) for a food reward in a "Skinner box." As pointed out earlier, even the subjects in these examples (pigeons or persons) are engaged in behaviors which are controlling the significant others in their environment (experimenters, parents, teachers and friends). It is therefore only in special cases where one person has such control over another that he can significantly manipulate another's behavior against his will by use of rewards. This issue will be addressed more fully under the topic of Self-Control.

A third difference between the everyday conception of reward and positive reinforcement lies in what constitute effective rewards. Food, water, oxygen, sex, and money to buy those things can often serve as effective reinforcers, in the defining sense that people will behave in certain ways in order to earn them as consequences. Such items are conspicuous

Photo 6.1. Climbing or social climbing? The power of attention.

in their effect, especially those that satisfy biological needs, but that is not all that controls our behavior. Once our biological and safety needs are satisfied (e.g., Maslow, 1954), then social reinforcers such as praise or attention from others become important reinforcers, if only because they affect our self-esteem needs (in Maslow's terminology). Attention from another person would seldom be called a reward, especially if the attention is a reprimand. But such attention is often the most powerful reinforcer in an environment operating to maintain behavior.

Consider the beginning of each 47-minute high school class in English in which the teacher introduced class with a "search-and-deposit" mission: "Wrap that gum up in paper. Don't throw it naked into the basket."[3] The teacher was searching for gum chewers who, in addition to having to deposit their gum in the wastebasket in front of their peers, were fined 5 cents (the money was used to buy get-well cards for students or facial tissues for the

Anecdote 6.1

Unwitting Reinforcement for Attention-Seeking

Tyler, a preschooler, walks up to his teacher, for the fourth time this morning, and taps her repeatedly on the leg. "Teacher, teacher," he says while looking up at her pleadingly. "Yes, Tyler?" says his teacher, always striving to be very patient with her young students. "Ummmm, what can I play with?" asks Tyler. His teacher leads him to the Legos and walks away once she is certain that he is fully absorbed in building a train. Several minutes later the tapping Tyler has returned, this time with a request to help him get a puzzle, even though he is perfectly capable of reaching it himself. By now the teacher's patience is beginning to wane and she decides that Tyler has had enough of her attention for one day. She resolves to ignore Tyler's future pleas for assistance. Sure enough, a few minutes later, Tyler comes up to her and begins tapping her on the leg and calling "Teacher, teacher". She continues her conversation with her classroom assistant and then helps another child tie her shoe, all the while fiercely gritting her teeth, pretending that she doesn't hear Tyler. Finally, she can take it no longer and she looks down and says, "What is it, Tyler" "Is it lunch time yet?", he asks while looking up at her and smiling. This happens repeatedly throughout the week. Tyler's teacher tries her best to ignore him, and sometimes she succeeds, but often she responds to his calls for assistance on the third, fifth, or even the eighth time that he calls her. Much to her dismay, it almost seems that Tyler is seeking her attention more frequently than before she started ignoring him!!!

Linda Licata
Teacher

Author's Note: The teacher solved the problem by a combination of techniques from this chapter.

students to use). What was alarming to the observer and evidently overlooked by the teacher was that the students enjoyed this game and used it to avoid beginning their studies: class was delayed an average of 15 minutes per class when the topic was grammar and 5 minutes per class when it was literature. Among other things going on, it is clear that the teacher's and peer group's attention for chewing gum was a much more powerful reinforcer than the lesson, and completely overrode the presumed punishing effects of the fine or losing the chewing gum. The teacher was reinforcing, through her attention to it, the very behavior she sought to eliminate.

Americans, in particular, are extremely prone to reinforce unwanted behavior by their very attention to that behavior. How many adults have not had the experience of trying to carry on a conversation with another adult when, as soon as a child comes into the room, the adult interrupts the conversation to fulfill a request of the child? The adult's attention serves as a very powerful positive reinforcer to the child who learns a valuable lesson: interrupting other's conversations is not only all right, but will get me what I want immediately.[4] (See also anecdote 6.1)

Positive reinforcement, in sum, must be defined by its effect on behavior which, in turn, can usually be assessed only over some extended period of time. When that is done for most humans—at least those whose basic needs are already being satisfied—the most powerful reinforcer turns out to be attention from significant others. But attention does not have to be praise and adulation in order to reinforce behavior; disagreements, arguments, reprimands and even yelling and fighting, can serve to increase the probability of a behavior that has those consequences. In extreme cases it is perhaps as though the person is saying, "Say anything to me, just so long as you do not ignore me." Our attention, wittingly or unwittingly, does much to affect others' behaviors and teach them how to behave toward us.

Negative Reinforcement

As already defined, *negative reinforcement is the escape or avoidance of an aversive state (or stimulus) as a consequence of some behavior.* The prototypical experiment for the study of such behavior is the shuttle box, in which an animal is placed in one side of an experimental space with a barrier in the middle separating it from the other side (e.g., Sidman, 1953). If the floor, which is electrically wired, delivers a continuous shock, the animal begins to scurry around until eventually it leaps the barrier and discovers the other side of the compartment to be free of shock. If the animal is now placed back in the aversive, shocking side of the box, it will again leap the barrier only this time much faster. Repeat this procedure ten times and the animal's latency of jumping the barrier will become shorter and shorter. The probability of the animal's response of *escaping* the aversive situation is increasing. Diagrammed, the situation looks like this:

(2) $S^{AV}_{Shock} \longrightarrow R_{jumps\ barrier} \longrightarrow NoS^{AV}_{No\ Shock}$

If we now turned on a yellow light which preceded the onset of the shock by 10 seconds, it would not take very many trials before the animal would use this predictive cue to jump the barrier before the shock came on. The anticipation of this aversive stimulus and acting to prevent it is called *avoidance* behavior and can be diagrammed as follows (where S^D = Discriminative Stimulus or Cue):

(3a) *early trials*
$S^D_{yellow\ light} \longrightarrow S^{AV}_{Shock} \longrightarrow R_{jumps\ barrier} \longrightarrow NoS^{AV}_{No\ Shock}$

(3b) *later trials*
$S^D_{yellow\ light} \longrightarrow R_{jumps\ barrier} \longrightarrow NoS^{AV}_{No\ Shock}$

Avoidance, in other words, is a more complex form of escape behavior; both are based on negative reinforcement.

Note that, as in positive reinforcement (defined as the presentation of a stimulus as a consequence of a behavior), the frequency of the escape behavior must be increased or maintained in order to conclude that negative reinforcement did in fact occur. Note also that, contrary to popular opinion, *negative reinforcement is not synonymous with punishment.* Whereas negative reinforcement occurs when an aversive stimulus is terminated contingent upon a behavior, punishment occurs when an aversive stimulus (e.g., a slap or shock) is the consequence of the behavior (e.g., talking back to your parent). The procedure of punishment is, therefore, the behavioral opposite of that for negative reinforcement. And so is the intended effect. Through punishment the behavior is expected to decrease, while in negative reinforcement, where the key word is reinforcement, the behavior will increase. Punishment will be discussed in more detail shortly. For now, let's consider some common examples of negative reinforcement under two general topics, "Escaping Tension" and "Peace at any Price."

Escaping Tension

It used to puzzle me that the students who made the most mistakes and got the worst marks were so often the first ones to hand in their papers. I used to say, "If you finish early, take time to check your work, do some problems again." Typical teacher's advice; I might as well have told them to flap their arms and fly. When the paper was in, the tension was ended. (Holt, 1964, p. 66).

Many students feel a tremendous amount of tension in classrooms, particularly when they do not understand what is being said or when they cannot do an assignment. If this is a chronic problem as in cases of math anxiety, learned helplessness, or the like, then any behavior that relieves or escapes the tension is likely to be repeated. A way of relieving the tension that reading brings, for example, is to close the book. A way of relieving the tension that long assignments evoke is to do them quickly and sloppily or turn them in incomplete; in either case, the tension is ended, as John Holt astutely observed. A way of avoiding the tension that a test will bring is to have a stomach ache that day, so that Mom lets you stay home or so that the teacher sends you to the nurse. A way of escaping the tension that a teacher's questions evoke is to play dumb and say "I dunno" so that the teacher calls on someone else.

In all of these cases, the students are perceiving something in their environment as threatening—every bit as threatening from their point of view as the shock for the dogs in the shuttle box—and thus their primary goal is to escape the threat. Their teachers might tell them that the easiest way to reduce the threat is to study, but to many students such advice would be no more effective than telling them "to flap their arms and fly." In fact, many teachers reinforce these escape behaviors by not making the students re-do incomplete or incorrect papers, or by letting another student take over when one is playing dumb and saying, "I dunno." Why teachers let students off the hook in these ways is a point we'll come to in a moment, but first let us be clear that the students are learning that the consequence of these behaviors is to escape an aversive situation. Such situations might be diagrammed as follows:

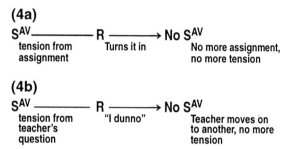

Of course, the ultimate in escaping is becoming a school drop-out. Slightly less severe variations on this are (1) dropping or avoiding tension-producing courses (e.g., math or statistics for a math anxious student) or (2) being obnoxious to your teacher so that you are suspended from class. If such behavior succeeds in escaping or avoiding the tension, then the student is more likely in the future to quit when the work is too hard or to be obnoxious to get thrown out of class.

(4c)
S^{AV} ———— R ————→ No S^{AV}
tension from   quit or   No class or
course   be obnoxious   suspension

"Peace at Any Price"

As the last section shows, students will engage in behaviors that in the long run are not good for them for the short-run gain of escaping undesirable or tension-producing situations. The question remains: why do teachers let them escape?

The somewhat surprising answer is because the teachers are also escaping. Consider first the student who not only does not do his work, but is also belligerent about it. It definitely brings relief to suspend that student from class.

(5a)

S^{AV} ——— R ———→ No S^{AV}
obnoxious   throws out   peace and quiet
student   of class

Moreover, in the future it is likely that the teacher will be waiting for the student to "make another wrong move, and you're history."

If the above teacher behavior brings peace without solving the student's underlying problems, at least it is usually apparent that the teacher had just cause. A more insidious variation on this can be seen when people give in to unreasonable behavior in order to stop it. Tantrums and bullying are excellent examples. A tantrum being thrown by a child is an aversive stimulus to the adult in charge. To stop the tantrum adults often give the child what the child wants, thus positively reinforcing the child's tantrum. Bullies likewise often get what they want, in this case using a more sophisticated form of tantrum—namely, physical intimidation. The people who give tantrum throwers or bullies what they want are also escaping aversive situations—the "peace at any price" syndrome.

(5b)

S^{AV} ——— R ———→ No S^{AV}
Tantrum or   gives in   Tantrum stops
Threat   or Threat is removed

Peer pressure follows a similar form, and acceptance-seeking adolescents are particularly vulnerable to it. "What are you, chicken?" is a threat to the adolescent's self-esteem. To be accepted by peers, many adolescents will do what the group wants and thus escape the "chicken" label.

In general, when we give in to someone because they are "bugging" us, we are being negatively reinforced by them (they cease to bother us). We are ever so more inclined to do what they want us to do in the future. You

Cartoon 6.2.

may now wish to re-examine Anecdote 6.1 and ask why the teacher eventually gave in to the student's demands for attention. This situation clearly portrays reciprocal determinism at work: the teacher is positively reinforcing the student's attention-seeking, while the student is negatively reinforcing the teacher's attention-giving by ceasing to nag (for a while at least). We shall return to more of these issues later, particularly in chapter 8 on "Discipline."

Extinction

We have already encountered extinction in the chapter on respondent conditioning, where it was described as a process that weakens the relationship between CS and CR by nonreinforcement—i.e., by the nonoccurrence of the US. An analogous process operates in regard to operants when the behavior does not achieve the desired consequence—a previously reinforced behavior is no longer reinforced. As a teacher technique the procedure of extinction is also known as *planned ignoring*. The teacher in anecdote 6.1 was attempting to use the procedure of extinction to stop Tyler's continual attention-seeking. On previous occasions she had attended to his behavior, thus reinforcing it. On the current occasion, she ignored his pleas for attention. The situation can be diagrammed as follows:

(6) *Previous Reinforced Trials*

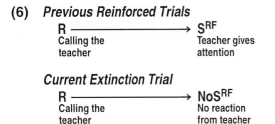

Current Extinction Trial

Unfortunately, the teacher eventually gave in to the child, thus providing positive reinforcement. Thus the planned ignoring became a kind of intermittent reinforcement (which, as we shall see, is a powerful way to produce behavioral persistence).

Teachers' behaviors can also be extinguished as when students feign stupidity and answer "I dunno," when they answer at all. Teachers need positive reinforcement, too, and they obtain it from students who are alert and can answer their questions. Students who seem never to know what is going on are not reinforcing their teachers. Thus the teachers' behavior of calling on those students will likely decrease, and they will direct their attention to the students who are responsive. In some cases this may even be planned ignoring by those students (who are escaping work by having the teacher off their backs).

Extinction of a negatively reinforced behavior is similar in that the behavior does not achieve the desired consequence. Since the desired consequence is escape or avoidance, the extinction process would be a case in which the behavior did not bring about escape. To use the immediately preceding example, if a student expects the teacher to stop calling on him by saying, "I dunno," then extinction of that escape behavior will be to continue calling on him.

Photo 6.2. Who's affecting whom and how?

(7) *Previous Negatively Reinforced Trials:*

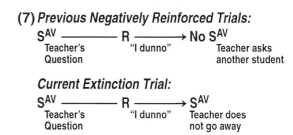

Current Extinction Trial:

One way this is commonly done is by giving the student another task: "I am going to call on someone else, and then I'll be back to you to paraphrase what the student said and to analyze the comment."

As used above, the word *extinction refers to the procedure of nonreinforcement* and not to the effect of reducing the frequency of the behavior to zero, as when we say the behavior was "extinguished." The latter use of the word can lead to some confusion since it is rare that a behavior is totally extinguished (i.e., reduced to zero) as fires are extinguished. The process of extinction does, however, reduce the frequency of the concerned behavior, though not always or immediately to zero.

Parents have often used the procedure of extinction to put an end to undesirable behaviors. For example, when their four-year-old learns his first curse word, everyone laughs or chuckles, even while scolding the child. The positive reinforcement this attention gives is usually immediately apparent in the increased frequency of this behavior. When the parents realize this, they decide that everyone in the family should ignore the behavior: no laughing. If indeed no one laughs, the behavior will become less and less frequent—at least in the presence of the parents. But the result will seldom be either immediate or antiseptic because extinction has some side effects.

The Frustration Effect and Spontaneous Recovery

When the child first emits a swear word and is ignored, he feels like you do when your last coin disappears into the pay telephone and you have not gotten through. He feels frustrated and may actually say the offending words more frequently or "once more with feeling." This immediate increase in frequency or magnitude of the behavior following the first extinction trial (often with accompanying kicks or shakes in the case of telephones or vending machines) is appropriately enough called the *frustration effect*.

If the parents continue to ignore the behavior despite the increased outbursts, they will eventually succeed. The frequency of the behavior will continue to decrease. But this will not be a smooth, continuous process. A *spontaneous recovery* of a higher rate may occur after a few days of decline, so named because its cause is usually hard to predict. It was probably because some cue that was present when the behavior was being learned, but was absent for a while, was reintroduced. Whatever the reason, the rate will again fall with consistent nonreinforcement of the behavior.

The procedure of extinction, then, can reduce the frequency of a behavior to zero or near-zero via long-term consistent nonreinforcement. That's the good news. One piece of bad news is that it is likely to take much longer to eliminate a habit by extinction than to acquire it in the first place. A second piece of bad news is that *behaviors that have been extinguished have not been forgotten*. The child still remembers the swear words, but he has learned not to use them, at least in this time and place.

Finally, for practical use in classroom settings, a teacher's use of extinction will be effective only if (1) the teacher does not forget and reinforce the behavior every once in a while (as was done to Tyler in anecdote 6.1) and (2) the other students are not reinforcing the very behavior the teacher is ignoring. For those reasons, extinction is a technique that is best used in combination with other techniques, such as reinforcement of a more appropriate alternative behavior. For example, instead of trying to eliminate children's attention-getting behavior by ignoring it, teach the children a new and better way of requesting help, reinforce them for doing that, and ignore their old inappropriate behaviors.

Punishment

Of all the types of operant conditioning, punishment needs the least introduction. It is probably the strongest and quickest way known for changing behavior, but it is also associated with the most unpleasant experiences people have. As in our daily experiences, *punishment is defined as an aversive consequence of a behavior*. Diagrammed, the situation is as follows:

(8a) $R_{\text{breaking rule}} \longrightarrow S^{AV}_{\text{Slap}}$

(8b) $R_{\text{breaking rule}} \longrightarrow S^{AV}_{\text{paying fine}}$

Slapping, yelling, or shocking a behavior or taking something away[5] (i.e., as a consequence of the behavior) usually result in an immediate suppression of the behavior. In general, the more severe the punishment—that is, the more intense and/or the longer the duration of the punishment—the greater the suppression of the behavior (e.g., Church, 1969). By suppression is meant the temporary cessation of a behavior as opposed to a permanent reduction in its frequency to zero or near-zero.

Anecdote 6.2

The Coffeehound's Guide to Positive Reinforcement, Extinction and Punishment

Positive Reinforcement: You insert coins in the coffee machine in order to obtain coffee and you succeed.

    R ⟶ S^{RF}
    insert coins   coffee

Extinction: You insert coins expecting coffee, but the machine swallows your coins and gives you no coffee.

    R ⟶ No S^{RF}
    insert coins   No coffee

Punishment: You insert coins expecting coffee, but instead a boxing gloves comes out of the machine and punches you in the face.

    R ⟶ S^{AV}
    insert coins   punch in the face

There are a few strange exceptions (to be described later) to the general rule that punishment suppresses, but does not eliminate, behavior. In daily life though, the punishers that are considered legal and moral are neither sufficiently strong nor delivered close enough to the behavior to act to eliminate the behaviors or, for that matter, to deter others from doing them. Thus if you are speeding on the highway, you may slow down when you see a policeman because of having previously paid a fine or seeing others pay one. Upon getting past him, you are likely to speed up again. This is the suppression effect of punishment.

Before we ask the logical next question—namely, why aren't parents, teachers and policemen equipped with punishers that really hurt?—the truth is that stronger punishers probably do no more than suppress the behavior either, or perhaps the behavior is eliminated only in the presence of the punishing agent. Moreover, punishment has widespread side effects (as we saw in the last chapter) and, at least in humans, breeds resentment and revenge-oriented behavior. So if we did shock our students for making noise with a tetanizing voltage, so that they could not breathe and their body just shook, they might be quiet in our classes. But they would also plot how to steal our cattle prod or invent one of their own. We are existing in an interdependent, reciprocally determined world after all, and if we use greater and greater force to control students, they will have to also. And what do we do when their chemistry class gets the bomb?

Discrimination Learning

To learn anything implies some discrimination of the conditions under which it is appropriate. We have already seen how emotions are attached through classical conditioning to certain previously neutral stimuli—but not all stimuli. That kind of differential response according to the conditions is discrimination learning. In adjusting our operants or motions to the appropriate conditions, we are making differential responses to different stimulus events.

The child's use of swear words, described earlier, provides a good example of how discrimination learning occurs on the operant level. On the playground, saying those words is likely to obtain positive reinforcement in the form of attention, giggles, additional swearing by others, etc. When the child tries those same words with the parents or teacher, the adults may follow an extinction procedure to attempt to eliminate the swearing, or at least to decrease its frequency. We thus have the defining features of a discrimination learning procedure: in the presence of one set of cues (people or situation) the behavior is reinforced; in the presence of another set of cues, the behavior is not reinforced.

The cues that come to signal the likelihood of reinforcement are called *discriminative stimuli*, symbolized as S^D or S^+ (to indicate reinforcement will be added as a consequence of the behavior). A certain friend, or a peer group, could therefore become an S^D for swearing, since the group is likely to condone and contribute to that behavior. The cues that come to signal nonreinforcement—all other cues—are symbolized S^Δ (s-delta, the Greek letter for D) or S^- (to indicate that reinforcement will be subtracted as a consequence of the behavior). Diagrammed, the situation looks as follows:

(9)
S^D —————— R ——→ S^{RF}
peer group　　　swearing　　　attention, approval

S^Δ —————— R ——→ No S^{RF}
adults (or people　swearing　　No attention or
not in peer group)　　　　　　disapproval

The above diagram is quite a general one, since people behave differently on different occasions (classes vs. sporting events; church vs. home, etc.) or with different people (teachers vs. peers; clergy vs. parents, etc.). Particularly for pre-adolescents and adolescents, the peer group serves as a cue for behavior that would never occur in the presence of other people, or even when the person was alone. The behavior comes under habitual control of the discriminative stimulus, much like our stopping or going comes under the control of red and green traffic signal lights.

It is also possible to describe punishment situations in discrimination learning terms since, as noted earlier, we are likely to modify our behavior in the presence of punishing agents, like police or principals. That is, people who are speeding on the highway or writing on the walls of the school will likely stop these behaviors if the appropriate authority is in the vicinity. In this case, the authority who would punish us is the S^D and everyone else is S^Δ.

(10)
S^D —————— R ——→ S^{AV}
authority　　　misbehavior　　fine or suspension, etc.

S^Δ —————— R ——→ No S^{AV} (or S^{RF})
no authority　　misbehavior　　No fine; gets away
　　　　　　　　　　　　　　　with the behavior
　　　　　　　　　　　　　　　(or gets something wanted)

In general, discrimination learning occurs whenever different behaviors are appropriate to, and receive different consequences in, different situations. The cues present in those situations may then come to exert stimulus control over the behaviors.

It should also be noted that discrimination learning, as just described, is also a major component of cognitive learning. Learning to recognize that □ is a square and ▢ is not, for example, requires that □ become the S^D for saying "square" and all other shapes be S^Δ.

(11)
S^D —————— R ——→ S^{RF}
□　　　　　　"It's a square"　"That's right!"

S^Δ —————— R ——→ No S^{RF}
▢ or ○　　　"It's a square"　"Not correct"

Table 6.1 Summary of types of operant behavior.

Name	Procedure	Expected Effect
1. Positive Reinforcement (Reward Training)	$R \rightarrow S^{RF}$	An increase (or maintenance at a high level) in the frequency of the behavior that led to that consequence.
2. Negative Reinforcement (Escape Training)	$S^{AV}-R \rightarrow NoS^{AV}$	An increase (or maintenance at a high level) in the frequency of the behavior that led to escaping the noxious event.
3. Extinction	(a) $R \rightarrow NoS^{RF}$ (b) $S^{AV}-R \rightarrow S^{AV}$	A decrease in the frequency of the behavior because it does not lead to a reinforcing consequence.
4. Punishment	$R \rightarrow S^{AV}$	A decrease in the frequency of the behavior because its consequence is an aversive event.
5. Discrimination Learning	$S^D-R \rightarrow S^{RF}$ $S^\Delta-R \rightarrow NoS^{RF}$	A differential response rate, with an increase of the behavior when S^D is present and a decrease of the same behavior when S^D is absent (i.e., S^Δ is present).
6. Negative Reinforcement (Avoidance Training)	$S^D-S^{AV}-R \rightarrow NoS^{AV}$	Discriminated escape training in which an increase in the behavior occurs when S^D is present so that S^{AV} can be avoided.

As we shall see in Unit 4, much more is involved than just this, but discriminations are a major component of cognitive processes. In fact, from one point of view it is possible to think of education as the process of learning finer and finer discriminations, which implies that a teacher or athletic coach reinforces closer and closer approximations to a desired level of knowledge or performance.

Having now presented the basic types of operant behaviors, a succinct comparison of them is possible and it is presented in table 6.1. The procedure or process for obtaining each type is shown along with the expected effect of that process.

Generalization and Discrimination

We have already seen how fears (and other emotions) can generalize beyond the particular stimuli directly associated with the fear to other, previously neutral, stimuli. Analogous processes occur in operant and cognitive behavior as well. Learning concepts is a case in point.

When young children receive their first pet dog, whom they may name Snoopy, they are quite likely to generalize and call all dogs "Snoopy" for a while. If their experiences with Snoopy were pleasant, they are probably also prone to approach other dogs, to the consternation of their worried parents. The children are generalizing their behavior (naming, or approaching to pet) from one stimulus to other stimuli.

For our purposes, a technical definition of generalization of operant behavior, then, might be the following: *generalization is the performance of the same (or a similar) response in the presence of different stimuli.*[6] In the case above, saying "Snoopy" is the response that was first learned to the original pet, but is now extended to other dogs.

The tension between generalization and discrimination is a natural developmental process: as we learn new responses we consciously or nonconsciously try them out in new situations. Learning to speak provides many examples. When a child first utters the sound "da-da," he or she receives a tremendous reaction from significant others, repeating and modeling the phrase and praising the child for saying it. This adult attention has the desired effect of increasing the frequency of the child saying "da-da" compared with, say, "ga-ga" (discrimination learning). Once "da-da" becomes an established part of the child's verbal repertoire, he or she may use it when mail carriers or deliverymen come to the door, etc. (generalization). If for no other reason than to avoid embarrassment ("No, that's not your father"), the parents now embark on a program to teach the child how to use "da-da" only in the presence of father (discrimination).

When children are learning to read, there are many opportunities for stimulus generalization. For example, teach children to say "dog" to the printed stimulus DOG and then provide them with these printed words several times in random order: DOG, GOD, DOT, DUG, HOP, HAT. If, as is likely, the children respond "dog" to stimuli other than the correct one, the errors are more likely to occur to similar (e.g., GOD, DUG) than to dissimilar stimuli (e.g., HOP, HAT). The curve that can be plotted from these responses is called a *generalization gradient*, and it demonstrates that the more similar a new stimulus to the original (reinforced) stimulus, the more likely the response will be emitted.

If the process of generalization can be described as a natural *developmental* process, then perhaps it is the case that discrimination—its behavioral opposite—is the major *learning* process of the developing individual. As noted above, parents and teachers seem to require finer and finer discriminations as the child ages. From the first uttered "da-da," children have to learn to say it only in certain appropriate instances. Later they learn that father is a noun, though sometimes a verb, and to discriminate nouns from verbs from adverbs and conjunctions. Where it was once appropriate to call all pets "Snoopy," Snoopy becomes a particular dog to be distinguished from cats. Cats and dogs become vertebrates to be distinguished from invertebrates, etc.

In the process of learning discriminations, the shape of the generalization gradient changes dramatically. Before the organism is reinforced for a discrimination, its generalization curve is approximately flat: in other words, the response is the same to all stimuli. As the organism is reinforced for discriminating—that is, one stimulus becomes the S^+ or

S^D and all others become S^- or S^Δ—then the appropriate response occurs with higher frequency in the presence of S^+ and with less frequency to other stimuli. And the less similar the stimulus to S^+, the fewer the responses (e.g., Jenkins and Harrison, 1960; Guttman and Kalish, 1956; Reese, 1966).

To take a hypothetical example (see figure 6.1) consider the generalization gradient for the concept of circle. As children first learn to say "circle," they may say it with almost equal likelihood to each of the symbols. As they learn to discriminate curved lines from straight lines, they may say it with less frequency to squares and triangles than to ovals and octagons. Eventually they will say it only to true circles and ambiguous circular figures.

Reinforcer Effectiveness

At various times the preceding discussion emphasized the importance of attention from significant others as a powerful reinforcer. Armed with that knowledge, a teacher or parent may rush right in to lavish attention on every approximation of an appropriate behavior: after all, if a little immediate positive reinforcement is good, a lot is better, right? Would that it were so. In this and the next few sections we shall encounter some of the complications involved in the efficiency with which positive reinforcement regulates behavior.

Types of Reinforcement

Some stimuli have the power to regulate behavior from the day of our birth. This is because they satisfy a biological need; oxygen is a prime example. If oxygen were not available for a few seconds, all of our attention and behavior would be purposefully directed to finding a way to obtain oxygen. Not only would our success in obtaining oxygen maintain our life, but it would also develop and maintain the behavior that had the desirable effect. Other examples of reinforcers that satisfy biological needs are food, water, sleep, and sexual stimulation. Reinforcers of this type do not need to be learned; they are reinforcing because of the biological nature of humans and animals. For this reason they are called *primary reinforcers*. As is well known, however, behaviors can also be affected by stimuli other than primary reinforcers, such as money, praise, or a smile. These stimuli are *conditioned* or *secondary reinforcers*, so called because they acquire reinforcing properties by being paired with primary reinforcers.

Money, for instance, is not reinforcing to a newborn baby, but it is not too many years later that money comes to be able to affect response rates. Let us consider how money may come to acquire reinforcing properties. A child in a store sees candy (the stimulus) and responds "Candy, please." The adult then provides the child with money, which he exchanges for candy (reinforcer).

Two aspects of this process should be noted carefully. First, the stimulus money became associated with the reinforcer candy by being paired with it. But second, the stimulus money not only accompanied the reinforcer but preceded it. For a neutral stimulus such as money to acquire reinforcer status, it must eventually be exchangeable for the primary reinforcer. Notice that, if the neutral stimulus occurred after the reinforcer, the response would already have been reinforced and the neutral stimulus would be irrelevant to the process. Thus it could never come to reinforce the response. Notice also that since discriminative stimuli (S^Ds) precede and come reliably to predict that reinforcers will follow, those S^Ds may acquire secondary reinforcer status. After many pairings of neutral stimulus and reinforcer in this manner, the previously neutral stimulus (money) acquires reinforcing properties, and people will respond in ways that will increase their chances of receiving money as payoff. This, of course, is just another way of

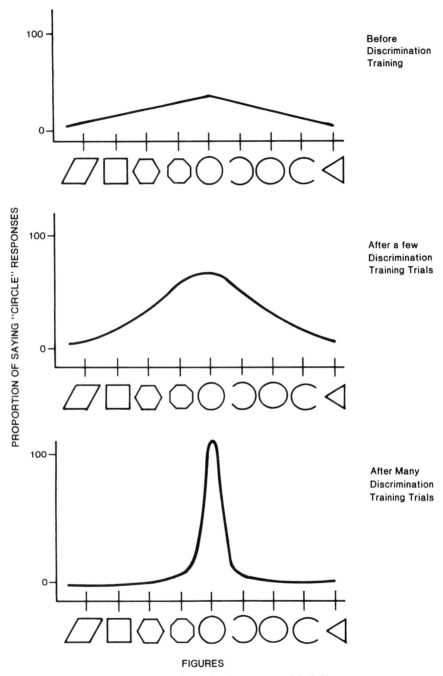

Figure 6.1. Hypothetical generalization gradients for the concept "circle".

saying that money has acquired the defining properties of a reinforcing stimulus—it increases the rate of some kind of responding.

But what would happen if, all of a sudden, all the governments of the world decided that money would no longer be exchanged for goods or services? It would not be long before people stopped working for money. Money would have lost its secondary reinforcing qualities because it would no longer be connected with such primary reinforcers as food. The implication of this is that secondary reinforcers must be backed up by primary reinforcement, at least occasionally.

Secondary reinforcers have come to be classified into three broad classes: social reinforcers, tokens, and activities. *Social reinforcers* include attention, praise, social acceptance, smiles and other human interactional stimuli. It is not actually known for sure whether many of these social reinforcers are not actually primary reinforcing stimuli, and the question will not be resolved here. For convenience, we shall include them under secondary reinforcers.

Tokens are a second class of secondary reinforcers, and they include physical objects or records that increase or maintain response rates. Examples are money, grades, points, stars, and happy faces drawn on student papers.

Activities are a third type of reinforcer, and they provide a great variety of potential reinforcers that can be tailored to individual students' preferences. Thus television-watching can be a reinforcer for doing homework, as can free time for completing an assignment. An important point to keep in mind is that any one activity may or may not be an effective incentive for a given child. The teacher or parent who wants to find effective reinforcing stimuli, therefore, will take care to find out what the child's individual preferences are at any given moment. One efficient way of doing this, often forgotten, is to ask the student what would be an adequate incentive for him to do a certain task—that is, a rudimentary contract is negotiated.

Photo 6.3. Snack time: A preferred activity?

More on Activities: The Premack Principle

If you think about it, an activity is a behavior, not a stimulus; thus in using television-watching as a reward for completing homework, one behavior follows as a consequence of another behavior. David Premack (1959) was the first to state explicitly how this works, in what has now become known as Grandma's Law or the *Premack Principle: of two activities, if the more preferred is the consequence of the less preferred* (e.g., if TV-watching is the consequence of doing homework), *it will act to reinforce the latter* (e.g., to increase the probability of doing homework). But not vice-versa—that is, doing homework will not be a reinforcer for watching TV.

Premack did not stop there, however. He reinterpreted the whole reinforcement relation, pointing out that it is not just the stimulus food that is reinforcing to a hungry organism, but the activity of eating. Hungry rats in a Skinner box engage in one behavior, bar pressing, in order to be able to engage in a more preferred behavior, eating. Children who are deprived of stimulation or attention will engage in behaviors that allow them to interact with other people or activities. Of course, if you have just eaten, eating will not be a preferred activity for a while. Thus the reinforcement value of a given activity shifts from time to time. In some cases, as with water for all of us, drugs for an addict, or bodily movement for a hyperactive child, the preferences may shift quickly, almost moment to moment.

For most behaviors there will be longer term preferences, what perhaps induced Premack into thinking of his principle as a theory of values (e.g., Premack, 1971a). Those behaviors in which we engage most frequently, given freedom of choice (without any coercion), are those we value most. A person who listens to rock music more frequently than classical music can be said to value or prefer rock music more than classical, given freedom of choice. (As pointed out earlier, however, there may be considerable peer pressure to listen to rock music to the exclusion of other music, in which case the purity of the *freedom* of choice is questionable.)

So far I've presented the Premack Principle as a one-sided case—more preferred behaviors reinforce less preferred behaviors, but not vice versa. It is actually more complicated than that. When appropriate conditions are established to make it necessary to engage in a less preferred behavior as a consequence of doing something more preferred, then the more preferred behavior is punished and becomes less preferred (e.g., Papp, 1980; Premack, 1962; 1965; 1971a; Terhune and Premack, 1970).[7] In this light perhaps we can see how having to write a report after reading a book could be seen as a punishment for the act of reading by many children. Perhaps this also suggests how to get children to stop watching too much television: after every show, they must mow the lawn or scrub the bathtub, etc. (I'm just joking . . . . Hm, on second thought . . .).

Some Applications

The practical uses to which the various types of reinforcers have been put are, of course, many. Praise and attention, as we have seen, have powerful effects on behavior, and unwary teachers may have their time monopolized by students. In an extreme case, which was also one of the earliest reported behavior modification studies in a special education classroom, an eleven-year-old boy of normal intelligence was able to dominate his teacher's attention during spelling by the following behavior. Zimmerman and Zimmerman (1962, p. 59) described the situation in these words:

> . . . when [he] was called upon to spell a word which had previously been studied and drilled, he would pause for several seconds, screw up his face, and mutter letters unrelated to the word. Following this, the instructor (E) consistently asked him to sound out the word, often giving him the first letter and other cues, encouraging him to spell the word correctly. Only after E had spent considerable time and attention would the boy emit a correct response.

On the assumption that the teacher's attention was maintaining this behavior, a new strategy was designed. The boy was called to the board and given a spelling word to write on the board. At first he wrote it wrong, and asked for help, but the teacher sat at the desk ignoring his request. After about ten minutes, he wrote the word correctly. The teacher said "Good, now we can go on," and gave him a second word. Similar histrionics occurred, but for a shorter period, following which the teacher went to a third word. With each successive word, up through ten, the latency of the correct response decreased along with the number of inappropriate behaviors. After the tenth correct word, the teacher wrote an A grade on the spelling chart and spent time with him on an art project. After a month of this kind of treatment—and it did take a month to break these disturbed behavioral habits—the frequency of these bizarre antics declined to a level close to zero per class session and the child was able to make better academic progress.

The effectiveness of selective attention by significant others has now been demonstrated repeatedly in many settings. As the title of an influential article by Madsen, Becker and Thomas (1968) stated it, rules, praise and ignoring are the prime elements of classroom control, at least in elementary classrooms (see also Becker et al., 1967; Hall et al., 1968; O'Leary and O'Leary, 1972; Krumboltz and Krumboltz, 1972; Madsen and Madsen, 1981; McIntire, 1970).

Attention is also important for teenagers, but often the significant others shift from parents and teachers to peer groups. This often makes teachers rely on grades as a motivator for teenagers. Grades, as we have seen, fall into the class of secondary reinforcers called tokens. But they are anything but "token" for the majority of students: the implicit economic contract existing in schools is the exchange of grades for schoolwork. Unfortunately grades are often used noncontingently, in the sense that they are not given for the performance of a particular behavior but for the relative performance of one student in relation to the norm provided by the performance of other students. This type of competitive grading means that one student can succeed only at the expense of other students, which makes the reinforcer not contingent on each student's individual performance. In addition, teachers often give grades to punish a student for behaviors that are irrelevant to the objectives of a course. Because of this, course grades are usually not a direct consequence of performance.

A better way to use tokens in the schools is like college or professional football teams do. Many of these teams award stars (which are pasted on the player's helmet) to a defensive player who makes a certain number of unassisted tackles or interceptions. Each player who earns the stars receives them—yes, even some of the most macho of our idols will do almost anything for a star! In classrooms a similar use of tokens is applied with a mastery-learning approach, in which students' grades are contingent on their own learning of the course objectives—a criterion-referenced, as opposed to a norm-referenced, grading system (see chapters 13 and 14 for further discussion of this issue).

When things are going badly in secondary classrooms, it is often because students cannot perform prerequisite skills. If they are forced to compete for the teacher's praise and high grades with students who have attained the prerequisite knowledge, they are likely to come up short. This has emotional effects, of course, and also shows up in refusals to work appropriately. In such cases, an individual contract between student and teacher can be very helpful.

In one study of high school dropouts (Kelley and Stokes, 1982), thirteen students between the age of 15 and 21 were receiving about minimum wage on a government program for attending vocational educational classes, which could eventually lead to a high school equivalency diploma. Since their pay was not a consequence of work performed, but contingent only upon attendance, the students did the minimum work with a very low accuracy rate. When the students contracted with the teacher to receive their pay contingent upon successful completion of specified academic assignments, the quantity and quality of work increased dramatically. Analogous procedures can be followed with grades instead of money as the reinforcer.

Classroom uses of the Premack Principle are also many and varied. Many elementary teachers schedule a free play period sometime during the day. Unfortunately, it is often scheduled rigidly to occur at a certain time each day for all students. This free period could be better used by allowing each student to select activities at natural breaks in the classwork, such as when a student has successfully completed a unit of work or has been task-oriented for some reasonable period of time (e.g., Osborne, 1969).

In a variation on this idea Hosie, Gentile and Carroll (1974) observed fifth and sixth graders during free time in the classroom. From among several alternatives, several students reliably chose either painting or modeling clay on two successive days. On a third day neither of those activities was available, but in their place was a reading task on dinosaurs which included a brief written report. None of the children chose to do that report. On the next day half the students who preferred painting and half who preferred modeling were told if they did the dinosaur report, they could then paint. The other half of each preference group were promised that they could model clay as soon as they completed the dinosaur report. Of course, no one *had* to do the report at all. As the Premack Principle predicts, significantly more students completed the report when the consequence was their preferred activity than when it was their non-preferred activity.

Other classroom applications of the Premack Principle are to provide enrichment activities, such as math games, as reinforcers for completing other, perhaps prerequisite, math assignments (e.g., Taffel and O'Leary, 1976). Most current teachers use some of these approaches already, though they may not have known the name for the procedure or the research on which it is based. One of my student teachers, for example, reported the following solution to a discipline problem in an inner-city high school physical education class. The curriculum called for a unit of instruction on soccer, but the students threatened a strike if they did not play basketball instead. The teacher established a mutually agreeable contract which allowed playing basketball toward the end of each period (in some weeks at the end of the week), contingent upon their learning the soccer unit in other times.

Schedules of Reinforcement

Up to now we have been discussing reinforcement as though it is *continuous*—that is, for every correct behavior there is a reinforcement given. In real life, as well as in many experimental studies, behaviors are seldom if ever continuously reinforced. Rather, sometimes a behavior is reinforced and other times the very same behavior is not (which to say, it is being extinguished). This naturally occurring state of off-and-on reinforcement for the same behavior is called *intermittent* or *partial reinforcement*. Continuous and intermittent are two terms used to describe *when or how often a behavior is reinforced*, the general term for which is *reinforcement schedule*.

Continuous Reinforcement and Shaping

When every correct response is followed by a reinforcing consequence, *continuous reinforcement* is occurring. As we have seen, reinforcing a response every time it occurs is especially useful for increasing the frequency of new behaviors. In the early stages of learning, whether it be learning associations, concepts, or skills, immediate and continuous reinforcement allows students to repeat and improve upon correct, or partially correct, behaviors. In the very beginning, of course, the behavior is unlikely to be totally correct, and the sensitive instructor looks for approximations to the correct final behavior and reinforces those. As practice continues, the instructor will raise the standard for what is correct, thereby reinforcing only *successively closer approximations* to the final correct behavior. This procedure of reinforcing only closer and closer approximations to the correct response is called *shaping*.

It is difficult to imagine most new learning occurring without such small-step improvements and continuous feedback and encouragement from a parent or teacher. But if later stages of learning required continuous reinforcement, teachers would quickly burn out and students would be too dependent, never learning-how-to-learn on their own. Besides, they would never learn to perform in the face of frustration and would develop no persistence.

Intermittent Reinforcement

Consider what is learned in a situation in which reinforcement is delivered intermittently rather than continuously. On reinforced trials, clearly you are learning to continue the behavior and, as a side effect, you are probably feeling confident that you are doing the right thing and on the whole feeling good. On nonreinforced trials, however, you probably first feel frustrated (like what happens when you put a coin in a machine, but do not get your coffee or soft drink). But if you try again and again, getting reinforced only sometimes, you are also learning a very important lesson—namely, to engage in that behavior despite occasional nonreinforcement and feelings of frustration. Your behavior is beginning to be able to *resist extinction* or, to put it another way, to become *persistent* despite periods of nonreinforcement.

The height of persistence probably occurs in gamblers working on slot machines or playing lotteries. Gamblers continue depositing coins in spite of the fact that only a small proportion of these responses receive payoffs. Thus gamblers learn to continue responding in spite of the frustration of nonreinforcement. The reinforcement schedule they are on is a kind of *variable ratio schedule* (called *ratio* because the reinforcement is programmed to occur in a ratio of 1 reinforcement to every so many responses, say 50, and called *variable* because it is not exactly 50, but varies around it). This kind of schedule is known to produce great amounts of responding for minimal reinforcement. Those casino owners are not dummies!

At the opposite end of the persistence continuum is a continuous reinforcement schedule—that is, a *fixed ratio schedule* of 1 reinforcement for one behavior. This is analogous to putting a coin in a coffee machine. If you are used to continuous reinforcement, your behavior will not persist beyond one or two nonreinforced trials: how many additional coins do you put in the machine after it gave you no coffee but swallowed the first coin? Much more could be said about the various types of schedules, the sequences in which they can occur, and their resultant effects on behavior, but it will be more profitable to go on to some classroom issues that are intimately tied to schedules of reinforcement.

Shaping from Continuous to Intermittent Schedules

Attention Spans

A common problem for teachers, particularly teachers of special education classes, is the student with a short attention span. Most often a male child, he is usually easily distracted from what he is doing, and overly active or restless. Without getting into diagnosis or labeling at this point (as the saying goes, "Will the Real Hyperactive Child Please Sit Down?"), it may be instructive to consider that there is only so much time for behavior. Thus the bigger the slice of time taken up by inappropriate behavior, the less time there is for appropriate behavior. Conversely, if you can increase the attentive behavior, the proportion of behavior left for inattentive behavior must decrease accordingly. We mention this because when the typical classroom consequences of the child's (let's call him Johnny) short attention span are analyzed, they usually show aspects of the following:

1. Johnny attends to some task, at which time the teacher is happy that he is occupied, since now she can work with some other children. Thus Johnny is being ignored; the consequence of Johnny's working is to be ignored by the teacher.

2. Johnny stops working at the task and does something else, at which time the teacher reminds Johnny that he should be working and often takes him by the hand and leads him back to his work space. Thus the consequence of Johnny's not working is to receive the teacher's attention.

Looked at in this way, the first step in increasing Johnny's attention span is to have the teacher attend to his working behavior—not his inappropriate behavior. At first, the teacher will have to praise Johnny (or find some other effective reinforcer) for working for very short periods of time. The schedule of reinforcement here will be short intervals—very nearly continuous reinforcement. As the child begins to attend to his work for longer periods, the teacher can then lengthen the intervals between reinforcements. But consistent with the principles of intermittent reinforcement, she must attend to Johnny's appropriate behavior. Instead of catching the child being bad, she must *catch the child being good*. By considering the problem as one of shaping to an intermittent reinforcement schedule, the teacher can slowly increase Johnny's attention span.

One way this has been done in special education classes (e.g., Alexander and Apfel, 1976; Wolf et al., 1970) is to use a simple timer, such as a kitchen timer, and set it for, say, two minutes. When it goes off, the teacher praises the student if he is working appropriately, or ignores him if he is not. The timer is again set for two minutes and the procedure is repeated. The schedule for reinforcement in this case is known as a fixed interval schedule. As the child begins to respond appropriately, the teacher then may set the timer for varying times, sometimes two minutes, sometimes five minutes, etc; the schedule is becoming longer and more variable.

With many special education classes or other severe behavior problems, a discrete event such as the timer bell is useful to remind both the teacher and student of the new reinforcement contingency in the classroom. In more regular classes, a teacher can often achieve a similar result by nonobtrusively walking over to a disruptive student at increasingly longer intervals when he or she is behaving appropriately. Just a look and a smile, sometimes a touch or a few words, can increase the attention span of a disruptive student.

Student/Teacher Ratios

From the previous example, it is obvious that one teacher would not be able to deal effectively with a class of 30 Johnnys. Since Johnny needs to be on a continuous (or nearly continuous) schedule of reinforcement at first, it will be physically impossible for the teacher to be adequately spread around to more than a few such students. Except in the generally smaller classes for exceptional children, this fact is often ignored in schools today. Class size is usually determined for fiscal and administrative convenience and not for the recognized educational needs of students and teachers.

This fact is recognized in programs for disadvantaged learners, such as Headstart, where there is a very small student/teacher ratio. When the students graduate into regular classrooms, however, they are competing with a greater number and variety of learners for the teacher's attention. If they have not been properly shaped from the relatively continuous reinforcement of the special program classroom, they may not be resistant to extinction. Their lack of persistence will show up in a variety of ways: extreme teacher dependence, no frustration tolerance, short attention spans, and little work output, to name a few. Inadequate provision was made for the generalizability of the student's behavior from the training environment to the regular environment. This is the "Train and Hope" method of preparing students for the real world (Stokes and Baer, 1977).

Figure 6.2. Typical learning curve relating response strength (magnitude or probability) to number or amount of reinforcements.

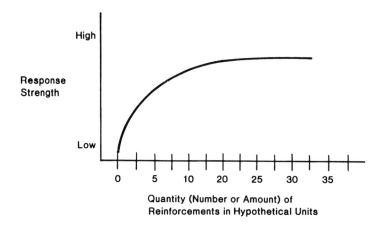

We are not naive enough to expect that the schools will ever reduce the teacher/student ratio to some optimal level—it will probably always be less than optimal. What teachers need to do, therefore, is to recognize the problem in terms of reinforcement schedules, recognize their own limitations in providing more than a few students with nearly continuous reinforcement, and get help. Surprisingly, help is almost always available for the asking. Paid teacher aides and student teachers are one source. Parents as classroom helpers are another. Older or more advanced students in the school system are yet another. Finally, perhaps the least tapped resources in our society are senior citizens. If I had my way, senior citizen housing would be built on the premises of schools, perhaps as high rise apartment complexes on the upper floors of elementary and middle schools. Under programs managed by teachers, old folks could help students practice their assignments and could provide more frequent reinforcement. There would also be benefits for the senior citizens in giving them something worthwhile to do with their time, and the students could do things for them, as adoptive grandparents.

Adjacent facilities exist in only a few places, but it is still possible for inventive teachers to reach out to senior citizens and others for help.

Quantity of Reinforcement

We have seen how several factors are involved in reinforcement effectiveness. The quantity of reinforcement is also important, and it can be explored through the number of reinforcements (i.e., practice trials on which reinforcement is received) and the amount of reinforcement.

Effects on Learning

Not surprisingly, the number of reinforcements affects operant behavior as it does respondent and cognitive behavior: in general, the more times the behavior is performed correctly and reinforced, the greater the strength or probability of that behavior (e.g., Hovland, 1937). The greatest increment in the probability or magnitude of the response occurs after the first few reinforcements, with each succeeding reinforced trial providing less of an increment. The last sentence describes the typical learning curve, as shown in figure 6.2.

The same basic finding also applies to the amount of reinforcement. In general, the first few increments in amount of reinforcement make the biggest difference in responding, with succeeding increments having a smaller effect. In practical terms, going from zero pay to $1.00 per hour has a major effect on your behavior. So does doubling your pay from $1.00

to $2.00, or going from $2.00 to $3.00 per hour. But when you are earning $20.00 per hour, a $1.00 raise is not likely to have the same effect on your behavior that it did earlier.

Effects on Persistence

Perhaps by now you're thankful that behavioral psychology has this nice general, uncomplicated law, given the complexities of behavior we have discussed throughout this book. If you are feeling that way, sorry, but rapanoia's got you again! The general effects described need to be qualified, especially with regard to amount of reinforcement but also, to a lesser degree, with regard to number.

The problem is that nothing occurs in a vacuum. Behavioral events have histories and each new situation is viewed by the organism in relation to that history or other events which provide a *context* or *contrast* for current behavior. Continuing with our previous examples, $10 per hour is quite attractive if contrasted to your previous $2 per hour, but is a punishment to someone accustomed to earning $20 per hour. Analogously, to nonhuman organisms the *deprivation-satiation history* of the organism and the current context make tremendous differences in performance, differences that can markedly change the shape of the curve in figure 6.2 (e.g., Bower, 1961; Crespi, 1942, Reynolds, 1961). Similar effects have also been shown in respondent learning (e.g., Amsel, 1971).

Even that is not all. Schedule of reinforcement interacts with quantity in an important way. You may recall that someone who has been exposed to intermittent reinforcement will resist extinction longer than someone who has previously been continuously reinforced.

How does this relate to amount of reinforcement? Well, it turns out that in the context of prior continuous reinforcement, the greater the amount of reinforcement, the faster an organism will quit responding when reinforcement is no longer forthcoming. This lack of persistence makes sense if you consider that the organism accustomed to large rewards will have greater frustration, but will not have learned frustration tolerance.

On the other hand, if the organism has a prior history of intermittent reinforcement, then the larger the rewards obtained, the longer the organism will persist when reinforcement is no longer forthcoming (e.g., Hulse, 1958).[8] This is because the organism had already experienced great frustration from not receiving large amounts of reinforcers, but learned to tolerate that frustration and continue with the behavior.

In sum, the greater the amount of reinforcement during early stages of learning, the faster the learning. But unless some frustration tolerance is built into the training, through frequent nonreinforcement, then the experience of receiving large reinforcers could lead to a lack of persistence. Larger is not always better.

Finally, let's return to the problem of number of reinforcements. You may now be anticipating that once we get past some minimum number, it is the proportion of trials that are reinforced that is more important than the total number of reinforced trials, at least with regard to the persistence of the behavior. Since we are seldom getting reinforced by all persons in all situations, it may be that the development of persistence should be a major educational objective. You may also recall that this same advice was given as a suggestion for preventing learned helplessness.

Delay of Reinforcement

It would be difficult to imagine teaching a new response to a rat or a pigeon if the food reinforcement were not delivered immediately after the response occurred. Once the response has been learned and practiced a while, however, the reinforcement may be delayed for longer and longer periods (but there is probably always some optimal interval beyond which delays would not maintain the response).

Anecdote 6.3

Teaching Patience Patience

During the first two months of kindergarten, Patience showed little patience. When we told her she needed to do something (stand for the pledge, get in line, sit on the rug, etc.) she would begin to argue. When we explained that Kindergartners do not argue with the teachers, she would scream and work her way into a tantrum—cry, wiggle on the floor, hit and kick anything near her—for up to 45 minutes. When her mother was called, she was not surprised, answering "Oh, it figures, she does it all the time. I just let her do what she wants and let her have her own way to shut her up."

Having diagnosed that Patience was being positively reinforced and her mother negatively reinforced (the "peace at any price" syndrome), her teacher and I needed a plan. After one of her tantrums, we sat Patience down and explained that crying will not get her what she wants and that she must listen. If she has a problem, she needs to discuss it with us, not cry.

She continued to have tantrums, but we moved her to the back of the room and ignored her. She screamed louder and louder, interfering with class, but we ignored her, and eventually after a few days we began to see a change in her behavior: she cried less and less and "got her act together" sooner. When she was in control of herself—and only then—she could join the class. The procedure, though not reducing tantrums to zero by the end of the school year, was successful. Unfortunately, Patience's mother was apparently not able to follow our advice and she reported that the tantrums were still frequent at home.

Heather McDivitt
Teacher

Humans similarly need to receive immediate reinforcement, at least in the beginning of learning a new skill. Imagine a novice learning to hit a tennis ball if his instructor did not praise or correct his strokes for five or ten minutes after hitting the ball. The more reinforcement is delayed, the less effective it is. But in the more advanced stages of learning, reinforcement can and should be delayed for longer periods, in successively small steps of course. This will allow continued improvement. More importantly, it will increase persistence by allowing the student to tolerate the frustrations of waiting. In addition, it will increase generalizability of the behavior to other settings (e.g., Fowler and Baer, 1981; Kazdin and Bootzin, 1972, Renner, 1964; Stokes and Baer, 1977).

Reinforcement Contingencies

When reinforcement is consistently (not necessarily continuously!) made available as a consequence of one behavior, then we say that the *reinforcement is contingent upon that behavior*. Another way of saying this is that reinforcement is dependent upon, or brought about by, that behavior. We can then speak of a causal relationship between the behavior and reinforcement as a *reinforcement contingency*. A rat who earns his food by pressing a lever is operating on contingent reinforcement. But if food were simply dropped into the cage every minute irrespective of what the animal was doing, we would say the reinforcement was *non-contingent*.

Loosely speaking, it is possible to think of a reinforcement contingency as the *rule* that exists between the behavior and the reinforcement. The typical parental exhortation "no TV until you finish your homework" makes TV-watching a contingent reinforcer for doing homework. But many everyday rules are not consistently enforced and therefore lose the causal relationship implied in the word contingency. In addition, a contingency may be operating despite the fact that no rule may be able to be stated verbally, either because we are not consciously aware of the contingency or because the controlling factors have not been discovered yet. There are many species-specific behaviors that are controlled by what might be called contingencies of survival, yet the organism itself is probably unaware of the operating rule. For example, rats learn aversions to the taste of certain foods if illness is induced even up to 3 or 12 hours later. If illness does not follow, the organism learns that the food is safe and will eat it again. Birds, on the other hand, similarly learn to avoid foods that are associated with illness, but through sight instead of taste (see, Hulse et al., 1980, pp. 65–67 for a good introduction to this topic).

Language behavior in humans offers many instances of the operation of complex contingencies despite our typical unawareness of the rules. For example, we learn to say "please" and "thank you" at an early age because doing so gets us the ice cream we want, as well as praise for being polite (Skinner, 1957). Or consider the following linguistic combinations (from Leeper, 1970, p. 242):

(1) old coat plus brown coat = old brown coat
(2) expensive dress plus red dress = expensive red dress
(3) beautiful sky plus azure sky = beautiful azure sky

Perhaps the linguistic rule is to place the color adjective second when combining the adjectives. But then what about these?

(4) coronation gown plus blue gown = blue coronation gown
(5) brick wall plus red wall = red brick wall
(6) utility room plus brown room = brown utility room

In these last three cases, the rule seems to be to place the color adjective first. It is grammatically incorrect in phrases 1–3 to place the color adjectives first and in phrases 4–6 to place them second. Almost all native speakers of English will agree with that—their linguistic behavior is being controlled by some contingency—yet a verbal rule is hard to come by (except perhaps by English teachers, who might explain that descriptive adjectives precede nouns modifying nouns).

Contingencies, in other words, can be simple and rule-like at times and at other times can be difficult, if not impossible, to state. Moreover, behavior can often be controlled by reinforcements which are not really causally related to the behavior, but are nevertheless *perceived* by the organism as though they were. Superstitious behavior can be produced in the pigeon by dropping food into the experimental space randomly. But many pigeons then behave as though their behavior was responsible for getting the food, and they repeat certain stereotyped behaviors over and over (Skinner, 1948). Similar behaviors occur in humans. A professional baseball player's wife, for instance, wore the same article of clothing throughout a world series because her husband hit a home run the first day she wore it. Likewise, in the *Peanuts* comic strip, Linus' belief in the Great Pumpkin is maintained by unexplained movements he perceives in his "sincere pumpkin patch." These random events serve as reinforcers for his expectation that the

Great Pumpkin will appear, and they maintain his belief in the Great Pumpkin, despite the fact that he never receives any objective evidence (such as toys or candy) that the Great Pumpkin exists.

In complex school situations, teachers may often be unaware that what they do or say to a student may serve to reinforce the behavior the student was engaged in. In other words, the teacher's attention may randomly reinforce a behavior that was occurring. For example, intending to be warm and sincere, an attractive teacher may unknowingly reinforce a student's sexual advances. Such events, often leading to unpleasant confrontations later, demonstrate that the control chance reinforcement has over behavior is difficult to overestimate. The actual contingency—not the purpose of the reinforcement agent or teacher— is the important variable.

For practical purposes, few have ever stated the advantage of contingent over noncontingent reinforcement better than Benjamin Franklin (1969) in his advice to a Presbyterian minister. It seems that the enlisted men in the chaplain's outfit had been promised a gill of rum a day as an enlistment bonus. And while they were always on time for the serving of rum, few attended the prayers and services conducted by the chaplain. Franklin simply suggested that the rum be given out only immediately after prayers. The chaplain tried the idea with this result, in Franklin's words:

> Never were prayers more generally and more punctually attended; so that I thought this method preferable to the punishment inflicted by some military laws for non-attendance on divine service (p. 247).

As we have seen, contingent reinforcement does not necessarily mean continuous reinforcement, because the effects of intermittent reinforcement can be even better for maintaining behavior in the long run. Contingencies do imply that inappropriate behaviors will *not* achieve reinforcing consequences. In this sense, contingencies in the practical situation are like well-enforced rules. In dealing with humans in practical situations, therefore, it is often helpful to state the contingency as a rule. The following list may provide helpful advice in that regard (see anecdote 6.3 for an example).

1. Choose a rule (contingency) that can be understood and followed by the student. (Note: There is no reason why a democratic method or students themselves should not decide what the rule should be. Rules do not have to be—and indeed will often be less effective when—imposed by an autocrat.)
2. Choose a rule that can be described clearly and objectively.
3. Choose a rule that can be enforced.
4. Make sure that the reinforcement is given consistently only when, but not necessarily always when, the correct response occurs.
5. Never present reinforcement before, or without satisfactory, completion of the task.
6. Ignore irrelevant behavior that is used by students to get you to relax the contingency requirements (they are testing the limits of the rules).
7. Do not devise or enforce unnecessary or unreasonable rules.
8. Introduce and enforce rules one by one, rather than presenting several rules at once (especially with young children).

Contingencies and Honesty

It should go without saying—but I'll say it anyway—that praise and other reinforcers should be given honestly by teachers. Many students lose respect for their teachers because everything they do receives gushing praise, ("Oh, isn't that beautiful," "aren't you doing great work," etc.) when the students know that the work was not their best, or that the teacher doesn't really mean it. Teachers establish the

> **Box 6.2**
>
> ### Contingencies and Schedules: a Further Explanation
>
> Contingent reinforcement, as described, means that *only* correct behaviors receive reinforcement. When we use the terms continuous or intermittent reinforcement, it is implied that the reinforcement is contingent upon correct behavior. Thus continuous reinforcement means *every* correct behavior receives reinforcement, and incorrect behavior is not reinforced. Likewise, intermittent reinforcement means that no incorrect behaviors are reinforced, but that correct behaviors *will* be *sometimes* reinforced.
>
> Consider a child who shouts out answers without first raising his hand to be called on. If the correct behavior is defined as raising the hand, then
>
> 1. contingent reinforcement will be given for correctly raising the hand, but not for any other behavior.
> 2. continuous reinforcement implies reinforcing the child every time he raises his hand, but not for any other behavior.
> 3. intermittent reinforcement implies reinforcing the child sometimes (but not always) when he raises his hand, but not for any other behavior.

standards of performance in a classroom and, whether the contingency is stated verbally or not, students will adopt those standards (see next chapter) and adjust their behavior to meet those standards.

As we have seen (and will pursue further in the next section), students are not adversely affected by intermittent reinforcement. On the contrary, they develop persistence by exposure to it. Likewise, students are not harmed by teachers who withhold praise when work is shoddy, or even when it is good but could be better. When withholding praise, teachers do not need to be cold. Rather, they should provide warm attention to the students and their work and give good honest feedback on the good and bad points of it. Moreover, they should make suggestions for improving the weak points and have the students correct the work.[9] They will then be establishing high standards as well as teaching the students to discriminate between good and poor quality work. Equally as important, they will be providing reinforcement for the student in the form of *careful, honest attention*.

Token Economies

In a nontechnical sense, almost all schools are already token economies, since grades are dispensed as a result of classroom achievement or other behaviors. Grades, however, are not strictly contingent upon day-to-day behaviors; are often given days or weeks after the behaviors; and are often contingent upon a student's performance relative to others, instead of an absolute performance. In a more technical sense, then, grading systems do not qualify as token economies.

What does qualify as a token economy is a system in which tangible secondary reinforcers are distributed immediately following and contingent upon certain prescribed behaviors. Those secondary reinforcers, usually plastic tokens or points, are exchangeable at a later date for a wide variety of other reinforcers, such as privileges, activities, foods, grooming aids, etc. The advantages claimed for token reinforcers used in such a system are the following (e.g., Kazdin and Bootzin, 1972): (1) they bridge the delay between the behavior and the eventual reinforcement; (2) they allow reinforcement at any time during any activity, including sequences of behaviors; (3) they can be parcelled out when back-up reinforcers are unavailable; (4) they are not subject to deprivation or satiation states; (5) they provide the same reinforcer for individuals who may choose very different back-up reinforcers; and (6) since, like money, they become associated with a wide variety of other reinforcers, they may take on a greater incentive value than any single back-up reinforcer.

When such advantages get translated into advice for teachers they often take the form of the following kinds of rules for implementation (e.g., Stainback et al., 1973, chapter 4);

1. Learn behavior modification techniques, both general and those specific to token economies. The message is that a little learning can be a dangerous thing.
2. Arrange the setting so that you can observe students' behaviors no matter what you are doing, and so that you can distribute reinforcers quickly and easily (without, for example, tripping over desks).
3. Obtain tokens which are appropriate, not easily counterfeited or stolen. If actual tokens are not desirable, it is possible to have a personalized card taped to each child's desk or notebook, on which a tally mark can be placed for appropriate behavior.
4. Establish a store, in which tangible items (e.g., foods, school supplies) or activities are for sale, or can be rented (e.g., tapes and tape recorders, games, free time). Pricing must be done with attention paid to the desirability of the objects or activities.
5. Collect other necessary materials which will assist the implementation of the program (e.g., banks to store tokens).
6. State the rules of the class on which contingent reinforcement will be based. These should be few in number and should be written clearly and positively—i.e., tell what behavior will be reinforced, not what behavior is undesirable.
7. Determine the specific behaviors of individuals that will also be reinforced with tokens—that is, develop individualized goals for behaviors to be modified to complement the classroom goals in point 6.
8. Collect baseline data on the frequencies of the behaviors to be modified (i.e., those in points 6 and 7), so that the results after implementation of the program can be compared to the behaviors prior to implementation.
9. Secure trained help to implement the system.

Perhaps the most obvious feature of the above list is the immense behavior modification required on the part of the teacher. For most teachers, a token economy requires a substantial change of roles and daily activities, so much so that it is tempting to implement tokens as an afterthought to the ongoing activities. Such an approach will probably contribute further evidence on "How to make a token system fail" (in the apt title by Kuypers et al., 1968). Stainback and colleagues (1973, p. 5) made the following points in that regard:

It is discouraging when some teachers remark that they have tried a token system and it didn't work, when later we find their idea of a token system was handing out a token a week, or at best, a token a day for good behavior or for completing the arithmetic assignment. One of the first things that must be perfectly clear is that if you have not given out at least twenty-five tokens per child per day, you haven't used a token system. In order for the token system to work, you must communicate and communicate often. The same is true with praise.

It may indeed be the case that the major effect of a token economy—or perhaps of any school behavior modification program—is on the teachers. To the extent that teachers are re-educated to pay attention to students' positive, normal and achievement-oriented behaviors

Cartoon 6.3.

instead of to the negative, disruptive and achievement-evading behaviors, then the token economy is probably half-way successful already. For those teachers who need such redirection of their attention, a considerable investment in time and effort is required. Often no reinforcement is offered the teachers for this changed behavior, or the decision to implement a token economy is imposed from the top. It is easily understandable when teachers' behaviors do not persist through these periods of nonreinforcement. A few programs have recognized the token economy staff with reinforcers such as increased pay, vacations and workshift preferences (Kazdin and Bootzin, 1972). One study even reinforced teachers with tokens that, at the end of the day, were exchangeable for beer (McNamara, 1971).

An extensive literature now exists on token economies, their uses and mis-uses, in educational and other settings, and with various categories of people from elementary school children to adults, and from normal to retarded, hyperactive and emotionally disturbed (Kazdin, 1982; Kazdin and Bootzin, 1972; O'Leary and Drabman, 1971). Most research on classroom token systems has been done with special education students. There is now evidence that such programs are effective in (1) decreasing disruptive behavior, (2) increasing study and attentive behavior, and (3) to a lesser extent increasing academic achievement (O'Leary and Drabman, 1971). If it seems "obvious" that these behaviors should change together, it turns out to be not necessarily so. A study by Ferritor and associates (1972) suggests that the relationship between task attention and correctness of performance is not that simple. In their studies of arithmetic-drill exercises in third-graders, they found that (1) reinforcing attending behavior alone increased attending and decreased disruptions but had little effect on correctness of work; (2) reinforcing correctness of work alone increased accuracy with little positive effect on attending and disruptions; and (3) reinforcing both attending and correctness was necessary to improve accuracy, increase attention, and decrease disruptions. Thus reinforcement effects may be more specific than we would hope for, and, in order to understand the behavior, strict attention must be paid to the actual reinforcement contingency operating.

Anecdote 6.4

Life in the 90'S: A Token System

I teach sixth grade special education students, mostly with learning disability or emotional disturbance diagnoses. When they come to me at the beginning of the year their outlook on school is very poor. Most of them want nothing to do with learning, homework or tests. Therefore, my main goal at the onset of the year is to work towards making school a positive atmosphere for them.

One of my techniques is "Life in the 90's"—a technique to encourage the children to perform the best they can on all their tests and quizzes. At the beginning of the year we have a discussion and later a poll on fun things we can work towards: a pizza and pop party, trips to an amusement park or bowling, etc. We then agree on the first one and write it on a poster which has all children's names on it. I then tell them that every time someone in the class scores a 90 or above on any test, quiz or homework assignment, I will put a sticker next to their name. When every student has earned at least one sticker and the whole class has earned fifty, then we share the prize. Throughout the year I increase the number of stickers needed to earn the prize; however, the prizes usually increase as well.

You would be surprised how well this works. First, they love to see stickers next to their names. More importantly, I have kids begging me to stay after school with them to study for tests and quizzes. It can be expensive, but if you can get support from your principal, it can be manageable. But what a change in children who previously lacked motivation!

Kelly E. Block
Teacher

Regarding the effects of token systems on academic behaviors, O'Leary and Drabman (1971, p. 385) had this to say:

> If token programs serve as a priming or incentive function, one would certainly expect academic behaviors to be more difficult to change than social behaviors, since children in token programs frequently have the appropriate social behaviors in their repertoire but not the academic skills necessary to progress without considerable instruction.

They then went on to make these the first three of their ten recommendations:

1. Provide a good academic program since in many cases you may be dealing with deficient academic repertoires—not "behavior disorders." (p. 395)
2. Give the child the expectation that he is capable of doing well by exaggerating excitement when the child succeeds and pointing out that if he works hard he *can* succeed. (pp. 395–396).
3. Have the children aid in the selection of the behaviors to be reinforced, and as the program progresses have the children involved in the specification of contingencies. (p. 396).

Token Economies: For "Ordinary" Classrooms?

Token systems, in sum, have been shown to be successful for a variety of purposes, especially in special education (e.g., see Anecdote 6.4). But they are not without their problems, two of the most difficult of which are staff training and transfer of behaviors beyond the environment of the token system (Kazdin, 1982; Resnick, 1971). Transfer can be resolved by shaping to intermittent schedules (a point discussed earlier in this chapter), by training parents and significant others to use similar techniques in other environments, by teaching students how to transfer their behaviors (e.g., by teaching self-control), and by weaning students from tangible reinforcers to the more wide-spread social reinforcers (Stokes and Baer, 1977). There is even a report of a system allowing persons to earn their way off the token system by meeting high standards of performance (Kazdin and Mascitelli, 1980). While this should help transfer behaviors, it nevertheless strikes me as strange that an incentive system should provide negative-reinforcement through "earning your way off."

Kazdin (1982, p. 432) also makes another point that is troublesome, to wit:

A significant development over the last decade is recognition that lack of responsiveness to the token economy may reflect more on the program than on clients who fail to respond. Lack of responsiveness usually refers to the failure of some clients to respond to a set of contingencies that is standardized across all clients.

Clients sometimes fail to respond, but often they actively resist. Precisely because a token economy restructures the extant system of reward, ". . . the potential for coercion is great," as Kazdin (1982, p. 434) cogently argues.

It is for reasons such as these that I agree with Ryan (1979), that token economies and

Photo 6.4. A pretty picture of self-control.

other explicitly extrinsic reinforcement systems should be avoided in the "ordinary" classroom.[10]

If token systems are helpful with special classes, it is often because (1) the teachers are more likely to have been properly trained to use these techniques; (2) the main target behaviors are usually disruptive or attentive behaviors and not achievement per se; (3) most, if not all, students in the class are in need of immediate tangible reinforcers and specific contingencies in order to show improvement; and (4) most students in the class have known academic deficits which need correction before regular classroom objectives can be attained.

None of these four problems is true of the vast majority of "ordinary" classes. Each class has its clown, its disruptive student, its underachieving student, etc., but teachers can deal with these individual problem cases with special contingency contracts. The majority of students will respond to a teacher's attention, praise, corrections and grades if provided in appropriate ways (such as suggested in the rest of this book). Thus, while token systems can be useful, I would recommend their adoption only in special circumstances.

The Development of Self-Control

At a typically American birthday party for a one-year-old, all will be amused when the guest of honor literally digs in to the cake with both hands. The same observers would be much less amused if their children attacked the cake in the same manner at their fifth birthdays. By this time children are assumed to have acquired the means to control their own immediate impulses in the interests of propriety. But how do they learn such behavioral self-management or, as it is usually called, self-control?

Before attempting an answer to that question, let's define more precisely what is meant by self-control and then consider a typical adult's reaction to a determined need for self-control. *Self-control is displayed when, in the relative absence of immediate external constraints or reinforcers, a person engages in a behavior which was previously less likely than some alternative available behavior.* This definition, which is based on that of Thoresen and Mahoney (1974), can be better understood through an example. A person who was trying to lose weight would demonstrate self-control if he or she ate fresh garden vegetables and skipped the fattening foods and desserts at a buffet luncheon when dining alone. In this case, the unlikely behavior is eating the vegetables, the alternative and perhaps more probable behavior is eating the fattening foods and desserts, and the absence of immediate constraints is given by no one else being present and lots of other available foods.

It would be sensible to advise an adult with a self-control problem to do three things (e.g., Gross and Drabman, 1982, Kanfer, 1970): to *self-monitor* the behavior of interest, in this case, eating; second, to *self-evaluate* the behavior in terms of some standard of performance; and third, to *self-reward* for meeting the behavioral standard. Self-monitoring might take the form of observing and recording how often, what and how much you eat, by counting calories or even by counting bites of food in a day. To evaluate your own performance you need a standard. This might be derived from some optimal number of calories per day for your height suggested by a nutrition expert or some other model. Then, when you meet this standard each day, you reinforce yourself with praise or some special activity you reserve for that occasion—hopefully the reward is not eating a big piece of chocolate cake.

Using these three components of self-control in this order is a logical and oft-suggested intervention technique to effect change in behavior. But now let's return to the question of how self-control behavior is learned by normally developing children. Clearly young children do not learn to monitor, evaluate and then reward their own behavior in that order. The sequence is the reverse, as Harter (1982, p. 173) cogently argued using a real example of a young girl whose mother is trying to teach her to pick up after herself:

> *She has previously learned to imitate mommy's approval in the form of "good girl," which leads to an experience of positive affect. However, she next must learn to discriminate between those actions which are good and those which are bad; she must learn how to evaluate her behavior. Mommy initially serves as the evaluator, telling her that she is a good girl when she puts her dirty clothes in the hamper, and that she is not a good girl when she doesn't. The child internalizes these standards for self-evaluation. As a next step in the process, Mommy begins to set the stage for self-monitoring, by initially monitoring the child's behavior.*
> *Mommy, as monitor, says things like, "Now you know what you are supposed to do with your dirty shirt," setting the conditions for the child. Eventually, this component of the process becomes internalized, such that the child can monitor her own behavior. The developmental acquisition sequence then is self-reward, self-evaluation, and then self-monitoring.*

What Harter is describing is the natural process of acquiring self-control or, more generally, what might be called self-motivated behavior. It is *internalized* by the child as a result of social interaction with significant others, as in Vygotsky's theory. Moreover, it is a parallel developmental process to the kind of competence motivation (e.g., White, 1959) that we mentioned earlier as the cure or prevention for learned helplessness. Internalized control of one's own behavior is a form of mastering skills and controlling environmental consequences and, therefore, it is a prime component of purposeful behavior.

What is important to remember is that the acquisition process for this kind of self-regulation moves from external to internalized control. Children first self-reinforce by modeling the way they are reinforced by their parents (and how they reinforce each other and themselves). Next, children self-evaluate according to the internalized standard they model from the parents. Finally, they can monitor their own behavior to remain consistent with that standard.

Punishment and Its Amazing Effects[11]

Masochistic Behaviors

Earlier in this chapter, I defined punishment as an aversive consequence of a behavior ($R \rightarrow S^{AV}$), pointing out that its usual effect is to suppress behavior, at least temporarily. Suppose, however, that you visited a laboratory in which you witnessed an organism behave in the following strange way. A green light goes on, the organism quickly presses a bar, and then receives a strong shock (S^D—$R \rightarrow S^{AV}$). The light goes on again, the bar is pressed, and the shocking consequence is repeated. For the next hour, this sequence of events is repeated with no diminution in the organism's response rate or latency. This is truly masochistic behavior since the organism is causing itself to be shocked by pressing the bar. It is also opposite to what is expected from punishing consequences: the organism should stop pressing the bar—if it is followed by strong shock. What is maintaining this behavior? How did the organism acquire this self-punitive behavior?

Consider possible answers to the question before I provide a likely behavioral history. The behavioral episode in question is of potential importance as a prototype for studying masochistic behavior in humans, though it is also of interest in comparative psychology. As Seligman (1975, p. 29) quipped, ". . . some experimenters will not believe that a phenomenon is real until it has been demonstrated in the white rat."

The answer, or at least one simple answer,[12] to how to induce the masochistic behavior described above is to have the green light go on, *followed ten seconds later by a strong shock.* This establishes conditions for avoidance learning, so that the next time the light goes on, the organism will do all sorts of things that might work to keep the shock from arriving. Finally the organism will stumble on the bar press, the consequence of which will be to receive a *mild shock,* but avoid the strong shock that would have followed within ten seconds. The organism will now perfect his avoidance behavior, responding more quickly and vigorously each time the light goes on, accepting the mild shock.

But the story does not end there. Through a process of *habituation,* we become more tolerant of noxious stimuli. For example, if you work near loud noise, you begin to adapt to the noise and it is not nearly as bothersome after a while. Similarly, the organism adapts or habituates to the mild shock. Thus the voltage can be slowly increased over several trials until, after some time, the organism is now pressing the bar and receiving the consequence of considerably more shock than he originally learned to avoid. In other words, he would be much better off not pressing the bar, but—and this is a critical point—he will probably never find out because, without some other kind of intervention, his avoidance bar-pressing behavior will be extremely persistent. How persistent it will be depends on a number of factors, the most important of which is probably the severity of punishment.

Before going into specific effects of variables like severity of the punishment, consider another example of masochistic behavior. An organism is trained to leap a barrier from one side of a small room to another. If he does so within ten seconds of the onset of a green light, he avoids the shock; of course, he learns this avoidance response very quickly. But now lets reverse things. If the organism crosses the barrier, he receives shock; but if he stays where he was, he avoids it. After their first experience jumping into the shock ($R \rightarrow S^{AV}$), organisms stop jumping and simply stay put when the green light goes on, right? Wrong. There is now considerable evidence (e.g., Church, 1963) showing that few organisms learn to reverse their behavior. Instead, they punish themselves by continuing to jump the barrier into the shock. In fact, jumping into punishment produces more persistence than continuing to jump into a safety zone after shock has been removed from the original side of the room.

What is going on here? Conventional or common sense explanations might stress the fear factor (e.g., Mowrer, 1960). If the original shock was severe enough, avoidance would occur and be maintained because whenever the S^D (the light) came on, the conditioned fear would recur and the organism would respond. Then why doesn't the organism have even more fear when jumping into shock and stop jumping? Because, it seems, there is more to it than that.

For one thing, there are apparently *species-specific defenses* that impel organisms—in different ways for different species—into "flight or fight" behaviors whenever they are punished (e.g., Bolles, 1975). Shock, loud noises, and

Cartoon 6.4.

other aversive stimuli seem to propel organisms into action, rather than into passiveness, as a survival mechanism. Sometimes, if another organism is present when shock is delivered, the action will take the form of aggression.

In addition to fear and species-specific response patterns, there is also a more cognitive factor—the necessity of learning the particular contingency involved. Organisms whose emotions and motions are so fully engaged (i.e., they are fearful *and* running or jumping) are less likely to be cognizant of which event predicts safety and which predicts danger, a finding which is as true of humans as other organisms (see Hulse et al., 1980, for a good review). Thus punishment may produce cognitive confusion, especially when the conditions under which it is administered are changing.

Factors Contributing to Punishment's Effects

The above examples require some moderate to severe pain to produce such bizarre effects. A mild reprimand would surely not produce such masochistic behavior in normal humans, though it might produce conditioned emotional responses and other side effects. But painful shocks or other physical blows might, if conditions were confusing as in the cases above. In this section, however, we shall consider the more straightforward case of punishment—namely, the case in which an aversive stimulus is delivered following a behavior (R→S^{AV}).

Severity of Punishment

The first factor contributing to the behavioral effects of punishment is its severity. In general, the greater the intensity and/or duration of punishment, the greater and more permanent the suppression of the punished behavior (Church, 1969).

As usual, this general statement must be qualified according to the context provided by past history. Prior exposure to punishment of a certain type and severity affects how organisms will respond to subsequent punishment. Church (1969) summarized the research on this problem and concluded that organisms tend to persist in the performance of what they have learned in their previous exposure to noxious stimuli. This may help explain the masochistic tendencies we just discussed. If organisms learn vigorous escape or avoidance responses after exposure to a punishing consequence, then they are likely to persist in that behavior. The stronger the original punishment, the less likely they are to discover that their behavior is no longer adaptive.

Delay of Punishment

Analogous to the effect of delay in reinforcement, the more immediate the punishment, the greater the suppression of the punished behavior. This can also be extended to sequences of behavior. Church summarized the research evidence as follows (1969, p. 154): "Punishment of the first response in a behavior sequence produces greater response suppression than punishment of later responses in the behavior sequence."[13]

Punishment Contingencies

Punishment that is contingent upon a response produces greater suppression of the behavior than the same punishment provided noncontingently, or randomly according to time. In addition, if a discriminative cue is presented prior to the noxious stimulus, the suppression becomes limited only to that condition. That is, there is little or no suppression of the behavior in the absence of the warning signal (Church, 1969). Neither does it seem to produce as much emotional behavior, such as generalized anxiety, depression and helplessness, as is likely in noncontingent punishment (see Seligman, 1975, and the discussion of learned helplessness in chapter 3).

Punishment as a Cue for Reinforcement

As a final effect of punishment, let's consider what happens if punishment and positive reinforcement are sequentially related. But first, let's review. The procedure for positive reinforcement is to present a desired stimulus contingent upon performance of a behavior (R→S^{RF}), with the expected effect of increasing the probability of the behavior. The procedure for punishment is to present an aversive stimulus contingent upon the behavior (R→S^{AV}), with the usual result of suppressing, or decreasing the probability of, the behavior. Now, let's combine these so that a behavior receives the consequence of an aversive stimulus followed by a desired stimulus, diagrammed as follows:

(12)   R→S^{AV}→S^{RF}

Will the behavior increase or decrease in frequency? There is some evidence in animals that, at least for mild to moderate shock as the S^{AV}, behavior under R→S^{AV}→S^{RF} occurs almost as frequently as under R→S^{RF} (Church, 1963).[14] It is, in other words, as though the aversive stimulus acts as a signal or as feedback that reinforcement is coming, so your response is correct. It certainly does not deter the response.

Extrapolating from such results to difficult and complex human situations is always risky, but I see a parallel that is so striking that it should at least be mentioned. First an example from a typical adult-child supermarket interchange. The child, reaching from the shopping cart seat, grabs a package of candy from the just-reachable shelf. The parent takes it from the child and scolds or slaps, following which a tantrum ensues. This embarrasses the parent sufficiently that a deal is made and the child receives candy, gum, or something equally desirable.

A more serious human problem may also be considered via the $R \rightarrow S^{AV} \rightarrow S^{RF}$ prototypic model. This is the battered child syndrome. In some of these cases, children seeking attention (often in less-than-desirable ways, but perhaps the only ways they learned) receive physical beatings way beyond what is justified by their behavior. Immediately following the attack, the parent feels guilt and remorse and then lavishes attention and love on the child. This may also be one of the few times such children receive that kind of warmth and they may come to accept it and even feel that the beatings are proof that the parent loves them. If others of us do not understand the attachment of child to parent (or wife to husband, or pet to master) in wanting to return for more abuse, because we do not have similar behavioral histories, we can at least understand their behavior through the metaphor of the punishment-reward sequence research.

Punishment: The Moral of the Story

There are three stories about punishment I am particularly fond of. The first is about the teenager who comes to breakfast and says to his father, "Pass the goddamn cereal," whereupon his father slaps him across the face and says, "What did you say?" So the kid says, "I said, pass the goddamn cereal." His father slaps him again and says, "Now what do you want?" The kid says, "Well, I sure don't want any of the goddamn cereal."

The second story, from a Peanuts cartoon, has Charlie Brown explaining to Linus that the best way to teach a dog is to punish him with a rolled up newspaper. His dog Snoopy, overhearing the conversation thinks, "Sure, but it also tends to give you a rather distorted view of the press."

The third story is about the behavioral psychologist who was trying to toilet train his new puppy. But every day when he came home from work there was a mess on the living room carpet. So he stuck the dog's nose in it, then threw the dog out the window. This went on for thirty days without any change. But on the thirty-first day, do you know what happened? The psychologist opened the door and the dog ran over to the mess he had made, stuck his nose in it, and jumped out the window.

The morals of these stories are, first, that punishment teaches what not to do, but does not teach what to do. Second, punishment has emotional side effects. Third, punishment may have quite varied and unexpected effects or, as Guthrie (1935, p. 160) put it, "To train a dog to jump through a hoop, the effectiveness of punishment depends on where it is applied, front or rear." Guthrie's comment, like the above jokes, are humorous, but not frivolous. Punishment may suppress behavior, but probably only if the aversive stimulus produces behavior that is incompatible with the punished act. If the aversive stimulus releases behaviors similar to the punished act (e.g., hitting a child for fighting), punishment may facilitate the act (Church, 1963). When we strike children to suppress their fighting behavior we are also providing models who physically strike others to suppress annoying behaviors. What are we teaching?

Indeed, what *are* we teaching by punishment, especially revengeful, retribution-types of punishment? Does discipline require us to pay attention to every inappropriate behavior, or does such attention simply increase the frequency of inappropriate behaviors? If it is

Anecdote 6.5

An Alternative to Punishment: The "Restitution Solution"

In my position as youth counselor, I provide counseling for youthful offenders and their parents. The traditional approach to these youngsters in trouble with the law has been to counsel the people so they could understand *why* they did what they did (and sometimes to fine them, although usually the parents pay most fines and lawyers fees). Although counseling sometimes worked to change *some* kids, attendance at the prescribed sessions (usually 10) was considered a punishment, but an insufficient one: Some even told the counselor they'd probably commit the offense again.

The most significant problem with the program is the fact that the wrong isn't righted in any way. Thus I proposed a revised plan to the court system which provides restitution to teach responsibility for their behavior.

Example: *Becky was arrested for harassment of a police officer after she was found drinking at the Town Park. The officer confiscated her alcohol and was going to bring her home when she proceeded to harass him calling him obscene names. When she was placed in the women's cell block she carved her name and several obscenities on the bench in the cell block. She was charged also therefore, with criminal mischief—defacing Town property.*

The Restitution Solution

Since empty beer cans/bottles are a growing problem at Town Park, Becky was to be required to pick up bottles and papers at the park along with the park maintenance employees. This would result in a dismissal of the harassment charge. In order to satisfy the criminal mischief charge she was to be required to sand the bench in her cell block to prepare it for refinishing.

Mary Eisenhauer
Youth Counselor

clear that punishment has quite varied effects, it should be equally clear that humans are too quick to use it to the exclusion of other methods of control. We are not just trying to control children's behaviors; we are trying to teach them how to learn, how to control themselves, how to create, how to love, etc. We are trying to "influence" them, to use Friedenberg's softer words (1959, p. 59):

> But influence does not mean pushing people around; it means leading them to want to do what you want them to do . . . it requires real awareness of what other people need and some skill in helping them get it. More than anything else, it requires a clear understanding of what is going on and how things actually work. An influential person is no bully; he is a sculptor who works in the medium of human situations. He must respect his tools, his materials, and his market.

In this chapter, we have explored "what is going on" and how behaviors "actually work." In the next chapter we will broaden our outlook to include imitation, among other topics, and in chapter 8 we shall draw practical implications from all of this and apply them to problems of discipline.

Emotional and Cognitive Interactions with Operant Behavior

Operant conditioning in both basic and applied research settings is probably the best studied field in behavioral research. So perhaps it is fitting to end this chapter with an emphasis on the interdependence of the operant level of behavior with the respondent and cognitive levels.

Dealing first with the operant-respondent or motions-emotions interaction, there have been innumerable variations of cartoons and jokes on the following basic theme. A secretary, sitting at her desk when a man walks by, says to her office mate, "I can't imagine why I like Mr. Peterson. He's not handsome or rich, and he's not my type at all. But just the sight of him makes me feel good." And, of course, it turns out that Mr. Peterson is the company pay clerk. The negative side of that is even more compelling because we are usually better aware of people or settings that make us fearful, angry or guilty. The point is that it is probably impossible to be emotionally neutral about people and events. Our mutual interdependencies of behavior not only condition observable physical and verbal operant behaviors, but also condition feelings to the people and settings in which our interactions occur.

Vis-a vis operant-cognitive interactions, it is also quite improbable that any operant conditioning—whether it be positive or negative reinforcement, extinction, or punishment—can occur without also setting many thought processes in motion. What is going on here? How can I change the situation? Shall I hit the other person, ignore him or explain something to him? What extenuating circumstances might be causing him to act as he is? Thoughts such as these occur, sometimes in parallel and sometimes as interacting processes with our operant behaviors.

Consider the following discrimination-learning problem: train a chimpanzee (or even a lower animal) to respond to the larger of two squares until the subject comes to respond correctly 90 or 100% of the time. Now give him a new discrimination, with the previously correct stimulus having to be compared with a still-larger square. Which stimulus will the organism judge to be the correct one?

This is an old problem in psychology, known as a *transposition* experiment. What is the answer? The chimps choose the larger of the two stimuli. Despite being positively reinforced for choosing a specific stimulus, the organism was learning a *relationship* between the stimuli. In other words, if the chimps could think aloud, we might have heard them saying, "the larger one is correct" instead of "that particular one is correct."

While this problem and others like it were much debated in the literature, the debate centered on theoretical explanations and whether chimps and rats become lost in thought over such problems (e.g., Krechevsky, 1932; Spence, 1937; 1940). What was never at issue was the following: *when a specific behavior is reinforced, the organism learns to perform that behavior, but it may also learn more than that specific response.* What the more is, is often difficult to specify, especially in nonhumans, but it falls under the category of cognition.

More recent and quite exciting extensions of this point have been seen in the literature on teaching chimpanzees to use sign language or communicate in other ways (e.g., Gardner and Gardner, 1969; Premack, 1971b). In these studies the chimps were positively reinforced for using appropriate symbols. For example, the first chimp to use sign language, Washoe, had to use the American Sign

Language sign for "more" before the consequence of more food or more play was achieved. But much more than this was learned by the chimps. Once they learned the appropriate responses (via operant conditioning), they combined the symbols in grammatical or logical ways beyond the specifics taught. Washoe, for example, after separately learning the words for bird and water, signed "water bird" when she saw a duck (described on Public Broadcasting's TV show Nova entitled, "The First Signs of Washoe").

In sum, while much of our teaching/learning goes on at the operant level through the social learning and feedback of student-teacher interactions, parallel analytical and synthesizing activities are going on within the student. Those cognitive, emotional and motivational processes, meanwhile may be manifesting themselves in verbal and nonverbal interactions between students and teacher. ♦

Practice Exercises

A. Practice Items

For the following multiple-choice items, select the alternative choice which *best* answers the question. (Note: Answers are in Note 15).

1. Positive and negative reinforcement
   a. both lead to an increase in response frequency.
   b. have opposite effects on response frequency.
   c. are unlikely to teach harmful or inappropriate behaviors.
   d. both require the presentation of a desired stimulus as a consequence of the behavior.

2. "The occurrence of a reinforcing stimulus *only following a correct or appropriate behavior*" is the definition of _____ reinforcement.
   a. intermittent
   b. negative
   c. secondary
   d. contingent

3. Which of the following procedures defines extinction?
   a. $R \rightarrow S^{AV}$
   b. $S^{AV}-R \rightarrow NoS^{AV}$
   c. $CS-US \rightarrow UR$
   d. $S^{\Delta}-R \rightarrow NoS^{RF}$

4. Which of the following is most true of continuous reinforcement?
   a. It produces great frustration tolerance.
   b. It is better for shaping a new behavior than for maintaining an already learned behavior.
   c. It produces great persistence through periods of nonreinforcement.
   d. All of the above are true of continuous reinforcement.

5. Which of the following is an example of negative reinforcement?
   a. A child steals something when his peers tell him he is a chicken and a wimp.
   b. A graduate student becomes tense whenever he looks at his statistics book.
   c. A teen-ager receives her allowance contingent upon washing the dishes.
   d. An adolescent boy is grounded (cannot go to the weekend dance) because he received a failing grade in school.

6. Which of the following is the *least likely* effect of mild or moderate amounts of punishment (e.g., yelling)?
   a. relatively permanent suppression of the punished behavior.

b. an immediate suppression of the behavior in the presence of the punisher.
c. no suppression of the behavior in the absence of the punisher.
d. all are equally likely

Items 8–12 are definitions or situations that are to be matched to the following:
   a. positive reinforcement
   b. negative reinforcement
   c. extinction
   d. punishment
   e. discrimination learning

____ 8. A person takes a drug to relieve stomach distress. But, after taking it for a week with no improvement, he stops taking the drug.

____ 9. Johnny B. Good works hard in Dr. Dixon's Room 222, because Dixon rewards completion of assignments with "funny money" which can later be exchanged for cakes and cookies. Johnny hardly ever completes his assignment in Ms. Love's class, however, despite Ms. Love's prodding and yelling.

____ 10. $S^{AV} - R \rightarrow NoS^{AV}$

____ 11. Frieda Scream throws a tantrum at the store until Mom buys her candy or ice cream. Frieda's tantrums are receiving _____.

____ 12. Agnes is so afraid of statistics that even looking at the textbook makes her anxious. Thus when she has a homework assignment, she works quickly, writing something—anything—so she can put the book away.

B. For Cooperative Study (in or out of class):

1. In small groups, take turns teaching your colleagues one or more of the following concepts, giving examples:
   a. the types of operant behavior as shown in Table 6.1. (p. 172).
   b. the difference between continuous and intermittent reinforcement and the types of intermittent reinforcement schedules.

2. Discuss how well some of the "amazing effects of punishment" fit cases of child abuse, spouse abuse, or other strange behavior of which you are familiar.

3. Ask students of different cultural backgrounds to describe their child rearing practices in terms of the principles of this chapter. For example, discuss the issue raised in Note 4.

4. Discuss the following issue: should token economies or other tangible reinforcers be used in normal classrooms? in special education?

5. Compare Harter's description of the development of self-control via modeling and reinforcement with Vygotsky's description of internalization of control (Chapter 2).

C. **For More Information**
1. View one or more of the following films showing operant procedures at work:
   a. *The Miracle Worker* (about Helen Keller).
   b. *Harry: Behavioral Treatment of Self-Abuse* with Richard Foxx (Research Press).
   c. *Behavior Modification: Teaching Language to Psychotic Children* (one of the earliest behavior modification programs, with O. I. Lovaas; Appleton-Century).
   d. *The First Signs of Washoe* (the Gardner's project to teach a chin sign language).
2. Read, and perhaps make a written or oral report on, an empirical study on one or more of the concepts in this chapter. For example, you may wish to consult the following journals: *Journal of Applied Behavior Analysis, Behavior Modification*, or *Journal of the Experimental Analysis of Behavior*. Alternatively, you could seek out one of the sources cited in this chapter.
3. Survey teachers in your area regarding their use and understanding of some of these principles. Are their uses and understandings consistent with what is presented in the chapter?

CHAPTER
Study Questions

1. Analyze the following components of a modeling episode:
   a. the model (M)
   b. the observer (0)
   c. direct consequences (reinforcement or punishment)
   d. vicarious consequences (reinforcement or punishment)

2. What is the distinction between *learning* and *performance?* Upon which do reinforcement and punishment have their effects?

3. Describe each of the following three effects of modeling:
   a. the learning effect
   b. the inhibitory or disinhibitory effect
   c. the response facilitation effect
   Give examples.

4. What are some of the characteristics of people whom we are most likely to model?

5. What is the authors' opinion on the relationship between TV violence and subsequent aggression by viewers?

6. Compare the effects of TV-modeled pro-social and anti-social behaviors.

7. Describe some of the ways that advertisers attempt to manipulate our behaviors as consumers.

8. Why is logical persuasion an inefficient means of changing attitudes and behaviors? Include the concept of cognitive dissonance in your answer.

9. What is meant by vicarious emotional learning? How is it learned?

10. What is meant by habituation? Describe how it might explain increasing tolerance for violence or for what your author described as "nude, lewd, crude or rude."

11. What does the research evidence cited have to say on the following aspects of conformity?
    a. the individual vs. the group
    b. assuming the behaviors of the role you play (e.g., guards vs. prisoners)
    c. obedience to an authority
    d. norms

SEVEN

12. What is meant by sociometric wealth (the sociodynamic law)?
    a. How is it related to friendships in classes?
    b. How is it related to intergroup rivalries in classes?
    c. How does it apply to ability grouping or tracking?
13. What is meant by goal structures? Define the following kinds of goal structures and describe their likely classroom effects:
    a. cooperative goal structures
    b. competitive goal structures
    c. individualistic goal structures
14. Review each of the nine recommendations provided as a summary from this chapter. Describe ways to apply them to real classroom situations.

Modeling and Social Processes

Introduction

1. "By not exalting the talented you will cause the people to cease from rivalry and contention.
   By not prizing goods hard to get, you will cause the people to cease from robbing and stealing.
   By not displaying what is desirable, you will cause the people's hearts to remain undisturbed." (from the Tao Teh Ching, "The Way" in Murphy and Murphy, 1968, p. 158)
2. "There is only one way to improve ourselves, and that is by some of us setting an example which the others may pick up and imitate till the new fashion spread from east to west. Some of us are in more favorable positions than others to set new fashions. Some are much more striking personally and imitable, so to speak. But no living person is sunk so low as not to be imitated by somebody." (James, 1904, p. 142)
3. "Parents who beat their children for aggression intend to "stamp out" the aggression. The fact that the treatment does not work as intended suggests that the implicit learning theory is wrong. A beating may be regarded as an instance of the behavior it is supposed to stamp out. If children are more disposed to learn by imitation or example than by "stamping out" they ought to learn from a beating to beat. That seems to be roughly what happens. . . ." (Brown, 1965, pp. 394–395)
4. On one of her daily runs to junior high school, school bus driver Gloria Arsenault caught the aroma of marijuana. She told the children to stop smoking. When they did not, she drove directly to the local police station who found two joints and two hashish pipes among the students. None of the students confessed to smoking and no one "squealed." Appearing to have no other recourse, town officials and the police suspended the bus service for three days.

Did the students—some of whom lived as far as six miles from school—have to walk as a consequence of their behavior? None did. Their parents, many of whom "complained loudly about the suspension," drove them to school.
(*Time*, January 17, 1983)

In a strange way each of the above four items, from the Taoist philosophy of ancient China to a common American news item, is an example of and helps define the scope of the concerns in this chapter. We are not only affected by the direct antecedents and consequences of our behavior, but we are also greatly affected by the behaviors of others. Humans are social beings—survival of the species depends upon social interactions—and it is therefore not surprising that our most efficient way of learning to approximate complex behaviors at any age is imitation. The phrase "Monkey see, monkey do" is probably at least as apropos of humans as monkeys.

Consider how much more efficient it is to teach someone to hit a golf ball by demonstrating it and saying do that, compared to trying to describe all the facets of the stance and swing. Even more preposterous would be to treat the various facets of the golf swing as operant chains of behavior (which they nevertheless are) and positively reinforce each successive approximation of the correct behavior. Bandura (1962) humorously described the hypothetical application of shaping principles to teaching a person to drive a car. This is not to say that the operant and respondent principles we have studied in the last two chapters must be discarded; rather, it is to say they must be viewed in a larger context, that of groups.

Indeed, the fourth item above is a case in point. The breach of discipline would have been unlikely to occur if students had been separately driven to school in their own individual school buses. People behave differently in groups than they do as individuals for a number of reasons, among which are the following: (1) there is a lower likelihood of any person's

Photo 7.1. Filling mommy's shoes.

behavior being directly related to a consequence—a factor of anonymity; (2) there are competing reinforcement contingencies—some persons will be reinforced for breaking the rules; and (3) powerful peer pressures can be brought to bear on anyone who opposes the behavior of a subgroup—the negative reinforcement of avoiding the censure of peers can be much stronger than the positive reinforcement from authorities for "squealing." As if this were not sufficient to describe a no-win situation for such law-abiding citizens as the bus driver, the parents protested the action taken and the students received none of the aversive consequences intended for them by the authorities.

Whatever your thoughts on the merits of this relatively innocuous case, similar principles operate in more severe cases as well. A news item that hit the national press in 1981 (e.g., Buffalo Courier-Express, November 25, 1981), for example, reported that a teen-ager murdered his 14-year-old girl friend and then took a procession of more than a dozen of his schoolmates to view the corpse. After the police were finally notified, twenty-four hours after the first "viewings," a policeman interviewed thirteen of those who viewed the corpse. He said that none of them reported the murder because their primary objective was "to cover up their friend."

From minor disciplinary incidents to covering up a murder, from selling toothpaste to status symbols, from learning sex roles to learning to be violent—all these involve models to be imitated and/or other social complexities. This chapter will focus on these topics and, to bring some order to them, we begin with some basic definitions and principles involved with learning by imitation.

Modeling

Marc, a ten-year-old, had been occupying the attention of his visiting aunt and uncle for the better part of an hour with his postcard collection, a good portion of which had been sent to him by them over a period of three or four years. His sister, Sara, aged four, sat with them throughout. As the last cards were being inspected, Marc pointed out that he had a duplicate of one and might give it away. Sara immediately said, "I'll take it, Markie," and announced that she would add it to her postcard collection. Of course, when Marc obliged by making her a gift of the duplicate, her collection consisted of that one card.

This common developmental process, known to every parent, serves to illustrate the basic components of a modeling episode, as well as providing some glimpses of the factors controlling such behavior. Marc was, of course, the *model* (M) whose behavioral interaction with aunt and uncle was being witnessed by the *observer*, Sara.[1]

Vicarious Consequences

The behavior of both children is easily understandable, at least at the general level of parental discourse. Through his postcard collection, Marc was monopolizing the adults' attention—his behavior of showing his postcards was being *directly reinforced* by that attention. And promises of future reinforcers were made for additions to the collection on the aunt and uncle's current trip. During this period Sara was observing the reinforcement her brother was receiving and was therefore being *vicariously reinforced*. Vicarious means through someone else's experience, in the same way that we say we had the vicarious experience of seeing China by viewing a friend's pictures of China. In symbolic terms, the model (M) received direct reinforcement, while the observer (O) received vicarious reinforcement. Despite the fact that O did not personally engage in M's behavior, the probability of O's performing that behavior has increased as a result of witnessing M's behavior and its attractive consequences. Vicarious learning of this sort, since it requires no performance by O, is a case of what Bandura (1965a) called "no trial learning."

The fact that modeling can occur with no-trial learning requires that we introduce a distinction, long recognized by learning theorists, between learning and performance. (Note the similarity of this distinction to that between competence and performance mentioned in the discussion on Kohlberg's moral reasoning.) Important research by Bandura and his associates (e.g., Bandura, Ross and Ross, 1963c; Bandura and Walters, 1963) demonstrated that children observers learn many of the details of a witnessed act, though they may suppress performance of such imitated behaviors until they are more likely to be reinforced than punished for emitting M's behaviors. Those research studies typically had children observe a film in which some M engaged in unique kinds of aggressive-destructive behaviors against, for example, an inflated Bobo doll. A third of the subjects saw a film in which M's aggressive behaviors were severely punished, another third saw M lavishly rewarded for the same behaviors, while the film shown to the remaining third saw no consequences of M's behaviors. Later the subjects were placed in a setting just like that in the film and were scored on which behaviors of M were imitated, how frequently, and under what conditions. As expected, when O witnessed M's behavior being punished, there was little imitation in the real-life situation. This would be suppression according to a *vicarious punishment* effect.

However, there was no difference between the no-consequence and positive reinforcement groups in performance of the behavior. Apparently they *learned* and *performed* the behaviors equally well. Most importantly, when all O's were asked later to reproduce the behaviors they saw in the film and were given attractive rewards for doing so, there were no differences among any of the groups. All groups including those who witnessed M being punished, had *learned* the acts equally well. Whether they would *perform* the acts depended upon the situation. Vicarious reinforcement and vicarious punishment, in other words, have their effects on subsequent performance of behaviors. The behaviors will be learned observationally so long as they are novel and appropriately attended to. Bandura (1965b; 1969) has gone further in explicating *three effects of modeling*. First, there is the *learning effect,* as we have just seen. New behaviors, never before occurring in O's repertoire, may be acquired as a result of witnessing M. Second, there is an *inhibitory* or *disinhibitory effect* of modeling. O is likely to inhibit or suppress the performance of a behavior as a result of M's being punished for the same behavior; in contrast, if M's behavior was reinforced, O's performance of a similar behavior may be disinhibited, or increased in probability. Third, there is a *response facilitation effect,* in which M's behavior simply serves as a signal (a discriminative stimulus, or cue) to facilitate the performance of a behavior already learned and socially sanctioned. Examples of the response facilitation effect of modeling are applauding after someone begins to applaud, trying new foods when others do, or pledging money to a benefit fund because others are doing so.

Reinforcement Reconsidered

On the basis of what we have now discovered about the relationship between modeling and reinforcement, it is worth spending a moment to reemphasize the definitions of reinforcement and punishment learned in the last chapter. Positively reinforcing and punishing consequences were defined as increasing (or maintaining) or decreasing, respectively, the frequency of a behavior. This can now be seen to imply that such consequences affect performance of an already acquired behavior more than they teach a behavior. Learning can occur in the absence of a reinforcing consequence, as has been widely known for many years.[2] Learning can also occur, as we have just seen, without any overt performance and therefore with no direct consequence to O. In fact, it may be impossible not to learn things if conditions are right, such as in vivid images on television (to be discussed shortly).

To say that learning occurs whenever we pay proper attention to something is not to say, however, that reinforcement and punishment cannot facilitate or hinder the learning. The consequences of a behavior often help make the learning more memorable cognitively and affectively. Thus while learning can occur in the absence of reinforcing or punishing consequences, such consequences may facilitate (or hinder) the learning and will certainly affect when and whether the learned acts or facts are performed. *Another way of saying this is that reinforcing and punishing consequences are sufficient but not necessary for learning; they primarily affect the performance of behavior once learned.*

Cartoon 7.1

Whom Do We Model?

Often to the chagrin of the parents, children model their behaviors too well as, for instance, when they are frustrated or hurt themselves and utter a parent's favorite expletive. Children obviously model their parents, older siblings, and significant others with whom they interact in person or on television. As children grow older, teachers become dominant models and are then displaced by peers and media and sports personalities.

To say that such factors as age, sex, prestige, wealth, talent and/or popularity of models affect the likelihood of observers reproducing their behavior is probably true, but not very informative. Only Charlie Brown of the Peanuts cartoon strip has a baseball hero—Joe Shlabotnick—who was a major league failure. Other children identify with and model their baseball swings after successful players and "superstars."

Why is that? What are the factors responsible for the efficacy of a model in inducing imitative behaviors? Part of the answer has to do with *power* or, more specifically, with *control of desirable resources*. People are more likely to imitate a model who has the power to bestow favors and give rewards than someone who is the recipient of those favors (Bandura, Ross and Ross, 1963b). As stated in the chapter 2 cartoon perversion of the Golden Rule: "They who have the gold make the rules." This fact seems not to have been lost on advertisers, a point to which we will return later. Nor has it been lost on women's rights or minority group advocates who promote a greater number and variety of women and minorities in positions of power and competence on television shows.

But all modeling is not based on the power of the model. As William James said in quotation 2 at the outset of this chapter, no one is so low as to be imitated by no one. We imitate the behaviors of siblings younger than we, if they may be getting some attention we are not ("Mommy always liked you best!"). We may even imitate siblings of the opposite gender, even if we are not being reinforced for such behaviors.[3] Moreover, we may model aggressive behavior even if the consequences of it are negative—a point we shall turn to next. It is not yet entirely clear, in summary, whom we model or why, though social power of the model, vicarious consequences of the model's behavior, the likely consequences of performing the model's behavior, and perceived scarcity of resources (see the Tom Sawyer anecdote) are all important determinants of modeling.

Modeling Aggressive Behaviors and TV Violence

From time to time a unique suicide, bombing or arson will occur and soon afterwards be followed by several more, enacted in a strikingly similar manner. In parallel fashion the evening news is semi-regularly dominated by a bizarre murder or other aggressive act that was almost a carbon copy of a TV or movie scene, or a recent real-life crime. Such bizarre episodes reach the point that the police and others worry continually that publicity for a crime may have the unintentional side-effect of stimulating a rash of "copycat" duplications of the feat. It seems that no matter how insane an act or actor appears to the general public, there always seems to be someone who will imitate the behavior.

Aggressive behaviors, in particular, are extraordinarily ripe to be modeled from sources such as movies and TV, as well as real-life persons. Or so it seems. From time to time, therefore, there are investigations into the effects of TV violence on aggressive behaviors, some of which have been sponsored by the U.S. Senate.[4] Before delving into the findings and implications of these studies, let's become a subject in one of the earliest and most famous of the experiments.

If you were a three-to-five year old attending the Stanford University Nursery School in the early 1960's you may have participated in this study. A female experimenter escorted you from your classroom to a special room. On the way in you met another adult who was also invited to come along and join the game. You were then seated at a table which contained such artistic materials as potato prints, stickers, and colored paper, and given instruction on how to create pictures with those materials. The other adult, the Model, was taken to a table at the far corner of the room to play with tinker toys, a mallet, and a 5-foot inflated Bobo doll. Then the experimenter left the room.

After about a minute of tinkering with the tinker toys, M spent the remainder of the ten-minute period aggressing against the Bobo doll in a number of highly novel ways, including sitting on the doll and punching it in the nose, pommeling it on the head with the mallet, and tossing it in the air and kicking it around the room. M repeated these acts in sequence about three times interspersed with verbal comments appropriate to the acts—e.g., "Sock him in the nose," "Kick him," and "Pow."

Following this, the experimenter returned and led you to another room full of a number of attractive toys to play with. But shortly after you became involved with one or more of the toys, she announced to you that because these were her very best toys, she decided not to let you play with them and to keep them for other children. Then she took you to a third room, which included a wide variety of toys, like a 3-ft. Bobo doll, a mallet and peg-board, dart guns, a tea set, crayons, dolls, stuffed animals, and so forth. She stayed inconspicuous in the room and let you do whatever you wished. In this third room, unknown to you, you were being observed through a one-way vision screen and scored every five seconds for various types of aggressive behavior.

Before telling you the results, we'll now introduce you to the other conditions in this study. You were in the Real-Life Model condition. Other children witnessed the same aggressive acts by the same model, but shown on a ten-minute Movie in the same room. Still other children saw the same behaviors performed by a cartoon figure called Herman the Cat. The last fourth of the children were a control group

Anecdote 7.1

Modeling and the Law of Supply and Demand

That astute observer of human behavior, Mark Twain, gave us the classic image of Tom Sawyer not only getting others to *want* to do what he *had* to do, but also making a handsome profit from their gullibility. When Ben asked Tom if he wouldn't rather go swimming than whitewash, Tom answered:

"Like it? Well, I don't see why I oughtn't to like it. Does a boy get a chance to whitewash a fence every day?"

That put the thing in a new light. . . . Tom gave up the brush with reluctance in his face but alacrity in his heart. And while the late steamer Big Missouri *worked and sweated in the sun, the retired artist sat on a barrel in the shade close by, dangled his legs, munched his apple, and planned the slaughter of more innocents. There was no lack of material; boys happened along every little while; they came to jeer, but remained to whitewash. By the time Ben was fagged out, Tom had traded the next chance to Billy Fisher for a kite, in good repair; and when he played out, Johnny Miller bought in for a dead rat and a string to swing it with– and so on, and so on, hour after hour. And when the middle of the afternoon came, from being a poor poverty-stricken boy in the morning, Tom was literally rolling in wealth. . . .*

Tom said to himself that it was not such a hollow world, after all. He had discovered a great law of human action, without knowing it—namely, that in order to make a man or a boy covet a thing, it is only necessary to make the thing difficult to attain.

The Adventures of Tom Sawyer, chapter 2

The law of supply and demand is both economic and psychological truth: the value of an activity or commodity is inversely related to its availability and ease of attainment. This law is well-exploited by advertisers. Is there an implication for educators? If being in class were a *privilege* (perhaps earned by having done required homework and/or being prepared) instead of a right, then (1) those who earn it would be higher status models than those who are defiant, and (2) education would be more in demand.

---

who did not witness any modeled aggression, but went directly to the second room. Finally, half of the subjects in the Real-Life and Movie conditions observed a male model, while the rest observed a female model.

The results were quite convincing in showing that over all, the real-life, human film and cartoon film Models induced approximately equal amounts of aggressive behaviors by the child observers and that amount was almost twice as much as that which occurred in the control group. The effect was even greater for the imitative aggression scores—that is, the specific acts of aggression performed by the models. Clearly, the observers learned the aggressive acts.

Other notable findings concerned the gender of both M and O. Boys exhibited more aggression than girls, especially of the type that involved hitting and gun play. Girls, in contrast, sat on the Bobo doll more frequently. This tendency was even more pronounced when sex of M was taken into account. Boys who observed the female M were more likely to sit on the Bobo doll without punching it, while those who observed the male M were more likely to punch it. Girls, on the other hand, were likely to imitate the male M's sitting on the doll, but less likely to punch it. Thus even for three-to-five-year-old youngsters there is a "sex-appropriate" behavior pattern that makes a model more or less likely to be imitated.

Bandura, Ross and Ross (1963a), the authors of this famous study, contrasted their design and results with some other conceptions of aggression and modeling. One important aspect of their experimental design was the inclusion of a frustrating experience in the denial of opportunity to play with the attractive toys in the second room. They reasoned that people would be more likely to reproduce aggressive responses if they had encountered a frustrating experience, based on Dollard and colleagues' (1939) *frustration-aggression hypothesis*. Since they were not concerned with a frustration vs. no-frustration comparison, they did not include a no-frustration control group in their study. Their control group experienced frustration equal to the other groups, but did not witness the prior aggressive acts by a model. As a result, they did not act nearly so aggressively when presented the opportunity.

The Bandura et al. results also contrasted strongly with other alternative explanations of the effects of filmed and real-life aggression on modeling. There was, and perhaps still is, a view that filmed violence has a cathartic effect, allowing observers to vent their frustrations vicariously (e.g., Feshbach, 1955, 1964, 1970). While there may indeed be occasions on which violence fantasized or observed vicariously produces a reduced tendency to be aggressive—the so-called catharsis effect—most researchers in the field would agree with Huston-Stein's assessment (1978, pp. 80–81):

> . . . the results of the theory-based laboratory studies of Bandura and Berkowitz[5] do apply to the naturalistic effects of television violence on real aggressive behavior. Heightened aggression occurs after children or adolescents watch violent television under many conditions; such aggressive behavior can be suppressed by situational constraints, but often it is not. Other factors related to television viewing, particularly deprivation of programs that children like to watch, can also lead to aggressive behavior. Finally, aggression is especially likely to increase for children and adolescents who are already aggressive. The net result is that the people with the greatest potential for harm to other people are the ones most likely to be inspired to violence by television.

Lest you draw the conclusion that it is only a "violence-prone personality type" who succumbs to the aggression portrayed by television or other models, consider that the nursery schoolers at Stanford were not a particularly violent or deviant group. And besides, whenever we are labeling a group for research purposes as "more aggressive," that is simply their current status. We do not know how they developed that status, which may also have been influenced largely by modeled violence. We do know that there is evidence from naturalistic settings which shows (1) that violence at school is correlated with the amount of violence watched on TV at home, and (2) that television viewing at primary school age predicts later aggressive child-rearing practice on any other family characteristics studied (Huston-Stein, 1978).

Photo 7.2. Prosocial behavior in Nigeria.

Cartoon 7.2

Modeled aggression, on TV or elsewhere, can indeed be a dangerous commodity. Even when the "bad-guy" gets caught and punished in the end, the aggressive acts are learned by the observer. Even when the modeled aggressive acts can be rationalized by laudatory motives, as when superheroes punish villains, the aggressive acts are learned by the observer. Whether these aggressive behaviors are subsequently manifested or suppressed by the observers depends, among other things, on the similarity of the modeled and real situations and the likelihood of positive or negative consequences in the current situation. Nevertheless, the model—villainous or pious—of these aggressive behaviors is teaching the moral equivalent of "might is right."

Modeled Prosocial Behaviors

To be fair to the television industry, there have been shows developed especially for children that attempt to model pro-social behaviors such as cooperation, empathy, sharing, tolerating frustration, and so forth. Sesame Street and Mister Rogers Neighborhood on Public Television come to mind first, but there are other shows on both public and commercial TV which model socially sanctioned behaviors. Incidentally, most shows model some pro-social and some anti-social behavior, including Sesame Street, though the ratio and vividness of violent acts is usually of concern to critics.

As might be expected, there is considerably more research on TV violence than on TV pro-social behavior. The evidence that exists indicates that the observers of programs like "Mister Rogers" do indeed model some of the pro-social behaviors, and perform fewer aggressive acts than control groups of children not watching the show (e.g., Friedrich and Stein, 1973; Stein and Freidrich, 1972; Shirley, 1974).

It is ironic that pro-social behaviors such as cooperation are not as vivid as many aggressive acts. Thus they may not be as easily recalled or modeled. On the logic that that is essentially accurate, Friedrich and Stein (1975) added role playing and verbal labeling of the pro-social behaviors being modeled on TV to enhance the probability that the acts would be recalled and imitated. They concluded that each enhances a different aspect of behavior: role playing increased the probability of the behavior in a test situation, while labeling

Anecdote 7.2

Power Rangers in Preschool

One little boy in my pre-K class plays Power Rangers constantly and tends to kick and punch while imitating the program. Although he doesn't try to hurt the other children, they tend to get in the way of his punches. I try to encourage him to play something a little less violent or appropriate with little success. Just about anything in our room can be turned into a gun, sword or knife. As a result the other children do not play with him. No matter what they are doing he enters the area and immediately begins cutting them with a sword or shooting at them. He talks about Mortal Combat, Terminator and Tales From the Crypt. From the way he speaks about these shows they obviously upset and scare him. Unfortunately, he continues to watch them with his older brother. He acts out the moves and tells his friends about blood squirting from his eyes at the lunch table. It is sad for me to think how different this boy might be if he watched nothing but Barney or Sesame Street.

Tracy Sievenpiper
Teacher

(e.g., "helping") facilitated subsequent recall of the concepts modeled, but did not affect their behavior.

A Tentative Conclusion

More needs to be learned about the effects of modeling on behavior, but much is already known. A report written for the Scientific Advisory Committee of the Surgeon General on Television and Social Behavior inferred from the available data as early as 1972 that viewing violence on television can induce aggressive behavior in adolescents (e.g., Chaffee, 1972). As I write this second edition in late July 1996, President Clinton has called a summit meeting of TV executives to discuss the continuing problem of violence (and also sex) which dominate the airwaves. The problem has not gone away and even the arguments on all sides of the debate sound just like the original battles of the 1960's and 1970's.

While TV violence is obviously not the sole cause of aggressiveness, modeling in general is perhaps the primary means of learning specific aggressive behaviors, verbal and non-verbal. It is therefore very difficult to overemphasize the importance of modeling. Thus the parent or teacher who spanks or yells at a child may be modeling the very behaviors intended to be stamped out (see also quote number 3 by Brown, 1965, in the beginning of this chapter). Elementary school teachers of the early 1990's have complained about their children's imitation of the "Power Rangers" karate chops and other moves, and how those aggressive acts dominate play (see anecdote 7.2). Regarding sex, one first grade girl was observed singing "When I think about you, I touch myself" and gyrating with all the masturbatory moves that a rock singer made famous on MTV.

People do not imitate only aggressive or anti-social behavior, of course, although that is what is likely to receive the most media attention. People also imitate pro-social behaviors (for one example, see anecdote 7.3). Prosocial behaviors such as conflict resolution and mediation, however, are not as exciting to watch

Anecdote 7.3

> ### They Don't Learn It from Strangers
> One can often obtain a glimpse of the behaviors parents model for their children from the children's own behavior. On such example—a case of pro-social modeling—occurred at a family gathering.
>
> Father had just finished serving drinks to all the guests and was about to sit down with his own drink, when he accidentally knocked over the full glass. He was angry and berating himself all the while he was trying to sop up the drink from the carpet. At this point 2 1/2 year-old Shannon came over to him, put her arm around him and said, "It's all right Daddy; we still love you."
>
>

and apparently attract smaller audiences even when available. The result, according to a 1992 investigative video reported by Edwin Newman,[6] is that today's children will have witnessed 20,000 murders and countless other violent acts by the time they graduate from high school. Such statistics are not likely to change much in the near future, if ever. Thus, if parents want to protect their children from learning some information or behaviors before those children are developmentally ready, parents will have to control access to the TV. In addition, what do we parents and teachers have to lose by modeling the behaviors we are attempting to induce?

Advertising

P. T. Barnum was reputed to have said that a sucker is born every minute. If you watch commercial television long enough, you'll not only overdose on violence, but you'll come to understand why it is called "commercial" television. TV is not the only medium for advertising, of course, and modeling and vicarious reinforcement are not the only selling techniques used. For example, coupons and rebates that come with the purchase of certain products are designed as direct positive reinforcements for behavior that is loyal to the sponsor. On top of that, some supermarket chains double or triple the value of product coupons to reinforce the behavior of shopping at their store. But if modeling is not the only psychological technique used to modify the behavior of generation after generation of "suckers," it is nevertheless a major technique. A sexy movie star slinks into view, runs her hands over fanny and thigh and, in appropriate bedroom voice, whispers "Nothing comes between me and my _____," advertising a brand of designer jeans. A small, average looking man in a locker room full of big, handsome, muscular jocks announces that he has an advantage over these guys: his advantage is not looks or brains, but the razor blade he uses. Sure enough, up comes a beautiful blonde in a sports car, to whisk away our frog-transformed-into-a-prince-by-the-kiss-of-a-razor, as he announces smugly to the jealous macho-men, "So who said life was fair?" If most reasoning can be said to use either inductive or deductive logic, much current advertising seems to rely on seductive logic.

Famous people—sports figures, film and TV personalities, musicians and artists—are shown using "the only" product able to stop their hemorrhoidal itch, relieve their headache without stomach upset, or transport them to their party in a car sporty enough to maintain their glamorous lifestyle. Ordinary people who use the advertised product are the envy of the neighborhood for their shiny floors, the absence of ring-around-the-collar, or their newly discovered attractiveness to the opposite sex. The formula is the same: a model uses our product and is highly reinforced. We observers should be vicariously reinforced and, therefore, ever so slightly more disposed toward purchasing the product.

The story, however, does not end there. In addition to direct and vicarious operant reinforcement, advertisers also use music and jingles that may come to be uniquely associated with and evoke certain feelings appropriate to the product. They also associate their product with words and emotional states of the actor/models that will elicit the feelings desired for their product (see Higher-Order Conditioning in chapter 5). Finally, they advertise on programs that fit the image they are trying to convey: beer is advertised most often on sporting events, cereals on cartoon shows, gospel records on religious shows.

Consumers are often unaware of the many ways they are being manipulated, but products, musical groups, and styles begin to capture larger shares of the market as a result of these techniques. Walt Disney was a master of similar techniques in creating lasting positive feelings toward his creations. For example, in the Hall of the Presidents at Disleyland and Disneyworld, a very patriotic feeling is induced in the observers as they watch various life-like versions of the presidents move and speak. But as the show climaxes with Lincoln giving a stirring address, the sunset in the background slowly changes to a red, white and blue American flag while appropriate patriotic music fills the theater. For those old enough to recognize the music and know what the flag is, hardly an eye remains dry.

I mention these techniques for two reasons. First, all of us are subjected to such manipulations whenever products, lifestyles, ideas and beliefs (yes, even religious, educational and political products and beliefs) are being sold. Thus, we can better understand our own feelings and behaviors by learning about how others attempt to manipulate us. Second, it helps us understand our children—why they "desperately need" certain sports shoes, jeans, rock records, and hamburgers, but would rather die if seen by their peer group with the wrong brands. The advertisers create a "need" for their product through media models and, if successful, peers follow through by using the product, providing models closer to home as well as differential consequences to those who conform and those who are too different.

A nagging question may remain: why don't advertisers (and others) simply provide us with a logical presentation of the facts to convince us to use their product? The answer is that such "convincing" does not work very well and often gives rise to counterarguments that, if anything, make it harder to change the belief and behavior. Facts contrary to one's beliefs create what Festinger (1957; Festinger, Rieken and Schachter, 1956) called *cognitive dissonance*, which people can resolve to cognitive consistency by changing their beliefs or, more likely, by marshaling support—social or logical—for their current beliefs. Try to convince a smoker to give up smoking or a "junk-food junkie" of the benefits of broccoli. Behavior change by persuasion seldom works though it is universally and repeatedly attempted. As Varela (1978, pp. 121–122) described such direct persuasion,

All the arguments favoring a certain position are marshaled as strongly as possible, the dire consequences of not following that course of action also being presented. The target of our persuasion attempt usually proves to be very refractory, something that leaves us nonplussed, "How is it," we wonder, "that in spite of all these clearly logical reasons, our subject remains, if anything, more adamant in what is often a pigheaded position that is not only wrong, inconsistent, inconsiderate, but often damaging to him as well?" We focus the problem on the subject, seldom doubting that perhaps what needed improvement was the procedure that we used.

If we observers/consumers still haven't learned that convincing and persuading are inefficient means of changing attitudes and behaviors, the message has not been lost on those forces—companies, promoters, certain religious organizations and politicians— whose livelihood depends on shaping our attitudes and behaviors. And so, to paraphrase the Taoist verse (No. 1 in the Introduction to this chapter), they display what is desirable and cause many people's hearts to become disturbed.

Vicarious Emotional Learning

The vicarious learning processes we have discussed so far have been mostly concerned with behaviors most observers would call operants—aggressive acts, purchases, imitations of a model's motions. But emotions and respondent conditioning can also occur via the indirect route of witnessing a model.

Our common experiences tell us that this is true from observing actors portray various emotions which induce observers into a similar emotional state. Often, however, we observe not only the actor portraying the emotion, but also other situational cues that may directly induce the emotion in the observer. For example, if an actress playing a mother begins to scream and cry just after her child falls off a bridge into the river, the audience may feel a similar emotion, too; however, it may not be the excellence of the acting that induced the observers' reaction, but the horror of seeing a child fall from a bridge. The most convincing evidence of vicarious conditioning of emotions, therefore, occurs when the only stimuli available to the observer are those of the model.

Fortunately or unfortunately, life is full of such situations.[7] If young observers see a parent react with intense fear to an unseen something they later learned was a spider, it is not surprising if the observers develop a fear of spiders. Through the vicarious experience of witnessing a model's fear, the observer associates a similar reaction to the feared object, even though that object has never been directly experienced.

As described, vicarious and direct classical conditioning are governed by the same processes (as Bandura, 1969, cogently argued). In fact, the process looks remarkably like higher-order conditioning (see chapter 5). Consider its likely history. The initial experiences children have with parents showing fear reactions may have occurred in the presence of an actual US for fear, such as fire, falling, or some other pain-producing consequence for the children (observers), as well as the parent (model). Then the parent's emotional reaction can become CS for producing that reaction in the child. As we know, once a stimulus becomes a CS_1, it can be used to condition other stimuli via second-order conditioning. In the above example, the spider is a CS_2 which gains its strength to elicit a fear reaction by being paired with the CS_1—namely, the parent's emotional reaction.

Similar but more subtle vicarious respondent conditioning may occur in children learning to feel tense and uneasy with, say, mathematics through a parent's, teacher's, or peer's dis-ease. Attractions to rock music, for example, may also be learned this way: an older sibling's or friend's facial expressions and emotional reactions appear to be happy and excited after listening to a new musical group. The younger child then takes an immediate liking to the group, though there was not direct experience with the music.

It is possible that this kind of vicarious emotional arousal is the basis for understanding how others feel—a process usually called *empathy*. Observers are not intuiting what another feels; they actually feel, or can at least imagine how they would feel, if they were in the same situation as the model (Bandura, 1969).

Other, Subtle Vicarious Learnings

In addition to all of the above, there are some very subtle effects of modeling that are difficult to measure but likely powerful. Consider first the effect of repeatedly watching violence or pornography on television. At first it is shocking, but after repeated exposures it becomes less and less so. Eventually a person who has grown up with it cannot understand the shock and outrage of someone seeing it for the first time; likewise, the latter person cannot understand why the former is not shocked and outraged.

The process by which this works is called *habituation*, as noted in the section on masochistic behaviors in chapter 6. Habituation is often described by noting that if you drop a frog in hot water, it will jump out. If you put it in cold water and slowly increase the temperature, however, it will not jump out but remain the water until it eventually expires. Habituation has a useful side, as when doctors and nurses learn not to feel revulsion at the sight of blood and can therefore do their jobs. But it can also be harmful as when we learn to accept increasing levels of violence. This is one of the arguments that is often made by those who speak of the moral decay of civilizations, both past and present (e.g., Moynihan, 1993/94).

"In olden days," as the song goes, "a glimpse of stocking was looked on as something shocking." Now string bikinis are in vogue and few people are outraged anymore. Similarly, parents, women, older people and people in authority used to receive honorific treatment and special politeness as conventional etiquette. Now children openly ridicule and disobey teachers and parents as part of the regular fare of prime time situation comedies; men treat women as sex objects and women eagerly seek the role on music videos and popular movies. As Edwin Newman reported (see Note 6),

> . . . in a typical television season, the average adolescent views 14,000 instances of sexual contact or sexual innuendo in TV ads and programs. Less than two percent make any reference to any possible consequences. Soap operas average 35 romantic encounters per hour.

Does our acceptance of violence, sex, and ridicule as a normal part of our culture arise because we have habituated to what is nude, lewd, crude and rude?

Conformity

The Individual vs. the Group

Perhaps it is not too big a leap from models and habituation to a more obvious way in which we humans are susceptible to the influences of others—namely, the pressures of a group to conform to their behaviors and standards. Some famous studies have been done in social psychology to uncover how group consensus and norms become established (e.g., Sherif, 1947), the impact of group norms on an individual's behavior (e.g., Asch, 1956; Krech et al., 1962) and the impact of authority on obedience (Milgram, 1963).

To make the point most vividly, assume that you are a subject in Dr. Asch's experiment on visual judgment. You are brought into a room, seated as the seventh of eight subjects and told that you will be seeing a card (A) with a vertical line drawn on it. Next

Modeling and Social Processes 219

Given the existence of a generation gap, and different conflicting norms among generations, then why is it that children who don't get along with their parents get along so well with their grandparents?

Simple. The children and grandparents have a common enemy.

Cartoon 7.3

to it would be another card (B) with three vertical lines on it. The job of everyone is to decide which of the three lines on card B is the same length as the standard on card A. Furthermore, you are to state out loud your opinion in turn. After everyone agrees to participate and understands the directions, the first trial begins.

Card A's line is 10 inches and the lines on card B are 8 3/4 inches, 10 inches and 8 inches. It is apparently an easy judgment for all, because each subject in turn (the six before you and the one after you) all state that the middle line matches the standard. On the second trial there is also unanimity. On the third trial the match appears to you to be as easy as the first two and you are prepared to say it is the third line on card B which matches the one on card A. To your great surprise, however, the first subject calls out "number 1." You double-check your perception and conclude he must have made an error just about the time the second subject also says "number 1." In fact, all six subjects before you agree that number 1 matches the standard. It is now your turn.

What do you say? Do you conform to the others or do you continue to trust your own judgment and resist the temptation to be agreeable?

As you may have gathered, the other seven subjects were stooges following a script of the experimenter. You were the only real subject, being tested not on visual judgment, but on resistance to conformity. Would you have conformed? You were, as Asch's title suggests, a minority of one against a solid majority of seven who were obviously wrong; and yet one-third of the 50 subjects tested yielded to the social pressure and agreed with the majority on at least half of the test trials.

The results of variations on this type of research show that the amount of conformity is markedly decreased when there is *just one other person* who disagrees with the majority and/or when the judgments can be made privately or anonymously. Conformity can be increased by increasing the difficulty of the test items or judgment and by having the reference group be significant others (e.g., colleagues or supervisors). The extent to which yielding to pressure can go is seen by some comparisons on opinion items using Crutchfield's variation on Asch's procedure (e.g., Krech, Crutchfield and Ballachey, 1962). Military officers, for example, all disagreed with the statement "I doubt whether I would make a good leader" when tested privately; under group pressure, however, 37% agreed with the statement. Only 19% of college students privately agreed that "Free speech being a privilege rather than a right, it is proper for a society to suspend free speech whenever it feels itself threatened;" when confronted with unanimous group pressure on that point, 58% agreed. The same technique can induce people to agree to such facts as "male babies have a life expectancy of only 25 years," "the USA stretches 6000 miles from San Francisco to New York," and "men are 8 or 9 inches taller than women on the average." See anecdote 7.4 for another example.

Anecdote 7.4

Conformity in Children's Questions

It is one of the principles of brainstorming and other creative processes that ideas should be neither praised nor criticized. Praise tends to increase conformity to the idea which received it, and criticism tends to suppress further creative expression in favor of "safe" ideas. Safe ideas, of course, are those which conform to the group, as in the Asch experiment.

An example of such conformity arose following a performance of a children's opera for a large number of elementary school children.[7] The singers, dancers, orchestra players, conductor, and my wife and I (as authors/composers) were invited on stage to answer any questions the children might have about the opera. The mistress of ceremonies took the questions by running around the auditorium Phil Donohue style to let the children speak into the microphone. The first question was "How long did it take to make the horse heads" (costumes)? This was followed by another dozen or more "How long did it take. . . ." questions (. . . to make the scenery, etc.) By the time the MC was sick of such questions and tried to model a different kind of question, it was too late. Conformity had interfered with thinking.

Guards vs. Prisoners

If you were too young to be recruited for Asch's study and/or you think those findings ancient history, perhaps you might have responded to an advertisement for male college students to participate in a two-week mock-prison experiment in the early 1970's. If so, you would have been extensively interviewed and tested to assure that you were more-or-less normal. Then you would have been randomly assigned to be either a guard or a prisoner. If you were a guard, you were randomly assigned to one of three eight-hour three-man shifts and were outfitted in appropriate uniform and night stick, which you were told was not to be used but was just for "show." If you were one of the twelve prisoners, you were unexpectedly "arrested" at your home by regular police officers who transported you to the make-shift jail in a 35' corridor in the psychology building at Stanford University. Upon arrival, you were stripped of your clothes, sprayed for lice and made to stand in the cell yard alone naked for a while. Then you were given a prisoner's uniform and a cell.

When all were there, the warden came to greet all prisoners with the standard speech of your lack of responsibility and citizenship in the real world, which the prison staff would teach you. He then read you the rules of the prison which, if followed along with the proper penitence for past misdeeds, would lead all to get along fine. Some of the rules follow:

1. Prisoners must remain silent during rest periods and meals and whenever they are outside the prison yard.
2. Prisoners must eat at all mealtimes and only at mealtimes.
8. Prisoners must call guards "Mr. Correctional Officer."
16. Failure to obey any of the rules is punishable.

Except for the admonition not to use physical punishment, the guards were given no

Anecdote 7.5

> ### More Prisoners and Guards
>
> From time to time there have been informal replications of the prisoner-guard study in high schools around the country. One of those that made the national press in 1983 was conducted by two Catholic high schools in Chicago (e.g., Buffalo News, Oct. 18, 1983).
>
> The weekend program, initiated to teach 95 participants about prisons and behavior, began with much levity but quickly deteriorated.
>
> > "It was all 'ha, ha' until we lined them (prisoners) up against the wall and said, "Take your clothes off!" said Mr. Blake, "The humiliation was just painted across their faces."
>
> The prisoners, segregated by gender, had to strip to their underwear in front of same-gender guards and turn over all of their belongings.
>
> In parallel with the Haney-Zimbardo study, but apparently unanticipated by the faculty, was the extent of "overacting by the guards," who insulted prisoners, flashed lights in their eyes in hourly bedchecks, took away communal meal-time privileges for such minor offenses as failing to say "Sir" or "ma'am," etc. If anyone talked back, they received solitary confinement. At least one student had to run the gauntlet of guards en route to solitary confinement.
>
> At least one "prisoner" escaped by climbing a ladder to the school roof ("I couldn't stay here another night," he said) and jumping down. Others attempted escape, one by jumping from a second story window. She was later cornered and recaptured when a passer-by, who noticed her prison garb, pointed her out to the searchers. She spent the rest of the weekend in solitary confinement.
>
>

other specific instructions, but were told only to carry out whatever activities were necessary to interact with the prisoners and staff members.

Haney and Zimbardo (1977), who conducted the study, described the results in the context of socialization of roles. Their results were classical examples of the ways institutions and environmental settings shape behavior into the stereotypical behavior patterns expected for the role. The guards gave directives and became physically and verbally abusive in the name of maintaining "law and order." Macho exercises of power by guards were respected and modeled by other guards. Prisoners, on the other hand, resented their treatment and sometimes rebelled. The guards taunted and harassed them more. The prisoners became angry, even enraged at each other when, for example, guards took privileges away from the group because of defiance by one. Eventually most of the prisoners became passive, initiating no activity, and reflecting symptoms of learned helplessness. One even had to be released on the second day because of stress.

In this experiment no one was told how to behave. Assumption of roles led to one social group reinforcing its own members for struggling against the other group. That increased

> **Box 7.1**
>
> ## More on Milgram's Obedience Study
>
> Milgram's (1963) experiment had some other interesting features and results. For example, Milgram asked 14 Yale seniors in psychology to predict how 100 subjects age 20–50 would respond when asked to administer shocks. The unanimous prediction was that only 0–3% would "obey" to the end and administer Very Strong Shocks.
>
> Regarding the belief that shocks were painful, the subjects rated the shocks they believed they were administering on a 14-point scale from "Not at all painful," the lowest rating, to "Extremely painful," the highest. Their modal response was the maximum 14, with the mean (average) being 13.42
>
> Subjects' emotional behavior was consistent with their belief that they were administering painful shocks. One sign of their tension was nervous fits of laughter shown by 14 of the subjects, with 3 of them having uncontrollable seizures of laughter. In the post-experimental debriefing these subjects were embarrassed by their laughter and took pains to point out they were not sadistic and did not enjoy administering the shocks.
>
> If I may be excused for a bit of black humor, Milgram's experiment was truly a case where the punisher could say to the victim, "This is going to hurt me more than it hurts you."

the other group's conformity to perceive the situation similarly, to become more cohesive as a group, and to resist the other group. In addition to the dynamics within a group, pressures from outside groups increase conformity. Ironically, in Haney and Zimbardo's words (1977, p. 219),

> Because they have been socialized to see each other exclusively as 'enemy,' guard and prisoner groups cannot appreciate the degree to which their individual plights are actually common ones.

Authority vs. Morality

Perhaps the most vivid experimental example of conforming behaviors occurred in a study by Milgram (1963), which was an attempt to understand the kind of obedience which allows crimes to be committed by people who were just "following orders," as occurred in such events as the holocaust. Had you been one of the paid subjects, you would have been told you were to help the experimenter administer a study of the effects of punishment on learning. Your job was to read a list of word pairs to another subject (a confederate of the experimenter), whose duty was to memorize them. The latter was taken to another room where he would be out of sight and strapped into what resembled an electric chair. Whenever the learner made an error, you were to administer a shock to him from a real shock-generator. After each error, the voltage of the shock was increased one level (from a low of 15 to a high of 450 volts). Unknown to you, the shock was not connected to the learner in the other room.

The learner, of course, made many errors and you were told by the cold, matter-of-fact experimenter to increase the level and administer the shock. The learner regularly screamed and, by 300 volts, pounded on the wall and then fell silent. The experimenter nevertheless told you to treat the silence as an error and press on. If you complained and asked to discontinue in the experiment, the stone-faced experimenter told you to please continue.

If the study does not sound sufficiently convincing to believe that the shocks were real, you should read Milgram's report. The subjects administering the shocks were not only convinced that they were hurting an innocent subject, but many were highly stressed themselves, muttering such phrases as "Oh, God, let's stop." And yet—and this is the frightening result—26 of 40 subjects showed continued obedience until the end.

As in conformity to other norms, yielding to pressure to obey can be reduced if the experimenter were not an authority figure (in this case he wore a white laboratory coat of a scientist or physician), or if he were not in the same room as the subject, or if the learner receiving the shocks were in closer proximity and visible to the subject.

While such research would not be permitted under the current strict guidelines for human research, it was then supported by grants from the National Science Foundation and Yale University. Its procedures and results are significant for helping us understand the subtle and not-so-subtle pressures we are under to conform. These studies also show how difficult it is to resist and remain independent of such pressures.

If there is good news from these studies, it is that not everyone succumbs to the pressure of malevolent authority. Thirty-five percent of Milgram's sample, for instance, were able to resist obeying the experimenter's orders because they felt the orders were wrong. But it would be a much too simplistic conclusion to draw from these studies that there are simply two kinds of people in this world—those who blindly obey and those who don't.[8] The impelling conclusion from these studies in my view is that pressures from our reference groups can be very powerful determiners of our behavior in given situations.[9] It is simply not a viable notion that evil is perpetrated by evil people and that good people are not perverted or sadistic. Good people can become sadistic and perpetrate evil when they are placed in a situation which expects, requires and reinforces otherwise unthinkable acts. One reason that this can occur is because the socialization process into accepting one's own unacceptable behavior occurs gradually ("and besides, everyone else is doing it!").

In fact, it is interesting to contemplate that the goal of most parents, teachers, ministers, etc. is to produce "good" children, meaning those who obey laws and orders. Military recruits, to take it a step further, have blind obedience to (sometimes ridiculous) orders "drilled" into them so that they will be willing and able to carry out unpleasant orders under the stress of battle conditions. Then, paradoxically, we expect these same "good" children and soldiers to resist evil orders from the same authorities they were trained to obey.

None of us is immune from such pressures, though some have learned how to assert our independence in ways that are self-protective and still supportive of the best interests of the group. It is also true that group pressure is not always subversive of the individual: sometimes it is clearly in the interests of the individual. In either case, we will better understand ourselves and the people with whom we interact if we can properly assess the group pressures under which we are all acting.

Norms and Classrooms

In one of my classroom observations in Japan in 1976, an interesting discussion occurred in an eighth grade girls classroom. It seems that a discipline situation had occurred: two of the girls had skipped classes early to meet boyfriends but told their parents they were in school. As a result, they had to stand in the teachers' room instead of going to class until the class decided that one class period should be set aside for class reflection on the problem.

Photo 7.3. Norm-building in Japan.

A student led the meeting (called "hansei kai"), with the teacher sitting to the side taking notes, but otherwise not commenting. The two "deviants" were in class to present their side of the issue and to comment on agreements. After a short presentation by the leader, the class broke up into five groups of 6 or 7 members each. After a few minutes, the large group was formed again and spokeswomen from the groups presented arguments. Popular views were greeted with spontaneous applause. Formation of small groups occurred twice more for a minute or two each time. The total time for the meeting was about 30 minutes, during which time the "deviants" presented their side, all arguments were heard, and an agreement was reached.

The observer was not privy to the solution reached; but that is not the point here. The situation is in itself interesting because it is an overt demonstration of group norms in operation. By having individual or small group views expressed, debated and eventually adopted by the larger reference group—in this case the class—we have the process of norm-building occurring before our eyes. *Norms, at least in classroom settings, have been defined as ". . . shared expectations or attitudes about what are appropriate school-related procedures and behaviors."* (Schmuck and Schmuck, 1983, p. 198).

The Japanese are justly famous for their attempts at reaching consensus in all parts of their society. Here we see one way they build a consensus, which in no uncertain terms informs all what the classroom norms are. It can build an esprit de corps for all the participants in the group, since each individual contributes to and is affected by the eventual agreement. It also applies direct group pressure on any "deviants" in the group to conform.

If Japanese groups are often more overt in their group processes, group pressures in western societies are just as real. Deviates from reference group norms can receive much pressure to conform, followed by outright rejection and hostile criticism if they do not conform. Of course, if there are several deviates who have been rejected from a group, they may now have a common enemy which can form the basis for a new group with its corresponding set of norms.

Tracking systems, undertaken with the best of good will by teachers and administrators, can also fall prey to this adversarial group norm problem. Like the guards and prisoners in the Zimbardo-Haney (1977) study, the students in the "fast lane" will develop shared expectations and behaviors that are different from those in the lower tracks. Life would be simple if all these groups could be kind to and tolerant of each other, but often that is not the case. It is never the case when one of the groups is given the label "buzzards," as described in the preface of this book.

If Teachers are Guards, What Are Students?

In Bel Kaufman's (1964), *Up the Down Staircase*, Miss Barrett permits a student to go to the lavatory during an examination. The student is returned by a livid Administrative

Assistant, McHabe (whom she calls "Admiral Ass") — livid because she had not followed the rules and let the student go without a hall proctor accompanying him. The student, in Miss Barrett's words,

> . . . has become a moral issue by which I stand or fall. The incident of the lavatory has brought into focus my values against McHabe's—everything I believe in as opposed to all that is petty, regimented and rote in the school system; all that degrades the dignity of my profession, and consequently, of my pupils; my desire to teach well, as opposed to bureaucracy, trivia and waste. (p. 270).

The Funky Winkerbean comic strip has continually portrayed a similar scene: Funky as a hall monitor with a machine gun. The illustration is only partly comic: most city schools have the doors locked, and any student walking the halls without a teacher had better be able to flash a hall pass. If school is run like a prison, how are the inmates—er, students — likely to behave? What role will teachers have to assume?

There is, of course, at least one good reason for locking school doors—to protect students and educators from neighborhood criminals. This is realistic judging from the signs outside saying "Drug-Free and Gun-Free School Zone" (and these are probably right down the road from signs which say "School-Free Drug and Gun Zone"). On the other hand, some of those same neighborhoods house hospitals. And when there is a crime problem in or around the hospital, are doctors and nurses required to monitor the halls and protect everyone, or do we hire security guards for such purposes?

More importantly, would doctors and nurses tolerate the "mission creep" which added guard duty to their roles? I think not. So it is an interesting question why teachers accept the role of guard, especially since it is totally incompatible with the roles of teacher/mentor/counselor/facilitator. And if required to act as guards by malevolent authority (as Milgram and Bel Kaufman might describe it), why do they succumb to such pressure and conform to this unnatural role? Would physicians? Nurses? Professors?

Classroom Groups

Sociometry and Interpersonal Relations

It may strike you that the previous section on groups and their conflicting norms paints a rather dismal picture for a teacher who wants to see both individual achievement and cooperation in the classroom. Looked at from a different perspective, however, perhaps it is not so dismal. Each student, like each teacher, wants to be considered a normal person, possibly better than average in some ways, but still a normal, not too deviant person. To be normal is to be like the others and also to be liked by the others.

Unfortunately, the number of friends and amount of respect people have are not equally or even randomly distributed. Rather, this *sociometric wealth* (the *sociodynamic law* as it is called by Moreno, 1953), is distributed much as economic wealth is distributed: a few are wealthy and many are poor. Likewise with friends: when students are asked to name the three classmates they like the most, a few students will be chosen as friends by many other children. Unfortunately, the least popular children are not just ignored or isolated, though that is often the case; they are also, in contrast to popular children, more likely to be frequently mentioned in a list of the three persons disliked most. To give an example, Bill will choose Harry as his most-liked classmate, while Harry will not mention Bill in any of his most-liked choices, and may even place Bill at the top of his personal least-liked list.

Research by Dilendik (1972) in two sixth grade racially integrated classrooms confirmed this basic pattern. In one of the classes none of the isolated students—those at the bottom of the sociometric ladder—chose their "best liked" people from within their group. All chose upward and, of these, only 19% were chosen reciprocally by their more popular peers. In contrast, of the popularity leaders 78% named friends from within that clique, with 71% reciprocity. The other 22% chose downward with reciprocity of liking returned at 100%. The data from the other class were similar.

This situation can be bad enough for the individuals involved. For the group, however, it can have other implications. In Moreno's words (1953, p. 705):

> . . . conflicts and tensions in the group rise in proportion with the increase of the sociodynamic effect, that is, with the increased polarity between the favored ones and the neglected ones. Conflicts and tensions in the group fall with the decrease of the sociodynamic effect, that is, with the reduction of the polarity between the favored ones and the neglected ones. This hypothesis has been brought to an empirical test and confirmed by many investigators.

No classroom is so cohesive that it has no cliques and 100% reciprocity of friendships. The social world in which we live is much too complex for that. Friendships and cliques are often in existence from previous years and they may carry over into a current classroom. Norms and values of one group may be quite different from those of another and, as we saw in the prisoners and guards study by Haney and Zimbardo (1977), members of one group may reinforce each other for giving the other group trouble. Moreover, there is a tendency to overgeneralize on the good points of the group of which you are a member as well as on the bad points of a separate group. Heider (1958) makes this perceptual principle a central part of the balance or homeostasis of an individual when he says,

> For instance, liking and admiring go together; the situation is unbalanced if a person likes someone he disrespects. In other words, the unit of the person tends to be uniformly positive or negative. This is known as the halo phenomenon. To conceive of a person as having positive and negative traits requires a more sophisticated point of view; it requires a differentiation of the representation of the person into subparts that are of unlike value. (p. 182)

Groups are often formed for the purpose of being different from others. Thus their norms will emphasize the similarities of their members and the differences between them and everyone else. Thus the "best sorority" at a college has the prettiest, brightest, most desirable women on campus as members (by their own definition) and tremendous group pressures are placed on the sorority sisters never to date men who are not fraternity members, but rather to date only "big men" from the most exclusive fraternities.

In these gestaltist tendencies to oversimplify our relationships with others, however, also lies a solution to the problem. To paraphrase an example of Heider's, where are you most likely to find a Kansan boasting about the Empire State Building?

a. in Topeka
b. in New York
c. in Tokyo
d. in Chicago

The obvious answer, Tokyo, implies that Kansans can overcome their regional competition with New Yorkers when they are representatives, not of Kansas, but of the USA. Similarly Democrats may vehemently criticize a Republican administration in Washington when discussing politics with other Democrats or Republicans; but they will temper their criticisms with praise when having such a discussion with a Communist party member.

Psychological theorists are not above these group dynamics games either. But the situation is not hopeless; we've already seen that people can view themselves as members of a small separatist group or of a larger group, inclusive of the smaller factions. Teachers can take advantage of this fact in planning their approach to the classroom, the topic to which we shall turn now.

Teachers and Groups

Teachers do not create in their classrooms the kinds of group dynamics we are discussing; rather they inherit them. Teachers nevertheless can facilitate group cohesiveness or contribute to factionalism by their reactions to the different individuals and groups in a classroom. Factionalism becomes a de facto part of classroom life when ability grouping is instituted. It is further encouraged when the groups are given "good" or "bad" labels, or when teachers treat the students differently on the basis of their group membership.

Beyond grouping, however, there is a more general point to be emphasized. Teachers model respect or disrespect for various students by what they say to them or about them in front of others. We have witnessed the kinds of "death at an early age" that Kozol (1967) described in classrooms—namely, children hearing teachers make derogatory statements about them within earshot of others. Aside from the direct devastation that such behavior has on the affected child, the teacher is additionally modeling how other students may behave toward that person. Moreover, if the object of the teacher's comments is a social isolate, it will further isolate the child. If the object of the criticism is a member of an alienated group, it will tend to further alienate the group to treat the teacher and those students who receive the teacher's favor as the enemy.

Fortunately few teachers are as insensitive as portrayed above; but all of us are prone to momentary lapses which may produce the same unwanted effects unintentionally. Good and Brophy (1978) provide an interesting example of this under the topic "teacher expectations." The teacher asks a complex question of the class, pauses, and then calls on Johnny Bright. Johnny remains silent, scratches his head, and wrinkles his brow, behaviors the teacher interprets as "working out the problem." When Johnny asks for the last part of the question to be repeated, the teacher happily obliges on the assumption that the Bright boy has the problem partially worked out, and then waits patiently for the answer. "If someone interrupted the teacher at this point to ask him what he was doing," say Good and Brophy (1978, p. 89), "he might respond that he was challenging the class to use creativity and logical thinking to solve problems!" If the teacher had called on Sammy Slow, on the other hand, the same silence, head-scratching and furrowed brow might be interpreted as further evidence of Sammy's being hopelessly lost again. After a short pause, the teacher may say, "Well Sammy?" to which Sammy may request to have the last part of the question repeated. But this might only serve to confirm the teacher's suspicion about Sammy and he might have the student sit down and call on someone else. In Good and Brophy's words (1978, p. 89), "If interrupted at this point and asked what he was doing, the teacher might respond that he was 'making it clear that the class is expected to pay close attention to the discussion, so that they can respond intelligently when questioned!"

Such subtleties of differential treatment are not lost on the students as individuals or as classroom subgroups.

Cooperation, Competition and Individualization

. . . in the first few hours of a game as played in the land of After-Africa both teams were engaged in a desperate attempt to establish . . . "a monotheistic lead." The ultimate ambition was to separate oneself from one's opponents by a single goal. In the first few minutes of a game therefore, attack was the imperative. But once the goal had been scored, the victorious team then shifted its entire strategy to defense. The commitment was a commitment against equalization. A small margin of superiority by one team over the other was supposed to be aesthetically more satisfying than a wider measure of separation.
But the defeated team had to attempt equalization whatever happened. If the defeated team succeeded in establishing parity with its opponents, both teams resumed attack as the strategy of action on the field. Both teams became once again engaged in the relentless pursuit of a 'monotheistic lead.' The lead was still monotheistic if one side had two goals to its credit and the other had one. But the totality of three goals was at a lower level of purity than the single match goal. (Mazrui, 1971, pp. 35-36).

The conception of a competition as a dedication to win without humiliating the opponents is not something with which most people grow up in the United Sates of America; perhaps nowhere, since the event Mazrui described occurred in African Heaven.[11] It is used to introduce this section because it may serve to induce a reconceptualization of competition. (See also chapter 13.)

Sport, of course, exists for the primary purpose of competition between individuals or groups (secondary purposes might be competition against oneself or physical fitness). But contrary to many of our aphorisms about the "dog eat dog world" we live in, each culture socializes its citizens to be cooperative for the most part. Competition is reserved for special occasions and then usually based on strict regulations or norms of fairness.

Schools, in contrast to sporting events, exist for the primary purposes of the improvement of individuals and of socializing those individuals to society's goals—a cooperative venture. Secondarily they have the goal of teaching people to compete better, but that is intended to be a consequence of the individual growth and within the cultural norms of cooperation. Few would dispute this and yet many of the teaching methods and events in classrooms appear designed to foster competition: grading on the curve, homogeneous groupings, and recitations based on the game "who knows the answer?"

One analysis of the problem suggests that we have not adequately attended to the student-student interactions in developing our teaching plans. As Johnson and Johnson (1975) introduced it, teachers must not only specify their instructional goals, but they must also specify the *goal structures*, defined as the type of interaction that will exist among students while working to attain the goals. Three types of goal structures cover the range of school situations—namely, cooperative, competitive and individualistic:

Cooperative Goal Structures: require that individual student behaviors are coordinated to achieve the educational goal; if one student in the group succeeds, all succeed.
Competitive Goal Structures: require that an individual student's success comes at the expense of the others; if one student succeeds, others cannot, at least not relative to the best.
Individualistic Goal Structures: require that students achieve goals without interaction with others whether the goals are the same or different for each individual; if one student succeeds, it has no bearing on another's success.

Modeling and Social Processes 229

Photo 7.4. Student teacher establishing cooperative teams.

Learning specific knowledge and skills is an individual process. Each person's nervous system, conditioning history, and manner of interacting guarantees that that is so. When one member of your group learns something, the learning does not transfer to the other members by osmosis. Teachers teach groups, but individuals learn. Having said that, however, does not imply that each individual in the group is independent from the others, even in individualized instruction. This chapter in particular, and this book in general, has presented evidence to the contrary: we are all interdependent, reciprocally determining each other's behavior and highly influenced by the groups of which we are members.

Thus it is difficult to disagree with the claim that there are some times in which individualized or competitive goal structures are desirable in class, but that "Beyond all doubt, cooperation should be the most frequently used goal structure" (Johnson and Johnson, 1975, p. 66). To decrease classroom anxieties, to encourage creativity, to bring social isolates into the mainstream of the classroom, to encourage friendships, to reduce the felt need for cheating, to encourage adoption of modeled standards, to reduce aggression and discipline problems, to encourage each other—all these and more require a cooperative classroom climate.

Specific research evidence on such claims will be presented in chapter 13, but it should be clear from the thrust of this chapter that these claims must be generally true. When people feel alone and against the group they are anxious and easily manipulable (e.g., the Asch studies). They are easily distractible and therefore less frequently on task. They have little opportunity to discuss ideas with peers, to clarify and elaborate what they have learned, in part because helping another student might be at their own expense, and thus their learning, retention, and transfer of training cannot help but suffer.

This does not make cooperative learning a panacea. It does not guarantee that students will not compete at times. Nor does it guarantee that learning and retention will be maximum, that all regardless of race or creed will be friends, and that there will be no discipline or motivation problems. What it does is allow more possibilities for these desirable outcomes. And the teacher, either explicitly or implicitly, sets the kind of goal structure that will exist in the classroom. Specific techniques for using cooperative learning in classrooms are described in chapter 13.

Anecdote 7.6

> **Turning a Competitive Situation into Cooperation**
>
> Everyday I heard the phrase, "I wanna be line leader! Please, can I be?" Just think of 45 three-year-olds charging at you. And honestly, does it matter? Surprisingly, it did to the ladies I work with and, therefore, to the children of our early childhood center.
>
> Since I couldn't abolish the idea, I needed to change the reasoning and format before I could live with it. The new and improved version is that the line is a train. The front, still the line leader, is the engine; the middle of the train the cargo; and the end the caboose. If all the children work together, the entire train will arrive at the destination, but if any portion of the train isn't doing its part, the train will fall apart.
>
> This makes all the difference. We have gone from pushing and hitting, crying and pouting to helping and sharing roles. The middle and end of the line, previously an undesirable location, is now desirable. It hasn't eliminated all the attention-seeking or competition, but it's a start.
>
> Amy Green
> Teacher

Modeling and Social Learning: Some Recommendations

It should be obvious by now that difficult problems such as racial integration and equality do not disappear simply by desegregating classrooms and busing poor black children to affluent white neighborhood schools. The racial attitudes of all can change in positive, accepting directions, but they do not just happen because the children are in the same classrooms. If, in fact, each separate racial group becomes cohesive but antagonistic to the other group, then the social experiment of busing can be a social disaster. Academically it will also likely be a failure since the higher achieving, but socially antagonistic students, are unlikely to be models the lower achievers will want to imitate. On the other hand, there is some evidence that integrating classrooms can bring about better academic performance by the minority group, but only when they are accepted as friends by the majority group (e.g., Lewis and St. John, 1974).

It is true that problems of racial, sexual, or other kinds of equality have political, legal and economic overtones in this society, and thus the schools cannot be held totally responsible for solving them. It is nonetheless equally true that schools—and more specifically teachers—do immensely affect student interactions and behaviors in classrooms. They do this by the academic standards they set for the class, by how they treat students in class, by how they allow students to treat one another, and by how they practice what they preach. To be more specific, let's review some of the major points of this chapter and infer some recommendations for classrooms.

1. Teachers, by virtue of their position of knowledge and authority in the classroom, can be powerful models for students. The students will likely learn to adopt the

teacher's standards in the level of performance required for self-reinforcement and will likely model the teacher's treatment of others (e.g., whether teacher's comments are kind, honest and constructive; or whether they are destructive or derogatory).

2. Teachers not only model social and emotional behaviors, but also model cognitive behaviors, such as logical thinking and problem-solving. Thus if teachers speak of encouraging creative thinking and problem-solving but ask only "Who knows, or what is, the answer?" they are modeling "answer-grabbing" (to use Holt's (1964) terminology). To be a model of process instead of only product, they must ask "How can we find the answer?" (e.g., Good and Brophy, 1978) and think aloud whenever possible for the students, as well as encourage it among the students.

3. If teachers want cooperative behaviors in classrooms, they cannot model competitive behaviors by rewarding one student at the expense of another. Thus grading on the curve is incompatible with cooperation. So is ridiculing a student's contribution, or calling on a student whom you suspect is unprepared to answer, and then moving to another student who appears to succeed at the first student's expense.

4. Teachers can reduce the sociometric distances in the group by reinforcing the natural peer group leaders (those who are liked by more isolated students) for modeling appropriate academic and social behaviors. Some of these natural leaders can also be peer tutors (with appropriate training) who may also help others increase their academic performance. This will also relieve the teacher from being the sole person in the classroom reinforcing goal-oriented behavior.

5. Teachers also model emotions and how they can be controlled. Honesty in expressing these emotions is important both for the teacher's own mental health and for the student observers. Thus if certain behaviors are making you angry, say "What you are doing is making me very angry. What can we both do to keep this situation from getting out of hand?" The feeling is thus expressed in a nondestructive way and the students observe a self-controlled, honest model of how that can be done without an aggressive confrontation.

6. Teachers and parents should recall that witnessing violence on television, or perhaps elsewhere, is unlikely to have a cathartic effect of "draining people of their aggressive energy" (to use the apt phrase of Berkowitz, 1962). Rather it may (1) teach techniques of aggression, (2) provide cues for arousing previously learned aggressive behaviors, and (3) affect an individual's cognitive justifications for aggression.

7. Aggressive acts—by children or adults—against the cause of someone's frustration can reduce hostile tension, but only if the other person does not counter-attack. In any case, the act of aggression, if repeated and practiced often enough to the exclusion of other ways of solving interpersonal conflicts, can become a dominant habit. An "aggressive personality" is being formed. As Berkowitz (1962, p. 256) proposed, ". . . frequent aggressive behavior can be regarded as arising from aggressive habits and that such habits may be strengthened by whatever rewards the attacker receives through injuring others." Adults, therefore, need to model and systematically to teach cooperative ways of resolving conflicts.

8. Because of the tendency to habituate to shocks—both physical and psychological—it is very easy over time to tolerate intolerable conditions and even come to accept them as natural or inevitable. This has led, as Senator Patrick Moynihan (1993/94, p. 12) put it, to our ". . . redefining deviancy so as to exempt much

conduct previously stigmatized, and also quietly raising the 'normal' level in categories where behavior is now abnormal by any earlier standard." Educators need to model and reinforce high standards of achievement, work ethic, decorum, and even artistic taste to combat habituation to the destructive, lewd, crude, and rude. If new generations rebel against these more traditional values, at least they have something to compare their new behavior with or rebel against.

9. Teachers may often be able to turn interpersonal conflicts, peer pressures, or group rivalries into instructional training exercises by encouraging role-reversals and honest evaluations of what is going on. This is not to say that teachers should step into each controversy. Many controversies, especially young children's, are short-lived and may actually be prolonged by adult attention. But in some cases students can learn to analyze their own and others' feelings and behaviors with a little help from role-playing and teacher behavior as a model.

10. It should be recognized that the roles that are thrust upon us are major determiners of our behaviors. If teachers are required to assume the roles of guards by, for example, checking hall passes or searching for weapons or drugs, then they will begin to treat their students as prisoners. If students consider themselves inmates in a prison—and many do—then we should expect them to act like prisoners, by resisting regulations and trying to escape, among other actions.

Practice Exercises

A. Practice Items

For the following five multiple-choice items, select the alternative choice which *best* answers the question. (Answers are in Note 11.)

1. If a model is seen being punished for a certain behavior, and an observer therefore suppresses the same behavior, we can say the observer was
   a. also being punished.
   b. receiving negative reinforcement.
   c. receiving vicarious emotional conditioning.
   d. being vicariously punished.

2. Three-year-old Barbie watches a horror movie in which a psychopathic character rips the legs from a dog. The character is later caught and punished. But a few days later, for no apparent reason, Barbie breaks the arms and legs off her doll. This provides an example of
   a. vicarious emotional conditioning.
   b. the response facilitation effect of modeling.
   c. the learning effect of modeling.
   d. the inhibitory effect of modeling.

3. According to the evidence in the text,
   a. reinforcement and punishment regulate the performance, more than the learning, of behaviors.
   b. behaviors must be practiced at least several times to be learned.
   c. direct reinforcement is more powerful than vicarious reinforcement.
   d. all of the above are true.

4. From the evidence presented in the text, self-control
   a. is an internalized behavioral control that occurs as a result of interacting with significant others.
   b. is unlikely to occur unless an authority is present to enforce it.
   c. is replaced in adolescence by peer pressures.
   d. is a stage of development that occurs by maturation with minimal input from the environment.

5. According to the evidence in this chapter, most persons
   a. will conform to group pressure under any circumstances.
   b. will resist conforming to group pressure as long as there is at least one other person resisting.
   c. will resist conforming to group pressure as long as at least a majority of those present are resisting.
   d. will resist conforming to group pressure under any circumstances.

For the following five items, fill in the blank with the word or words which best completes the sentence (Answers are in Note 11).

6. Shared expectations about what are correct behaviors or procedures are known as _____.
7. The type of interaction pattern existing among students who are working in teams or discussion groups to complete certain instructional objectives is known as a _____.
8. Facts presented which are contrary to one's beliefs are likely to produce _____ and are seldom, by themselves, convincing in changing attitudes and beliefs.
9. In any stable group of people a few will have many friends and admirers and the majority will have few friends and admirers. This is a statement of _____.
10. A person attaches a feeling to an object or situation through another person's experience, without ever being in that situation itself. The technical name for this kind of learning is _____.
11. _____ is defined as the process by which, through repeated exposure to something (e.g., noise or destructive behavior) a person comes to tolerate it.

B. For Cooperative Study (In or out of class):

1. In small groups, give some examples of real situations in which group pressures were placed on people to do inappropriate things and in which
   a. everyone conformed, or
   b. someone resisted.
   What seemed to make the difference?
   What were the outcomes?
2. Discuss a copycat suicide or crime that was recently in the news. How closely do the facts of this chapter conform to the facts of the case? What can be done to prevent such events?
3. Analyze the goal structures of the classes you are presently taking to determine if they are cooperative, competitive, individualistic, or some combination of those. How will you plan to use these ideas in your own classrooms?
4. In small groups, explore further the ten recommendations that conclude this chapter. Do you disagree with any? Why? Would you expand the list?
5. Have you ever seen examples in which teachers have (purposely or accidentally)
   a. modeled how to ridicule a social isolate?
   b. reinforced antagonism among rival cliques?
   c. modeled how to bring a social isolate into the mainstream?
   d. reinforced cooperation among rivals?

Share these examples with your colleagues and analyze them according to the principles in the chapter.

6. Discuss the Tom Sawyer incident in Anecdote 7.1. What do you think of the author's conclusion?

C. For More Information

1. View one or more of the following films:
    a. Obedience (about Milgram's study);
    b. The Bizarre Trial of the Pressured Peer (a film about high school peer pressure and how to cope with it; Research Press).

2. Read, and perhaps make a written or oral report on, one or more of the classical studies described in this chapter.

3. Analyze some television commercials or television evangelists to ascertain what techniques they are using to sell products or encourage donations.

4. With assistance from your instructor and proper approval from the appropriate human subjects review committee at your school and/or college, collect data on the sociodynamic law in a real classroom. That is, have each student name and rank his or her three "best liked" and three "least liked" persons in the class. Then plot the distribution of sociometric wealth.

5. Write a report on one or more of the following texts: Darryl J. Bem's *Beliefs, Attitudes and Human Affairs* (1970), Thomas L. Good and Jere E. Brophy's *Looking in Classrooms* (1978). David W. and Roger T. Johnson's *Learning Together and Alone* (1975), Vernon F. and Louis S. Jones' *Responsible Classroom Discipline* (1981), and Richard A. and Patricia A. Schmuck's *Group Processes in the Classroom* (1983).

CHAPTER

Study Questions

1. What is the book's definition of misbehavior?
2. Analyze a discipline problem in terms of the interaction between student and teacher. Whose behavior is being positively or negatively reinforced, extinguished or punished—and with what effect on the other?
3. Contrast the amount of unstructured free time for physical activity in Japanese, Chinese and American schools. What are the logical consequences of littering or vandalism in these schools?
4. What is meant by each of the following (reality therapy) concepts? Give examples.
    a. logical consequences
    b. accepting no excuses
    c. reality therapy needs
        (1) for love
        (2) for self-worth
    d. asking "what?" instead of "why?"
    e. ignoring past failures
    f. committing to a new behavior
5. What is meant by each of the following concerning rules?
    a. How many rules should there be?
    b. What are "reasonable rules?"
    c. How should teachers express their emotions when rules are broken? Give examples?
6. What are the effects of punishment in discipline situations?
7. Distinguish between each of the following in purpose, procedure and likely effects. Give examples.
    a. retribution and restitution
    b. physical restraint and corporal punishment
    c. time out and solitary confinement
8. What are characteristics of a good *contract*? How can contracts help develop self-control?
9. What is meant by each of the following aspects of conflict resolution?
    a. a win-win situation
    b. focus on process rather than outcome
    c. the cadre or peer mediation approach vs. the total student body or whole-school approach
    d. listening to and understanding the other's view of the dispute
10. What is meant by
    a. the relationship between curriculum decisions/teaching quality and discipline?
    b. the distinction between *spending* time and *investing* time?

EIGHT

Discipline: Learning Responsibility for Behavior

Introduction

If I ordered a general to fly from one flower to another like a butterfly, or to write a tragic drama or to change himself into a seabird, and if the general did not carry out the order that he had received, which one of us would be in the wrong?" the King demanded. "The general, or myself?"
"You," said the little prince firmly.
"Exactly. One must require from each one the duty which each one can perform," the King went on. "Accepted authority rests first of all on reason. If you ordered your people to go and throw themselves into the sea, they would rise up in revolution. I have the right to require obedience because my orders are reasonable."

(from the *Little Prince* by Antoine de Saint Exupery, 1971, p. 45).

From all that we have learned so far about (1) the interactions of emotional, motivational and cognitive processes within individuals; (2) the social interactions between people on all of these levels; and (3) the influences of groups and models on all of these social learnings, it should be clear that discipline problems are just special, and perhaps more complicated, cases of normal interactions among students and teachers. As such, we should be able to analyze some of the interaction patterns with the hope of discovering what conditions are maintaining the behaviors of each person involved. Thus, after a definition of misbehavior, this chapter will explore the social learning of some prototypical discipline problems, provide a cross-cultural perspective in which to view misbehaviors in schools, survey some of the analyses that others have made to prevent or solve discipline problems and suggest some viable, field-tested techniques for dealing with actual or potential discipline situations.

Definitions of Misbehavior

First, a definition is in order. *A discipline problem, a misbehavior, or a case of indiscipline* (I have always favored this British term) *shall be considered to be "any action taken where it is not wanted"* (following Gnagey, 1968, p. 5). This definition emphasizes the behavior itself and avoids questions of moral transgression, safety, courtesy, etc., which are often bound by culture, social class, or religion and which therefore lead to disagreement. For example, one teacher may find classroom talking to be objectionable and another may find the same level of noise to be a sign of contented and constructive activity. Who is to say what absolute standard is to be imposed on all classrooms or all teachers?

If a discipline problem is simply any action taken where it is not wanted, then such an action is like a weed: any plant growing where it is not wanted. A dandelion in a lawn is a weed to some homeowners, but so may be a rose in a wheatfield to a farmer. It depends on the context, the purpose, and the preferences of the person(s) responsible.

A second definition is more substantive. As Burden (1995, p. 15) phrased it, *"Misbehavior is any student behavior that is perceived by the student to compete with or threaten the academic actions at a particular moment."* This gets to the core of the issue—namely, disruption of instruction and/or other students' learning.

The teacher is, of course, central to the definition of misbehavior, though teachers operate in the larger context of school and community expectations and definitions. There is nothing in these definitions, however, that prevents the inclusion of students in the process of defining misbehavior. As we shall see, if students are to develop responsibility for their behavior and learn to resolve conflicts productively, then it will be profitable for teachers to learn how to include them in the processes of legislating and adjudicating the rules.

But make no mistake about it: schools are not democracies, or else students would vote on whether and when to come and what to study. Thus it is a teacher decision on how much control the teacher should maintain and how and how much it should be shared. Discipline techniques vary along this degree of control dimension (e.g., Burden, 1995) and there is probably no issue more important for new teachers than establishing their own philosophy regarding such control.

Discipline Situations: Interactions Gone Sour

However established, classroom rules serve to establish the context in which interactions occur. If a rule has been established of no talking unless called upon by the teacher, then any student talking is likely to be viewed as an annoyance—at least by the teacher. Of course, students may find reasons to talk anyway: to make fun of the teacher who is writing at the board, to get a laugh out of another student, to ask for an interpretation of what was said, or for many other reasons. When the talking first occurs, it may be diagrammed as follows for teacher and student, where arrows show the sequence of events and boxes portray completed sequences of operant behavior.

(1a)

In the presence of the classroom rules and other students the student should not talk. But he does anyway and his talking serves as an aversive stimulus for the teacher.

The teacher angrily acts to correct the situation by yelling at the student, which has the effect of punishing the student, as follows:

(1b)

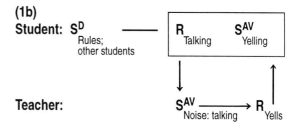

Now the effect of a moderately aversive punishment like yelling is usually to suppress the behavior, so the student immediately stops talking. As we know, however, punishments of this small magnitude do not serve to eliminate the behavior forever; rather, they suppress the behavior only for a short while in the presence of the punisher. This immediate suppression, nevertheless, has an effect on the teacher, diagrammed as follows:

(1c)

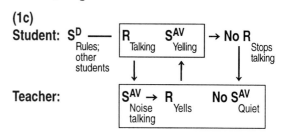

This is a classic case of negative reinforcement (i.e., escape) on the teacher's part. That is, the teacher finds that yelling removes the aversive stimulus, as aspirin removes a headache or pulling a plug removes shock. The student is negatively reinforcing the teacher for yelling.

What we have in this mutual interaction, then, is the teacher punishing the student, while the student is negatively reinforcing the teacher. The punishment has no long-term effect on the student. The negative reinforcement, on the other hand, has a great effect on the teacher: the frequency of yelling in similar situations is likely to increase.

At first the student would not plan this effect; nor would the teacher. But if it continues and becomes a habitual pattern, the teacher is likely to be yelling more and enjoying it less. In fact, it won't be too long until the students notice how emotionally upset the teacher becomes (and how much entertainment value that can hold, especially if they are not interested in, or prepared for, class) and begin to plan how they will get the teacher angry each day. When the situation reaches this sorry state, the teacher has lost any semblance of control over the class.

Consider the example mentioned earlier (chapter 6) about the student thrown out of math class, which he hates. Chronic discipline cases can be a thorn in the side of a teacher. Another way of saying that is that they are aversive stimuli. But the class or the teacher is likewise an aversive stimulus to the student. Diagrammed, it looks like this:

(2a)
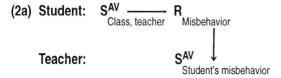

There is only so much teachers can take, so after the final straw is dumped on them, they send the student out of class (to go to the principal or stand in the hall). This has the immediate effect of escaping from the aversive stimulus for the student, providing negative reinforcement (like escaping a fire). He is likely to behave that way again if he wants to escape the class. Extending the diagram, it appears as follows:

(2b)
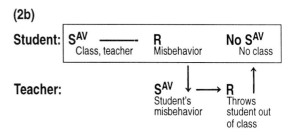

The effect is not only on the student, however, because as the student escapes the class, he removes himself from the teacher—another instance of negative reinforcement for the teacher.

(2c)
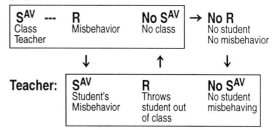

This is a classic case of mutual interaction based on negative reinforcement. It is very destructive of any potential for teaching or relating, but it is nevertheless a very strong pattern of interaction since each person is reinforcing the other. The student is being conditioned to misbehave in the presence of the teacher and the teacher is being conditioned to do something to get rid of the student.

There may, in fact, be more going on than this. Often a student who is sent out of class, in addition to escaping the teacher, receives positive reinforcement in the form of praise from his peers or attention from the principal (recall that the principal is unlikely to have

Cartoon 8.1

any really effective punishment at his disposal). If this is the case, there is a kind of double reinforcement for the student.

However the interaction is diagrammed, it is clear that this type of interaction develops into an ever-widening spiral of reciprocal determinism which degenerates rapidly. To develop a positive teacher-student relationship requires that this interaction pattern be interrupted in some way. In an Adlerian approach to this sort of problem, Dreikurs (1968, p. 47) analyzed this type of interaction in the following way.

It requires alertness not to succumb to the child's goals when he expresses them through disturbing or inadequate behavior. Yet if the teacher falls for the child's provocation, she plays into his hands and fortifies his belief that his methods are effective. When in doubt about a child's goal the teacher can find a helpful guide in watching her own reaction to his behavior. It is good policy not to do what the child expects; this means not to follow one's first impulse, but to do the opposite. Such a procedure is particularly helpful if a teacher does not know what to do. Then she can simply watch herself and see what she would first be inclined to do—and do something else.

Dreikurs makes it a major principle of his approach to discipline that the teacher must be sensitive to his or her own bodily responses to the interaction. The teacher verifies the child's goals in part by observing the teacher's own affective behaviors, both operant and respondent. What the teacher feels inclined to do, "almost with impulsive coercion," is the behavior the student would like as a consequence of the misbehavior. If the teacher feels annoyed and feels inclined to scold or coax, the child is probably seeking attention. If the teacher feels challenged or threatened and feels like authority must be invoked, then student and teacher are probably in some kind of power contest. If the feeling is one of "I don't know what to do with you," the student is probably trying to get the teacher off his back by behaving as though he has no ability or willingness to do the tasks assigned. For these reasons Dreikurs concludes (p. 45) that,

It is of great importance that the teacher learn to observe her own emotional response to the child's disturbing behavior. Not only does such observation provide her with a training in understanding the child's goal, but it is an

Anecdote 8.1

The "I Dunno" Syndrome

The following situation was experienced by a teacher during her student teaching experience:

The first example of negative reinforcement that hit home with me was the "I dunno" syndrome. I ran into this situation my first week of student teaching. My cooperating teacher had warned me that his first-period ninth-grade math class was very frustrating because they were so quiet they would hardly answer, even when called upon. They would usually answer with, "I dunno" or give such an obviously wrong answer I would wonder what they were up to. My cooperating teacher had told me that he had almost given up on even trying to get them involved because it was so frustrating.

When I took over, one of my objectives was to get the students more involved. Not only by calling on them and having them answer, but by also getting them to volunteer some answers, or even asking some questions. I could not understand why they were so resistant to getting involved. For the first couple of days, I would call on a couple of students, they would shrug, and I would end up just giving them the answer that I was looking for. This was also when I realized how much patience is needed in the classroom. I finally realized that the students were getting exactly what they had wanted, the teacher not calling on them anymore.

Finally, I figured out that the students were just playing a "game" with the teacher: "If I do not answer or if I give a stupid answer then the teacher will just let me be and I won't have to deal with math any more". The next day I decided that that was going to change. I called on the "I dunno" students and did not leave them until they were able to answer one of my questions. If they could not answer my first question, I would give them a simpler question, if they did not answer that one, I made an even simpler one, and so on until the student could not help but answer correctly. I did not leave that student until he/she was able to answer at least some part of the question correctly. After doing this to a couple of students, the rest of the class began to realize that they could not avoid math any more by responding "I dunno" or acting stupid just to get out of doing something. I still wonder sometimes if the students do this subconsciously or consciously. If they were taking that much time to avoid math, I wonder what would happen if they put the same amount of effort into doing math.

Nancy A. Holdsworth
Teacher

---

indispensible prerequisite for a more adequate approach to the child. For as long as the teacher gives in to her impulsive reaction, unaware of its meaning, she will fortify the child's mistaken goal instead of correcting it.

The previous two discipline examples are of the acting out variety. A common problem, especially for elementary teachers, is the case of the student who does his work, but too quickly and, almost invariably, inaccurately. There may be several complex factors operating here, and one of them may be that assignments have come to produce conditioned emotional responses. If this is plausible, then whenever and however the respondent conditioning occurred, it is reasonable to expect that assignments (math ditto sheets, tests, writing assignments) are conditioned stimuli. That is,

(3a) $\underset{\text{Assignment}}{\text{CS}} \longrightarrow \underset{\text{Emotional Response: Anxiety}}{\text{CR}}$

On the operant level that same assignment may be an aversive stimulus and lead to any behavior that reduces the anxiety (an interpretation originally suggested by Mowrer, 1960), in this case, escape or avoidance. If avoidance is precluded—after all, there are only a few excuses for missing school or skipping class without getting into big trouble—then escape is all that is left. One way of escaping is to do the work, but quickly to get it over with. In symbolic form, the two levels of behavior interact as follows:

(3b)
Respondent Level:

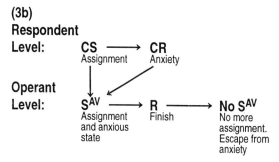

Operant Level:

Photo 8.1. Students cleaning a Japanese school at the end of the day.

To solve a problem like this probably requires much shorter assignments, with an emphasis on correct behavior, not fast behavior. But if this escape condition really exists, it is unlikely that simply being correct will act as a positive reinforcement for completing the behavior (this was one of the myths of programmed instruction!). To complicate matters further, if there is anxiety attached to such assignments, then direct intervention may be in order for that problem. For instance, relaxation training may be helpful: the teacher can work with the child to do deep breathing exercises,

or to take a short break from the assignment to tense and relax muscles at his or her seat, then to return to the assignment (see chapter 5 for other suggestions).

As these examples show, often what seems to be a misbehavior is a complex interaction between person and environment, or between levels of behavior within a person. The teacher's own behavior and feelings play a large role in discipline incidents because teachers are as much controlled as they control (see anecdote 8.1 for another example). Nevertheless, teachers are responsible for the classroom and must remove themselves from the fray at times to interrupt negative interaction patterns or to recognize that there are often anxious students beneath those cases of indiscipline.

A Cross-Cultural Perspective

One of the wonders of the educational world is what happens at the end of the school day in many of the classrooms of Japan.[1] When the last lesson has been completed, one

Anecdote 8.2

> ## Memories of School Cleaning in Japan
>
> In Japan school cleaning is regarded as one of the most essential homeroom activities. I remember cleaning classrooms, windows, floors, stairs, toilets and gardens from corner to corner under the supervision of the teacher. This activity was held for fifteen minutes every day and forty minutes once a month. The teacher had to be involved in it. This presented the opportunity to communicate between the teacher and the student or among students themselves.
>
> On winter days I had a hard time dipping and squeezing a floor cloth into cold water, putting up with the chilblain. Students were divided into several groups according to their cleaning position. A leader was appointed to take responsibility of the group. After cleaning, we had a short meeting standing in line, while our work was checked.
>
> What was the value of this? Though I was an unwilling participant at times, I believe school cleaning helps students develop self-discipline, etiquette and manners, in addition to strengthening communication and cooperation in the classroom. It also helps students recognize the value of labor in the Buddhist sense, which is probably why countries with a great Buddist heritage require it of students and other countries do not—namely, that cleaning not only improves the environment, but it cleans the mind. Thus monks use cleaning as part of their self-discipline training.
>
>
>
> Yukiko Taki

team of students move the desks and chairs, and clean the classroom from top to bottom. They wash the blackboards, wash the floors, realign the desks, and then rearrange everything to be ready for the next day. Meanwhile other teams of students wash the hallways, stairs, toilets, and other common areas.

An American visitor, after recovering from the initial shock, may have had several reactions. One negative reaction might have been "Aren't there any child labor laws in Japan?" Another, more positive, reaction: "Gee, they must save a lot of money on janitorial staff." After some reflection a quite different reaction may have emerged: "Students are unlikely to write on the walls, litter or otherwise vandalize their school if they are responsible for cleaning and repairing it later the same day. Ingenious, those Japanese."

What about the rest of the school day? In some ways it was just as remarkable. Before school, students could be seen milling around the school building, talking or playing sports or games. Particularly in the elementary schools, the children were likely to be engaging in a game of dodge ball or the ubiquitous jump rope games they play. When the bell rang, all ran—they seldom walked—in total disarray to their classrooms to take their seats. A few minutes later their teachers entered and signaled to the class leader to call the 30–40 students to attention. The leader then said something to the effect that, "We are all ready for the lesson, Sensei,"[2] This was followed by "Oneigaishimasu" or "Hajimemasho" ("let's begin") and "Rei" the command for all to bow to the sensei and sensei to them. Then classes (or homeroom activities) began.

When the bell rang to signal the end of the class period, perhaps 40 minutes later, the teacher again nodded to the class leader who called all to attention, thanked the teacher for the lesson, and initiated the bowing. Class was then dismissed for ten or fifteen minutes and all hell broke loose. Children grabbed their sports or play equipment and ran outside, or they stayed inside and played musical instruments, talked, or whatever. The teachers meanwhile took their own break or talked with individual children. They did not monitor halls or playground activities, at least not in any active way. When the bell rang, the whole process repeated itself.

Lunch was a similarly interesting experience, with lunches served in classrooms by students (often draped in white coats and surgical face masks). The teacher ate with the students. After all had eaten and cleaned up the food and dishes, which might have taken 30 minutes, the remainder of the lunch break (30–45 min.) was available for more free activities.

Chinese schools had many similarities to what has been described in Japan. There classes were even larger, in the 40–50 range. Each class began with a formal greeting from the teacher, standing and bowing. This was followed by the lesson. When the bell rang after 40 minutes or so, again students ran everywhere to play games or sports (in China table tennis, basketball, and a different kind of rope game are popular activities). When the next bell rang after 10–15 minutes, the students scrambled back to class to repeat the sequence. In addition to these regular interclass interludes, exercise periods were scheduled twice a day, once in the morning and again in the afternoon. These were held in the playground/sportsfield with the entire school, teachers included, in attendance. Then to the cadence of a recorded voice and background music, calisthenics and eye exercises were done for ten to fifteen minutes. (Such exercise periods were also common in factories and other institutions in China.) At

Photo 8.2. Eye exercises in China.

the end of the day student clean-up crews cleaned the building.

Contrast the above Japanese and Chinese school routines with a current typically American school routine. Students sit on a bus on their way to school, get off the bus and are expected to go fairly directly—quietly and without running—to their classrooms. When they arrive they must sit at their desks and be silent or talk quietly in approved ways. Between classes they may have 3–5 minutes during which (if they change classes) they must *walk* relatively quietly until the process repeats at the next class. At lunch time they must walk to the cafeteria, supervised by teachers or others, stand in line quietly, and sit at their (often) prescribed place at the table until dismissed, often to return to the classroom within 30–40 minutes to begin the afternoon session of more sitting.

In which culture do you think the diagnosis of hyperactivity has reached almost epidemic proportions? In which culture is there an all-day school rule against running? against play? against physical activity? In which culture is school vandalism rampant? In which culture is "teacher burnout" a major concern?

Granted there are other reasons for the differences between Oriental and American discipline problems than the ones just presented, such as differences in respect for teachers, involvement of the parents (in fact, the extended family and even the police) in the schools, and totally different political and economic policies for education. In addition, Chinese teachers at the secondary level teach only two or three classes per day six days a week, although their class sizes are close to 50. This is only half the class periods most American teachers must handle in a day, though their class sizes are likely to be considerably smaller and they have Saturdays off.

Nevertheless, we have seen that if you randomly assign people to be prisoners or guards (Haney and Zimbardo, 1977), they assume their roles. And compared to Japanese and Chinese schools, American schools have many unnatural rules for children and adolescents against physical activity. Moreover, we have assigned our teachers the role of policing those unnatural rules. And as we learned from *The Little Prince* in the opening quote, "I have the right to require obedience because my orders are reasonable." But if the orders are not reasonable, can we expect them to be obeyed? If school is perceived as a jail and teachers as guards, will not students adopt the norms and behaviors of prisoners? If students do not have to repair or clean up what they destroy or make dirty, and in fact adults (parents and taxpayers) make reparations for them, what consequences are controlling their behaviors?

The Scope of the Problem

Sometimes one can see one's own culture best by visiting another. This vicarious excursion to other cultures may help us understand why discipline continues to raise such problems in American schools and suggest some of the issues that must be faced if these problems are to be solved. But what is the magnitude of the discipline problems American schools face?

Problems prominently mentioned in reviews are truancy, lateness to class, profanity, fighting, disruption, drugs and alcohol, violence, vandalism, assaults on students and teachers, rape and robbery (e.g., Feldhusen, 1978). Interestingly, the severity of the problem is in the eye of the beholder. Teachers, administrators, students and parents are likely to perceive different problems as those of prime importance. Predictably they would be those that most directly affected their own lives (e.g., absenteeism would be of much concern to teachers, vandalism to administrators, and robbery or fighting to students, with some overlap, of course). All would probably agree that there is a problem. Certainly many polls echo the concern that we hear directly from teachers that discipline is their number one problem, though few would go as far as DeCecco and Richards (1975) who speak of "civil war in the high schools."

In historical perspective it is possible to see that discipline was of equal concern to teachers around the turn of the century. Doyle (1978) surveyed recent and 1890-era educational literature and found many problems common to the list above. However, he also pointed out that in that age (a) less than 50% of the total school-age population enrolled in schools; (b) anywhere from 25–50% of those enrolled were absent for substantial portions of the year; (c) enrollment was highest in the first four grades, with fewer than 40% of those who finished eighth grade going to high school and only 10% of those graduated; and (d) the poorest of society were most likely to be truant.

Compulsory attendance laws, designed to bring universal literacy and accessibility to the American dream, ironically also took crime off the streets and brought it into the schools. This may have been done somewhat consciously since Americans often expect the schools to solve broader social problems. Thus "incorrigibles," who were dealt with by the police before universal education, became the province of school personnel once education became the primary occupation of youth. Doyle (1978) concluded that, in the aggregate, youth are no worse than they have ever been. However, the venue has changed: violent and criminal behaviors that occurred in the streets now occur also in the corridors and classrooms.

What has changed since Doyle's review is the availability of automatic weapons and the illicit drug trade. The President of the American Federation of Teachers, Albert Shanker (1995) described the current problem as one

Photo 8.3. So many attention-seekers, so little time.

> . . . of extreme danger, where we are dealing with violence or drugs in the schools. Often the schools living with these threats are at a loss about . . . the guns, knives, and drugs coming into their schools. They say they've tried everything they can think of and nothing helps. (p. 8)

A second problem is disruption, which though not life-threatening is "deadly to learning." Shanker suggests that disruption is at least as serious because we seem to have developed a tolerance for it:

> Occasionally, kids who are violent are suspended or removed for periods of time, but little ever happens to kids who are "only" disorderly. (p. 10)

In fact, as Shanker (1995) argues (see also Johnson & Immerwahr, 1994/95, Moynihan, 1994/95; Shanker, 1994/95; Toby, 1993/94) we have been too eager to absolve the disruptive child and blame society instead in a "Menendez brothers mentality: 'We had a right to murder our parents because they gave us too much money and we resented it'" (p. 12).

If the perception is even partly true that violence and disorder are rampant in many public schools, then something must be done. Cognitive learning may only be possible once other threats and disruptions are removed. Safety takes precedence over learning, self-esteem, self-improvement and other motives for self-actualization (Maslow, 1954).

If law and order is needed—the so-called "zero tolerance" policy—to make a school safe, then I suppose that is where we must start. But this is a job for law enforcement officers: violence and drug sales, after all, are crimes not just classroom interruptions. Besides, as noted in the last chapter, there are major difficulties of assigning teachers the role of guards—searching lockers, apprehending drug dealers, disarming threatening people— even if the teachers were skilled enough to carry out this role (which few are).

What educators *can* do, however, is make students responsible for their own behavior as well as teach—and practice—more acceptable, pro-social solutions to conflicts. Thus we turn to the following crucial issues: logical consequences and restitution, reality therapy, and conflict resolution.

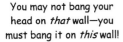

Cartoon 8.2

Logical Consequences and Reality Therapy

Case 1. Psychotherapist to patient who has delusions of being Adolf Hitler: "I've been told you have experience handling wall paper."
Patient (taken aback): "Yes."
Therapist: "Good, we're decorating the dayroom and need experienced help."
Case 2. Psychotherapist to patient who has delusions of being Jesus Christ: 'I've heard you're quite a good carpenter."
Patient: "Yes."
Therapist: "Good, then you won't mind building a bookcase for me."

Aside from the productive labor involved in assigning the above psychiatric patients to useful jobs, the therapist was making the patients accept the logical consequences of their behavior, albeit unexpected consequences.[3] The cartoon provides another example.

As Dreikurs (1968) explained, *natural consequences*, which I shall call *logical consequences*, emphasize the power of mother nature or the social order, not the power of a particular authority. The teacher simply makes the students responsible for their behaviors, both verbal and physical. For example, a student was constantly getting out of his seat, leaning on his desk in a half-standing position in such a way as to bother the teacher. Rather than reprimand the child, the teacher asked whether he would prefer to sit or stand while working at the desk. He said he preferred to stand, whereupon the teacher said, "Then the seat would no longer be needed," and removed it from the room. The next day the teacher asked his preference again and he chose to sit. According to Dreikurs (1968, p. 103) this solved the problem.

Glasser (1965) gave a similar example, all too well recognizable by parents. His five-year-old was asked whether he wanted to bathe in the regular bathtub, which was full and ready for him. He said, "No," preferring to assert his independence and bathe in his own tub. At that point his ten-year-old sister took over the ready and waiting water. Little brother immediately became incensed, wanted to take the big tub. Glasser bodily picked up his "fifty pounds of tantrum" and placed him in his own tub. After the tantrum was spent and all was quiet, the psychiatrist Glasser said to him (1965, pp. 17–18): " 'Let me give you some good advice. Do you know what advice is?' He did, so I told him, 'Never say no when you mean yes.' "

Glasser's advice is sound for all ages. Responsibility is learned by accepting—sometimes suffering—the consequences of our choices. Unfortunately parents and teachers often want to spare children the negative consequences of their own behaviors. Many would give in to the child's tantrum and let him take his bath in the big tub despite his earlier negativism. But what they would be teaching, if giving in to the child's tantrum were a frequent occurrence, would be (1) that what you say doesn't matter very much, since you can always reverse yourself; and (2) that tantrums get you what you want.

Glasser's behavior as a parent, at least in the above instance, is true to his advice to other parents, teachers and psychotherapists. He calls his method *Reality Therapy* (1965) because it emphasizes the client's own behavior and its consequences in the here and now. Glasser believes that all psychiatric patients and chronic discipline problems have a common characteristic—namely, that they deny the reality of the world around them and the part they play in making their world. Their own behavior is not just willful self-destruction or wanton aggressiveness, however. Rather it derives from unsuccessful efforts to fulfill their needs.

In Glasser's view there are only *two basic human needs: the need for love* (to love and to be loved) *and the need for self-worth* (to feel worthwhile to ourselves and others). The differences between humans, then, are conceived not as differences in our needs, but differences in our ability to fulfill those needs. When we have someone who cares about us and we about them, then the love need is satisfied. But we must also behave at a high standard (in terms of competence and values), according to Glasser, or we will not fulfill our need to be worthwhile.

In applying his ideas to classrooms, Glasser suggested that the two needs for love and self-worth are really so intertwined as to be inseparable, being reducible to what we usually call *identity*: "the belief that we are someone in distinction to others, and that the someone is important and worthwhile" (1969, p. 14). Then love, which in schools is really social responsibility or the golden rule, and self-worth become two pathways to an identity. Self-worth in school means academic success. A student who does not achieve success in school must find it elsewhere, possibly through withdrawal, through delinquency, or power games.

As described to this point, Glasser's ideas should sound like variations on Erikson's and Maslow's theories, as well as what is known about emotions, motivation and social learning in general. But Glasser's work provides a fitting framework for dealing with these concepts in a discipline chapter because he takes an additional, practical step—namely, *accepting no excuses*. No matter what terrible conditions children grew up under, from poverty to broken homes, this does not excuse unsuccessful behavior. The schools must help the children learn successful, responsible behavior.

In helping children, we must work to make them understand that *they are responsible* for fulfilling their needs, for behaving so that they can gain a successful identity. No one can do it for them. If they continue to choose pathways

Anecdote 8.3

Excuses, Excuses!

Surviving a divorce, never easy, affected the two late-elementary school boys of one family quite differently, at least in regard to school work. The older became more and more rebellious, including refusing to do his homework and turning in sloppy work when he did do it. The problem became even worse in secondary school. The younger seemed to use school as perhaps his one place of refuge, being meticulous and excelling in his schoolwork.

The interesting thing about this was the teachers' reactions. When speaking of the scholastic difficulties of the older boy, his teachers used variations of the excuse, "Well, what do you expect? He's from a broken home." When speaking of the scholastic achievements of the younger boy, however, teachers never said, "Well, what do you expect? He's from a broken home."

You can't have it both ways, which of course is Glasser's point about accepting no excuses.

that lead to failure, that diminish their self-worth, that are without love, they will continue to suffer and continue to react with delinquency or withdrawal (Glasser, 1969, p. 16).

In a reality therapy approach, then, there is little interest in the client's past history, family background, or the reasons for the unsuccessful behavior. This is not because they have not had an influence, but because dwelling on them—particularly while the misbehavior is occurring—will not help solve the child's problem. The therapist *does not ask why* the behavior is occurring. The question, rather, is *what*. What are you doing? How is that helping you satisfy your needs? This focuses the question on the behavior in relation to the person's goals. Focusing on why, in contrast, usually leads people to find excuses for the behavior (e.g., "He made me do it," or "I was bored," "The teacher's a jerk," etc.). Being in touch with reality means accepting no excuses for a failure—just commit yourself to a new, better behavior and try again.

If the responsibility of students is to make a value judgement about their inappropriate, unsuccessful behaviors and commit to new, better behaviors, then school personnel have a parallel responsibility of not holding a student's past negative behaviors against them. (see anecdote 8.3). The title of Glasser's book, *Schools Without Failure* (1969, p. 20) emphasizes that point as follows:

> *The only worthwhile information . . . to be gleaned from the past concerns the child's successes; this knowledge can be used to help him in the present. The past of people who fail is filled with failures. It is useless to work with failure because the teacher (or the therapist) and the child become deeply involved with failure . . . By ignoring the past failures, we encourage the child to change his present behavior.*

Specific Recommendations Based on Reality Therapy

Consistent with his approach for dealing with unsuccessful behaviors, Glasser (1977) recommended ten steps for teachers to follow in solving discipline problems. In a very important sense these steps are really changes in teacher behaviors. The steps teachers should follow are these.

1. Consider a specific child with whom you are having a difficult problem and make a list of what you do when the child disrupts. Don't ask "why," just ask "what" do I do?
2. Consider each behavior on the list and ask "Is this technique working?" It is likely that it isn't or you would not be worrying about the problem. (If you're not sure, you may want to do a social learning analysis as suggested earlier in this chapter). Resolve to stop responding in the ineffective ways.
3. Commit yourself to making the student's life better in class, being warmer, finding appropriate behaviors to reinforce, and special things for the student to do that can show his/her self-worth. Whether or not this makes an immediate change in the student's behavior, which is unlikely, resolve to continue this behavior for the long-term.
4. When problems arise, as they inevitably will, do not behave in ways which you've shown don't work (steps 1 and 2). Instead, recall your newly developing relationship with the student (step 3) and ask "What are you doing?" If the student responds by blaming someone else, press on in a matter-of-fact manner until the answer includes a statement of the actual behavior, at which time simply ask that the student stop it. Recognition of the problem by the student is often sufficient to engage self-control and the problem may disappear. This is especially true of a student with whom the teacher has a good relationship.
5. If the problem persists, follow the question "What are you doing?" with "Is it against the rules?" and then with "What should you be doing?" (Glasser, 1977, p. 62) The matter-of-fact manner of the teacher should convey warmth and helpfulness, but also firmness.
6. If the problem still persists, again ask "What are you doing? and "Is it against the rules?" but then tell the student that we need a plan to work out this problem. The student must come up with the plan of positive action that includes specific behaviors over a short time period. Resolving never to forget my homework again, for example, is not specific, not positive and unrealistic (never is a long, long time). Resolving to do my homework as soon as I get home and then placing it at the door of the house for the next three days is specific, positive and short-term. Part of the plan is a logical consequence of what should happen if the student violates the rule again. This plan for direct positive action and the consequences of not fulfilling the plan constitutes a *contract* between teacher and student. No excuses can be accepted for not fulfilling the contract. The students must suffer the consequences they agreed to and must recommit to a new plan. Note that the teacher does not "punish" the student—just enforces the contract.

For almost all problems, steps 1-6 will provide an adequate solution. For severe and chronic disruptions additional steps may be needed. Glasser recommends the following:

7. You may need to have an in-class suspension, or isolation of the student from the rest of the ongoing activities. This "time out" tells the affected students that they have not responsibly carried out the contract and may therefore not participate in class until they have devised a totally new

plan to which teacher and student can agree. When the new contract is approved, the student can rejoin the class.
8. If recommitment in the class does not work, in-school suspension is the next step with the plan being made by the student with the principal, psychologist, or other school personnel. As soon as the new plan is developed, the student is readmitted to class.
9. Students who take recommitment plans too lightly, who refuse to draw up a plan, or who are otherwise totally out of control must be suspended to go home with their parents for the rest of the day. But tomorrow is another day and they may return with a plan.
10. Students who cannot learn to be responsible for successfully meeting their needs in these ways (Steps 7–9) may have to be barred from attending school or referred to other agencies until at that level commitment to a whole new contract can be made.

Reality Therapy and Social Learning

Glasser's system has become quite popular through his books, films and articles (e.g., Glasser, 1986; 1992).[4] Apparently many schools have adopted many of his ideas. In this section I will further analyze his suggestions in light of other principles in this book and other methods of solving discipline problems.

Reasonable Rules, Responsibility and Reinforcement

Glasser's first steps ask teachers to deal with defining a real problem in light of the classroom rules and the ultimate goals. If there are too many or unreasonable rules, then there will be much conflict. If the rules are few and reasonable, then students and teacher will have fewer conflicts by definition. While students who break rules may be technically in the wrong, teacher reactions set the stage for the long-term relationship. Glasser's advice in step 3, therefore, is to commit to making the student's life better tomorrow. Though teachers seldom start a discipline problem, they have the power to defuse it, maintain it or aggravate it by their reactions. Through their reactions they also model the actual contingencies of reinforcements and punishment in the classroom as well as the norms and standards for treating others. Perhaps more importantly, they have the capability by their reactions of helping students get through minor problems or see their problems spiral into larger crisis.

For example, when a student is late, some teachers might say, "Why are you always late? Why can't you get here on time like everyone else?" A more productive response might be, "We're on page 256." Of course, if this is a chronic problem, then it may be necessary to confront the student *individually* and have the student commit to a new behavior. During the individual conference teachers may also assert their own feelings on the topic: "Although I try not to show it in front the class, it really annoys me when you come to class late." This honest and fair response is much better than, "Why do you constantly disrupt the class by coming late?"

Glasser's procedure, then, has the goals of making students responsible for their behavior. It does so by neither adding to an already emotional situation nor by denying honest emotions. It simply moves on to having the student commit to a new, better behavior and the teacher commit to looking for the student's appropriate behavior, not dwelling on past errors. This procedure is not unlike suggestions made by others (e.g., Canter and Canter, 1976; Charles, 1981,

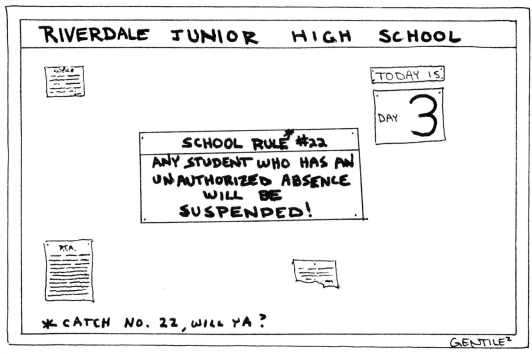

Cartoon 8.3.

Dreikurs, 1968; Dreikurs et al., 1971; Ginott, 1972; Gordon, 1974). Ginott (1972, pp. 15–16) summed it up in his own personal philosophy:

I have come to a frightening conclusion. I am the decisive element in the classroom. It is my personal approach that creates the climate. It is my daily mood that makes the weather. As a teacher I possess tremendous power to make a child's life miserable or joyous. I can be a tool of torture or an instrument of inspiration. I can humiliate or humor, hurt or heal. In all situations it is my response that decides whether a crisis will be escalated or de-escalated, and a child humanized or de-humanized.

Punishment, Retribution and Restitution

In earlier chapters we have seen some of the problems with punishment, some of which are worth reiterating in the present context. First, punishment has emotional by-products, including classically conditioned feelings to subjects, situations and people. Second, it seldom works to eliminate the behavior it is intended to stamp out; rather it suppresses it for a while usually only in the presence of the punisher as a cue. Third, punishment informs the victim what not to do, but does not teach what the appropriate behavior is. Fourth, if punishment is followed by reinforcement, it may act as cue for reinforcement and increase the probability of the subject working to attain punishment (e.g., masochistic behavior). Fifth, if nothing the subject does can avoid the punishment (noncontingent punishment), learned helplessness can result. Sixth, punishment delivered by a teacher or other significant person provides a model for the observers of how to treat others and solve problems. Seventh, punishment for an act does not correct the problem for which the person was punished—that is, there is no restitution. Finally, punishment engenders revenge, especially if a group reinforces its members for retaliation against the punisher.

Given all the above, it is no wonder that authors on the topic of discipline argue for nonpunitive resolutions to conflict. As the cartoon portrays, the typical punishment is to suspend students who make trouble, though the students are more likely to appreciate the holiday (escape from distasteful work) than to consider that punishment.

Punishment, in sum, seems to serve only two purposes—namely, to stop inappropriate behavior and to vent the punisher's anger. It can eliminate behavior, but only if the punishment is strong (in which case it is outlawed by civilized societies) and the victim cannot escape or reduce its effects. But even rats learn how to reduce the effects of aversive stimuli. One rat, pictured by Azrin and Holz (1966, p. 385), learned to lie on its back to distribute strong shocks across his entire furry back instead of on his sensitive feet, all the while pressing the bar to continue receiving his food as if having "Breakfast in Bed." If rats are intelligent enough to dilute the effects of punishment, can we expect less of students? The only punishments we are left with, in other words, are ineffective. That leaves the second purpose of punishment—venting anger—also unfulfilled, since the problem will not have been eliminated and there will be a continual need to vent anger.

Why, then, do teachers and others continue to punish? The answer, it would appear, is that they mistakenly believe it works: that is, the teacher is being negatively reinforced for punishing students and those behaviors are simply becoming habitual, as smoking or drinking can become habitual responses to stressful events.

In light of this, advice on how to avoid punishing is welcome indeed. Logical consequences, such as those involved in suspending students (Glasser's steps 7–10) for not keeping their contracts are much preferable to punishments or continual arguments. The teacher is simply enforcing a contract suggested by and agreed to by the student.

In cases when students lose control and become aggressive, *physical restraint* may become necessary (e.g., Foster, 1986). It differs from corporal punishment in the following ways: (1) its intent is solely to cease the aggressive behavior of the child; (2) it uses the minimum force necessary to stop the behavior; and (3) it is used only during the behavior for as long as needed. As described, physical restraint is useful to a teacher when students are aggressing against each other. Like football team members "holding back" an enraged teammate from fighting against an opponent, there is no enmity built up between the aggressor and the restrainer (e.g., the teammates or teacher). The intent is important here.[5] Were the teacher to punish the student instead, the force would likely be greater than necessary and would continue after the aggressive behavior ceased. This would likely maintain hostility in the form of "getting even."

The final point to be made in this section concerns the distinction between retribution and restitution (e.g., Gnagey, 1968). *Retribution* can be thought of as retaliation—"an eye for an eye;" "don't get mad, get even." It is very difficult to punish someone in such a manner and keep the immediate problem from growing since the loser of the battle will harbor resentment and plot a new retaliation. The problem may also grow in another way, by spreading out to include the observers in the class if they feel the punishment was unfair or too harsh (what Kounin and Gump, 1956, dubbed "the ripple effect"). *Restitution*, on the other hand, is making right what is wrong. If you have broken a contract or commitment, restitution is completing the contract even though late and/or recommitting to a new contract (see anecdotes 8.4 and 8.5).

Restitution strikes people as being reasonable, as being a logical natural consequence of an inappropriate behavior or error. Therefore, it is not likely to engender revenge. It is not even likely to be considered punishment. Moreover, it is effective in teaching people to be responsible for their own behavior.

Anecdote 8.4

Logical Consequences? Food (Fight) for Thought

Once upon a time, not very long ago, in a not very far off school district, a gaggle of high school students got into a food fight. All who participated were suspended from school immediately for a three-day period. In addition, they were barred from making up their work for the missed school days and, since final exams for the ten-week grading period were to take place then, the suspended students were to have zeroes for the exams averaged in to their grades. The suspended students immediately screamed "Unfair!"

Now it happened that the parents were not enthralled about the entire episode and one of the fathers asked his son what happened.

Son: "Well, somebody at another table started throwing food."
Dad: "What did you do?"
Son: "I just tried to stay out of it."
Dad: "But?"
Son: "Well, somebody hit me with some food. So I *had* to get him back."
Dad: "Couldn't you find another alternative than getting involved?"
Son: (in disbelief): "Like what?"
Dad: "Like, for example, moving to another table when the food fight began."
Son: (in exquisite macho tone of voice and mannerism): "Naw, it was the only thing I could do. I *had* to do it!"

So much for the power of right over might. Father was now convinced that his son was guilty and deserved penance through some kind of logical, restitutive consequence. But suspension and the inability to maintain schoolwork? Determined to get to the bottom of this, he telephoned the principal.

Father: "It's clear to me my son was guilty, but why suspension from school with no opportunity to take their tests?"
Principal: "It was the only thing I could do. I *had* to do it."
Father: "What a minute! That's the same logic I just heard from my kid. Why not have the guilty parties clean the cafeteria?"
Principal: "There's a law against that, and, besides, it wouldn't be clean in time for the next lunch period."
Father: "I don't believe there's a law against that, but if there is (and I plan to check), then why not suspend them from the cafeteria and/or bill them for the costs of cleaning up."
Principal: "Our policy is to suspend students and that's what I did."
Father: "In that case, I assume that the next time you get a traffic ticket, you would find it appropriate punishment to be suspended from work and have your pay docked for three days."
Principal: "That's different."
Father: "We'll see how different. If my son and the others are not allowed to take their exams, I will be appealing this decision to the superintendent and the school board. Thank you."

Following their three day suspension, all the students were allowed to take make-up tests, no further appeals were necessary, and they all lived happily ever after—or at least until the next food fight.

Anecdote 8.5

Retribution vs. Restitution

I have often wondered about the tactics used by some teachers as forms of punishment. Expecting a student to write a sentence one thousand times is ridiculous. I have witnessed a teacher keep students after school for not completing an assignment or misbehaving in class, then give them the choice of completing the assignment or doing fifty push-ups before giving them permission to leave. Others keep students after school only to have them sit quietly in the classroom without expecting them to complete a previous assignment.

I do not understand how any of these methods can possibly suppress or decrease the probability of an inappropriate behavior. I have tried to encourage students to take responsibility for their actions. Absenteeism was never an excuse for not completing an assignment or an exam. Students who threw papers across the room were expected to sweep the floor (I keep a broom and dustpan in the classroom). If a student wrote on his desk he would inevitably find cleanser on the desk and would be expected to clean it.

Denise E. Clarke
Teacher

Time Out

Glasser called his in-class suspension (step 7) a brief "time out," whose purpose was to have the student devise a new plan before rejoining the class. In essence this provides a reinforcement contingency between fulfilling the contract and participating in the class activities: if the appropriate behavior occurs, participation follows; if inappropriate behavior occurs, participation is not allowed until the student is ready to behave appropriately.

Time out, as used by Glasser, is quite a sensible and useful procedure. But no behavioral procedure has been more mis-used in practice than time out (See anecdote 8.6). Thus it is not uncommon to visit schools or other institutions in which a time out box or room is proudly displayed. Students who break a rule or annoy the teacher are sent there as a kind of solitary confinement. And since it feels so good to the teacher to have miscreants out of their sight, it is easy to keep them out of mind and forget about them for 30 minutes or, in some cases, much longer. This long time period is a misuse of the "time out" idea.

Originally known by its longer title, *time out from positive reinforcement*, the procedure was first used in pigeon training experiments as an alternative to punishing incorrect behaviors. In discrimination learning studies, for example, correct choices led to food, while incorrect choices delayed the next problem to be presented and thus delayed the availability of food (e.g., Ferster and Appel, 1961). In variations of the procedure used on humans, institutionalized delinquents, who were fighting or otherwise breaking rules, were briefly isolated to interrupt the attention they were receiving for this inappropriate behavior (e.g., Brown and Tyler, 1967). Time out lasted from half a

Anecdote 8.6

> ### Time Out or Just Out?
>
> I believe time out is extremely misused in many schools. I have seen students spend anywhere from thirty minutes to three hours in time out. Three of my own students had to spend forty-five minutes in time out because the policy requires that the school psychologist, who had to be called from another building, has to have an exit interview with them. By the time they were interviewed, they had to be reminded of why they were in the time out room in the first place.
>
> In addition, children learn to push the limits, especially if the staff does not understand the technique. For example, one little boy was able to convince his aide to let him stop for a drink and bathroom break on the way to time out.
>
> Cheryl Aldrich
Teacher
>
> P.S. Ms. Aldrich's current procedure is "keeping children in time out long enough for the children to regain control and not talking them to death in an exiting interview."
> Chronic problems that need talking ". . . will be addressed with the child later at a more appropriate time," consistent with Glasser's theory.
>
>

second to ten minutes in prototypical pigeon studies and less than 15 minutes in corresponding human studies.

Time out was made contingent on a response in such a way that when the undesired behavior occurred, all stimuli that might be reinforcing that behavior became unavailable for a time. Since it is not always clear in practical situations what reinforcers are maintaining the behavior (e.g., other students' attention, etc.) isolation to a somewhat stark room can be effective. *But the isolation must be brief.* In fact, it will be less effective if it has durations beyond 15 minutes (Johnston, 1972) and is likely to be (perhaps accurately) perceived by the student as a retributive act by the teacher if it is longer than a few minutes. Then students may spend the extra time plotting revenge. Hall and Hall (1980, p. 14) advise that a "time out period should last from two to five minutes and certainly no longer than a minute for each year of the person's age."

Time out was very effective when used in the following way to teach good manners in the Gentile household:

> *Doug* (aged 4, speaking in a nasty tone of voice): "Dad, get me a drink."
> *Dad* (calmly): "Doug, please go back to your room. And when you can ask me nicely, come back and ask me again."

The first times this happened he would go (or be escorted) and complain about unfair treatment. Later, he would smile (Dreikurs' "recognition reflex"?), turn around, walk in and out of the room in a few seconds and try again.

Glasser's time out procedure is similar. It sets the stage for a change in behavior by the child, promises reinforcement for that acceptable behavior, and does not get into an argument about why or who is fair to whom. I believe that American parents and teachers spend too much time arguing and explaining, thereby reinforcing and modeling the behavior of arguing. The child, of course, complains about the adult's unfairness, but what about the unfair treatment to the adult? The adult has the right to expect children to live up to their contracts, too (Canter and Canter, 1976). Thus an unemotional time out can provide the needed withdrawal from the attention that may maintain arguing or other inappropriate behavior, while allowing the child to recommit to doing better next time. Meanwhile the adult can remain (or become) calm and focus attention on the child's forthcoming appropriate behavior.

Perhaps the most creative time out procedure I have ever witnessed was in a primary school classroom, where the teacher had built a small log cabin. Among other uses, she told her students that any time they got upset—with their work, with another student—they could go into the log cabin for a *self-imposed time out*. The rules regarding this were that only one child was allowed at a time and they could only go for about 5 minutes. What happened when I observed the class was that students would become frustrated with something, grab a favorite book, and disappear into the cabin and snuggle up in a corner of the cabin on a pillow. A few minutes later they would emerge and rejoin the group. No emotional contagion occurred and no teacher time was needed. The children were learning emotional and behavioral self-control by deciding when they needed a time out.

Contracts

Dr. Haim Ginott once relayed in a lecture that the best way for solving child-child problems was for the parent to act as arbitrator with a rule that only written complaints would be accepted. Thus if one of your children whines, "He hit me," you say "Here's some paper and pencil. Write down everything that happened." If the child does so, then you show the other child the written accusation and ask the other child to respond in writing. What happened almost always, in Ginott's story, was that after one trial with this procedure, the kids would say to each other, "Let's make up 'cause if we complain, we'll just have to write it all down." Ginott was also fond of advising parents not to try to "get to the bottom of a problem" because there is no bottom—everyone just sinks into a murky abyss.[6]

The moral of the story is that putting behavior—whether past, present or future—into writing may solve most of the problem without involving the teacher or parent in emotional conflicts. The act of writing out a plan committing oneself to a new behavior does several positive things: (1) it makes people aware of their behavior and its consequences, (2) it provides a permanent record of the new agreement, so that (3) the consequences of the successful or unsuccessful behavior can occur in a manner that is productive for the future relationship between the parties to the agreement.

Written agreements or *contracts* are already widely used in education and behavioral self-management (e.g., Jenson, 1978; Sulzer-Azaroff and Reese, 1982; Watson and Tharp, 1985). They always include a statement of the objectives, often include a recording technique for monitoring the person's behavior, and usually include consequences for appropriate and inappropriate behaviors. They are especially useful for persons over twelve years old because, properly negotiated, they provide informed consent and maximum participation of the students in learning responsibility for and self-control over their behaviors. At the same time they prescribe certain behaviors for the teacher.

Some commonly stated rules for contracts include the following (not all of which are necessary for all contracts).

1. Specific objectives must be stated clearly so that both student and teacher (and perhaps administrator and parent) will know exactly what the goal is.
2. The behaviors wanted (and perhaps not wanted) must be specified clearly. Emphasis should be placed on what to do instead of what not to do.
3. The time frame (usually one week or less) and conditions within which the behaviors are expected to occur must be specified.
4. For many problems, records should be kept by both students and teachers vis-a-vis the behaviors.
5. The consequences of completing appropriate behaviors, as well as engaging in inappropriate behaviors, must be specified.
6. The consequences must occur as specified.
7. If there are several behaviors that are targeted for change, it is probably best to deal with one at a time with others added later. This may be stated at the beginning so the student knows what he or she is getting into.
8. The student must agree to the contract, should write the contract or at least contribute to the wording of it, and all parties to the agreement must sign it.

Many of us are mostly unaware of our own behaviors, their frequency, the conditions under which they occur, and their effect on others. Until we systematically count the number of mouthfuls of food we take each day, for example, we may not be aware that our overweight condition is a result of a large number of snacks. Children with behavior problems may similarly be unaware of how little assigned work they do, how frequently they miss class or come late, how often they ridicule others or talk out of turn, and how their behavior makes others feel. A good discipline procedure, especially for difficult problems, must help the students come to grips with their own behavior and bring it under their own control. Such *self-control* is the purpose of the record keeping in point 4. For many problems therefore, it should be considered indispensible.

Most of us, after having been largely unaware of our own behaviors, make global resolutions when we finally realize the extent of our errors. Thus many an overweight person, to continue the analogy, resolves to stop snacking and to lose 20 lbs. in the next 20 days. Such grandiose plans for self-control hardly ever continue past the first few days, however, because we find that we only lost two lbs. the first week. So we give up. The problem is that the goals are too remote and difficult to reach.

It is apparently not at all uncommon for adolescents in trouble with the schools to be truly remorseful and willing to promise anything for "one more chance." But the teacher who lets the student agree to an impossible dream is not helping that student learn self-control of behavior; rather they are both contributing to the student's very likely next failure. These problems are addressed in rules 3 and 7.

Exactly what a contract should look like is difficult to prescribe, given the range of possible problems and our emphasis on students suggesting the wording. Hall and Hall (1982) suggest, however, that each contract should include a column headed "Behavior" and one headed "Consequence" with spaces for "Who," "What," "When" and "How Much" under each to specify who does what behavior under what conditions to what standard (e.g., 4 out of 5 days next week). This is probably good advice for most situations.

Choices, Delay of Reinforcement, and Self-Control

One of the problems people have with fulfilling contracts, and self-control in general, is that the choices that have to be made involve a conflict between short-term and long-term gains. Mazur (1986) gives the example of a college student who has the best of intentions of going to every early morning lecture. Thus she sets her alarm each evening to allow herself plenty of time. She has chosen going to class, which should improve her chances for getting a high grade, over getting an extra hour or two of sleep. By the time the alarm sounds, however, the immediate reinforcer of sleep is much more attractive than the potential long-term reinforcement of a high grade, and thus she turns off the alarm and goes back to sleep. The immediate small reinforcer wins over the potentially larger but delayed reinforcer (a result that is predicted by the *matching law*, which states that our behavior tends to occur in proportion to the amount, frequency, or immediacy of the available reinforcement; see Mazur, 1986, for a good explanation).

When she wakes up having missed her class, she feels remorseful and vows never again to sleep through her alarm. But "never again" hardly lasts until the next early morning class, and the problem persists. One way of looking at this problem is that two choices were involved. The first was at night when the student had to set her alarm clock. The second was in the morning when she had to get up. As this example shows, from a distance the small reinforcer, sleep, loses in comparison to the large reinforcer, high grades. This is because both reinforcers are delayed when viewed from the perspective of the night before.[7]

Thus the solution to the problem is to allow the choice of behaviors to be made only once, in this case the night before, as a *precommitment* which is virtually impossible to change. To continue this example, the woman could have another student meet her for breakfast on class days, so it would be embarrassing not to go, as well as providing another immediate reinforcer for going.

All of this is to say that another way to help students fulfill their contracts and gradually develop self-control is that after they have committed to a plan, help them find ways to avoid backsliding. Here is where peer reinforcement (and even a modest amount of peer pressure) can be helpful, encouraging the person for meeting the commitment and (gently) accepting no excuses for reneging.

Conflict Resolution and Peer Mediation

by
Kay Johnson-Gentile[8] and
J. Ronald Gentile

Perhaps the most exciting development in dealing with interpersonal difficulties has been the introduction of conflict resolution skills into schools. Although this field can boast of a distinguished history, leading to some of its finest actors receiving the Nobel Prize for Peace, the principles on which conflict resolution are based have only recently been adapted to and widely practiced in schools. In this section we hope to elucidate those principles and describe some of the ways schools have successfully implemented them.

The American Heritage Dictionary defines conflict as "(1) a prolonged battle, a struggle; clash; (2) a controversy, disagreement; quarrel or opposition; (3) the opposition or simultaneous functioning of mutually exclusive impulses, desires, or tendencies. With such images as battle and quarrel, it is no wonder that most people view conflicts as unpleasant and therefore to be avoided or suppressed. As Smith, Johnson and Johnson (1981) noted,

The degree to which most people and organizations avoid and suppress interpersonal conflict, furthermore, indicates that large parts of the general public may not believe that conflict can be constructive. (p. 660)

Long-time researchers in the field have discovered, however, that avoidance and suppression of conflict is counterproductive (e.g., Deutsch, 1973, 1994; Pruitt & Rubin, 1986). To resolve conflicts it pays to work from a more optimistic, constructive definition. Thus Pruitt and Rubin (1986) emphasize that conflict is a *perceived* divergence of interest or *belief* that aspirations are mutually exclusive. The typical perception identifies a conflict as a zero-sum or competitive game, in which one person must lose for the other to win, or both must give something up. Since perceptions and beliefs can be changed, then it is possible to redefine conflict as an opportunity:

- to find a win-win solution
- for personal edification and growth
- to prevent stagnation or rigidity in thinking
- to become more creative
- to walk a mile in someone else's shoes
- for restructuring self, family or organization

It is not the fact that conflict occurs, in other words, but our response to it that proves beneficial or harmful, functional or dysfunctional (Deutsch, 1973; Johnson, 1970; Johnson & Johnson, 1979; 1991; Kreidler, 1984).

Common sense requires the separation of process from outcome in such matters. That is, although dysfunctional processes are likely to yield negative outcomes (as when marital conflicts escalate to fighting and abuse), it is possible for quite healthy processes to result in negative outcomes (as when married couples decide, after appropriate mediation and counseling, that the marriage should not be saved). The other permutations are possible, too, (both functional and dysfunctional processes leading to positive outcomes), but the focal point must be process instead of outcomes. This is not because outcomes are not important, but because our *perception or interpretation* of the outcome is likely to be colored by the process (e.g., divorce in the above case is likely to be perceived by all as a positive outcome if it was a consensual decision arrived at by a healthy rather than a dysfunctional process).

School-Based Conflict Resolution Programs

A growing number of schools are using conflict resolution programs as a major component of their discipline plan. The main purpose in most of these programs is to reduce or prevent violent and other negative confrontations by teaching negotiation skills. The focus of most of these programs is student-student conflict, though there is no logical reason that the same principles cannot be used for most student-educator or educator-educator conflicts.

Conflict resolution programs are basically of two types: a cadre or a total student body approach, although they can overlap (Johnson & Johnson, 1995; Rosenthal, 1995). In the *cadre or peer mediation* approach, a small number of students are trained in mediation techniques. They then serve as peer mediators, usually in pairs, for their school helping resolving interpersonal conflicts that occur among the students. Selection of student mediators requires some care: they must be respected by their peers and be in good academic standing, so that they can spare the time. Selection should also provide a team of mediators that is representative of the sex, race, or other politically important categorizations of the school. Anecdote 8.7 summarizes one such program.

In the *total student body* or *whole-school* approach, every student and staff member is taught negotiation and mediation skills (Johnson & Johnson, 1995; Kreidler, 1984, 1990). This has the disadvantage of being more costly and time-consuming, but it has the obvious advantage of teaching much-needed pro-social skills to all, while making a public commitment to conflict resolution as a way of life.

As Kreidler (1984, 1990) describes it, most conflicts are of three basic types: conflicts over resources, needs, or values. Conflicts over resources occur when two or more people want something that is in short supply, such as the same book, the class gerbil, a

Anecdote 8.7

Peer Mediation in a Middle School

As part of her research project, Gwen Rosenthal (1995) studied the conflict resolution programs in several schools in western New York. One of them, a suburban middle school of 450 students, runs a cadre model which exemplifies the issues described in this section.

Teachers nominate students as peer mediators and 10–12 are chosen, though they had 16 one year. Criteria for selection are having the respect of peers, good verbal skills, passing grades in all academic subjects, and a positive attitude. Once nominated, students must still volunteer and they may resign at any time.

For two days in the summer, students are trained in the theory of conflict resolution, given video-taped practice role playing and reflecting on effective practices of a mediator. They then receive a notebook to use as a guide, as well as a certificate and a Peer Mediator T-shirt. Early in the school year, they attend further practice sessions and sign a pledge to keep all mediations confidential, to follow the mediation rules they are learning, to remain impartial (or be replaced in any conflict in which they are involved), and when to refer problems to others. They also develop plans to educate the other students in the school about peer mediation and their role (creating videos, posters, demonstrations, etc.).

Referrals come from anyone (currently 80% from students), including anonymously by friends of people in conflict. A faculty supervisor then contracts the referred students and, if they sign a contract to participate, a pair of peer mediators—one boy, one girl, usually from different grades—schedules meetings with the disputants.

Mediation has five steps: (1) opening, to establish the rules; (2) listening, to hear all sides of the story, and what each person wants; (3) mutual understanding, to get each side to summarize the other side's complaints and hopes; (4) creating options, in which the peer mediator helps the people brainstorm alternative solutions and seek win-win solutions; and (5) planning, which is to provide a written agreement, steps to implement the agreement, planned follow-up, and an evaluation of the peer mediation process.

computer or a friend. These conflicts tend to be the easiest to solve by widening the circle to include more people, by taking turns, or sharing in some other way. Conflicts of needs (e.g., for respect) or values (e.g., a religious conviction) are more difficult to solve because defining the specific problem is more elusive.

Conflict Resolution Skills

Whatever the cause of the conflict, the process is all important: emphasis is on helping people perceive conflicts as *mutual problems* (not just "your" problem). This view has the potential to be resolved in ways which allow all participants to be successful, though success at the conclusion may not be what each participant thought he or she wanted at first. Though the techniques for negotiating such win-win outcomes require participants to focus initially on the problem at a personal level (e.g., What do I need in this situation? How do I feel about this situation?) *they must also listen to, as well as explain, the other person's point of view* (e.g., the person I am in conflict with feels this way and needs this. . . .). Finally, both participants must try to find solutions which foster win/win outcomes (e.g., How can we both get what we need in this situation?). Time and energy is focused on finding creative solutions, not on being defensive, name calling, and reiterating the problem over and over.

It should not go unnoticed that the mediation skills described above are the same skills that counselors and therapists need to learn. For example, among their *Elements of Counseling*, Meier and Davis (1996) list these:

- If you want to change something, process it (that is, talk about the problem, but emphasize negotiation processes, not content).
- When in doubt, focus on feelings.
- Listen closely to what clients say.
- Do not assume that you know clients' feelings, thoughts, and behaviors.
- Avoid advice.
- Avoid premature problem solving.
- Be concrete.
- Do not assume that change is simple.

Perhaps the last is most important of all, because it puts many of the others in context and suggests that solutions to problems require empathy, exploration, self-discovery and patience. None of these traits is in abundant supply in modern society. This is why Johnson and Johnson (1995) and Kreidler (1984; 1990) have developed a number of curriculum activities to help alleviate this problem (See anecdote 8.8), and why we believe conflict resolution programs are so essential in today's schools.

Teaching and Discipline

Third Grade School Teacher to parents at the first PTA open house of the year: *We have a problem. For the first time at this school we have a number of students who are reading below grade level. Thus they are having trouble with the books. As a result, they get frustrated and cause discipline problems. Then I'm forced to take their free time and other privileges away from them and we work on the reading more. So, if your children come home tired and frustrated at the end of the day, I hope you'll understand, because I'm the same.*
Parent: *If the reading level is so different this year, why don't you just use other books?*
Teacher: *We'd like to, but the committee on new text books won't meet until next year to order books for two years after that.*

The above interchange actually took place some years ago in what is considered a "good school district." Almost everyone accepts that there is a causal relationship between teaching/curriculum and discipline, but still we accept less than adequate teaching or curricula which do not match the students' entering knowledges or skills.

If students enter a particular class without the proper prerequisites (e.g., knowledge of facts and skills that will be built upon, a level of anxiety that is not too high, etc.), then *it is the teacher's responsibility either to teach them the prerequisites or have the student placed in a class in which the prerequisites will be learned.* Teachers are the professionals society trusts to make educational diagnoses and prescriptions. If teachers do not take this responsibility or carry it out improperly, then students will quickly feel frustrated, have difficulty understanding what is going on, pay less and less attention to the task, and sooner or later become a discipline problem.

Student success is central to a well-controlled classroom because it is central to the develop-

Anecdote 8.8

Curriculum Activities to Help Develop Communication Skill

The following curriculum activities for introducing some of the skills needed for conflict resolution are from Kreidler (1984):

1. Discuss paraphrasing with the children. Then assign each child a partner, designating one as Pete and the other as Repeat. Tell Pete that he is to paraphrase everything Repeat says. Pete must then say, "okay," if it is paraphrased correctly, or try again.
2. Have students role play both nasty and peaceable ways to say the following:

   You're not following the rules.
   You are messing up this project by doing that.
   You are getting on my nerves.
   I don't want to play with you now.

   Discuss if it is easier to talk in a peaceable or nasty manner. Why is talking and behaving peaceably often difficult? List reasons that might make it worth the effort.
3. As a class, make a list of ways that children often express anger. Look at each item on the list and decide if the expression is hurtful or dangerous to others. Cross out all hurtful and dangerous expressions. Finally, describe to the class situations that could provoke anger and have them role play appropriate responses (i.e., responses that are not hurtful or dangerous). Better yet, have the class create the situations and then role play appropriate responses.

ment of self-control, to competence vs. helplessness, to emotional development, to social power games—to everything in the individual's growth. The curriculum must be built around the student's needs and abilities, both collectively and individually. Teaching methods must be flexible, varied and perceived as directly related to important instructional outcomes. Students must know what those outcomes are. And students' work must be assessed and graded uncompetitively against a high standard of achievement. That is, each student must be required to master these objectives to a high level of achievement with no excuses, but with additional attempts and instructional assistance as needed. The alternative is to use teaching as the ultimate punishment.

In this sense good teaching is integral to a good classroom management plan: it includes both the particular content as well as whether the learning is *time spent or time invested*. Time, like money, can be used so that it is gone with little or nothing to show for it, or it can be used so that it returns a dividend in the future. For instance, a person can spend many hours and much money learning to play a video game, the long term effect of which is essentially nil. In a few months there will be a new game to replace it. If a person spent the same amount of time and money interacting with a

264 *Chapter Eight*

Cartoon 8.4

word processor, the long term effect would be a skill that is either marketable or useful in many ways at home. Similarly, a person can spend time watching television or investing it in learning to play a musical instrument or a sport. The latter two skills open up possibilities for careers or hobbies later in life, while TV-watching has little, if any, long-term value.

School teachers, wittingly or unwittingly, often reinforce behavior which both they and the students know is "busy-work." Endless dittoes, given both to students who need the drill and those who do not, as well as assignments which are neither graded nor handed back for the students to correct, are two examples of time spent. It is possible to modify people's behavior so that they do such tasks, but probably only by threatening punishment or manipulating with rewards. This is where there are "hidden costs of reward" (e.g., Balsam & Bondy, 1983; Lepper & Greene, 1978): when students receive tangible reinforcers for doing activities, even activities they like, that are essentially useless. Once reinforced for such behavior, students will wonder why they ever did it before for no payoff.

On the other hand, time invested in mastering valuable tasks—such as learning to read, do mathematics, program a computer, and understand our own behavior—will eventually, if not immediately, become valued by students. Even if you have to use tangible reinforcers in the beginning to motivate such skill development, this can be phased out without losing the behavior, since the behavior is becoming an integral part of the person's self-concept. The non-reader is now a reader; the musically non-talented person is becoming a guitarist, the math-anxious person can now do algebra (e.g., Gentile, Frazier and Morris, 1973, pp. 45–46). The person's self-image changes when important competencies are developed. As Friedenberg (1959) put it, people's self-esteem is tied directly to their competencies: people know who they are by what they can do. It is our opportunity and responsibility as teachers to arrange the school environment to teach students what it takes to become successful. That is the ultimate reality therapy.

But we need to retain a sense of humor about it, too, because we teachers also misbehave

Anecdote 8.9

"Hidden Costs of Reward?"

There has been a continuing debate on the "hidden costs of reward" since Lepper & Greene (1978) first popularized the issue. For the latest skirmishes in this thirty-years war, the interested reader is referred to the following sources: Cameron & Pierce (1994; 1996); Kohn (1993; 1996); Lepper, Kearney & Drake, (1996); and Ryan & Deci (1996). For the practical purposes of teachers, however, I believe the debate mostly misses the point which, as stated in the text, concerns the perceived usefulness of the activity to the student. It is just not true that paying a budding musician makes him or her less willing to perform, as the proponents of the "hidden costs of reward" argue. In contrast, paying a child to take out the garbage, or do a math assignment the purpose of which is obscure, will surely make him or her less willing to do it for free. In the former case, the task is perceived as proof of self-efficacy; in the latter case, the task is perceived as useless.

at times. No one ever described his own self-control better than Mark Twain (Buffalo Express, August 21, 1869):

I am simply going to do my plain, unpretending duty, when I cannot get out of it; I shall work diligently and honestly and faithfully at all times and upon all occasions, when privation and want, shall compel me to do it; in writing, I shall always confine myself strictly to the truth, except when it is attended with inconvenience; I shall witheringly rebuke all forms of crime and misconduct, except when committed by the party inhabiting my own vest; I shall not make use of slang or vulgarity upon any occasion or under any circumstances, and shall never use profanity except in discussing house rent and taxes.

There was an honest man whom we can model!

Cartoon 8.5.

Practice Exercises

A. Practice Items

Items 1–4 describe discipline situations that relate to either retribution or restitution. Identify each by writing the letter corresponding to the appropriate choice in the space provided next to the discipline situation (Answers are in Note 9).

      a. restitution
      b. retribution

____ 1. A child breaks a neighbor's toy and has to save his money to buy him a new one.

____ 2. Mary is absent for a quiz and is assigned a grade of zero.

____ 3. George removes a record from the choral library without permission and is suspended from chorus.

____ 4. A child whose homework is always late is asked to draw up a written plan for how he is going to correct the problem.

For the following multiple-choice items, select the alternative choice which *best* answers the question (Answers are in Note 9).

5. When a student misbehaves, Glasser says the teacher should first ask
   a. "Why are you breaking the rules?"
   b. "Is that behavior in your contract?"
   c. "Who gave you permission to do that?"
   d. "What are you doing?"

6. Tony Graffiti, a high school basketball player, is caught painting slogans on the wall of his high school. According to the principles of this chapter,
   a. Tony should have to clean off the wall.
   b. Tony should be suspended from the basketball team.
   c. Both a and b should be done.
   d. Tony's parents should be billed for the costs involved in cleaning the wall.

7. The first time Peter talked without raising his hand the teacher yelled. The second time she scolded even more. The third time she ridiculed him. Later still she physically punished him. *Peter's talking out loud became continually more frequent* despite the teacher's attempts to control him. From this information, it can be seen that the teacher's controls are _____ Peter's behavior.
   a. reinforcing
   b. extinguishing
   c. punishing
   d. having no effect on

8. Chuck Himout, a tenth-grade trouble maker, is often thrown out of biology class for obnoxious behavior. When that happens, he avoids doing the lab exercises which he needs because he does poorly at them. In addition, he meets his "macho" friends at the principal's

office. What is the most likely reason that Chuck gets thrown out of class?
   a. His appropriate work is being extinguished by the teacher.
   b. He is receiving both positive and negative reinforcement by being chucked out.
   c. He is receiving both positive reinforcement and punishment from the teacher.
   d. He has a conditioned fear of the principal.

9. Continuing with the situation in question 8, why is the teacher chucking Chuck out of class? Because the teacher's behavior of throwing Chuck out is being
   a. punished.
   b. extinguished.
   c. negatively reinforced.
   d. positively reinforced.

10. Conflict resolution is best conceived as
   a. an opportunity for compromise between disputants.
   b. a student judiciary system to replace teachers as police or judges.
   c. a systematic program to teach mediation skills.
   d. all of the above.

11. What are the two definitions of misbehavior adopted in this book? Misbehavior is
   a. _____
   b. _____

B. For Cooperative Study (in or out of class):

1. In small groups recall or make up some discipline incidents and see if you can diagram "who did what to whom with what effects," as in the beginning of the chapter.

2. Discuss Glasser's ten steps for discipline through reality therapy. Are there any problems that are likely not solvable through those steps? What further steps, if needed, should be taken?

3. Ask students of different cultural backgrounds to describe the ways discipline was handled in their schools. Contrast those comments with the issues raised about oriental schools, and other experiences in the group.

4. In the last paragraph of the section entitled, "A cross-cultural perspective," the author states "Moreover, we have assigned our teachers the role of policing those unnatural roles." Should teachers assume the role of the police, in, for example,
   a. breaking up fights?
   b. discovering who is using or dealing in drugs?
   Or should undercover police be employed to arrest these people? These are, after all, not just misbehaviors, but crimes.

5. Discuss Study Question 9 at the beginning of this chapter. Give examples from your own experience, if any, with conflict resolution programs.

C. **For More Information:**

1. Write a contract for yourself to develop self-control on some behavior of importance. Consider the rules for contracts, as well as the issue of choice and delay of reinforcement, in your plan.
2. Read, and perhaps make a written or oral report on, one or more of the following books on discipline: Alschuler (1980), Burden (1995), Canter and Canter (1976), Charles (1981), Dreikurs (1968), Dreikurs et al. (1971), Foster (1974; 1986), Ginott (1972), Glasser (1965, 1969, 1977, 1992), Gnagey (1968), Gordon (1974), Hunter (1990), Jones and Jones (1981), Madsen and Madsen (1981).
3. Survey teachers in your area regarding their own personal classroom rules and means of enforcing them, as well as their school's official policy. What advice would you give prospective teachers regarding discipline?
4. Survey teachers in your area regarding the use of conflict resolution programs. What procedures does their school use? Are there similarities or differences with those procedures described in this chapter?

UNIT FOUR

Cognition: Memory, Transfer and Thinking

Having dealt with emotional and behavioral processes in previous chapters, this unit considers the various processes which fall under the label cognition. Although cognitive processes do not occur in the absence of emotional and behavioral concerns, they have been studied by different methods and appear to function according to different principles, at least most of the time. The next three chapters explore a variety of cognitive processes, the principles by which they operate, and their implications for instruction and curriculum development.

We begin in chapter 9 with problem solving and the difficulty of transferring what we know from the learning situation to another situation—a test or practical experience, for example. This is accomplished by having you, the reader, try to solve a number of problems to experience some of the feelings and interfering effects that the text is describing.

Since it is impossible to solve problems or transfer knowledge or strategies without adequately acquiring and retaining them, chapter 10 explores cognitive learning and retention processes. A long history of research on learning and retention has provided a number of theoretical principles about memory processes, as well as sound advice about how to improve memory. In addition, research since the 1970's has provided some results that may surprise you; in any case, they provide some reason for optimism about retention by slow learners and about very long term retention, to name two areas. Chapter 11 describes the processes of knowledge, its construction and organization, along with studies of how novices become experts and how knowledge is structured. The chapter ends with a description of approaches to increase intellectual skills.

CHAPTER
Study Questions

1. What is meant by each of the following:
   a. perceptual or mental set?
   b. anticipatory set (or advance organizer)?
   c. learning to learn (or learning set)?

   How can the structure of a problem or instructions lead to either positive or negative transfer?

2. What is meant by each of the following?
   a. learning
   b. memory
   c. transfer
      (1) positive transfer
      (2) negative transfer
      (3) zero transfer

3. What is meant by each of the following? Give examples.
   a. proactive interference
   b. retroactive interference
   c. proactive facilitation
   d. retroactive facilitation

4. Describe the kinds of experimental designs necessary to demonstrate proactive and retroactive interference. What is meant by "rest" in the control groups of these designs?

5. How can similar or identical elements provide
   a. positive transfer?
   b. negative transfer?

6. What is meant by situated cognition? Why is the culture or context in which knowledge is acquired important? Relate this theory to cognitive constructivism.

7. What is the difference between "low road" and "high road" transfer? Give examples.

NINE

8. How are each of the following factors likely to affect transfer?
   a. adequacy of original learning
   b. practice on perceiving distinctive features
   c. practice with several methods
   d. practice on principles
   e. emotional/motivational factors
   f. speed in learning vs. transfer
   g. drugs in learning vs. transfer

9. What is meant by each of the following?
   a. near vs. far transfer
   b. warm-up

10. Describe the differences between "fast" and "slow" learners in regard to learning, transfer and retention.

11. What is Murdock's formula for measuring the extent of transfer? What information is needed to solve the equation? What do the symbols E and C stand for? What are each of the following scores resulting from the formula?
    a. maximum scores (range)
    b. most likely score

12. What is meant by insight? Why does the author find it to be of little use?

13. What is the relationship between the *structure of the material* and the *readiness of the student?*
    a. What does it imply about curriculum development?
    b. What does it imply about students' cognitive development and cognitive reorganization?

14. How can all of the above points be transferred to classroom teaching? Why should teachers "retain humility?"

Learning, Problem Solving and Transfer

Introduction

The day after the orangutan's first inspection an avalanche of new tests descended upon us, the first at mealtimes. Instead of putting our food in the cages as they usually did, Zoram and Zanam, the two gorillas whose names I had finally learned, hoisted them to the ceiling in baskets by means of a system of pulleys with which the cages were equipped. At the same time they placed four fairly big wooden cubes in each cell. Then, stepping back, they observed us. It was heart-rending to see my companions' discomfort. They tried to jump, but none could reach the basket. Some climbed up the bars but, having reached the top, they stretched out their arms in vain since they could not get hold of the food, which was some distance away from the sides of the cages. I was ashamed at the stupidity of these men. I, needless to say, had found the solution to the problem immediately. One merely had to pile the four cubes one on top of another, then climb onto this scaffolding and unhook the basket.

The above description of humans having difficulty solving problems that were elementary for apes is from Boulle's *Planet of the Apes* (1963, pp. 95–96). The joke Boulle perpetrated on his readers in using the example was that it came from Köhler's studies on *The Mentality of Apes* (1925), in which humans had apes solve such problems to obtain food. Turnabout is fair play.

Whether it has been people testing apes or vice versa, the problem solving process has always been of interest. I shall use it to introduce this unit on cognitive processes and, more specifically, to explore the issue of transfer of training. *Transfer* involves the processes of using material or skills previously learned to facilitate (or hinder) new learning or problem solving. One of the easiest ways to illustrate the principles of transfer is to have students observe their own successful and unsuccessful attempts to solve problems, along with their emotional side effects. Thus I shall begin by asking you to solve some classical problems, which will then serve to prepare us for the discussions to follow. You will get the most from the discussion if you try all of the problems, no matter now frustrating some might seem at first, because that is part of the lesson to be learned.

Some Problems to be Solved

For a good deal of what follows, you will need pencil and paper. And to make it even more interesting, time yourself.

Problem 9.1

Unscramble the following words in the order given:

LECAM
EZGRA
ALVIO
SDLEN
PACHE

Problem 9.2 (Sample Problem)

You have two jars available to you as measures, one that is known to be of size 29 units (e.g., ounces) and the other of 3 units. Your task is to obtain exactly 20 units of water. How can you do it? Think about the problem and how you might express the solution mathematically before reading on.

Well, if the first jar were filled to the rim and then you poured out enough to fill the second jar, emptied the second jar, and then repeated that process twice, you would be left with 20 units in the first jar. As an equation this could be stated as follows:

(1) First Jar minus Second Jar minus Second Jar minus Second Jar = Required Amount

Alternatively, we could say:

(2) $29 - 3 - 3 - 3 = 20$

Or, more abstractly, we could let the first jar = A, the second jar = B and the required amount = X. Then we could say,

(3) $A - B - B - B = X$

or more efficiently,

(4) $A - 3B = X$

Now solve the following problems, in order, in the same way, as fast as you can. The only difference with these and the sample above is that these have three jars.

Problem Number	(Jar A)	(Jar B)	(Jar C)	Obtain the following amounts of water (X)	Solution
Sample (done above)	29	3		20	$A - 3B = X$
1.	21	127	3	100	
2.	14	163	25	99	
3.	18	43	10	5	
4.	9	42	5	23	
5.	20	59	4	31	
6.	23	49	3	20	
7.	15	39	3	18	
8.	18	48	4	22	
9.	28	76	3	25	
10.	14	31	8	6	

Please do not go on until you have solved all problems.

Perceptual or Mental Set

The two types of problems above are designed to induce a phenomenon known in the literature as *set*, as in being "set to respond" or in "mental set" or "perceptual set." The unscrambling problem was adapted from Farnham-Diggory (1972, p. 99). If you discovered a system for solving the problems which led to the last word being unscrambling as CHEAP you have been victimized by *set*. Why didn't you unscramble the last word as PEACH?

The answer, apparently, is that people in finding a solution to a problem—an act of discovery and personal creativity—usually become fixated on that solution. Their novel solution, in other words, soon becomes ritualized by the process of being reinforced for that solution so many times. A habit has set in that interferes with seeing other, sometimes simpler, solutions to the same problem. You are *set* to respond in a certain way.

The water jar problems are classic illustrations of set, attributed to Luchins (1942). If you solved the first eight problems by pouring them from B into A once and into C twice (i.e., by the formula $B - A - 2C = X$), then you were victimized by set by the time you got to problems 9 and 10, which cannot be solved that way. And it becomes especially disconcerting to learn that when you realize that problems 6–8 can also be solved in much simpler ways. For example, problem 6 can be solved by filling A and pouring it into C (i.e., $A - C = X$).

In demonstrating the Luchins water jar problems dozens of times in classes of teachers, where I often leave off the last two problems, the following results never cease to amaze me (not to mention the victimized teachers):

- a. a large number of people become immediately paralyzed by having to solve math problems ("My God, he expects me to do math.");
- b. a few people cannot solve even one problem in the 10 or so minutes allowed;
- c. of those who solve the first eight problems, more than three-fourths do not see the simpler solutions in the last three problems; and
- d. of those who do not succumb to the set—that is, who do solve all or some of the last problems in the simpler way—many of them "cheated" by not solving the problems in the order given.

Not surprisingly, the math anxiety of those who are suffering is never relieved when we say to them, "Ye gods, what heads! You've had all of this before," or "My son was doing more complicated work than this in fifth grade," or "You've got one minute left."

The rigidity that comes with sets has been known to increase with the pressure of time. One theoretical account of phenomena like this, (attributable to Spence, 1958; Taylor, 1953; see also Glucksberg, 1962, 1964) is that a time limit increases the anxiety (motivation) level, which has the effect of increasing the probability of a person's use of whatever habit is most available (i.e., highest in the hierarchy of habits). In the water jar problems, once you've learned how to solve the problem one way, increased pressure to finish will make you rely on that method to the exclusion of other methods. Rigidity sets in.

More Problems

For the next problems, as before, time yourself as you try to solve them.

Problem 9.3

What is the area of the square in the figure shown?

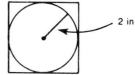

Problem 9.4

What is the diameter of the circle in the figure?

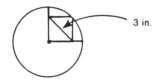

Problem 9.5

Make both sides equal by moving one match.

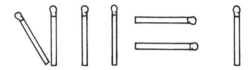

Problem 9.6

How can a person build a house so that it has southern exposure on all four sides simultaneously?

Problem 9.7

John and Mary are lying dead on the floor. There is water, broken glass and pieces of fur lying around. How did they die?

Problem 9.8

Connect all 9 dots using exactly four straight lines without lifting your pencil off the paper and without retracing.

Problem 9.9

A policeman was walking down the street when he heard a woman scream, "No, Jim, No!" then he heard a gunshot. When he rushed into the apartment, he found the victim surrounded by a doctor, a lawyer, and an accountant. He immediately arrested the doctor. Why?

Problem 9.10

Using six matchsticks of equal length, make four triangles of exactly the same size (i.e., equilateral triangles) so that each side of a triangle is the size of a matchstick.

The Structure of the Problem

If you are satisfied that you have solved all of the problems, or if you're satisfied that you've solved as many as you can without them becoming an obsession for the next few days, let's move on. These problems demonstrate a number of important principles about mental sets—variations on themes already mentioned—as well as some ideas about the structure of the problem.

Problem 9.3, for instance, is much simpler for most people when portrayed as follows:

Problem 9.3a

What is the area of the square in the figure shown?

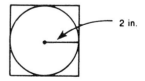

Of course there is still some prerequisite knowledge—namely, that to calculate the area of the square you multiply the length of one side by itself. Since half of one side is 2 inches, then the area of the square is 4 × 4 or 16 square inches. In the earlier drawing of the problem you first had to realize that the radius of a circle is the same in each direction.

Problem 9.6 is similar, though the structure has been verbally established. In asking "How can the house be built?" it is likely that verbal associations about construction were stimulated. But let's restate the problem:

Problem 9.6 Restated

Where can a person build a house so that it has southern exposure on all four sides simultaneously? Thus prompted, the search for the solution becomes oriented toward directions or locations. The answer, "at the north pole," is likely to occur to you much more quickly.

An extreme example—at least to many of the students in my classes, who argue vehemently with each other about the solution—of the way problem statement can interfere with finding a solution can be seen in the next problem.

Problem 9.11

If a man walked up a mountain path one day from 3–6 P.M. and returned on the same path the next day at the same time, is there a point on the path that he would pass at exactly the same time of day during ascent and descent?

In this problem, most people become distracted by some irrelevant features of the problem, such as the rate of walking or the question of what time it would be that he would pass at the meeting point. If you have been confused by these issues, stop for another moment to reconsider your solution.

In a restatement of the problem, the solution becomes obvious to some people. For others it appears obviously contradictory to the previous statement, so much so that it seems a different problem altogether. To illustrate:

Problem 9.11 Restated

If there were two climbers, one starting at the bottom at 3 P.M. and the other starting at the top at 3 P.M., would they meet on the path? We assume they will both be off the path by 6 P.M. and they had to stay on the same path.

The answer to the restatement, most everyone readily agrees, is "yes." Hence there must be a point on the path that our "unsocial" climber would pass at exactly the same time of the day during ascent and descent. (It may help you to see that by noting that the same point at the same time is redundant, at least in this problem). Clearly the statement of a problem structures the problem in such a way as to facilitate or inhibit finding a solution.

Moving on to *Problem 9.4* the radius of the circle jumps out at you when you realize that the diagonals of a square are of equal length (assuming you remember what a radius is).

Problem 9.4

What is the diameter of the circle in the figure?

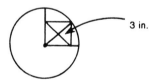

Thus the radius is 3 inches, and the diameter is 6 inches.

Problem 9.5 requires a restructuring, too, but of a slightly different sort. One might say it requires a *radical* solution (Note: radical is a hint). Most people read the equation VII = I as Roman Numeral seven equals one. They then look for ways to move one of the matchsticks from the left side to the right, or even try to make an inequality such as VI ≠ I. But the problem is to "make both sides equal by moving one match," which can be done by perceptually restructuring the left side of the equation so as to visualize a square root sign. Then the solution looks like this:

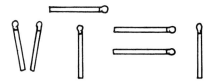

Problems 9.7–10 are all similar in a way: they all require you to get beyond a self-imposed set or rigid structure that will be debilitating in terms of finding a solution. Sometimes a problem's solution can be facilitated by a hint. For mathematicians and others who know that the word radical means square root sign, then the hint was a virtual give-away of the solution. For those whose previous experience did not include that piece of information, or for those whose memories are good but short, the hint was probably no help at all.

Moving on to *Problem 9.7*, about John and Mary lying dead on the floor with water, glass and fur lying around, a useful hint might be the following:

Problem 9.7 (Hint 1): Who were John and Mary?

If that doesn't help much, consider another hint:

Problem 9.7 (Hint 2): Were John and Mary people?

More explicit hints could be given, but by now you might have reasoned that if John and Mary were goldfish, a cat could have knocked their bowl down and had a good portion of them for lunch. The set that we impose on ourselves in this problem is that of assuming that things with names like John and Mary are people.

Does that solution suggest the answer to *Problem 9.9?* Feminists like to use problems like this, which provides a hint.

The nine dots in *Problem 9.8* can be connected by four straight lines without retracing or lifting the pencil off the paper only when you realize that the outer dots do not define a boundary. The lines can—indeed, must—extend beyond the rectangle formed by the dots. Then one correct solution is this one:

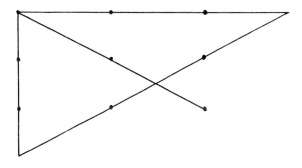

Similarly, *Problem 9.10* requires that you go beyond the natural tendency (for most people) to find a two-dimensional solution. If you think about a three-dimensional solution, an answer is more likely to occur to you: a pyramid.

Some Preliminary Conclusions

What conclusions can be drawn from the above attempts at problem solving?

1. Just because you have *had* something before does not mean you remember it.
2. Just because you remember something (i.e., it is available or even accessible to you) does not mean you can apply it to a new problem.
3. Just because you understand all the parts of a problem does not mean you will perceive it in a way that facilitates finding the solution.

Many problems require for their solution an associative or perceptual restructuring not unlike the figure-ground reversals involved in perceptual illusions. While there are undoubtedly wide individual differences in the ability to avoid rigidifying mental sets and to restructure problems, it is also the case that the statement of the problem and our previous experiences with it affect our solution processes. The conclusions, so far, are decidedly negative—that is, they state how difficult problem solving is, but do not establish the conditions for making it easier. To understand those, we shall need to consider transfer theory, to which we now turn.

Transfer of Learning and Teaching For Transfer
by
J. Ronald Gentile and Colleen McNeil[1]

The paradox of learning a really new competence is this: that a student cannot at first understand what he needs to learn, can learn it only by educating himself, and can educate himself by only beginning to do what he does not yet understand. (Schön, 1987, p. 93)

When students ask their teachers the inevitable question, "Why do we have to learn this stuff?" teachers always answer with some variation of the following: "Because you'll need it to be able to do (or understand) X later on." This is seldom a satisfactory answer to students for any number of reasons, including: it requires an understanding of the structure of knowledge and how this piece fits in, it requires imagination of how ideas can transcend situations, it requires delayed gratification, and it requires trusting that one's teachers know what is good for you. None of these qualities exist in abundant supply in most late-twentieth century American students.

Such issues may, in fact, epitomize the fundamental tension between teacher and student. To continue with Schön's elaboration of the above quote in the hypothetical words of master to novice,

"I can tell there is something you need to know, and with my help you may be able to learn it. But I cannot tell you what it is in a way you can now understand. I can only arrange for you to have the right sorts of experiences for yourself. You must be willing, therefore, to have these experiences. Then you will be able to make an informed choice about whether you wish to continue. If you are unwilling to step into this new experience without knowing ahead of time what it will be like, I cannot help you. You must trust me."

Schön was speaking, of course, of complex learnings requiring higher order skill or cognitive processes that can only be acquired over a significant period of time. Moreover, he was speaking of skills or cognitive processes that will *transfer* beyond the particulars of the learning experience to new materials, examples, or situations.

Transfer vs. Learning vs. Memory

Transfer, the central issue of this chapter, depends upon learning and memory for what was learned, but it goes beyond those. *Learning* implies the acquisition of *new* skills, information, strategies, or ways of thinking (such as initially coming to understand how and why we need to invert and multiply in dividing fractions). *Memory* implies that those newly-acquired skills and rules have been retained past the initial learning session and are accessible at some later time (such as to do homework that evening or to pass a test at a later date). *Transfer* implies being able to use

Cartoon 9.1

the material in new and different problems or settings, including the ability to recognize when and where the learnings are appropriate (such as on word problems requiring decisions about whether multiplication or division is necessary, or recognizing the usefulness of the information or skill in a different course or in a real life problem). Whereas learning and memory can be accomplished without understanding—as Madeline Hunter joked, "Ours is not to wonder why; just invert and multiply"—transfer is a higher order thinking skill. If you don't understand why, you cannot reconstruct your knowledge. If you forget a step, you cannot see commonalities or differences among situations, and your knowledge is isolated and inert. Therefore you will see little reason for having had "to learn this stuff."

The above account strikes some as portraying a bleak outlook for transfer which, as we shall see, has been amply supported by a century of empirical data and theorizing: *spontaneous transfer*, after learning is apparently extremely rare. The disappointing empirical evidence, furthermore, is not limited to children transferring school learnings, but includes teachers—and professors—applying new teaching techniques, as well as the general population in, for example, thinking metric (as Linus in the Peanuts comic strip once complained, "How can you do new math with an old math mind?"). This creates a dilemma for educators who must believe that "this stuff" will be useful, or why bother to teach at all? Perhaps educators can relate to the sign Prof. Thomas Shuell had in his office: "I'm not a pessimist; I'm an optimist who suffers a lot."

Indeed, we would not be writing this if we had lost hope. Thus the purpose of this chapter is to provide a brief history of transfer, including the so-called behaviorist and cognitive approaches; a description of current trends; and some conclusions and suggestions for teaching and curriculum development. You may have noted that our conclusion in the previous paragraph that transfer was rare italicized *spontaneous*. This implies that there must be ways to plan and teach for transfer to remove it from the endangered thinking list. On this belief we reject pessimism and shall try to document our case for being suffering optimists.

Photo 9.1. Transferring biology lessons to the aquarium?

A Century of Transfer Research

The seminal studies of transfer were conducted by one of the founding fathers of the field of educational psychology, E. L. Thorndike, in collaboration with R. S. Woodworth. They set out to test the dominant educational theory of their time—namely, a belief that if one studies certain "formal disciplines" such as mathematics or Latin, the benefits would be to impose order on the mind that would make the student a better thinker in general. In a series of experiments (Thorndike & Woodworth, 1901; Thorndike, 1923); they found that whatever benefits accrued from studying these formal disciplines (such as greater facility with that discipline), they did not transfer to other disciplines or to improvements in thinking in general.

Measuring Transfer

Before considering theoretical explanations or other issues, you may be wondering how transfer effects are measured. The standard research design for studying transfer effects uses the same logic as drug or toothpaste studies. An experimental group uses the product for a while (A) and is subsequently tested on blood pressure, number of cavities, etc. (B). Meanwhile, a control group does whatever they normally do or receives a placebo (during part A) and is subsequently examined in blood pressure or cavities (B). Assuming random assignment of people to the groups (or some other way to equalize the groups at the start), then if the experimental group does better than the control group, the drug or toothpaste is judged effective and estimated efficacy is often reported as "x reduced cavities by 16%."

In parallel with the drug study logic, transfer designs tend to take either of the following two forms (e.g., Bugelski, 1979; Ellis, 1965; Ferguson, 1956):

(1) Experimental Group: Learn A   Learn B
    Control Group: Rest (i.e.,   Learn B
                                normal activity)

(2) Experimental Group   Learn A   Learn B   Test on B
    Control Group   Rest   Learn B   Test on B

In both forms of the design, "rest" for the control group is interpreted to mean "the normal routine" or "an activity that keeps the students occupied and gives them an amount of teacher attention equal to that of the experimental group." In the first design, rate of learning task B is the outcome measure. In the second design, some kind of test or demonstration is given to compare how much of B was learned or remembered either immediately after task B was completed or at some subsequent time. In either case, the following conclusions are possible:

Positive transfer: The experimental group learns B faster, or scores higher on the test of B, than the control group.

Negative transfer: The control group learns B faster, or scores higher on the test of B, than the experimental group.

Zero transfer: There is no statistically significant difference between the experimental and control groups in rate of learning or amount recalled of B.

In parallel with the drug studies, it is also possible to estimate extent of transfer by the following formula (Murdock, 1957):

$$\text{Percent of Transfer} = \frac{E - C}{E + C} \times 100$$

where E and C are the mean scores of the experimental and control groups, respectively. Thus if students learn Logo (or some other computer assisted system) before studying geometry, they can be compared with a control group who studies geometry without the technological introduction on (1) rate of learning specific geometry principles and (2) score on a test of what was learned. If the Logo group averaged 85% correct, while the control students averaged 65%, then the conclusion would be that positive transfer occurred, and furthermore, that Logo boosted performance by about 13%. If the numbers were reversed, then negative transfer would have occurred, with the conclusion that learning Logo had a 13% interference effect. Whether or not such a study has been done, it may be noted that Logo has been touted as a tool for increasing the depth of thinking about geometry and, by some disciples of Logo, of thinking in general (e.g., Papert, 1980). Formal discipline theory isn't dead: it's alive and well and living in the promoters of curricula for technology, whole language, critical thinking, cognitive strategies, and even Latin and the classics. With the proper experiments, however, these claims can be tested.

An Early Theory of Transfer: Identical Elements

In parallel with his landmark experiments, Thorndike proposed an influential theory of transfer, known as "identical elements" theory, to account for the empirical data. As its name implies, transfer was argued to depend upon the number of identical (or highly similar) features or stimuli that exist both in the learning environment and in the environment in which the newly learned knowledge or skill was to be used. For example, a mathematical principle or thinking strategy would be more likely to be considered relevant and applied to a problem never before seen if the new problem (1) occurred in the same teacher's class than with another teacher, (2) in another math class than in science or social studies, and (3) in problems structured in similar ways to those originally learned than in very different ways.

One exception to such predictions—that is, a situation to which identical elements transfer theory did not transfer—is the case in which identical elements exist, but have contradictory or antagonistic meanings or behaviors associated with them in the original and new environments. Common educational examples include the following:

- false cognates in languages: e.g., bekommen, which in German means to receive, not to become; or constipado in Spanish which means to have a cold, not to be constipated, as their nearly identical spellings would predict.
- homonyms: e.g., their, they're and there; its and it's; and to, too, and two all sound identical and thus make it difficult for students to use the appropriate word in their own writing.
- multiple meanings of the same word or symbol: e.g., in different subjects or formulas, v = velocity, volume, versus, or five; negative reinforcement in behavioral psychology means learning to escape or avoid a situation rather than implying bad behavior or punishment as it is used in general parlance.

To incorporate these kinds of exceptions, Osgood (1949) developed a more complex model of identical elements theory, though it seemed to be most applicable to paired-associates learning, like vocabulary building, than to transfer generally.

Anecdote 9.1

An Example of a Common Theme or Principle in Two Problems

Perhaps the most celebrated problem of all time is the following:

Problem 9.12. A father and his son were driving along a highway when the father suddenly lost control of the car and crashed into a telephone pole. The father was killed instantly and his son was seriously injured. The boy was rushed to the hospital where it was found he was suffering from serious internal injuries. A prominent surgeon was immediately summoned. Upon seeing the boy, the surgeon gasped, "I can't operate on this boy. He is my son!" How can this be?

The reason the above problem is so famous is because it was widely publicized by the women's rights movement some years ago, which should provide a hint for the solution (same hint as in Problem 9.9). If you've discovered the principle, then you should be able to solve the following problem:

Problem 9.13. A mayor was going into a room to meet a secretary, a nurse, and a cheerleader, whom he had never met before. On the way into the room, he was told that one of them, named Mary, had just won the lottery.

As soon as he walked in the room, he said to the cheerleader, "Congratulations on winning the lottery, Mary." How did he know the cheerleader was named Mary?

Note: The answer is in Note 2.

Nevertheless, the thrust of the empirical research was confirming, in general, the central point—namely, with the exceptions noted above, that the greater the similarity between the learning and test environments, the greater the likelihood of positive transfer (e.g., Bugelski, 1979; Deese & Hulse, 1967; Hilgard & Bower, 1966; Ellis, 1965; Travers, 1977). Also, the theory was not limited to micro-level stimulus-response elements, but was able to include thinking and principles (e.g., Hendrickson & Schroeder, 1941; Judd, 1908; Perkins & Salomon, 1989; Travers, 1977). For example, if a student learned a principle concerning, say, light refraction, that was similar to the kind of reasoning needed to solve a new problem, then that was an even better identical element than a stimulus-response commonality. (See anecdote 9.1 for another example.)

Despite an implicit optimism in the above paragraph, the empirical evidence has been decidedly pessimistic since, as it turns out, the vast majority of tasks and situations have only a few elements in common. Parts 1 and 2 of Figure 9.1 represent this situation in Venn diagram form. According to identical elements theory, positive transfer is impossible in the case represented in part 1 and unlikely in part 2. Furthermore, what counts is not the actual proportion of common elements between the tasks, but the perceived common elements. Deese and Hulse (1967) made the case this way:

If there is in fact zero commonality between the requirements of a task, but the individual, because of previous experience, brings elements from previous tasks to bear, there will be negative transfer. Therefore it is theoretically possible, at least, for negative transfer to occur when there is no relation between tasks whatever. (p. 358).

But even when many common elements make positive transfer potentially likely, as in Part 3 of figure 9.1, people can choose the wrong elements to apply and turn even positive transfer into negative. Deese and Hulse (1967) put it this way:

. . . the misapplication of previous experience to a given task is, in theory, unlimited. That becomes obvious when we realize that the set of conditions which do not satisfy effective performance on any given task is infinite. In theory, people can go on forever trying out the wrong habits in the attempt to learn some new skill. (p. 358).

In other words, they summarized,

. . . the limit on negative transfer is not set by the commonality between the requirements of tasks; it is set by the conditions which induce human beings to try to give up the application of old habits. (p. 358).

Interference Theory

By the time Deese and Hulse were writing, identical elements theory had evolved into a somewhat broader conception known as interference theory. Still including the identical elements arguments from above, it incorporated both transfer and memory into the equation, allowing a more complex view of the cognitive processes involved and with additional instructional implications. Including memory meant among other things expanding the experimental design to include a test on what was remembered about task A after task B intervened (as when teachers try in May to get

1. No Identical Elements Between Tasks A and B:

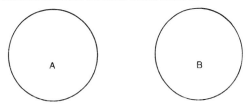

2. A Few Identical Elements Between Tasks A and B:

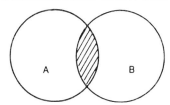

3. Many Identical Elements Between Tasks A and B:

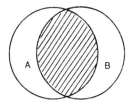

Figure 9.1. Schematic representations of the amount of transfer possible.

students to remember something they studied in October). The experimental procedure was called the *retroactive* design, in the sense of being a retrospective, and had at least the following groups (e.g., Bugelski, 1979; Ellis, 1965; Ferguson, 1956):

Experimental Group   Learn A   Learn B   Test on A
Control Group   Learn A   Rest   Test on A

Rest for the control group is interpreted as an activity that keeps the mind occupied and prevents rehearsal, much as in the transfer design described in a previous section.

To have parallel terminology, the second transfer design (in the section on Measuring Transfer) was called a *proactive* design, since the early experiences from task A were acting in a forward direction to affect memory for

Table 9.1 Proactive and retroactive designs and possible conclusions.

Proactive Design

Experimental Group:	Learn A	Learn B	Test on B
Control Group:	Rest	Learn B	Test on B

Possible Conclusions:
  If E>C, then A enhances recall of B (proactive facilitation)
  If E<C, then A inhibits recall of B (proactive interference)
  If E=C, then A has no effect on recall of B

Retroactive Design

Experimental Group:	Learn A	Learn B	Test on A
Control Group:	Learn A	Rest	Test on A

Possible Conclusions:
  If E>C, then B enhanced recall of A (retroactive facilitation)
  If E<C, then B inhibits recall of A (retroactive interference)
  If E=C, then B has no effect on recall of A

task B, in the sense of being a prospective. Table 9.1 reprints the designs along with a summary of possible conclusions.

What the proactive-retroactive conception points out, perhaps better than earlier theories, is that any experience occurs in a continuous historical sequence, affected by previous experience. At the same time, each experience influences subsequent experiences, as well as the recall of previous experiences. In the experimental psychological literature, this insight stimulated a plethora of research and analysis on such questions as whether proactive or retroactive interference (also called inhibition) effects were more potent (e.g., McGeoch & Irion, 1952; Schulz, 1960; Underwood, 1957). Such research—perhaps both mundane and esoteric in retrospect—was also most notable for its absorption with the interference side of the coin, to the exclusion of possible facilitation effects. But it could handle each and could easily be applied to questions about curriculum sequences. Consider the following common experiences (and anecdote 9.2):

Proactive Interference: previous experience makes it more difficult to learn or remember new material, as when people accustomed to feet and inches have to learn (or fear learning) the metric system.

Proactive Facilitation: previous experience makes it easier to learn or remember new material, as when learning a visual imaging technique helps people remember names and faces or states and capitals.

Retroactive Interference: subsequent experience makes it more difficult to learn or remember previously learned material, as when recent classes interfere with recall of students from early in the teacher's career.

Retroactive Facilitation: subsequent experience makes it easier to learn or remember previously learned material, as when the

Anecdote 9.2

Proactive Interference in a Spanish Classroom

I sometimes read a list of words one by one and had the students repeat them after me as a group. Great, no problem. But when the time came for them to say a word individually as I went around the room, it was difficult to get three correct pronunciations in a row—all because they had reverted back to pronouncing the Spanish vowels like English vowels.

One of the biggest pronunciation problems, for example, concerns the syllable *con.* In Spanish this syllable is pronounced like the English word "cone", but no matter what the situation, the students pronounced it "con" as in "pro and con". *Contestar,* which means "to answer" in Spanish is forever pronounced with that English sound. Another problem is the word *de* which means "from" or "of". This is pronounced like the English word "day", but I hear "dee" 90% of the time.

Semantic construction is another source of interference from English. In order to say "Spanish class" in Spanish you must say *clase de español,* or "class of Spanish", but the students have a hard time doing this. On many exercises I still get *español clase.* The same goes with possessives. In order to say "John's book" in Spanish you must say *el libro de Juan* or "the book of John", but someone will invariably write *Juan's libro.*

Joseph Walter
Teacher

biological classification system helps us understand and categorize the animals (e.g., dogs, cats and dinosaurs) we learned as children.

Educational Implications of Early Theories

The implications of the above theoretical arguments and empirical findings were obvious to the researchers, many of whom published suggestions for teachers. Specific suggestions included the following (e.g., DeCecco, 1968; Ellis, 1965; Gagné, 1970, Hunter, 1971; Shuell & Lee, 1976; Travers, 1977):

1. Knowledge or skills cannot be transferred unless first mastered to a high level.
2. Since all new learnings are forgotten (i.e., suffer interference effects), practice must

Cartoon 9.2

be distributed over time (instead of massed or crammed) and retrieval cues provided so that the material is accessible from memory when needed.
3. Since practice with one method or strategy not only increases the ability to do similar problems (i.e., learning to learn) but also reinforces the notion that that method is the "one best method," it is important to learn multiple methods or strategies for solving problems. This avoids the rigidifying effects known as mental or perceptual set and emphasizes the problem solving behavior over the outcome (i.e., process over product).
4. Because many facts or skills are specific to certain topics or situations, focus should be on general principles and strategies which are likely to be useful in (i.e., have identical elements with) many situations.
5. Arrange the learning/practice and transfer environments to be as similar as possible.
6. Sequence the curriculum so that each new unit to be studied (1) reinforces, reviews and incorporates what was learned in previous units and courses; and (2) anticipates and sets the stage for what is going to be learned in subsequent units and courses.

Such advice is, of course, general and not likely to be transferred by teachers or professors to their own classrooms by just reading about it, as the advice itself prophesies. But we'll reserve the implications for staff development to the end of this chapter. Meanwhile, two additional comments seem worth making in the context of the above suggestions.

First, consider how easy it is to violate principle #6 in actual teaching practice. For example, in teaching fractions to young children, it is quite common to use pies and cakes, or the like, to demonstrate the whole and fractions of the whole. When the curriculum evolves to addition and subtraction of these fractions of a pie (3/4 minus 1/5 = 11/20 or slightly more than half a pie), commonality of the concept seems to be preserved. But what happens when students, who have learned in that way, ask the teacher what it means in multiplying or dividing fractions to divide 3/4 of a pie by 1/5 of a pie; furthermore, how can division lead to the larger answer, 3 and 3/4, when division leads to smaller answers with whole numbers? Many teachers, not fully understanding the reasons themselves, fall back on such excuses as, "Well it doesn't work with pies" or "Ours is not to wonder why; just invert and multiply."

Such answers, however, undermine the kind of trust that is needed by students for their teachers (see the opening quotes by Schön, 1987): "Learn it this way because you'll need it later on" becomes "Forget everything you learned previously because it doesn't work here."[3]

If teachers do not know how to build on previous knowledge, methods and examples, then interference effects will run rampant and, it could be argued, it would be better if pies had never been used at all in teaching fractions. Of course, it *is* possible to link pies and division of fractions in a way that provides proactive and retroactive facilitation (see Figure 9.2), but if teachers themselves, are not familiar and competent with the entire curricular sequence—first through sixth grades, say—then they are not likely to be able to identify and solve such problems.

Finally, returning to principle 5, consider what Thorndike, Bregman, Tilton, & Woodyard (1928) had to say in a book entitled, *Adult Learning*:

Children now learn about voting in civics in grades 7 and 8, seven years before they can vote. They learn the arithmetic of notes years before they will probably have any occasion to borrow or lend money on a note. Certain facts of history and geography they learn only to have forgotten them when the occasion to use them arrives. Other things being equal, the best time to learn anything is just before you have to use it. (p. 191)

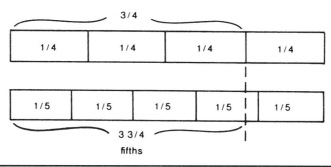

Figure 9.2. Division of fractions: Easy as pie or a piece of cake.

Identical elements theory, combined with a series of investigations on adults as learners, convinced Thorndike et al. that formal schooling much beyond elementary school was wasteful for many reasons, including that school learning is separated from the work, or transfer, environment. What is necessary, they said, is to apply "The Dewey doctrine of 'First the need then the knowledge or technique to satisfy the need'" (p. 190). They go on to say:

> We can of course, devise forms of schooling which bid fair to be much better for inner growth than the average forms of labor open to boys and girls in their teens. But we could also devise forms of labor which would be so. It is significant that the changes made in schools to improve them from this point of view often seek to duplicate the "real world" in general in the school. Why should the chief activity of the real world be so rigorously excluded? The history of schooling does not warrant a bigoted optimism concerning schools as benefactors to inner growth. They have indeed been chief sinners.

> According to the best present theory, the silent, motionless, memorizing elementary school, which was in vogue until about a generation ago, repressed, thwarted and deformed mental growth. (p. 187).

To truly satisfy the Dewey doctrine as well as transfer theory, according to Thorndike, we should not have spent our tax money on secondary schools, but on work environments which provide education on what is needed, when it is needed, in the situation in which it is needed.

Cognitive Constructivism and Situated Cognition

The last quote by Thorndike may seem to have been a radical one, if only because it would have prevented much of secondary education as we know it from becoming societal practice. Ironically, the most dominant current

Anecdote 9.3

> # "The Thinker" in Greeno's Pastures
>
> In a comparison of the prior cognitive or behavioral and new situated conceptualizations of learning, Greeno (1994) presents the earlier conception as analogous to the great sculpture of "The Thinker". The figure, seated alone, chin on hand, represents the solitary, passive, silent student lost in abstract thought. New conceptions of learning in the theory of situated learning present a different view. Where the "Thinker" is solitary and silent, we must now reconceptualize thinking, learning, and knowing as social and active. The learner is not quietly absorbing knowledge, but is actively constructing it, applying his own prior experience to create a unique interpretation. He is explaining and arguing with others, listening to and incorporating those parts of their ideas that he feels are valuable.
>
>

theory—known as situational cognition (Brown, Collins & Duguid, 1989)—is at least as radical:

> *Unfortunately, students are too often asked to use the tools of a discipline without being able to adopt its culture. To learn to use the tools as practitioners use them, a student, like an apprentice, must enter that community and its culture. (p. 33)*
>
> *. . . If we take learning to be a process of enculturation, it is possible to clarify this distinction and to explain why much school work is inauthentic and thus not fully productive of useful learning. (p. 34)*

So how did situational cognition theory come to reach a conclusion to which Thorndike would have subscribed? From very different kinds of evidence, it turns out, associated with what has come to be known as the "cognition revolution."

Although the emergence of the field of cognitive psychology is usually traced to Neisser's (1967) book of the same name, there were influential predecessors, including Ausubel (1963), Bruner (1960), Spearman (1923), and of course a number of Piagetians and the more recently popular Vygotskians. To understand their findings and the educational implications they draw from them, let's turn first to their methods.

Some of the most informative and influential contributions to the cognitive revolution were studies comparing relative experts and novices in their learning and memory strategies. We shall discuss this body of research in chapter 11, but for now, we shall just ask the question of how people develop from novices to experts. The answer, according to situated cognition theorists (Brown et al., 1989; Brown & Duguid, 1993), is through authentic activities experienced in the culture of the practitioners of that field.

There are three major components, all interrelated, to the acquisition of knowledge in the theory of situated learning. The first is that knowledge, in both a qualitative and quantitative sense, is largely determined by the activity through which it is learned. This ties into the idea that learning must be active rather than passive (as in the still-all-too-prevalent didactic methods to which Thorndike also objected in the passage cited earlier). See anecdote 9.3 for Greeno's reconceptualization of activity in thinking.

The second component is that learning is seen as dependent on the context in which it occurs. In a naturally occurring setting, knowledge is not developed by an isolated individual; it is a part of a long history of prior knowledge that arose from social negotiations and is learned with the social support of the community of users of that knowledge.

The final component of situational learning theory is the culture in which the knowledge is developed and used. Concepts learned abstractly are unlikely to be recalled, even when prompted, as the recall is too dependent on the irrelevant (to the real world) cues found in the classroom. Educational activities need to be designed to "enculture" the learner in the field of the information to be learned. Information, concepts, and thinking strategies are the tools of real world practitioner, which ". . . can only be fully understood through use, and using them entails both changing the user's view of the world and adopting the belief system of the culture in which they are learned" (Brown et al., 1989, p. 33).

As noted above, the educational implications of this view are authentic activities which (1) provide an environment for learners to actively explore and develop their own learning, (2) provide social support and information about the types of support available in that real world situation, and (3) provide the cultural context of the information to be learned, including the vocabulary of the domain of study and the types of work situations in which practitioners are placed. These activities are theorized to promote better original learning, a higher degree of retention, and an increased likelihood of transfer.

If authentic activities exist in continuum, the most authentic would probably occur in the world of "just plain folk" (according to J. Lave as cited in Brown et al., 1989) doing their work and solving problems in their own domains of expertise: masons finding ways to build a wall that will withstand erosion in a wet environment, teachers finding ways to overcome a student's frustration, etc. At this end of the continuum, the learner would have an on-the-job apprenticeship with an expert (at the construction site, in a school, etc.). A little further down the continuum would be individual or small group tutorials, as are often done with private music or tennis lessons (Schön, 1983; 1987).

At the other end of the continuum would be classrooms in which learning is competitive, the subject and nature of the problems change every hour (or 42 minutes), the teacher is the primary source of knowledge, and the topic is broken into artificially small, discrete parts (Brown & Duguid, 1993; Young, 1993). Authentic activity, in contrast, suggests that knowledge resides outside the academy in a myriad of sources, including other students (e.g., Damarin, 1993; Pea, 1989), in large composite problems. The task for students is not to learn first how to add, subtract, multiply and divide and later to use them on real problems; rather the task is to encounter the real problems, learn to break them into their component parts and learn to add, subtract, multiply and divide in that context (Brown et al., 1989; Brown & Duguid, 1993).

To be able to do this in current schools would fall somewhere in the middle of the continuum, with classroom environments created to resemble those in the real world. This would include social groupings, peer tutoring, and modeling of expert reasoning strategies on large life-like problems with which experts concern themselves. Brown et al. call this kind of learning a cognitive apprenticeship, give several examples, and summarize the approach with this analogy:

Cognitive apprenticeship methods try to enculturate students into authentic practices through activity and social interaction in a way similar to that evident—and evidently successful—in craft apprenticeship. (p. 37)

Educational Implications of Situated Cognition

Situated cognition, although it has little direct empirical evidence to support it and some critics (e.g., Anderson, Reder & Simon, 1996), is clearly in the mainstream of the popular cognitive constructivist movement. Supporters advocate the following: constructed knowledge, based on activities that are authentic and mediated by experts in the cultural context in which the knowledge naturally resides and will be used.

The irony of this, as noted earlier, is that situated cognition theory, even more than identical elements theory, predicts that learning is situation specific. Transfer from one domain of expertise, field or craft to another is unlikely because the knowledge base is fundamentally situated or contextualized. Therefore, even general tools like thinking strategies, heuristics or indeed chisels are nontransferable:

Thus, carpenters and cabinet makers use chisels differently. Because tools and the way they are used reflect the particular accumulated insights of communities, it is not possible to use a tool appropriately without understanding the community or culture in which it is used. (Brown et al., 1989, p. 33).

What, specifically, then are the educational implications? In the greatest irony of all, the theory predicts that there can be no implications for educators unless those educators actively constructed such implications by being enculturated in mediated situated cognitive studies. But ignoring that irony, the implication is that learning contexts must be created to simulate as closely as possible the target culture and practices of the folks who use the knowledge to be learned. Biology classes should resemble medical labs, or the like; literature classes should resemble the apochryphal coffee houses where poets and novelists ex-

Of course you'll have culture shock! What else *can* you have in a country where you drive on parkways and park on driveways!

Cartoon 9.3

change ideas, or the like; and methods classes in education should resemble, or better be apprenticeships in, actual on-going classrooms. Anything less borders on inauthentic activity with little or no transfer value.

A Synthesis and More Optimistic Conclusion

It is difficult to resist the overwhelming converging evidence from all of the scientific approaches described above that transfer, even when teachers try to teach for it, is a rare commodity. Nevertheless, whenever such arguments are made—recently, for example, in a volume edited by Detterman and Sternberg (1993)—someone comes up with counter-examples (e.g., Pressley & Yokoi, 1994, in a review of Detterman & Sternberg's book). In fact, the ability to come up with counter-examples may be a prime exemplar of a transferable skill that philosophers try to teach, as Perkins and Salomon (1989) argued, thus snatching hope (if not victory) from the jaws of defeat.

Of course, it is one thing to find counter-examples and another to prove transfer. Perkins and Salomon provide such other anecdotes as Schoenfeld's and Polya's research on use of heuristics in mathematical problem solving, but point out that ". . . such observations do not make the empirical case that these skills can be decontextualized and applied more broadly;" that is, they offer ". . . no evidence of transfer" (p. 21). But that is the last bit of bad news we shall present.

The good news is twofold. First, all of the above theories probably underestimate the potential for transfer (Anderson et al., 1996). Ability to find counter-examples, discover logical fallacies, or use the scientific method are certainly examples of thinking that are not directly tied to specific contexts. The least context-dependent skill of all, of course, is reading; reading's positive transfer is certainly the reason it is so central to all education schemes.

A second bit of good news is that teaching techniques continue to be invented which take advantage of the suggestions arising from the last century of evidence and theorizing on transfer. Perkins and Salomon (1989) have been in the forefront of helping us transfer those principles of transfer. Specifically, they distinguish between two mechanisms of transfer:

- The "Low Road" to Transfer: ". . . much practice, in a large variety of situations, leading to a *high level of mastery and near-automaticity*" (p. 22).
- The "High Road" To Transfer: ". . . deliberate mindful abstraction of a principle" (p. 22).

On the "low road" we learn to practice driving, for example, to the point of such automaticity that we can eventually generalize to other cars with different transmissions, and so forth. There are limits to this transfer, such that driving cars may not easily transfer to backing up in a tractor trailer. In addition, we may not have a good understanding of the principles underlying our skill (e.g., speed vs. distance ratios for stopping). Nevertheless, we have taken advantage of suggestions 1,2,3 and 5 (in the section entitled Educational Implications of Early Theories) and thereby increased the probability of transfer of this skill.

On the "high road" we focus on generating the principles, recognizing their operation and connectedness in many situations or fields, and accumulating knowledge about and experience with these principles in various domains, so as to learn when and where they might be relevant. This is the kind of *general transfer* which Bruner (1960) linked to attitudes or dispositions as well as principles, placing them at the

> . . . *heart of the educational process—the continual broadening and deepening of knowledge in terms of basic and general ideas.* (p. 17)

As promised, there are exemplars of both "low road" or specific and "high road" or general teaching techniques which have been shown, empirically as well as theoretically, to have considerable promise. The use of what has variously been called an *anticipatory set* (Hunter, 1982; Gentile, 1993) or an *advance organizer* (Ausubel, 1960; 1963) is a case of the former. At the beginning of a lesson, the teacher can introduce an activity that requires students to retrieve from their memories information that is congruent with the lesson. For example, to set the stage for a lesson on light refraction, place a pencil in a glass half full of water and have students draw what they see. Show students an excellent and a poor performance of a skill (e.g., volleying in tennis) and have them discuss the differences in position before trying the shot themselves. Have students, in pairs, review their homework to agree how they might teach the process to a beginner; then have a lesson on the use of that principle or method on a new class of problems.

The invention of reciprocal teaching (Palincsar & Brown, 1984; Rosenshine & Meister, 1994) is an exemplar of the "high road" to transfer for reading comprehension. In this case, students take turns leading a dialogue on pertinent features of a text, learning to summarize (including self-review), question, clarify, and predict. Such techniques become general strategies because they teach children to monitor their own cognitive processes—when they understand and what to do when they don't—and how to identify whether the difficulty is in their own understanding or is an incongruity in the text. Of course, transfer will still be better the more knowledge you have in the domain—that is, you cannot easily summarize, question, clarify or predict if you are reading about advanced physics and know none of the prerequisites.

Thus, the teacher needs to establish the following conditions for "high road" transfer (Perkins & Salomon, 1989, p. 22):

- Learners must learn to see how problems resemble each other.
- Learners must become familiar with the problem domains (i.e., must have sufficient knowledge or experience in that field).
- Learners must have examples of and practice with rules or principles, not just with facts and skills (although principles without facts and skills are probably also useless). Whether these principles are best "discovered" is still an open question, although it certainly cannot hurt to discover them.
- Learners should negotiate all of the above in a social context ". . . whereby justifications, principles, and explanations are socially fostered, generated, and contrasted." (p. 22)

If, furthermore, both high road and low road transfer can be combined into a spiral curriculum which continues to revisit and reorganize concepts at higher levels of complexity, then we shall reap the additional benefits of scaffolding (e.g., Glaser, 1984), learning hierarchies Gagné (1970), and proactive and retroactive facilitation. Perhaps then we would be on track to making Bruner's (1960) famous hypothesis come true:

> . . . any subject can be taught effectively in some intellectually honest form to any child at any stage of development. (p. 33)

Transfer, Teaching, and Staff Development

"Why", we educators might ask, "do we have to learn this stuff?" The answer, according to the above account, is so that we educators can take the "high road" to teaching for transfer. Without knowing the history of transfer, we are destined to repeat the mistakes. Without knowing the basic facts and research methods of transfer, we are likely to be at the mercy of educational entrepreneurs with their "one best way," when what is needed is practice with a variety of techniques. Without knowing the principles of transfer, we are not likely to discuss learning sequences with educators at all levels to design spiral curricula.

Finally, without knowing the principles of transfer, we are likely to settle for less than adequate staff development programs. If we educators want to continue learning new techniques and transfer them to our own classrooms and curricula, then our own staff development programs must include:

- learning the new material to a high level
- learning the principles on which the new material is based
- observing experts and practicing and receiving feedback in their presence
- practicing under a variety of conditions distributed in time
- learning more than one way to accomplish the same ends

- practicing the new material in the target environments
- reflecting on our own practice
- discussing, justifying, explaining, coaching and debating in a collaborative environment of peers

Fortunately, the staff development literature has long included many of these suggestions (e.g., Joyce & Showers, 1980; Joyce, Hersh & McKibbin, 1983). If our own staff development programs do not incorporate these principles of transfer, we probably need to reflect on whether we practice what we preach. Why *do* we have to learn this stuff, anyway?

Some Special Topics in Transfer

The preceding sections on transfer and teaching for transfer traced the major trends of the field for the last hundred years. A few specialized topics were left out, however, and in this section I hope to correct those omissions.

Learning to Learn: Efficacy Plus Rigidity

If a succession of problems is quite similar, as might be found in an exercise workbook for practicing arithmetic skills, students will show improvement over time in the ease and speed with which they can solve the problems (as you may have in solving the water jar problems). We might say that over the course of learning how to solve them, the students were *learning how to learn*.

Harlow (1949) investigated this *learning-to-learn* phenomenon systematically over a wide age-range in longitudinal studies of monkeys learning successive discrimination problems. On the first problem the monkey moved one of two common objects (e.g., a block and a cup) to find which one hid a food reward. The monkey then had to make this same discrimination

Photo 9.2. Piano recital: An example of transfer.

(with position of the block and cup randomly changed from trial to trial) for a number of other trials until they were reliably anticipating where the food was hidden. Then they were shifted to a new problem (e.g., a cylinder and a plate). On successive problems different objects were used, but the goal was the same. After studying many animals solving hundreds of such problems, the results consistently showed that in the initial stages the monkeys responded by trial-and error for many trials before finally "catching on." After experience with many such problems, however, their response to a new problem was correct by the first or second trial. That is, if they chose the correct object the first time, they stuck with it on the next trials; if they chose the wrong one the first time, they switched on the next trial and then stuck with the correct choice. The monkeys had learned how to learn and now had a *learning set*, a set to respond which was facilitative of solving the new discrimination problems.

Similar studies have been done on humans solving problems (e.g., Duncan, 1960), showing similar learning-to-learn results. What seems to be required for learning-to-learn to occur is (1) a number of successive experiences on (2) the same kind of problem. For example, a new song to be played on the piano may be based on identical chords, or have similar fingering of arpeggios to previously learned songs. Or, we may practice applying the same algebraic formula to a wide variety of problems. We are becoming more efficient at learning new songs or solving new problems. Learning to learn, in such cases, is a good example of "the low road to transfer."

It should not be forgotten, however, that the better people become on a particular style of learning or problem solving, the more mentally rigid they become as well. The old joke is that if you give a child a hammer, everything looks like a nail. The more he uses it, the better he becomes at using it, but also the more he thinks that hammering is the solution to each new problem. To transcend such rigidity the child needs additional tools to learn-to-learn with, and then (1) learn to discriminate when and where each is most appropriate, or (2) how to solve the same problem in more than one way. This can be facilitated by the "high road to transfer."

Adequacy of Original Learning

It is well-documented that the better something is learned, the better the performance on a transfer task, whatever the task may be. Conversely, if negative transfer is likely, then better learning can reduce it (e.g., Jung, 1962; Postman, 1962b). In addition, the more practice on the transfer task, the less interference there will be, resulting in a reduced amount of negative transfer (Hovland, 1951). In learning a second or third language, for example, interference from the native language to the new language has been demonstrated for a number of grammatical and semantic constructions. As students get more experience with the new language, however, interference from previous languages decreases (e.g., Ahukanna, Lund and Gentile, 1982; Selinker, Swain and Dumas, 1975).

One type of prior experience that can often be given to students is a kind of perceptual discrimination practice. To take a kindergarten example, children who are later to learn the names of various geometric forms (e.g., square, circle, triangle, hexagon, etc.) will learn to name them faster if they have already been exposed to those forms as objects through, say, a puzzle. The students are getting experience with the *distinctive features* of the objects (Gibson, 1967; 1968). Once the relevant features of each form are distinguished perceptually (what learning psychologists call stimulus predifferentiation or acquired distinctiveness of cues; see Arnoult, 1957), then it is easier to use those features in solving later problems.

Practice discriminating distinguishing features of concepts can help in learning those concepts, as we have seen. It is also the case that verbal labeling can help to organize or cluster concepts according to similar features and thus improve the retention and transfer of those concepts (Wittrock, 1968). Calculating the area of geometric figures, for example, is facilitated when figures are grouped and labeled according to their relevant and distinctive features (e.g., rectangles defined as all 4-sided figures joined by 4 right angles) as opposed to other less relevant ones (e.g., size or color). Thus the better we have learned—and the better we can perceptually and conceptually discriminate the relevant features of—the material, the greater the likelihood of positive transfer.

Looked at another way, practicing distinguishing features before doing the complete task is a kind of *part-whole* sequence which fell into disrepute in situated cognition theory. Their argument (e.g., Brown et al., 1989) was that we learn best by having cognitive apprenticeships with experts in their natural setting doing the whole task in all its complexity. Anderson et al. (1996) brought a better balance to this conception pointing out, first, that situated cognition theory probably underestimates the amount of part-whole training that goes on in the real world and, second, ignores the large body of evidence (such as described above) on the effectiveness of some kinds of part-whole training.

I would add that, in any case, a spiral curriculum—in which concepts continue to be revisited at more complex and inclusive levels—guarantees that each new learning will subsequently be seen as a part of a larger whole. Thus part-whole learning sequences are inevitable. The question for teachers—and a difficult question it is—remains how to decide which sequences are effective and which are not.

Practice with Several Methods and Cues

The rigidifying effects of set can be overcome by successively practicing different methods of applying previous learning to a new task (e.g., Hovland, 1951). However—and this is a crucial however—extensive practice must be attained with each method. The best way to master several methods to avoid interference effects has not been adequately studied, but we might profitably speculate that the following should help. If you want to teach two methods of solving problems or performing a skill, you might teach Method A on Monday. On Tuesday, teach Method B and review A. On Wednesday, reteach A and review B. On Thursday review both A and B and give practice transfer problems. On Friday, have a mastery test on using and applying both methods. This scheme provides much repetition, in successive practice on each method, and over a sequence of days allows for distributed practice which, we shall see in Chapter 10, should increase retention.

Another way recommended to increase transfer is to learn to solve the same basic task under a variety of circumstances and stimulus situations. Travers (1977, pp. 417–418) pointed out that

Transfer of a principle is facilitated if the situation in which it is learned involves many irrelevant cues and if it is to be transferred to other situations involving also many, but different, irrelevant cues.

The reason for this is to keep the learner from becoming dependent on specific cues to find the solution to the problem. For example, in learning to drive, more transfer should occur if you practice on standard shifts of all types (3-, 4- and 5-speed) as well as on automatic shifts, than if only one car is driven. More transfer of your strokes in playing tennis should occur if you play against a variety of opponents instead of just one. Practice solving a variety of problems may be analogous.

Principles vs. Habits

Consider the following experiment that you science teachers may wish to replicate in your class. One group of students is given practice shooting targets which are under water, until they master the task of adjusting for the variable of light refraction through trial-and-error. A second group is given instruction on the principles of light refraction and then allowed to practice shooting targets until they, too, master the skill. Then the target depth is changed, which constitutes a transfer task. Which group do you expect will more quickly master the new task?

Judd, who first reported this study in 1908 (see also Hendrickson & Schroeder, who replicated the study more carefully in 1941), found that the group exposed to the principle (the "high road to transfer") was more quickly able to adjust to the new conditions. The practice-only group required extensive extra practice (the "low road to transfer"). The logical conclusion is that knowledge of an abstract principle can facilitate transfer. But note that the principle group also had practice. *It is extremely doubtful if knowing principles in the abstract can make up for a lack of concrete knowledge and practice.* Principles become assimilated through active manipulation of objects and the environment, a point made by theorists along a continuum from Skinner to Piaget. The latter stated it as well as anyone (1970a, p. 29): "To know an object is to act upon it and transform it . . . ."

Speed of Learning

Consider the following hypothetical elementary school experiment using flash cards for reading or arithmetic times tables. Students in one class are taught to give a correct response within one second, at which time the teacher moves on to the next card. In another class the students are taught to be more deliberate—to respond within five seconds. After both classes have mastered the correct words or arithmetic facts to a criterion of 100% correct, the classes are brought together in a TV-game-like competition in which the winner is the first person to answer correctly the problem posed by the card. Assuming that the two classes are competing, either in groups or one against one, which group of students do you think will have the advantage?

Your common-sense answer has been subjected to experimental study in ways not too different from our hypothetical study, though on adults. Logan (1963) interprets the results as indicating that people learn not only facts and habits, but they also learn response speed. Moreover, they learn-to-learn at a particular speed.

The speed that they learn, of course, can facilitate performance on a later task (positive transfer) assuming that that task is to be done at a rate slower than or equal to the speed used in learning. If the transfer task requires a faster rate of response than that involved during learning, then performance will be upset and negative transfer will occur. This principle (Logan's micromolar theory) may help explain, among other things, some reflective person's inability to perform well on timed tests, and some impulsive person's seeming inability not to blurt out answers before considering the question carefully. Their past learning may have been adequate, but their response speed does not transfer to the task at hand. (See anecdote 9.4 for another interpretation of transfer and "speed").

Many people who have studied a foreign language in school experience a kind of culture shock when they visit the foreign land. Despite the considerable knowledge they have acquired, the natives speak so quickly that they are dumbfounded. The classroom experiences were at a pace that was too slow to transfer to the natural linguistic environment. Of course, it is often necessary to learn new material (a language or a musical passage) at a slow, deliberate rate, but eventually practice must be conducted at the speed required in the target environment if transfer is to be facilitated.

Emotions

Although described in various places in this book, it is worth mentioning again that cognitive processes like solving problems and transferring knowledge and skills do not occur without also engaging our motivational and emotional processes. In fact, if our motivation is to protect our egos, we may try to escape from attempting any problems, with such attributions (excuses) as "I was never any good at those kinds of problems." Or if our emotional reaction is one of fear, we may just freeze or panic at the sight of a problem.

In discussing the learned helplessness phenomenon, Seligman (1975) pointed out that these motivational/emotional factors provide a kind of proactive interference because they prevent the person from discovering that the current situation is within their power to control.

Anecdote 9.4

Transfer and Drugs

Most of us have met people who claim, or seem, to perform certain tasks better under the influence of alcohol or drugs than in their absence. Dartshooters, pool sharks or pianists who honed their skills in bars, provide some stereotypical instances. Without dealing with the question of the long-term effects of such behavior, or the absolute effects of drugs on skill development, there is some research evidence on drugs and transfer—namely, the dissociation of habits practiced under drugged and nondrugged states. The phenomenon deserves further study in this day of increasing concern over drugs, but it has been known for some time. Hilgard and Bower summarized the results this way in 1966 (p. 476) speaking of research using sodium pentobarbital ("truth serum") with rats:

The curious fact is that habits learned during this drugged state do not transfer to nondrugged state, although the habit can be reactivated after putting the animal back into the drugged state. The dissociation works as well in the other direction: a habit learned in the non-drugged state is not available to the subject while he is in the drugged state. The habits are drug-state specific.

As Hilgard and Bower went on to say (same paragraph), the results were directly related to drug dosage ". . . with larger dosages yielding a greater degree of dissociation."

Even in the improbable case that there were no harmful physiological effects of the drugs, these findings provide a different kind of evidence that habits learned under one set of conditions are unlikely to transfer to other conditions. For this reason, if for no others, physicians, parents and teachers should be wary of prescribing drugs to hyperactive children and students should be wary of going to class high.

Freezing from fear, not trying, or attempting to escape are all mental rigidities which interfere with cognitive processes. From this point of view, the teacher has an added responsibility of trying to optimize stress levels and helping students learn to persevere through multiple-step or other difficult problems.

Near vs. Far Transfer

A distinction many have found useful is that between near and far transfer. As their labels imply, *near transfer* refers to target tasks which are quite similar to the original learning. In math, for example, if you learn to solve some problems using x for the unknown, then using a or v or some other letter to solve for the unknown would be a case of near transfer. If you learn a mnemonic technique to visualize interacting images for memorizing, say, states and capitals (e.g., Annapolis-Maryland is visualized as two apples getting married), then using the same technique in memorizing states and flowers or countries and capitals would be near transfer.

Far transfer, then, is the ability to apply past learnings to quite different problems or situations. To continue the above examples, people will show evidence of far transfer on solving for x if they are given word problems not before seen and (1) can decide which formulas or operations to use and (2) correctly use them.

Likewise, people who can apply the visual imaging technique, described above, to learn foreign language vocabulary or names and faces are giving evidence of far transfer.

As described, then, near and far transfer are points on a continuum. The teacher's task, in addition to teaching the material in the first place, is one of helping the students move as far along the continuum as possible. We shall see other ways of looking at this issue when we study Bloom's taxonomy of educational objectives, particularly the Application level, in chapter 12.

Warm-up

At any program of symphony orchestras when the concert A is sounded, it is common for the musicians to go beyond tuning their instruments by playing scales or some other idiosyncratic exercises. These individual flourishes, producing a most recognizable cacophony, are seldom related to the music that is about to be played. Rather, they are done as warm-up exercises. Singers, dancers, gymnasts and other sports men and women, and even lecturers sometimes go through analogous exercises to limber up the body and, in some cases, reduce anxiety in preparation for the event to come.

Warm-up should not be confused with learning-to-learn. The latter has long-term positive transfer effects on problems with many identical elements, as we have seen. The former can be done on a very unrelated task and for shorter-term goals; for example, jogging around the court before you play tennis, or memorizing numbers before you memorize word-pairs.

In one sense warm-up is hardly, if at all, related to transfer. Travers (1977, p. 386) holds this position when he says that warm-up ". . . resembles transfer but is not a true learning phenomenon." Others have included both warm-up and learning-to-learn under the concept of *general transfer* (e.g., Hulse, Egeth and Deese, 1980). This is then contrasted with *specific transfer*, defined in terms of the identifiable elements that are common to the tasks to be learned. General transfer, then, is the catch-all for effects which are not easily specified, though believed to facilitate transfer.

The usefulness of the general vs. specific transfer dichotomy is probably debatable,[4] but it does serve to point out some of the holes in our knowledge. Warm-up is probably better understood in motor-skill learning than in cognitive tasks, but it is widely believed that warm-up exercises could be helpful in such tasks. For example, if you are going to present words or test questions at a two-second rate, a good warm-up might be simply to have students count at that rate for a while to become accustomed to the rate. Many experiments have such tasks built into them, especially so as not to disadvantage control groups at the test phase of the study. It is not too far-fetched to suggest that teachers might find this idea helpful to their students, particularly in preparing for timed tests.

Individual Differences

There is much evidence to suggest that, as in probably everything else, there are wide individual differences in solving problems and ability to transfer. One investigation of such differences looked into the relationship between IQ and Mental Age (MA) and learning-to-learn on a task not unlike Harlow's monkeys' discrimination problems (Harter, 1965). Harter found the expected relationship—the higher the IQ and MA, the faster students approached 100% correct. However, once slow students "caught on" to the problem, inferred by a sudden rise in the percentage of correctness of their choices, they kept on improving until the criterion was reached. The main difference between the faster and slower children was in the length of the period prior to their sudden improvement. The slower children take longer, but they do learn how to learn.

In a similar study, Duncan (1960) used a paired-associates task to study individual differences in learning-to-learn. He compared the upper and lower quartile of students and found results quite parallel to Harter's: the slower learners took longer to get started, but eventually performed about as well as the faster learners.

Apparently once people master a task to the same high standard, their original differences in rate of attainment of that standard are no longer predictive of performance—at least on learning-to-learn types of tasks. A similar conclusion is drawn from research on the *retention*, learning, and organizational strategies of fast and slow learners in later chapters, and so this is a point we shall consider again.

Why slower learners, or those with low IQs, have the lengthy period of what looks like little or no progress is not clear. Zeaman and House (1967) posited an attention deficit for retarded children—namely, that they need more experience with the task just to figure out what to attend to. Once they attend to the relevant stimuli they learn at the same rate as normals. Ellis (1969) made a similar point about attention in a more general context. Or perhaps the slower learners are not good at finding verbal labels to describe their experiences (a point made by DiVesta and Thompson, 1970), or perhaps there is a production deficiency (Flavell, 1979) as described in chapter 4. Whatever it is, teachers need to realize that the extra time it takes with slower students to help them achieve the high standard is worth it, since they will then maintain it. As we saw with ourselves in attempting to solve problems like those that introduced this chapter, we cannot transfer knowledge and skill we do not know well. And that is true of old and young, fast and slow alike.

Insight

I went through an entire chapter (almost) on problem-solving and transfer without once mentioning insight—the "aha" phenomenon. In many of the early pieces of research on problem solving, particularly the gestalt psychologists, insight was taken as the mechanism for the fact that a solution occurred (e.g., Hilgard and Bower, 1975). This is understandable since all of us have occasional experiences in which the light seems to go on in the head and all dark corners of the problem are momentarily illuminated. The problem is those kinds of experiences as often as not result in a feeling that someone pulled the plug just when we turned to look. You may have experienced several "aha" experiences yourself in solving the problems earlier. The question is how many of those occurred when you found the right solution and how many were false leads?

The problem with insight as it has classically been defined is not that we do not experience any such thing; it is just too vague a concept to be of much use to a psychologist explaining problem-solving or transfer. It is even less use to a teacher trying to teach it.[5]

Structure of the Material/Readiness of the Student

It follows from all of the preceding that the act of transfer is an interaction between (at a minimum) a person's previous knowledges (or skills) and a problem or subject matter. The person's maturational readiness and prior experience combine to establish the cognitive structure of mental capabilities that can be brought to bear on the task at hand.

By cognitive structure is meant, following Ausubel (1963, p. 76), ". . . the stability, clarity, and organization of a learner's subject-matter knowledge in a given discipline." This cognitive structure in part determines what aspects of the current task will be attended to, and certainly provides limits on how much of the task can be understood.

Subject matters and tasks can likewise be analyzed with each subtask considered in relation to its contribution to the whole. If it is necessary to be able to add one-digit numbers before two-digit numbers can be summed (or single-digit numbers can be multiplied), then it can be said that a *learning hierarchy* (Gagné, 1970) exists between these two skills or knowledges: summing single-digit numbers is prerequisite to summing double-digit numbers. How does this relate to transfer? Each subsequent skill in the hierarchy will be more easily learned if the subordinate (prerequisite) capabilities have been adequately learned—and are available for recall. In Gagné's words (1970, p. 239),

> *A learning hierarchy, then, identifies a set of intellectual skills that are ordered in a manner indicating substantial amounts of positive transfer from those skills of lower position to connected ones of higher position.*

Not all tasks or subject matters can be analyzed into a neatly ordered set of hierarchies, although it is often possible to do task analyses in more fields than might be immediately apparent. Gagné and his collaborators (1970; Gagné and Briggs, 1974; Gagné and Paradise, 1961) have done much to show how such hierarchies can be used in designing curricula in relation to the learning that has been attained by students (according to Gagné's hierarchy of eight types of learning).

A similar point about the relation of curriculum and readiness was made by Bruner in a very influential book called *The Process of Education* (1960). Bruner acknowledged the distinction between specific and general transfer, linking the former to the learning of useful, but limited skills. The latter, nonspecific or general transfer, he linked to the transfer of principles and attitudes and properly placed them at the "heart of the educational process—the continual broadening and deepening of knowledge in terms of basic and general ideas" (p. 17). See anecdote 9.5 for another example.

Learning such general principles implies first of all a well-structured curriculum, one which shows the relationships among the fundamental concepts of the field. Second, the student must overlearn these fundamental concepts in as rigorous training as is possible in early stages of learning. Bruner's famous hypothesis (1960, p. 33), that "any subject can be taught effectively in some intellectually honest form to any child at any stage of development" speaks directly to this point, because he continually argues that rigorous and relevant training on the fundamentals of a field makes later learning easier. Scientific topics cannot be taught abstractly through mathematical equations in the elementary years, but many of the fundamentals of science can be taught through concrete operations. This is likely also to be true for most beginners in new fields.

Curriculum experiences, then, must be structured in a way so that students are prepared for them, in the sense of having overlearned the prerequisites or fundamentals. Then they can acquire the new material in that context. But that is not enough. Any new learning should be accomplished in a way that it can allow the learner to restructure their schemata in a Piagetian sense. This allows old and new facts, concepts and principles to be related, reconstructed, and reorganized for better access in memory (a point we shall encounter in the next chapter) and for better transfer.

Anecdote 9.5

> ### Teaching for Transfer in Reading Comprehension
>
> Palincsar and Brown (1984) reported an ambitious approach to teaching for transfer in the area of reading comprehension. They argued that one of the reasons poor readers have difficulty is that they have poor strategies for monitoring their understanding while they are reading. They thus undertook to teach some poor-comprehending seventh-graders some better strategies by a method of *reciprocal teaching* where the tutor and students take turns leading a dialogue on pertinent features of the text. The active strategies were ". . . summarizing (self-review), questioning, clarifying, and predicting" (p. 120). These activities were expected to teach the children to monitor their own learning process (what we shall call a "metacognitive process" in later chapters). This is not only important in its own right, but is also expected to be quite generalizable as a skill. Their results were quite encouraging. Students did, in fact, learn the new strategies with good results on tests of comprehension. More important in the present context, the students were able to transfer these strategies to some very different tasks, such as detecting incongruities in stories. A recent review by Rosenshine and Meister (1994) supports the view that such strategies of thinking may be effective ways of increasing transfer.
>
>

To take an example from chapter 6 of this book, certain facts about reinforcement and punishment were presented in a sequence designed to build on most people's prior experiences. Repetitions of the fundamental ideas were given through various practical anecdotes, and throughout it was stressed that these ideas would be transferable to the problem of discipline. To the extent that I succeeded in my presentation and you succeeded in mastering these fundamentals, you should have been prepared for the discussion about discipline in chapter 8. You should also have been reorganizing your ideas about common rewards and punishers, social processes and so forth, as you were learning those new facts. And, if all went well, you were learning new cues for recalling those ideas (e.g., thinking about negative reinforcement as escape).

Continuing the example, when you started analyzing discipline problems via the principles of reinforcement and punishment, that should also have set in motion a reorganization of the original learning and the facts in memory. You get some idea of the applications and limitations of reinforcement and punishment in real-life discipline situations, as a result of which you derive a new conception of that knowledge. This after-the-fact restructuring of the knowledge through transfer may then facilitate further transfer in a kind of a bootstraps operation.

To say all of this another way, if knowledge is simply the accrual of facts, then those facts will soon become overwhelming, often contradictory, and eventually incomprehensible. To be able to transfer knowledge we must (1) have a sense of where we're going and what the applications might be, (2) learn fundamental facts systematically and to a high standard, (3) reorganize our previous knowledge as we add new facts and applications, (4) practice applying our ideas to new situations, and (5) use effective learning and thinking strategies. When students get lost along the way—and lost many will be—it is the teachers' privilege and responsibility to find out where in this forest of curriculum and cognitive structure the student is lost. Not all will be saved all of the time. But as Holt (1964, p. 103) put it, "To rescue a man lost in the woods, you must get to where he is."

Teaching for Positive Transfer

What have we learned from this chapter that might, in principle, be transferred to classrooms?

1. First, and foremost, positive transfer is rare since in principle there are an infinite number of ways to misapply knowledge or skills. Therefore, one must *teach for positive transfer*, not just expect that it will occur.
2. Although there are large individual differences in ability to solve problems and transfer knowledge and skill from one task to another, the overriding concern is to ensure that the material to be transferred is adequately mastered. As Shuell and Lee put it (1976, p. 73), "Students frequently fail to transfer material to which they have been exposed, simply because they have not adequately learned it in the first place!" The more adequately material is learned, the more likely it is to obtain positive transfer in tasks with identical elements, and the less likely to obtain negative transfer in tasks with no commonalities.
3. The structure of the problem, as we have seen, establishes the direction of the problem-solving effort. Either by verbal direction or by the physical representation of the problem, a teacher can make it more or less probable that prerequisite associations and strategies are engaged by the present problem.
4. It is not insight which allows us to solve novel problems, and thus transfer, although we may feel insightful when we've discovered a solution; rather it is the following:
   a. knowing well the specific prerequisite concepts, principles, or skills required by the problem;
   b. recalling those at the time the problem is posed; and
   c. having experienced successful solutions to problems by many different methods (to avoid the rigidifying effects known as mental or perceptual set).

   To a great extent all of these components are part of a teacher's responsibility.
5. Having done all of the above, a teacher is still not sure that a student will properly transfer to solve the problem, since problems are only interesting if they require something above and beyond the normal. Thus a perceptual restructuring may be necessary and that may require additional hints.
6. A teacher can facilitate all of the above functions by a well-planned curriculum that not only requires mastery of prerequisite concepts, but that also encourages creative processes—a topic that will occupy us in later chapters. In addition, if we wish to take "the high road to transfer," students need to practice finding commonalities among problems and tasks, including underlying principles. Moreover, they probably need to practice doing these things in a social context that resembles the environments in which professionals in those fields work.
7. In addition, the teacher can begin instruction on each new topic by using what David Ausubel (1960, 1963) called an *advance organizer* and what Madeline Hunter (1982) called an *anticipatory set*. An anticipatory set is an exercise which actively engages the student's prior knowledge and

experiences which are congruent with the current lesson's objectives. In other words, the teacher plans an activity or asks a question which evokes the student's relevant skills and knowledges in the context of the current lesson. This should decrease the probability that students will misapply, or forget to apply, past learning to the current task.

8. Find ways to help students to relax so that emotional and motivational factors do not interfere with the cognitive task at hand.
9. Above all, a teacher needs to retain humility. Students, like their teachers, will more often than not fail to transfer their knowledge and skills to situations which, to an observer or expert, seem obvious and straightforward. We all, as teachers, need to be humbled on occasions by taking a course in, say, Japanese or by trying to solve the kinds of problems with which this chapter began.

Transferring the Information in this Chapter

Finally, if you expect the material in this chapter or, more broadly, in this book to transfer immediately into your teaching, you overexpected transfer from yourself and this material (another case of rapanoia?). For each of us to transfer material from one setting to another requires considerable help and practice, as we have discovered. There is little automatic transfer. With regard to the transfer of psychological principles to education, William James may have said it best nine decades ago (1904, pp. 23–24):

> . . . *you make a great, a very great mistake, if you think that psychology, being the science of the mind's laws, is something from which you can deduce definite programmes and schemes and methods of instruction for immediate schoolroom use. Psychology is a science, and teaching is an art; and sciences never generate arts directly out of themselves. An intermediary inventive mind must make the application, by using its originality.*
>
> *The science of logic never made a man reason rightly, and the science of ethics (if there be such a thing) never made a man behave rightly. The most such sciences can do is to help us to catch ourselves up and check ourselves, if we start to reason or to behave wrongly; and to criticize ourselves more articulately after we have made mistakes.*

Educational psychologists find rereading William James to be a humbling experience, especially in regard to transfer. Just in case you have gotten smug and think it will be easy to transfer the information in this chapter to a teaching situation, consider the following real problems from John Holt's *How Children Fail* (1964).

Example 1

Holt had been using the Cuisenaire rods (named for the inventor) to teach some arithmetic skills. Each rod is a wooden stick one centimeter (cm.) wide, and one cm. high, and varying in length from 1 to 10 cm. and painted in colors which are correlated with their length. Thus, the 1-cm. long rods are white, the 2-cm long rods are red, and the 10-cm. long rods are orange. As Holt described it, his fifth-graders had been using the rods for at least three weeks and knew the lengths of the rods well enough to call them by name (e.g., if they were shown an orange rod, they would call it "the 10 rod.").

Presuming the children knew the prerequisites, Holt asked (p. 142), "How many white rods would you need to make a row all the way across your desk?" About half of his 15 students began using the 10-cm. orange rods to measure. All but one of the rest lined up white 1-cm. rods until they ran out of them.

Then they lined up the red 2-cm. rods, but sideways, so they also acted as 1-cm. measures. When they got all the way across, they counted the number of rods.

Holt then asked, "How many whites would you need to cover up one sheet of pad paper (about 9" × 6")?" Again, about ten students began covering the paper with white rods. A few finally realized that each row was the same length and they could multiply by the number of rows. Two children tried to cover the entire paper with rods, using all colors, but standing the longer ones on end so that each still covered only 1 sq. cm. of paper.

How does one help these students transfer their knowledge to a situation which would make their work easier?

Example 2

One day Holt (1964, p. 133) asked his students, who had previously learned about place value many times, "Suppose I go to the bank with a check for $1437.50, cash it, and ask them to give me as much of the money as possible in ten dollar bills. How many tens will I get?" When most students could not get the answer and were guessing wildly on even third or fourth tries, he erased the original number and asked how many tens would he get with $75. All knew. Then $175.00. A few got it, most could not answer correctly. Holt then pointed to the 7 digit and asked what it meant. They knew it meant 70 dollars or 7 tens. He asked about the 1. They knew it meant $100, but it took a while until they could transfer that $100 plus the $70 into 17 tens. When he was satisfied that they understood, he went back to the $1437.50 and considered the problem digit by digit. By this time the students were saying, "Oh, yeah, I get it; I see; it's easy; it's cinchy."

But the "insight" faded, because two days later he asked how many hundred dollar bills he could get if a check were cashed for $14357.50. Holt claims (p. 134)

> *some answers were 43, 17, 107, 142, 604, 34, 13100, and 22. Only one student got the answer the first time. Four more eventually got it, before I worked it on the board. The other eleven were completely stumped.*

How does one help such students transfer their knowledge? Is it likely that the students mastered the prerequisites?

Example 3

Holt (1964, p. 182) had the following conversation with a second grader out of school (not his student).

> *"What sort of stuff do they teach you?" Pause. "Oh, stuff like the difference between 'gone' and 'went.' "*
> *"I see. By the way, can you tell me which is right? 'I have gone to the movies' or 'I have went to the movies.' "*
> *Long, thoughtful pause. Then, "I don't know; I can't tell when it isn't written on the board." We both laughed at this.*

How indeed does one teach for transfer? It should be clear by now that it is not easy.

Nevertheless, there has been a growing interest in teaching general thinking strategies which may increase the probability of positive transfer. In chapter 11 a number of those teaching programs and strategies will be presented. But first it is important to master some fundamentals of learning and memory, which are the subject of chapter 10.

Practice Exercises

A. Practice Items

Items 1–5 are definitions or situations that are to be matched to the following technical terms by placing the letter of the term on the appropriate line. (Answers are in note 6).

   a. retroactive facilitation
   b. retroactive interference
   c. proactive facilitation
   d. proactive interference
   e. zero transfer

___ 1. An Englishman who learned to drive on the left comes to America and has trouble driving here.

___ 2. Winnie Brown was well-known in the community before she married Ian De Pugh and became Winnie De Pugh. Years after her name was changed, people who knew her before marriage continued to call her Winnie Brown.

___ 3. The experimental group first learned A, then B, then was retested on A. The control group learned A, then rested, then was retested on A. Both groups remembered A equally well.

___ 4. Lizzy Taylor has been married so often that people have trouble remembering how often. It even affects her own memory. Once when asked to describe her first husband, she couldn't recall his name. This is most likely due to _____.

___ 5. The experimental group learned some Chinese characters, then learned Japanese characters, and was later tested on the Japanese characters. The control group just learned the Japanese characters and, like the experimental group, was later tested on the Japanese characters. The experimental group remembered the Japanese characters better than the control group. This result demonstrates _____.

For the following five multiple-choice items, select the alternative choice which *best* answers the question. (Answers are in Note 6).

6. In which of the following cases will similarity of elements be most likely to lead to negative transfer? You learn the names and faces of all twenty-five students in your class. Then

   a. you learn their nicknames (e.g., John becomes Jack; Christine becomes Chris).
   b. you give them totally different names in Chinese (e.g., John becomes Ying; Christine becomes Chen).
   c. you learn other things about them, such as their address (e.g., John lives on Sweethome Road; Christine lives on a farm).

d. You have them trade names (e.g., John becomes Christine; Christine becomes Fred; Fred becomes John).

7. In order to ascertain the amount of transfer between learning logic and learning a language, you exposed an experimental group to experience both subjects in sequence (logic then language), while a control group only learned the language. Which of the following results according to Murdock's formula $\frac{E-C}{E+C} \times 100$ shows the most positive transfer between logic and language?
   a. +27% transfer
   b. zero transfer
   c. −13% transfer
   d. −100% transfer

8. POSITIVE TRANSFER is to NEGATIVE TRANSFER as
   a. perceptual set is to learning to learn
   b. advance organizer is to anticipatory set
   c. anticipatory set is to perceptual set
   d. anticipatory set is to learning to learn

9. Ed Syke's students learn the defining characteristics of positive reinforcement, negative reinforcement, extinction and punishment. Then they are given a test in which they must observe actual human interactions on videotape and classify them into the above categories. Since they had no classroom practice on this, this sequence of events would provide
   a. a test of far transfer.
   b. practice for low road transfer.
   c. a test of the adequacy of original learning.
   d. an authentic situated cognition activity.

10. Learning refers to
    a. a change of behavior due to experience.
    b. the effect of past experiences on the present.
    c. material that remains over a relatively long period of time.
    d. the rate at which material can be placed into memory.

B. For Cooperative Study (in or out of class):

1. Divide into groups of size 3–5 according to subject matter and level (e.g., math or elementary math and secondary math, languages, social studies, etc.) and discuss the following topics:
   a. What are some common misconceptions students have that lead to their having difficulty learning certain concepts (proactive interference effects)?
   b. Brainstorm some ideas for teaching those concepts to minimize the negative transfer in (a) and maximize proactive facilitation.

2. In small groups discuss any concepts in this book for which your own past experiences have provided negative transfer (e.g., how about the concept of negative reinforcement? any others?).
3. Discuss study question 13 about the structure of the curriculum and the readiness of the student. How do you feel about Bruner's famous comment that "any subject can be taught effectively in some intellectually honest form to any child at any stage of development"?
4. In small groups, consider John Holt's students described at the end of the chapter. How would you diagnose their problems? What would you do to remediate those problems?
5. Share some of your own experiences of proactive interference and facilitation, and retroactive interference and facilitation.

C. **For Further Information**

1. Read, and make a written or oral report on, one or more of the classical problem solving studies in the literature: for example, those in Note 1.
2. Do a curricular task analysis of a particular instructional objective to decide what prerequisite knowledge is assumed and what order, if any, must the prerequisites be learned. For example, suppose you had to teach a child how to multiply or divide fractions. How would you go about planning your teaching to maximize transfer?
3. Find or invent a problem to share with the class which demonstrates one or more of the kinds of perceptual sets or mental rigidities described in the early part of the chapter. For example, what principles are involved in the following problems (Answers are in Note 7).
   a. How can you plant four trees so that each is equidistant from every other?
   b. A farmer must plant ten trees in five rows so that there are four trees in every row. How can he or she do it?
   c. Name an important 4-letter city in Czechoslovakia.
   d. If I have two US coins which total 55 cents and one of them is not a nickel; what are the two coins?
4. Make up some hypothetical data (or get real data) on an experimental and control group, in either a proactive or retroactive design, and calculate the % of transfer using Murdock's formula.
5. Discuss study question 6. Can you give personal examples of the kinds of cognitive apprenticeships that illustrate (or question) the theory?

CHAPTER

Study Questions

1. Describe the active "analysis by synthesis" interpretation of perception.
2. How is attention "selective"? Give examples.
3. What is the distinction between *automatic* and *controlled* attentional processes? How does stress affect each?
4. Define each of the following and give examples:
   a. sensory register or memory (e.g., visual or echoic memory)
   b. short-term or working memory
   c. long-term memory
5. How does "chunking" help to increase short-term memory? Explain by reference to the Peterson-Peterson and Murdock research.
6. Describe the acquisition of memories in terms of the following phases:
   a. encoding
   b. storage
   c. retrieval
7. Describe each of the following memory issues and relate each to the phases in question 6.
   a. interference (proactive or retroactive)
   b. cue-dependent retention
   c. availability vs. accessibility
   d. subjective organization
8. What is meant by elaboration? Give examples of
   a. verbal elaboration
   b. imagery elaboration
9. What is a mnemonic technique? Give examples.
10. What is meant by dual coding theory? What does it predict about the relative efficacy for memory of
    a. verbally coded material?
    b. imagery coded material?
    c. both a and b?

TEN

11. What is the effect of each of the following on both learning and retention?
    a. amount of practice
    b. overlearning
    c. distribution of practice

12. What is the "savings score"? How can it be used to provide evidence that unrecallable material is still available in memory?

13. What is the relationship between rate of learning and forgetting? What methodological requirement must be fulfilled in order to answer the question?

14. What is meant by each of the following?
    a. metacognitive processes
    b. production deficiency

15. How do "fast" and "slow," normal and retarded, nondisabled and learning disabled differ in
    a. spontaneously using memory strategies?
    b. using elaboration strategies or other mnemonic techniques in which they have been instructed?

16. In what ways are memories
    a. reproductive?
    b. reconstructive?
    Give examples from childhood memories or "how lies become memory's truths."

17. What is the implication of Bahrick's research on very long-term memory (i.e., memory that lasts for decades) on how material should be learned?

18. Using summary points 1–9 at the end of the chapter, describe some implications for instruction from the principles in this chapter.

Cognition and Memory

Introduction

I can still remember the traumatic experience I had in my first paired-associated experiment. It was part of a sophomore class . . . experiment that involved learning 16 memorable pairs such as DAX-GIB. That is, our task was to be able to recall GIB when prompted with the cue DAX. I was determined to outperform other members of my class. My personal theory of memory at that time, which I intended to apply, was basically that if you try hard and intensely you will remember well. In the impending period I would say (as loud as was seemly) the paired associates over and over again, as fast as I could. My theory was that by this method the paired associates would be forever "burned" into my mind. To my chagrin, I wound up with the worst score in the class. (Anderson, 1980, p. 123)

Perhaps this experience led John R. Anderson into the study of cognitive psychology where he has subsequently become one of the foremost researchers in the field. His personal trauma, shared by many college students each year, shows how unsophisticated most people are with regard to some common principles of learning and memory. Anderson's assessment of the above experience, written years later but described in his next paragraph, was as follows (1980, p. 123):

My theory of "loud and fast" was directly opposed to the true means of improving memory. I was trying to commit a meaningless auditory pair to memory. But . . . I should have been trying to convert my memory task into something more meaningful.

Lest you think that Anderson's advice should be construed to be "Stay away from learning nonsense syllables" or "Only learn what is already meaningful," consider the following pair: ANO-HON. For most people these trigrams (3-letter combinations) are nonsense words. For students of Japanese they mean "that book." Most learning of novel material, particularly verbal material, begins with the first exposure looking and sounding like nonsense syllables. It is only upon repeated exposure that the materials begin to seem meaningful, though (as we have already seen and will see further) there are ways of expediting the process of turning lists of unrelated items of apparent nonsense into more related and memorable items. That is one of the purposes of this chapter.

More broadly, the purpose of this chapter is to describe systematically the cognitive processes that are involved in learning and memory. This will include such factors as perception and attention—though we will certainly not cover these topics comprehensively—as well as many of the cognitive components of short-term and long-term memory. As we proceed we shall also encounter some further explanations for the phenomena of problem-solving and transfer described in the previous chapter. Throughout I shall emphasize that such cognitive processes as memory are the active, constructive or reconstructive efforts of people trying to make sense of and have an effect upon the world with which they are interacting. This is certainly consistent with the social cognitive viewpoint expressed throughout earlier portions of the book. It is also very much influenced by the "analysis by synthesis" approach to cognitive processes championed by Ulric Neisser's 1967 landmark book *Cognitive Psychology*.

Attention and Perception

No one ever had a simple sensation by itself. Consciousness, from our natal day, is of a teeming multiplicity of objects and relations, and what we call simple sensations are results of discriminative attention, pushed often to a very high degree. (James, 1890, p. 219).

There is great survival value in our capacity to respond quickly to certain stimuli—for example, smoke or fire, shock, human screams, and the like. We are probably natively endowed with "fight or flight" reaction patterns to such stimuli without the necessity of taking time to process the information coming in. The vast majority of our perception of stimuli, however, is not nearly so reflexive as it is reflective. That is to say, under normal conditions stimuli do not force responses, rather our processing of them defines the stimulus.

Consider, for example, the following:

(1) A 13 C   12 13 14
(2)   THE CAT

Almost everyone interprets the middle item at the left in (1) to be the letter B and the middle right to be the numeral 13, despite the fact that they are (nearly) identical physical stimuli. In (2) we read "THE CAT" despite the identity of the stimuli that we interpret first as H, then as A.

From these demonstrations (the first attributed to Bruner and Minturn, 1955; the second to O. G. Selfridge, in Neisser, 1967) it is clear that past experience and present context influence our interpretation of the stimuli.

Interpreting the sounds of speech is likewise a constructive perceptual act. Warren and Warren (1970) presented taped sentences in which only the last sound (phoneme) of a crucial word was presented. The first sound,

Photo 10.1. Faces and vases.

the critical consonant sound, was omitted. Parts of three of those sentences follow, where * indicates the omitted sound:

(1) the *eel was on the axle.
(2) the *eel was on the shoe.
(3) the *eel was on the orange.

As you may have guessed, though no wh, h, or p, sounds were on the tape, subjects reported hearing wheel, heel, and peel, respectively, in the three sentences.

The subjects in such experiments are not hallucinating, of course. It is not even fair to say that their mind is playing tricks on them, because this is the way of our cognitive processes—namely, to impose meaning on the stimuli or information that comes our way. At times the meanings we impose can greatly facilitate our understanding of the sensory impressions we are receiving, as in reading "THE CAT" or in hearing "the wheel" (instead of something else) was on the axle. At times, however, these same constructive perceptual processes can lead us astray, as when we do not have the appropriate knowledge to interpret the stimuli in the way it was intended (and it provides proactive interference). Often this occurs with humorous results, as when students in the 1990s were asked to write about George Gershwin's "Rhapsody in Blue" which, for many, came out as "Rap City in Blue."

To summarize, a *sensation* is the stimulation of one of more of our senses—sight, hearing, touch—by some external event. Since it implies neurological activity, sensation is precursor to, but not yet a cognitive act. *Perception*, in contrast, is the active cognitive process of making sense of sensations. To take our last example, a child first hearing "Rhapsody" has a sensation and immediately sets out to understand it by supplying a meaning he or she has for those sounds—namely, "rap city."

Attention and Its Selectivity

If perception can be thought of as the active process of making sense of sensations, then it is equally clear that we can actively seek or ignore sensations. The process by which we do this is called *attention*.

The cacophony of conversations at a cocktail party provides an oft-used example of how selective attention can be. We are capable of tuning out most of the ongoing conversations, while concentrating all of our energy on only one. If the one we engage in is not too demanding on our attention, we can even selectively tune in to other conversations to find one that is of more interest. This capability is not just limited to cocktail conversations, but is also widely used (to the chagrin of teachers) to tune out a teacher's lecture to attend to a peer or, more generally, to "do some serious thinking while someone is talking at you."

Some interesting experiments have been able to show how we can so divide our attention. Through headphones, two different messages can be transmitted to the listener, one in each ear. The subjects are asked to "shadow" one of the messages; in other words, to report the words from that message as they hear them. As we would expect from the "cocktail conversation capability," most people have little trouble tuning out the one message and shadowing the other. They tune out the non-shadowed message so effectively, in fact, that they often cannot tell if the unattended message was in the same language as the other message or even whether it was the same word repeated over and over. They can usually discriminate the gender of the speaker or whether it was a voice, as contrasted with just noise (e.g., Cherry, 1953).

Tuning out is not just done by turning off one ear. As two Oxford undergraduates were able to show, subjects could shadow the message if it crossed from one ear to the other (Gray and Wedderburn, 1960). In this experiment, digits were simultaneously presented with syllables or words which, at half-second intervals, were alternately presented in each ear. Thus a subject heard, for example, the following in the two ears:

Left	Right
Mice	3
5	eat
cheese	4

Although there were other issues involved in the experiment, the relevant point here is that people attend to messages not by the input channel (i.e., ear), but more centrally by tuning in to the message they are following. Triesman (1960) provided other evidence for this and also pointed out that when her subjects shadowed according to the meaning, they were seldom even aware that the message switched ears.

Automatic vs. Controlled Attention

Of course there is more to attention than already described. It takes all of our energy to monitor two or more messages at once or to remember all of the items in a visual display. But it is also well known that humans can do more than one thing at a time. Those who are reputed not to be able to do more than one thing at a time are usually the butt of such jokes as, "_____ can't walk and chew gum" (you'll have to supply your own candidate). But how do we come to be able to walk and chew gum simultaneously?

The answer, apparently, is that one of the tasks must become so well-practiced that it becomes automatic. As usual, William James anticipated the importance of this expert-novice distinction in an 1890 essay called Habit (p. 119):

> *When we are learning to walk, to ride, to swim, skate, fence, write, play, or sing, we interrupt ourselves at every step by unnecessary movements and false notes. When we are proficients, on the contrary, the results not only follow with the very minimum of muscular action requisite to bring them forth, they also follow from a single instantaneous 'cue.' The marksman sees the bird, and, before he knows it, he has aimed and shot. A gleam in his adversary's eye, a momentary pressure from his rapier, and the fencer finds he has instantly made the right parry and return. A glance at the musical hieroglyphics, and the pianist's fingers have rippled through a cataract of notes.*

Increased skill makes *qualitative changes* in the performance of perceptual and cognitive tasks. Those tasks which are so well-practiced as to allow *automatic processing*, take very little of our energy, do not interfere with whatever else we are doing, function consistently at a low error rate and are exemplary schemata. As Schneider and Shiffrin (1977, p. 2) put it ". . . once learned, an automatic process is difficult to suppress, to modify, or to ignore." Once driving a car becomes automatic, for example, the driver can carry on a conversation (as well as chew gum if it is also an automatic process). Yet no matter how animated or interesting the conversation, a red light will cue the automatic processes for hitting the brake, and certain speeds or engine sounds will cue the automatic processes for engaging the clutch and shifting gears (in a standard shift vehicle).

At the opposite extreme of the continuum are what are called *controlled processes,* which are fully conscious and effortful. They require purposeful attention, occupying our attentional and cognitive capacity almost fully, as James described. They also, therefore, show tremendous improvement with practice, requiring less attentional effort as skill improves.[1]

Common experience tells us that automatic processes do not easily stand up to the attentional scrutiny of controlled processing. If you ask skilled drivers of standard shift cars to explain the steps they use in driving, they probably cannot. To do so, they will probably have to perform the steps automatically and pay attention to the steps to "learn" what it is they've been doing habitually. Similarly, if you ask skilled pianists to explain the fingering of a passage, or to define the chords they are playing, you will probably significantly interfere with the performance. You have reduced the pianist to the level of the proverbial centipedes who can no longer walk once you ask them how they manage to coordinate all their legs. Under these conditions centipedes would certainly find it difficult to walk and chew gum.

As we shall see, the automatic-controlled processing distinction is very useful in understanding the development of rather complex learning and memory processes. To be able to read, for example, we must be able to recognize each individual letter, and also to understand the syntax of the sentences at least sufficiently to infer who did what to whom. Yet there now exists much evidence that people do not read one letter at a time; furthermore, they recall the semantics, or meaning, of a sentence, but not the syntax, or structure (e.g., Anderson, 1980, Neisser, 1967). Novices in reading must consciously attend to letters, sounds and syntactic structures. In so doing they cannot easily comprehend the larger meaning the sentence conveys. As skill in reading develops, recognition of letters, words, phrases and syntactic structures become more and more automatic.

Photo 10.2. Attentiveness in class.

Thus we can focus our attention on the meaning of the sentence (e.g., LaBerge and Samuels, 1974).

Attention and Emotion

Many of the automatic processes described in the previous section have been described elsewhere in this text as operant processes. The red light, for example, that controls the automatic perceptual processes can also be called a discriminative stimulus for the operant behavior of stopping. The difference resides not in the stimulus itself, but in the level of behavior—operant or cognitive—with which we are concerned.

Another overlap of levels of behavior is that which exists between attentive processes and emotional behaviors. The theory of Hasher and Zacks (1979) addresses this issue directly by pointing out that attentional capacity varies both between and within individuals. People who are depressed, highly aroused or stressed, or aged, for example will show reduced attentional capacity. However—and this is the important point—the evidence supports the view that *stressful events take their toll by reducing performance on tasks that require controlled processing; automatic processes are not (or hardly) disrupted by stressful events or old age.* This is similar to results we have seen in the transfer literature, as well. The stress of a recital on a beginning piano student, whose playing is under conscious control, is likely to disrupt the performance. The same recital would not at all affect the performance of a skilled pianist whose playing is on automatic pilot.

The Acquisition of Memories

With this brief background in perception/attention, we are ready to consider more generally the processes of learning and memory. Our attentive processes provide our sensory organs with stimuli which, as rapidly as possible, are perceived as meaningful in some way. To enable this to happen, we must have various memory functions. It is currently fashionable to divide these functions into three distinct types of memory, though there are many overlaps among them. We shall consider each of these types—the sensory, short-term, and long-term memories—in turn.

Sensory Memory

Imagine yourself a subject in a now famous experiment in perception, published by Sperling in 1960. You would have been seated in front of a device (called a tachistoscope) in which you were shown an array of letters on a slide exposed very briefly—for example, 50 milliseconds (1/20th of a second). One of the arrays might have looked like this:

```
Q   Z   P
N   S   K
R   D   T
```

Immediately after this extremely brief presentation—much briefer than the 200 msec or 1/5th of a second it takes to move the eye from one focal point to another in, say, the saccadic movements used in reading—you are asked to recall as many of the letters exposed as possible. If you were a typical subject, you would recall four or five letters correctly from the display.[2]

After several attempts at the task as described, suppose you are given these instructions:

As soon as exposure of the array of letters has been terminated, a tone will sound. If it is a low-pitched tone, please report the letters from the bottom row. If it is a high-pitched tone, please recall the letters previously shown in the top row. If it is a tone of intermediate pitch, please report the letters from the middle row.

After hearing samples of the three tones, you are shown a new array of letters, immediately followed by one of the tones. How well do you think you would do? Take a moment to construct an answer before going on.

Considering that the array is no longer physically present when the tone is sounded, it may seem incredible that the typical subject is close to 100% correct in reporting the letters. Yet that is the case when the tone sounds immediately upon the termination of the array's exposure (i.e., a zero-second delay). As the tone's onset is delayed for increasing lengths of time, the accuracy of reporting also decreases. When the interval between the end of slide and the sound of the tone is about one second, accuracy of recall is about the same as for the whole array—about 4 or 5 letters. Why?

Through this technique Sperling provided the first scientifically replicable demonstration of an after-image phenomenon with which we are all familiar—for example, the streak of light that appears when a lit match is waved in a dark room. He showed that the visual sensation persists longer than the actual physical stimulus and thus provided evidence that there is a *visual sensory register or memory* which can hold the information of a visual display for up to a second (even up to five seconds when the visual field is dark). The image, or *icon* (Neisser's 1967, term for it) which is maintained for this period is now available to the person to rehearse, or process in some manner. Thus we can see the utility or evolutionary significance of such a mechanism: it allows us to consider longer what just flashed by us.

An analogous mechanism occurs in the auditory system, which is probably the explanation for a person's ability to understand speech; to recognize a melody; and to take notes on, or to simultaneously translate, a lecture. This auditory after-image provides a kind of *echoic memory* (in Neisser's, 1967, terminology), but it is sufficient for our purposes to recognize (1) its existence and (2) that its utility parallels that of the visual icon—namely, to extend in time a physical stimulus until we can more fully attend to and rehearse it.

Short-Term Memory[3]

Rehearsing an item, by repeatedly paying attention to it or saying it over and over, is the prototypical experience of most people in learning the names of a room full of people or in remembering a new telephone number. We look up the number, then repeat it continuously until we dial it. But if the line is busy, the odds are good that you will have to consult the directory for the number before dialing again. This is *short-term memory*: the active but transient memory processes that keep small amounts of information in a working state while we attend to them for a short period of time—a period of seconds or perhaps a minute or two. Short-term memory is to be contrasted with *long-term memory*:[4] a relatively permanently stored large body of information which is temporally measured in hours, days, months or years and which is not actively being used.

By these definitions one can see, first of all, that there is no clear boundary between short-term and long-term memory. It is not possible to say with certainty that anything kept in memory for, say, two or ten minutes, has passed from short-term into long-term memory. Like the difference between sensory and short-term memories, short-term and long-term memories co-exist on a continuum and it is not the time, but what occurs during the time, which is presumed to transfer information in one system to the other.

Second, short-term and long-term memories overlap in another way, as well. Information in long-term memory can be called up to be actively processed in the working short-term memory. When that happens it is not erased from the permanent store. Thus one should not think of them as opposites, but rather as complementary and overlapping functions. Figure 10.2 shows a schematic representation of the interaction of the memory functions.

With these distinctions to guide us, let's again take the part of a subject in an experiment, in which a portion of the instructions from the experimenter went like this (Peterson and Peterson, 1959, p. 194):

I will speak some letters and then a number. You are to repeat the number immediately after I say it and begin counting backwards by 3's . . . from that number in time with the ticking [of a metronome] that you hear. I might say, ABC 309. Then you say, 309, 306, 303, etc., until the bottom or red light comes on. When you see this red light come on, stop counting immediately and say the letters that were given at the beginning of the trial.

You were then given a large number of trials in which the length of time during which you were to count backwards varied from 3-18 seconds. The results were as you might expect: the longer you had to count backwards before repeating the three letters, the less recall there was. After only 3-sec., recall was close to 80% on the average. After 18-sec., recall was less than 10% on the average. The counting backwards, of course, prevented rehearsal and thus allowed a relatively pure measure of the decay that occurs in a short-term memory over a brief period of time. When rehearsal is prevented, as these results show, short-term memory is quite short indeed.

Murdock (1961) replicated these findings with several important additions. The addition of most interest here is the type of material to be learned. Subjects in the experiment first tried to recall a triad of consonants (CCCs) such as KDP with the counting backwards procedure to prevent rehearsing. At a later session they were given a single 3-letter word (e.g., HAT). At a still later session they were given three unrelated 3-letter words (e.g., COW, TAP, BED). At each of these sessions they had a number of experiences recalling the test items at various intervals of time, ranging from 0 to 18 seconds.

One might speculate that the single 3-letter word might be easier to recall than three consonants or random letters that do not make a word. This would definitely be the case if the word were somehow processed as a single item (or bit) of information, while the consonant triads had to be processed as individual letters. If this were true, would three 3-letter words be as easy to remember as three letters that do not make a word?

Murdock's (1961) study provided a neat test of this hypothesis. His results (from his Table I on p. 619) can be succinctly graphed as in figure 10.1. They demonstrate rather convincingly (1) that a single word is much easier to recall than three consonants or three unrelated words, and (2) that the forgetting curve of three consonants is remarkably similar to that of three unrelated 3-letter words. Clearly the capacity of short-term memory does not depend solely on the number of stimulus items being processed. But processing a word, compared with an equivalent number of unrelated letters, requires much less of a memory

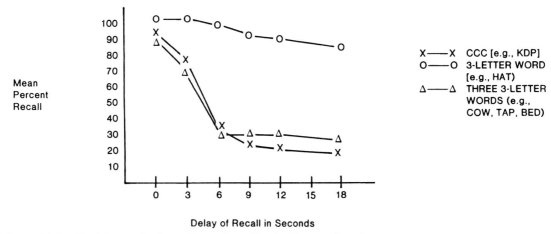

Figure 10.1. Short-term retention of items from Murdock's experiment.

load, presumably because it reduces the amount of information to be processed. That is, one word may require only one item of information to be processed, while three unrelated letters or words each require the processing of three items of information.

What, then is the capacity of the short-term store? Other studies suggest that it is about 7 (*plus or minus* 2) unrelated items of information such as individual consonants, digits or words (G. A. Miller, 1956). But as we have seen, the letters that form a word are no longer recognized as individual stimuli, rather they are treated as one meaningful item. Similarly, three 3- letter words such as COG, NIT, and ION can sometimes also be combined into one meaningful chunk, COGNITION, which reduces the items of information and thus the processing load. The same would be true of making a meaningful chunk out of digits, such as 1,4,9,2, or 1,7,7,6, becoming the dates for the discovery of and independence of America, respectively.

The process of combining isolated bits of information into meaningful items is called *chunking* (G. A. Miller, 1956). This process allows us to increase vastly the amount of information that can be held in short-term memory. Thus the capacity of short-term memory depends upon the meaningfulness of the material or how much chunking or other organizing we are able to do to material to make it meaningful. As Anderson (1980, pp. 167–168) points out, we are probably able to recall about

a. four, but not six, nonsense syllables such as DAX;
b. six, but not nine, one-syllable words such as JUMP;
c. three, but not six, four-syllable words such as OPTIMISTIC; or
d. a nineteen-word sentence such as "Richard Milhous Nixon, former president of the United States, wrote a book about his career in the White House."

Long-Term Memory

Whatever number of items are being processed in the working short-term memory, they decay rapidly, as the Peterson-Peterson and Murdock studies demonstrated. When rehearsal is not prevented, on the other hand, material can pass from the short-term store to the long-term store. Exactly how this occurs is not yet well-understood. In fact, whether material *passes* from one state or place to another is anyone's guess. It is more likely that a continuum operates between what we are calling

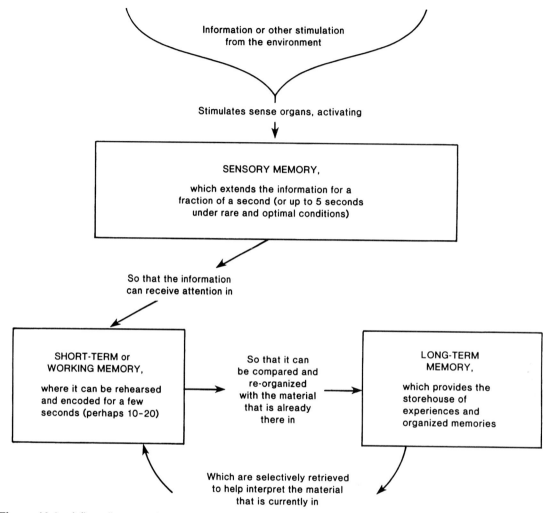

Figure 10.2. A flow diagram of memory functions and interactions.

short- and long-term memory (e.g., Melton, 1963) and that the major difference between them is how much time the learner had to process the incoming information. Many researchers would agree with the view expressed by Bugelski (1979, p. 311):

At present, there appears to be no reason to consider short-term memory as anything but a label for what happens when one has a brief exposure to some unfamiliar sequence of materials that one cannot rehearse because some other activity follows immediately.

In that case, the term long-term memory simply implies longer, and perhaps better, exposure to the material. (e.g., Ellis & Hunt, 1993). Let's turn to this issue.

Encoding, Storage and Retrieval

How does information which is normally so transient that it decays in a half minute or less become stored more permanently? Repetition of the material, as in saying a telephone number over and over, is probably not very helpful in creating a permanent and accessible memory, while organizing the material in some way is.

The process of depositing information into a long-term store has often been described via a filing system metaphor. When a letter or other information comes in, it must be processed and then stored in a filing cabinet. If it is to be accessible at a later date, the filing cannot be haphazard. Each incoming item must be categorized or labeled in some way that will distinguish it from other letters (they can't all be filed under miscellaneous or in the circular file). This processing or categorizing of information is called *encoding*.

Once information (or a document) is encoded, it can be placed in an appropriate file folder and stored in a filing cabinet. This phase of processing information is called *storage*. Like nonliving storage systems (filing cabinets and computers), human memories are assumed to be relatively safe and permanent while in storage. Photographs may fade and paper may yellow with time, but short of a fire or other damage to the system, the information remains where it was placed. Most theorists make a similar assumption about memories: while they may fade somewhat over time, disuse is at most a minor cause of forgetting.[5]

There would probably be no memory problem if you had only one file folder in your cabinet. Problems arise because there is a continual proliferation of letters and files. Each new addition to the file cabinet makes it more difficult to find those stored earlier—a case of *retroactive interference* (as described in the previous chapter). Simultaneously all the old files make it difficult to access those more recently filed—a case of *proactive interference*. Once material has been stored, in other words, its *retrieval* is directly affected by the amount and organization of the rest of the stored material.

To summarize before moving on, the filing system provides a useful metaphor for memory processes. This is not because human memory works in similar ways physically (with file drawers, computers, etc.) but because some of the same functions—namely, encoding, storage, and retrieval—are performed by both mechanical and human memories. Of course, humans invented filing systems so perhaps that is not too surprising. In any case, to continue the analogy, files must be organized in some way (by category, alphabetical order, etc.) as they are being encoded if there is any reasonable hope of retrieving them later. Moreover, the manner in which they are encoded must be known at retrieval time. The next few sections deal with some of these issues.

Availability vs. Accessibility: Cue-Dependent Recall

Let's follow an item of information on a hypothetical trip into our memory system. Let's say that we are a typical university professor who has met a new student for the first time. We look at the face and concentrate on the correct pronunciation as the student introduces himself. We perhaps repeat the name to ourselves while trying to pair it with facial features or create some obvious or bizarre association that might help us recall it later. The first day of class we might learn quite a few students' names that way. By the next class we might have forgotten some, but then we relearn them, and by the third class we know them fairly well.[6] Then comes an interesting and totally unexpected quiz: we meet the student at a shopping mall with his spouse and children. He greets us and, though we know we have seen him before, we cannot recall his name and cannot even recall where we met him.

The student's name is *available* in our memory, but it is *not accessible* to us at this time or under these conditions. *Availability* refers to its storage in the memory. Since the information was adequately learned, it must be available. *Accessibility* refers to our capacity to retrieve

Cartoon 10.1.

the information. That depends on the current cues. In this case, the chance encounter provides none of the cues that have been encoded with the student's name—for example, the classroom, other students, the position in the room in which he sits, or the clothes he typically wears. In the mall his face is a fact out of context. Since you never saw him there before, and never met his wife and children, those stimuli do not provide you with any cues for his name. When you see him in class the following week, however, his name will likely occur to you without difficulty, demonstrating it was available but not accessible under these conditions.

A laboratory demonstration of this cue-dependent effect was provided by having subjects learn sentences such as, "The boy earned a *GOOD GRADE* on the test" (Light and Carter-Sobell, 1970). Later an extensive list of adjective-noun pairs was shown to the subjects whose job was to identify whether they had previously seen that *noun* in the sentences they had learned previously. In this experiment the preceding adjective "good" as well as the entire sentence were expected to provide a biasing context, or situational cues, that

could facilitate or hinder subsequent recognition of the nouns. When the adjective-noun pairs in the list provided the same situational cues (or semantic bias in the authors' words) as in the original sentence, recognition accuracy was highest. When the test list included not "good grade," but "steep grade" or "bad grade," accuracy of recognizing whether they had seen the noun in previous sentences was significantly reduced.

The results of such studies[7] demonstrate that memories for specific facts are not stored as isolated facts. They are stored along with the conditions, cues, organizational or categorical biases that existed when they were encoded. If different cues are present when the person's memory is tested, then it is likely to fail. We encountered many instances of this in the chapter on Problem-Solving and Transfer since, almost by definition, what makes a problem interesting is its unique differences from our previous learning. A large part of the transfer process, then, depends upon how many cues (i.e., similar or identical elements) present at original learning are also present at the time of the transfer test.

Tulving and Thompson (1973, p. 369) have called this the *encoding specificity principle*, which they defined as follows:

Specific encoding operations performed on what is perceived determine what is stored, and what is stored determines what retrieval cues are effective in providing access to what is stored.

A rose is a rose is a rose—well, perhaps, but only if the conditions under which "rose" is encoded are the same each time. Otherwise, remembering "rose" when called upon may well be a thorny experience.

Organization in Memory

We have repeatedly alluded to the need to impose an organization on incoming information if it is to be retrieved at a later date. Suppose you were shown the following words one at a time in random order by categories:

TREE	COOKIE	MOTHER
FLOWER	PIE	UNCLE
WEED	CRACKER	BROTHER
BUSH	CAKE	COUSIN

Then for additional practice you were shown them twice more in different random orders, but together by categories. Following this you were asked to recall as many words as possible from the list. Suppose further that other subjects not only learned this list, but then learned anywhere form one to five additional but similar lists. Following each list all subjects were asked to recall the words for that list. After the last list was learned, you were to recall as many of the words from all of the lists that you could. This was the *non-cued recall condition*. Finally, you were given a new answer sheet which was organized by category names—that is, it had the name of a category (e.g., "Plants," "Foods," or "Relationships") followed by four blank spaces for all of the words in all of the lists. This was your task under the *cued-recall condition*.

Cartoon 10.2.

Tulving and Psotka (1971) actually conducted such a study, but with six categories of four words each, for a total of 24-words, in each list. Among other things, they plotted the recall scores for each list as a function of the number of intervening lists. As expected, retroactive interference reared its ugly head in the first or non-cued recall test. The more lists learned, the less that was recalled of earlier lists. For example, when subjects only learned one list they recalled about 70% (a mean of 16.6 out of 24 words) of the words. If they learned six lists, in contrast, they recalled fewer than 40% of the words in list 1. But this was under non-cued recall conditions. What happened on the cued-recall test?

When subjects were finally asked to respond with the category cues present, performance was markedly different. Subjects recalled 75% of the words in list 1, if they had learned only that one list, but they recalled almost 70% (a mean of 16.1 of 24 words) of the words in the first list even after learning a total of six lists. *The category cues almost eliminated retroactive interference in this study*. Please note also that the category cues provided for the retention test had never been part of the lists to be learned. It was the organization of the lists by categories that facilitated the encoding and subsequent better retrieval by category cues than when such cues were not explicitly provided (the cues provided retroactive facilitation).

This experiment shows (1) the powerful effect of cues in recall and (2) the effectiveness—indeed, the necessity—of organizing material for its retrieval. Categories imposed by an experimenter or teacher provide one obvious kind of organization. Materials that are learned more-or-less randomly, however, are only treated randomly by learners if they can impose no organizational structure on the materials themselves. For example, they may invent an organization, possibly by associations with previous learning, by alphabetizing, or by some other perhaps totally idiosyncratic means. Self-imposed structures have been called *subjective organizations* (e.g., Shuell, 1969; Tulving, 1962). They imply, as we pointed out earlier, an active person trying to make order out of a confusing barrage of stimuli. To the extent that they can do so, learning and retention are improved, perhaps amazingly, as anecdote 10.1 shows.

One Long-Term Memory, or Two?

When we discuss the differences between experts and novices (chapter 11), it is useful to distinguish between the information that is stored in memory and the procedures that we use to act on that information. In adding 247 + 493, for example, we have such number facts in storage as 7 + 3 = 10 and 9 + 4 = 13. This basic factual information is known as *declarative knowledge* and can be contrasted with *procedural knowledge*, such as is needed to perform the several steps in the above problem (such as: add 7 + 3, write 0 in the ones column, carry 1 to the tens column and add it to 9 + 4 to get 14, write 4 in the tens column, etc.).

One very detailed and explicit theory of cognition (Anderson, 1983) suggests that declarative (knowing *that*) and procedural (knowing *how*) knowledge actually arise from two separate components of long-term memory. In Anderson's view, when people work on a problem like the one given above, they do not find at the same site in their long term memory both the number facts and procedures for combining the facts. Rather, they call upon two separate long term memory stores—one which yields the declarative knowledge and the other the procedures and skills for operating on that knowledge.

Whichever postulate—the one or two (or maybe more) long-term stores—is eventually supported by the preponderance of evidence, the differentiation of the two types of knowledge is now widely accepted.

Memory—Who's Tending the Store?

If the last sections have given the impression that what happens at encoding determines what can later be retrieved, that seems true, but only partially. Each encounter with new stimuli occurs in short-term memory, while activating items from long-term memory. These are somehow retrieved and interact in the working memory with the new information. As items seem to fit into an existing organization, they may be rehearsed together with the other items already there and stored in the same file (to use our earlier metaphor). If the new information doesn't seem to fit neatly into one of our categories, or contradicts other facts in our store, we may need to reorganize our knowledge. Presumably this is also what happens when a child develops from one of Piaget's cognitive stages to another.

Information in memory, therefore, is not static, but may be continually reorganized. This may be purposely planned as in a teacher's spiral curriculum which recycles old facts through successively more complex theoretical interpretations of those facts. Or, it may

Anecdote 10.1

The Power of Organization in Memory

An otherwise average college student, S. F., was able to increase his memory span from the typical level of 7 to a remarkable expert level of 79 digits. He did this by practicing about one hour a day for three to five days a week for over 18 months, or a total of 230 hours. At these sessions, S. F. had random digits (e.g., 7, 9, 1, 3 . . .) read to him at the rate of one per second, following which he repeated the sequence. When he was correct, the next sequence was increased by one digit; when incorrect he received one fewer digit on the next trial. Among other things, a typical session included many trials on these sequences, with a verbal report of his thoughts immediately after half of the trials.

How did S. F. increase his average digit-span from 7 to 79? At first he began to categorize the digits into 3- and 4-digit groups, labeled as running times for various races. Since he was a long-distance runner, this was a mnemonic device for which he already had some experience. "For example, 3492 was recoded as '3 minutes and 49 point 2 seconds, near world-record mile time' " (p. 1181). Digits he could not categorize that way, such as 893, were classified as ages (89.3, a very old man). For the first seventy-five days or so S. F. perfected this technique and his memory span increased to between 25 and 30 digits. Theoretically this would be the maximum one could expect by chunking into 3- and 4-digit groups: the magical number $7 \times 4 = 28$.

How did S. F. exceed even this remarkable achievement? Ericsson et al. (1980; also see Chase and Ericsson, 1981), who reported the study, did not provide the specific images S. F. used in creating his hierarchy. They did, however, describe some of the associations that S. F. used. For example, he often broke running times into those for various kinds of races: the mile, 10,000 meters, 100-yard dash, etc. (a first level). He further divided those into near-world-record times, average times, and practice times (second level). His third level included specific features, such as "my old coach's best time." This hierarchical structure seems analogous to remembering that robin, sparrow and eagle (level 1) can all be called birds (level 2). Still later he was able to create a three-level hierarchy as he was encoding the digits, perhaps analogous to the category animals (level 3) with subcategories of birds, reptiles and mammals, each with specific instances in the next subordinate level in the hierarchy. With such a hierarchy, in principle, there is no known limit to the digit span or, more generally, what can be stored in memory. And S. F. was still increasing his digit span when the study was discontinued. That's the good news. The bad news was that this incredible skill didn't transfer to such other stimuli as letters, where his memory span was about six consonants. Apparently he would need to develop a hierarchical mnemonic system specific to letters to achieve the same results. But who would expect practice in golf to perfect a tennis stroke as well?

Cartoon 10.3.

be serendipitous, where isolated facts come together in such a way as to allow a new interpretation of those facts. In either case, this is a major difference between a computer or filing cabinet and a human memory—the organization of the store in humans may undergo change from within as well as from without.

Learning vs. Retention

Most textbooks on the subject treat learning before going on to discuss memory. I have chosen to maintain that tradition but, as must be obvious by now if not previously, there could be no learning if the memory processes just described were nonexistent. The converse seems just as true: memory cannot exist without learning. In much of our daily lives a distinction is seldom made between learning and retention, and current cognitive psychology deemphasizes the distinction. Traditionally, however, psychologists have felt the necessity of delineating the differences between them, partly because (1) analytical thinking is one of the methods of science and (2) there are some factors which seem to affect learning and retention in different ways (e.g., massed vs. distributed practice). In any case, the kind of learning that is under discussion in this unit is cognitive as opposed to operant or respondent. And although the term learning can be applied to all three of those levels of behavior, the term retention is traditionally reserved for cognitive learning (we speak of operants and respondents as being increased or decreased in frequency or intensity, not as being remembered or forgotten).

As introduced in chapter 4, I shall adopt a constructivist definition of learning for the cognitive, academic kinds of experiences which are the focus of this unit. Specifically, and somewhat in contrast to operant and respondent learning, *cognitive learning is defined as a change in knowledge or competence in a learner who is actively and purposefully seeking meaning from the experience.*

This definition, following Brown (1994) and Shuell (1992), allows the learning to be experienced alone, with a teacher/mentor, or in social contexts. It also implies that the memory functions deriving from cognitive and information processing theory—e.g., attention, encoding, organization, negotiation between working and long-term memory, and so forth—are integral to, but separable from, the learning functions. Finally, it implies that to be effective, teachers must find ways to activate those functions (e.g., Driscoll, 1994; Shuell, 1996).

Elaboration in Encoding

This chapter began with John Anderson's personal trauma of trying to learn pairs of nonsense syllables like DAX-GIB by brute force of diligent repetition. Suppose, instead, that he had used a learning strategy that had made the pairs more meaningful. One way might be to make meaningful associations to the presumed non-meaningful nonsense syllables and then *elaborate* those further into a sentence. Such a *verbal elaboration* might be done as follows: DAX are funny ducks which gib (GIB) or taunt each other; or, more simply, DAX always GIB each other. One might even go further and imagine a scene in which several daffy DAX were teasing and taunting each other amidst loud honking GIBS and physical sword-fights with their beaks. This would be a kind of *imagery elaboration.*

Two papers by Rohwer (1971; 1973) sparked a considerable amount of research on the topic. Rohwer defined *elaboration* broadly as the placing of items to be associated into an episode, process or relationship, and provided evidence that elaboration is an effective strategy to facilitate learning and subsequent retention. He also suggested, among other things, that there is a normal developmental process of learning to provide oneself with these more meaningful contexts for associating items: adolescents (who are presumably in Piaget's formal operational stage of cognitive development) are more likely to benefit from or to use spontaneously elaborative strategies than pre-adolescents (in the concrete operations stage).

Meaningfulness of Material and Mnemonics

The results of such experiments on elaboration strategies, particularly with such materials as nonsense syllables or lists of words, raise an important practical question—namely, what is the important factor, the meaningfulness of the materials to be learned or the process by which they are learned? The answer seems to be both, but in a rather interesting way.

It has long been known that words and concepts differ remarkably in their ability to elicit other word associations (e.g., the word "kitchen" evokes an average of about ten responses in 60-seconds while the nonsense word "gojey" elicits less than one). This was one way of calibrating the *meaningfulness* of materials (Noble's *m*, 1952). Other approaches were to ask people to rate words for their *pronounceability,* their *familiarity,* or *emotional value,* or even to rate larger groups of words for their *associability* or *semantic relatedness* (e.g., the pair chair-table is judged more related than chair-kitchen). A third way of calibrating materials is the extent to which they evoke *images* (e.g., most people can easily form an image of "kitchen" or of "fatigue", but would have a harder time visualizing "virtue").

It turns out that *the more materials to be learned evoke imagery or meaningfulness* in one or more of the above ways, *the easier those materials* are to learn. This is an important general rule, but it only begins to approach the crux of the matter, which becomes clear when you realize that someone who speaks only Chinese would find no differences in meaningfulness or imagery among any of the above English words, real or nonsense. Thus the *meaningfulness of material* is only partly inherent in the material, and is *mostly a function of the previous experience of the learners in regard to that material.*

Today, it is fair to say that, though cognitive scientists still calibrate their materials for meaningfulness, the emphasis is now properly placed on the learners (Shuell, 1988). After all, it is they who actively imagine, provide associates and relationships, and judge material pleasant or unpleasant, easy or difficult. And whatever the ease or difficulty of materials, learners must encode them in some way to be able to remember them or even to understand the stimuli that their senses are receiving. The evidence is now mounting that all strategies for encoding are not equal, as least for long-term memory: that imagery elaboration techniques are more powerful than verbal-elaboration techniques which, in turn, are much better than simple rote-learning ("burn them in" by repetition) techniques. This is probably one of the reasons for the recent rise in popularity of various *mnemonic techniques,* or memory aids.

Consider the *keyword method,* perhaps the most popular mnemonic system researched for use in schools, since it can be used to associate any pair of items: language translation equivalents, states with capitals, or famous people with their accomplishments (e.g., Atkinson, 1975; Levin, 1981; Miller, Galanter, & Pribram, 1960; Pressley, Levin, & Delaney 1982; Pressley & Dennis-Rounds, 1980). In this system, a keyword is identified in each word or idea to be associated. For example, if you must learn that Annapolis is the capital of Maryland, then key words might be "apple" and "marry." Then you visualize the keywords interacting in some way — two apples, dressed as bride and groom, getting married. Later, when asked what is the capital of Maryland, you recall the keyword "marry", visualize a marriage of two "apples," which is a cue for Annapolis. Or, if Annapolis were given and you had to name the state, you would reverse the process by starting with your image of "apples".

It is surprising to many people that such techniques are worth the effort. After all, it seems like more trouble to remember to find keywords, add images, etc. But that, apparently, is the point: mnemonic strategies work at the encoding phase to organize material and provide retrieval cues for subsequent recall. Elaboration of the information, verbally or visually, helps link that material to something already in storage. If it can be linked to something already meaningful in the long-term store, these additional cues add further organizational structure to make the material that much more complete and/or useful. If the new information is not currently meaningful or interesting—which is often the case from the student's point of view—then mnemonic strategies provide a temporary meaningful scaffold to help get the material in memory so that later instruction can build on it. We'll revisit this idea in the next chapter.

Do mnemonics really work? There is now a very large and growing literature suggesting that elaboration techniques, particularly imaginal ones, add significantly—up to double the amount—to what is recalled from a learning experience (for summaries of such research, see Gentile, 1987; Levin, 1981; Pressley & Levin, 1983a, 1983b). Furthermore, imagery techniques seem to reduce interference effects, even in studies in which multiple lists of similar items have to be learned (e.g., Bugelski; 1968; Bugelski; Kidd, & Segmen (1968). Finally, these effects are generalizable across children and adults, retarded and nonretarded, learning disabled and non-disabled (e.g., Pressley & Levin, 1983 a&b; see also anecdote 10.2).

Dual Coding Theory

The fact that both images and verbal associations appear to play central roles in learning and retention raises the question of how best to account for these processes. Some possibilities include the following: (1) that there exist separate and independent systems to encode words and images, (2) that images are translated into words, (3) that words are transformed into images, (4) that both are transformed into something else (e.g., in a computer, words and numbers are recorded into a series of on-off decisions). Certainly the first three of these appear to be commonly experienced by most of us. For example, you may retain a vivid image of a beautiful sunset, but no adequate words to describe it. On the other hand, if you are asked to describe your living room, you can probably do a good job of mentally scanning the room and verbally

Anecdote 10.2

Mnemonics for Learning Disabled

Sixty junior high school students, half classified as learning disabled (LD) by their school and half nondisabled (NLD), participated in a memory study. Half of each of these groups, the mnemonic groups, were taught the peg-word rhyme "one-bun; two-shoe, three-tree, . . . ten-hen" until each participant showed in a variety of ways that he or she knew the jingle. These same students were then given imagery practice. For example, they had to imagine a surfboard paired with the number 1 by visualizing a surfboard sandwich (one-bun: surfboard in a bun). After practicing doing this with a list of ten words, so that they could recall at least 8 of the 10 correct word pairs, they were then given three other lists to learn using the same technique.

The other half of the LD and NLD groups did not receive the jingle nor the imagery instruction, but they were given an equal amount of practice on the first list. Their instructions were to learn the words as well as they could. After that they also learned the same three lists as the students in the mnemonic groups.

Immediately following the fourth list, and again 7 days later and 5 months later, all students were surprised with a retention test on all four lists.

Since one criterion for classification as LD is poor memory ability, it was not surprising that the NLD controls recalled more words than the LD controls. However, both the NLD and LD mnemonics groups had more than double the recall of their respective control groups. Furthermore, the LD students who learned the mnemonic peg-word system did better than the NLD control students who were left to their own devices. The results are portrayed in graphic form below:

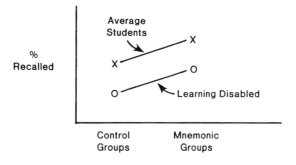

The results of this study (Elliott and Gentile, 1986) replicated previous studies by Bugelski (1968; Bugelski, Kidd and Segmen, 1968) on college students.

describing the positions and colors of the objects. Your listener can probably visualize your living room, somewhat accurately, from your verbal description. How are these experiences to be best accounted for theoretically?

An account of these phenomena which incorporates the first three of the above-mentioned possibilities is known as *dual coding theory* (Paivio, 1971; 1975; Paivio and Begg, 1981; Paivio and Csapo, 1973).[8] According to dual coding theory there exist *two independent but interacting systems* for encoding, storing, and retrieving information. One of these systems specializes in *words*, or more generally, in processing and generating verbal behavior. The other specializes in *images*—in the processing and generation of perceptual information about pictures, objects and other nonverbal stimuli. Since these systems are considered independent, either can be activated without engaging the other system—for example, when we watch and remember a sunset without describing it, or when reciting the Pledge of Allegiance without visualizing it. The interactive nature of the two systems implies that the verbal system can, and usually does, arouse images, while images can be translated into words. The living room example in the previous paragraph (from Paivio and Begg, 1981, p. 69) refers to a common experience of the interconnections of the verbal and non-verbal systems.

Some evidence that dual coding theory is correct in its essentials arose from studies showing that, when stimuli are presented both verbally and nonverbally (i.e., when students see and name pictures), recall is better than when the stimuli are presented as words alone, or as pictures alone. If one system were translated into another system, then there should be no additive advantage of presenting stimuli in more than one modality. Another finding in such experiments is that memory is better for images than for the same stimuli processed verbally.

It should also be mentioned that dual coding theory has also been extended to the issue of bilingualism. In this interesting case, separate verbal systems such as Spanish and English are independent of, but interconnected with, each other, as well as with the imagery system. The interested reader is referred to the following sources: Arndt and Gentile (1986), Paivio and Begg (1981), Paivio and Desrochers (1980) Paivio and Lambert (1981).

To summarize and draw some conclusions, dual coding theory postulates (1) that memory traces aroused by images are likely to be stronger than those aroused by words (the more concrete the image, the greater the effect), and (2) that generating images of words engages two memory systems—the verbal and nonverbal—and increases the probability of recall over stimuli encoded as either images alone or words alone. These findings underscore and explain an important curriculum principle: that *concrete operations are more memorable than formal or abstract operations.* That is, through manipulating objects drawing graphs, and the like, more imagery will be evoked than by dealing with the same material in a purely verbal, mathematical or symbolic way. But I am not just speaking of the teacher manipulating or drawing, though that may help; it is the student who must do the encoding. Piaget told us why pre-adolescents need concrete experiences to understand concepts and principles; Paivio informs us that concrete experiences will make those concepts and principles more memorable for adults as well as children.

Amount and Distribution of Practice

Perhaps the most ambitious experimental study of learning and retention ever conducted was the first. Hermann Ebbinghaus (1885) was both the experimenter and the sole subject in this epochal study, in which he subjected himself to years of learning and then relearning lists of nonsense syllables, as well as portions of Byron's poem *Don Juan*. In search of material he could learn, Ebbinghaus invented the nonsense syllable by creating 2300 unique consonant-vowel-consonant combinations that were, first, relatively devoid of meaning and, second, could provide a large population of similar items from which small samples could be randomly drawn to be memorized.[9]

Another of his inventions was the *savings score*, a measure of retention which measures the *time needed to relearn* something after some period of time *subtracted from* the *time originally needed to learn* it.

In one of his studies, Ebbinghaus systematically assessed his retention as a function of the number of repetitions in original learning. He studied a series of six 16-syllable lists as one group and discovered that it took an average of, let us say, x-seconds.[10]

At another time he studied another comparable series of six lists, repeating them eight times; then twenty-four hours later he relearned those same syllables until he could recite them perfectly and recorded the time as y-seconds. The difference x-y, if any, was the savings score. Ebbinghaus found the difference to be 103 seconds which, divided by the 8 original practice trials 24-hours previously, meant that each original practice trial saved an average of 12.9 seconds in relearning time.

Not content with this simple but important finding, on other days he went on to practice for 16, 24, 32, 42, 53, and 64 repetitions on original learning days and then to relearn those same lists 24-hours later. The time saved in relearning was a direct function of the amount of practice during original learning. For Ebbinghaus learning nonsense syllables, the savings averaged between 12- and 13-seconds for each repetition during original learning (for 32 repetitions it was a total of 407 seconds saved; 64 repetitions saved a total of 816 seconds). As Ebbinghaus summarized (p. 57):

> *In other words: for each three additional repetitions which I spent on a given day on the study of a series, I saved, in learning that series 24 hours later, on the average, approximately one repetition. . . .*

Original Learning and Overlearning

The Ebbinghaus study described above clearly showed the advantage of extra practice for learning and retention, but did not directly deal with the issue of mastery of the material. To be more specific, it matters tremendously for retention how well material is originally learned. Material that is 100% learned for the first time will obviously be better remembered than learning that is less than 100%, but it will still be vulnerable to all of the many forces which produce forgetting, chief among them interference. *When material is practiced beyond its first perfect recall—technically called overlearning—its retention is markedly increased.*

Although Ebbinghaus estimated the effect of each additional repetition to be about constant, more recent research has qualified that slightly. The first few additional trials may have larger effects on retention than later trials—in other words, a kind of diminishing returns may set in with multiple repetitions of the material (e.g., Krueger, 1929; Postman, 1962a). Even if this is so for many kinds of material, however, it must be recognized that the point of diminishing returns "will be reached slowly" (e.g., Postman, 1962a) since additional rehearsals are having a number of indirect effects even if they are not directly strengthening retention. For example, each time material is relearned it is occurring under slightly different conditions, therefore creating additional cues for recall. Each time it is rehearsed allows an opportunity for it to be reconsidered and

Cartoon 10.4.

reorganized. Such "re-cognizing" may also establish some of the conditions for positive transfer, especially if the overlearning is done in imaginative ways (such as by enrichment activities, elaboration, and the like) instead of simply relearning in the same way.

Why do teachers have such good memories for the material they teach? The answer is that they relearn the material—overlearn it—each year. By the twentieth year they may remember the material quite well and be beyond the influence of most interfering factors but, unfortunately, the one thing they may have forgotten is how difficult the material is to remember during original learning. Thus in becoming masters they may have lost empathy with their students.

Figure 10.3 summarizes these issues. Since forgetting is the inevitable result of trying to learn something the first time (panel 2 in both curves), then amount of original learning is critical. When original learning is high (panel 1 in curve B), then there is considerable savings in relearning and all relearning can be considered overlearning. When original learning is not high (part 1 in curve A), such as when the teacher moved on before many students mastered the material, then there is little or no savings in relearning and additional practice is not considered overlearning. If this process continues, the students in A will be "at risk" of low achievement, while those in B will be "at promise" to consolidate and reorganize their memories and benefit from new learning.

To end this section, I can't resist retelling the old story of the tourist, lost in New York, who approaches a street musician and says, "Excuse me, sir, but can you tell me how to get to Carnegie Hall?" The musician answers, "Practice, man, practice!"

Massed vs. Distributed Practice

"Practice makes perfect." "If at first you don't succeed, try, try again." "If at first you don't succeed, you're about average." Advice, aphorism, and satire are full of allusions to practice. But the evidence is that *how* practice is done determines the outcome. Making the task more meaningful by imagery or verbal elaboration is much more effective than repetitious rehearsal, though rehearsal is much more effective than "wishing for a better memory."

Another concern is how practice should be distributed in time. Let's experience this issue by joining the second-level French students in

A. WHEN MATERIAL IS NOT MASTERED TO A HIGH LEVEL:

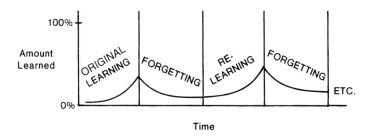

Moral:
When material is not originally learned to a high standard, it is quickly forgotten, and there is no savings in relearning; and if it is not relearned to a high standard, it will be quickly forgotten, etc.

B. WHEN MATERIAL IS MASTERED TO A HIGH LEVEL:

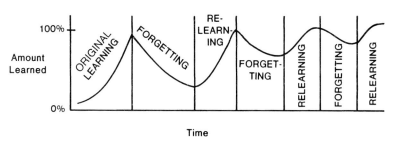

Moral:
When material is originally learned to a high standard, it is quickly forgotten, but (1) there is considerable savings in relearning and (2) subsequent recall is greater, leading to (3) considerable savings in relearning, leading to (4) greater recall, etc.

Figure 10.3. Hypothetical shapes of forgetting curves under various conditions of mastery.

a high school class. The objective of the instructional unit was to learn the French equivalents of twenty occupations (e.g., lawyer—l'avocat), typed on a sheet of paper for study only during scheduled class time. In addition, three different exercises were prepared, each scheduled for ten minutes. The first was a multiple-choice exam to be taken as practice "(e.g., fireman: le proviseur, le facteur, le pompier)." The second provided recall practice in supplying the correct occupation from context "(e.g., Il cultive les legumes et les fruits. _____)." The last was like the flashcard procedure of supplying the correct equivalent (e.g., lawyer—_____). At the completion of the three exercises loomed a vocabulary test which counted toward the course grade.

Half the class were taken to a different room and given each ten-minute exercise on three successive days. These students were in the *distributed practice* condition. At the conclusion of the third practice exercise, they received their exam. The rest of the class did unrelated work on the first two days, and on the third day worked for 30-minutes on all three practice exercises in succession. These students were in the *massed practice* condition. Following those experiences, they had their immediate retention test. Four days later a surprise delayed retention test was administered to all students.

The authors of this study (Bloom and Shuell, 1981) report that on the immediate test, which assessed the degree of original learning, the mean retention scores were 16.85 and 16.12 for the distributed practice and massed practice groups, respectively. This small difference was not statistically significant. On the delayed retention test, however, there was a statistically and educationally significant difference: students who received distributed practice scored 15.04 while their peers receiving massed practice scored 11.15. Distributed practice, though it had no effect on original learning, was a potent force for maintaining retention.

This major finding that the spacing of practice has a significant effect on long-term retention has been replicated many times (e.g., Cain and Willey, 1939; Ebbinghaus, 1885; Keppel, 1964; Leith, Biran and Opollot, 1969; Reynolds and Glaser, 1964). Sometimes it has a significant effect on amount originally learned as well, though such results probably depend upon the task to be learned and the particular time periods involved. For instance, if you have to memorize a long poem or play that will take hours, then such factors as fatigue will militate against massed practice even during the original learning phase. For briefer texts or lists that take only a few minutes, there may be no difference between massed and distributed practice on original learning and yet, as in the Bloom-Shuell results, a difference may emerge in retention.

Why? There is no firm answer at present, but we can make a reasonably educated guess based on the rest of the information in this chapter. On the second occasion of practicing something, we are not only dealing with the immediate stimuli in working (short-term) memory, but we are induced to dredge up the items that are already in long-term memory. In addition to providing possible additional cues or ways to reorganize the material, distributed practice may also be providing experience in retrieving information from the long-term store. This should provide positive transfer to a subsequent retention test, as Bloom and Shuell so succinctly suggested (1981, p. 247):

> *Individuals learning materials under conditions of massed practice only have the opportunity to recall information from short-term memory during learning. Yet on a test given at some later time they must recall the material from long-term memory, something they have not practiced.*

This position is also supported in a study by Bahrick (1979) who found that accessibility of material from long-term memory is optimal when practice sessions are spaced at approximately the same time intervals as the learning-to-testing intervals. For example, "if information is likely to be retrieved only once each month, training sessions should not be spaced much more closely than one per month" (Bahrick, 1979, p. 302).

Whether the last suggestion is optimal for all kinds of materials and learning situations may require further research. The main point, however, appears to be firmly established—namely, that retention, if not original learning, is facilitated by conditions of distributed practice (see anecdote 10.3 for another example). For school learning this is of major importance, since learning is seldom considered to be an end in itself but, rather, is the means to an end. The residue of learning—as it shows up in such measures of retention as recall, recognition and savings in relearning—is the main interest for educators.

Learning Rate and Forgetting

Consider the following potential test question (who knows, your instructor may even use it):

Item: Which of the following is the best answer? Fast learners forget _____ slow learners.
a. more quickly than
b. less quickly than
c. at the same rate as

Before revealing the answer, let's participate in another experiment. The experimenter shows you a stack of five 3 x 5 inch cards and explains that each contains two lines of a poem which will be shown to you for 5-seconds. After you've seen all five cards, you will be asked to recite as much of the poem as you

Anecdote 10.3

Cumulative Effects of the Keyword Method Plus Distributed Practice in Eighth Grade Social Studies

As stated in the text, empirical evidence favors imagery over rote memorization and distributed practice over massed practice. What happens if you combine them? Are the effects (1) mostly independent and cumulative, so that distributed practice adds to keyword effects; or are other interactions possible, such as (2) the keyword technique compensates for and makes distributed practice unnecessary or less helpful?

Baehre and Gentile (1991) set out to evaluate such questions on students learning facts of social studies that were part of their eighth grade curriculum. Three different 12-item lists were learned: (1) states and capitals (e.g., Frankfort, Kentucky), (2) countries and capitals (e.g., Canberra, Australia) and (3) famous people and their accomplishments (e.g., Harry Truman ordered use of atomic bomb on Japan). Four different classes of eighth graders, relatively equal on average standardized achievement scores, were randomly assigned to one of the following four groups:

A. *Keyword with Distributed Practice:* On Monday, students were introduced to the keyword method, practiced using it by drawing interactive images, and then learned a list using the drawing technique. On Tuesday, students recalled list 1, practiced the technique and learned a second list. On Wednesday, recall and further practice took place on both lists.
B. *Keyword with Massed Practice:* The same procedures were used as with group A except that all three learning/practice sessions were done in one class period on Wednesday.
C. *Control with Distributed Practice:* Students were given the same lists, spaced over three days as in group A, but without imagery instruction; instead they were told to learn the items the best way they could (and were given a scratch pad to use).
D. *Control with Massed Practice:* Students had the same instructions as group C, but learned the lists on Wednesday (as Group B).

Seven days later, all students were given a surprise retention test on both lists and then asked to learn list 3, as a transfer test.

The results were quite straightforward. First, students in the keyword groups were able to invent images within the thirty seconds allowed per item and use the same sketches on recall tests on about 75% of the items. This use of images resulted in the keyword groups (A&B) obtaining recall scores that were 44% better than the control groups (C&D). Distributed practice (groups A&C) resulted in a 19% improvement over massed practice (groups B&D). Finally, these effects were independent and cumulative (group A was 61% better than D) and easily transferred to the third list.

As the authors note, one may question whether such facts should be part of a social studies curriculum. But as long as they are part of the curriculum, why not teach students to use the most efficient means available to learn them?

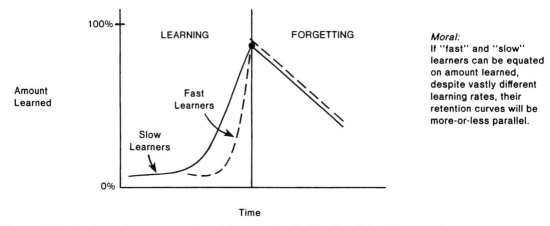

Figure 10.4. A schematic representation of the retention by "fast" vs. "slow" learners in learning poetry.

can remember. When you are ready, you begin, seeing either a poem by A. A. Milne (two lines of which are "And there I saw a white swan make another white swan in the lake") or a poem by G. Awooner-Williams (the last two lines of which are "Alas! the travelers are back all covered with debts"). After the first trial through the five cards, you do not remember too many of the words. But the experimenter repeats the presentation a second and a third time, and so on, until you have learned it satisfactorily.

Satisfactory performance in this case was reciting 75–90% of the poem's words correctly. For a few of these college-age subjects this was as few as three trials; but for at least one subject, it was 17 trials. Unknown to you, the rate of learning to this standard was an important consideration in this study, because the top third and bottom third, in rate of learning, were classified as "fast" and "slow" learners, respectively, and were due to receive a surprise retention test. The retention test occurred during a regular college class that had nothing to do with the experiment and occurred either 24-, 48- or 72-hours after you learned the poem.

Before presenting the results, another significant point must be raised. The learning criterion of 75-90% was established for two reasons. First, it did not allow anyone to master the poem completely and thus begin to overlearn it; thus anyone who scored above 90% was discarded from the study. Second, it equated "fast" and "slow" learners within a narrow range of words recalled. Only if their original learning was approximately equal could a fair test of retention be conducted.[11]

The authors of this study (Gentile, Monaco, Iheozor-Ejiofor, Ndu and Ogbonaya, 1982) present results for both American college students and Nigerian secondary school students. Despite the large differences in rate of original learning (the "fast" third took from 3–5 trials compared with 8–17 trials for the "slow" third of the American sample; the same trials-to-criterion data were 1–5 and 8–10 for the "fast" and "slow" thirds in the Nigerian sample), there were no significant differences between "fast" and "slow" learners in retention. Figure 10.4 presents these results graphically.

Other studies of this sort were conducted on materials comprised of lists of unrelated words, including two other experiments reported by Gentile et al. (1982) that were stimulated by Shuell and Keppel (1970). Other studies that have replicated this basic finding, using a variety of techniques but all equating original learning, are the following: Gregory and Bunch, 1959; Schoer, 1962; Stroud and Carter, 1961; Stroud and Schoer, 1959; Underwood, 1964).

The answer to the test item, therefore, is C. *"Fast" and "slow" learners forget at the same rate once they have been equated in original learning.* In classrooms, it is probably impossible and undesirable to equate "fast" and "slow" learners, since students who master material can and should go on to overlearn it and use it in new ways in a good spiral curriculum. It should not be a goal of education to hold up the progress of faster learners so that slower learners can catch up. The fastest student in class may learn a poem, as one of the subjects did, in one trial. The slowest, on the other hand, took 17 trials. In other studies, it took five or six times as much practice time for the average student in the bottom third to learn to the same level as the average student in the top third. We are speaking of normal classrooms with students of average intelligence, not including especially gifted or retarded students.

If students cannot be equated in original learning, nor should that be the goal, then why are such laboratory findings as these important? I think the answer is that they present a new optimism for educating people. "Slow" learners may take longer to learn, but they are not stupid: they will retain what they learn, they will benefit from overlearning, from mnemonic techniques, elaborations, and thus reap the benefits of having learning-forgetting-relearning curves that resemble those in B, rather than A, of figure 10.3 and so forth. Campione and Brown (1978a) have also concluded that even with many retarded individuals, the problem is not availability of what is learned, but transfer (see also Zeaman and House, 1967). Thus as Gentile et al. concluded (1982, p. 137):

> . . . *teachers may be happy to know that the time and effort required to teach "slow" learners to a high standard reaps the benefit of retention that is at least no worse than that of "faster" learners attaining the same standard.*

Relearning by Fast vs. Slow Learners

As the research in the previous section shows, there is now abundant evidence that amount remembered depends on amount learned, not rate of learning it. What happens, however, when faster and slower learners are asked to relearn and then recall the same material?

Gentile, Voelkl, Mt. Pleasant and Monaco (1995) set out to answer that question. First, in what they called Phase 1, they had fourth and fifth graders learn the same poem and attempt to recall it seven days later under the same conditions as before, and replicated the findings of Gentile et al. (1982). Then, in what they called phase 2, the students were asked to relearn the poem to the same 75–90% correct standard and then tested for recall seven, and again twenty-one, days later. Among other purposes of the study, the investigators wished to answer the following questions:

- Would faster learners also be faster relearners?
- How much savings would occur in relearning, and would faster and slower learners benefit about equally?
- If faster and slower learners can be equated on amount relearned, would their recall also be equal?

What do *you* predict happened?

Regarding the first two questions, the average number of trials to memorize the poem to criterion was 5.3 for the fast third and 17.4 for the slow third at original learning. In relearning, averages were 1.4 and 2.1 for fast and slow learners, respectively—a remarkable absolute savings. Furthermore, although faster learners remained faster in relearning, note that the ratio of fast:slow, which was about 1:3 at original learning, was reduced to 1:1.5 at relearning. Is it worth the effort to a teacher to achieve high levels of original learning for all, including the slowest learners, when such savings can be expected when this material is re-encountered?

Regarding the last question, the results were a bit more complicated because the fast and slow learners were not equated in amount relearned, despite the narrow 75–90% standard. The fast learners, on average, were at the top of this range in words recalled while the slow learners at the bottom, which turned out to be a significant difference. That difference was, in turn, reflected in the recall scores, with the difference increasing with length of retention interval.

Why might fast and slow learners differ, even after they were originally equated in amount learned? Gentile et al. (1995) had no way of answering that question directly, but they noted that there must be a reason that fast learners are faster, and speculated that it resides in their greater facility with and use of cognitive and metacognitive strategies.[12]

Cognitive and Metacognitive Strategies

Research from a wide variety of sources (see Worden's 1983 review) is locating the differences between fast and slow learners not in long-term memory, but during short-term memory. You will recall that while information is being held in the short-term store, it must be encoded in some meaningful way in order to go into long-term storage and, more importantly, to be accessible when later needed. We have already seen that many of us use quite inefficient strategies for organizing material as it comes to us piece by piece. Might the efficiency with which people organize material be a primary determinant of their differences in rate of learning? Evidence is mounting that this is so. Fast and slow learners in college classrooms (i.e, the top and bottom thirds of the classes) differ in their spontaneous use of categories in lists of words. When instructed in how to organize the material, Shuell (1983) found that the slow learners gained on the fast learners. Similar evidence exists that many memory differences between learning disabled and nondisabled,

Photo 10.3. A eager learner.

as well as between retarded and normal, individuals can be traced to their *rehearsal strategies*—or lack of them (e.g., Bauer, 1977; 1979a; 1979b; Borkowski and Büchel, 1983; Kopfer, in press; Torgesen, 1977; 1980; Torgesen and Goldman, 1977; Worden, 1983).

The strategies people use to recall information and/or transfer knowledge to new situations are receiving an increasing amount of study by educational and cognitive psychologists. Sparked primarily by some early studies by Flavell and his associates (Flavell, 1979; Flavell et al., 1970; Keeney et al., 1967; Moely et al. 1969), researchers are now asking not only (a) *what* and *how much* people can acquire and remember, but also (b) *how* they try to remember (i.e. their strategies), and (c) how they monitor their strategies—that is, their metacognitive processes.

As introduced in chapter 4, younger children tend not to be very good at monitoring their own thinking processes. Subsequent studies of this developmental difference suggest that the direction "to memorize" or "to remember" is understood more as "to examine" or "to look at" by younger children (e.g., Appel et al., 1972; Yussen et al., 1974). Thus, in contrast to older children, many preschoolers do not spontaneously rehearse the material to be learned, despite the directions. This does not mean, however, that they are incapable of rehearsing the material or benefiting from such rehearsal; rather it is a transfer problem, or what Flavell calls a *production deficiency*, in that the children do not utilize a strategy which is known to them.

Keeney, Cannizzo and Flavell (1967) provided an experimental demonstration of this process. Six-and seven-year-olds were asked to learn the serial order of blocks or pictures and, while they were trying to learn, an observer rated them for whether they appeared to be rehearsing. Those children who spontaneously rehearsed recalled significantly better than those who seemed not to be rehearsing. Then the nonrehearsers were given a brief training session on how to rehearse. On recall tests immediately following this training the trained rehearsers did as well as the spontaneous rehearsers. Subsequently, when left to their own devices they reverted to nonrehearsal. For whatever reason, they had not yet incorporated this rehearsal strategy into their normal use, though it was available and could be elicited by good instruction.

Consider a more complex task in which you are given a stack of 24 picture cards in no systematic order, as follows: bear, bicycle, chair, jacket, tie, table, truck, horse, crib, camel, mitten, boat, cow, dog, purse, shoe, lamp, sink, bus, car, sock, stove, train, goat. You are given three minutes to study them so that they can be recalled in any order. During that time you may arrange them in any order, make piles, take notes, etc. What strategy would you use for learning all 24 words? When Neimark et al. (1971; see also Moely et al., 1969) gave three trials on this task to students in grades 1, 3, 4, 5, 6 and college, they found systematic differences in both number of words recalled and how the materials were processed. The youngest children did deliberately rehearse with some rearranging of the cards, but there was no systematic organization of the cards. By grade 4, systematic sorting of the cards into categories (e.g., animals, items of clothing, vehicles of transportation, household furniture and appliances) was becoming common. In addition, some children began sorting into items previously recalled and those needing extra practice, since they had been forgotten previously. By college age, students not only organized by category, but were also organizing within categories, and could tell you what sort of item they were trying to recall. This latter self-monitoring of what is known and not known is like the tip-of-the-tongue phenomenon (e.g., Brown and McNeil, 1966) in which we search our memories for cues that might help us recall.

The research just cited provides us with some generalizations concerning individual differences and the development and use of learning strategies. As we have already seen in our discussion of verbal and imagery elaboration, there is a developmental trend in the use of any kind of strategy: older or more experienced persons are more likely spontaneously to use systematic strategies in a wider variety of learning/memory situations than younger or less experienced persons.

Interacting with this developmental trend, however, are some situation or task variables. Memory strategies are more likely to appear when tasks or materials encourage their use—e.g., when the words to be learned are on cards which can be physically manipulated and sorted, or when the teacher calls attention to, and provides practice with, a useful strategy.

Continuing on with the practical applications, Pressley et al. (1984) argue that people will utilize strategies to the extent that they understand not only how the strategy works, but how and why it is useful. By this argument our metacognitive processes direct our cognitive processes. Speaking of cognitive processes by which we monitor our memories—what has come to be known as "metamemory"—they argue that

> ... the more children know about a strategy, the more likely they will use it on a later occasion. That is, strategy use is tied to knowledge about the strategy—including information about its utility, knowledge about when and how to use the strategy, and insights about the ways in which a particular skill relates to other strategies. (Pressley et al., 1984, p. 94)

Thus a particular mnemonic technique, such as the keyword method, is increasingly likely to be used as people gain experience with it with various kinds of materials in various settings. The more successful practice people have with a strategy, the more automatic it becomes, the less affected it is by stressful conditions, and the more likely it is to transfer to new situations.

Good teaching, then, cannot stop with giving the objective and even a good strategy for reaching the objective. It must include specific knowledge and practice on the strategy, its areas of usefulness, and its range of applicability. This is another area in which faster and slower, and younger and older, learners differ from one another: in the extent to which they are aware of their own memory limitations and the efficacy of the strategies they utilize. As we have seen, however, even relatively brief instruction on mnemonic techniques and rehearsal strategies facilitates memory. Systematic and continuing classroom instruction on how and why certain memory strategies can be used should prove even more beneficial. (See anecdote 10.4 for a classroom example).

Although we cited studies in the second paragraph of this section that the memories of retarded, learning disabled, and normal individuals seem to be affected in similar ways by instruction in memory strategies, it seems worth returning to that point for a moment. Two of the foremost researchers in the field of retardation, Joseph C. Campione and Ann L. Brown (1978b, p. 410) stated the general problem as follows:

> *It has become clear that mature memorizers use an impressive array of strategic devices when faced with the problem of trying to commit material to memory, and that these strategies vary considerably with subtle changes in the task demands and requirements. It is by now also apparent that immature memorizers in general, and retarded individuals in particular, do not generate such strategies when faced with tasks in which they would be appropriate. The educational implications of this state of affairs are straightforward. Given that poor performance reflects, at least in part, a failure on the part of retarded individuals to employ task-appropriate strategies, it becomes an obvious next step to see if teaching them such strategies would result in enhanced performance. The answer to this question is a clear and emphatic "yes."*

Some of the first direct tests of this hypothesis were provided by Jensen and Rohwer (1963a and b). They found that retarded adults (IQ about 55) could significantly increase their recall of picture-pairs if sentences were provided which linked the pairs (e.g., "The HAT is on the TABLE"), rather than if subjects simply named the pairs (HAT-TABLE). These conditions provided for verbal elaboration and demonstrated that retarded, like normal individuals, could benefit from elaboration strategy training.

Turnure et al. (1976) further elaborated on elaboration training in which Belmont (1978, p. 170) called an "almost perfect demonstration of the point." Turnure and his colleagues

Anecdote 10.4

Teaching Memory Organization Skills to Eight-Year-Olds with Reading Problems

The first summer I taught summer school to elementary students with reading problems, I was shocked to find that reading was not their main problem. Rather, it seemed to be organizing their knowledge. For example, when questioned about the names of the months, one child responded, "Monday," and another said "seven." Concrete exercises on organization of knowledge to provide imagery seemed important to combine with reading.

To start, I filled an empty laundry basket with an assortment of socks, shirts, towels, shorts, and pants. In school the next morning, I gathered my class in a circle and dumped the contents in the middle, explaining that this is what some people do with information in their minds. They just throw it all in one big unorganized pile. Then I asked the children to help me sort the laundry so it could go in the right drawers, modeling first by sorting the socks. After we finished, I explained that although our minds do not have actual drawers, we have to put information that goes together in the same place in our minds. Then when we need it, we can find it quickly and easily—like our socks.

We also did an exercise sorting candy in which the children had the task of deciding the sorting categories. Another activity combined reading with organizing. Students reached into a bag and pulled out an index card on which was written a word, such as apple, horse, or July. The students, in groups of three, had to read the word and then decide into which bag (labeled months, days of the week, fruits, animals, continents and seasons) the card belonged. For some, reading the cards and the bags was the greatest hurdle: once the words were deciphered, categorization was all right. For five of the students, however, the categorization was much more difficult than the reading: apparently they had never learned strategies for organizing before.

Armed with the above diagnostic information, I now find myself constantly devising new tasks which combine reading and organizational strategy training. Grids in which reading material can be categorized and recategorized (e.g., by beginning consonant sound as well as by concept), tacked on a poster board, and then rearranged have proven interesting. Practice elaborating categories and subcategories (foods, then vegetables) in brainstorming is another activity. My plan, which is now extending into the school year, is to combine the regular reading activities with these learning-to-learn organizational activities, constantly challenging the students' comprehension and metacognitive processes.

Gretchen Gerstle
Teacher

matched retarded 7.5 year-olds (mean IQ = 67.5) in mental age with normal five-year-olds. They then exposed the two groups to the Jensen and Rohwer conditions, and added a unique condition in which the subjects were questioned in such a way as to make them further elaborate the pictures. For example, the picture-pair "soap-jacket" had the experimenter-elaboration "The soap is hiding in the jacket." Under questioning subjects were asked "What is the soap doing under the jacket?" or "Why is the soap hiding in the jacket?"

The results were extremely important. First, there were no differences between the normal and mental age-matched retarded subjects under any of the conditions. Second, of 21 test pairs of pictures, the mean number correct was 1.3 and 2.0 (for normal and retarded, respectively) under the labeling condition, 3.0 and 4.0 for self-generated elaborations, 8.3 and 8.4 for experimenter-generated elaborations, and ranged from 12.3 to 16.1 for the various question-induced elaborations. Among other things, these results provide strong evidence for the benefits of a good educational program on memory strategies for "fast" or "slow," normal or retarded individuals. They also support the contention that poor performance of immature learners is a *production deficiency* rather than a problem of capability—that is, they may not be able spontaneously to *generate* good memory strategies, but they are able to *use* them effectively if provided by a teacher.

Campione and Brown (1978b) also pointed out that the difficult part is to get immature or retarded memorizers to transfer their strategies to other appropriate tasks. Transfer problems, as we saw in the previous chapter, are not unique to retarded individuals but are endemic to learners of all species. As with transfer of operant behavior one cannot simply "train and hope" in the words of Stokes and Baer (1977). One must train for the generalization. A good start has been made in finding cognitive strategies that retarded individuals can transfer (e.g., Belmont et al., 1978; Borkowski and Büchel, 1983; Butterfield et al., 1973; Campione and Brown, 1978b). Some of them are extremely simple (e.g., "stop-check-study-recheck") which is perhaps why they can transfer to other situations.

Research in this area is just beginning, but it promises to enrich our theories of intelligence as well as our practical teaching techniques not only for retarded individuals, but for everyone.

Memories: Reproductive or Reconstructive?

Consider the following story:

At first they seemed the perfect match, but the longer one observed them, the more obvious was the mismatch. He began to attack more frequently which, in turn, seemed to elicit more defensive reactions from her. The outcome was inevitable.

Before going on, cover the above story and write out as much as you can recall of it. What *was* the inevitable outcome? Divorce? War? A six-love (i.e. six to zero) set of tennis? Ambiguous information is difficult to encode. Therefore, people tend to reduce the ambiguity by imposing meaning on the material by, for example, categorizing or labeling what the passage is about. That, in turn, affects their recall of the passage. Perhaps in recalling the above passage (shall we call it "Love Games"?) after reading it just once, it is likely that your recall of it would have included embellishments consistent with your overview of it. Thus, if you thought it was about a man-woman relationship, your reconstruction may have included words like "argument" or "accusation". If you thought it was about tennis, you may have included words like "strokes," or "rushing the net." See anecdote 10.5 for another example.

Anecdote 10.5

What is this Story About?

Read the following story (from Bransford & Johnson, 1972, p. 722); then cover it, and write a brief synopsis and give it a title:

The procedure is actually quite simple. First you arrange things into different groups depending on their makeup. Of course, one pile may be sufficient depending on how much there is to do. If you have to go somewhere else due to lack of facilities, that is the next step. Otherwise you are pretty well set. It is important not to overdo any particular endeavor. That is, it is better to do too few things at once than too many. In the short run this may not seem important, but complications from doing too many can easily arise. A mistake can be expensive as well. The manipulation of the appropriate mechanisms should be self-explanatory, and we need not dwell on it here. At first the whole procedure will seem complicated. Soon, however, it will become just another facet of life. It is difficult to foresee any end to the necessity for this task in the immediate future, but then one never can tell.

If you wish to see what it was about, see Note 15. What does such an exercise imply about what will be remembered from instruction? About advance organizers? Have you ever felt "clueless"?

The classic demonstrations of memory reconstructions of this sort were provided by Bartlett (1932), who asked people to read a story called "The War of the Ghosts" and then tested their recall at intervals ranging from 15-minutes to ten years. His major findings, which have intrigued investigators for years, were that (1) the story is likely to be considerably shortened; (2) words and style are likely to be changed to conform to the language habits of the reader (e.g., canoe might be changed to boat or seal-hunting to fishing); (3) the story is likely to be strikingly elaborated or changed according to how they interpret it or recall the main theme—what Bartlett calls "effort after meaning"; (4) the people recalling are likely to be most pleased and certain about those features of the story that were purely their own inventions; and (5) with frequent reproductions, the form and what is remembered become stereotyped and suffer little change thereafter.

While there are a number of personal idiosyncracies in Bartlett's interpretations and no objective data in his report, many of his findings—especially those regarding reconstructions—have been observed in such situations as eye-witness accounts of accidents, crimes, or what are called "flash-bulb" memories.[13] Flash-bulb memories are those that accompany a powerful (usually traumatic) event such as the assassination of Dr. Martin Luther King, Jr. The event seems to be frozen in time, like a flash picture, so that many people swear they can *reproduce* everything they were doing and wearing, whom they were with, etc. At least two problems arise with regard to the self-reports of such memories. First, they are difficult to confirm, but often when investigators do track down the persons who shared the experience, they have equally vivid, but different accounts of what they were doing, wearing, and even whether they were with the person who identified them. This is not unlike

Anecdote 10.6

Piaget's Childhood Abduction

Jean Piaget used to relay the story of a memory from his second year of life (e.g. Huyghe, 1985). He was being wheeled down a street in Paris in his baby carriage by his nurse when some would-be kidnappers attacked. Somehow she fought them off, having her face scratched in the process. This vivid memory, however, turned out to be the recollection of the story his nurse told him. When Piaget was a teenager she confessed to having fabricated the whole thing.

the problem the police or teachers have in the conflicting eyewitness accounts of an accident or crime.

Second, as time passes the actual experiences and conversations about those experiences become entwined. Subsequently, the memory of the event may be reconstructed to include those discussions, pictures, etc. For this reason people's memories for their own childhood experiences are at least as likely to be from what parents or grandparents told them than from the actual experience. See anecdote 10.6 for an example from Piaget's childhood memories.

Whether and how memories are *reconstructed* has recently become a very hot topic in the national news, particularly with regard to allegations of sexual abuse which were said to have occurred years earlier when the accuser was a child. Early childhood memories—before age three—are particularly troublesome because proof that such memories survive at all has been difficult to produce (Ceci and Hembrooke, 1993, provide an interesting history of this research). Consider the problem of verbally reporting an incident that presumably occurred before you had the linguistic capacity to talk about it and you can understand the difficulty researchers are confronting. And hypnosis is no help, first because the mechanism by which it elicits memories has not been discovered and, second, because it is based on suggestibility. Suggestibility itself is part of the problem of discovering the veracity of memories, particularly with young children (Ceci, Ross & Taglia, 1987).

As Elizabeth Loftus (1992), one of the leading researchers in this field, states the problem, when does "a lie become memory's truth?" To study this phenomenon, she and her colleagues (Loftus & Hoffman, 1989; Loftus & Ketcham, 1991), expose people to a simulated violent crime or accident. Sometime later half the witnesses receive new and subtly misleading information about the event (e.g., a stop sign is referred to as a yield sigh, an intruder is suggested to have had a mustache). Finally, when all witnesses are asked to recall the events, including the particular points about a stop vs. yield sign or mustache vs. no mustache, the group exposed to misinformation is usually 30–40% less accurate than the control group. Furthermore, they report their distorted memories as though they are true. It takes little to imagine what an experienced lawyer can do with such discrepancies: for example,

In your initial report you said you saw the accused run through a stop sign. When I asked you about it yesterday, you swore he ran through a yield sign. Just what did you see, or did you in fact witness this event at all?

Loftus suggests that the only reliable way to keep lies from becoming your own personal truth is to detect the discrepancy immediately. Otherwise, the new misinformation will be mixed in with the old episodes, reorganized and reconstructed to become our "indelible memories." Thus we see how our memory plays tricks on us: our "effort after meaning" causes us to fill in the blank spots with plausible "facts." The more plausible our invented "facts," the more sure we are that they must have been what really happened, as Bartlett's research confirms.

But memories for prose passages are not always distorted reconstructions; often they are quite accurate reproductions. One of the critical determinants seems to be the ambiguity of the passage. When the theme of the passage is known, it facilitates recall of specifics in the passage (e.g., Dooling and Lachman, 1971) and does so better if known prior to reading the passage (e.g., Bransford and Johnson's, 1972, passage in anecdote 10.5). Similarly, suppose you thought the above passage was about a lovers' quarrel while reading it, and later were told it was about tennis and asked to recall it. Both reconstructive and reproductive processes would be at work (Hasher and Griffin, 1978; Spiro, 1980); the additional cues provided by the new theme could serve to access the supposedly forgotten details.

Permastore: Very Long-Term Memory

Earlier I credited Ebbinghaus (1885) with the most ambitious studies of retention ever undertaken. Recently, however, Harry P. Bahrick and colleagues (1983; 1984a; Bahrick, Bahrick and Wittlinger, 1975) have published data which may be destined to have an impact equal to or greater than that of Ebbinghaus. Perhaps the greatest testament to the impact of his work was given by the most outspoken critic of traditional learning approaches to the study of memory—namely, Ulric Neisser (1984, p. 32), who said:

> Harry Bahrick's (1984) study of the retention of material that was originally learned in Spanish classes is a fundamental contribution to the psychology of memory. Taken together with his work on memory for places, former students, and high school classmates . . . it is surely the best corpus of data on retention in natural settings that has ever been collected.
> Not only has he invented a new methodology to study the natural course of forgetting, but in the study of recall of Spanish he has applied it to a problem significant for educators—namely, the retention of material for periods up to 50 years following school learning.

If you think about the difficulties involved in monitoring the course of forgetting over 50 years, you are likely not to pursue the project. For example, you need to know how well material was originally learned before you can describe a forgetting curve. But how do you find out how well someone learned something 50 years ago? In addition, you need some knowledge about the rehearsal of the material, if any, in the intervening years.

Bahrick solved the problem by taking a cross-sectional approach. He obtained 773 subjects for his study, 146 of whom were currently studying Spanish in high school or college. Another 587 persons were those who had taken Spanish in high school or college anywhere from one to 50 years previously. They were assigned to one of eight groups, in increasing numbers of years since completing the course. The final 40 participants had had no Spanish instruction and served to control for incidental learning of Spanish and for difficulty of the test items.

Subjects were further categorized into training levels on the basis of number of Spanish courses completed. One year of high school was equated with one semester of college

Spanish and adjustments were made to account for overlap of courses (e.g., taking one year of Spanish in high school and one semester in college: this counted as only one course). Thus, the equivalent of three college semesters was scored at training level three. The range of training levels for the entire sample was 0–10, which he combined into three levels for analysis purposes. Since memory for courses taken, grades received, and other such data are also subject to distortion over time, Bahrick did a verification check on 14% of the sample (making sure that there was proportional representation from each of the eight retention intervals). Errors occurred, of course, but their magnitude was not sufficient to distort the general shape of the retention curves to be tested. Thus he used both grades and level of training to categorize the subjects into three levels of original learning. These measures correlated highly with test performance and thus proved valid for Bahrick's purpose.

The retention measure was a non-timed test which had ten sub-tests, as follows: reading comprehension, Spanish-English vocabulary recall, Spanish-English vocabulary recognition, English-Spanish vocabulary recognition, English-Spanish vocabulary recall, grammar recall, grammar recognition, idiom recall, idiom recognition, and word order.

What were the results? By this point in this chapter you would certainly predict that the better the material was learned in school, as reflected by number of courses completed and/or grades received, the better it was remembered after a given retention interval. That, in fact, is what Bahrick found. But what was the shape of the forgetting curve from 0 to 50 years, and was it the same or different for individuals who had achieved different levels of training? Before answering, I'll throw in one additional necessary fact—namely, that Bahrick found no significant amount of rehearsal by his subjects during the intervening years between the courses and the test. Thus his results are not confounded by, say, more rehearsal by higher level students.

Although there were slight differences in the shape of the curves for each of ten subtests, Bahrick found a remarkable consistency: *the losses of material occur during the first five-year interval, with the percent retained at that time remaining constant for at least the next 25–30 years.* Around 30–35 years from the last course, when the individuals are 55 or more years old, there is an additional loss of material.

Bahrick interpreted his data as follows (1984b, p. 36):

The data demonstrate that the level of Spanish training determines not only the amount of acquired knowledge, but also the proportion of knowledge which survives for 25 years or longer. This proportion, that is, probability of survival, is close to zero for the knowledge of students whose training is terminated at level 1, but it increases steadily with training at Levels 3 and 5 to over 70%. . . . This function is independent of conditions during the retention interval, within the limits of variation encountered by 587 individuals. The probability of 25-year survival reflects simply the degree of training, that is, the state of the memory traces at the beginning of the retention interval.

Bahrick (1984a and b) goes on to discuss his retention curve as consisting of discontinuous parts. The first, from zero to five or six years, is the portion in which the material is either lost or not. Whatever remains after this period goes into the second part which he named the "permastore," since the material seems to be more-or-less permanently available for the next 25 years or longer. The third part of the curve, reflecting new downturns of the curves after 30 or more years, did not elicit extensive comments from him. It certainly deserves further study.

As one might expect, empirical results as unique as these are likely to be met by more than one interpretation. His previous words of praise notwithstanding, Neisser (1984) took issue with Bahrick's interpretation of the results (cited above). Neisser categorizes Bahrick's description of the data the "reappearance hypothesis," since Bahrick implies that retention occurs simply by reproducing material acquired at an earlier time. Neisser prefers a "reconstruction hypothesis" similar to that of Bartlett's (1932), described in the previous section. How would this work for Bahrick's data? Neisser (1984, p. 33) assumes

> ... that instead of acquiring a set of isolated responses, students of Spanish discover a structured system of relationships. Their knowledge of vocabulary, their ability to recognize idioms and to state rules of grammar, and especially their ability to understand Spanish text depend on their mastery of that system. Bartlett might have said that they acquire a schema for Spanish.

Two paragraphs later (p. 34) he concludes,

> In other words, knowledge of Spanish does not persist because previously learned responses are still in permastore but because subjects can generate the right responses from a cognitive structure that they still possess.

In reply, Bahrick (1984b) did not reject Neisser's interpretation. Rather, the fact of the discontinuity between parts of the curve suggest to him that there must be organizational restructuring of the material by the learners. He then goes on to embrace a truly eclectic view of the learning/memory process (p. 37):

> No one has demonstrated, to my knowledge, that learning does not involve the gradual strengthening of associative connections. The findings of cognitive psychologists show only that learning in many situations involves far more than this. Cognitive psychology has not wiped out the contributions of Ebbinghaus, Pavlov, Thorndike, Skinner, and other associationist psychologists. Their empirical findings regarding the strength of associative connections remain as valid as ever, and we have no reason to believe that such associative processes are irrelevant to language learning.

Since Bahrick's view is quite close to the overall them of this book—namely, the interdependence of the three levels of behavior, motivation, emotion and cognition—it is worth mentioning here. But I shall not belabor this theoretical point. No matter how these data are ultimately interpreted, Bahrick has reemphasized a point made earlier: the better material is learned, the better it is remembered. He has added to that generalization the important finding that material well learned (which implies well organized) will remain for decades.

Since Bahrick's work, there has been much interest in the topic of very long term memory, as well as memory for what is learned in school. Semb and Ellis (1994) reviewed 96 studies of classroom learning and long-term retention—defined for their purposes as at least one week. On a number of issues relevant to this chapter, they concluded the following:

- Although retention curves generally show a decline over the years, on some content, tasks and skills a substantial amount of classroom learning is retained.
- The higher the original learning scores, the greater the retention.
- Recognition memory is generally higher than recall.
- Instructional strategies that promote (1) more active involvement by students and (2) higher levels of original learning produce greater retention.
- While high ability students learn more than low ability students, there is no evidence for differential forgetting (when their original level of learning is controlled).

Finally, Winograd (1993) reviewed some additional evidence on very long term retention which suggests, not surprisingly, that

Photo 10.4 What will they remember from school?

there is still much to be learned about memory over decades and in natural settings. The most amazing cases are those with a pathology (e.g., Korsakoff's syndrome) who show a retrograde amnesia. In one well-documented case, where facts of the patient's life were recorded in an autobiography, the forgetting curve was reversed:

He seems to remember nothing about events of the past 20 years but shows increasing access to memories the older they are. (Winograd, 1993, p. 60)

Memory for This Chapter

In this chapter we have encountered a wide range of approaches to the study of memory, along with many time-honored, as well as some quite recent, facts about memory processes. Because of its central role in all levels of human behavior, memory will continue to occupy the attention of both biological and psychological scientists, not to mention practitioners like physicians and educators.

Because the goal of this book is application, the topics covered have been those which appear to have the most direct relevance for teaching-learning interactions. In chapter 11 we shall see other aspects of some of these topics—particularly, encoding and organization of memory—when we consider how a person progresses from novice to relative expert in any given field or whether and how it is possible to increase a person's intellectual skills. Meanwhile, what might we remember from this chapter that will be useful in teaching?

1. Cognitive processes in general, and memories in particular, are the active, constructive efforts of individuals attempting to make sense of, and have an impact on, the world with which they are interacting. Our strategies, mental structures which arise from our past experiences, and the present context, assure that our attention will be selective and that we will perceive some kind of meaning from almost all stimulation.
2. Much of learning consists of becoming sufficiently skilled so that performing or processing of information becomes automatic. This reduces the level of attention required and makes the performance less subject to stressful events.
3. It is useful to define three overlapping, but relatively distinct memory systems:
   (a) sensory memory—a visual or auditory register holding information for rehearsal for up to a second (or a few seconds under proper conditions);
   (b) short-term memory—an active, but transient store which holds information while it is being worked on; and
   (c) long-term memory—a relatively permanently stored body of information.

   Information that (a) is perceived by the senses can be (b) rehearsed in some way while it is categorized for (c) storage and later access.
4. In order for learned information to be accessible at a later date it must have been encoded in a meaningful way, which implies that there must be some cues available that can help retrieve the material. A filing system metaphor is didactically useful for this because it emphasizes the processing, categorizing and labeling that must go on when information is coming in. Teachers have a major role to play in helping students organize and label what they are learning.
5. Encoding of material for subsequent recall can be markedly facilitated by verbal elaboration, visual imagery, mnemonic techniques, and categorization of the material.
6. Probably the single most important variable for maintaining high retention is overlearning—learning that occurs beyond first mastery. But optimal additional practice should be distributed instead of massed because, among other things, that provides practice retrieving items from long-term memory, allows reorganization of the material, reduces the effects of interfering factors, and increases opportunities for positive transfer.
7. Despite the tremendous individual differences in learning rate, once material is mastered to the same standard, forgetting rates are about the same. Furthermore, research is now confirming that the major differences between younger and older, retarded and normal, learning disabled and nondisabled learners are in their encoding strategies. Educators will never be able to eliminate such individual differences, but all can be improved tremendously by instruction in effective categorization and mnemonic techniques, as well as in monitoring their own knowledge and strategies (metacognition).
8. Memory for the gist of a story or for some personal experience is somewhat different from memory for specific details. It is especially susceptible to reconstructive inventions on the basis of a perceived theme when content is ambiguous, or when too many facts have been forgotten to reproduce the episode exactly. In the latter case, reconstructions are likely to occur, with

people being perhaps more sure of their inventions (because they seem so plausible) than of the original events.

9. Evidence now available on very long term memory of classroom material suggests that the losses occur during the five years immediately following the last class. Material remaining after that period has probably been sufficiently rehearsed and organized to be accessible (in a "permastore") for up to 25 years, before further forgetting may occur. This argues strongly for learning to a high standard while in class.

10. It seems there was another point to be made here, and it's on the tip of my tongue. . . . Well, maybe I'll think of it later. ❧

Practice Exercises

A. Practice Items

INSTRUCTIONS FOR ITEMS 1–5: Match the following terms with their appropriate definitions by placing the letter of the term in the space provided. (Answers are in Note 14.)

   a. retention
   b. cognition
   c. learning
   d. transfer
   e. attention
   f. perception
   g. sensation
   h. metacognition

____ 1. The process of actively seeking or ignoring stimulation.
____ 2. A relatively permanent change in behavior as a result of experience.
____ 3. The process of making sense of stimulation.
____ 4. Material that is remaining after some period of time.
____ 5. Knowing what it is that you know.

For items 6–12 select the alternative choice which *best* answers the question. (Answers are in Note 14.)

6. The best way to avoid forgetting is by
   a. massed, intensive practice to a high standard of mastery.
   b. being reinforced for work correctly done.
   c. being reinforced for work correctly done and punished for errors.
   d. overlearning the material under a variety of conditions.

7. Why should material be *originally learned* to a high standard?
   a. because you will not forget the material if you learn it well the first time.
   b. because you can relearn quickly.
   c. because this removes the effects of proactive interference.
   d. because that guarantees transfer.

8. If cues that were associated with the material when it was being learned are also present when the material is to be remembered, which of the following is most likely to occur?
   a. Recall will be facilitated.
   b. Recall will be adversely affected.
   c. Transfer will be facilitated.
   d. Transfer will be adversely affected.

9. When memory for auditory or visual information lasts for 20 or more seconds it is probably because
   a. the information has been encoded in some way.
   b. it did not exceed the limits of sensory memory.
   c. the intelligence of the subject was high.
   d. the student was paying close attention.

10. Assuming fast and slow learners attain the same degree of learning of some particular material, then
    a. they will forget at about the same rate.
    b. they will forget in the same ratio that they learned (e.g., if fast learners were twice as fast in learning, they will forget twice as much in a given period).
    c. they will forget in the inverse ratio that they learned (e.g., if fast learners were twice as fast in learning, they will forget half as much in a given period).
    d. there will be no forgetting.
11. S.F. was a college student whose memory for digits was shown to be about 79. Which of the following statements is true about this memory?
    a. He was born with a photographic memory.
    b. He was able to accomplish this feat by inventing an idiosyncratic strategy for encoding the digits.
    c. He was also able to recall close to 70 unrelated words and pictures when presented at the same rate as the digits.
    d. All of the above are true.
12. According to dual coding theory which of the following is true for memory, where I = Image coding, V = Verbal coding, and B = Both image and verbal Coding?
    a. B > I = V
    b. I > V > B
    c. B > I > V
    d. B > V > I

For items 13–15, fill in the blank with the word or words which *best* complete(s) the statement. (Answers are in Note 14.)

13. The first time Betty memorized her part in the play, it took her four hours. Some years later she memorized the part again in only two hours. this 2-hr. difference demonstrates _____.
14. Fred is told to memorize the following words: apple, six, nine, house, orange, hotel. . . . As the words are presented, he classifies them as fruits, buildings, or numbers. His behavior is best classified as _____.
15. Despite performing his piano piece correctly, Peter continues to practice the piece. This additional practice is known as _____.

B. For Cooperative Study (in or out of class):

1. Obtain two volunteers: one who has tied a tie for many years and one who never tied a tie. Have the former instruct the latter, using only *verbal* instructions, in front of the class. Discuss the results in terms of the automatic vs. controlled attention distinction.
2. Have someone read a list of 12–15 unrelated words out loud at a rate of one every five seconds. Then have the students write down as many as they can remember. Discuss the various techniques students use to memorize lists in light of the suggestions in the chapter.

3. In small groups discuss the learning and instructional issues raised in study questions 13, 14 and 15 for
   a. "fast" vs. "slow" learners,
   b. older vs. younger learners, and
   c. normal vs. retarded or disabled learners.
4. Discuss study question 16. What does this imply about (a) the affects of previous misinformation on what students get out of instruction and (b) what they remember from a course years later? Give examples from, say, science courses you took or courses you teach.
5. Discuss study question 10. What are the curricular implications of dual coding theory for
   a. children in Piaget's concrete operations stage?
   b. adolescents or adults in Piaget's formal operations stage?

C. **For More Information:**

1. Learn one of the mnemonic strategies mentioned in the text (consult the references) and practice it for several weeks in the semester. Keep records on your relative ability to memorize as you progress from novice to relative expert. Make a written or oral report on this personal experiment.
2. Explore some of the interesting case studies of remarkable and everyday memories by consulting, for example, Neisser (1982), Gruneberg et al. (1978), Ericsson et al. (1980). Make an oral or written report on your findings.
3. Read one or more of Bahrick's studies and make a report, orally or in writing.
4. Read some news reports on childhood memories, including memories of abuse, and compare to research evidence (e.g., studies by Loftus or Ceci).

CHAPTER

Study Questions

1. What is the difference between experts and novices in
   a. memory for chess positions?
   b. memory for written music?
   c. declarative knowledge (factual knowledge, knowledge that)?
   d. procedural knowledge (performance, heuristic knowledge, knowledge how)?

2. What is meant by each of the following terms?
   a. heuristic
   b. algorithm

3. Describe how integrated knowledge is likely to be structured in a hierarchical manner. How can learning be viewed as "remodeling a knowledge structure"?

4. What is a schema? What is meant by each of the following assumptions of schema theory? A schema assumes
   a. prior knowledge
   b. important ideas as large units
   c. reconstructive memory (but what about reproductive memory?)
   d. active, developmental processes
   e. cultural specificity

5. What is meant by each of the following parts of the IDEAL Problem Solver? Give examples.
   I =
   D =
   E =
   A =
   L =

6. What is meant by lateral thinking? How can the following techniques facilitate lateral thinking?
   a. the "why" technique
   b. the "fractionation" method
   c. the reversal method

7. What is meant by the following?
   a. brainstorming
   b. unusual uses or uncommon associates

ELEVEN

8. Describe each of the following intellectual development activities and give examples:
   a. dialogical thinking
   b. thinking aloud
   c. using novels to stimulate inquiry
9. What is meant by each of the following?
   a. domain-specific or embedded teaching strategies
   b. domain-general or detached teaching strategies

   How can a program use both strategies to teach thinking?
10. What does the author mean when he says (p. 382) that "expertise is subject-matter related"? What does this imply about expertise in teaching (see also Anecdote 11.2)?

Nurturing Knowledge and Intellect

Introduction

1. [Our kindergarten teacher] placed before each of us a board with various shaped holes and a packet of pegs. She told us to place the pegs in the correct holes. "And remember," she said staunchly, "it is impossible to put the wrong peg in the wrong hole." There was something about the way she said "impossible" that convinced me to prove her wrong. With dogged determination, I began to pound the round pegs into rectangular holes. When the time was up, the teacher collected each board, and, as mine was carried away, one round peg could be seen standing proudly from a partially accepting square hole.

2. The subject sat in front of a TV screen and was shown a short videotape of a person trying to play a phonograph record, without success. Unseen by the actor, but visible on the videotape, was that the stereo was not plugged into the wall socket. The last scene was frozen on the screen and the observer had to select one of two pictures from a box—for example, a picture showing just a plug in a socket vs. a picture of a hose on a faucet. The subject's task was to select the correct picture, place it at a specific location, and call the teacher by ringing a bell (the teacher was not in the room during the test).

3. For one class of problems the teacher placed a yellow card, say, on a green one and queried, "Is yellow on blue?" The task of the student was to examine the

cards, compare them with the version related by the sentence, and answer "Yes" or "No" in appropriate fashion.

One student, Sarah, did this very well, also introducing a striking innovation on some of the occasions on which the cards and sentences did not agree. In these cases the appropriate answer was, therefore, "No." Other times, however, she changed the cards in such a way as to make a "Yes" answer appropriate. For example, if the question were "Is yellow on blue?" when the yellow card was actually on a green one, she would remove the green one, replace it by a blue one, and answer, "Yes."

4. The mathematician A. C. Aitken was given a number of mental calculations to report while being tape-recorded. For example, multiplying 123 × 456 took him two seconds until he gave the answer, from left to right, 56088. His explanation: "I do this in two moves: I see at once that 123 times 45 is 5535 and that 123 times 6 is 738; I hardly have to think. Then 55350 plus 738 gives 56088." When asked to calculate the decimal equivalent of 1/851, Aitken commented, "The instant observation was that 851 is 23 times 37. I use this fact as follows. 1/37 is 0.027027027 and so on repeated. This I divide mentally by 23. 23 into 0.027 is 0.001 with remainder 4. In a flash I can get that 23 into 4027 is 175 with remainder 2. And 2027 is 88 with remainder 3. . . . And so on like that. Also, before I even start this, I know that there is a recurring period of sixty-six places."

Do these situations give evidence of intelligent behavior? Are there any of them so elementary as to not deserve the label "intelligent"? Are any so advanced as to be obviously intelligent—no further discussion necessary?

Most cognitive scientists, for example, would consider mental flexibility to be a component of intelligence. In that case, the child in #1 (Dowling, 1985, p. 72) may be a budding Thomas Edison, refusing to believe that anything is impossible and, moreover, being ready to challenge dogmatic assertions about what is true. One can only wonder whether her teacher could take such a generous view of her unorthodox behavior.

What shall we make of the other stories? The second seems not unlike a scene that might occur on a children's television show such as Sesame Street, designed to teach young children about cause-effect relations. If fourteen-year-olds were not able to reliably select the picture which is most closely related to solving the actor's dilemma, we might conclude that they were retarded. Would we draw the same conclusion if we know the fourteen-year-olds were from a recently discovered tribe of people who had never seen either phonographs, records or electricity? What would we say about the intelligence of the fourteen-year-old who could solve the problem, but was a chimpanzee? The second problem was indeed solved by a now-famous chimpanzee named Sarah (Premack and Woodruff, 1978), who could also see the cause-effect relation involved in the need for a key to help a cage-rattling actor escape captivity and a need for a flaming torch to warm a shivering man. This is the same Sarah, who seven or eight years previously, learned to communicate by reading and composing sentences of the form described in example 3.

Chimpanzees cannot learn vocal language, but they (and other species of apes) have learned sign language (e.g., Gardner and Gardner, 1969) and learned to communicate via symbolic plastic words (e.g., Premack, 1971; 1976a; 1976b). The plastic symbols themselves were invented to stand for words or concepts, such as the name of a person, but were made not to be iconic replicas of the objects for which they stand. For instance, the symbols for colors were all an achromatic grey with only the shapes of the plastic discs to discriminate them, just as the shape of the letters r-e-d and b-l-u-e are what distinguish colors for readers of English. Similarly the symbols for shapes—square, circle, etc.—were deliberately not shaped like the concepts they were to represent. Thus when Sarah read the sentence "Is yellow on blue?" (Premack, 1976b, p. 30) she was actually reading four plastic discs from top to bottom and then responding "Yes" or "No" or, as we have seen, sometimes first rearranging the test items so that she could answer "Yes." Most of us would consider this evidence of intelligent behavior in children aged six or seven, and it was performed by Sarah at around that same age.[1]

Perhaps #4 was the clearest example of intelligent behavior, at least, in the western academic context. Here we see a recognized mathematical expert showing the extent of his well-organized knowledge and the variety of ways he has of accessing that knowledge. The report, from I. M. L. Hunter (1978, p. 341), is not just a glimpse of a prodigious mathematical memory, although Aitken had clearly developed that. It is mostly about an insatiable curiosity for numbers and the manner in which an expert goes about encoding and processing problems and information. For example, Aitken commented as follows (Hunter, 1978, pp. 343–344):

> *It is a good exercise to ask oneself the question: what can be said about this number? Where does it occur in mathematics, and in what context? What properties has it? For instance, is it a prime of the form 4n+1, and so expressible as the sum of two squares in one way only? . . . And so on. Sometimes a number has almost no properties at all, like 811, and sometimes a number, like 41, is deeply involved in many theorems that you know.*

Hunter goes on to point out that this comment could only be made by people who already know much about mathematics and use their knowledge to acquire more. I would extend that to say that the organization of knowledge allows new information, examined in such ways, to be encoded for ready retrieval at a later date. Clearly the expert is attending to incoming information in a way that is different from the novice. But novices do become experts, so much educating does occur and it behooves us to ask how.

This chapter, then, is about intellectual processes, from the mundane to the extraordinary, from the beginner to the expert. If one goal of education is to make us better thinkers—more critical, more creative, more systematic—then educators need to understand (1) the different capabilities of people at different stages of expertise; (2) the different structures of knowledge at each of these stages, which presumably account for these different capabilities; and (3) the variety of educational programs that are available for nurturing these cognitive processes. We begin with some relevant studies of experts and novices in several fields.

Experts and Novices

As mentioned above, one way cognitive scientists have been studying the growth of knowledge and skill is by comparing the thinking and performance of experts and novices. The purpose is not just to show that experts are quantitatively faster or more accurate than beginners (which, after all, is tautological); rather, the quest is for the qualitative differences—their memory structures, strategies, and the like. Experts were once novices, too. If we can understand what they had to learn to be transformed from frog to prince, then we can develop teaching strategies that more efficiently help others achieve the princely status of expert.

Chess Masters' Memories

Assume that you are a beginner in chess: you know the names, placement, and moves of the pieces on the chess board; you have played a few games; and you are interested in playing it more. Thus you are intrigued by an advertisement requesting a beginner for an experiment in memory for chess. When you arrive, the experimenter seats you at a table with an empty chessboard in front of you, with all the black and white pieces beside the board. Just to your left is another chessboard with some pieces on it, but it is hidden behind a screen. On cue, the experimenter lifts the screen to allow you to see the placement of the pieces on that board, but only gives you five-seconds before replacing the screen. You are asked to reproduce what you have just seen on the empty board in front of you, taking as long as you want.

Since you can reproduce only a few of the pieces, you are given additional trials conducted as before—five-second peeks at the model and as long as you wish to reproduce the placement of the pieces. As expected, you improve considerably over the first five or six trials, showing evidence of learning how many pieces there were and where they all go. Later you are shown additional problems like this, with additional learning trials. Some of the problems have 24–26 pieces on the board, such as might be found at the middle of a typical chess game, while some have 12–15 pieces on the board, as might occur near the end of a game.

After you finish all the problems, you find that your performance in recalling pieces is being compared to two other persons. One is a very experienced player on the Class A level in competition. The other is a world class chess master. The research question, it turns out, is whether memory for chess positions is related to skill in chess. How do you, as a beginner, expect to do compared to these more experienced players? How will the master compare to the experienced Class A player?

As you think about those questions, we'll add another complication in the study—namely, that some of the board positions came from actual games between advanced players. Others were random arrangements of the pieces on the board. Should memory for real game positions be different from memory for random positions? Which should be better? Should the different skill levels of the memorizers be affected by the real vs. random distinction? How?

I've asked a lot of questions in the last two paragraphs. To simplify and summarize the problem, which of the following do you think is correct?

Problem 11.1

a. Masters' recall will be more accurate than Beginners' for both real and random positions.
b. Masters' recall will be more accurate than Beginners' for random positions, but there will be no difference between them for real positions.
c. Masters' recall will be more accurate than Beginners' for real positions, but there will be no difference between them for random positions.
d. Masters' recall will be no different than Beginners' for either real or random positions.
e. Beginners' recall will be more accurate than Masters' for both real and random positions.

Chase and Simon (1973) conducted such an experiment, replicating and extending earlier research by de Groot (1965, 1966). Their findings were that when the pieces were positioned from real games, there was a positive relationship between memory and skill level: the Master was more accurate than the A player who was more accurate than the Beginner. The difference in recall was evident on the first trial, as well as on each subsequent trial until perfect scores were obtained, first by the Master, then by the A player, and last by the Beginner.

Different results occurred, however, for the randomly placed pieces: Chase and Simon (1973) found no relation between accuracy of recall and playing skill. Furthermore, the performance of all (the Master, A Player and Beginner) on the first five-second exposure to the randomly placed pieces was worse than the Beginner's performance on the first trial of actual game positions.

The correct answer to problem 11.1 is therefore c: *the memories of experts are better than those of novices, but only on tasks that are directly related to their expertise.* Perhaps you anticipated the results. Memory of positions, especially to an expert, depends on the recognition of familiar clusters or configurations of pieces. Certain pieces characteristically belong together by virtue of some offensive or defensive purpose. Often these configurations have a name; e.g., castling, in which the king is protected by a rook and usually three pawns. The advanced player can recognize such a configuration and recall the placement of all of the appropriate pieces as one memory chunk—in the case of castling, at least 5 pieces could be remembered as one memory item. Randomly placed pieces, in contrast, look "unreasonable," especially to an expert, and therefore each piece must be remembered as a separate item.

What distinguishes experts from novices, then, is not better memory spans in general; rather, experts have many well-practiced configurations that can be recognized at once and chunked together. Chase and Simon (1973, p. 80) summarized this point as follows:

> *The data suggest that the superior performance of stronger players (which does not appear in random positions) derives from the ability of those players to encode the position into larger perceptual chunks, each consisting of a familiar subconfiguration of pieces. Pieces within a chunk are bound by relations of mutual defense, proximity, attack over small distances, and common color and type.*

If experts immediately encode positions by chunking them into recognizable configurations, then they are also immediately engaging their long-term store and freeing their short-term memory to scan the board for other pieces. This implies that their memory for actual positions should be less susceptible to retroactive interference than, say, their memory for random positions or a novice's memory for actual positions. Charness (1976) tested that assertion in an ingenious procedure which showed the chess positions for five-seconds followed in some conditions by 30-seconds of various intervening activities such as summing random digits. Chess experts' memories were relatively impervious to such interference effects, which argues that within five seconds they had already stored the information into long-term memory.

In sum, the more expert a chess player, the more easily he or she can scan a board to extract meaningful chunks of information from it. These chunks are meaningful in the sense that they are already in long-term memory because they have been seen before and are well-practiced under many varied conditions. The memories of novices are still relatively unstructured in those ways. Practice in recognizing common configurations should, therefore, be a helpful instructional device.

Other Expert-Novice Differences

When one chess master was asked how many alternative moves he considers before making his choice, he allegedly replied, "Only one, the right one." Although this expert's reply is not very instructive to non-experts, it shows another way in which experts and novices differ—namely, they are likely attending to different aspects of a problem. But let's explore how in the domain of music.

Consider the following partial melodies:

Musicians and nonmusicians were exposed to melodies like them for 5-seconds; then, after a 15-second wait, they had to recall the melody in written form. As might be expected, musicians recall both types of melodies better than nonmusicians. Nonmusicians, moreover, recalled both the A and B melodies equally well. Musicians, on the other hand, recalled the A melodies much better than the B melodies. Is the reason obvious?

Musicians, in contrast to nonmusicians, are more literate in musical notation. Part of that literacy may include the ability to sing or hear the melody (in the "mind's ear"?) and perhaps analyze the chord pattern underlying the melody. Thus musicians are more likely to recognize a melody such as that in A as a typical or "good" melody for western culture. The B melody is more discordant or "bad" to those reared in western culture.

The subjects who participated in the study, being westerners, did indeed show those results. Halpern and Bower (1982) conducted the study to see whether some of the same differences between chess experts and novices could be found among musicians and nonmusicians.[2] Nonmusicians, apparently, could not distinguish between "good" and "bad" melodies in their written form, though they agreed with musicians' judgments about the melodies when they could hear them played.

Photo 11.1. Toward becoming expert musicians in Japan.

Musicians can remember more notes than nonmusicians because they are processing the information at different levels of abstractness. For example, the first three notes of melody A would be recognized immediately by most musicians as comprising a C-major chord. Thus not only are the specific notes being processed (at a concrete or surface level), but the musicians are processing information at a deeper, more abstract, level as well. This is analogous to the chess expert's recognition of "good" moves.

As we first saw in Hunter's (1978) description of the mathematician Aitken, experts have many more ways of approaching a problem than novices. They not only have access to information (i.e., *declarative knowledge* or *what* they know), but they have strategic knowledge (i.e., *procedural knowledge, how to* apply what they know). In mathematics, for example, it is always correct to add any quantity to both sides of an equation, but it is only in a few problems that it is useful to do so. As Lewis (1981) showed, experts distinguish themselves from novices in their strategic knowledge much more than in their perfection. They still make calculation errors, although perhaps not as many as novices. In some extremely complex tasks, they may even show worse recall than novices for specific concrete facts (e.g., Adelson, 1984), especially if they were expecting to be tested on more abstract or general material.[3] In certain cases, therefore, experts' strategies can be counterproductive, but these cases are rare.

Through practice, experts develop large amounts of specific knowledge and the cases to which the information applies. This information, when reorganized with pre-existing information, becomes better and better practiced until it emerges as an automatic sequence, requiring little attention or thought—that is, a schema.

Experts, with little effort, recognize a problem (or some part of it) that is familiar to them, which automatically engages one or more schemata for solving the problem. Experts do little searching and less "trial-and-error" behavior, unless of course, they are working outside of their area of expertise.

It cannot be overstressed that such automatic processing and problem-solving comes about through practice. As Larkin (1981, p. 311) pointed out in regard to solving physics problems,

Individuals who have become skillful in such tasks usually report a relatively small amount of

Cartoon 11.1

time spent studying textual materials or listening to lectures, but a much larger amount of time spent practicing solving problems.

We have seen the importance of practice in the last chapter. We recognize its importance for musicians and sports figures. It is equally important in intellectual endeavors and probably necessary for advancing from controlled to automatic processing.

Heuristics v. Algorithms

Another way in which experts and novices differ is their use of educated guesses and approximations vs. the more rigid or unquestioned following of formulas. The former, called *heuristics* (heuristic methods, heuristic rules), are general strategies, rules of thumb, or ways of estimating or checking whether answers or approaches to a problem are sensible (e.g., estimating that 8243 divided by 205 will be about 40, since 8000 divided by 200 is the same as 80 divided by 2). The latter, called *algorithms*, are rules or formulas which when applied correctly are guaranteed to solve the problem, given enough time (e.g., using the long division formula for dividing 8243 by 205).

Anecdote 11.1

Automaticity in Reading

Benjamin Bloom (1986, pp. 72–73) provides the following account of the importance of automaticity, and the differences between experts and novices, in the act of reading.

Suppose . . . you were to spend a few minutes timing how long it takes to read the first letter on each line of several pages. You would find that you can read about 80 letters a minute. Similarly, if you were to read only the last word of each line of several pages, you would find that you also read about 80 words a minute. But if you were to read two or three entire pages of this article, you would discover that you read about 300 words per minute. How does one go from reading 80 letters a minute to 80 words (400 letters) per minute to 300 words (1,500 letters) per minute?

The great speed of word reading, versus letter reading, is possible because most of the words read are now sight words for the adult who can process them without paying attention to the individual letters. The even greater speed of reading connected discourse is because the adult is now reading phrases, sentences, and ideas rather than letters or individual words. While we are in the process of reading connected discourses, we may also be making judgments about the ideas, enjoying the story, getting new ideas and insights, or being involved in other conscious processes. The point is that the reading process has become automatic for capable adult readers, and much of our conscious attention is now on the ideas, insights, plot, and characters rather than on the mechanics of the reading process. Again, as adults we may contrast our reading with that of a child in the 1st or 2nd grade of school to see how reading has changed from a slow and difficult process to a rapid and highly automatic one. Or, we may contrast our reading in the mother tongue with reading in a foreign language studied for less than a year.

To imply that experts use heuristics to advantage while novices use algorithms does not warrant the conclusion, however, that algorithms are bad or are less useful than heuristics. There are times when this may be so, but it is also true that algorithms, when appropriately used, are efficient means for solving problems and carrying out many daily duties. Consider the following examples:

1. When writing a declarative sentence, capitalize the first letter of the first word and place a period after the last word.
2. When pluralizing a common noun that ends in "y", change the "y" to "i" and add "es." (e.g. story → stories).

3. When dividing fractions, find the reciprocal of the divisor and multiply the fractions (e.g., 3/4 ÷ 1/5 = 3/4 × 5 = 3 3/4).

Applying algorithms like these provides correct answers in an efficient manner and experts, as well as novices, use them.

There are, however, many problems for which algorithms do not exist. Translation from one language to another is an excellent example, since individual words usually have more than one meaning and the meaning depends in large measure upon the context. Humorous examples of word-by-word translations abound, as in the (probably apocryphal) translation of "the spirit is willing, but the flesh is weak" into Russian. When translated back to English from the Russian, it came out as "The vodka is plentiful, but the meat is spoiled" (R. L. Thorndike, 1984, p. 30). Translation does not lend itself to algorithmic formulas, requiring instead a strategy of decoding the context as well as various word definitions to find a suitable match.

Heuristics also allow people to check on whether the results they obtained in applying an algorithm make sense. While most of us can apply the division of fractions algorithm in #3 above, we feel like Peppermint Patty in the Peanuts cartoon: after stating the "find the reciprocal" rule, she said "Why?". Her friend Marcie asked "Why find the reciprocal?" Peppermint Patty said, "No, why was I born?" If we have forgotten, or never learned, the reason for finding the reciprocal, we are simply blindly applying the algorithm and we have no way of using a strategy to check our results. Recall that the reciprocal rule is a short hand for the following sequence:

$$\frac{\frac{3}{4}}{\frac{1}{5}} = \frac{\frac{3}{4} \times \frac{5}{1}}{\frac{1}{5} \times \frac{5}{1}} = \frac{\frac{3}{4} \times \frac{5}{1}}{1} = \frac{3}{4} \times \frac{5}{1} = 3\frac{3}{4}$$

Photo 11.2. Teaching a long division algorithm in China. (Photo courtesy of Dr. Thomas J. Shuell)

For many people the question still remains, "Why does division of fractions result in a number that is larger than either of the fractions?" The answer is more intuitively obvious if you begin with whole numbers. For example, 6 ÷ 2 can be restated as how many 2's are there in 6? Then 3/4 ÷ 1/5 can be restated as how many fifths are there in 3/4? A useful heuristic for understanding the problem and estimating the answer then emerges by making the rough kind of drawing described in chapter 9 (figure 9.2).

We similarly use heuristics to estimate the square root of, say, 47. Since 7×7=49 and 6×6=36, the answer is between 6 and 7 and closer to 7. Even if you know how to apply the square root algorithm, it is a good idea to use the above heuristic strategy to check whether your calculated answer makes sense.

Experts therefore do indeed use algorithms, but they are more likely to apply them after heuristic searches have shown the algorithm will provide a sensible answer. Novices, on the other hand, may have memorized a number of algorithms, but they lack the integrated knowledge necessary for deciding (1) when to use them and (2) whether the results obtained make sense.

Toward Becoming Experts

Before drawing some pedagogical lessons from this foray into experts and novices, let's do another problem. You are shown four cards, as follows:

1 [T]   2 [6]   3 [5]   4 [E]

Problem 11.2

Your instruction as a quality control worker at a label factory is to check labels, each of which has a number on one side and a letter on the other. Your specific duty is *to ensure that every label with a vowel printed on one side has an odd number printed on the other side*. Which of the labels, 1, 2, 3, or 4, must you turn over to be certain that the label was correct?

As you are thinking about the problem, and perhaps perusing further down the page looking for a cue, consider that only 13% of the subjects of Andrade's study (reported in Rumelhart and Norman, 1981) obtained the correct answer. Try to find the correct answer by circling Yes or No.

Problem 11.2

If vowel, then odd number on the back. I must turn:

Card 1.	Yes	No
Card 2.	Yes	No
Card 3.	Yes	No
Card 4.	Yes	No

Problem 11.3

As part of your job at Sears, you must *check all sales receipts to make sure that any sale over $30 has been approved and signed on the back of the receipt by the manager*. The amount of the sale is written on the front. Which of the following receipts must you turn over to be sure that the rule has been followed?

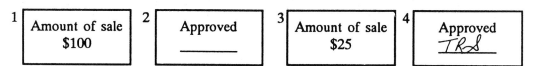

Problem 11.3

If total is greater than $30, then signed on the back. I must turn

Card 1.	Yes	No
Card 2.	Yes	No
Card 3.	Yes	No
Card 4.	Yes	No

Again, as you consider this problem, about 70% of the subjects obtained the correct answer. What are the correct answers? In problem 11.3 both 1 and 2 must be turned over: card 1 because it is over $30 so we must be sure it is signed; and card 2 because it is not signed, so we must ensure it is not over $30. The other cards do not matter.

In problem 11.2, which is the logical equivalent of problem 11.3, the answers are cards 2 and 4: card 4 because it is a vowel and, therefore, must have an odd number on the other side; card 2 because it has an even number and thus must be checked to make sure there is not a vowel on the other side. Since the rule says nothing about consonants, card 1 can have any number on the other side; likewise, a card with an odd number can have either a vowel or a consonant on the other side. Thus neither cards 1 nor 3 need be checked.

The question is, why is this basic problem so much more difficult for most people when stated as problem 11.2 than as problem 11.3? Rumelhart and Norman (1981, p. 340) analyze it this way:

> *The first case of the label factory represents a relatively unfamiliar case in which we cannot rely on specific knowledge and must, therefore, rely on general reasoning processes. The second case more nearly approximates our "real-life" problem-solving situations. Once we can "understand" the situation . . . our specific knowledge can be brought into play, and the problem readily solved. It is as if our knowledge representation already contains all the reasoning mechanisms ordinarily required.*

In the previous section it was pointed out that experts have both *factual or declarative knowledge (knowledge that)* and *procedural knowledge (knowledge how)*. I believe that is Rumelhart and Norman's position in the last sentence cited. In other words, in the situations or tasks on which we are relatively expert, we have strategies for thinking about the problem, as well as available relevant facts. In the situations or tasks on which we are relative beginners, however, we may have neither facts nor heuristic strategies, or some of one or the other, but likely not enough of either to solve our problem. Chi, Glaser, and Rees (1982) put it another way: novices, they said, are "data driven," responding to the problems by immediately trying this fact or unknown in that equation, etc. Experts, in contrast, are "schemata driven," in that a problem for them evokes a search through their knowledge repertoire for a number of possible solution methods before plugging in the data.

What will help us on the road to thinking as experts? Let us count the ways:

1. A thorough knowledge about the subject matter must be obtained, with many facts at the fingertips, so to speak. Recall the incredible array of number facts, multiplication tables and roots of numbers that Aitken could call upon at any time.
2. The knowledge must be organized so as to be accessible via many cues. This implies how information is chunked together with its purposes, uses and effectiveness.
3. In addition to the above, which might be considered *declarative knowledge,* is knowledge of procedures. That is, the information must be practiced in many, many varied situations for its transfer and heuristic value. Only by practicing these many ways can multiple, abstract strategies begin to emerge and then they will probably emerge only slowly.
4. Practice must continue until it becomes automatic and whole chunks of knowledge, procedures, and images arise where

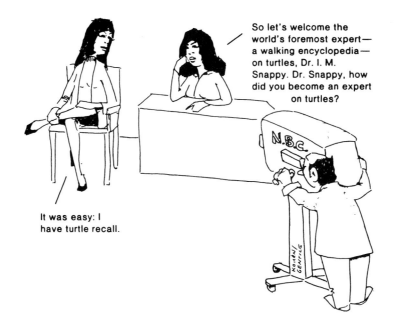

Cartoon 11.2

a problem is presented. In this sense the old adage "practice makes perfect" does not mean 100% correct; rather, it means developing schemata—organized, automatic past experiences—to fit many situations or occasions.

Structures for Knowledge

The preceding sections of this book have suggested two conflicting trends: (1) as more knowledge is acquired, each fact will be harder to retrieve (by interference effects), and (2) experts have acquired many facts and nevertheless have less trouble than novices in accessing these facts. These conflicting trends have become known as the "paradox of the expert." Preceding results have also strongly implied a resolution of this paradox—namely, that experts integrate new material into the old by reorganizing and finding larger superordinate themes (or chunks) under which all relevant facts can logically fit, and therefore from which retrieval should be faster and more accurate.

Consider the following pairs of sentences from Smith, Adams and Schorr (1978, p. 444):

(1) Marty broke the bottle.
    Marty did not delay the trip.
(2) Herb played a damaged bag pipe.
    Herb realized the seam was split.

With each additional fact that you must learn about Marty, for example, there should be an increase in the amount of time to recognize that it is indeed something you know about him (in contrast to a false sentence about him). Thus adding a third fact, "Marty was asked to address the crowd," increases the amount of time to recognize any of the three facts over the time required when only two facts were known. However, suppose the third fact were, "Marty was asked to christen the ship," which supplies a theme for the other two sentences. Now the third fact is integrated with the other two, forming a kind of hierarchical network concerned with christening a ship by breaking a bottle on the bow and then going on a voyage.

A similar finding was obtained when the third sentence was an additional fact that

Anecdote 11.2

Expert vs. Novice Teachers

Taking their cue from studies of expert-novice differences in other fields, a number of educational researchers have been studying relatively expert and beginning teachers (Berliner, 1986, provides a good review). One of the not unexpected findings is that expert teachers have two well-formed domains of knowledge: in their subject matter field and in pedagogical principles (which includes how to teach content and how to organize and manage classes).

To examine further how the experts and novices differ in their knowledge and its application to a real problem, teachers were asked to plan the first two lessons of a class that they had been asked to take over from another teacher. Berliner (1986, p. 12) describes some of the differences as follows:

> *Most of the experts saw the problem as consisting of two integral parts: finding out what students already knew and starting the classroom over from scratch. The experts also had established routines to introduce themselves, explain new rules, get lots of student information and to "groove" the students. . . . Furthermore, in this situation, the experts all made much out of starting the class over. New rules and new instructional systems were seen as needed. New relationships had to be established.*

Beginners, on the other hand, dealt with the situation by:

> *Simply moving on—taking the old material and lessons and getting the class moving on in the tracks of the old teacher . . . [they] seemed to want to know where the class was, and not what the students knew.*

In addition, Berliner reported that beginners and postulants worried about discipline and classroom management; experts took that for granted as an automatized function so that they appeared:

> *unconcerned about management and discipline when planning instruction. This kind of confidence allowed one expert teacher to plan for a personal talk with the class about his beliefs, hopes ambitions, and the like in order to purposely be "vulnerable" in front of them. His confidence in his management skills allowed his humaneness to be featured in his introduction. We do not think novices and postulants could have dared to be so open about themselves in their planning of introductory activities with their students.*

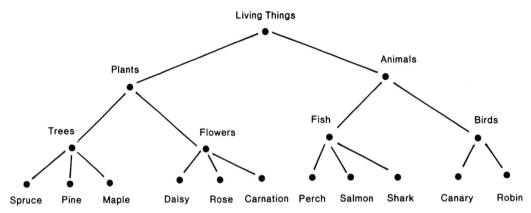

Figure 11.1. Hypothetical partial knowledge hierarchies.

already fit under a theme. A third sentence about Herb does not add to the recognition time of the three sentences if it can be integrated into the knowledge structure already there (e.g., "Herb produced sour notes"), but does increase recognition time for each sentence when it is irrelevant to the previously acquired facts (e.g., "Herb painted an old barn").

Evidence such as this provides support for the idea that knowledge is represented according to a hierarchical structure. We already explored (anecdote 10.1) the evolution of such a structure in S.F.'s increasing skill in digit span by developing running time hierarchies (Chase and Ericsson, 1981, Ericsson et al., 1980). Other theorists have suggested that knowledge is structured or integrated via hierarchical networks, with different hierarchies for separate knowledge domains and interconnections among many of the domains.

Consider the knowledge we have about trees and flowers as categories, under which fall such specific items as pine, spruce and maple vs. daisy, rose, and carnation. Now consider how we might have to search our memory to verify the truth of such statements as "A spruce is a tree" and "A carnation is a tree." Contrast those to what would have to be done to verify a statement like "A pine is a plant" or "A rose is an animal." These latter statements require climbing the hierarchical ladder to more superordinate categories, perhaps as shown in figure 11.1.

What each of us learns over the course of our lives, according to such formulations, is new facts or interconnections regarding such hierarchies. These structures define our general world knowledge. As we study a field in depth, becoming expert in it, we not only add more facts, but we learn them better, interconnect them in more and more ways, providing easier and speedier access to them (Hayes-Roth, 1977). This is not to say that tree diagrams can be drawn to describe all of our knowledge. They are used here only as a didactic technique (and are used in the literature often as the way researchers have attempted to simulate memory processes via computers). More likely, human knowledge structures are so complex and interconnected as to defy easy diagramming. Nevertheless, it is becoming clearer that we must use something like hierarchically integrated networks to allow the extraordinary, as well as the ordinary, feats of memory we witness every day.

Schema Theory

What, then, is *schema theory?* What are we assuming about cognitive processes when we suggest that a child has a conservation schema or an expert is schema-driven? Ellis and Hunt (1993) summarize schema theory in eight assumptions:

1. *Prior knowledge:* New information or experiences are interpreted in terms of prior knowledge already stored in long-term memory. The amount of new information that can be assimilated is directly related to the amount of relevant knowledge already in storage. However, "Mere possession of prior knowledge is insufficient; it must be *activated* at the time of encoding new information" (p. 249). The parts that are activated enable encoding to be selective, since only portions of encountered material are stored.
2. *Important ideas:* Ideas that are most central or meaningful to the individual are those which will likely be assimilated into the existing structure of knowledge and therefore remembered best.
3. *Reconstructive Memory:* Recall is seldom simply reproduced verbatim (but see #8), but is more likely reconstructed and reorganized to make previous and current episodes of one's life make sense.
4. *Development of schemas:* Reconstruction of schemas occurs by attempting to make sense of prior episodes in light of current experiences.
5. *Active process:* Schema development does not just happen; it is an active, constructive process of attempting to make sense of one's experiences of the world.
6. *Culture specific:* While schemas are individualistic, they are so within cultures; cultures differ perhaps even more than individuals in what a schema is (e.g., gourmet dining).
7. *Large units:* A schema is a whole unit (conservation or hitting a backhand in tennis), not the components (identity or eye-hand coordination).
8. *Verbatim memory:* While some memories—particularly for life episodes and stories—are reconstructive, other memories are reproductive and verbatim (story details, poems, and purposely learned school materials, for example).

Knowledge Structures, Schemata, and Teaching

Knowledge structures undergo continual development as children grow and learn. At any given point in development, children attempt to assimilate new facts or to solve new problems on the basis of the knowledge they already have. In that sense experts and novices are exactly alike: both are using their current knowledge structures or schemata as a theory of the world to allow them to understand the situation they are facing.

We have encountered this developmental view of schemata in chapter 2 in discussing nonconservers' and conservers' solutions to Piaget's problems. A variation on this view was provided by Glaser (1984), who considers a schema to be analogous to a scientific theory. When new observations occur they are compared with what is expected on the basis of the theory (or schema) and the theory can then be confirmed, modified slightly, rejected, or replaced with a better theory.

Assuming the analogy between schema and theory is even partially correct, then education can be viewed as a systematic procedure for erecting and remodeling knowledge structures (Glaser, 1984). For rank beginners in a topic, the teacher must provide a temporary structure or scaffold through some kind of overt organizational scheme. Then as instruction continues, we expand, refine and qualify the original structure, perhaps eventually replacing the temporary scaffold with a more-or-less permanent structure of knowledge. Effective teachers already do this to some extent in categorizing, for example, living and nonliving things, plants and animals, and so forth into hierarchical structures such as that in figure 11.1. To make schema development and change an explicit goal of teaching, Glaser suggests the following as pedagogical principles (1984, p. 101):

First, one must understand an individual's current state of knowledge in a domain related to the subject matter to be learned, and within which thinking skills are to be exercised. Second, a "pedagogical theory" can be specified by the teacher that is different from, but close to, the theory held by the learner. Then third, in the context of this pedagogical theory, students can test, evaluate, and modify their current theory so that some resolution between the two is arrived at. Thus, the stage is set for further progression of schemata changes as the students work with, debug, and generate new theories.

Teaching, in this view, becomes a matter of, first, understanding something of the students' current levels of understanding, which may be quite surprising at times (see anecdote 11.3 for instance). Next the teacher's job is remodeling the student's knowledge structure, by laying the foundation and erecting the main supports (main facts and principles). Only later can the teacher complete the structure (supporting facts and principles) and add creative touches (nice to know information, creative approaches, etc.), remodeling the temporary scaffold into a more permanent edifice.

Teaching to Increase Intellectual Skills

Given the recent societal interest in increasing standardized test scores and so-called "critical thinking," along with the recent research on novice-to-expert cognitive processes, it is not surprising to find that there are a number of people who have designed methods which they hope or claim can increase intelligence. In the following section, I shall summarize some of these systems, beginning with a general strategy for increasing problem solving ability—namely, the IDEAL Problem Solver (Bransford and Stein, 1984). Then we shall explore components and metacomponents of intelligence, Philosophy in the Classroom, and several other ideas that not only have the purpose of increasing intellectual skills, but are also interesting ideas for diversifying the curriculum. Interspersed among these systems will be other approaches which are relevant, such as de Bono's lateral thinking.

The IDEAL Problem Solver and Lateral Thinking

The IDEAL approach to solving problems does not mean it is "the best" or a "perfect" approach. IDEAL is an acronym in which each letter stands for an important component of a systematic problem solving process, as follows (Bransford and Stein, 1984):

I = Identify the problem.
D = Define the problem and find a way to represent it verbally or physically (e.g., drawing it).
E = Explore alternative strategies for solving the problem.
A = Act on the strategies.
L = Look at the effects of each strategy to see whether it has resolved the problem.

It seems strange that the first step should be *identifying* that a problem exists, since that would appear to be obvious. When you consider how often we humans take situations for granted; accept things as they are instead of asking how they might be improved; or actively avoid problems instead of solving them, then identifying the problem appears to be an important first step. For example, people often

Anecdote 11.3

A Child's Conception of Living and Nonliving Things

As part of her studies of changes in scientific concepts in childhood, Susan Carey (1985) concluded that the categorization living vs. nonliving things (as implied in figure 11.1) is not part of young children's knowledge structures.

For young children, the salient contrast is not between alive and inanimate, but between alive and dead. However, since these children do not yet understand death as the cessation of bodily functions, they conflate this contrast with others, such as the contrasts between real and imaginary, existent and nonexistent, and functional and broken. This is shown both by young children's patterns of judgments and justifications (as when they say that a button is alive because it can fasten a blouse, or that a table is alive because you can see it) and by what they list when asked to name some things that are not alive (George Washington, ghosts, dinosaurs . . .). (p. 182)

Carey also provided the following exchange with her daughter at about age 3 1/2 (p. 27):

Mommy (Susan):	What do you have in you?
Daughter (Eliza):	Skin.
S:	Inside?
E:	Bones.
S:	Anything else?
E:	Blood.
S:	Does your (teddy) bear have bones and blood inside her?
E:	No, because she's not a big, real person.
S:	Are you?
E:	Yes, well, not very big—she can never die, she'll always be alive!
S:	Is she alive?
E:	No—she's dead. HOW CAN THAT BE?
S:	Is she alive or dead?
E:	Dead.
S:	Did she used to be alive?
E:	No she's middle-sized—in between alive and dead. She moves sometimes.

Anecdote 11.4

How Many Cans of Tennis Balls?

A very popular but disorganized person was elected director of a school fund-raiser, the first of what was hoped to be an annual single-elimination tennis tournament. Not being a tennis player himself, he found himself with a number of problems, including reservation of tennis courts, refreshments, and so on. His previous experiences with such things made the resolution to these problems seem automatic.

But one problem baffled him completely. It had been agreed that the tournament would furnish a new can of tennis balls for each match. With the single-elimination format (that is, when you lose, you play no more matches) and 100 entrants, how many cans of tennis balls were needed?

Can you help the director decide?

complain, "I seldom forget a face, but I just can't remember names." When such people identify this as a problem to solve, then the person can attempt to find solutions (such as learn a mnemonic technique) instead of remaining content with the fallible memory. People who are continually late for appointments or disorganized when they get there often seem oblivious to their problem. To change, they must first identify their disorganization as a problem.

To have a specific case to deal with, consider the problem in anecdote 11.4, *identified* as follows:

Problem 11.4

How many cans of tennis balls do you need (1 for each match) for 100 players in a single-elimination tournament?

The next step is to *define* the problem and figure out how to represent the solution. Will you set up a flow chart for the progress of the matches? Will you represent the problem as a mathematical formula? Can the problem be defined in a simpler way than either of these?

Before, moving on to the next step in the IDEAL Problem Solver, consider how the definition and representation of a problem affects the ease of solving it.[6]

Problem 11.5

What is 2/3 of 1/2?

Problem 11.6

Inside of three equally large boxes are two separate, smaller boxes. Inside of each of those two boxes are four even smaller boxes. How many boxes are there all together?

Problem 11.7

A man had four chains, each three links long. He needed to have them joined into one closed chain. At the local hardware store, he was told it cost two cents each to open a link and three cents each to close a link. He paid the man exactly 15 cents to obtain his single, closed chain. How did he do it?

Most people attack the fractions problem by setting up the algorithm 2/3 × 1/2 = 2/6, which is then reduced to 1/3. But consider how much simpler the problem becomes by defining it as "What is 1/2 of 2/3?"

The boxes problem is not very complex, but it provides a heavy memory load. Thus it is much easier to solve it, if you represent the problem as a drawing. If you have not yet solved the problem, try it with this definition of the problem.[7]

The chain link problem is more complex yet, because it requires more than one step to solve it, and thus taxes the short-term memory. In addition, the representation as a drawing may suggest solutions.[8]

Returning to the tennis tournament problem (problem 11.4), it should now be obvious (if it wasn't before) that how you define and represent the problem will affect your solution attempts. Seeing more than one way of defining the problem is not bad, however. It is in fact, desirable because it helps us to explore alternative approaches, the E in IDEAL.

In exploring alternatives, much can be gained by adopting what deBono (1970) called *lateral thinking*. The emphasis at this stage is not on finding the best alternative; rather it is on generating as many *different* alternative approaches as possible. In groups this can be accomplished by brainstorming (Osborn, 1957; Meadows and Parnes, 1959) a large number of ideas without evaluation. Individuals can use this concept to generate and write down ideas (so as not to have to remember them), always suspending judgment until later. Ways of generating alternatives include the following (de Bono, 1970):

1. *The "why" technique:* always asking why x is so, much as a child does. The purpose is not to find a comfortable answer, but to create discomfort with each answer and thus keep us flexible enough to look for other alternatives. In the above problem one might ask oneself "why would a flow chart help?" The answer "to get all possible matches." "Why?" "Because I can't think of anything better to do." At this point, even though you know the procedure will work, you also know there must be another way. And besides, would you draw a flow chart of all matches if there were 10,000 entrants?

2. *The "Fractionation" method:* breaking a problem into some usable parts. Note: deBono (1970, p. 135) points out that "One is not trying to *find* the true component parts of a situation, one is trying to *create* parts." It is the creativity of inventing possible parts that allows us to break out of our rigidity of thinking. Fractionating the tennis tournament would allow us to take four players, for example, and see how many matches we would need to declare a winner. Whether or not the answer to the four players problem is proportional to the 100 player problem, we may still learn something of importance.[9]

3. *The Reversal Method:* finding a way to see the problem from the end, upside down, inside out, or backwards. The idea is to provoke a rearrangement of the information to see what happens (to make water run uphill, to make a car drive a person, etc.). In the tennis tournament we have been asking "how many matches?" Since continued matches depend on winners, the reversal method tells us to find a different focus: How many losers will there be in a 100-match tournament?

Using such techniques as these (from de Bono, 1970, and Bransford and Stein, 1984), we can begin to see what *exploring* alternative approaches means. Coincidentally, the Reversal method above presents us with the easiest and perhaps most elegant solution to the tennis tournament problem—namely, that there must be 99 losers in a 100-player single-elimination tournament. Thus 99 cans of balls are needed. Nevertheless, even if no good solution had arisen from any of those techniques, they would have served to keep our minds flexible, to eliminate unworkable solutions, and possibly to generate still more alternatives.

Having explored alternative strategies to solve problems, the next two steps are to *Act* on those strategies and *Look* at the effects (the A and L of Bransford and Stein's IDEAL Problem Solver). For example, suppose you have the following problem:

Problem 11.8

Eight people at a party are each going to receive 2/3 of a pint of champagne. How many pints of champagne do you need?

As Holt (1964) reminded us in *How Children Fail*, many people will decide on a strategy, act on it, and not bother to look at whether the answer makes sense. Some might reason that since the pints are to be divided among eight people, it is a division problem. Thus they act to apply the division algorithm as follows:

$8/1 \div 2/3$ or $8/1 \times 3/2 = 24/2 = 12$ pints.

Looking at this answer to see whether it makes sense, however, forces the person to confront the original question. Such a confrontation might occur in this form: "If each person is getting less than one pint, then the answer must be less than the number of people—in this case, less than 8. Thus the previous solution process is in error."[10] Most teachers preach that students should check their work, but unfortunately the students have not adequately practiced how to do that, nor are they reinforced for doing so. Perhaps less emphasis on the correct answer—by requiring checks, justifications, or alternative solutions in order to obtain credit for the problem—would help. Of course, teachers need to model such processes for the students, not just tell them to "do as I say . . ."

It is sometimes a good strategy in a multiple-step problem to *act* on the initial step and then *look* to see what has been learned before taking the next step. In the tennis tournament problem, for example, a first step that may have occurred to you is to notice that after the first round of 50 matches, 50 people would be left. Before acting again, it is worth assessing what was learned, perhaps by talking to yourself and using the "why" technique as follows:

"One lesson learned is that the field has been cut in half after one round."
"Why is that useful?"
"Because I am getting closer."
"Why?"
"Because there may be a trend where each step simply divides the number in half."

So far so good. Acting on the next round we find there are 25 matches and 25 players left. Assessing, you might continue:

"The trend is correct, but now there are an odd number of players left."
"Why is that important?"
"Because now I can't simply keep taking half and add up the numbers, like 50 + 25 + 12.5 etc."
"Why?"
"Because you can't have half a person."
"Suppose I start again from a different point of view. What would happen if instead of starting at the beginning with 100 hopeful players, I reverse things and start at the end?"
"In that case, there is one winner—and 99 losers. That's it: to have 99 losers you need 99 matches and 99 cans of tennis balls."

Acting, then looking (1) may force you to consider what has been learned at each step, (2) may make you confront the adequacy of your answers and solution processes, and (3) may facilitate your awareness that you need to explore other alternatives or even redefine the problem.

The IDEAL Problem Solver, in sum, provides a useful general vehicle for creative and critical thinking. Why do most of us need such a procedure? The evidence in chapter 9, you'll recall, points to the extreme difficulty of transferring knowledge or skills from one situation or problem to another. Often we are unaware that our definition of the problem is limited, that we are making unwarranted assumptions, or (in deBono's turn of the phrase, 1970) that we are being dominated by the dominant idea in the problem. In addition, as Bransford and Stein (1984, p. 26) put it:

> . . . people may be so personally involved ("ego involved") in their own approach to a particular problem that they have difficulty considering alternatives. They therefore keep trying to show they were right all along rather than attempt to find alternative ways a problem might be defined.

Some people, moreover, are convinced they are not good at solving problems and will not even try (learned helplessness?). A system such as the IDEAL Problem Solver, if it is well-practiced can potentially overcome these difficulties while having great generalizability in areas as diverse as discipline problems, statistics problems, or disarmament. See anecdote 11.5 for other examples.

Metacognitive Strategies

Another way of teaching intellectual skills is to identify or develop exemplary tasks which can remediate known deficiencies. Three very influential programs based on this idea have been undertaken by Howard Gardner, Reuven Feuerstein, and Robert Sternberg, which have already been presented in chapter 4. To illustrate further what is meant by emphasizing metacognitive strategies, I shall use Sternberg's approach to show what is meant by this. First, you may recall that Sternberg identified three components of intelligence, as follows:

(1) *metacomponents*, which are the executive or metacognitive processes which control and monitor allocation of time and energy, define the problem and find a mental representation, check solutions to see if they make sense or if more information is needed, etc.
(2) *performance components*, which carry out plans, draw inferences, solve algorithms, etc.
(3) *knowledge-acquisition components*, which encode and organize information, find ways to get more information (from contexts, for example), etc.

Consider Sternberg's (1986) suggestions relating to those executive planning and monitoring functions he calls metacomponents:

1. Define the nature of the problem.
2. Select the components or steps needed to solve the problem (e.g., decide the first step and make it a small one; consider alternatives).
3. Select a strategy for ordering the components (consider the full problem; don't assume the obvious; establish a systematic, logical order for following the steps).
4. Select a mental representation for information (write or draw, use verbal or graphical methods to portray the information).
5. Allocate your resources carefully (spend extra time planning your approach and understanding the task before trying to solve the problem; resist impulsive random attempts to get the answer).
6. Monitor your solution processes (be aware of each solution attempt, what process it is using, and what information it is obtaining; persevere at a strategy long enough to be sure it is unsuccessful; but don't stick with a strategy that did not work just because you've invested a lot of effort into it).

Using these metacomponents, try solving the following problem and monitor your own solution process.

Anecdote 11.5

Ideal Ideas

The IDEAL Problem Solver can be put to a wide variety of uses in classrooms, as the following educators suggest in their examples and comments.

1. THE CASE OF THE LOST KEYS by Sharon Milliken, Teacher

    Identify: Teacher's keys are not on her desk where they should be.

    Define: Teacher asks the class for suggestions. A diagram is made of the desk, the area, and who was close to the desk (represented by drawing).

    Explore: These approaches were considered: When and where were the keys last seen? What was the last thing the keys might have been used for? Who could have touched the keys?

    Act & Look: These were acted upon by retracing steps, checking cabinets that might have been opened, etc. Keys were found on top of a filing cabinet where the teaching assistant inadvertently left them.

    Comments: Luckily the teacher did not try to place blame for the lost keys (I've been in situations where teachers say things like, "Okay no one leaves the room until I find my keys"). So instead of defining the problem as a discipline incident, making anyone defensive, and still not solving the problem, IDEAL made everyone a problem solver and gave practice with using a cognitive strategy.

2. THE FIGHT OVER TOYS by Kathleen Girton, Teacher

    Identify: Two preschool children are fighting over a toy.

    Define: Teacher asks each child to tell or draw the problem (e.g., one child drew himself with a sad face and the other with the toy).

    Explore: Suggestions were "Since I had the toy first, give it back," "Play together with the toy," or "I have it for a while, then you have it."

    Act & Look: Students then tried a solution. (If someone was still not happy, I reminded them to try one of their other solutions).

    Comments: Young children are not only struggling to learn the concept of sharing, but also learning self-control and how to solve problems. If I step in, they continue to rely on adults to impose order. Since I started having them go through the steps of IDEAL, they learn to solve their own problems and I rarely have to become involved anymore.

Anecdote 11.5—(continued)

3. AN IDEAL WRITING STRATEGY by Reneé Gravelle, Teacher

   Identify: Community college students have a writing assignment.

   Define: Students brainstorm possible perspectives to take, who is the intended audience, and what the goal of the writing is.

   Explore: Should the task be broken into parts, with several steps or components to be completed before combining into a whole? Should the reversibility method be used, focusing first on a climax or conclusion and then working backward to conceptualize the piece? Should there be role playing or other cooperative methods used to stimulate divergent thinking on the topic before writing?

   Act & Look: Try one of the strategies, and write. Then read, edit, revise, and look again.

   Comments: IDEAL offers a language for students and teachers to use in their interactions. The flexibility and creative thinking built into each component of the model are good for experienced as well as novice writers, but having permission to see tasks in a variety of ways unchains the novice in particular from formulaic limitations. There may also be embedded in the IDEAL principles some strategies for overcoming writer's block.

Problem 11.10

Bob and Ray were standing in the driveway of Bob's house discussing their families. Ray asked the ages of Bob's three girls. Bob, being a fun-loving math teacher, answered, "Well, the product of their ages is 72."
Ray answered, "That's not enough information."
Bob said, "OK, the sum of their ages is equal to my house number."
Ray looked at the house number and said, "That helps, but it's still not enough information."
Bob said, "All right. My youngest daughter loves strawberry ice cream."
Ray said, "Oh, now I know their ages."
What were the daughters' ages?

When confronted with the Three Daughter problem, most people take the product of their ages = 72 to be an important fact and set out to discover some possible factors of 72. Unfortunately, it is common to find a few factors (e.g., 1 × 1 × 72; 1 × 2 × 36; 2 × 3 × 12) and then to see whether any of those could solve the problem. This is a form of "answer grabbing" which, since it is unsystematic, is unlikely to solve the problem (or even if it is correct, the problem-solver cannot say why it is). When this attempt to escape from the problem fails, the problem-solver often gives up on this strategy. Sternberg (1986, p. 81) cautions us to:

Avoid impulsiveness in solution monitoring. Sometimes, in problem solving, you will realize

> **Box 11.1**
>
> ## Solution to the Three Daughters Problem
>
> | Nonredundant Factors of 72: | SUMS |
> |---|---|
> | 1 × 1 × 72 = 72 | 74 |
> | 1 × 2 × 36 = 72 | 39 |
> | 1 × 3 × 24 = 72 | 28 |
> | 1 × 4 × 18 = 72 | 23 |
> | 1 × 6 × 12 = 72 | 19 |
> | 1 × 8 × 9 = 72 | 18 |
> | 2 × 2 × 18 = 72 | 22 |
> | 2 × 3 × 12 = 72 | 17 |
> | 2 × 4 × 9 = 72 | 15 |
> | 2 × 6 × 6 = 72 | 14 |
> | 3 × 3 × 8 = 72 | 14 |
> | 3 × 4 × 6 = 72 | 13 |
>
> Since, among all of the factors, only two of the sums are the same, then the house number must be 14. The two combinations which sum to 14 each have a set of twins. Since there is a youngest daughter (who loves strawberry ice cream), then the twins must be older, leaving the daughters' ages to be 2, 6, and 6.

that something is wrong and that some course of action needs to be taken to correct whatever problem has arisen. . . . Avoid the tendency immediately to withdraw from your first path or solution and to jump at the second.

Returning to the Three Daughters, it may not be immediately obvious how the house number and strawberry ice cream are relevant to the problem. Thus, it is tempting to dismiss one or both of those facts as irrelevant. If the problem is defined, however, as having all facts relevant, then the question is why are such unlikely facts all relevant? Further attempts to understand the nature of the problem will suggest something like the following: (1) the factors of 72 provide a list of alternatives; (2) the sums being equal to the address reduces the alternatives to two or more possible alternatives, but some ambiguity remains; and (3) the youngest liking strawberry ice cream removes all ambiguity.

Then, even if the mechanism by which the house number and the strawberry ice cream work is still unknown, the following have been established:

1. the first step—namely, to find the factors of 72.
2. the mental representation—namely, to write them out.
3. the strategy—namely, to find all the non-repeating factors of 72, calculate their sums, and see if there is any ambiguity remaining.

Having done all of the above provided a considerable allocation of time in the defining and planning stages. What remains is to carry out the plan and to monitor how systematic and successful it is. Recall that even unsuccessful efforts provide useful information. If you have still not solved the problem, try it again (the solution is in the box).

It is important to acknowledge that Sternberg is *not* claiming, as some popular psychology books seem to do, to "raise your IQ in ten-minutes a day." He is, rather, attempting to go "Beyond IQ" (Sternberg, 1985) to identify the important components of intelligence and then help people improve on those. In fact, Sternberg (1987) argues that the very strategies that are often used to teach people to achieve higher intelligence test scores—such strategies as "work as quickly as you can," "read everything carefully," "memorize vocabulary," or "use all the information in the problem"—may help in the short run on the immediate test, but will be counterproductive in the long run in increasing intellectual skills. As we have seen, *good metacognitive processing requires working slowly at certain stages, provides for allocating reading time on the basis of purpose, emphasizes inferring meanings of words in context, and requires selective encoding of what information in a problem is relevant.* Sternberg emphasizes these basic components because he, along with many other current cognitive psychologists, considers them to have wide generalizability in daily life (e.g., reading, shopping, understanding claims of advertisers or politicians), as well as on standardized tests and in-school tasks.

Given the converging types of evidence presented in the previous three chapters—namely, evidence on improving memory strategies of slower or disabled learners, on the differences between experts and novices, and on organizing knowledge—it is clear that Sternberg's suggestions are consistent with the evidence and current theorizing. For example, experts have automatized much of their routine work, which allows them to concentrate on the novel features of a problem (Berliner, 1986; Bloom, 1986). This is also a likely explanation for the surprising finding that speed of performance on elementary tasks is often correlated with IQ score (e.g., Hunt, Lunneberg and Lewis, 1975; Jensen, 1982; Thorndike, 1984). By this view, those who have automatized a number of components of intelligence will solve problems faster and more accurately than those who have not. Therefore, just as a pianist or basketball player works to improve speed and automaticity, we can all improve in the intellectual domain (though as Thorndike, 1984, points out, differences among individuals may increase, not decrease, as a result of such practice).

Philosophy in the Classroom

> . . . *one reason children cannot read better than they do is that we do not teach them reasoning. And without reasoning, they cannot figure out what they're reading. (Lipman, Sharp and Oscanyan, 1980, p. 19)*

Matthew Lipman and his colleagues have devised yet another unique approach to the teaching of reasoning skills. Called *Philosophy in the Classroom*, it is a comprehensive curriculum from kindergarten to twelfth grade. The most novel aspect (pun intended) of this curriculum is the use of the novel to introduce problems for discussion. At the earliest grades stories are used to teach certain language and logical concepts, recognition of perceptual and linguistic ambiguities, classifications, and ways of reasoning. By grade 5, students read a novel entitled *Harry Stottlemeier's Discovery* (Lipman, 1974), in which Harry and his classmates begin to acquire and practice some of the principles of logic through the cooperative use of inquiry methods. Additional novels, in later grades, introduce the topics of scientific inquiry, ethical inquiry, social inquiry, and aesthetics, among other topics. The teachers' manuals provide exercises, questions and procedures for conducting class discussions consistent with what the characters in the stories are experiencing.

Consider the following passage for upper class high school students from Lipman's novel, *Mark* (1980, p. 75), in which street corner con-games evoke an argument among

Casey, Sandy, and Link about "gambling as human nature." Casey continues,

> "Sure it's only natural to want to compete. But it's also only natural to want to cooperate. We've got natural tendencies to do both, and there's nothing wrong with those tendencies. But that's where the Big Switch comes in."
> "The big switch?" Sandy demanded, mystified. Link laughed and took another portion of pizza. "That's what we call it. It happens in every society. If they have cooperative institutions, they'll claim it's because people are born *cooperative*. And if they have competitive institutions, they'll claim it's because people are born *competitive*."
> "But that makes sense!" Sandy cried out. "Societies adjust their institutions to suit human nature!"
> Link's voice was bitter now. "Sure, that's what people *claim* they do, so they don't have to change things and make them better. But in fact, *although people are all born with the same tendencies, certain tendencies are rewarded and others are punished. That's why kids born into hunting tribes turn out to be warlike and kids born into peasant families turn out to be peaceful."*
> "And boys are taught to be aggressive and girls are taught to be docile," Casey added. "Sure they're all born with both kinds of tendencies, but society screens one kind out and the other kind in."
> Link gulped down the last bit of the piece of pizza he'd been nursing. "Either way," he said, "society blames the result on human nature, never on itself. But the fact is, social institutions aren't the way they are because of human nature. It's the other way around: human beings are the way they are because of the social institutions they live in."

In the teacher's manual accompanying the novel (Lipman and Sharp, 1980, pp. 347–352) various "leading ideas" are suggested for conducting classroom discussions about social processes. The first explores whether there is such a thing as human nature and how it can be contrasted with cultural universals. For example, how can we tell if toilet training is due to human nature or to social practices that occur in all nations? What about what, how and when people eat? A second leading idea contrasts the ideas of cooperation and competition as being genetically or environmentally determined. For example, do sports foster cooperation, competition, or both? How about grades in school? Are boys naturally more competitive than girls? The third leading idea on this passage concerns the "big switch," in which causal explanations for behavior are examined for some common fallacies or overgeneralizations.

For each of these "leading ideas," Lipman and Sharp provide some additional examples or vignettes to prepare the teacher for a discussion, along with a number of examples or questions to be explored.

To conduct Lipman's program competently in the classroom—just as to conduct any other program competently—requires considerable expertise on the part of the teacher. For most teachers, this would entail considerable retraining to refocus their emphasis from a factual orientation to one based on such questions as "How do you know?" and "What are the implications or consequences of that belief?" It would affect the teacher's own cognitive processes, and it would affect virtually every aspect of schooling including, for example, how we teach and assess reading and the kinds of materials to be read.

Intellectual Skills in the School Curriculum

As the preceding examples suggest, there are now available a large number of good ideas for teaching a variety of intellectual skills. Though we are short of any definitive research on any particular system, there is support for the principles underlying most, if not all, of these systems (as the last several chapters have attempted to make clear).

What I can advocate, therefore, is *a curriculum which includes much active participation, much questioning, and at least as much emphasis on process as product*. This does not replace factual knowledge, of course, because expertise is in large measure dependent on well-organized, accessible knowledge. Nor does it replace the practice of skills to the point of automaticity, which is also a feature of expertise. What it does is attempt to provide a knowledge structure which continually questions (1) how our present facts and skills can be used in a given situation.; (2) whether those facts and skills need to be revised or refined as a result of new information; and (3) whether those facts and skills could be interfering with our flexibility to solve some problems and, indeed, retarding our mental growth.

The bad news is that it is not easy to provide such a curriculum, especially since few teachers have themselves been exposed to such a curriculum. The good news is that much of this can be done with existing curricula. The difference, according to the view being advocated, is not in the particular story being read, but in how students think while they are reading it. As Lipman (1987) argued, Sherlock Holmes could be a vehicle for teaching thinking.

> When Holmes examines a footprint and tells Watson what sort of person it was who made such a footprint, we are impelled to reenact Holmes's thought processes, for only by going through his reasoning can we explain his conclusions to ourselves. If Holmes tells us that the man who made that footprint must have weighed 200 pounds, we cannot help asking ourselves what such a footprint must look like to be able to infer from it the weight of the man who made it. (Lipman, 1987, p. 156)

So could films such as *Raiders of the Lost Ark* (Bransford et al., 1987). In fact, most current curricula in most schools could be a vehicle for teaching thinking skills as long as there is a major emphasis on "why?", "how do we know that?" and "what are the implications or consequences of that?"

Teaching intellectual skills within the domain of the curriculum of each subject matter is technically known as *domain-specific* or *embedded* teaching strategies (see Derry and Murphy, 1986, for a review of this issue). This is contrasted with *domain-general* or *detached* strategies, in which the intellectual skills are presumable broadly applicable to many fields and can thus be taught as a separate curriculum. An example of a domain-specific mnemonic system is Every Good Boy Does Fine for the names of the notes on the lines in the treble clef in music.

Sometimes a technique appears to be domain-specific when it actually has broad applicability. For example, if Bransford and Stein's IDEAL Problem Solver were taught by the math teacher as a technique for solving math problems, then it is a good bet that few students will spontaneously transfer it to other subjects. The other extreme is to teach the IDEAL Problem Solver in a course by itself, entirely detached from other subjects and teachers. In this case, the students will have limited practice using the newly acquired skills in the regular curriculum. It is also likely that the teachers in the separate disciplines will not know the IDEAL Problem Solver well enough to model it and incorporate it in their fields. Again, transfer will be limited.

The position of most promise is the compromise position—namely, to provide a structured program to develop intellectual skills as a separate class, meeting perhaps one hour per week. In addition, the teachers in the various disciplines also receive in-service instruction and practice using these techniques in their own fields, and then build those intellectual skills into the objectives of their curricula. This position of teaching intellectual skills as both domain-general and domain-specific skills has the highest probability of eventually showing positive transfer.

Many programs now exist for teaching intellectual skills, some of which were the topics of previous sections of this book—namely, Bransford and Stein's IDEAL Problem Solver, deBono's Lateral Thinking,[11] Feuerstein's Instrumental Enrichment, Lipman's Philosophy in the Classroom, Gardner's Multiple Intelligences, and Sternberg's Teaching Components of Intelligence. But there are many other good ideas left unmentioned and I shall close this section of the book by briefly describing a few of them.

Dialogical Thinking

Consider some cold, hard historical facts about the Boston Massacre in 1775 (Paul, 1987):

1. A colonist gave sworn testimony that the first shot was fired by the British.
2. A colonial British sympathizer wrote an official letter saying the colonists fired the first shot.
3. A British lieutenant wrote in his diary that the colonists fired one or two shots before the British returned fire.
4. The commander of the colonial troops ordered his troops to disperse and not to fire; then the British fired without provocation.

Most people assume that their own personal account of events, or the account most favorable to their nation or reference group, is accurate. Such dubious "facts" get reported in a nation's history texts and students are asked to commit them to memory. As Paul (1987, p. 133) reminds us,

> By not grasping that all history is history-from-a-point-of-view, the students do not recognize appropriate logical parallels, such as, for example that all news is news-from-a-point-of-view.

Biases will be with us always, but suspending judgment and seeing that alternative logical positions exist as intellectual skills can be practiced in class. One way in which this can occur is to have students choose sides from which to debate a particular topic. Then assign the students to *defend a different position* than they chose. Another way is to have each student argue, orally or in writing, from more than one point of view. Paul calls this technique *dialogical thinking* since each person must reconstruct points of view on more than one side of a question, as would occur by opponents in a debate or lawyers in a courtroom. Dialogical thinking, since it requires empathy for other points of view, is important to maintain flexible and lateral thinking, as well as to appreciate the fact that most issues are multilogical—that is, there is more than one way logically to solve the problem.

A new method for teaching reading comprehension (see also anecdote 9.5), particularly for learning disabled students, seems parallel in some ways to the dialogical thinking procedure. Developed by Palincsar and Brown (1984; see also Brown, 1994) to teach the comprehension-fostering activities of *questioning, clarifying, summarizing,* and *predicting,* the procedure has the following as guiding principles. First, the teachers model the procedures whenever they are leading the discussion; all members of the group serve, in turn, as leaders. Second, the strategies are modeled in the context of the dialogue about a particular text. Third, the discussion focuses on comprehension of both the text and the goals of their strategies. Fourth, the teacher provides feedback on both text comprehension and strategy use. Fifth, responsibility for the discussion and the strategies is shifted as soon as possible from the teacher to the students.

Thinking Aloud

In 1950 Bloom and Broder asked college students to think out loud while solving problems. They then tried to ascertain some of the differences in strategy between good and poor problem solvers. Among other discoveries was the following (p. 28):

It seemed, then, that the ideas which the nonsuccessful problem-solvers possessed were huge, unwieldy things, figuratively capable of fitting into only one particular space—that in which they had originally been formed. The ideas of the successful problem-solvers, in contrast, were many faceted things which could be turned this way and that, expanded or contracted, and made to fit the space in which they were needed.

More recent research supports and extends their findings, as we have seen in studies of experts and novices.

Another major program that was designed to teach intellectual skills uses thinking aloud protocols from experts as well as thinking aloud as an instructional activity for the learners. This program, Whimbey and Lochhead's Short Course in Analytical Reasoning (1980; see also 1986), first exposes students to how experts solved problems, using transcripts of their thinking aloud sessions. These protocols provide models of efficient ways to solve problems, as well as familiarizing students with how to think out loud (which is a skill that must also be learned).

In the next phase of instruction, students work in pairs, solving problems while thinking aloud. While one solves problems aloud, the other listens; on later problems they reverse roles. The listener, however, is a very active participant, fulfilling two major functions: (1) checking the accuracy and comprehensibility of each step, without regard to speed; and (2) ensuring that all steps are vocalized and no step is skipped. Students learn that this role is not one of being overly critical; rather, it is because completeness and explicitness are important in solving problems. (Note: if you've ever had to program a computer to solve a problem, you know the value of completeness and explicitness.)

In a third phase of instruction, students devise problems which are similar to those they have been working on, so that problems can be understood from the point of view of the author as well as the solver.

Whimbey and Lochhead's method is another one that deserves more extended treatment and analysis. For the present purpose—namely, to describe another instructional technique—it is perhaps sufficient to offer just two editorial comments.[12] On the positive side, thinking aloud appears to be a good way to give students practice making metacognitive assessments of their strategies. On the negative side, if student pairs are obsessed with finding one strategy which works, they may succumb to the dominant idea (as deBono, 1970, called it) and still need other practice generating alternative strategies. A possible way around this is to have students practice thinking aloud on the same problem at least twice, using different approaches each time.

Practicing Mental Flexibility

Consider the kindergarten experience of Maureen Dowling, with which this chapter began. Pounding round pegs into square holes is often considered the epitome of stupidity, but most of us would applaud this child's creative, though perhaps misguided, efforts. One can only wonder whether the teacher applauded the effort.

Despite the negative connotation of "placing round pegs in square holes," it is the behavior precisely of challenging the clichés, the labels, and the familiar functions of objects which is considered creative. The point is to avoid taking familiar objects and events for granted, to see them as though it was the first time, and thereby overcome mental rigidity.

Consider the following lines which most Americans have overlearned:

My country 'tis of thee
Sweet land of liberty
Of thee I sing

Have you ever noticed the redundancy that is built into this verse? We concede poetic license to the lyricist of the song, but we may be surprised to have sung those words hundreds of times and never noticed the problem. This is similar to the following classical problem in perception in which it is easy to overlook the redundancy.

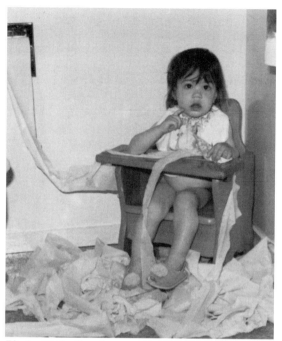

Photo 11.3. Creative expression or naughty behavior? (Photo courtesy of Dr. Robert D. Gentile)

Children often learn things they do not understand. Ask a seven year old, after he or she can proudly cite the Pledge of Allegiance what the words "pledge" and "allegiance" mean. If they answer at all, their answers may surprise you. But that is the beauty of taking a fresh look at the world. One child drew a picture of the manger scene at Christmas. The Sunday School teacher said it was quite nice and recognized Mary, Joseph, Jesus, and other figures in the picture. But there was a large, round figure with a face on it. So the teacher asked, "But what is this?" The child indignantly replied, "That's round John Virgin."

Such children's conceptions should not be considered creative, since they were probably only memorized misinformation, but they do serve to make us aware that there is more than one view of a thing.

Some of the earliest training for mental flexibility used tasks such as unusual uses of common materials (e.g., Guilford, 1950) and originality of word associations (e.g., Maltzman, 1960). The unusual uses task presents people with a common object, such as a brick, and requires them to continue to think of uses for bricks long after they have exhausted the normal uses. For example, at first people tend to respond with "build a house, build a garage, build a bookshelf," etc. After those are exhausted more original ideas may occur: "tie a note to it and throw it through a window to send a message," "use as a paper weight," etc. Later still more original uses may occur: "Keep several bricks in the toilet tank to displace water and therefore save money on the water bill" or "Scrape with sandpaper to provide rhythm for a jug band."

The word association originality task is similar, in that you keep free associating to the same words, but must give a different response each time. Under these conditions, the responses become more and more uncommon.

It is wise to be skeptical of the transfer value of such tasks, since they seem to have so little relation to the kinds of problems we are likely to encounter (in this book or elsewhere).

They could serve in instruction to provide some early practice in lateral thinking. Like brainstorming, these techniques require that we generate as many new ideas as possible, evaluating them later. Thus they can still provide practice in going beyond first reactions and in suspending judgment.

More recent approaches to stimulating originality are likely to be related to particular kinds of problems. For example, Sternberg (1986) has developed a set of *novel analogies*, in which there is a novel condition for solving the problem. In the following problem, you must solve the analogy as though the opening statement were true:[13]

Problem 11.11

Villains are lovable.

HERO is to ADMIRATION as VILLAIN is to
   a. contempt
   b. affection
   c. cruelty
   d. kindness

Problems like this can force us to go beyond our common word associations and experiences to solve the problem according to the logic of another point of view.

This brings us to what deBono (1970) calls breaking out of cliché patterns and labels. Whenever a statement is taken as a truism, or a practice is defended because it is traditional, it is good practice to question the conditions under which it is true or may not be true. That goes for the conclusions in this book, as well. Regarding labels, which deBono says are likely to rigidify our thinking into narrow and convenient categories, we should regularly challenge them.

Now, challenging labels does not mean that you disagree with them or you have a better alternative. It just means you want to answer such questions about the labels as these: "Why am I using this label?" "What exactly does this label mean?" When this is done you can continue to use the label, but you will have a better understanding of its meaning and limits. In an earlier chapter we saw some of the difficulties of labeling on the basis of IQ. Many other labels that we use in education and psychology could profitably be challenged regularly. I nominate "hyperactive," "dyslexic," and "learning disabled" as some of my favorites. But, to be honest, I must tell you to challenge the beliefs and labels I use in this book: for examples you may want to start with "learned helplessness," "positive and negative reinforcement," "short-term and long-term memory," and so on.

Do such techniques as these increase the number of creative products? Possibly not, but when used as part of an intellectual skills development program, they may (1) help students focus on the rigidifying effects of various categories they use frequently, and (2) provide practice exploring alternatives.

Expertise Revisited

The emphasis in the last two-thirds of this chapter has been on general problem solving strategies or component processes that are presumably transferable to many subject matter domains. It bears repeating, nevertheless, that *expertise is subject-matter related*. Thus it is not just general problem-solving skills that experts possess, but problem-solving skills within their field—both declarative and procedural knowledge. What separates the expert musician from the expert psychologist from the expert mathematician, then, is their knowledge and the structure of that knowledge—in their respective domains. This is one important reason for teaching thinking within the subject fields.

Not only do novices have to learn effective problem-solving techniques in a field, they must also learn or relearn the structure of knowledge of that field. There is quite a bit of evidence that students go through science classes in high school and college earning B grades or better, for example, and still have limitations or basic misconceptions about the material they covered (e.g., Chi et al., 1982). In addition to providing a very readable review of such evidence, Susan Carey (1986) also suggests a reason for this intractability. Students do not come to a course with zero knowledge schemata. If they did, they could not understand the new instruction, since new information is interpreted in terms of the existing knowledge. They come, instead, with *some* knowledge structures. If their teachers teach them new facts, but the schemata for organizing those facts do not change, then there will simply be new facts hanging on in random places to the old structure (to continue Glaser's, 1984 remodeling analogy described earlier). Carey (1986) provides the following examples from Newtonian mechanics:

Problem 11.12

If a coin is tossed into the air, in what direction are forces acting on that coin (a) on the way to the top of its trajectory and (b) on the way back down?

Novices, even many who have had relevant instruction, often answer that there are upward and downward forces in both parts of the trajectory. The misconception, apparently, is that the toss provides an upward force ("no motion without a force") and a weaker counteracting gravitational force. On the downward side, gravity is the stronger force winning against the upward force of the toss. However, this logic is a violation of Newton's laws, which recognize only the force of gravity in this problem. The reason is that the force that sets the coin in motion is a force of *acceleration*. But once the coin is in motion, it continues in motion without a force. Most of us who are not physics experts have not remodeled our knowledge structures vis-a-vis such facts and, thus, additional facts are really not well-understood.

Consider two other scientific facts which most of us know, but probably do not understand—namely, the facts that light travels at a speed of 186,000 miles per second and that time is relative. How did Einstein remodel his knowledge structures to build a theory of relativity? One way was to conduct a thought experiment like the following:[14]

Problem 11.13

Suppose you were on a train traveling at the speed of light going away from a clock which nevertheless remains visible. What time would it appear to be on that clock as you continue to move away from it?

The answer, which is counter-intuitive in a pre-Einsteinian sense, is that the image of the clock will always appear the same, because light is traveling at the same speed as you. If that is true then,

Problem 11.14

What will appear to happen to the time if the train is traveling away from the clock faster than the speed of light?[15]

Problems such as this require, for most of us, a substantial remodeling of our knowledge structures. Teachers can facilitate such remodeling or, if they just emphasize the learning of new facts, have essentially no long-term effect on students' understanding.

A Churchillian Epilogue

We have now come to the close of both the chapter, and the section on cognition. Among other things, we have seen the importance of structuring knowledge, for metacognitive strategies, and for automatizing such strategies. Unfortunately for seven-year-old Winston Churchill, his teachers did not know about those things in planning his curriculum. The headmaster of his new school asked him if he had done any Latin yet. When Winston answered, "No, sir," the headmaster opened a Latin grammar book and told him to learn the following:

Mensa	a table
Mensa	O table
Mensam	a table
Mensae	of a table
Mensae	to or for a table
Mensa	by, with or from a table

What could it possibly mean, he wondered. But he could not worry about that, because the master was to return in thirty minutes to see what he knew. At his return, young Winston was, indeed, able to recite the list. The master seemed satisfied, but Winston was not, so he asked (Churchill, 1965, pp. 21–22):

"What does it mean, sir?"
"It means what it says. Mensa, a table. Mensa is a noun of the First Declension. There are five Declensions. You have learnt the singular of the First Declension."
But," I repeated, "what does it mean?"
"Mensa means a table," he answered.
"Then why does mensa also mean O table," I inquired, "and what does O table mean?"
"Mensa, O table, is the vocative case," he replied. . . . And then seeing he was not carrying me with him, "You would use it in speaking to a table."
"But I never do," I blurted out in honest amazement.
"If you are impertinent, you will be punished, and punished, let me tell you, very severely," was his conclusive rejoinder.

When questioning is considered impertinent behavior, thinking is suppressed in favor of regurgitating correct answers, and children's natural curiosity is stifled. But perhaps I am being too hard on the teacher who, if he really did regularly speak to tables, could have modeled that behavior for young Winston. ❧

Practice Exercises

A. Practice Items

INSTRUCTIONS FOR ITEMS 1–5: Match the following terms with their appropriate definitions by placing the letter of the term in the space provided. (Answers in Note 16).

- a. schema
- b. heuristic
- c. algorithm
- d. cognition
- e. metacognition
- f. procedural knowledge
- g. declarative knowledge
- h. intelligence

___ 1. The process of monitoring your own thinking or remembering.

___ 2. An automatic, well-organized behavioral sequence or structured thought process.

___ 3. Knowledge of how a thing is done.

___ 4. A general strategy for solving a problem.

___ 5. A step-by-step application of a formula to solve a problem.

For items 6–11 select the alternative choice which *best* answers the question. (Answers in Note 16).

6. Chess masters, in comparison to novices, have been shown to have
    a. better memories for all kinds of things (chess, music, poetry, etc.).
    b. better memories for anything having to do with chess, but no better on anything else.
    c. better memories for real games of chess, but no better on anything else.
    d. no better memories for anything.

7. According to the logic of schema theory, a teacher's job is
    a. first, to lay a groundwork of facts upon which knowledge structures can later be built.
    b. to begin a new topic with creative projects so that students will become motivated to discover the discipline's structure.
    c. to provide a partial structure and a few central facts which are close to the student's current structure and later to add facts and revisions to the structure.
    d. first, to elicit from the students the facts and organizing principles they currently have and then to compare them with the correct structure as shown by the teacher.

8. Which of the following is a metacognitive process?
    a. Deciding how much time to spend on each part of a problem.
    b. Encoding, or elaborating on, a word in order to learn it.
    c. Using a mnemonic strategy.
    d. All of the above are example of metacognition.

9. In Bransford and Stein's IDEAL Problem Solver, finding a way to represent a problem (e.g., verbally or by drawing it) falls under the
   a. A
   b. E
   c. I
   d. D

10. When students are asked to choose sides on a debate and then are required to defend the opposing point of view, they are being given practice in
    a. the fractionation method.
    b. the reversal method.
    c. lateral thinking.
    d. dialogical thinking.

11. Students are given instruction in critical thinking skills in a one-hour-per-week special class, but then the teachers in math, science and social studies also give practice using the technique in their own classes. This is known as teaching thinking skills via
    a. the embedded (or domain-specific) curriculum.
    b. the detached (or domain-general) curriculum.
    c. a combination of a and b.
    d. a lateral thinking curriculum.

B. For Cooperative Study (in or out of class):

1. Have people self-nominate on the basis of their expertise in some area (e.g., music, chess, football, mathematics, etc.) and then take a problem in their field and explore the differences between how the experts and novices think about the problem. (In football, for example, a play can be observed or drawn and the expert will call attention to things the novice didn't see).

2. Discuss the author's assertion in study question 10. What does this imply for teachers' continuing education? What does it imply for research studies comparing teaching methods? What is your opinion?

3. Discuss the parts of Bransford and Stein's IDEAL Problem Solver. Take a problem and, in small groups, go through the steps until you reach a solution. If you need a problem, try this:

Problem 11.15: Find a number which has a remainder of 1 when it is divided by 2, 3, 4, 5, and 6, but which has no remainder when it is divided by 7.

4. Can the IDEAL Problem Solver be used in solving mysteries? in exploring personal problems? Give examples.

5. Practice some of the lateral thinking, brainstorming and other techniques mentioned as class or small group exercises.

C. For More Information:

1. Read some of the original sources for the methods of teaching intellectual skills described in this or chapter 4—for example, Sternberg, Bransford and Stein, Feuerstein, deBono, Lipman, and Paul—and make a written or oral report on their systems.

2. Using some of the problems in this or previous chapters, or problems of your own, teach a friend or a class what it means to use the IDEAL Problem Solver or a componential approach to improve higher order thinking skills. You may also wish to make an oral or written report on your experience.

3. Interview someone who is a recognized expert in some field to begin to find out (1) how his or her memory is structured; (2) how he or she thinks about problems in that field and, perhaps, other fields; and (3) how the person describes his or her own expertise. You may also wish to make an oral or written report on your findings.

UNIT FIVE

Expanding the Repertoire For Teaching

In the previous units, basic principles about development, emotions, behavior and cognition were presented. These were presented, for the most part, in the context of their application to home and school environments, but the emphasis was nevertheless on the principles. This unit addresses some of the same issues, but from the vantage point of instruction. The goal is to lay a foundation of instructional procedures and teacher decision making upon which can be built a continually expanding repertoire of teaching skills and, most importantly, a commitment to life-long growth as a teacher.

Chapter 12 begins the process by providing a comprehensive view of the kinds of decisions teachers need to make, using Hunter's essential elements of instruction. Next, other models of teaching are shown to be congruent with this view (e.g., Glaser's Gagné's, Rosenshine's and Shuell's) though each approaches the learning-teaching functions from slightly different angles. Next we consider Carroll's model of school learning and some of its implications for mastery learning (to be considered in more detail in chapter 13). Finally, we reconsider what it means to become an expert teacher, using Shulman's formulation. This presentation has the advantage of revisiting most of the concepts presented in previous chapters, but reorganized to fit into a structured view of what it means to teach. These models also allow us to pick up a few elements left out of previous discussions—for example, Bloom's taxonomy of educational objectives and such concepts as feedback.

Chapter 13 goes into some detail on instructional procedures in three important areas: (1) cooperative learning, (2) mastery learning, and (3) creative and critical thinking processes.

CHAPTER
Study Questions

1. What is Hunter's definition of teaching? What are the three decisions teachers need to make?
2. What is meant by each of the following major categories of essential elements?
   a. Selecting objectives at the correct level of difficulty
   b. Teaching to those objectives
   c. Monitoring progress and adjusting teaching
   d. Using principles of learning
3. What are the component parts of a good behavioral objective according to Mager?
4. What is a task analysis? How is it done?
5. What is Bloom's Taxonomy of Educational Objectives? What is meant by each of the following levels of cognitive complexity? Give examples.
   a. Knowledge
   b. Comprehension
   c. Application
   d. Analysis
   e. Synthesis
   f. Evaluation
6. What is meant by each of the following teacher actions?
   a. providing information
   b. asking questions
   c. designing activities
   d. giving responses
7. Give some examples of monitoring progress and adjusting teaching during a lesson.
8. What are the three parts of a good *anticipatory set*? Give examples of its correct use in classrooms.
9. Distinguish between *feedback* and *reinforcement*. Provide some correct and some incorrect examples of feedback.
10. What is meant by *active participation*? Explain by reference to the following, and give examples:
    a. overt vs. covert participation
    b. continual vs. eventual participation
11. Consider the following components of Glaser's instructional psychology:
    a. Specification of what is to be learned.
    b. Diagnosis of students' entering capabilities.

TWELVE

   c. Achievement of those objectives.
   d. Assessment of the direct and indirect effects of instruction.

   Compare these steps to Hunter's essential elements.

12. What is meant by each of the following ideas from Gagné's conditions of learning?
    a. learning hierarchy
    b. events of instruction
       (1) gaining attention
       (2) stating the objective
       (3) stimulating memory
       (4) presenting information
       (5) guiding the learning
       (6) eliciting performance
       (7) providing feedback
       (8) assessing performance
       (9) ensuring memory & transfer

    Compare these to Hunter's and Glaser's components of good instruction.

13. What is meant by a teaching-learning function in Shuell's conception? Give examples.
    a. Why is each function different for the teacher and the learner?
    b. How do Shuell's conceptions compare with those of Hunter, Glaser and Gagné?

14. What is meant by each of the following of Carroll's model of school learning?
    a. Time Needed To Learn
       (1) Aptitude
       (2) Quality of Instruction
       (3) Ability To Understand Instruction
    b. Time Actually Spent Learning
       (1) Perseverance
       (2) Opportunity to Learn

    How can these be used to estimate percent of learning attained?

15. What do each of the models of instruction—Hunter's, Glaser's, Gagné's, Shuell's, and Carroll's—say about which teaching methods (e.g., lecture vs. discovery) must be used to achieve satisfactory learning in their model?

16. What does Shulman mean by the following?
    a. pedagogical knowledge of teaching
    b. subject-matter content knowledge
    c. subject-matter pedagogical knowledge
    d. curricular knowledge

    Give examples from various fields.

Teaching Decisions and Functions

Introduction

". . . perhaps there are teachers who think they have done a good day's teaching irrespective of what pupils have learned."

"I represent that remark," thousands of us could answer. We want credit for our successful students, but not the blame for unsuccessful ones. After all, many students come to school from broken homes or from poverty conditions. Others, when they come to school at all, are in a chemical or psychological state that is not conducive to learning. Still others have not mastered prerequisite fundamentals, have poor work habits, or miss school so frequently that they have no continuity in their instruction. Potential excuses for unsuccessful learning, in other words, are not hard to find.

John Dewey, among others, might agree that the above paragraph is accurate, but he would still not let the teacher use these excuses. The more complete context of the opening quote is as follows (Dewey, 1933, pp. 35–36):

> We should ridicule a merchant who said that he had sold a great many goods although no one had bought any. But perhaps there are teachers who think they have done a good day's teaching irrespective of what pupils have learned. There is the same exact equation between teaching and learning that there is between buying and selling.

Teachers, like merchants, can be satisfied that their efforts were successful only for those who leave the encounter with a newly acquired package of skills or knowledge. Regarding those who leave empty handed, teachers as well as merchants must conclude that their efforts were not successful, at least not yet. Another tactic may be required.

If the merchant-teacher analogy breaks down, it is because the teaching-learning process is much more complex than the selling-buying process. You can buy and use something without understanding it, or even misunderstanding it, but knowledge or skills superficially learned or misunderstood will eventually be a liability. These facts make Dewey's point even more cogent for learning than for buying. Complex products can be sold with neither salesman nor customer understanding them. But complex fields can be taught only by experts, who can arrange conditions, often somewhat different for each learner, so that the learners acquire not only the fundamentals, but also the strategies, skills and motivation to continue refining and transferring those fundamentals to their lives beyond the classroom.

Educational psychology has long recognized the importance of a holistic approach to the teaching-learning process. Emotion, behavior (motivation), and cognition are widely recognized as three separable, but interconnecting and interdependent systems which affect the social-learning event we call teaching. It is therefore true that some classroom events are beyond the capability of teachers to affect. Heredity, home environment, and social conditions, after all, still account for more of the variance in student ranks on scholastic achievement than any teacher is likely to attain. Nevertheless, teachers can and do have important effects on students—their emotional, motivational and cognitive development.

WE NEED A HISTORY OF EDUCATION COURSE IN OUR DEPT. WHENEVER I MENTION DEWEY IN CLASS, STUDENTS THINK I AM GIVING THE WEATHER REPORT.

Cartoon 12.1

Although there is much we do not yet know about teaching, particularly what Shulman (1986) refers to as principles of instruction that are "subject-matter specific" (to which we shall return at the end of this chapter), there is much agreement about some of the generic principles of learning and instruction. We shall begin with some of the instructional models which incorporate those principles.

Madeline Hunter's Essential Elements of Instruction: Teaching as Decision-Making[1]

Hunter (1982, p. 3; see also 1979a; and 1984) defines teaching as a *"constant stream of professional decisions made before, during and after interaction with the student; decisions which, when implemented, increase the probability of learning."* Hunter would probably agree with Shavelson (1976) that many teacher decisions are made by forfeit—that is, by having too few alternatives available or by not recognizing that a decision can be made. This is all the more reason she stresses that we need to make these decisions consciously. Shavelson (1976, pp. 411–412) likewise wants teaching to be considered ". . . a process by which teachers consciously make rational decisions with the intention of optimizing student outcomes."

The professional decisions that comprise teaching occur in three major areas (Hunter, 1967e; 1971b; 1979a; 1982): (1) what to teach—the content; (2) how the students will learn and then demonstrate what they have learned; and (3) what teacher actions will be needed to accomplish (1) and (2). Each of these decisions is equally important. A learning task is an interaction of learner with material to be learned. Learning to fly a new airplane is a different task for an experienced pilot than for a novice (Hunter, 1967d), and the teacher's actions would therefore be quite different depending upon the objectives, the learner, and the manner in which learning will be demonstrated.

Before describing these three categories of decisions in more detail, it is worth noting that Hunter is most misunderstood on this point. Critics and supporters alike continue to define her model as a direct teaching method (e.g., Gibboney, 1987) or a series of steps in lesson design (e.g., Stallings, 1985; Stallings and Krasavage, 1986; Stallings et al. 1986; Slavin, 1986a; 1987; 1989), despite Hunter's repeated protestations. For example, she defended the definition of her model as follows in 1986 (p. 174):

The Hunter Model is a model of teacher decision making based on three categories: (1) content—what to teach, (2) learner behavior—what students will do to learn and to let the teacher know they have learned, and (3) teacher behavior—the teacher's use of research-based principles of learning that accelerate achievement. This model undergirds all models of teaching (discovery, cooperative learning, computer-based instruction, individualized instruction, auto instruction, etc.), not just direct teaching.

The first decision—what content to teach—is more complex than it may first appear. It is a decision about *selecting objectives to be taught at the correct level of difficulty.* Thus it goes right to the heart of the curriculum as it interacts with the entering behavior and knowledge of the students. It requires a *task analysis* of the curriculum, to break a given topic into its component parts and, further, to order those components incrementally in order of difficulty so that students are not struggling with more advanced concepts before prerequisites are mastered. It also requires a *diagnosis* of the student's ". . . present status in relation to that objective" (Hunter, 1966, p. 546). It is sometimes presumed that the content decision has either been already made by the textbook publisher, a school board, or a legislative body such as a board of regents. But textbook writers and legislative bodies can only provide a general outline for a course. It is the teacher who interacts with the student and who, therefore, makes day-to-day *content decisions.* Likewise, it is sometimes possible for students to have input into the content to be studied, and how independently (Hunter and Brown, 1979). Nevertheless, Hunter reminds us (1971c; 1982) that in all these cases, the teacher maintains the responsibility for the results of content decisions, whether they were delegated or not. If student learning suffers, then the teacher is responsible for correcting the problem.

The second decision—what students will do to learn and to demonstrate their learning—requires the teacher to specify before instruction begins how learning will be assessed. This will also have implications for how the material is to be presented; for example, if students will be expected to converse in a foreign language, much of the material should be practiced in dialogues, not presented solely through lectures. If students are expected to solve problems, then perhaps guided discovery or inquiry may be the learning mode. Student performance also requires a decision about the *level of cognitive processing* to be required in learning each objective. For example, students may be asked simply to memorize definitions, to apply their knowledge in a new situation, or to evaluate two or more courses of action. These different levels of thinking—known as knowledge, application, and evaluation, respectively—are part of a hierarchy of possible levels of complexity of instructional objectives (e.g., Bloom's, 1956, taxonomy). More will be said on this later. For now the important point is that how students learn and then demonstrate their learning is another important teacher decision.

The third teacher decision—and Hunter emphasizes that it must follow the other two—is what teacher actions will be taken to facilitate the student's learning of the objectives. Teacher actions fall into four basic types: (1) providing information, (2) asking questions, (3) designing activities, and (4) responding to students. Each of these is important, but variations of some of them will be more or less important depending on what is to be taught and how students will demonstrate it has been learned. In other words, teaching method—dialogue, inquiry, direct instruction, etc.—depends on the content objectives and student performances required. In any case, Hunter stresses, it is critical that important principles of learning be known and appropriately used by teachers. These fall under the general headings of reinforcement, retention, motivation, and transfer.

The flow diagram in figure 12.1 is one way of portraying Hunter's model to show how all the parts interact with one another. Thus, despite considerable planning for a lesson, a teacher may discover as it is being taught that

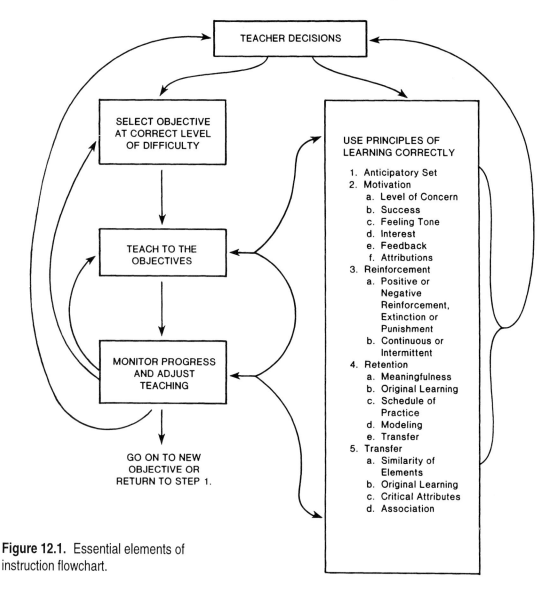

Figure 12.1. Essential elements of instruction flowchart.

it is not being well-received by some students. This produces a need to diagnose the problem:

- Is it a motivation problem?
- Do the students have prerequisite knowledge?
- Is there a transfer problem?
- Etc.

Based on the diagnosis, the teacher may decide to change the content (e.g., review prerequisite material), to change the classroom activities (e.g., from lecture to small groups), to deal with a discipline problem, or whatever. In such ways all four essential elements interact to produce teacher decisions which, hopefully, increase the probability of learning.

The complete list of essential elements, as figure 12.1 shows, is quite formidable and we shall not have the space to consider each variable in detail in this chapter. Nor is it necessary, since we have already devoted a chapter each to reinforcement, retention, and transfer. Thus I shall refer to those concepts only to point out how they fit into Hunter's model and to show their relation to other essential elements. For a more complete account of Hunter's model of instruction, her approach to clinical supervision, and a critique of her model and her critics, see Gentile (1993) and Hunter (1994).

Selecting Objectives at the Correct Level

If you ask teachers what they are teaching, they may say, "statistics" or "medical terminology," or "Julius Caesar." Most educational researchers would wish to clarify such statements by pointing out that one does not teach broad topics, except via the specific subcomponents of those general goals. The specific skills, knowledges and attitudes which comprise the goals of a unit can be succinctly stated as behavioral objectives.

Writing Objectives

In their most general definition, objectives provide a description of what the student will be able to do at the end of a lesson. This includes the specific content to be learned, as well as the observable behavior that the student will perform to demonstrate mastery of the objective. In a more narrow definition (e.g., Mager, 1962) behavioral objectives have at least three parts—they state (1) the behavior to be performed (in clear observable terms); (2) the level of performance required, and (3) the conditions under which the performance will occur. For example, "Given ten distributions of scores (whole numbers), the student will be able to identify correctly the medians in at least nine of the ten." In this example, the behavior is calculating the median, the standard is 90% correct, and the conditions are given ten distributions of scores.

Other variations on how to write behavioral objectives are also widely used. For example, Kibler, Barker and Miles (1970) suggest that each objective include the following five parts: (1) who is to perform, (2) the actual behavior, (3) the result (i.e., product or performance), (4) the relevant conditions under which the behavior is to be performed, and (5) the standard to be attained. The above example for calculating the median has all five of these parts: (1) the student (2) will calculate (3) the median of the scores, (4) when given a set of ten distributions, (5) to an accuracy of 90%.

Hunter and her advocates place great stress on objectives because they provide a blueprint for the teaching decisions described in the previous section. They adopt the simpler definition of objectives, consisting of two major parts—namely, the specific content to be learned and the observable behavior with which the student will demonstrate that learning occurred. The standard remains implicit in the student's demonstrable behavior. See table 12.1 for examples of poorly-stated and better-stated objectives.

Task Analysis

Objectives, no matter how expertly stated, facilitate instruction only if they match the entering capabilities of the students. To achieve a match between any given student and the objective requires an assessment of the student's capabilities in relation to the planned curriculum. That, in turn, is based on a task analysis.

Workshops on the Hunter model give practice doing task analyses through the following four steps:

1. Set an instructional objective that you wish students to achieve.
2. Clarify the meaning of that objective by defining it, as in the previous section, to be sure what is to be included and what isn't.

Table 12.1 Poorly-stated and better-stated objectives.

Poor	Better
1. The student will understand the events leading to the Civil War.	1a. *As a Behavioral Objective:* The Student will list in writing three major differences between the North and the South which led to the Civil War. 1b. *As a Study Question:* Identify and explain at least three major differences between the North and South which led to the Civil War.
2. The student will know the concepts of symmetry and line of symmetry.	2a. *As a Behavioral Objective:* Given pictures of ten objects, the student will be able (1) to sort them into symmetrical piles, and (2) for those which are symmetrical, to draw the line(s) of symmetry. 2b. *As a Study Question:* Draw at least two symmetrical and two nonsymmetrical figures, and for the symmetrical ones fold the paper along the line(s) of symmetry.

3. Make a list of essential sub-objectives which appear to be prerequisite to the major objective by a brainstorming or free association technique. Then go through the list and purge those which are not necessary for this objective.
4. Order the essential sub-objectives in their necessary sequence (i.e., x must be learned before y), if there is one.

The final ordering is a *task analysis: a list of the essential objectives in the necessary (or best) sequence for the achievement of a final objective.*

For example, if the concept to be taught is negative reinforcement, then one clarification of the objective might be stated as follows: Given descriptions of behavioral interactions, the student will be able to discriminate those which demonstrate examples of negative reinforcement from those which do not, with an accuracy of not less than 80%. Brainstorming the prerequisites might include defining or recognizing stimuli, reinforcing stimuli, aversive stimuli, responses, positive reinforcement situations, extinction situations, punishment situations, etc. Purging the list would probably eliminate extinction and punishment, and would probably keep the rest. Ordering the list would probably require that stimuli and responses be learned first, followed by types of stimuli, and then by the sequence of events known as positive reinforcement. Positive reinforcement may, in fact, not be necessary for learning negative reinforcement (though that is an empirical question), despite the fact that it is traditionally taught before negative reinforcement.

Once the task analysis has been completed, then the teacher can begin the lesson by reviewing what the students know (to jog the memory and facilitate transfer) and introduce the new concepts at the appropriate point in this sequence of objectives.[2]

It may be noted that there is no necessary contradiction between the task analysis described above, and the more constructivist idea of spiral curriculum (after Bruner, 1960). In the spiral curriculum, students revisit concepts in math, say, at increasing levels of complexity commensurate with their developmental and instructional readiness throughout the math curriculum. In addition, well-planned programs may have the same math concepts appear in science, social studies and other subjects as well, so that students are less compartmentalized in their thinking about the subject. While there are probably few programs actually doing this well, it is a goal that, as far as I can see, all "task analysis" theorists (see note 2) would find laudatory. They would probably also go on to point out that the ordering of the various spirals would benefit from a task analysis.

Bloom's Taxonomy

The final issue regarding objectives concerns the complexity of the cognitive processing to be required. For this purpose, Hunter (1982) adopts Bloom's taxonomy of instructional objectives. Bloom's (1956) taxonomy distinguishes six levels of complexity in cognitive processing. These follow:

1. *Knowledge:* Knowledge objectives mostly emphasize the cognitive process of remembering: recall of specific facts, terminology, and procedures, and ways of organizing and classifying (e.g., When did Columbus discover America? Define positive reinforcement. What are the six levels of cognitive complexity in Bloom's taxonomy?).
2. *Comprehension:* Objectives at this level emphasize the beginning stages of understanding of the material, including the capacity to translate or paraphrase, interpret or extrapolate material (e.g., What is the central idea in the paragraph? Translate this sentence from English into Japanese. From a graph of average heights and weights in one-inch increments from 5' to 6', predict what the average weight would be of a person who is 6' 1" tall).
3. *Application:* Objectives at this level involve the transfer of knowledge to a new situation, usually involving some abstraction of a general principle (e.g., How much carpeting is needed to cover a 10' × 13' room and a 4' x 12' hallway? How might a teacher use the procedure of "time out" to stop a child from swearing in class?).
4. *Analysis:* Analysis objectives require students to find the constituent parts of a larger whole, so that the structure and relationship of the parts become explicit (e.g., Describe the molecular structure of carbohydrates. Given a real discipline situation between student and teacher, identify how the behavior of each acts as stimulus for the other—i.e., do a "social learning analysis." Classify each word according to the grammatical function it serves in a given sentence.).
5. *Synthesis:* Objectives at this level engage the capacity to structure component parts into a (logical) whole, including literary or artistic compositions, and the production of a plan or blueprint (e.g., Write a report on the legal, psychological, economic, and physiological effects of taking cocaine. Propose a plan for dealing with severe discipline problems in your school. Write a 32-bar musical composition in the key of Db in 3/4 time for string quartet).
6. *Evaluation:*[3] Evaluation objectives require judgments about the value or utility of materials, methods or courses of action for given purposes, in terms of the internal consistency of the position or some external criteria (e.g., Compare drug vs. biofeedback treatments for a hyperactive child in terms of their side effects and probable success. Rank your state's congressmen in terms of their voting record on environmental issues. Compare the claims made by advertisers of two competing products).

Examples of appropriately written objectives for each of these categories for three general goals are provided in table 12.2. Such examples make explicit what teachers recognize implicitly—namely, that for any type of knowledge at any entering level, there are still great variations in the complexity of cognitive processing required by the teacher. Making these levels explicit has the major advantage of forcing the teacher to identify and develop the kind of student activities, projects and test items that will provide evidence that they can perform at that level. This is central to the "essential elements" approach since it is part of all three of the teaching decisions Hunter identified. Furthermore, it avoids the all-too-common situation in which teachers glibly claim to be teaching higher-order thinking, while their tests assess learning at a much simpler level.

As the examples in table 12.2 make explicit, it is possible to teach all levels of thinking in all areas of the curriculum and at every age level. It is certainly easier to teach at the lower levels of thinking, particularly in primary school, and leave the higher levels of thinking for later grades. Such an approach, however, conditions teachers and students alike to consider schooling as little more than the accumulation of isolated facts; whatever organization and thinking skills the students have will surely atrophy under such instruction.

Recent scholars (e.g., Baron & Sternberg, 1987; Costa, 1985; Feuerstein et al., 1980) emphasize that thinking skills may be more basic than facts, and rules—an idea that permeates the new math standards (NCTM, 1989). All recognize that thinking at higher levels—whether using Bloom's taxonomy or not[4]—must be integral to the curriculum. Moreover, in the spirit of the taxonomy, lessons can sometimes start with basic knowledge and proceed to higher levels of thinking, but lessons will often be more exciting if they begin with application or analysis and provoke the need to discover information.

As mentioned in note 3, Hunter's conception of the Evaluation Level of Bloom's taxonomy is different from the one I presented above. In my experience, many educators take Evaluation to be a more affective, opinion-like objective than Bloom meant it to be in the cognitive domain. In commenting on an earlier draft of this review, Hunter said that what I called Evaluation was mostly Analysis. Because there is so much general confusion on this, I shall rest my case on the original source, Bloom (1956), who states:

Evaluation is defined as the making of judgments about the value, for some purpose, of ideas, works, solutions, methods, material, etc. It involves the use of criteria as well as standards for appraising the extent to which particulars are accurate, effective, economical, or satisfying. The judgments may be either quantitative or qualitative, and the criteria may be either those determined by the student or those which are given to him.

Evaluation is placed at this point in the taxonomy because it is regarded as being at a relatively late stage in a complex process which involves some combination of all the other behaviors of Knowledge, Comprehension, Application, Analysis, and Synthesis. What is added are criteria including values. Evaluation represents not only an end process in dealing with cognitive behaviors, but also a major link with the affective behaviors where values, liking, and enjoying (and their absence or contraries) are the central processes involved. However, the emphasis here is still largely cognitive rather than emotive. (p. 185)

Later:

For the most part, the evaluations customarily made by an individual are quick decisions not preceded by very careful consideration or the various aspects of the object, idea, or activity being judged. These might more properly be termed opinions, rather than judgments.

Table 12.2 Example of objectives for each of the six levels of cognitive complexity for three general educational goals.

The following are examples for three different curriculum areas of how general educational goals can be translated into instructional objectives for each level of the cognitive domain taxonomy.

A. **GOAL:** The student will comprehend and appreciate (the Disney version of) "Beauty and the Beast."

   1. **Knowledge:** After reading or seeing the story, the student will be able to identify the following characters: Beauty, the Beast, the Prince, Gaston.
   2. **Comprehension:** After reading or seeing the story, the student will be able to tell in his or her own words how the Prince came to have a curse on him, what the curse is, and how he can have it removed.
   3. **Application:** After discussing the various meanings of "beast" and "beauty," the student will be able to give an example of when he or she was a "beast" to someone else and when he or she was a "beauty" to someone.
   4. **Analysis:** After discussing how the Beast captured first her father and then Beauty, the student will describe at least two things in the Beast's life which might have contributed to the Beast's behavior.
   5. **Synthesis:** Upon reconsidering the story up to the point where the townsfolk discover the existence of the Beast, the student will write a different ending that includes cooperating with the Beast instead of killing him.
   6. **Evaluation:** After discussing the meanings of brotherhood and self-esteem, the student will give examples from the story which compare the extent to which Beauty, the Beast, and Gaston have high self-esteem or practice brotherhood.

B. **GOAL:** The student will grasp the importance of exploration and the discovery of the New World.

   1. **Knowledge:** Given a list of dates and explorers, the student will be able to match the explorer with the correct date.
   2. **Comprehension:** After studying the scientific context of the Fifteenth Century, the student will describe in his or her own words why Columbus believed he could sail west to reach the East.
   3. **Application:** After reading about the Columbus voyage and a recent manned space voyage in the news, the student will list at least three similarities between the two missions.
   4. **Analysis:** After reading about the economic climate and trade policies of Spain, Italy, and Portugal in the late Fifteenth Century, the student will be able to write at least two reasons why Columbus, an Italian, sailed under the banner of Spain.
   5. **Synthesis:** After studying a unit on exploration of the New World, the student will write a dialogue between a European explorer and an American aboriginal, incorporating at least two arguments that each could have used to defend the following proposition: "What do you mean you discovered us? We discovered you."
   6. **Evaluation:** Considering the different religions, types of governance, and treatment of humans and the environment, the student will compare the post-Columbus development of the new world with what might have happened had one or more aboriginal cultures dominated until the Twentieth Century.

Table 12.2 *(Continued)*

C. GOAL: The student will understand the calculation and uses of the mean and standard deviation.

1. **Knowledge:** Given the formulas, the student will be able to match each symbol with its meaning.
2. **Comprehension:** Given a set of scores, the student will be able to calculate the mean and standard deviation, correct to within two decimal places.
3. **Application:** Given classroom scores on a test, the student will be able to calculate the mean and standard deviation of the scores and show in standard deviation units, the relative standing of the students.
4. **Analysis:** By inventing hypothetical data, the student will be able to demonstrate that the sum of the squared deviations from the mean will be smaller than the sum of the squared deviations from any other point in the distribution.
5. **Synthesis:** Given the mean and standard deviation, the student will be able to draw three plausible plots of the distribution of scores.
6. **Evaluation:** Given two or more distributions of scores, the student will be able to calculate their means and standard deviations and describe their relative variabilities for norm-referenced vs. criterion-referenced purposes.

Customarily, opinions are made at less than a full conscious level and the individual may not be fully aware of the clues or bases on which he is forming his appraisals. For purposes of classification, only those evaluations which are or can be made with distinct criteria in mind are considered. Such evaluations are highly conscious and ordinarily are based on a relatively adequate comprehension and analysis of the phenomena to be appraised. It is recognized that this may be far from the normal state of affairs. It is, however, based on a recognition that educational procedures are intended to develop the more desirable rather than the more customary types of behavior. (p. 186)

Hunter's (1982) chapter on this topic is entitled "Extending Their Thinking," because she points out that teachers need to make a special effort to elicit the higher levels of thinking. To do this requires that the various levels can be distinguished and objectives written for them. In Staff Development workshops, Hunter and her colleagues provide supervised practice writing such objectives, and then teaching to those objectives (the subject of the next section). Practice writing well-stated objectives at the different levels of Bloom's taxonomy is extremely useful, at least until the teacher finds that converting a general goal into an objective is becoming an automatic process. When the teacher is expert at this, shortcuts might be taken, such as (1) leaving out the standard of performance, because you have a general standard for an instructional unit, or (2) writing the objectives in the form of study questions. Teachers for whom writing objectives is not yet an automatic process, however, would be well-advised to practice being explicit about the cognitive level and completeness of each objective, at least until their teaching and testing is consistently congruent with the stated objectives.

Teaching to Objectives

If selecting objectives at the correct level of difficulty is the first step in teaching, the second step is *teaching to those objectives*. This means that *the teacher's actions and students' behaviors must be congruent with the objectives of*

Photo 12.1. Planning a lesson with a supervisor.

the lesson. "Congruent with" implies leading directly toward, not just "related to" or "associated with." While this may appear too obvious to mention, there are many teachers, who (in Hunter's words) "birdwalk" all over the place pecking at each interesting idea with what is to them an interesting and informative digression. The student (or a classroom observer) is often left wondering, "How did we get on this topic?"

As noted in the last chapter, constructivist theory often uses a construction metaphor to describe the knowledge acquisition process (e.g., Glaser, 1984). This seems appropriate for teaching congruently with the objectives because:

- The new structure of knowledge must be adapted to the foundation on which it is to be built.
- Temporary structures may need to be built to even begin.
- To reach higher and higher, old scaffolds will have to be replaced with new ones through the course of several lessons.

There is no "best method" for accomplishing the above and Hunter was an advocate for continual expansion of the teacher's repertoire of methods. Thus discovery learning, cooperative teams, individualized instruction, writing projects, and active participation even during lectures were all advocated (e.g., Hunter, 1986; Hunter & Brown, 1979; see, for example, anecdote 12.1). Whatever method is chosen, too many diversions will make it more probable (to continue the construction metaphor) that people will fall through the cracks.

This does not mean that there is no room for spontaneity in a classroom, nor that teachers should ignore students' questions. But an irrelevant question or comment by a student will interrupt the logic of the lesson and therefore interfere with other students' attempts to organize the information in the lesson. Thus the questioner's comment needs to be "dignified," as Hunter phrases it, without causing a digression. "You're way ahead of me. You've just given an example of something I planned to get into later." Then, after the lesson has been completed, bring up the issue and give credit to the student for raising it. Regarding spontaneity in general, there are indeed times when the lesson needs to be postponed in favor of something of immediate and higher priority. For instance, the teacher may discover that too many students are confused on a prerequisite concept, or a very emotional event, such as the death of a classmate, may disrupt plans. In such events, the teacher's decision to reteach a concept or to deal with the disruptive event constitutes a change of objectives. This, again, is an example of what Hunter means by teaching as decision-making.

In a way, such exceptions prove the rule. If there is to be time for genuinely useful spontaneity and student-generated examples, then the crucial informative lessons need to be that much more efficient; thus the importance of congruence between the objective and the classroom activities. In the Hunter model, classroom

Anecdote 12.1

Contrasting Methods for Teaching to Objectives

Consider this lesson. The teacher shows a series of objects (or pictures or drawings) one at a time, and begins to sort them. She places the letter A, a square, and a star on one table and the letter P, an irregular polygon, and a cutout hand on another table. As she does so, she asks her elementary students to think of the rule that makes all the objects on the first table different from those on the other. She then continues with new objects—a dog, a Valentine's Day Heart, a circle, the number 2—and has the students think alone or in small groups to agree on the rule. When they have mostly discovered the critical attributes of symmetry, perhaps without anyone voicing the word, the definition is considered. The students are then given application/transfer exercises by classifying objects in the room.

An alternative approach would be to ask if anyone knows what symmetry is, define the word, and announce how today's lesson will help them categorize real-life objects as symmetrical or not. Then the same examples could be given with students working alone, in small groups, or as a class, along with the follow-up transfer task.

These two contrasting methods—the first a *concept attainment* method, the second a direct instruction method—are both congruent with the objectives. Both have much active participation. Both lead naturally to subsequent lessons on lines of symmetry; geometrical flips, turns, and slides; and creative projects. In the first method, the students had to discover the purpose and objective of the lesson; in the second the teacher announced the purpose and objective.

activities are described in relation to four types of *teacher actions,* in no necessary order:

1. *Providing Information* on the concepts in the lesson.
2. *Asking Questions* designed to cause the information to be reprocessed, organized, discovered, etc.
3. *Designing Activities* that will allow students during class to learn, practice, and transfer the material, as well as to demonstrate what has been learned.
4. *Giving Responses* to students' questions and providing feedback on their practice attempts and thought processes.

Not all of these teacher actions will occur in every lesson, but whatever ones are used in a lesson should be congruent with the objectives. When they are, instruction can hardly help but be facilitated (as research on teaching effectiveness indicates; e.g., Brophy and Good, 1986; Rosenshine, 1986; Rosenshine and Stevens, 1986). Moreover, as many have argued (e.g., Cronbach, 1966; Gentile, 1993; Hunter, 1986; Joyce, Weil & Showers, 1992), the search for "one best method" is elusive, counter-productive, and sometimes downright silly. Consider the following exchange I have often heard:

Student: "But if a student doesn't discover a concept, he or she won't really learn it."
Professor: "Where did you learn that?"
Student: "My professor told us in a lecture."

The solution, therefore, is to have many methods in your repertoire to hook into each child's styles and backgrounds, or just to maintain interest.

Monitoring Progress and Adjusting Teaching

The third essential of teaching is to monitor the students' progress and adjust the teaching accordingly. Because they have to give grades, if for no other reason, most teachers monitor student learning, at least periodically in midterm and final examinations. Such infrequent and formal assessment of student learning may appear to be both necessary and sufficient for monitoring progress. *Unfortunately, it is neither necessary nor sufficient.* It is not necessary because there are other, better methods for assessing learning and grading students, such as formative and mastery testing (as we shall explore in Chapter 14). Infrequent exams such as midterms and finals are not sufficient because they come much too late to allow the teacher to adjust the teaching to correct misconceptions, provide additional practice, and so forth. Whether or not midterms and finals are used, in other words, teachers must monitor progress from hour to hour, and perhaps minute to minute, to be able to be most facilitative of student learning.

This is the essence of what is meant by *monitoring progress and adjusting teaching: immediate responsiveness to what students are digesting and what they are not.* In athletic and artistic fields regular monitoring of whether the lesson is being absorbed is much more common than in academic fields. For example, after demonstrating the forehand groundstroke in tennis, no self-respecting tennis coach would move on to the backhand before giving students practice and helping each correct errors. The same would be true of a piano teacher. After a brief lesson on expression or technique, the students will have to demonstrate their understanding with appropriate adjustments made by the coach. Similarly, academic teachers need to interrupt their lectures to find out whether anyone other than the teacher is learning the material. Obviously this is more easily accomplished in small classes than in large ones, but useful techniques are available to monitor student learning, even in large classes.

Hunter (1979b; 1982) describes several ways to monitor progress in large classes. One way is to pose a basic question or statement and then have every student *signal the answer*. With their fingers students can make the first letter of the word which best answers the question, or they can raise one hand if a sentence provides an example of x. As Hunter recognizes, signaling answers in this way may be considered "baby stuff" by many, or may allow students who do not know what is going on to copy those who do, and may even be dangerous (e.g., if you ask young teenagers to wave one finger in the air, you are asking for a riot). Thus, to counteract the "baby stuff" objection she recommends explaining that the purpose is for the teacher to check understanding. To keep students from copying each other, the students can be asked to close their eyes. And to avoid "the finger," teachers can have students write answers on individual slates or hold up previously constructed flash cards, or be more creative in the kind of signal required.

Other techniques are (1) the age-old *choral response,* in which students vocalize together the answer to a question; (2) *sampling individual responses,* where you ask a question of the whole class, then call on an individual to answer; (3) a *one-minute paper,* brief written response, mini-diagnostic test or exercise. All these allow the teacher to sample quickly what students have learned or how they are thinking and make a decision during the instruction about what to do next.

Another technique, that is especially useful and effective for large classes at the secondary and tertiary level, is to arrange students in pairs and *have each member of the pair teach the other member* one of the concepts. This technique is based on the assumption that you find out if you really know something when you try to teach it. While the students are practicing their learning by teaching it, they will also discover what they know and do not know and thus formulate good questions. The teacher, meanwhile, can rotate through the class and discover which concepts of the lesson were well-understood and which were confusing and need additional examples. Note that small groups are not used for this exercise because it is too easy for them to be dominated by one person. In pairs, in which each person has a specific teaching assignment, the dominance problem can be minimized. This technique has several advantages: (1) it takes only a few moments out of a lesson; (2) it keeps the students actively participating and practicing what they need to know; (3) it allows the teacher to monitor student learning; (4) it generates questions which are congruent with the lesson's objectives; and, therefore, (5) it allows the teacher to adjust the teaching by finding new examples and responding to

Photo 12.2. Cooperative pairs in a Chinese classroom. *(Photo Courtesy of Dr. Thomas J. Shuell)*

questions that were generated by serious students. Besides, students claim to enjoy the technique.

We shall return to some of these issues in later sections, but it should be clear that good teaching requires diagnosing what is being learned *during the lesson* (Good, 1983; Rosenshine and Stevens, 1986). Otherwise, by the time the teacher discovers students' misconceptions, they may have become habitual and all the more difficult to change. A major error in this regard is made by teachers who rush to complete a lesson at the sound of a bell and then assign homework problems for practice. But the teacher did not find out if anyone can do the problems correctly in the first place. For those who can, practice may provide useful

Anecdote 12.2

Which Teacher Would You Hire?

Madeline Hunter provided the following scenario to a conference of school administrators (Buffalo, NY, March 20, 1987).

Two prospective English teachers were asked to be prepared to teach a lesson on the uses of the colon and semicolon to an actual class, while being observed by the hiring committee.

Teacher A efficiently gave the definitions, had students open their books to problems 1–6, and called on six students, one by one, to see whether they could identify if the sentences needed colons or semicolons. Teacher A then asked if there were any questions. When there were no more questions, A assigned the class problems 7–20, which they could begin now and continue for the remainder of the class.

Teacher B efficiently gave the same definitions, and likewise had the students open their books to problems 1–6. But B had the entire class signal the answers by making colons and semicolons with their fingers (demonstrating how). Then Teacher B asked students to close their eyes and signal for the next sentences, using problems 7–20 as a test. B then assigned the class to write 5 sentences—some with colons, some with semicolons—about themselves for homework, which they could begin now. B then took four students who had done poorly during the eyes-closed test to the back of the room to give more instruction on the distinction. She used personalized examples designed to enhance these slower learning students' fragile egos. For example, she gave Mary the following sentence to punctuate: "Mary is very attractive: she dresses with good taste."

Which teacher would you hire?

overlearning and transfer to new problems. For those who cannot, practice may be stamping in a bad habit, may be a frustrating experience, and may therefore be counterproductive. While the teacher can reteach the misunderstood concepts after the homework assignments are corrected a day or two later, it is much more efficient to have students practice correctly in the first place (see anecdote 12.2).

To summarize what it means to monitor progress and adjust teaching, consider that you have just presented information congruent with the lesson's objectives. Then the "monitor and adjust" steps might be the following:

1. Have all the students perform some observable behavior congruent with the objectives.
2. Check the behavior.
3. Interpret whether the behavior is sufficiently accurate and complete to go on, or what might be necessary to correct errors of omission or commission.
4. Act accordingly—that is, move on to the next concepts, reteach, provide additional practice, and so on.

Cartoon 12.2

Using Principles of Learning

The fourth major component of the "essential elements" is *correctly using principles of learning*. By this Hunter means all of the items in the righthand box of figure 12.1, which is essentially everything in a general educational psychology text: knowing the principles and uses of reinforcement, motivation, memory, transfer, etc. Since we have already covered those issues in some detail in previous chapters, I shall not repeat them here. However, three principles of learning—stressed heavily in Hunter's staff development workshops—seem so important for improving both novice and expert teachers that they deserve to be highlighted here. Those principles concern anticipatory set, feedback, and active participation.

Anticipatory Set

The beginning of each new lesson provides the challenge of how to change the focus of students' attention from previous classes and the social agenda toward the current objectives. Most teachers want their students to be prepared with texts, notebooks and sharpened pencils, when the lesson is about to begin. In addition to these physical signs of preparedness, it is important to have students mentally prepared for the lesson. This means that the students should have retrieved from their memories the relevant terms, facts, principles and organizational structures with which the current lesson is most related. The teacher's opening comments and routines may hinder or facilitate the current lesson by the associations they elicit from the students. Rather than allow this to be unplanned, the opening of each lesson should be a conscious decision of the teacher.

Creating the proper *anticipatory set*, then, is the teacher's plan to stimulate the students to retrieve from memory the prior skills and knowledge that are relevant to the current lesson. This means (1) that the student must actively do something, overtly or covertly; (2) that the student must have the prerequisites in memory and those concepts must be elicited by what the teacher asks the students to do; and (3) that what is elicited is congruent with the lesson's objectives.

Marilyn Bates[5] tells the following story of a second grade classroom she observed. Taking advantage of the fact that the circus had recently been in town, the teacher opened the lesson by asking, "Did you go to the circus? What did you see?" Various children answered, "I saw a lion," "I saw the clown," etc. The teacher responded, "Good. Anything else." Finally someone said, "I saw the ringmaster." The teacher said, "Great. I was hoping someone saw the ringmaster, because ringmaster is a *compound word*." Imagine the students' emotional letdown when they discovered that the circus was introduced to trick them into studying compound words. The introductory comments established a set which quite likely provided cognitive and emotional interference for the lesson's objectives—that is, the kind of perceptual or mental set known to produce proactive interference on problem-solving and transfer (Ellis, 1965; 1969; Luchins, 1942; Schulz, 1960; Underwood, 1957). Use of a good anticipatory set, then, is the antidote for such interference and is therefore part of the process of teaching for positive transfer (see chapter 9).

The positive effect of eliciting relevant associates and prerequisite principles just prior to presenting a lesson is also similar to research on the comprehension of prose (e.g., Bransford and Johnson, 1972; Dooling and Lachman, 1971). Finally, the research on *advance organizers* is relevant here, since Ausubel (1960; 1963) provided empirical support for the notion that the learning of facts and principles is greatly facilitated when prerequisite concepts and organizing principles are, first, available in memory and, moreover, retrieved in the context of the new lesson.

What are some exemplary anticipatory sets? Often they can be quite simple, as by posing a problem that is similar to one the students have solved before and asking them to identify the component parts of it. Then you might check the students' behavior and, when ready, point out how today's lesson builds on one or more of those parts. For example, "Last week we learned to conjugate the German verb `machen.' Take one minute to do that again now." After sampling their recall, the teacher can say, "Today we will study two other verbs which follow the same pattern and one which does not." As another example, if you are going to study the refraction of light, place a pencil in a glass of water and ask the students to draw what they see.

Before leaving the principle of anticipatory set, a few words should be said about the entire start-up process for a class. Hunter (1982) calls the early moments of each class "prime time" which should not be wasted on administrative trivia or "soap opera activity." She recommends giving the students a review activity to do while papers are being passed out, roll is being taken, or other "settling in" is occurring. This is most easily accomplished by a routine in which an assignment is on the board. If the review assignment evokes recall of material relevant to the day's lesson, a good anticipatory set has been set in motion even before the teacher's opening comments. At the close of the anticipatory set the teacher can then tell the students the objective for the lesson and further focus their thinking. Or, if the students are to discover the objective, the teacher can focus their thinking by informing them of that.

Feedback

Knowledge of results or feedback, as presented by Hunter (1982), is *specific information on which parts of a performance were correct and which were not, along with how to correct or improve them.* Returning a student's paper with a grade, but no comments on it, obviously does not provide feedback. *Specific information* is required: "Your spelling and punctuation were correct; however, you used x incorrectly. Instead it should be y." "Your position at the net was OK and you held your tennis racket correctly, but to return a ball below your waist, you should bend your knees to get down to the ball. Like this (and demonstrate)." With general feedback ("You're doing a good job" or "That was terrible") or none at all, progress will be slow, if there is any at all.

Probably the earliest research on knowledge of results was done on the acquisition of motor skills. In reviewing that research, Bilodeau and Bilodeau (1961) concluded that feedback was the most fundamental determinant of performance—that there is no improvement without it, that there is progressive improvement with it, and that there is deterioration if it is withdrawn. Indeed, any classroom demonstration can convince you that performance of a skill (e.g., mirror drawing, ring tossing) does not improve if visual and auditory feedback is deliberately withheld. Although there is not as much research on feedback's effects on cognitive tasks, there is every reason to expect that it is at least as important, particularly in this age of breaking complex intellectual tasks into their component skills.[6]

Similarly, feedback should be received as close in time to the performance as possible—that is, it should be immediate. Hunter recommends active class participation, brief tests and one page papers to allow the teacher to provide such immediate knowledge of results. This is not because humans are not able to remember from hour to hour or even day to day, but because intervening activities are likely to interfere (retroactive interference) with recall (Bilodeau and Bilodeau, 1958). To return to a tennis example, if your coach commented on a stroke you made five minutes ago, it might be helpful if you had not hit a shot since. However, if you had been hitting shots continuously since then, the delay in the feedback would be fatal. In parallel fashion, giving feedback on problems the students completed days ago, is much less helpful than more immediate knowledge of results, especially if they have done intervening problems.

We cannot leave the topic of feedback without mentioning its similarities to and differences from reinforcement. Feedback really has two components: (1) it provides specific information—a cognitive component; and (2) it can provide reinforcement—a behavioral, motivational (operant) component. Since any consequence of a behavior that increases the likelihood of that behavior occurring again is, by definition, a reinforcer, a teacher's attention ("That's good," "Um-hm," etc.) can provide reinforcement without giving information. Similarly, specific information about an error and how to correct it may provide feedback, but if the student refuses to try again, that feedback can hardly be said to be reinforcing (since the definition of reinforcement requires that the behavior increase or be maintained in frequency). Nevertheless, specific knowledge of results often does fulfill both the cognitive and motivational functions. Because the two functions do not always overlap, it may be didactically useful to think of feedback as usually operating on the cognitive level and reinforcement on the behavioral (operant) level.

Active Participation

Throughout the preceding "elements," active participation of the students has been stressed. This is not because learning without doing is impossible (most people learn that rattlesnakes are dangerous without handling them), nor because doing is always sufficient for learning, but ". . . in most cases active involvement in that which is to be learned accelerates learning" (Hunter, 1971c, p. 163). Theorists as diverse as Piaget and Skinner make active participation central for education: "To know an object is to act upon it and to transform it . . . " (Piaget, 1970a, p. 29); "A good program of instruction guarantees a great deal of successful action." (Skinner, 1984, p. 952).

Active participation means *continually involving all* the students in the lesson (Hunter, 1967d). Involvement can be overt (observable) or covert (such as thinking), but it can never just be assumed. From the cognitive psychological point of view, this means that the students must be encoding the material, and then structuring or reorganizing this new material with what is already in their memories (as we saw in the last chapter).

To clarify this definition in terms of classrooms, consider some common cases of less than adequate participation and how they might be improved. First is the ubiquitous lecture. No matter how stimulating, a straight didactic presentation is not active participation by the above definition, even if students are continuously taking notes. In fact, it is usually the case that the less people understand in a lecture, the more notes they take. This is because they do not have the material organized in their own minds and are clutching for any straws that might allow them to understand later. Those who are truly "with" the lecturer take notes designed to fit new information into their previous knowledge structure. The lecturer can facilitate this process for all learners by regularly interrupting the lecture to ask a question, such as, "How does this fact relate to _____?" The question can be rhetorical, thereby eliciting covert active participation by the students, or the lecturer can obtain overt answers by having students discuss it in pairs, or by other means.

However teachers handle questions, two important features of the questioning process should be carefully understood. The first concerns the level of cognitive processing elicited by the question (from Bloom's taxonomy)—namely, that questions designed to tap higher-order vs. lower-order processing directly and significantly affect the quantity and quality of learning from the same lesson (Redfield and Rousseau, 1981). Questions such as "Why did Columbus sail to the East?" elicit more learning than "When did Columbus discover America?" A related concern is the post-question pause. The questioner must pause long enough after a question to allow students time to think (e.g., Berliner, 1984; Tobin, 1987).

Shortly after the students have become actively engaged in the above ways, the teacher may then profitably return to lecture mode and model their own way of thinking about and organizing the material, and then again to ask a question that will allow the students to consolidate the points learned (see Bonwell & Eison, 1991, for other ways of doing this). At this point, a student's note-taking might indeed be active participation, not to mention being more meaningful upon a subsequent re-reading.

A second case illustrates the difference between what is called *continual* and *eventual participation*. When a teacher calls on a person and then asks a question, the odds are great that only the teacher and the unlucky student will pay attention to the question. The rest have received the message that their participation is not required at the moment, to their great relief. A similar effect occurs in classrooms in which the teacher has a distorted view of democracy that implies that everyone should be called on at least once, or equally often, per class period. As soon as students answer their obligatory question, however, they know that they can relax for the rest of the class period, since the others need to have their turn. Such *eventual participation* is the antithesis of keeping all students involved. Fortunately, the solution to this problem is simply to ask questions before calling on any particular person. Moreover, which students get called on should be sufficiently random to keep all students paying attention all the time. Another way to accomplish this is to announce that you are about to ask a question of someone, following which you will call on a second person to paraphrase the first person's statement, after which you will ask a third person to critique the answers given.

Active overt participation, of course, is necessary for practicing what has been learned, for the teacher's providing reinforcement and feedback, and for the teacher's monitoring student progress in order to adjust teaching.

Photo 12.3. Modeling how to use the abacus in Japan. What might the teacher do next to get more active participation?

Other Models of Instruction

Hunter's model identified a number of the critical attributes of good teaching. Like a good gymnastics coach or maestro, once you know the essential elements of the skill you are observing—whether it is performing a tumbling sequence, a sonata, or various teaching acts—then you perceive things that the unskilled observer or novice cannot see. You recognize, for example, not just that Teacher B is better than Teacher A (in anecdote 12.2), but you can pinpoint precisely the differences. For instance, among other things you can see that B had much more active participation, monitored the learning and adjusted the teaching to accommodate some who did not learn, used personal examples to add interest to the homework, required student behavior for homework which was congruent with the objective of using (as opposed to recognizing) correct punctuation, and found ways to provide success and positive reinforcement even for the students who were having difficulty. Teacher A did none of these things, despite equal competence with the content of the lesson.

Many so-called "born teachers" perform many of these functions unconsciously. Many others of whom it is said, "He really knows his subject matter, but he's teaching over my head," perform few of these functions, probably also unconsciously.

Models of instruction have always been concerned with such issues, bringing teachers to conscious awareness of the critical teaching-learning functions to increase instructional effectiveness. Some of the earliest models arose from research for the military, who need effective instructional methods to teach large numbers of recruits all manner of information and practical skills. Out of such work came instructional models like Glaser's and Gagné's.

Glaser's Instructional Psychology

As early as 1962, Robert Glaser (see also 1977; Glaser & Bassock, 1989) proposed that instruction was effective only to the extent that we could demonstrate that students learned (as in Dewey's sales metaphor in the beginning of this chapter). That, in turn could only be demonstrated if instruction had the following components:

1. Specification of what was to be learned—that is, the terminal performance of which the learner would be capable—and the sub-objectives, if any.
2. Diagnosis of the student's entering capabilities (knowledge, skill, motivational state) in relation to those objectives.
3. Achievement of those objectives—that is, the instructional methods that induce the learner to move from entering state to the desired capabilities.
4. Assessing the students' capabilities to see whether the instruction had the desired direct and indirect effects. If not, the process would be repeated.

Cartoon 12.3

As we discovered in the last chapter, Glaser (1984) has been in the forefront of the thinking on expert-novice differences in memory and knowledge acquisition, scaffolding, and the like. Thus his view of the above components includes a healthy dose of active construction of knowledge and student responsibility for their own cognitive and metacognitive strategies.

Gagné's Conditions of Learning

In the first edition of his theory, Gagné (1965) proposed eight types of learning, including classical and operant conditioning, verbal associations, and then more complex intellectual processes like concept, rule, and principle learning. These formed a pyramid of complexity with each new level incorporating at least portions of the previous levels which, in some ways, paralleled Bloom's taxonomy of levels of thinking.

From the beginning, Gagné was always concerned with how this translated to curriculum design (Gagné and Briggs, 1974, 1979; Gagné and Paradise, 1961). Thus was born his conception of the *learning hierarchy*, which is a task analysis of the order in which

Table 12.3 Gagné's events of instruction.

Instructional Event	Learning Process
1. Gain the learner's attention	Attention
2. State the instructional objective	Expectancy
3. Stimulate memory of relevant information	Accessing long-term memories, bringing to working memory
4. Present the stimulus, information, or distinctive features to be learned	Pattern recognition, perception
5. Guide the learning	Encoding, chunking, practice
6. Elicit performance	Retrieval, active participation, practice
7. Provide feedback	Correction of errors, reinforcement
8. Assess performance	Metacognition, retention*
9. Provide for retention and transfer	Overlearning, distributed practice, generalization

*Note: Gagné and Driscoll report this as responding and retention, but the real issue I believe is metacognition.

components of skills and intellectual capacities should be learned for maximum positive transfer from task to task. For example, the skill of identifying right triangles has such prerequisites as the following: students must learn the defining characteristics of triangles and, even prior to that, must be able to discriminate triangles from other shapes. As Driscoll (1994) explained,

> . . . if they cannot see a perceptual difference between triangles, and, say, squares, they will be unable to identify examples of triangles. Thus, the discrimination skill is a necessary (and sufficient) prerequisite to the identification skill. (p. 339)

By the fourth edition of his book, Gagné (1985, see also Gagné and Driscoll, 1988; Driscoll, 1994) had changed his types somewhat to incorporate recent cognitive theory and to emphasize (1) the learning processes that are associated with instructional events, and (2) the conditions which lead to optimal learning of various intellectual skills. Table 12.3 lists Gagné's events of instruction.

Like Hunter's essential elements of instruction, Gagné's list is not meant to be a checklist of what should go into every lesson. Rather, it is meant to help teachers make good instructional decisions. As Hunter put it, *the only thing a teacher should always do is "Think"*—that is, be conscious of the instructional decisions you are making and why. (She added that the only thing a teacher should never do is cause a student to lose dignity; Hunter, 1994).

In their review, Rosenshine and Stevens (1986) identified six teaching functions for which there is strong empirical evidence: (1) reviewing past material, (2) presenting new material, (3) providing guided practice, (4) giving corrective feedback, (5) scheduling

Table 12.4 A sampling of Shuell's teacher-initiated vs. student-initiated learning functions.

Learning Function	As Initiated by Teacher	As Initiated By Learner
Motivation	Encourage student interactions on interesting, relevant material	Find ways to make material relevant to your own life
Prior Knowledge Activation	Use anticipatory sets; remind students of previous lessons	Question yourself on what you know about the new topic
Encoding	Suggest relevant mnemonics, categories, and organizational cues	Use or invent mnemonics; practice verbal and imaginal elaboration
Comparison	Suggest criteria for comparisons, invent diagrams to highlight critical attributes	Ask what is similar and different about these
Feedback	Inform students on what is correct, what is incorrect, and how to improve	Analyze your own performances; ask for specific feedback
Monitoring	Assess regularly, especially during lessons to check understanding	Question yourself; practice metacognitive strategies

independent practice and (6) reviewing weekly and monthly. Rosenshine (1968) concluded:

> These six functions are not new. While all teachers use some of them some of the time, effective teachers use all of them most of the time and implement them consistently and systematically. (p. 64)

Gagné, Glaser, Hunter and their associates could not agree more.

Shuell's Teaching-Learning Functions

Perhaps the most recent attempt to integrate theory, empirical data, and practice on teaching-learning processes is provided in a series of articles by Thomas Shuell (1988, 1992, 1993, 1996). Building on Glaser's, Gagné's, and Rosenshine's work, Shuell combines basic learning processes with essential teaching functions to show how they produce meaningful learning. His unique contribution—in keeping with his definition of learning as being an active, constructive, cumulative, self-regulated, and goal-oriented search for meaning (cited in chapter 9)—is a comparison of those teaching-learning functions when initiated by the teacher vs. when initiated by the student. Table 12.4 gives variations of the kinds of examples he uses.

Consider prior knowledge activation. When initiated by the teacher, it takes the form of an advance organizer, anticipatory set, review of an old example in the context of a new lesson, or some such. When initiated by the learner, it becomes practice on searching your own memory for relevant cues, for connecting long-term memory to what you are working on, and establishing habits of metacognition: what do I know, and what don't I know about what is coming up. In any case, as Shuell (1988) put it,

> The goal of teaching is to facilitate student learning. . . . The relative importance of teacher-initiated and student-initiated activities depends on the situation—for example, the classroom vs. independent studying—but in all cases the student plays a critical role. In the final analysis, what the student does is more important than what the teacher does in determining the effectiveness of the teaching/learning process. (p. 282)

Teaching functions, in other words, exist for the purpose of inducing students to do what they need to do. All the better if the effective strategies teachers induce in learners become habitual and transferable, and that can only happen if the students become skilled with them and come to believe in them.

Like the previous models described in this chapter, Shuell's teaching-learning functions ". . . can be performed in a number of *equally valid and effective* ways" (Shuell, 1996). Thus they can be made part of any teaching method and, in fact, should be considered in making teaching decisions. A second point is that Shuell considers these functions neither exhaustive nor mutually exclusive. In addition to the six in table 12.4, Shuell (1988; 1992; 1996) gives teacher- and student-initiated examples of the following six functions: Expectations, Attention, Hypothesis Generation, Repetition, Evaluation, and Combination/Integration/Synthesis. It would probably be an instructive exercise to come up with additional ones. For example, how about one explicitly concerned with transfer and another for developing automaticity? Any other ideas?

Carroll's Model of School Learning

A very different set of ideas, arising from his interest in language learning, formed the basis for John Carroll's (1963; 1970; 1985; 1989) model of school learning. Five basic variables were identified, divided into two major components: time actually spent learning and time needed to learn.

Under *time needed to learn* Carroll defined the following:

1. *Aptitude:* the amount of time required by a student to learn a task, unit, or curriculum to a predetermined acceptable standard of mastery. Holding instruction and motivation equal, then a student who needs a small amount of time to learn can be said to have high aptitude, while someone who needs more time is diagnosed as lower aptitude for that task or curriculum.
2. *Quality of Instruction:* the extent to which material is properly sequenced and presented and congruent with objectives known to the students. The better the instruction, the less time needed to learn.
3. *Ability to Understand Instruction:* the extent to which learners comprehend the language and requirements of the task, including the capacity to figure it out for themselves and decide how best to learn it. Native language, culture and general intelligence are likely factors; in any case, the greater the ability to understand instruction, the less time needed to learn.

Anecdote 12.3

Carroll's View of Mastery Learning

John Carroll (1989, p. 28) relates the following discussion he had with a teacher about mastery learning:

. . . he wanted to consider how one might teach children the meaning of the word musket. Using mastery learning, he thought, he would have to concentrate on teaching the definition of the word, as found in dictionaries, and having children practice writing sentences or stories using the word correctly. In contrast, if he could ignore mastery learning ideas, he would prefer to take the children on a field trip to a museum where they could learn the full meaning of the word by seeing muskets on display and hearing something about their role in the American Revolution. . . .

It is obvious that this teacher, to the extent that he had been exposed to notions about mastery learning, had gotten the impression that it required analyzing learning tasks into small steps and then using drill and practice procedures to pound in the learning. I argued with him, however, that mastery learning, or at least the model of school learning, carries no such implication. The model of school learning requires clear specification of the task to be learned. But this specification need not break the task into small steps, and it makes no requirement that drill and practice procedures be followed.

Under *time actually spent learning* are the following additional variables:

4. *Perseverance:* the amount of time a student is willing to spend on the learning task.
5. *Opportunity to Learn:* the amount of time allowed or scheduled for learning the task, unit or curriculum.

All these variables come together in Carroll's model in a prediction that the amount of learning is a function of the ratio of time actually spent to time needed, as follows:

$$\text{Amount of Learning} = \frac{\text{Time Actually Spent}}{\text{Time Needed}}$$

For example, suppose we find that Allison Wunderland needs two hours to learn a set of vocabulary and comprehend it in context, estimated from previous lessons we taught. If the time allowed in the schedule for instruction and practice on this material is only one hour, whether or not it is sufficient for others, then Carroll's model predicts that only 50% of the material will be acquired by Allison (either 50% of the vocabulary learned well or all of it only partially learned). If, further, the student gives up after spending only half an hour, the model predicts 25% achievement (30 minutes spent divided by 120 minutes needed).

The clear implication of Carroll's model is that students will learn—that is, achieve a particular objective—if and only if they spend the time they need on the task. The teacher's task becomes one of beginning instruction commensurate with the students' entering capabilities; providing sufficient information, feedback, and time to learn; and finding ways to motivate students to persevere until learning is complete.

Carroll's model has been extremely successful in stimulating other lines of work. For example, as we shall see in the next chapter, Benjamin Bloom based his approach to mastery learning on Carroll's definition of aptitude. This is because, as he said in 1986, we could no longer accept aptitude as a predictor of the *amount* of possible achievement; rather it was better as a predictor of *rate* of achievement. Thus the job for a teacher is to arrange for instruction that is adaptive to the students' needs, including time needed, and then motivate each student to persevere long enough—and efficiently enough—to achieve the learning objectives. (anecdote 12.3 clarifies Carroll's view of mastery learning).

Carroll's idea of opportunity has also been extended in the direction of time management, including time on task. Berliner and Casanova (1993) summarized the findings of much of the research in these areas. Among their conclusions were the following:

- One elementary teacher spent an average of 16 minutes per day on math, while another in the same district averaged 71 minutes per day on math.
- One reading teacher spent 50 hours over the course of a year teaching comprehension skills, while another spent only 5 hours; one teacher spent 7 hours on fractions, while another did not teach fractions.
- Students observed in typical classrooms attend to the task about 70% of the time, but the range in various classes was from 35 to 90%.
- Time on task in transitions from topic to topic or to get a class started is usually zero. Teachers differ significantly in how smooth their transitions are and, therefore, how much time is wasted. Students in one classroom were observed to spend as much as 75 minutes per day in transitions.

With such great differences in opportunity to learn, no wonder there are great differences in achievement within and between

Photo 12.4. Time on task or transition time?

schools, districts, states and nations. Berliner and Casanova (1993) draw the following conclusion:

Time-on task does not mean that school should become a dreary chore for teachers and students, any more than keeping a budget should result in a joyless lifestyle. It does mean giving conscious attention to the use of the limited time available. Since opportunity to learn is one of the best predictors of achievement, teachers must ensure that, by managing time sensibly, their students have the opportunities to acquire the knowledge and skills that we ask them to learn. (p. 31)

The Expert Teacher Revisited

A teacher is called upon to play many roles and do many things: from counselor and friend to mentor and coach, from evaluator and record keeper to motivator and disciplinarian, from diagnostician to healer, and the list could go on. The roles of which we have been speaking in this chapter relate directly to instruction but they, being general, are only part of the instructional story. That is, all the models presented are content-free, speaking of general principles and ideas that all teachers, regardless of specialty or level, should know and consider when planning and conducting a lesson. The same can therefore be said of teachers' supervisors. Like anthropologists or psychologists observing a foreign culture without knowing the language or customs, they can still make many valid observations based on general principles about cultures.

But teaching is not content-free and, therefore, a complete account of a lesson requires that we analyze instructional decisions and lesson designs in interaction with the particular content being taught. That is, a discovery lesson in geometric motions may be quite different than a discovery lesson in history. And while a supervisor may be able to evaluate the common elements which allow them both to be called discovery learning, it will take a subject matter expert to decide whether the discovery lesson in geometry or history satisfies the requirements of those specific disciplines.

In his presidential address to the American Educational Research Association, Shulman (1986) distinguished four kinds of knowledge that teachers must have, one generic and three subject-matter specific. These follow:

1. *Pedagogical knowledge of teaching:* the knowledge of general principles of classroom organization and time management, including the principles of learning and instruction on which we have focused in this chapter.
2. *Subject-matter content knowledge:* the amount and organization of knowledge in the teacher's discipline be it math, biology, English. He points out that a teacher's expertise in this area should be at least the equal of the typical major in that field.
3. *Subject-matter pedagogical knowledge:* the best ways to represent the ideas in the field for students at different stages of expertise. This includes ways of putting general methods like lecture, cooperative groups, and discovery to best use in teaching the subject, along with an understanding of what makes certain topics easy or difficult and the preconceptions and misconceptions people have about these topics.
4. *Curricular knowledge:* the full range of available materials, texts, software, films, laboratory demonstrations, and so forth that have been developed.

The purpose of Shulman's address was to call attention to the paucity of emphasis on the subject matter specific knowledges, both in terms of research and teacher education. Methods courses in the disciplines (math methods, social studies methods, etc.) have been presumed to educate teachers about subject-matter pedagogical knowledge and curriculum knowledge, but Shulman argues that our teacher education programs do a poor job in that regard.

Regarding the research, there are a number of well-supported principles of generic pedagogical knowledge (as this chapter, in particular, and this text, in general, has attempted to show), but the research on subject-matter pedagogical knowledge is still in its infancy. One example of the benefits it is likely to show is provided in anecdote 12.4.

Given our current state of knowledge and needs, it seems clear that only a small portion of what teachers need to know will be learned in their preservice education. Of the rest, a small portion may come from graduate study, but the vast majority will have to come from a lifetime of professional development. That, in turn, is only likely to occur if their work environment encourages a collegial attitude of growth through coaching and clinical supervision. When teachers can reflect on their practice, and then reflect on their reflections (Schön, 1983; 1987) in a safe environment, then they and their supervisors can get on with the business of expanding their repertoires in all four of Shulman's areas of knowledge.

Joyce and Showers (1980) reviewed the literature on inservice training and found aspects of the following components to have beneficial effects: (1) description of the theory, skill and

Anecdote 12.4

How Expert Arithmetic Teachers Teach

Gaea Leinhardt (1986) reported a study of seven expert elementary school teachers teaching arithmetic, compared with four student teachers. The experts were discovered through a combination of high student growth scores for three years in a row, by principals' and supervisors' nominations and by interviews and classroom visits. The teachers were observed and videotaped for 10 to 25 consecutive topical lessons, along with extensive interviews of the teachers and their students. Some of Leinhardt's general findings follow:

Most expert math teachers have goal and action agendas that enable them to form lessons that have particular structures with different parts such as homework, drill, review, presentation, guided practice, monitored practice, and tutorials. Experts do not use all structures in each lesson, but they develop specific routines that allow the lesson to progress smoothly and to help set the stage for the particularly important presentation structure. Further, experts explain new information well.

Novices tend not to have these lesson structures, nor are their routines as effective. (pp. 29–30)

Some examples from second-grade expert, Dorothy Conway's beginning lessons on subtraction with regrouping follow:

On the first day of the sequence, she quickly reviewed sums with ten (10+4, 10+8 . . .) in order to (1) activate student's old knowledge and make it available, and (2) accentuate the base ten aspects of the task or the additive composition of two (or more) digit numbers. Conway then switched to a series of two-digit subtraction problems done at the board with students giving choral support. Finally, she gave them two problems that required regrouping. . . .

By the end of the presentation, the children had used sticks to solve regrouping problems and had become skilled at re-expressing two-digit numbers as tens and ones. . . .

Leinhardt went on to describe the variety of concrete manipulable items Conway used, including felt strips and banded sticks, pointing out that she invented many of these procedures since they were not part of the lesson book or teacher's manual. In a day and a half the students learned an algorithm for problems which require regrouping as well as one for those which do not, and learned several ways of representing regrouping, among other things. Over the next several days subtraction was seen in such contexts as word problems, using money, and correcting each other's work. The complete sequence of lessons provided mastery of basics for the very weakest students along with opportunities for the best students to "invent" ideas that would come later.

Among other conclusions, however, Leinhardt (p. 33) cautions that although experts have many skills in common, they do have their own styles and ways of doing things. A supervisor's job, therefore, must not be to change a teacher's style, but

. . . to locate where in the teaching repertoire support is most needed—in the structural, management, or content domain—and to see that it is provided.

strategy; (2) modeling of the skill; (3) practice in simulated and regular classes; (4) feedback on the practice; and (5) hands-on in-classroom coaching. They concluded (pp. 384–85):

The most effective training activities, then, will be those that combine theory, modeling, practice, feedback and coaching to application. The knowledge base seems firm enough that we can predict that if those components are in fact combined in inservice programs, we can expect the outcomes to be considerable at all levels.

Others have made similar arguments, particularly with regard to the necessity of providing regular feedback and follow-up (maintenance) support (e.g., Guskey, 1986; Joyce and Showers, 1982; Joyce, Hersh and McKibbin, 1983). But if this is done, there is reason for much optimism. Gage (1985), for example, summarized what he called hard gains in the soft science of pedagogy. He concluded that there is now excellent evidence that training teachers in specified ways does have significant and positive effects on both how the teachers subsequently teach and how much their students learn. He concluded that ". . . changing teaching practices *causes* desirable changes in student achievement and attitude. And the changes in achievement are substantial, not trivial" (p. 24).

Such expert teachers were lauded by Shulman (1986, p. 14) in this variation of George Bernard Shaw's famous aphorism:

Those who can, do.
Those who understand, teach.

Practice Exercises

A. Practice Items

INSTRUCTIONS FOR ITEMS 1–10: Fill in the blank using one of the technical terms of the "essential elements of instruction" or other models described in this chapter (Answers are in Note 7.)

1. "This next problem we shall do has occurred on every final exam I have ever seen." In saying this, the teacher is manipulating _____.

2. The English teacher wrote the following comment in the margin of a short essay by a student: "Excellent use of a dependent clause! However, note where I moved your comma." The teacher is providing _____.

3. The students are asked to recall the political situation in South Africa at the time of Gandhi, which they had studied the previous week. After reviewing that in pairs, the teacher tells them that today's lesson has a parallel situation, though it occurred in a different era and in a different country. This exercise can be called a(an) _____.

4. When the teacher suggests some ways of organizing the information in the lesson and/or the student finds a verbal or visual elaboration for the material, which learning function is being activated, according to Shuell? _____

5. Two forty-minute math class periods were scheduled for exponents. Tom, who always needs about twice as much time to learn math concepts as scheduled, was also absent for one of the class periods. What is the maximum amount of learning Carroll's model would predict for Tom? _____

6. In the previous example, the two forty-minute class periods devoted to the topic is called _____ in Carroll's model.

7. Knowing how to diagnose what prior knowledge was lacking by a student when she couldn't comprehend the classroom instruction is part of a teacher's _____ knowledge, according to Shulman.

8. _____ breaks a lesson, or series of lessons, into its components and most efficient sequence.

9. The teacher says, "All right. I want each of you to work problems 1–3 on the handout. When you've finished, raise your hand and I'll check what you wrote." The teacher is _____.

10. Hunter defines teaching as decision making, in which the decisions occur in three areas. Name them:
    a. _____.
    b. _____.
    c. _____.

For the following five multiple-choice items, select the alternative which best answers the question. (Answers are in Note 7.)

11. Consider the following behavioral objective: Given a number of examples of assessment situations (testing or grading) in multiple choice format, the student will be able to identify all the norm-referenced ones. This objective:
    a. is missing the standard of performance.
    b. is missing the actual behavior required.
    c. Is missing the conditions under which the behavior is to be performed.
    d. is all right as stated.

12. The previous item in this test mostly tests which one of the following levels from the taxonomy of educational objectives?
    a. application
    b. evaluation
    c. knowledge
    d. synthesis

13. Professor Gentile asked his students to summarize Madeline Hunter's position on negative reinforcement. This activity is best classified as falling into which one of the following levels of Bloom's taxonomy?
    a. knowledge
    b. comprehension
    c. analysis
    d. evaluation

14. According to Shulman, knowing how to maintain order during a physics demonstration is part of a teacher's
    a. subject-matter content knowledge.
    b. curricular knowledge.
    c. generic pedagogical knowledge.
    d. subject-matter pedagogical knowledge.

15. All of the theorists in this chapter believe that _____ is the best predictor of whether and how much learning occurs.
    a. what the student does
    b. how much knowledge the teacher has
    c. the amount of time allowed
    d. how much prior knowledge a student has

For the next five questions, answer True or False (T or F) according to Hunter's point of view (answers in Note 7):

___ 16. Active participation by the learners requires that they do something the teacher can see.

___ 17. When asking a question, the teacher should first call on a student, then ask the question.

___ 18. When a teacher says, "Nice job, but it could be better" the student is receiving feedback.

___ 19. Hunter is like Glaser and Gagné in believing that teachers must always tell students the objective at the beginning of a lesson.

___ 20. A funny joke or anecdote at the beginning of a lesson can stimulate interest and create a positive feeling tone and, for these reasons, acts as a good anticipatory set.

B. For Cooperative Study (in or out of class):

1. Observe a lesson, perhaps one in the course for which you are reading this book, and identify:
   a. the teacher's use of essential elements or teaching-learning functions (from the models presented in this chapter).
   b. the students' (or your own) activities and learning functions stimulated by the class.

   Compare notes with another student on what you observed and why you labeled it as you did.

2. Observe a class and keep records on the time:
   a. the teacher allocates to various activities and concepts.
   b. a particular student spends on task.
   c. spent in transitions.

3. In pairs or small groups, have someone practice doing an activity (e.g., teaching) and then giving feedback on the activity. Discuss what it means to give feedback vs. reinforcement. How can you encourage self-reflection so that the student gives himself or herself feedback?

4. Develop a lesson plan for something you teach based on one of the models in this chapter. What categories will you use to help yourself make sound teaching decisions? Share your plan with others in class and compare.

C. For More Information:

1. Read (and prepare a report) on one or more of the articles by Hunter, Glaser, Gagné, Shuell, or Carroll.

2. Madeline Hunter has suggested that when teachers are learning the essential elements, they should not be *evaluated*, but *clinically supervised*. Read about clinical supervision and compare it to the suggestions in this chapter. Some sources include: Acheson & Gall, 1980; Cogan, 1973; Gentile, 1993; Goldhamer, 1969; 1980; 1984; 1988; Hunter & Russell, 1989.

3. Search through some current teacher journals of interest to you and report on one or more articles you find on topics relevant to the models in this chapter.

CHAPTER

Study Questions

1. What does the author argue about the "one best method" conception of education? How does this relate to the notion of expanding the repertoire of teaching skills?

2. Relate the concept of scoring in cooperative teams to the idea of handicaps in bowling or golf? Why does this matter for what Slavin and the Johnsons call *incentive structure?*

3. How are teams formed (i.e., what is the composition of the teams in terms of ability, gender or ethnic considerations) for cooperative teams for academic objectives?

4. Give an example of at least two of the following cooperative teams methods:
   a. Student Teams—Achievement Division
   b. Teams-Games-Tournaments
   c. Team-Assisted Individualization
   d. Jigsaw
   e. Learning Together
   f. Group Investigation

   Which one (or ones) is best suited for learning of facts? For inquiry?

5. What is meant by *peer tutoring?* How is it the same and how is it different from cooperative games?

6. Devise a plan to use cooperative learning in one of your own classrooms based on the 18 steps of Johnson and Johnson.

7. What was the major step forward that Washburne felt "the Winnetka Plan" contributed to education in 1922?

8. What does the author believe to be the strand which links the Winnetka plan to current mastery systems?

9. Bloom's ideas for mastery learning are based on John Carroll's (1963) model of school learning.
   a. How did Carroll redefine *aptitude?*
   b. What is the basic idea of Carroll's model?

10. What procedure does Bloom recommend for setting standards for grades if you have no experience setting absolute standards (i.e., how did he start)?

THIRTEEN

11. What is meant by
    a. summative evaluation?
    b. formative evaluation?

    Which is always criterion-referenced? Which may be either criterion-referenced or norm-referenced?

12. Bloom claims that ". . . our educational efforts may be said to be *unsuccessful* to the extent that student achievement is normally distributed." What does he mean by that?

13. Bloom claims that mastery learning procedures eventually produce learners whose aptitude and motivation for learning become more similar. What is your author's view of that argument from the standpoint of stability of rankings and absolute growth?

14. Describe Keller's Personalized System of Instruction in terms of the following (anecdote 13.5):
    a. lectures as reinforcers
    b. proctors
    c. grading

15. Describe the similarities and differences between the Bloom and Keller systems.

16. How effective are mastery learning systems?

17. Devise a plan to use a mastery learning system in one of your own classrooms based on the 13 steps Gentile recommends.

18. According to your author, what is the relationship between teaching creativity and mastery learning?

19. How does the author define creativity?

20. Give examples of what is meant by the following in synectics:
    a. making the strange familiar
    b. making the familiar strange

21. The author asserts that a teaching technique that is fundamental to both direct and inquiry instructional methods is correct use of *questions*. Give examples of why this is true.

22. Cronbach said "A particular educational tactic is part of an instrumental system; a proper educational design calls upon that tactic at a certain point in the sequence, for a certain period of time, following and preceding other tactics." What does this imply for finding "one best method"?

A Repertoire of Teaching Skills

Introduction

1. We must beware of the fallacy of the good teacher and the good student. There are many good teachers who have not needed to learn to teach. They would be good at almost anything they tried. There are many good students who scarcely need to be taught. Put a good teacher and a good student together and you have what seems to be an ideal instructional setting. But it is disastrous to take it as a model to be followed in our schools, where hundreds of thousands of teachers must teach millions of students. Teachers must learn how to teach, and they must be taught by schools of education. They need only to be taught more effective ways of teaching. (B. F. Skinner, 1984, p. 950)

2. Can all students learn a given task to the same high level of complexity? Studies of aptitude distributions in relation to student performance indicate that there are differences between the extreme (1 to 5 percent at each end of the scale) students and the remainder of the population. At the top of the aptitude distribution there are likely to be some students who have a special talent for the subject. At the bottom, there are individuals with special disabilities for particular subjects. In between, however, are approximately 90 per cent of the students for whom we believe aptitudes are predictive of rate of learning rather than level or complexity of learning possible. Thus, we propose that 95 percent of the students (the top 5 percent plus the next 90 per cent) can learn a subject to a high level of mastery (for example, an A grade) if given sufficient learning time and appropriate types of help. (B. S. Bloom, 1968, p. 5)

3. . . . the active [teaching/learning] methods are much more difficult to employ than our current receptive methods. In the first place, they require a much more varied and much more concentrated kind of work from the teacher, whereas giving lessons is much less tiring and corresponds to a much more natural tendency in the adult, generally, and in the adult pedagogue, in particular. Secondly, and above all, an active pedagogy presupposes a much more advanced kind of training, and without an adequate knowledge of child psychology (and also, where mathematics and physics are concerned, without a fairly good knowledge of contemporary developments in those disciplines), the teacher cannot properly understand the students' spontaneous procedures, and therefore fails to take advantage of reactions that appear to him quite insignificant and a mere waste of time. The heartbreaking difficulty in pedagogy . . . is in fact, that the best methods are also the most difficult ones. . . . (J. Piaget, 1970a, p. 69)

4. The sort of thing you can do is to draw out from your students their real problems relevant to the course at hand, thus tapping the child's intrinsic motivation. You can provide resources, making them easily available, both practically and psychologically. You can use such techniques as inquiry, simulation games, programmed instruction. You may find student contracts useful to give security and responsibility within an atmosphere of freedom. You will look for ways in which children can

express their feelings, work through their own problems, become involved in evaluation of their own learning. You even trust the student's own feelings about himself enough not to force freedom upon him. However, as the child slowly begins to develop his own value system and becomes less threatened by responsibility, he will be able to accept and use freedom to a greater and greater degree. (C. Rogers, 1971, p. 66)
5. Research on cooperative learning and peer tutoring has shown that programs in which students help other students to learn can enhance their achievement. Further, the social benefits and increased self-esteem of students working together are considerable, and many schools use cooperative learning and peer tutoring primarily for these reasons. Both approaches are inexpensive, relatively easy to implement, and fun for teachers as well as students. In a time of increasing expectations and diminishing resources for education, we cannot afford to ignore a powerful, free instructional resource available in any school: The students themselves! (R. E. Slavin, 1986a, p. 13)
6. *Repertoire:* the complete list or supply of skills, devices, or ingredients used in a particular field, occupation, or practice. (Webster's New Collegiate Dictionary, 1973)

For those who have learned that the theories of B. F. Skinner, Carl Rogers, and Jean Piaget are in conflict, it may be surprising to discover that they agree on many practical ideas about education. That may be reason enough to introduce this chapter with the preceding quotes. The more important reason is that the purpose of this chapter is to emphasize, from several points of view, the need for teachers to be continually expanding their repertoire of teaching techniques. None of us can ever master "the complete list," as Webster's dictionary defines repertoire, since (1) new curricula, techniques and technologies are continually being created; (2) uncountable variations on old techniques are possible; and (3) skills as complex as these, no matter how well-learned, are nevertheless never complete. But this is not a reason for despair—rather, it is a reason for excitement about teaching as a profession. Teachers who expect their students to be eager and motivated should be eager, motivated learners themselves.

A corollary of the teacher-as-lifelong-learner idea is rejection of the search for the one best method. This is the problem with too strictly identifying with theoretical camps, such as Skinner vs. Rogers or didactic instruction vs. inquiry. Each of these theoretical positions is unfairly described when reduced to a label or a one-sentence (usually pejorative) summary. To take just one example, the *Freedom to Learn* idea of Carl Rogers (1969) is often misunderstood as being so non-directive as to allow the students to do whatever they want to do and, in contrast to Skinner, to disallow positive reinforcement. But Rogers reinforces by his very attention, as he realizes; thus he models ways of responding to students (or clients) which encourage the students to learn to express themselves, both cognitively and emotionally. In addition, as in quote #4, he is not rigidly nondirective, but is willing to provide direction to students who need it, later helping them to become more independent. This is not to say that the Rogerian and Skinnerian positions are indistinguishable; they are not, but they are more complementary than antagonistic, at least when it comes to teaching children.

The same is true of specific teaching methods—they are complementary, rather than antagonistic. Advocates of particular methods—didactic, inquiry, Montessori, mastery, cooperation, critical thinking, behavior modification, you name it—never seem to tire of debating the research evidence to demonstrate that their method is superior to all others. Joyce and Weil (1980, p. 8) summarized the situation this way:

> The research evidence dealing with this question is remarkably ambiguous. Several hundred studies compare one general teaching method to another, and most of these studies—whether curriculums are compared, specific methods for teaching specific subjects are contrasted, or different approaches to counseling are analyzed—show that differences between approaches are for specific objectives.[1] Although the results are very difficult to interpret, the evidence to date gives little encouragement to those who would hope that we have identified a single, reliable, multipurpose teaching strategy as the best approach.
>
> This conclusion annoys some people. Naturally it bothers those people who feel that they do know such a single broad method. They are likely to say that the reason one particular approach to teaching (their approach) has not yet been proven superior is that our ability to measure learning outcomes is not yet sophisticated enough to detect the true power of their preferred strategy.[2]

Although it is possible that one of those methods will eventually prove superior to all educational goals, to the objective observer the whole debate appears to be endless case studies in cognitive dissonance (see chapter 7). Any evidence showing that *their* preferred method is no better than other methods or, for some purposes, is worse than other methods elicits an immediate and elaborate defense to reduce the dissonance. Perhaps the advertisers of these methods—after all, these methods do produce profits—will adopt the strategies of toothpaste commercials: "Colgate is unsurpassed in reducing cavities" will become "Method X is unsurpassed in producing critical thinking." Few will realize that the word *unsurpassed* really means "there is no statistically significant difference between X and the other products tested."

Where there are products to be sold—books, curricula, technological equipment, tests—people will take liberties with the truth. This makes it all the more important that educators take these "one best method" debates with a grain of salt. We need to take Cronbach's (1963) advice about comparison studies of different teaching methods of curricula: we shall have gained no real understanding of the reasons for any significant difference that does occur, because we will still not know what ingredients made the difference. Joyce and Weil (1980, p. 8) concluded their argument on this point by suggesting that, instead of searching for a single best method, we use

> . . . the rich variety of models for teaching that our heritage has given us. No presently known single approach succeeds with all students or reaches all goals. Our task is to develop an environment in which the student is taught in the variety of ways that facilitate his or her development.

This brings us full circle to the problem of repertoire. If a teacher has mastered only the lecture technique, then inquiry, mastery, or active participation approaches are likely to seem threatening. Likewise, a teacher who uses inquiry exclusively is likely to be suspect of direct instruction, mastery, or skill-oriented approaches. Unfortunately, the behaviors and attitudes of such teachers are conditioned by their success with their method, to the point of rigidity. To overcome this one-best-way mental set, they must become skillful and have success with other methods. In other words, they must expand their repertoires.

We have already seen the importance of viewing learning as a complex emotional-behavioral-social-cognitive process in which the various components, while interdependent, have different environmental causes and effects (chapters 5–8). We have also seen several theoretically sound and interesting approaches to teaching cognitive objectives at a variety of levels of complexity (chapters 9–11). In this chapter I shall describe a few additional sound teaching methods and the kinds of objectives for which they are appropriate. While the aim is to expand the reader's repertoire, it bears repeating that before any method can become effective in a classroom, the teacher will have to develop at least a modicum of expertise with the method.

Cooperative Learning

Team Play vs. Team Learning: A Basketball Example

Suppose you were a physical education teacher in junior high school. The lesson plans for the day called for playing basketball games in both boys' and girls' classes. Previously, you had taught the rules of the game and had given some practice on shooting, dribbling and passing. Today was to be some actual games. As luck would have it, each class has exactly 30 students in it and the gym is large enough to allow three games to go on simultaneously. How do you select the membership of the teams? Consider a few alternative ways.

One approach might be to allow people to form their own five-person teams. The consequence of that teacher decision would probably be for teams to be formed on the basis of pre-existing friendships. A sometime group member—a sixth person—would probably be rejected and would have to join a group he or she perceives as less desirable. Some individuals would be excluded from all of the desirable groups and would end up bound together in the one or two remaining groups by the common thread that they are all rejects. Since friendships are partly determined by skills and interests people share, the teams thus formed are also likely to be quite uneven in the distribution of basketball skill.

A common and somewhat more systematic selection procedure is to select (or take volunteers or have nominations for) team captains who, in turn, select the other members of their team. In this case, athletic skill and, to a lesser extent, personal friendships will dominate the selection of team members, with the best athletes and best friends drafted early, while the unathletic and social isolates will be accepted grudgingly as the fourth or fifth person on each team.

A third method might be for the teacher to preselect the teams on the basis of their skill in basketball, or other athletic ability (e.g., by observing how well they learned the skills in previous lessons). Then the best student would be assigned to team 1, the second best to team 2, . . . the sixth and seventh best to team 6, the eighth best to team 5, etc. The point is to guarantee as much as possible that talent is equally distributed among teams. In class, however, you simply announce the composition of the teams without mentioning the criteria and method of selection.

These three selection procedures will likely produce quite different team compositions. In addition to composition, now consider what is likely to happen if the teams were randomly paired to play a real game. The first, and possibly to a lesser extent, the second selection methods are likely to produce games with quite lopsided scores. For example, those who self-select because they already play team sports together are likely to beat those who select because they live in the same neighborhood, or those who are thrown together because no one else wanted them (for being overweight, slightly disabled, etc.).

But even where two teams are fairly well matched in overall ability, how will the involvement of each of the players be determined? Will those who were selected last in method two, for example, handle the ball as much as those selected first or second? Not if the teams are trying to win. The best players will naturally pass the ball to each other and if, by chance, poor players get their hands on the ball, they will pass to a good player to shoot. Ironically, everyone will probably think that this is only fair, given our national obsession with sport stardom, first round draft choices, and with winning. But is it fair in a classroom where the goal is to have each student learn to play basketball? And if that isn't the goal, why have a unit on basketball, including a game, as part of the curriculum?

As you have probably noticed, we are returning to the problem of cooperative vs. individualistic vs. competitive goal structures (Johnson and Johnson, 1975; described in chapter 7). Basketball games, like many other sports, involve all three kinds of behaviors. The two teams are competing—only one can win. Among the team members, cooperation, if not necessary to win, is probably facilitative of their best effort. Finally, individuals may find rewards in achieving their own goals (as is built into professional players' contracts and bonuses). But professional, and even scholastic, sports are for a highly select few to demonstrate in competition what they have already learned how to do. This real game model is totally inappropriate for teaching the vast majority of students in regular classrooms. In such classrooms, including the physical education class we are discussing, all students must have an equal opportunity to handle the ball and contribute to the team effort. Furthermore, all contributions must be valued and reinforced by the other players on the team.

Is this a pipedream? Not necessarily, and partial solutions to the problem are already employed in such sports as golf and bowling, in which players receive handicaps according to their abilities. For example, a professional or expert amateur golfer who can shoot par, receives a zero handicap, while an average golfer who averages bogeys (one over par) receives one stroke per hole. When playing a match, then, if the better player has a 4 and the poorer one a 5, they tie on that hole. This makes for a fair and interesting game between people of unequal skill levels, with both players motivated to do their best at all times. To

Photo 13.1. Cooperative learning through competitive games?

do the same for teaching team play, as well as encouraging each individual to practice the various skills of basketball, requires a similar kind of handicapping system.

Suppose you, as teacher, had reason to believe (from previous games or from shooting practice) that the five players on one team would make the following number of baskets in a 30-minute game:

> Dave 7
> Pete 4
> Jack 2
> Ron 0
> Don 0

Now suppose team points were earned, not for making baskets, but for equaling or exceeding the student's own average. For instance, each person receives 5 points for making his average number of baskets, as long as he at least tried to make one. Already Ron and Don contribute 5 points each just for making an attempt to shoot, so the others will make sure that Ron and Don have that opportunity. Continuing our incentive structure, let's give an extra point for each basket over each student's average, up to a maximum of 5. Now each student will be able to earn a maximum of 10 points. Dave for shooting 12 baskets (5 points for 7 baskets and 5 points for the extra 5 baskets), Pete for shooting 9 baskets, Jack for 7 baskets, and Don and Ron for shooting 5 each. Now there is no incentive for Dave to shoot beyond 12 baskets. The maximum team points of 50 will occur only if the better players can find ways to help their teammates contribute—and thereby improve their own skills. Dave, meanwhile, can still be the team star by learning to be the complete team player (like Michael Jordan in basketball, or Wayne Gretzky in hockey).

Cooperative Teams for Academic Objectives

Student Teams—Achievement Division

I have no knowledge of such a system being used for physical education objectives, but such a system has been quite successfully used in classroom settings for a variety of instructional objectives. The system on which I based the above is called the *Students Teams-Achievement Division,* invented by Robert Slavin. Slavin (1986a), proposes that the technique is appropriate for grades two to twelve and for any subject matter in which students will be tested on whether they can recall information or solve problems (i.e., instructional objectives at the knowledge, comprehension, and application levels).

Composing the Teams. The first step is to assign students to teams, four students per team (with any extra students becoming fifth members of a team). Students are assigned to teams on the basis of previous academic performance, such as grades on test scores. Perhaps the easiest way to do this is to rank the students from top to bottom and divide the ranked list into quarters, placing any extra students into the middle quarters. For example, a class of 30 would have 7,8,8, and 7 in the quarters, top to bottom. Then make up each four-person team by selecting one student from each quarter, also balancing for gender and ethnicity across teams. Extra students become fifth members of teams. Notice that the selection is done by the *teacher* to achieve cooperative learning goals; allowing students to self-select would form groups with other agendas.

Determining Individual and Team Scores. Since points will be awarded to the teams on the basis of how well students do compared to their past performance, it is necessary to establish numerical base scores that are representative of their past averages. Students with A-grades or averages in the 90's could be given an initial base score of 90 = A or 80 = B, and so on. When students later take their unit quiz, they receive Improvement Points as follows (from Slavin 1986a, p. 11):

- Perfect Paper (Regardless of Score) = 30 points
- More Than 10 Points Above Base Score = 30 points
- Base Score to 10 Points Above = 20 points
- 1–10 Points Below Base Score = 10 points
- More Than 10 Points Below Base Score = 0 points

This system provides incentive for students to help each other to learn so that both individuals and the team can achieve the highest number of points. Team points are computed by averaging the individual Improvement Points (i.e., by summing the Improvement Points and dividing by the number of team members present).

Team Learning. The instructional objectives are mastered by the following activities. First, the teacher presents the lesson in whatever manner is appropriate—lecture, films, reading passages, etc.—taking as long as is required. Next is a period of team study, in which the members are to master the material themselves, as well as to assure that their team members have also mastered the material. To facilitate this process the teacher should have prepared worksheets or study questions so that students can quiz themselves and each other. Students work in pairs or trios while learning and practicing. If they are solving a math problem, for example, Slavin recommends that each student work the problem and then compare answers and processes with their partner(s). Where discrepancies exist, teammates are responsible for explaining the reasoning. Team members can then quiz one another—for correct processes as well as correct answers—in order to prepare for the unit quiz. During this time the teacher can circulate through the groups, answering questions that arise and, more importantly, encouraging the cooperative learning process. The point of this is, through active participation in this cooperative incentive structure, all students will aspire to obtaining 100% on the quiz.

Assessing the Learning. After the teams have had sufficient time to learn the material (usually not longer than one class period), students take the quiz—as individuals. Scoring should be completed as percent correct and converted to Improvement Points, according to the scale described above, and then to Team Points. While there are various ways of including both individual and team points into each student's course grade, I shall leave these to the interested reader to discover by reading Slavin (1983, 1986a).

Recognizing Team Learning. Slavin (1986a) presents two levels of award for team accomplishments. For an average Team Score of 18–22 points, he recommends an award for GREATTEAM. For 23 points or above, he recognizes SUPERTEAM. Such criteria *must* be adjusted to fit each classroom situation, of course. He recommends posting the accomplishments of each team on bulletin boards, with pictures, or in a regular newsletter.[3] Of course, how this is done will depend upon the age of the students and the subject matter, among other things. The important point is that all teams can achieve at the highest level—they are not in competition with one another—and therefore the teacher should use whatever incentive system that will encourage achievement of all at the highest levels.

Changing Teams. Slavin recommends that students be reassigned to new teams every five or six weeks. This allows the teacher to reassign new Base Scores on the basis of their more recent quiz scores, and also to allow students to work with other people.

Other Cooperative Methods[4]

In addition to the Student Teams-Achievement Division, Slavin and his colleagues have developed a number of other cooperative learning methods. One method, called *Teams-Games-Tournaments*, uses the same team compositions to learn academic objectives. Then fair competitions among the teams are arranged by having the highest performers from each of three teams compete at one table, three second-ranked students compete at another table, and so on, as in a tennis or wrestling tournament. The questions are covered as in a board game, by having students pick a numbered card, then answer the corresponding question from a question sheet. Points that individuals earn accumulate for their respective teams. Analogous to team tennis or wrestling, as individuals move up or down the ranking scale, they compete with other students on that level. Membership of teams is readjusted every few weeks. This method uses competition between teams to motivate students to prepare for the academic tournaments, but uses cooperation within the teams to help each student master the objectives on which the games are based.

Another method is known as *Jigsaw*, now available in multiple versions. As originally conceived, the idea was to get students to cooperate in studying a complex topic, such as a historical event or a social institution, by having each team member be responsible for one aspect of that topic, and teach the others about the component. After reading required material, members of each team assigned to common topics meet in "expert groups" to discuss the material. Later they return to their teams and each "expert" teaches the others about their component of the material. Since the whole picture emerges only from the sum of its parts, Jigsaw encourages people to attend to and to encourage each other. In this version, students' scores on subsequent quizzes were graded individually and not accumulated into a team score. In Jigsaw II (Slavin, 1980b), all students read all of the material; then they go to "expert groups" and return to teach their peers. On quizzes, students are given Improvement Scores to form team scores, as in the Student Teams-Achievement Division program.

The above game-like cooperative methods, all developed by a cooperative research team at Johns Hopkins University, conclude with an individual demonstration of learning, such as on a quiz. A team of brothers, David and Roger Johnson (1975), have developed an alternative method in which students receive grades based on the average of the performance of the group on quizzes or other projects. This *Learning Together* model is actually a collection of procedures that can be used in many classrooms for a variety of purposes. What is common to these procedures is that students learn basic interpersonal communications skills, such as how to ". . . ask relevant questions, give coherent explanations, challenge each other's thinking, provide effective leadership, resolve conflicts between ideas and conclusions, and seek to understand each other's reasoning and perspectives" (Johnson and Johnson, 1986, p. 12).

Finally, the *Group Investigation* method (e.g., Sharan et al., 1985; Slavin, 1983) is an inquiry-based method aimed specifically at teaching higher-level knowledge (synthesis and evaluation) via small groups. Particularly appropriate for literature and social studies, students work in groups of two to six. In this method, students choose topics from a unit being studied by the entire class, further subdividing the task into individual projects, which then are synthesized into a group report. The group presents its results to the whole class and is evaluated on that report. The adequacy of the final report obviously depends upon the individual contributions of the group members; the discussion within the group about those contributions, including the resolution of conflicting ideas; and a synthesis into a coherent final report.

Other group methods have been developed (see anecdote 13.1) along with many variations on the ones presented here (e.g., Kagan's, 1985, Co-op Co-op based on the Group Investigation method). Rather than go into detail on further variations, present purposes will be better served by studying more carefully the general principles on which these procedures are based, along with evidence on their effects. However, there is one method that from one point of view is a cooperative team method but, from another point of view, is not. That method, peer tutoring, deserves a few comments.

Peer Tutoring

Peer tutoring requires cooperation between students in order for them to meet objectives. However, the students involved are working on different objectives. The tutors' objectives may be (1) to assure that tutees learn the material, (2) to practice and thereby overlearn the material themselves, and perhaps (3) to practice teaching. The tutees' objectives are to learn the material for the first time. Since different objectives are at stake for the participants, peer tutoring most resembles the Team Assisted Individualization method described above, although there are no points awarded to the tutor-tutee as a team.

From a different vantage point, however, peer tutoring is a misnomer; neither is it a cooperative team. The reason is that the tutors are usually older and have been chosen because they know the material. The tutees, in contrast, are younger and are learning the material for the first time. Thus tutor and tutee

Anecdote 13.1

How to Encourage Cooperation When All Are Doing Their Own Thing

Slavin and his colleagues have devised a team process for extremely heterogeneous groups, such as for mainstreaming disabled students, in which all members of the class are working on different learning objectives. In such totally individualized classes, it is very difficult to develop esprit de corps or even to encourage normal pro-social interactions, since the students have little to talk about.

The method they developed, called *Team Assisted Individualization,* combines the motivation groups can provide with individualized instruction in, say, elementary mathematics. On the basis of a diagnostic test, students tackle an appropriate programmed unit on mathematics at their pace. Diagnostic tests are taken and exchanged with and scored by a team member. When students have scored 80% on the diagnostic check-out, they are deemed ready to take a final test on those objectives, scored by a student monitor, which then accumulates points for the team. The team score, then, is a combination of the accuracy on the tests, as well as the number of units completed per week, with awards given to all teams which exceed preset standards. Because the students themselves do most of the scoring, the teacher is free to assist students in their learning and avoid much of the record keeping which accompanies many individualized learning programs.

This system seems to have an analogy to track-and-field sports. Each team member may have a unique objective—one is a high jumper, one a discus thrower, one a sprinter—but since that person's score accumulates to a team score, all team members root for and encourage each other to reach their own personal goals. When this works well, we credit the coach with creating great team spirit.

are not learning together and, as Slavin (1986a, p. 11) pointed out, while adults may regard fifth grade tutors and second grade tutees as peers, "the students themselves assuredly do not." Of course, peer tutoring can also occur with students of the same age or within the same class, but it is more common that tutor and tutee have different roles than typically occur in the cooperative teams.

There is an old saying about statistics that may generalize to other fields as well: "I began to understand my first statistics course in the process of learning my second. I began to really understand my second statistics course as I was teaching my first." Such sentiments support the value of tutoring as a learning activity. There is evidence, in fact, that the tutors gain considerably by teaching, and so do the tutees (e.g., Devin-Sheehan, Feldman and Allen, 1976; Cohen, Kulik and Kulik, 1982). Even in cooperative groups, there is evidence that the specific facts, procedures, and arguments that a student remembers are the ones that the particular student contributed to the group discussion, even if the contribution was stimulated by the group (Peters, 1986; Webb, Ender and Lewis, 1986). Preparation, rehearsal and active participation are probably some of the active ingredients which make teaching (as a tutor or as a contributor to a team project) a superb learning activity.

A Repertoire of Teaching Skills 435

Photo 13.2. Learning by teaching.
(Photo Courtesy of Dr. Thomas J. Shuell)

Later, in this chapter and the next, we shall see ways of giving students academic credit for peer tutoring (as in Keller's Personalized System of Instruction) as well as for providing grading incentives for peer tutoring.

Cooperative Learning: Theory and Evidence

Whether the teacher establishes tasks to be learned which are based on cooperative, competitive or individualistic goal structures, it is important to realize that learning is an individual matter. It can occur alone or in groups, but it is always the individual who learns, remembers, thinks, and transfers. Place several individuals in groups who have learned complementary things and they may more readily solve problems than any of the individuals in the group, because they can brainstorm, compensate for one another's mental rigidities, forgotten facts, and poor strategies. This group productivity will be evidence that the whole is often greater than the sum of its parts; nevertheless, individuals may subsequently be able to reproduce only parts of the group's processes. Slavin put it this way (1983, p. 11):

Learning takes place only between the ears of the learner. If a group produces a beautiful lab report, but only a few students really contributed to it, it is unlikely that the group as a whole learned more than they might have learned had they each had to write his or her own (perhaps less beautiful) lab reports under an individualistic or competitive incentive structure. In fact, what often happens in cooperative groups that produce a single report, worksheet, or other group product is that the most able group members simply do the work or give the answers to their groupmates, which may be the most efficient strategy for group productivity, but is a poor strategy for individual learning.

To avoid these ways of cheating on the system, researchers in the field (e.g., Johnson et al., 1984; Johnson, Johnson & Holubec, 1993; Slavin, 1983) make *incentive structure* a crucial variable in producing cooperative learning. It is not sufficient to create a cooperative task structure—that is, to ask students to cooperate on a task—if students will be graded solely on their own performance on a task. In that case, why should students care about how others are doing, especially if they do not really know the others, or consider them different or inferior (such as with ethnic differences or in mainstreaming handicapped children)? Worse is the case where students are asked to cooperate on a task and then are graded competitively. In such cases it behooves students to conceal information from their peers. Even if a reward is given based on the final group production, irrespective of individual member contributions, the most able students have much to gain by doing all the work: they maintain their knowledge advantage for subsequent competitive tasks and grades.

One solution is to *base group rewards on the learning of all members of the group;* when group benefits are contingent upon the progress of all members, then cooperative behavior will increase in frequency. Students will, in fact, teach each other and help each other practice so that each will be able to achieve high test scores.

In general, the effects of cooperation on achievement are large and positive over a wide variety of studies (e.g., Johnson and Johnson, 1985; 1989; Johnson et al., 1981; Stallings and Stipek, 1986). Even more impressive is the research in which students studied the same material and in which group rewards were based on the learning of all members; of 25 such studies, 22 (88%) found gains over control groups (Slavin, 1983). And these achievement effects are not limited to just factual knowledge. Because students are sharing ideas, they can engage in higher level processing of information, ways of challenging ideas, and various kinds of critical thinking (Johnson et al., 1984; Sharan et al., 1985).[5]

What is more is that cooperative learning produces important affective outcomes as well—on liking classmates, on cross-ethnic friendships, on self-esteem, as well as on other measures (Johnson, Johnson and Maruyama, 1983; Slavin, 1983; Slavin et al., 1985). Such methods also show promise for helping to overcome some of the social stigma attached to handicapped students; however, more research is needed in this area (Slavin, 1983).

Why should working cooperatively in groups have such effects? First, they produce *face-to-face contact* among people. This, in itself, does not produce friendships. Nevertheless, people who spend time together, especially if they are working toward a common goal, tend to become friends more frequently than those who see each other only across a crowded room when a teacher is doing most of the talking. Second, a person who is being successful and is liked by others is likely to be psychologically healthier than someone who is a social isolate and/or academically unsuccessful. A person with high self-esteem is likely to have the confidence to befriend or assist someone who is unknown, different, or having learning difficulties. Since cooperative groups can set such prosocial processes in motion, then some would argue they should be used in schools even if they had no effects on achievement. The fact that they produce both affective and cognitive gains make them techniques that we teachers must include in our repertoire.

Implementing Cooperative Learning in Classrooms

It is truly ironic that schools, which are presumed to prepare students for the "real world," have evolved a social structure that is so unlike the real world. Perhaps it is because we pay lip service to what Johnson et al. (1984, p. 73) call "Myth 1: Schools Should Emphasize Competition Because It's a Dog-Eat-Dog World." Even if that were true, however, we would have a period of learning time in which our children would be spared from competition until they were ready for it, and then they would compete only against those of like abilities. Would you take your seven-year-old, who wants to learn to play baseball, out to a diamond and throw hardballs at him as fast as you can because "It's a dog-eat-dog world"? Of course not: you get a plastic ball and bat, throw it so that there is high probability of his catching and hitting successfully, and then slowly increase the difficulty of the task and similarity to actual game conditions *over a period of years.* School days should be a similarly protected period for learning and building self-confidence.

Anecdote 13.2

A High School Teacher's First Attempt at Cooperative Groups

I've had students work informally in groups for years, but in the past few years I had actually decreased the amount of group work. Whenever I had students working in groups, I spent all of my time and energy keeping the students on task. Frankly, groups were a pain to manage, and I couldn't see where they were enhancing learning the way I expected. So I decided that the kids just couldn't handle group work and began to abandon the practice. The idea that perhaps it might be the way I structured the activity that was the problem never entered my head. And yet, in theory, working together still seemed to be a sensible and educationally sound idea. . . .

I decided to try cooperative groups with my math 4 regents classes on a review assignment in analytic geometry which had caused students difficulty in the past. I chose the two days prior to Christmas vacation because traditionally not much gets accomplished on the days just before vacations and, thus if the experiment were unsuccessful, not much would be lost. To make group assignments, I ranked students according to their first quarter grades, then divided the list into three parts. A student from the top third was assigned as a leader, one from the middle third was assigned as the recorder, and a student from the last third was assigned as the researcher.

On the first day each group was given one packet including a direction/role-assignments sheet, research sheet, problem worksheet and evaluation form. Students were instructed to work with members of their own group during the class periods only, and that each member of the group would receive the same grade. The students were allowed to used their textbooks, notebooks and each other. I would answer questions about the requirements of the assignment, but would not explain the solutions to the problems while they were working.

I was utterly amazed at how hard and how cooperatively the students worked! They stayed on task, and as I moved around the room I heard excellent discussions of the problem and strategies to solve them. Also, the grades were excellent. The average grade by groups was 35 out of 40. All groups but one scored above 30. More important, both the students and I felt they had a good understanding of the material when they were done.

In addition to the gains in mathematical understanding, I saw many other positive results. Poorer students who had previously given up when confronted with hard assignments were encouraged by the others in the group. On student evaluation forms, every group reported that they had benefited from the group experience and wanted to do more group work in the future. They even said that they enjoyed, yes actually *enjoyed* the experience!

Janet Schachner
Teacher

It is just not true that the real world is mostly competitive. Johnson et al. (1981, p. 73) go on to say that "It is a person-help-person world." Even our most cherished capitalistic notions are more cooperative than competitive. Companies compete with each other, surely, but to have products or services to sell, they have large corporate enterprises designed to produce and distribute those products and services. The corporations are composed of interdependent networks of cooperative teams. Certainly individuals compete within these teams, but the entire enterprise depends primarily upon the team's success in rewarding individuals for cooperative, rather than competitive or individualistic, behavior.

Schools, in other words, are out of touch with reality to the extent that they are not using cooperative incentives and task structures. Because the typical school has evolved into the non-traditional individualistic or competitive social structures, it is not a simple matter to switch to cooperative processes. Educators, students, and parents alike must learn how to structure, and operate in, this new system. Thus extensive training and practice by teachers is necessary, initial fears and awkwardness by teachers and students will have to be overcome by success, parents will have to see that this will not reduce the quality of education, etc. All relearning of new behaviors in old situations is more difficult than initial learning, because of the interference from identical elements (recall the discussion on negative transfer in chapter 9). But the effects are worth it.

What then are the steps to be followed in implementing cooperative groups in the classroom? I shall summarize the advice given in the very practical books written for educators by Johnson, Johnson, Holubec and Roy (1984) or Johnson, Johnson and Holubec (1993). What follows is advice in the form of 18 steps, that are generally applicable, but which need to be adapted by teachers to fit their own unique requirements. (See also the advice in anecdote 13.3). The steps are subsumed under five general headings, which the authors call major sets of strategies, and which I shall label A through E. The steps follow.

A. Clearly specify the objectives for the lesson.
   1. Objectives are specified in two domains:
      a. Academic objectives, which need to be matched to the entry level of the students.
      b. Collaborative skills objectives, which specify the cooperative skills emphasized in this lesson.
B. Decide before the lesson how students are to be placed in the cooperative groups.
   2. Decide on the size of the group, from 2 to 6. If you are inexperienced with groups or time is short, use pairs or trios. It is probably never useful to go beyond six, and 2–4 is probably optimum for most purposes.
   3. Assign students to groups. For most purposes the groups should be heterogeneous in ability, ethnicity, gender, and task-orientation. If some student selection is desirable, place a student with one person he or she chose and the rest from among those not chosen to balance for the above considerations. Students can be reassigned for each new learning objective or after being together through several objectives. It is good practice to have students work with everyone in the class through the course of the year.
   4. Arrange the room to facilitate completing the objective, usually in circles so that every student can have eye contact with every other in the group.
C. Explain the task, goal structure and learning activity to the students.
   5. Use or distribute instructional materials which promote interdependence among the students. For example,

Anecdote 13.3

Managing Classes of Group Learners

Suppose you had a class of thirty language students whom you wanted to practice a conversation exercise, while remaining (mostly) on task. Which of the following ways of grouping students would you allow to monitor most easily whether each student was involved in the lesson?

   a. by having two groups of 15?
   b. by having three groups of 10?
   c. by having six groups of 5?
   d. by having ten groups of 3?
   e. by having fifteen groups of 2?

One teacher who has been grouping students for years at all levels of high school Spanish and French argues as follows:

Pairs are much better for several reasons. First, since a conversation can occur only if both people are involved, the probability is already higher from the beginning that all will be actively involved. With trios or more it is possible that one of two people will dominate, which prevents shy but willing persons from practicing and allows those who would like to avoid participating to do so. The probability of each person's participating is inversely related to the size of the group.

Second, it is much easier, therefore, to monitor the proportion of people participating in pairs than any other group size, again with the likelihood of determining any person's participation decreasing as the group size increases. And even though pairs of interacting students could be off task (talking of boy friends, etc.), it is surprisingly easy, and becomes easier with practice, to tune in to individual conversations to determine whether students are, in fact, avoiding the task. As you gain experience with the particular students in your class, you can also assign students to work together on the basis of their ability to keep each other on task.

Third, the real problem is that students do now know how to work in groups. It is easier to teach them how to do this in pairs than in larger groups.

For all of these reasons, I recommend that new teachers begin to experience group activities by working with pairs, and, later, experimenting with trios and larger groups.

Dr. Joseph Zampogna
Mentor Teacher

provide only one copy of the materials, give each student a different piece of materials, or establish a team format for intergroup competition (as in some of the procedures described earlier).

6. Assign roles which assure interdependence among the students. For example, one student may be the recorder, another the researcher, another the summarizer-checker, and another the presenter.

7. Explain the academic task so that students are clear about the assignment, so that they see how their past knowledge and experience is relevant to the current objectives, and so on. Ask specific questions to check whether students understand the assignment.
8. Structure the situation to provide positive goal interdependence—that is, to provide an incentive for making sure that all are responsible not only for their own learning, but also for the learning and task completion of all other group members.
9. Structure individual accountability by letting students know that in addition to the group task, each person's learning will be individually assessed in some way (practice tests, reading individual contributions to projects, etc.).
10. Structure intergroup cooperation. Unless one of the interteam competitive tournaments is being staged, it is effective to have each group's achievements contribute toward a goal for the whole class (for example, all students could receive bonus points for the grading period if all students in class achieve a preset standard of performance on a test or assignment).
11. Explain the criteria for success—the standard of performance required for certain grades. These are to be criterion-referenced, but may conform to the ideas described earlier for handicapping (as in the Students Teams-Achievement Division).
12. Specify the cooperative behaviors desired (e.g., stay in your own group, take turns, everyone should participate, listen to each person when he or she is speaking, and criticize ideas but not the presenter of the ideas).

D. Monitor the effectiveness of each group and intervene when necessary or desirable to answer questions or teach academic concepts or model interpersonal skills.

13. Monitor the behavior of the students in the groups. This can be done by counting instances of appropriate behaviors (time samplings) or recording interactions in order to give specific feedback on the group's processes and to reinforce desirable behaviors.
14. Provide task assistance—that is, help with the academic objective—if needed. However, do not be seduced into presenting to the group what they should do for or discover themselves.
15. Intervene whenever necessary to teach cooperative, collaborative skills. In the beginning the teacher may need to intervene more frequently than desirable; as the group learns to cooperate, the teacher can intervene by clarifying the problem, and turning it back to them for a solution. Intervene as rarely as possible, teaching communicative skills as the group needs them. Encourage cooperative, collaborative methods to solve interpersonal, as well as academic, problems.
16. Provide closure to the lesson by reconvening the class as a whole and having them summarize and organize what was learned, answer general questions, etc.

E. Evaluate the students' achievement and discuss the group processes.

17. Assess how well the students achieved the academic objectives, according to the previously announced criterion-referenced system.
18. Assess how well the students achieved the collaborative skills objectives. For example, the teacher may give feedback on task-orientation,

students' encouraging each other's contributions, the enjoyability of the experience, and so on.

These steps provide a useful structure for establishing cooperative groups in a classroom. Following these steps is a beginning. Perhaps implementing the experience with other colleagues who are doing the same will also be helpful. In any case, the first experience will not go as smoothly as the tenth. Remember the street musician's advice and "Practice, man, practice."

Mastery Learning

Consider the following two visionary statements about the role of testing in schools:

1. Time has been the one measurable factor in education until recently. Consequently, we have laid out our educational system in terms of time units. These have been constant, while the achievement of the pupils within these time units has varied according to individual ability. But with the development of the achievement test movement, it is becoming possible to reverse this order. We may now make units of achievement the constant factor, varying the time to fit the individual capacities of the children.

2. Advances in cognitive psychology and technology, however, make possible new kinds of measurement instruments. This new generation of tests will have three functions: (1) it will serve individuals more than institutions; (2) it will aim primarily at helping individuals learn and succeed rather than simply yielding scores for institutional decision-making; (3) it will guide instruction and self-development on a continuing basis rather than compare performance among test takers.

This new generation of tests will be *helping* measures, enabling individuals to keep pace with rising standards in education and the workplace.

The second statement was made by Gregory Anrig (1986), President of Educational Testing at their 1985 conference on *"The Redesign of Testing for the 21st Century."* The first, by Carleton Washburne, was made in 1922 in the opening paragraph of an article entitled "Educational Measurement as a Key to Individual Instruction and Promotions." In the 63 years intervening, the key difference between the two positions, as I see it, is that Anrig was speaking of computer-based technology, while Washburne couldn't even have envisioned computers.

The Winnetka Plan

Conceptually, the basic idea of using tests to assess a student's mastery of objectives, independently of other students' performances, was available over four decades before mastery learning became a popular idea. But Washburne, a superintendent of schools, was not just expressing a vision for the future. His article described the progress of his Winnetka, Illinois, school district in a three-year experiment with these new procedures.

The first step in establishing this mastery procedure was to decide what material was crucial to be learned and break that into specific "goals" or "achievement units" which were ordered into a logical sequence. Then tests and practice materials for each of these units were developed to complement each other. The tests, for example, were developed according to the following criteria: each test must sample from the entire range of skills in the unit; each test must be objectively scored; and each test must diagnose specific weaknesses to be remediated by turning to practice materials keyed directly to the answer choices of the test.

Corresponding to the tests were the practice materials which were developed according to the following criteria: they must (1) be understandable by the children themselves and self-instructional to the extent possible; (2) provide adequate practice on one element at a time; (3) allow the children to score their own exercises; (4) lead directly to practice tests which are alternative forms of the regular test, so that the students decide when they are ready to try the regular test again; and (5) be in one-to-one correspondence with specific items on the regular test.

The difference between the practice and regular tests was that the latter were corrected by the teacher. Students who passed the test received an OK in their "goal book," which students kept and which was sent home to parents once a month in lieu of a grade card. The goal book listed the objectives in simplified form. For example, for fifth grade language, some of the goals were correctly using a period at the end of a sentence and correct use of apostrophes. For arithmetic the goals were stated as standards of accuracy, as well as speed. They also included reviewing and becoming faster (automaticity goals?) on material learned in previous units. Thus to pass the multiplication of fractions test a student could pass by attempting a minimum of four problems in three minutes and get all correct, or attempt 10 and get nine correct.

The progress of students was individualized on major academic goals in arithmetic and language (including writing motor skills, grammar and punctuation) while tests and practice exercises were being developed on certain basics in history, geography, general science, and such special subjects as cooking and sewing. Thus it was not uncommon for a student to be working on fourth grade arithmetic and sixth-grade language in a fifth-grade classroom.

So much for the basic material on which every student was expected to achieve mastery. In Washburne's words (1922, p. 198):

There are no recitations; there is no grade repetition; there are no failures; there is no skipping. No child is held back to a slower rate than is natural to him; none is forced forward too rapidly for thorough work. Each "goal" must be achieved by each pupil before he can go on to the next goal.

If the description so far sounds like a totally individualized curriculum in which there was no social interaction among students, nothing could be further from the truth. These achievement units constituted only part of the curriculum. The rest—an equally important part taking from 1/3 to 1/2 of a school day, according to Washburne—was called *social work*. Social work was comprised of the entire range of subject matter which need not be mastered, but provided opportunities for students to express themselves, to develop social and communication skills, and to explore other fields of interest. These included class discussions, group projects, dramas, group singing, assemblies, sports and games. Since there were no required objectives to be achieved in social work activities, no testing or recitation was required on these activities.

From Winnetka to Today

The mastery learning idea did not die after Washburne described his program, but neither was it widely adopted. Perhaps the longest single thread of continuity from the Winnetka program to today's mastery systems is through the programmed instruction/teaching machines/computer-assisted instruction movement.

That movement started with Sidney Pressey's (1926; 1927; 1932) invention of a simple machine which could automatically administer and score tests—and teach, at least drill material.

A Repertoire of Teaching Skills 443

Photo 13.3. Social work: From parallel play to development of social skills.

The next major milestone was B. F. Skinner's invention of the teaching machine (Skinner, 1954; 1958; 1984). In small steps, these machines guided students through a curriculum at the student's own rate, advancing automatically when the student answered problems correctly, and requiring students to reconsider the problem when their answers were in error. Skinner was a pioneer in the technology of teaching, but he fully expected subject matter experts to write programs to take students along the road from novice toward expert. And while the teaching machine was clearly good at drill-and-practice exercises, it only remained for experts to write the programs which could teach novices to solve difficult problems and engage in expert-like thinking. This did not happen, however. Teaching machines became a commercially exploited fad and critics worried among other things, about (1) the emphasis on drill-and-practice and (2) the lack of social interaction in classrooms dominated by students individually working with machines. The first criticism was real but, to draw an analogy, one can hardly criticize the invention of television for the poor programming that is dominant. The second criticism is also unfair because

Skinner, like Washburne, expected these machines and programs to be a portion of the school curriculum, not to replace it. To take the most mundane use, the teacher could assign students, as needed, to work on a machine which patiently and repeatedly could give drill-and-practice that the teacher could not possibly have time to provide. This, in turn, would free the teacher to work individually or with small groups on other things, including more time for developing critical thinking and social skills.

About the time teaching machines were being stored in the supply closets of schools, a whole new technology was being ushered in. The computer and, with it, a new kind of programming—called computer-assisted instruction—was both praised and dammed as the newest teaching aide. In 1967, I reviewed the computer-assisted instructional (CAI) systems then available and drew the following conclusion (Gentile, 1967, p. 43):

The technical problem is virtually solved in the sense that more equipment is available with faster operating speeds than the educator knows how to use. The semantic problem is being solved with the development of languages which allow courses to be programmed relatively easily. What kinds of programs to write in order to use the equipment effectively *is, nevertheless, an almost untouched problem.*[6]

Now we have personal computers with an underlying electronics technology that seems light years from the technology of 1967, not to mention from Pressey's first machine. In contemporary classrooms, the predominant use of computer-assisted instruction is still drill and practice (Tobias, 1985). While effective, drill and practice has the smallest of the potential CAI effects in evaluation studies (e.g., Tobias reports that simulations and tutorial uses of computers have larger effects). To use any of these programs *effectively* requires a plan by the teachers to incorporate the computer programs into the curriculum, computer literacy on the part of teachers involved, as well as well-constructed, user-friendly software. Sadly, the more things change (e.g., computer technology), the more they remain the same (e.g., inefficient use of the technology).

This foray into one strand of the history of mastery learning was not to emphasize the technology of teaching. Whether the technology is textbooks, chalkboards-and-chalk or computers, the teacher will have to decide how and when it is used, and whether it needs to be modified or supplemented. But the programmed instruction-to-educational software movement was, and still is, a mastery learning movement that, in its essentials, connects both Washburne's system and the two most popular recent branches of mastery learning (Bloom's and Keller's, to be described shortly).

The most essential ingredient linking all these systems is the requirement that students will achieve certain crucial objectives to a high standard of performance, even if some students take longer than others. This implies decisions about (1) essential vs. nice-to-know objectives, (2) how to schedule time and resources to accommodate the needs and rates of different students, and (3) how to assess the attainment of those objectives. The next sections describe several approaches to solving these problems.

Bloom's Learning for Mastery

In 1968 Benjamin Bloom wrote a paper almost gleeful in tone, speaking of 90% of students in school achieving what only the top 20% could achieve previously, of better mental health in schools, and of renewed zest for learning. He had been influenced by John Carroll's (1963) Model of School Learning and, in particular, Carroll's redefinition of the term *aptitude* as *time needed to learn a given task*. Whereas aptitude had traditionally been considered an intellectual trait indicative of either the level or complexity of a person's potential attainment, Carroll reconceptualized it as indicating only the amount of time a person would require to achieve a certain learning outcome. Thus a person with high aptitude for a field (like math or languages) would require a short time to learn some objectives in that domain, while a person with low aptitude is merely relatively slower in attaining the same objectives.

Bloom deduced from this redefinition of aptitude, in the passage quoted in the Introduction to this chapter, that 95% of students should be able to achieve what only a few had previously achieved. What was required was to provide the proper *quality of instruction* and *opportunity* to have students *persevere*, or *spend the time they need, to learn the objectives* (all variables in Carroll's, 1963 model; see chapter 12).

How does one begin? Having no prior experience with such a method in his own courses, Bloom could not easily specify the absolute performances he would define as "mastery." Thus he tentatively based his criterion-referenced standards on the previous years' norm-referenced grades. That is, University of Chicago students were told what scores were required to obtain each grade, derived from the distribution of test scores on the normal curve from the previous semester. For example, in 1965 about 20% of his students received A's on the final exam. In 1966, however, students were told that if they achieved the same or higher scores as achieved by those who obtained an A in 1965, they would receive an A. They were not competing with their classmates, but with a standard derived from the past. Thus, all could surpass that standard, much as current world class track-and-field athletes, even those who do not win medals in world class competition, may all surpass the performances of previous generations of athletes. Furthermore, they would receive extra instructional help as needed, and multiple opportunities to pass the test "if at first they had not succeeded." The students rose to the occasion, and 80% of them surpassed the test scores that in the past only 20% achieved (Bloom, 1968). Those 80% all received A's on the final exam. By 1967 the instructor was adapting to the specific needs of the students better, with the result that 90% of that class achieved the "mastery" standard to obtain an A.

Fresh from this initial success, Bloom, his colleagues, and students embarked on an ambitious campaign to develop, publicize and assess "Learning for Mastery" (LFM) strategies at all levels and areas of schooling.[7] As a result, there are a number of entire school districts and many, many individual teachers using variations on the system from elementary school to graduate school, and in subjects as varied as reading, math, foreign languages and educational psychology.

What, then, are the essentials of the LFM programs? Lorin Anderson (1985) suggested that any program containing all of the following features could be properly identified as an LFM program:

1. Clearly specified objectives.
2. Assessment procedures which are short, yet valid for those objectives.
3. Preestablished standards for mastery.
4. Properly sequenced curriculum units comprised of the necessary facts, principles, and skills.
5. Feedback provided to the students concerning their learning.
6. Additional time and assistance for students who fail to meet the minimum passing standard, to correct misunderstandings.

Bloom's system, in other words, has no requirement concerning such issues as homogeneous or heterogeneous grouping, direct instruction or discovery, lecture or self-paced individualization. It is equally usable in small classes and large lecture halls, as long as the instructors (or aides) provide the feedback and extra assistance required by points 5 and 6.

Where such a mastery system cannot be used is in a class in which objectives are either unclear or unspecifiable. If they are unclear or too vague, the only educationally responsible action is to clarify them for the benefit of both students and teachers. Where they are originally unspecifiable—as in some exploratory research, artistic creation, or original essay—then the criteria for mastery cannot be established and mastery learning is not possible. But such classes are in the minority. Almost all classes have some clearly specifiable objectives which are considered essential for all to achieve. These can be taught according to a mastery system, while other enrichment work or projects that are chosen as individual preferences can be assessed in other ways, or not formally assessed at all, as was done with "social work" in the Winnetka Plan. Later, I shall suggest a procedure for grading such individualized, creative projects in a criterion-referenced manner, even if mastery standards cannot be pre-established.

Central to the assessment in LFM of whether students are mastering objectives is the distinction between *formative* and *summative* evaluation. Bloom, Hastings and Madaus (1971, p. 117) provided the contrast as follows:

perhaps the essential characteristic of summative evaluation is that a judgment is made about the student, teacher, or curriculum with regard to the effectiveness of learning or instruction, after the learning or instruction has taken place.

Later, on the same page:

Formative evaluation is for the use of systematic evaluation in the process of curriculum construction, teaching, and learning for the purpose of improving any of these three processes.

By their definition, *summative* evaluation could be used for either norm-referenced or criterion-referenced purposes and seems to imply a finality that is contradictory to the idea of mastery learning. Bloom et al. recognize that it is this "final judgment" characteristic of summative evaluation which is the root of anxiety and defensiveness among students and teachers alike. But rather than arguing for the abolition of the summative exam, they argue (p. 117), "We do not believe it is possible to escape from the use of summative evaluation, nor would we wish to do so."

The summative evaluation—or final exam—is used in the LFM system as the major, if not sole, way to obtain grades and certify a student's competence. They do want it to be criterion-referenced and use it to define what are de facto the course objectives. They do this systematically by establishing a *Table of Specifications* (e.g., Block and Anderson, 1975; Bloom et al., 1971) for the course. This is a listing of the content areas that a student is expected to master, along with the intellectual operations (e.g., from Bloom's, 1956, Taxonomy) students will be able to perform with regard to those content areas. For example, if the content concerns "negative reinforcement" and "punishment," test items may be drawn up that concern simple recall of definitions, creating or recognizing situations that fit the definitions, analyzing real-life situations into the component parts, and so forth (much as was done in table 12.2; see also table 15.1, p. 503). The items define what are, in fact, the objectives being measured and, therefore, intentionally taught.

Having established the objectives and the summative test for those objectives, the next step is to establish *formative tests* (Block and Anderson, 1975). These are test items on small clusters of objectives, such as in one chapter in a textbook, designed (1) to diagnose whether students have mastered those objectives, and (2) if not, to suggest the kind of study that would correct the misunderstandings. No grades are assigned to these tests; since this initial learning is at the formative stage, LFM proponents argue, feedback and assistance should be offered, but without the evaluative connotations that accompany grades (Airasian, 1971, Bloom, 1981). During this formative assessment phase, a number of techniques are recommended for helping students master the material, including independent reading, academic games, peer tutoring, cooperative groups, and specially designed remedial programs (Block and Anderson, 1975). Following such correctives, students demonstrate mastery of these objectives on a parallel formative test.

Proponents of the LFM system have written prolifically on their techniques and the belief system that surrounds it. The interested reader is referred to the following sources as a beginning: Anderson, 1985; Block (1971a; 1974a); Block and Anderson (1975) Bloom (1968; 1976; 1981); Bloom, Hastings and Madaus (1971). Rather than go into any more detail, our purposes will be better served by examining the evidence on the effectiveness of the system in general, and the claims in particular.

Claims and Evidence

Bloom's (1968) initial claim, that upwards of 90% of the students could achieve under mastery learning what only 20% had achieved previously under traditional instruction, was soon illustrated in a juxtaposition of curves,[8] as shown in Figure 13.1.

The shaded area was the presumed result of mastery learning. Bloom (1968, p. 3) made the point this way:

> *The normal curve is not sacred. It describes the outcome of a random process. Since education is a purposeful activity in which we seek to have students learn what we teach, the achievement distribution should be very different from the normal curve, if our instruction is effective. In fact, our educational efforts may be said to be* unsuccessful to the extent that student achievement is normally distributed.

In other words, he argued, the correlation between aptitude for a subject and achievement scores was .70 or above as an artifact of all students receiving the same time to learn

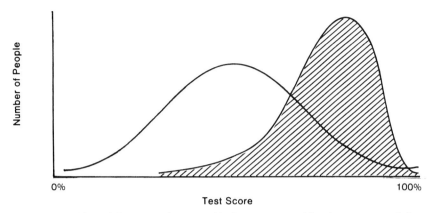

Figure 13.1. The juxtaposition of the normal curve with the curve resulting from successful completion of LFM programs (shaded area).

and the same quality of instruction (the fast students learn more than the slow, and thus the rank order from pretest to posttest does not change, as in the normal curve). Under a mastery strategy, on the other hand, the slow students would catch the fast students, with the result that the correlation between aptitude and achievement should approach zero.

This is true, by definition of mastery, since all students eventually pass a parallel form of a given criterion test. However, *it is true only for the limited objectives being tested.* If the faster students continue on with enrichment materials, or overlearn the material by, for example, tutoring their slower peers, then they will be expected to (1) organize the material better, (2) recall it better, and (3) have a higher probability of applying it to new materials. (On the other hand, if the faster learners are just given free time, then it could be argued that they are being held back in favor of teaching slower students; Arlin, 1982, presents data suggesting that teachers, particularly those who are new to mastery procedures, may indeed allocate time to help slower learners at the expense of faster learners). Thus a surprise retention test or a transfer test would virtually have to show another normal curve, with a high correlation between aptitude and these broader achievement measures. This does not, in the least, discourage most educational researchers. The implications are, as argued in the research on retention by fast and slow learners in chapter 10 (see also Gentile, 1987), that it is worth the effort getting people to learn to a high level of mastery because of the effect on retention. But no one expected mastery learning to eliminate individual differences in learning.

Almost no one, that is. By 1976, Bloom carried this "decreasing variability" correlation argument even further, declaring that the research he and his students had done (see also Block, 1974a) had led him to the view (1976, p. x, also in 1981, p. 135):

> *Most students become very similar with regard to learning ability, rate of learning, and motivation for further learning—when provided with favorable learning conditions.*

In essence, Bloom was arguing that in early units there would be great variation in the amount of time and assistance students need to attain mastery in a given subject, with low aptitude students needing perhaps 5 or 6 times as much time as high aptitude students. After repeated exposure to the mastery procedure, the slower students would learn how to learn and also would accumulate the relevant

Anecdote 13.4

A Study of Bloom's Decreasing Variability Hypothesis

Testing 376 graduate students, mostly teachers, from four semesters of a course on the psychology of learning and instruction, Livingston and Gentile (1996) tested Bloom's decreasing variability hypothesis—namely, that the differences between the faster and slower learners existing at the beginning of the course would disappear by the end. Those who passed the initial test on one try were classified as fast learners; those who needed more than one try were called slower learners. The individual scores, variabilities of each test, and correlations among the test scores were calculated for the three successive units for these students, as well as for six units (including a follow-up course) for a subsample of 85 students.

Contrary to Bloom's hypothesis, the variability (standard deviation) did not decrease over time, nor did the correlations between initial measures and later tests show declines. Rather, there was remarkable stability in the test correlations (from .22 to .48) for such a crude measure of rate of learning—namely, whether students passed or failed their first mastery test. That is, graduate students initially identified as fast learners tended to remain faster on subsequent units, while their slower counterparts continued to need extra time and assistance to attain the same level of achievement. With that extra time and assistance, usually one or two remedial sessions, almost all of the students passed all tests by the end of the semester.

The authors concluded ". . . that although LFM is effective as a philosophy and method for teaching (in this case graduate students), there is little evidence that it reduces initial differences in learning rates among students."

entry knowledge for succeeding units in a properly sequenced curriculum. Thus, on later units the time and help required by the slower students would be considerably reduced, high and low aptitude students would be much more alike in their learning, and the result could be a slow:fast learner ratio of only perhaps 1.5 to 1.0.

Assume Bloom and supporters are correct, so that the differences in learning rates of students become ". . . very difficult to measure except by the most exact measurements of time" (Bloom, 1981, p. 136). It follows, then that the previously slower students would now be able to relearn the material at the 1.5 to 1.0 ratio Bloom predicted (and reported in the study by Gentile et al; 1995; see chapter 10). It does not follow that a 1.5 to 1.0 ratio makes these students "very similar," even on the relearning. And on new units of material there is little evidence that the slower students have caught up with the faster in learning rate: rather there seems to be a rather stable correlation in the range of .35 for learning rate across tasks (e.g., Gentile et al., 1995; Livingston & Gentile, 1996; Stroud & Schoer, 1959). See also anecdote 13.4.

This should not be surprising. Students come to school with different behavioral, emotional and social histories (not to mention genetic differences), as well as specific knowledge structures. All school learning occurs on top of that. Thus, even if LFM or any other teaching technique should eliminate any further spreading out of the distribution of scores, it will certainly not cancel out the normal curve with which we began. (This should remind you of the dilemma in chapter 3 of how intelligence can at once grow and remain the same.) And if it should make the learning rate close to the same for all, it would do so only on material quite similar to the previous material. See also Arlin (1984) for similar arguments.

In summary, even if LFM somewhat homogenizes learners in the time and assistance needed in learning subsequent units, it will not substantially alter the students' relative class standing, even on other achievement measures on the same concepts (e.g., a surprise retention test or a transfer test). What, then, does mastery learning do if it does not assure equality of educational outcome? *It provides equality of educational opportunity* by assuring that students are prepared, by having mastered the essential prerequisites, for subsequent units. (Carroll, 1989, makes a similar argument concerning the philosophy behind his model). While this issue has received much space in print, and is perhaps important in its own right, *it is not central to the concept or usefulness of mastery learning as a teaching technique.*

Reviewers of LFM studies consistently conclude the following:

1. LFM programs are at least as effective, usually more effective, than programs not incorporating the defining features of mastery on both cognitive and affective outcomes (e.g., Anderson, 1985; Anderson and Burns, 1987; Arlin, 1984; Block, 1974a; Block and Burns, 1977; Block, Efthim & Burns, 1989; Bloom, 1976; Burns, 1979; Hyman and Cohen, 1979; Kulick & Kulick, 1991; Stallings and Stipek, 1986).[9]

2. LFM programs have their main effect by setting a high passing standard and then providing "correctives" and encouragement until students achieve those standards—and continue to expect to achieve those standards (Anderson, 1985; Stallings and Stipek 1986).

Mastery Learning: Some General Issues

We have now explored in some depth the first mastery learning system (the Winnetka plan), as well as two quite diverse modern approaches, one which emphasizes self-pacing (PSI, see anecdote 13.5) and one which emphasizes a more traditional group-based approach (LFM). We have also seen how some of the cooperative groups also include individual mastery requirements, and thus these provide further viable variations that can be used within a mastery framework (see also anecdote 13.6). Thus one firm conclusion to be drawn is that mastery is not *a* single system—it encompasses a wide variety of approaches which have at least the following in common:

1. a set of objectives broken into units (that are ordered sequentially according to a task analysis, where that is appropriate);
2. a requirement for demonstrating mastery to a high level (usually much higher than required to pass under traditional methods) on each unit; and
3. a grading method that is criterion-referenced, rather than norm-referenced.

A second conclusion is that mastery systems work. Block and Burns (1977) and Burns (1979) estimated that, on the basis of the comparative studies of mastery with more traditional methods, the typical mastery-taught student should move from the fiftieth to the eightieth percentile of the nonmastery group. Kulik et al. (1979) drew a slightly more conservative conclusion about size of effect, studying

Anecdote 13.5

A Totally Individualized Mastery System:
Keller's Personalized System of Instruction (PSI)

On the way into a college classroom, you are given a handout which begins as follows:

> *This is a course through which you may move, from start to finish, at your own pace. You will not be held back by other students or forced to go ahead until you are ready. At best, you may meet all the course requirements in less than one semester; at worst, you may not complete the job within that time. How fast you go is up to you. (Keller, 1968; pp. 80–81).*

The handout goes on to describe that the course has been divided into a number of units, perhaps 15 to 30, each of which is comprised of some readings and a kind of homework or laboratory assignment. Your job is to read the text materials and complete these exercises, which can be done in part during class time, and then to demonstrate mastery of each unit by passing a mastery test or properly carrying out an experiment. Achieving mastery on the first unit qualifies you for the second unit, and so on, in numerical order of the units. When you have passed all units, you are ready for a final examination, which may be taken at several times before the end of the semester, as well as during exam week, or later by appointment with the instructor.

Perhaps the biggest surprise of all is that lectures are optional and no examination is based on them. Furthermore, lectures and demonstrations ". . . will be provided only when you have demonstrated your readiness to appreciate them" (Keller, 1968, p. 80). That is, mastering prerequisite units earns you a ticket to the lecture—*the lecture is a reinforcer for appropriate achievement.*

More surprises. In this very large course, you are one of 10–15 students assigned to a *proctor,* who is another student who has previously completed the course. The proctor's role is to administer and score the mastery tests, to go over those tests with you, and help you learn any material that is difficult for you. Proctors are available during class time, and perhaps at other hours by arrangement. The proctors themselves may be receiving credit in another course, or they may just be volunteers (to learn the material better and for the experience teaching it).

These are the essentials of the Personalized System of Instruction, known more commonly as either the Keller Plan" or as PSI, which makes Fred Keller the father of *PSI*chology (Gentile, 1976).[10] Although Keller's PSI has not been as popular at the elementary and secondary levels, it has been adopted—and studied—in higher education classes. In reviewing the research evidence on teaching by any and all methods in higher education, Michael Dunkin (1986) came to the following conclusion about PSI (p. 759):

> *The single most significant conclusion to be reached from research on innovatory teaching methods in higher education is that the Keller Plan is clearly superior to other methods with which it has been compared. Indeed, the Keller Plan has been so consistently found superior that it must rank as the method with the greatest research support in the history of research on teaching.*[11]

Anecdote 13.6

Verbal Fluency as Part of a Mastery Requirement

When one of the aims of a lesson is fluency in discussing the material, student interviews may be a useful method. Developed by Ferster (1968; Ferster and Perrott, 1968), pairs of students must schedule interviews on the study questions of a unit. One person is the speaker, who practices teaching the material, guided by the study questions, to the listener. The listener's job is to listen, and when the speaker is finished, to ask for clarifications, discuss problem areas, etc., as a peer coach. Each student listens once for each time he or she is a speaker, but with different partners. This technique is sometimes suggested as a prerequisite for a mastery test (e.g., Keller, 1968), but it can also be used as evidence of mastery for some objectives if the teacher can find a way to be the listener.

only PSI systems. More recent research (Anderson & Burns, 1987; Block, Efthim & Burns, 1989; Guskey & Gates, 1986; Guskey & Pigott, 1988; Kulik & Kulik, 1991; Kulik, Kulik & Bangert-Drowns, 1990; Martinez & Martinez, 1992) has estimated that compared with more traditional instruction, mastery learning has an effect size ranging from .4 to .6, or about half a standard deviation. But even if the most conservative of conclusions is drawn, it would have to be—like Colgate toothpaste's old advertisement—that mastery learning is "unsurpassed." For example, after reviewing some favorable and some nonsignificant results on elementary school students, Stallings and Stipek (1986, p. 745) argue:

> In general, the evidence available suggests that mastery learning programs have a mildly positive effect upon student achievement and attitudes.

They then go on to ask, "Why then are these programs so controversial?" and describe some of the common criticisms of the approach, criticisms which are more philosophical than empirical.

One criticism concerns the holding up of brighter (faster) students while the slower ones are repeatedly attempting to master the unit. First of all, this criticism does not apply to the PSI system. But even within the LFM system, the faster learners would be waiting around only if the teacher did not provide other activities for those who finished earlier. One example of faster learner activities is helping the slower learners, with the benefit of providing overlearning, teaching experience, and cooperative social experiences. Other examples might be called "enrichment" activities. For example, extra reports; transfer activities; creative applications; working at the analysis, synthesis, and evaluation levels of Bloom's taxonomy—activities that are above and beyond the objectives to be mastered—can be given here. Such activities can also be built into the grading scheme as I show in the grading chapter.

Another criticism is that mastery learning is too structured and too skills-oriented, not allowing for creativity. It is indeed oriented to mastering basic skills, knowledges, and procedures which have been identified as the building blocks and scaffolding of an expert's knowledge structure. The point is not to allow students to escape mastering the essentials, but, as Carroll (1989) noted (see also chapter 12), what constitutes mastery does not have to be drill-and-practice on the smallest elements. Mastery of reading, often conceived as only drilling sounds and letters, might also be conceived as comprehension and writing of thought-sized units. Better yet, it could include some of each so that creativity and excitement are not divorced from mastery.

Is mastering the objectives the end state? Absolutely not. It is the beginning. Mastering the forehand stroke in tennis is not an endstate; it is the initial state for joining the exciting world of tennis players. This is where mastery systems in schools have tended to fail: by treating mastery of an objective as one more task to be checked off as having been completed, so we can move on to the next, and the next, ad nauseam. What is needed instead is a view of mastery as the initial step enabling students to explore the exciting world of advanced uses and creative thinking of those mastered skills—perhaps via enrichment activities—and a grading scheme congruent with such a view (see chapter 14).

A final criticism to be considered here is the extra work it requires of the teacher. In the beginning that is true, because the curriculum must be created or reexamined and broken into small units, parallel tests must be written, study guides and remedial activities must be designed, and the grading scheme must be reconceptualized. All of these tasks can be shared by teams of teachers. Happily, materials developed can be used in subsequent years and, like everything else, the task of teaching it becomes easier over time. If teachers still object because their experience has convinced them that there are too many children not sufficiently capable or motivated to learn, then indeed these teachers need to be convinced of the benefits of mastery learning. As Stallings and Stipek concluded (1986, p. 746):

Mastery learning advocates no doubt make an important contribution to student learning by convincing teachers that all children can master the curriculum. Indeed, the achievement gains observed for children in mastery-based programs may be explained as much by teachers' enhanced expectations, especially for the low-ability students, as by any other aspect of the program.

Have Stallings and Stipek hedged their bets by implying it is only teachers' expectations that change? Consider the following hypothetical conversation between two teachers:

A: I understand that Donna Dull has been scoring above 80 on your tests, when she hasn't passed any of mine all year.
B: That's right.
A: But, of course, you let your students take the tests over if they don't pass.
B: *Let* them! I *make* them take it over. I require all of my students to *learn* the material. Do you *let* your students escape without learning?

Mastery systems have high expectations backed up with high standards and, like the proverbial Japanese mother, do not allow students to settle for less.

Implementing Mastery Learning in Classrooms

Because of the wide range of possibilities for conducting mastery learning, it is impossible to create a single list of steps involved. The following is my attempt to list some of the steps that probably apply to whatever system you choose.

1. Divide your current curriculum into units, each perhaps two weeks in length.

Cartoon 13.1

2. Decide what information and skills in the curriculum are essential to know and which are "nice-to-know" or enrichment activities.
3. Consider the essential information and skills as the objectives for that unit and write them as "behavioral objectives" or as study questions. These are to be shared with the students (as a handout or a display on the board).
4. Write test questions (two or three at a minimum at about the same level of difficulty) for each objective.
5. Randomly assign the questions by objective to two or three parallel forms of a mastery test (and to a final examination if one is to be included).

Notes on Steps 4 and 5. If you are using non-objective style tests, such as essay, oral or performance tests, then devise a scoring key designed to assess attainment of the objectives.

6. Decide what the passing standard should be and what grades, if any, should be assigned to those who have passed and to those who have not yet passed.
   a. Set the standard as high as your ability to measure will allow (e.g., a passing score should probably never be below 75% correct, because then chance begins to play too much of a role; and rarely, if ever, should it be above 95%, because it is impossible to write perfect tests).
   b. Let the students know what the standard is, why it is set at that level, and what grades are attached to the passing standard.
   c. Let the students know that they will be expected to attain that standard, but they will receive additional help, if needed, and be given other opportunities to pass (as in an exam for a driver's license).

(For students' views on how it feels to retake mastery exams, see anecdote 13.7)

Anecdote 13.7

How Does it Feel to Retake A Mastery Test

As part of a mastery thesis, Kirsten Hoffman (1994) followed seven students throughout their first semester-long experience of mastery learning in a graduate course in educational psychology. The students ranged from 23 to 47 years in age and were majoring in various education specialties. They agreed to keep a diary of their experiences in class, studying, testing, etc. to be shared with and published anonymously by the researcher.

As the first mastery test approached, some students reported feeling more stressed than under other testing methods:

> Sandra: I have NEVER been a nervous test taker, so why was I for this one? . . . this is very definitely a very strange and foreign notion. I'm sure I wouldn't even consider the idea of blowing a test if I didn't have to retake it if I do . . . there's this feeling I might "never" be done studying for a particular test. (p. 52)

Others reported feeling so little anxiety that they were less inspired to study:

> Elena: Unfortunately, my study habits weren't up to par. The whole idea of only having to get an 80% to pass I found as not much motivation. (pp. 52–53)

Upon failing a test, there was also a range of reactions from a bit of guilt at having another chance to the following:

> John: Although it took me three tries, I feel like I know the material well. Overall, I feel good about retaking the test because I know that I have achieved my goal of learning the material. (p. 53)

> Douglas: I am now working on studying the material so I can do well on the make-up exam. I am grateful that this opportunity is available. I can see how this experience can be applied to a future student of mine. . . . (p. 54)

How do these reactions compare with your own experience in a mastery-based classroom? Among other findings, Hoffman (1994) concluded: ". . . all seven participants demonstrated a faith in the mastery learning system by suggesting its potential use in their own classrooms some day." (p. 64)

7. Optional: Use one of the forms of the test as a pretest to see which students, if any, have already mastered the material and/or to diagnose which particular parts of the unit are likely to cause the most trouble for some students.
8. Teach to the objectives by presenting information, providing activities, having discussions, responding to student questions, etc. NOTE: Many, if not all, of your previous teaching activities can be used here. In other words, as long as you are teaching to the objectives, you do not have to change your teaching style. On the other hand, you could adopt a totally individualized system such as Keller's PSI.
9. Optional: Use one of the forms of the test as a practice test, designed to give students feedback on how well they are learning the material. This test is, therefore, being used as a teaching exercise—a formative test.
10. Review and teach any concepts that are difficult for those who need extra help. For those who are well on their road to mastery, provide enrichment activities (e.g., the "nice-to-know" material in the unit).
11. Give a mastery test at a scheduled time, using one of the forms of the test.
12. a. For those students who pass, provide optional assignments as enrichment and/or to raise their grade.
    b. For those students who did not pass, provide remedial practice designed to help them pass (i.e., return to steps 10 and 11).
13. Move on to the next unit and repeat the process.
    a. If the next unit builds hierarchically on the previous unit, then students cannot move on until they have mastered the previous one. If it is relatively independent of the previous unit, students may work on mastering the old unit while beginning on the new one.
    b. Include in your new unit objectives from past units, first, to enhance retention and, second, to assist students in transferring relevant material from one topic to another.

Beyond Mastering Objectives: Encouraging Creativity in the Classroom

Suppose, having never before seen nor heard of a dolphin, you encountered one which had been trapped in a small, shallow pool by a disaster that closed off its escape route back to the ocean. As you approach to get a closer look, you find the animal also purposely (or is it "porpoisely") approaching you. To your amazement, you find yourself describing the animal as friendly, playful, and intelligent. The question is just how intelligent is this animal or, to put it another way, just what can it do?

If you continue to observe this big fish in a small pond, you will probably learn what it eats, how fast it can swim, and that it is capable of rising slightly above the surface of the water and of seeming to stand up in the water. However, you would not discover that it can learn (if it cannot already do so) to jump out of the water, do flips, and walk backwards on top of the water, as dolphins commonly do in aquarium shows. One reason you would not discover these creative behaviors is the limited habitat in which you found the dolphin. The shallow pool, in limiting the depths to which the dolphin can dive, also therefore restricts the heights it can attain. Another reason you would not discover the tricks of which the dolphin is capable is that your own expectations are limited: you expect only what you see, since you cannot imagine the dolphin in a more creativity-inducing environment.

To continue our imaginary problem, suppose your interest in this newly discovered creature is more than idle curiosity, because you are the animal trainer at an aquarium. Thus you can't wait to start training the dolphin for one of your shows. The problem remains: you still do not know what tricks it is capable of performing. How will you decide? Think about your options for a moment.

Most people agree it would be a very foolish trainer, indeed, who established specific objectives and mastery standards and tried to reinforce the dolphin for attaining those objectives. Having the dolphin poke an underwater button to ring a bell and release balloons might be such a trainer-defined objective. The dolphin could probably master it by being fed fish contingent upon poking the button, but we are left with at least two unsettling problems. First, we are still ignorant about the behaviors of which the animal is capable. Second, why have we chosen such a trivial task for the animal to master? It may show that we can manipulate our trainee, but of what use is it to the trainee to master that behavior?

Fortunately, for the dolphins and humans, the trainers of dolphins try to suspend their own judgment on the content of the show. What they do first is to catalogue the behaviors of the dolphins in various situations and plot the base rates of those behaviors. Armed with the knowledge of what behaviors were common or high frequency and which were infrequent, the trainers next encourage the dolphins to emit more uncommon behaviors. They do this at feeding time by blowing a whistle and giving the dolphins fish soon after any novel behavior, but not after common behavior. This procedure, as we learned in the chapter on operant conditioning, has the effect of increasing the frequency of novel behaviors. The next phase of training, then, is to keep raising the standard: as a previously novel behavior becomes more common, it no longer receives reinforcement and the dolphin has to introduce a still more novel behavior. For example, the first time a dolphin leaped partially out of the water, it would receive reinforcement. After it was doing that regularly, the trainer would withhold reinforcement until it came further, perhaps totally, out of the water. Later still, the dolphin would amaze the trainers by jumping out of the water and flipping, or jumping higher yet to grab a fish from the trainer's hand, and so forth. Continuing this process, the trainer would discover a number of "tricks" of which the dolphin was capable, all invented by the dolphin. Later, the trainers would have to bring these under their commands (discriminative cues) to have a sequenced performance, but the creativity of the show emerged from the trainer's establishing conditions for the trainee to attempt novel behaviors. In fact, this procedure is widely used to train dolphins (Pryor, 1969).

The moral of the above story is probably obvious but, believe it or not, there are some well-intentioned mastery learning classes in which students and teacher alike seem to be submerged in a sea of exercises whose only reward seems to be another exercise. These people need to be encouraged to leap out of the water and become more creative. Mastery learning was never meant to be a lonely task which dominates the entire day. When so used it deserves the label mechanistic. But note that it is not the system which is mechanistic, but the users (or maybe the curriculum publishers) who have made it so. Properly used, only the most important objectives should be tested for mastery (which is what Sizer, 1985, means by "less is more"). Many other educational goals, and a good portion of a typical day, should be invested in exercises of a social, creative nature. These may include creativity and intellect-developing exercises, transfer and enrichment exercises, and cooperative teams, to name only a few. In this section I shall describe some additional teaching procedures which have been recommended for developing creativity.[12]

So that there is no confusion, I shall interpret the term creativity in a very broad sense.

A Repertoire of Teaching Skills 457

Photo 13.4. Beyond mastery: Send in the Clowns.

A creative act will be defined as any behavior, idea, or invention that is novel, but repeatable, for that individual. This definition is similar to Young's (1985, p. 78), who defined creativity as the "skill of bringing about something new and valuable" and to Bruner's (1961, p. 22) definition of discovery as including ". . . all forms of obtaining knowledge for oneself by the use of one's own mind." Skill and repeatability imply that, although an accident may be responsible for a creation, the person can re-establish the conditions necessary to create the event or product again. Newness and value of a creation, by my interpretation, may be judged solely by reference to the individual. In other words, I do not wish to discriminate, for example, useful from useless inventions, or scientific breakthroughs from personal discoveries that other people discovered long ago. Nor do I wish to restrict us to thinking that creativity is what the gifted and talented do. The reason I wish not to restrict the definition to truly novel behaviors or to the gifted is because educators have the responsibility of encouraging all students to make personal discoveries and create (what for them are) novel behaviors or ideas. The child who writes her first story or poem is making a creative accomplishment every bit as important *for her future* as a scientist's discovery of a treatment for a disease is making for society's future. Both should be encouraged for their accomplishment, and for continuing to improve the quality and quantity of their creations. And, to return to the relation between the mastery of prerequisites and creativity, it is equally true for scientist and elementary school child that "Discovery, like surprise, favors the well prepared mind" (Bruner, 1961, p. 22).

Synectics

William J. J. Gordon devised an organized approach to developing creative ways of perceiving and solving problems, particularly for industrial use. He borrowed the word *synectics* from the Greek, which means ". . . the joining together of different and apparently irrelevant elements" (Gordon, 1961, p. 3). The idea was to invent a system which would guarantee that novel ways of stating or perceiving a problem would occur, thus increasing the probability of reaching successful solutions to problems.

One way of doing this is bringing a diverse group of individuals together—heterogeneous rather than homogeneous groups—with an optimal size of about five. Gordon (1961) argues that, even more important than intellectual diversity in composition of the group, is emotional and experiential diversity. This criterion for the composition of the group is based on fundamental beliefs about creativity.

Synectics theory holds that:

(i) creative efficiency in people can be markedly increased if they understand the psychological process by which they operate;
(ii) in creative process the emotional component is more important than the intellectual, the irrational more important than the rational; and
(iii) it is these emotional, irrational elements which can and must be understood in order to increase the probability of success in a problem-solving situation (Gordon, 1961, p. 6).

Synectics is not against rationality or an individual's creative act, however. The problem is that we are prone to jump to conclusions and want reasons for each new idea; if an early idea cannot be supported by evidence or logic, it is discarded before it is fully explored. Thus we need to avoid trying to express complete, rational ideas. "Ultimate solutions to problems are rational; the process of finding them is not." (Gordon, 1961, p. 11)

Regarding the individual vs. the group, properly operating groups can compress into hours the exploration of a number of ideas that might take months for an individual. For this to happen, of course, the members of the group must be committed to the group's goal more than to personal credit for ideas. This, in turn, depends on a non-threatening task-orientation for the group.

So much for the rationale. Procedurally, the synectics process has two components (Gordon, 1961, p. 33):

(i) making the strange familiar;
(ii) making the familiar strange.

Making the strange familiar means understanding a novel object or idea by analogy with something we already know. That is, we perceive and assimilate new experience according to the knowledge structure we already possess. This is the logical, rational means by which we add to our knowledge and skills and grow from novices toward experts in various fields. The problem is, as we have seen in earlier chapters, if each new situation is understood in terms of old experiences, we are prone to mental rigidity and proactive interference.

To overcome this, synectics exercises are based on ways of *making the familiar strange*— that is, to attempt consciously to invert or distort things, people, ideas, and feelings so that we view them perhaps as the proverbial extraterrestrial visitor would, uncluttered by our preconceptions.

Consider an example from art. Those of us who claim not to be able to draw (or perhaps we can only draw flies . . . or drapes . . . or paychecks) are often unknowingly too mentally rigid to see the object that is actually before us. For example, if you plan to draw a four-legged chair, whether you can actually see all four legs, or the apparent lengths of each, depends on your location relative to the chair. Our previous experience and logic tells us that all four legs are present and the same length, so we draw what we think the chair *should* look like, rather than *how it appears.* Our rationality interferes with our being able to draw what we actually see: the chair is so familiar to us that we disbelieve the sensation hitting the retinas of our eyes (perception overrides sensation). One way to overcome the problem is to make this familiar object strange by drawing it upside down (but note that taking a picture of it and turning the picture upside down is easier than drawing while standing on your head). Another way is to visualize the space around the chair and draw it. In her unique way of teaching the art of drawing, Betty Edwards (1979, p. 103) put it this way:

You probably have seen cartoons . . . where . . . Bugs Bunny, for example . . . runs down a hallway and smashes through a closed door, leaving a Bugs Bunny-shaped hole in the door.

Image this seeming paradox in your mind: what's left of the door is the negative space, and the inner edge of that shape is the edge of the negative space and also is the outline of the positive form (Bugs Bunny). In other words, the empty hole and the solid door share edges, and if you draw one you will have also drawn the other. With instructional assistance and this new way of drawing, people find they can draw much better than they thought.[13]

Synectics uses three metaphorical or analogical procedures for making the familiar strange: personal analogy, direct analogy, and symbolic analogy.[14] A synectics group practices using and analyzing, as part of the group process, each of these procedures.

Practice with *personal analogy* occurs by having the individuals imagine that they *are* the object or idea with which they are working. This is not to be merely role-playing, but is designed to provide empathic identification with the object. At first, most people feel self-conscious and anxious imagining they are, for example, a car engine. Their initial descriptions are likely to be just factual—"I feel greasy," "I have many moving parts." When pressed to identify with how it feels to be an engine, they may go slightly further and admit feeling "powerful." But the leader requires the individual to explore these feelings and facts further, which may elicit more empathetic statements, such as "It is difficult to maintain the proper temperature for efficient functioning—I'm constantly worrying about my hoses and circulating the anticoolant." Or, the individual might say "I feel exploited. I cannot determine when I start and stop. Someone does that for me." (from Joyce and Weil, 1980, p. 169)

Direct Analogy is practiced when the group sets out to find actual examples of how the idea works elsewhere in nature. To continue the automobile engine example, suppose you were trying to find an alternative way to cool the engine. The leader might ask, "How do other things we know about maintain temperature within a certain desirable range?" Various people might mention a dog panting, an elephant giving itself a shower at the water hole, a thermostat turning on the heat or air conditioner in the house. Each of these ideas can then be explained further until their mechanics are understood, and then the feasibility of using this idea for the current problem can be explored.

Synectics uses *symbolic analogy* to come up with a two-word description to capture the essence of the solution needed. Since this essence is often, but not necessarily, captured in two opposite or contradictory words, this type of metaphor is also called "compressed conflict" or "the essential paradox." Examples cited are Pasteur's "safe attack" to describe the immune system's response to invading microorganisms, or the Indian rope trick as the essence of a hydraulic jack (small enough to fit under the object to be lifted, which grows taller as the object is jacked higher).

Taken together, these techniques are a way of forcing us to suspend judgment and explore alternatives (much as we saw in de Bono's lateral thinking and Bransford and Stein's IDEAL Problem-Solver in chapter 11). In industrial settings, an expert is often one member of the group. There, however, the goal is usually an invention—a better mousetrap or more efficient automobile engine. In education, our goals would usually be novel ideas, rather than marketable products, and true expertise on, say, an automobile engine or hydraulic lifts would be less important. Nevertheless, a diverse group can bring many unique analogies to a problem, based on the backgrounds of the members. Thus, in any average classroom group, people can probably draw analogies to various sports, music, biology, foreign cultures, etc. on the basis of the diverse experiences of its members.

Joyce and Weil (1980) reproduced a partial transcript of a classroom use of synectics,[15] in which students were trying to get some new ways of understanding "The Hood," or gangster, preparatory to writing on the topic. During the exercise direct analogy was used with various machines. After such machines as washing machine, dishwasher, beat-up car, and pinball machine were named, the teacher asked them to choose the machine which would make the strongest comparison. The students voted for dishwasher. Then the teacher asked the students to explore what that means and, later, asked them to *be* a dishwasher and express how it feels. Still later the teacher asked for some "words that argue with each other" (as compressed conflicts or symbolic analogies) and received ideas such as used vs. clean, duty vs. inclination, and angry game. Settling on angry game as the best symbol, the students tried some new direct analogies which might express this idea: a lion in a cage, bullfight, and rodeo were some of the analogies. The class thought bullfight was the best to explore further in relation to "The Hood."

So went the introductory exercise. Then the teacher had the students write an introductory paragraph for their stories using the bullfight metaphor. Some wrote of "the hood" as the bull, others as the matador. They shared some of their introductory paragraphs in class before going on to write their stories.

The teacher's role in all of this was to keep the students from too quickly settling on one approach or, worse, using some stereotyped descriptions of gangsters in their writing. The classroom exercise, since it includes drafts of a paragraph, also allows the teacher to give some feedback. But notice that while the teacher may press students to go beyond the ordinary, there is no response that is criticized, and humor and farfetched ideas are encouraged. Notice also that this kind of synectics group could use a whole class, though the teacher must be careful to get maximal participation if this is done. For example, small groups could explore different direct analogies and make brief reports to the

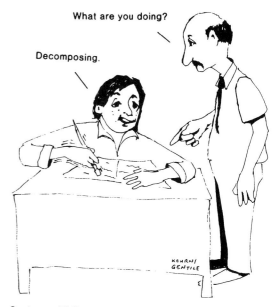

Cartoon 13.2

larger group on the ones they like best. Then the whole group would continue.

Joyce and Weil (1980) suggested the following six rules for making the familiar strange (or, as they also call it, Creating Something New). The teacher has the students do the following:

1. Describe the situation or object as they presumably see it.
2. Suggest direct analogies, select one of those, and then explore it further.
3. "Become" the object or idea they selected in (2).
4. Suggest several symbolic analogies or compressed conflicts, based on the above.
5. Generate other direct analogies based on (4) and select one of these for further development.
6. Return to the original task or problem, and use the last analogy and/or any of the ideas generated in the synectics exercise to complete the task or solve the problem.

It is difficult to find hard evidence on the effectiveness of synectics in producing more or better creativity. The evidence that exists is largely anecdotal, in which products were invented or people expressed satisfaction with the technique (e.g., Stein, 1975). Perhaps no additional evidence is needed for the purposes suggested here—namely, to avoid jumping to conclusions; to explore unique ideas from a wide variety of sources and points of view; and to show how one person's ideas can act as catalysts for others' ideas and thereby demonstrate that "none of us is as creative as all of us."

Creativity: Other Issues

In the Third Edition of the *Handbook of Research on Teaching*, there is only one entry in the index for the term creativity, and that occurs in Torrance's (1986) chapter on "Teaching Creative and Gifted Learners." In that chapter Torrance calls attention to the lack of research on such systematic programs for teaching creativity as Gordon's and deBono's. He goes on to describe the debates in the literature concerning creativity and its measurement. Ironically, most of the concern in this regard concerns identifying or selecting the gifted and talented. Those selected are given separate programs from the average student, but it is not clear that even the programs for the gifted and talented are designed systematically to produce more creative behavior. Torrance (1986) laments that many highly intelligent people are ineffective thinkers, and cites several studies to attack the fallacy that specific programs are not needed to help highly intelligent individuals learn to think.

Creativity has usually been discussed in relation to intelligence in the literature, as well as in the public mind. Even those who would have us believe that creativity is a separate entity from intelligence, such as Torrance and Guilford, have spent a good deal of their careers developing tests to correlate creativity with IQ. That debate rages on,[16] and we shall not resolve it here. But again, the irony is that if the tests are used solely to determine the creative status of individuals, we shall have ignored their possible growth (i.e., shifting the normal curve upwards, analogous to the problem in intelligence testing). To be fair, Torrance (1970) himself has been one of the most prolific proponents of creativity training for all.

From another point of view, it is possible to argue that creativity has not been disappearing from the general literature on educational psychology; rather, it has assumed a new name. By this view, creativity is being studied as one or more of the components of intelligence, critical thinking, instrumental enrichment, or inquiry training. I believe that this is what has happened in the field, and thus the separation of sections on developing creativity and developing intelligence is largely artificial.[17]

What, then, is the central component common to all of these? *From an instructional standpoint,* at least, I believe the *central component is the art of questioning.* Whether it be called inquiry training (Suchman, 1960; 1961), discovery learning (Bruner, 1961; Shulman and Kieslar, 1966), the inductive approach, or whatever, the central component seems to be the teacher's skill in systematically using questions to engage the student in thought. I am including here study questions and test questions, as well as those used in classroom discussions.

In a very thoughtful presentation, which should have put to rest the discovery vs. didactic learning polemic (but sadly, it did not), Lee Cronbach (1966, p. 77) put it this way:

> *I have no faith in any generalization upholding one teaching technique against another, whether that preferred method be audiovisual aids, programmed instruction, learning by doing, inductive teaching, or whatever. A particular educational tactic is part of an instrumental system; a proper educational design calls upon that tactic at a certain point in the sequence, for a certain period of time, following and preceding certain other tactics. No conclusion can be drawn about the tactic considered by itself.*

Anecdote 13.8

> ### "Nothing"
>
> There is a wonderful parody on the idea of personal analogy in the song "Nothing" from the musical "A Chorus Line." The scene is a high school for the performing arts and Morales is taking a course in acting. In the first verse, the class was to imagine they were a bobsled, then a table. But she honestly felt nothing in these exercises; her teacher, Mr. Carp, replied that "nothing" could get a girl transferred to another school.
>
> In the next exercise Morales dug deep to the bottom of her soul to become an ice cream cone and "tried to melt." But with the encouragement of her teacher, the other students gave her the nickname "Nothing."
>
> In the end she realized "This man is nothing. This course is nothing. If you want something, go find a better class."
>
>

With that, we've returned full circle to the point of this chapter—expanding our repertoire of teacher skills. If questioning behavior is important, it is important as a tactic for certain instructional goals at certain times for students and teachers who are ready for it. It is certainly inappropriate to use discovery learning to make you learn my address, the height of Mt. Fuji, or the date Columbus discovered America. Such exercises are the most trivial of pursuits. It is equally inappropriate always to answer a student's question with a factual statement which implies that no further questions are possible (though sometimes that tactic may be useful). A TV commercial satirizing this point shows a family asking questions of their all-knowing father.

Daughter: "Dad, why is grass green?"
Father: "Because of chlorophyll, Honey,"
Son: "Dad, Is the moon really made of green cheese?"
Father (laughing): "No, the moon is made of molecules."

I used to play a similar game with my son. He would ask questions to which I would answer, "I don't know." Then I would say, "But keep asking questions; it's the only way you'll learn anything."

"Chlorophyll" and "molecules" are not answers to the above questions any more than "I don't know" is. At best "chlorophyll," "molecules," and "I don't know" are the basis for further questions. But if students have been conditioned to quick answers, their most likely next question will be, "Is this going to be on the test?"

It is easy to describe how not to ask questions, as the above examples illustrate. It is harder to describe *how* to do it. Some good advice arises from a consideration of the level of our objectives (in Bloom's, 1956, taxonomy): questions asking "How does x apply to y?" and "What fundamental scientific law underlies x?" and "When might x not be true?" and "How is x like y?" are likely to generate better thinking and more creative responses than "Who is buried in Grant's tomb?" But even that is not certain. It depends on the skill of the teacher. If the teacher is looking for and rewards one and only one correct answer, then any of the above questions can become a game of trivial pursuit (see anecdote 13.8).

Practical suggestions for how to question so as to induce students to delve deeper have already been described in reference to the IDEAL Problem Solver, lateral thinking, and synectics. Other sources are Suchman (1960, 1961; also described in Joyce and Weil, 1980) and Brown and Walter's (1983) little gem of a book on problem posing in mathematics. Different curricula and approaches require different kinds of questioning behavior for the different objectives, and all require practice on the part of teachers and students.

No idea is foolproof since, to paraphrase an old saying, we can always find a fool to prove it. Questions designed to induce critical thinking can be asked in a threatening, evaluative environment and students will try to "psych out" what the teacher *really* wants to hear. Programs designed to assure that students master important concepts and skills before moving on to higher-order skills can be conducted so as to appear as a dull and never-ending sequence of trivial requirements, which students do for the negative reinforcement of escaping them. Activities designed to induce creative expression and cooperative behaviors can be turned into ridicule of those who are different. To paraphrase Cronbach (1966), no teaching technique can be judged independently of the system in which it is employed, and its success depends, in large part, on how well all the techniques in the system complement one another with respect to the ultimate goals.

Practice Exercises

A. Practice Items

For each of the first 5 items match the following three mastery systems with the characteristics of the system. If two or more of the mastery systems share a characteristic, place the letter of each on the line next to the item. (Answers are in Note 18).

    a. Washburne's Winnetka Plan
    b. Bloom's Learning for Mastery
    c. Keller's Personalized System of Instruction.

____ 1. The use of proctors to test and tutor.
____ 2. A requirement to pass each unit's mastery test before moving on to the next.
____ 3. Initial instruction that is usually group-based.
____ 4. Lectures that are reinforcers for students who qualify.
____ 5. The establishment of essential objectives to be mastered and nice-to-know objectives for enrichment or elective work.

For the following eight items, select the alternative choice which *best* answers the question. (Answers are in Note 18).

6. On the basis of the evidence concerning the wide variety of teaching methods available, the author argues
    a. that we should soon have one or two methods shown to be clearly better than the rest.
    b. that we now have a few methods shown to be clearly better than the rest and teachers should spend their time learning them.
    c. that no method is superior to any other.
    d. that teachers should abandon the one best method mentality and continue to expand their repertoire of methods.

7. Teams in most of Slavin's Cooperative Teams methods are formed by
    a. the teacher who balances the teams so that ability is equal on the average.
    b. the teacher who randomly assigns students to teams.
    c. the students who elect team captains who then choose their teammates.
    d. the teacher on the basis of academic tracks.

8. Which of the following is the best example of how *aptitude* should be interpreted in John Carroll's model of school learning?
    a. Barb takes less time than Bob to attain the same objective in math, but more time to attain the same physical education objective than Bob does.
    b. Barb perseveres at any learning objective for a much longer time then Bob.

c. Barb always scores higher than Bob on both standardized and teacher-made tests.
　　d. Barb has a deeper understanding of whatever is learned than Bob.

9. Which one of the following does not belong with the rest?
　　a. a minimum passing standard
　　b. criterion-referenced assessment
　　c. the normal curve
　　d. mastery-testing

10. Which of the following can be either norm-referenced or criterion-referenced?
　　a. mastery tests
　　b. summative tests
　　c. practice tests
　　d. formative tests

11. With which of the following statements would Bloom be likely to *agree*?
　　a. Probably more than 90% of the students in our schools can master what we now teach in the schools.
　　b. If student achievement on certain instruction objectives is distributed as a normal curve, then our educational efforts can be assumed to be unsuccessful.
　　c. A basic task of the teacher is to encourage each student to spend the time he or she needs to learn the material.
　　d. He would agree with all of the above.

12. According to the evidence cited by the author, creative behaviors
　　a. can best be taught by doing a task analysis of the objectives and establishing a mastery standard for achieving them in the correct order.
　　b. can best be taught by reinforcing successively more unique behaviors from the individual.
　　c. can best be taught in an evaluation-free environment.
　　d. cannot be taught.

13. Assume you were trying to understand how to transmute matter and send it through space, as in Star Trek ("Beam me up, Scotty, there's no intelligent life here"). *In synectics* which of the following is the best way to begin to explore this?
　　a. by imaging you were one of the characters in the show.
　　b. by discussing whether such things are possible.
　　c. by analogy with how voices are transmitted via telephone or radio.
　　d. by analyzing the component processes of laser beams, space travel, etc.

B. For Cooperative Study (in and out of class):

1. In small groups, discuss study questions 1, 21 and 22. How important are questions to all teaching techniques? How important is it to vary the teaching approach? Are students as likely to become bored with cooperative teams as with lectures?

2. In small groups, discuss some of the various approaches to forming and running cooperative teams (e.g., in study questions 2–4).

3. In small groups, practice some of the synectics techniques for "making the strange familiar" and "making the familiar strange," particularly the techniques of:
   a. personal analogy
   b. direct analogy and
   c. symbolic analogy

   It may help if the group takes on a particular goal-oriented task (e.g., how to solve a problem of current or historical interest).

4. Discuss the steps of implementing the following in classes:
   a. cooperative learning
   b. mastery learning

   What special problems are there in implementing these in elementary vs. secondary vs. tertiary classrooms? In normal vs. special education vs. gifted classes? In science vs. humanities vs. arts?

C. For More information

1. Design a unit for one of your own classes using either
   a. a cooperative learning approach,
   b. a mastery learning approach, and/or
   c. a creativity/synectics approach.

   If you are currently teaching, implement the plan. Then report either orally or in writing on your plan (and its problems and prospects, if you tried it).

2. Read, and perhaps prepare a written or oral report on, one or more of the articles or books by proponents of
   a. cooperative learning,
   b. mastery learning, or
   c. creative studies/synectics.

3. Read some of the evaluation research on one of the topics in this chapter. Prepare a written or oral report on
   a. the findings of the studies,
   b. the methodologies of the studies, and/or
   c. the implications for finding "one best method."

UNIT SIX

DEVELOPING ASSESSMENTS AND GRADING

This unit applies many of the psychological and instructional principles of the previous units to the problems of evaluating student learning. This includes, in chapter 14, an analysis of the purposes and practices of grading. A comprehensive grading scheme is proposed, with (1) a norm-referenced component for such selection/prediction purposes as obtaining rank-in-class, and (2) a criterion-referenced component for motivating students to master the essentials of the curriculum and go beyond.

In chapter 15 assessment tools are addressed—their psychometric properties (including validity, reliability, and other logical and statistical bases) as well as how to construct them. Both objective types of items (two-choice, matching, multiple-choice, and short-answer) and subjective types, (including so-called "authentic" essays, written reports, portfolios, and performance) are considered.

CHAPTER

Study Questions

1. What is the author's position on whether grades are necessary?
2. What is the difference between measurement and evaluation? Are grades measures or evaluations?
3. What is meant by each of the following purposes of grading?
   a. for prediction or selection
   b. for facilitating learning

   How do the terms criterion-referenced and norm-referenced assessment relate to these purposes?
4. Describe how each of the following is a problem in current grading systems:
   a. teacher variation
   b. significance of differences between scores
   c. averaging scores across classes or tests

   What is the author's proposed solution to these problems?
5. What is meant by between-class vs. within-class grading? How do these relate to criterion-referenced and norm-referenced assessment?
6. Why is the driver's test a good exemplar of the author's position on within-class grading?
7. What is the difference between *learning time* and *evaluation time*? Give an example (such as driving instruction).
8. How does the author recommend that each of the following be done?
   a. finding class ranks
   b. grading clinical or performance skills
   c. grading academic or cognitive knowledge
9. How does the author deal with the problem of numerical grades in a mastery system?
10. How is a failing grade in a unit to be averaged with other grades, according to the author?
11. How can *overlearning* be built into a criterion-referenced grading system to increase retention of material mastered at an earlier time?
12. What does the author say about the following?
    a. setting standards
    b. making evaluations more "objective"
    c. the instructor's "expert judgment"
13. Devise a way to build a grading system for your own classes or school based on the ideas in this chapter.

FOURTEEN

Grades and the Purposes and Practices of Assessment

Introduction

1. In the Peanuts comic strip by Charles Schulz, Charlie Brown's sister Sally received a C. She said, "A C? A C in coat-hanger sculpture? How can anyone get a C in coat-hanger sculpture? . . . Was I judged on what I learned in this project? Then are not you my teacher also being judged on your ability to transmit the knowledge to me? Are you willing to share my C?"

2. A few years ago, shortly after I took a class in spoken Japanese and received a grade of C, I mentioned it to a class of accelerated sixth graders. I asked what the "C" means. "It means you're average," was the response of one obviously above-average little boy. "You mean, I can speak Japanese like the average Japanese person?" I asked.
"It probably means you're average for your class," ventured one of the girls.
"Well, if you were my parent," I continued, "and I came home with this C, what would you say to me?"
"I'd say," piped up another boy immediately, "if that's the best you can do . . . well, keep trying."

3. In a discussion of grading disabled children who were being mainstreamed, a teacher described to me the extra care she took in grading a child known to be terminally ill. She wanted to make him work to his capacity, but she also wanted his remaining days to be as pleasant as possible. So, she said, she showed extra sensitivity to his feelings in grading him.

The opening vignette, though from a comic strip, was apparently based on a true experience, in which one of Charles Schulz's own children received a C in coat hanger sculpture (though I've lost the reference). Schulz wondered how a teacher could decide what grade a coat hanger was worth? Innumerable students have had similar questions, and not just regarding grades in the arts. For instance, how about the "83" that appears on the term paper without comments? Most of us, perhaps because we are satisfied with the grade or because we are afraid to question the teacher for fear of repercussions, do not hold the teacher accountable for this grade. A dialogue I would like to see in such cases might occur as follows:

> **Student (or Parent):** "83 what?"
> **Teacher** (surprised at the question): "83 percent."
> **Student:** "83 percent of what?"
> **Teacher:** "Well, I mean 83 points . ."
> **Student:** "Oh good, would you check off the points I got right, as well as those I missed?"

Most teachers would consider such questions to be impertinent beyond belief, but the true impertinence is the act of giving such a grade without also giving feedback (in the technical sense of the word). Such grades are cases of what I call "immaculate deception," since they seem to appear on the page miraculously.

Under the best circumstances, grades are not easy to interpret, as the episode of the Japanese grade (#2) shows. When grades are inscrutable, perhaps it is no wonder that Sally and many others consider their grades unfair (cases of rapanoia?). And even when the teacher is trying hard to be fair and sensitive, as in the true story in vignette number 3, there is an implicit dilemma. Why, for example, must a student be terminally ill before we find a way of grading that is both fair and kind? In any case, aren't we all terminally ill—some of us may just last decades longer than others.

Every adult I have ever asked about grades has what they consider at least one "horror story" like the above to tell. One might be tempted to dismiss the problem with such excuses as, "Well, in the long run it doesn't matter, anyway." It is my belief, however, that it matters greatly. Teachers, through the grades they assign and the processes by which they assign them, serve as models for how to give feedback, how to establish criteria for making evaluations, and how to be fair, among other things. Moreover, how students are graded is a major determiner of how they go about learning. Grading affects all aspects of the social learning process—the behavioral/motivational, the emotional, and the cognitive. In an important sense, then, grading should be one of the first orders of business in designing a course syllabus.

Sadly, grading is most often treated as an afterthought. Probably because people think of it as a necessary evil, the decision of how a paper is to be graded, for example, is left until the paper is written. Even courses and texts in educational psychology treat grading as a topic at the end of the course, often to be included if time remains. Then, while the text may present some basic facts about some relevant statistical issues, or the differences between norm-referenced and criterion-referenced approaches to grading, readers are left to draw their own conclusions about which approach is best for them. The implicit assumption is that the approaches are equally valid or, if they are not, teachers can do whatever they wish under the guise of tradition or academic freedom.

Cartoon 14.1

Although this book maintains the tradition of treating grades toward the end rather than at the beginning, the rest of the coverage will be much less traditional. This is for several reasons. First, it seems to me that all of the issues of the preceding chapters argue that certain approaches to grading are much more psychologically healthy than others (see also anecdote 14.1). We have already previewed some of these approaches in the cooperative teams and mastery learning discussions in the preceding chapter. Second, some fundamental statistical errors continue to be made by teachers grading students, and these need to be exposed and corrected.

Third, no teacher or assessment technique can be judged in the abstract. The question is, what purpose is to be served by the technique, or in what context is it to be used? There are only *two main purposes of educational assessment* (with a few possible subpurposes of each)—namely, the *purpose of selection (or prediction)* and the *purpose of facilitating learning (or diagnosis/remediation)*. The former is a norm-referenced purpose, while the latter is

Anecdote 14.1

Grading: Retribution or Restitution?

Madeline Hunter (1990) provides the following anecdote from a graduate class:

> . . . a high school English teacher asked, "If I have a student who cuts my class, doesn't turn in homework, and doesn't pay attention when he does come to class, doesn't he deserve an 'F'? Hasn't he earned an 'F'? Shouldn't I give him an 'F'?"
>
> The professor responded, "Let's change that example. Suppose that same student went to a party and saw someone empty a bottle of vodka into the punch. The student knows that punch is "spiked." He knows he shouldn't drink alcohol but he has never tasted vodka and he is curious so he tries some. The punch is sweet and he can't taste the vodka, so he drinks more and more until his vision blurs and his movement is unsteady. He realizes he'd better get home and as he weaves out the door he misjudges distance, hits his shoulder on the door frame and almost falls. He knows his vision and movement are not functioning well, but he gets in his car, drives off, misses a sharp turn, goes over an embankment, smashes his car into a tree, and is badly injured. A doctor comes along. Shouldn't he let the student die? The student knew he shouldn't drink, that he was not fit to drive. Isn't dying what he has "earned," [sic] what he "deserves?" Why doesn't the doctor drive on and let him die? Because the doctor's job is to save that student if he possibly can, not to give him his just desserts. Our job as teachers is to save the student if we possibly can. Neither we nor the doctor can save all of them but we must try." (p. 34)

fundamentally criterion-referenced. Since both are widely used in education, it is only a partial solution, at best, to advocate that grading on the curve should be forever eliminated from schools, even if that were a desired state of affairs (as many would advocate: for example, Holt, 1974; Kirschenbaum et al., 1971; Simon and Bellanca, 1976). Finally, therefore, I shall propose a comprehensive grading scheme which (1) is rational and statistically sound; (2) has provisions for both norm-referenced (e.g., class ranks) and criterion-referenced (development of knowledge and skills) assessment purposes; and (3) has provisions for grading academic knowledge, creative projects, and clinical skills.

Are Grades Necessary?

The history of grading shows that letter grades (A to F, or some variation on this) did not gain popularity until early in the twentieth century (Cureton, 1971). Interestingly, letter grades came to be used because people were dissatisfied with the 100-point numerical system, which implied that teachers could reliably categorize examination papers as 83, 84, or 85. A series of studies by Starch and Elliott (1912; 1913a; 1913b), however, destroyed the myth of interrater reliability, in which they found ranges of 10–50 points in grades for the same papers in history, English and, yes, even in arithmetic.

The 100-point scale itself had only been a relatively recent reporting system, becoming widely used only in the late nineteenth century. Prior to that, teachers were more likely simply to rank students in order of merit, or to categorize them into three or more groups, meaning high, average, or low achievement (Cureton, 1971).

Despite a continual century-long debate about the virtues and liabilities of each of these systems for grading, it appears that all of them have survived to today and, in many schools, they exist simultaneously. During that century, many other things have changed drastically, perhaps most dramatic of all being the transformation from optional, selective enrollment to mandated, universal enrollment. During that time also, letter grades became firmly entrenched, being used by over 80% of junior and senior high schools in the USA, according to a 1974 survey (as reported by Evans, 1976). The largest proportion of these schools used letter grades as the major, if not sole, summary report of students' progress.

Nevertheless, surveys indicated that few people seem very happy with current grading systems (Evans, 1976). One indicator of this unhappiness is the amount of committee time spent assessing grading practices. From universities to grade schools, committees are charged with recommending changes which, more often than not, are then reviewed by a new committee formed in the following year or two.

Part of the debate invariably centers on the question of whether grades should be abolished entirely. For example, consider the following statement from an essay by Sidney Simon (1976, p. 22):

When will teachers discover that without a grading system, there is no cheating? We all recognize that, without grades, certain teachers would leave the classroom, certain subjects would disappear from curricula, and useless memorization would die a natural death. All would go, as they should, into the valley of the forgotten.

Simon has been in the forefront of writers who have exposed the evils and weaknesses of common grading practices (see also Holt, 1974; Kirschenbaum, Simon and Napier, 1971; Simon, 1970; Simon and Bellanca, 1976; Simon and Hart, 1973). Although it may appear from the tone of the above quote[2] that Simon would be among those advocating abolition of grades, that is not the case. In the introduction to the collection of essays in Simon and Bellanca (1976), he explicitly states that the purpose of the book is ". . . to show that there *are* alternatives to the conventional system" (p. 3).

I mention this to point out that even those who make the most vitriolic attacks on conventional grading schemes seem to realize that abolishing grades is not a viable alternative. Perhaps grades, or some other single summary analysis of academic progress, would not seem to be necessary if each teacher were responsible for teaching only a few students as, for example, private music or tennis instructors have. In those cases, the teacher need only provide relevant feedback and encouragement; no one requires permanent records or diplomas of such informal teaching relationships. In a bureaucratic society of state certifications, diplomas, national assessments, etc., it is necessary for records to be kept. While some have used written evaluations, even they tend to be condensed by busy teachers and administrators into a few key words that may then (correctly or not) translate into "outstanding, average, or below average." The more students a teacher has, the more likely it is that the teacher will use or invent a standardized and shorthand way of keeping such records.

Given this, it seems to me that efforts toward reform of the grading system will be much more productive than efforts at abolishing it. The way most reformers have suggested is to reduce or eliminate the competition in

Photo 14.1. How will this activity be graded?

current grading schemes and move toward cooperative learning, mastery learning, and contracts (e.g., Block and Anderson, 1975; Bloom, Madaus and Hastings, 1981; Combs, 1976; Keller, 1968; Slavin, 1983). Such systems use A and B grades as reinforcers, de-emphasizing D and F grades as punishers (which do not work all that well anyhow). The systems to be described later incorporate these features. But before going into detail on them, a few more preliminary distinctions need to be made, first among them the difference between measurement and evaluation.

Measurement and Evaluation

In this age of massed standardized testing, computerized test scoring, percentile ranks, stanines, grade-equivalents and other means of score reporting, it is easy to allow scoring and grading to become a highly mechanized function. If the grades are reported by the computer as highly scientific-looking z-scores, percentile ranks, T-scores, or grade-level equivalents, how many of us are willing to argue with the assigned grades? But grades do not automatically flow from distributions of scores; there is a fundamental difference between the score itself and the interpretation of that score. In more technical terms, the distinction is between the processes of measurement and evaluation, defined for present purposes as follows.

Educational *measurement* is the process of *quantifying* performances or traits of persons, by means of a numerical description in the form of scores or ranks. As Gronlund (1985, p. 5) points out, measurement answers the question "How much?" Thus, to say that John is six feet tall, scored at the 84th percentile on the Scholastic Aptitude Test, and obtained 80% of his math problems correct is to provide numerical measures of John.

Evaluation, in contrast, is the process of making qualitative judgments or *value statements* about a person or measures obtained on the person. Evaluation, according to Gronlund (1985, p. 5), answers the question, "How good?" because it includes value judgments concerning whether a behavior or test score was good or bad, desirable or undesirable, passing or failing. Thus to say that John at six feet tall can try out for the basketball team, but Pete at 5 feet 10 inches is too short to try out, is to be evaluating on the basis of height. To say that John, at the 84th percentile is accepted into a college, but George at the 83rd percentile is not, is to be making an evaluation of those ranks. Likewise to give John a B in math on the basis of his 80% correct and to give Cynthia a C for her 79% correct is to be making a value judgment, or evaluation.

Throughout this text, it has been emphasized that teacher and student are inextricably bound together in a social interaction unit, in which part of the teaching act is to assess and give feedback on the student's progress toward the instructional objectives. If that is so, then teachers can never escape the process of evaluation—it becomes an integral part of their job. Sometimes evaluation includes measurement, as when test scores are obtained, but always it includes qualitative descriptions of students' progress—for example, does Mary understand this concept or should she be given more help and tested again?

Since evaluation is an inescapable part of the teaching function, it must be clear that *no matter how automated or traditional our grading practices are, assigning grades is always an evaluation process*. The teacher is making a value judgment that 80% is significantly better than 79% when the traditional system is used (i.e., 90–100%=A; 80–89%=B; 70–79%=C; etc.). The same is true when test scores are converted to z-scores. Wherever the cut-offs are made dividing the distribution of scores into A's, B's, C's, and so forth, the teacher is making a value judgment. Such judgments are statistically unsound, since there will never be a significant difference between adjacent scores on opposite sides of a cutoff—for example, between a score of 80% and 79%. This will be equally true if the scores are transformed into other measures, normalized, standardized, or "otherwised." In other words, no matter how scientific-looking we make our measures, we are still making evaluative judgments when we convert those scores to grades, whether pass-fail; A-F; or gifted, average, retarded; or euphemisms to that effect.

This means that teachers' judgments about student progress are professional judgments. Sometimes numerical information (measurements) can be used to assist the judgment, but the measures themselves should not automatically determine students' grades any more than blood pressure should determine whether an operation should be given. The teacher, like the physician, should interpret all those data, including the numerical measures, in forming a professional opinion. When such judgments are made fairly and sensibly, few people object. For instance, patients do not say to their physician, "Give me a few extra points on my blood pressure to raise my grade." Nor would anyone say that to their tennis coach who just told them that, in his professional opinion, their backhand needed extra work. Students have been conditioned to fight for extra points in classroom tests, I believe, because we teachers have tried

Cartoon 14.2

to substitute objective scores for what is essentially a subjective, evaluative, professional judgment. To avoid the quibbling for points requires an improvement in how we give students feedback and what our purposes are in grading.

Furthermore, professional judgments must always be made with utmost humility. Consider the immensity of the problem: how does one person (e.g., the teacher) know what another person (e.g., the student) knows or can do? This is a difficult problem about which test scores, projects, and the like supply evidence which can be helpful in drawing an inference, but teachers must be prepared for the possibility that their judgments were wrong, despite the evidence. Doctors would order another blood test and do other tests to see whether a mistake was made. Or if they did not, the patient could go to another doctor for a second opinion (see cartoon 14.2). The tennis coach or music teacher would allow students to demonstrate their skill again, perhaps in another way.

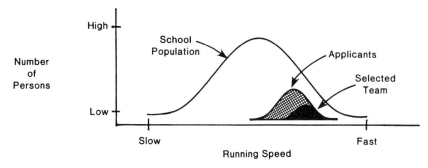

Figure 14.1. Selection of a track team from the entire school population.

So must academic teachers be ready to allow the student another chance to confirm or disconfirm their diagnosis.

The Purposes of Grading and Assessment

As stated earlier, *there are two fundamentally different functions or purposes of assessment—namely, (1) the purpose of prediction or selection or determining a person's status relative to others; and (2) the purpose of facilitating learning, or determining a person's status relative to a specific set of instructional objectives.*[3] Traditional grading practices have not kept these two purposes separate, but have attempted to use the same grade for both purposes. It is perhaps the major point of this presentation that these two distinct functions of grading must be accomplished in very different ways. A score on a single test or project cannot adequately fulfill both functions.

To make a point, let's take an extreme example. Suppose you gave a test and everyone got the same score. Or, suppose we held a race and everyone ran at the same speed. In other words, suppose there were no individual differences on any dimension of life that we examined. It is probable that the olympics would never have been invented, since such games depend on differential skills. It is also probable that the normal curve would never have been used to describe how individuals differ in intelligence or achievement. But the fact that stable individual differences exist—in everything from intelligence and academic achievement to physical strength and speed to personality traits—does not imply that they need to be considered in grading practices. Whether these individual differences should be reflected in assessing a person's performance depends on the purpose of the assessment.

Consider the problems of the women's track coach. First she holds tryouts for the track team, the purpose of which is to *select*, from all applicants, the fastest runners for the team. Now, those applicants are likely to have been a sample of the fastest runners from the entire school population, as shown by the cross-hatched area in figure 14.1. The coach will select even further, however, to get the fastest runners that she can (as shown by the dark area in figure 14.1). Her tryout trials served the function of predicting who would be the fastest runners and selecting members of the track team on the basis of that prediction. Note that there is a built-in assumption of reliability of measurement here—namely that a person's running speed is relatively stable over time, so that a person who ranks near the top of the distribution today will rank near the top tomorrow. In any case, the selection process requires a comparison of the students—a ranking from the best to worst. Testing in this way is technically called *norm-referenced testing,* because each person's score is interpreted in terms of the average, or norm, provided by the comparison group's scores.

Once the team has been selected, the coach has a different problem to contend with—namely, to field the fastest team that she can. A training program is established to help each student increase her strength, endurance and running speed. The coach, at this point, is not concerned with the rank ordering of the individuals—she already knows who is fastest and slowest—but rather with improving each student's performance. Now, of course, she is teaching the students, and her assessment of their performance should be concerned with *each student's improvement*. Testing to see whether each student has met the goals established for her is technically called *criterion-referenced testing*, since each person's score is interpreted relative to the achievement of certain objectives in a particular domain of behaviors (e.g., Popham, 1978b).

Academic subjects have their analogies with the situation just described. Students are often ranked to select a valedictorian or other prize winners, or to be placed in various homogeneous ability groups. For these purposes standardized or other competitive tests may be useful.

Once academic teachers have their assigned classes, however, they have no need to be concerned with the students' ranks. Their job—in fact, the purpose for which they were hired—is to help students achieve important cognitive and affective objectives. Assessment of whether these learning objectives have been attained is, by definition, criterion-referenced.

In closing this section, you may recall the discussion of how intelligence may simultaneously show both stability and growth (in chapter 3). This occurred because stability, or reliability, was a function of people's rank orderings remaining much the same over repeated testings, while the entire distribution of persons could significantly grow in knowledge and intellectual skills. The same statistical issue underlies the fundamental incompatibility of norm-referenced and criterion-referenced assessments described in this section. In fact, it is fair to say that the science of academic prediction has made such remarkable progress that, when appropriate measurements are taken, end-of-year rankings are almost entirely predictable (i.e., to within the standard error of the test) from rankings at the beginning of the year.[4] Thus the teacher who grades students on the basis of student rankings is doing little that could not have been done without ever having the students in class. Of course, teachers were not hired to rank students. If they were, they could easily be replaced by computerized statistical prediction (regression) equations. Rather, teachers were hired to help all students achieve their maximum capabilities. Teachers, in other words, are charged with moving the entire curve up. Whether the rankings of students change or not should be of little or no concern to teachers and, as we have seen, is probably statistically beyond their control in any case.[5]

Some Statistical Problems

Combining Scores

Problem 14.1

Consider the following midterm and final exam results:

	Midterm	Final
Charles	80	80
Diane	90	60
Class Average (Mean)	80	60
Standard Deviation	10	20

Assuming that these test scores are to be weighted equally, are the only source of evidence for a final grade, and that students will be graded competitively (i.e., in a norm-referenced fashion), then which of the following is true?

a. Charles and Diane should receive the same final grade.
b. Charles should receive a higher grade than Diane.
c. Diane should receive a higher grade than Charles.
d. Mean persons should receive higher scores than standard deviates.

This is a simplified version of the problem that confronts most secondary and college teachers every grading period. It is simplified because they have grades to calculate for many more than two students, often have more than two tests, and often have projects or other data to include in the equation. Nevertheless, the issue is central to any norm-referenced assessment process, and most teachers do not know how correctly to solve the above simplified problem, let alone more complex variations.

In surveys in my own classes, for example, most in-service teachers believe that Charles, who has a total of 160 points, should receive a higher grade than Diane, whose points total only 150. In making that judgment, the teachers are ignoring completely the information about test means and standard deviations because, having never before received instruction on these statistical concepts, they do not know what to do with them. But, as we saw in chapter 3, the mean and standard deviation describe the shape of a distribution of scores, informing us of the proportion of students falling under various portions of the curve.

For norm-referenced purposes it is statistically incorrect to compare Charles and Diane without also taking account of the norm provided by the rest of the students. Furthermore, it is statistically incorrect simply to add the raw scores of tests with different means and standard deviations. In a variation on an ageless metaphor, you cannot add apples and oranges unless you are making fruit salad. Adding test scores from two different tests is producing statistical fruit salad.

Fortunately, the solution to the problem is not very difficult, and you already know how to do it (from chapter 3). In general, it is to convert the incompatible scores into standard scores that are compatible, and can thus be added. This can be done, more specifically, by converting the raw scores to percentile ranks, or better, z-scores. Since the z-score is calculated by subtracting the mean from the student's score and dividing by the standard deviation, then the following are the relevant calculations:

Midterm   Final

Charles: $z = \dfrac{80-80}{10} = \dfrac{0}{10} = 0$ $z = \dfrac{80-60}{20} = \dfrac{20}{20} = 1$

Diana: $z = \dfrac{90-80}{10} = \dfrac{10}{10} = 1$ $z = \dfrac{60-60}{20} = \dfrac{0}{20} = 0$

Now the z-scores can be summed and, since both Charles and Di have one z=0 and one z=1, their sums of 1 are equal. Thus they must both receive the same grade in a norm-referenced grading system. The same conclusion is achieved graphically in figure 14.2.

This common error made by teachers within their own classes is perhaps compounded when grades in English, math, science, social studies, and what have you, are added together to determine students' class ranks. Add to this already complex fruit salad the problem that students did not all have the same tests from the same English teachers, and it becomes obvious that the manner in which class ranks in most schools are determined is nothing short of a statistical abomination. Fortunately, it is easily corrected by the procedures suggested above. Further, although the arithmetic procedures involved are relatively simple, most school districts also have such services available by computer.

478 Chapter Fourteen

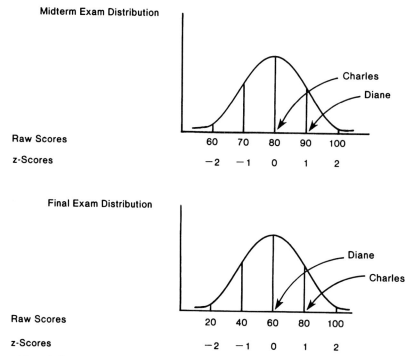

Figure 14.2. Graphic solution to problem 14.1.

Teacher Variation

As probably everyone has experienced, variation in teacher grading is quite wide, with some people having reputations as "easy graders," and others teaching the same course having reputations that cannot be described in polite company. For example, many teachers in secondary schools use plus and minus grades as a "fudge factor" to reward extra effort. Others use them as separate grades with numerical equivalents; for example, one teacher described a conversion as follows: A+ = 98–100; A = 95–97; A– = 93–94; etc. The fact that such differences exist make it extremely difficult to interpret the meaning of, for example, an A– compared with a B+. Yet grade point equivalents that give 4 points to an A– and 3 points to a B+, as often happens, operate as though the differences between them are real.

Significance of Differences

Another way of making the above point is to express it as a problem of statistical significance. Any assignment of different grades to scores (e.g. A to a 93 and B to 92), grade points to grades (e.g., 4 points to A– and 3 points to B+), or percentage distributions to grades (e.g., the top 7% get A, the next 14% get B) implies that there are significant differences between the adjacent scores. With so much variation between teachers, it is impossible to know whether the grades of two students are more a reflection of the students' performances or of their teachers' grading practices. But it is nevertheless the case that even with no variation between teachers (as on a single teacher's test) and a perfectly reliable test (which is probably impossible to write), *there is no significant difference between adjacent scores.*

If two scores, such as 80 and 79, are not significantly different from one another, then it is statistically unsound for *norm-referenced purposes* to give one of them an A and the other a B. Two things need to be said about the above comment. First, it is not statistically unsound just to rank the scores (or convert to z-scores, percentile ranks, or some other standardized score). Scores or ranks are simply measures and do not imply significant differences between adjacent scores whereas grades, as evaluations, do. On the other hand, whenever a cutoff is made, as in selecting ten persons out of 100 applicants for a team or a college, there is likely no significant difference between the tenth and eleventh ranked persons on the list. While the eleventh-ranked person may be upset at being excluded, he or she at least may be consoled by the fact that it is availability of positions, not a significant lack of talent, that caused the rejection. But when a distribution is broken into A,B,C,D, and F grades, there are four cutoffs, each implying significant differences between adjacent scores on each of the cutoffs when, in fact, the differences will not be significant.[6] The more grades given, the more arbitrary the cutoffs and, thus, the more errors of this statistical nature.

The second comment to be made about the practice of giving different grades to adjacent scores on opposite sides of a cutoff is that it is equally statistically unsound for criterion-referenced cutoffs. For example, where 80% = mastery and 79% or less means nonmastery, there is no statistically significant difference between 79% and 80% (or between 70% and 80% on a 10-item test). Such criterion-referenced decisions are legitimate, however, because (1) they are made for professional, not statistical, reasons and (2) they are temporary, not permanent, decisions. In other words, when teachers or coaches suggest that more work is needed to understand or perform at an acceptable level, they are making professional judgments which they defend not by statistics, but by reference to their experiences, models of expertise, and so forth. Students seldom object to such judgments and, if they do, they can simply try again and prove that they have, in fact, mastered the task. In that eventuality, the teacher or coach simply says "Congratulations! You have mastered it."

Variation Among Grade Levels

Of concern to many teachers is the lack of standardization of grading systems among grade levels. It is therefore difficult to understand a student's transcript from first through twelfth grade, since the grading scheme may go from comments or checks to the "+, ✓, –" system, to the A-F system. While I agree that this can be confusing, a single system often covers up the real underlying confusion that exists. For example, a rigidly adhered to A-F system implies that the same standard of performance is required for each grade for each class level and by each teacher. Not only have I never seen that to be true in practice, I do not think it is even possible. Thus, a totally different grading scheme for each grade level, since it forces the observer to learn what each teacher's standards and requirements are, seems to be superior to a widely-adopted system that allows a superficial expectancy of sameness.

The more important issue here seems to be that of the purpose of a grade at each level. Since each subject matter, age level and teacher is different, it seems necessary to be explicit about the meaning and purpose of each grade. If this can be done within a single grading system—and I shall suggest a procedure that I believe can do this—all the better.

Anecdote 14.2

From Grade Inflation to the Inflation of Grades

Everybody talks about grades, but nobody does anything about them. Except now and then. Some years ago at a great public university, the Faculty Senate was upset about grade inflation—that is, what they perceived to be too many A's and B's being awarded. So they established a grading committee to make some recommendations.

The committee met and after a year or more of deliberations recommended to the Senate that the following system be adopted (Senate Minutes, April 3, 1973):

Numerical grades will be used, on a continuous scale in intervals of tenths (.1) from 4.3 to 0.7 (e.g., 2.3, 2.4, 2.5, etc.), according to the following equivalents in terms of the "traditional" letter grading system:

A+ = 4.3	B+ = 3.3	C+ = 2.3	D+ = 1.3	F = 0.0
A = 4.0	B = 3.0	C = 2.0	D = 1.0	
A− = 3.7	B− = 2.7	C− = 1.7	D− = 0.7	

This system, it should be noted, inflates the number of possible grades from 4 (A,B,C,D) to 37 (.7 to 4.3 in one-tenth increments). Notice also that it inflates the number of A's and B's from 2 to 17, which is almost guaranteed to inflate the proportion of those grades given and defeat the purpose of having the committee look into grades in the first place.

Most importantly, with all of those possible discrimination cutoffs ("Mary is a 3.4 B+, while Joan is only a 3.3 B+), the more statistical errors that will be made (see text).

You may also have noticed that there was a 4.3 A+ which goes above the 4.0 maximum on the traditional grade point scale. This came as a result of the suggestion from an undergraduate, who as an invited representative of the student association, commented:

"Ladies and gentlemen, it's not a bad system [at that point the proposal had a 4.0 = A maximum]. But it doesn't reward the truly outstanding student. Thus I recommend a 4.1, 4.2, and 4.3 A+."

Clearly the students were no better informed than the faculty. There was a happy ending that year: the Senate voted to table the motion. A few years ago, however, another committee was formed and, you guessed it, we now have a system of A+ to D− grades, but without the one-tenth increments. I can hardly wait for the next grading committee to be formed.

But adoption of a single system should not be expected to alleviate the problem of interpretation of grades across teachers, subject matters or grade levels.

Mixed Purposes

The major problem with typical grading systems is their confusion of purposes. Every time teachers evaluate students they are presumably trying to tell who is superior, above average, average, and below average—norm-referenced judgments—and who has and has not mastered the material—a criterion-referenced judgment. Theoretically, it is quite difficult, though perhaps not impossible, to solve all of the problems raised above and still accomplish both of these purposes in one grade. In practice, teachers violate one or more of these precepts frequently. One of the most common violations has not yet been mentioned—namely, the practices known as "curving up" or "curving down." Misnomers both, the first refers to the practice of adding points to everyone's score when all, or the vast majority, of a class have not reached a minimum passing score on a test. If the range of scores on a test was 32 to 63, then the teacher adds 37 points to everyone's score, on the logic that the test was too hard. But if the test was too hard because the students do not know the material, then they need to be retaught. If they know the material but the test was too hard, a new test must be written. Adding points to the scores serves no educational purpose, though it may serve to protect the teacher from appearing to have failed to teach.

"Curving down" is equally bizarre. In this case a whole class may score at the highest levels, say 90–100% correct, but the instructor feels compelled to grade on a curve, often so that a certain proportion of people can be washed out of a competitive program like engineering or medical school (see cartoon 14.3). Thus people with 85 or even 90% may receive C or D grades.

Cartoon 14.3

Such practices are maintained, in my opinion, mainly out of tradition and the widely held, but mistaken, notion that there are no better ways of grading. It is now time to present a comprehensive grading system that addresses the criticisms raised above.

A Comprehensive Grading System

On the basis of the above considerations, there is much to recommend a school-wide grading system that has separate components for *between-class grading* (such as for calculating class standing in one's major, or overall in the school) and *within-class grading* (such as grading on a particular test or for a marking period in a given class). The between-class component as described here requires a norm-referenced procedure that includes some type of standardized score reporting. The within-class component would optimally be of the criterion-referenced variety with mastery testing procedures. The system suggested here is

Anecdote 14.3

Running the Race

Suppose we conducted the hundred meter dash the way we conduct our races for class rank. Then the students in Ms. Strait's class would be given practice and feedback on their running, and prepared with the proper equipment the day of the race. Sir Prize, however, believes in unannounced quizzes. Thus his students would show up one day, and whatever they were wearing, they would have to run the race.

Mr. Hy Standards believes that kids have it too easy nowadays, so he requires his students to run 105 meters up hill. Ms. Sweet, on the other hand, thinks grades interfere with students' self-esteem. Thus, although she has to make them run the race to conform to school policy, she subtracts a few seconds off many of her students' running times to compensate for their poor home situation or to reward them for good attendance.

Would we accept such variations as these in races? In any sporting event? Why should we accept such invalid procedures for determining ranks in academics?

based on that described in Gentile and Stevens-Haslinger (1983), Gentile and Murnyack (1989), and Gentile and Wainwright (1994).[7]

It may also be noted that this system is designed to supersede the arguments about whether summative grades are useful or destructive (e.g., Feldmesser, 1974, vs. Holt, 1974) or, more generally, whether we should adopt criterion-referenced over norm-referenced assessment procedures (e.g., Block, 1971b, vs. Ebel, 1971; and Ebel, 1978, vs. Popham, 1978a; see also Millman, 1970). It does this by incorporating each, for the purpose for which it is uniquely suited, into an all-inclusive system.

Between-Class Grading

As described earlier, there seems to be only one reason to combine grades from classes as disparate as mathematics, English, social studies, etc. That reason is to establish a person's class standing relative to his or her peers, usually initiated because schools are expected to provide information about students' ranks for prospective employers or colleges.

To provide such data in the most accurate form requires a system that avoids the problems raised earlier. Clearly, averaging grade points that arise from grades that have different purposes is compounding the errors at each level. A sensible solution requires a recognition of our purpose, and grade reporting consistent with that purpose.

Since the purpose is to provide a statement about each student's class rank, then data should be collected in each course vis-a-vis that goal. In other words, in addition to whatever other testing is occurring in each course, some testing should be scheduled for these norm-referenced purposes. The fairest way to do this is schedule at certain times during the year a comprehensive test on the course covered, which has the *purpose of comparing students*. All students from every section of the course would take the same test at the same time. This would be done even in courses using criterion-referenced grading, though it should have no bearing on the students' grades for those courses. The test should be developed by the department, not just by the instructor of the course, if more than one instructor teaches the same course.

Were there two or more such examinations per year for each course, the standing of students in the course would likely be quite stable—most important, the reliability and validity could be systematically checked and the tests improved, as standardized tests are. In addition, the students' standing would be on the whole uncontaminated by the different grading schemes, purposes, or "fudge factors" of teachers. The students would know that this was a test on which they were competing. It would not, however, affect their course grade. That is because this information is *not to be used as a grade or reported on a grade card*. It is information that may be made available to students or parents on request, and at appropriate times and with proper permissions, to prospective employers and colleges.

Much testing is already done for this purpose. Current midterm and final examinations which are graded on a curve already serve this function. What is added here is (1) to have department-wide exams where more than one instructor is involved, and (2) to convert the scores to z-scores. Then the norm-referenced data from English can be summed with the data from other subjects to provide an overall class rank, expressed perhaps as a percentile rank.

The astute reader may well have noticed that even these uses of exams in schools are not really necessary, since students are already inundated with standardized examinations which provide percentile ranks. Such tests are professionally developed and, since they compare students with national norms (and, usually, with local norms as well), they are much better suited for norm-referenced assessments than almost any test that is developed on a local level. Since such standardized data are already available, it is arguable that local norm-referenced testing is, at best, redundant and could be eliminated with little loss of information and a considerable saving of time, effort and money. If this last suggestion is not feasible in your system, the proposal in the previous paragraph certainly is.

Within-Class Grading

Having ascertained each student's class (and national) standing by appropriate and statistically sound norm-referenced procedures, then all that remains is to assess each student's progress toward mastering course objectives. All that remains, in other words, is to teach. Thus the recommendation is for each course to have a criterion-referenced grading system designed to motivate each student to, first, master the basic minimum objectives at a high level and, second, to go beyond those minima in a continuous development effort toward excellence. As promised, the recommendations are applicable, with slight modifications, to teaching academic knowledge, clinical skills, or creative projects.

The Driver's Test

Perhaps the easiest way to introduce the type of grading system I am advocating is through an example that almost everyone in this society has experienced first hand—namely, passing a driver's test. A driver's test typically has two parts. One part tests basic knowledge and comprehension of the rules of the road, appropriate use of signals, and so forth, primarily through an objective test (usually multiple-choice). The other part tests performance of the skills needed to operate the automobile safely and competently under simulated or actual road conditions. Together, both tests assess a wide range of basic objectives, which constitute the state's criteria for competent driving skills and knowledge.

Anecdote 14.4

If Driver's Tests Were Conducted Like Classroom Tests

Consider the absurdity of the following hypothetical driver's tests:

Case 1. Tester: "Well, I'm afraid you didn't pass. We require a score of 80% on the written test and you only got 73."

Student: "Yes, well when can I take it again?"

Tester: "Excuse me?"

Student: "I said, when can I take the test again?"

Tester (with a chuckle): "Take it again?"

Student: "Yes, I realize I need to study the book harder. When can I come again for the test?"

Tester (annoyed): "I'm sorry. You had your chance. You only get one chance at a driver's license. Maybe in your next life you can have a driver's license."

Case 2. Student: "How did I do?"

Tester: "Well, I'm afraid you didn't pass. Although you got a score of 85 on the test, that translates to a C+ because there were a large number of people who got higher scores than you. And since we give licenses to only those who get B or better, I'm afraid there will be no driver's license."

Case 3. Tester (to Administrator): I'm afraid this crop of students taking the driver's test didn't do too well. The range of scores was from 33 to 83% with a mean of only 54. Only 5% of the people passed. What are we going to do?"

Administrator: "Well, we can't fail 95% of the applicants. So let's curve the grades and give everybody above the median their driver's license."

Each test also has a minimum passing standard. The test of the cognitive domain, which can often be automatically scored, requires 80% correct for passing (at least in many states). The skill test requires judgments by the examiner as to whether a prospective driver is competent on each of the required subskills (parallel parking, stopping, turning around, etc.). While there are suggested guidelines for scoring each of those criterion subskills, scoring is accomplished by the examiner's professional evaluation of the novice driver's skills. In the end, there are two possible grades, Pass or Fail, which operate independently—that is, you can pass both parts, pass one part, or pass neither part. Notice also, contrary to anecdote 14.4, that failing either part is not a permanent status; rather, you have as many opportunities to retake a parallel form of the exam as you wish. When you pass, even on the fourth attempt, you get a real driver's license. The previous grades are not averaged with the latest grade. The license does not say "D-minus License," or "License for People Who Needed Four Attempts." It is the same license bestowed on those who passed on their first attempt.

To summarize, a driver's test provides a reasonable model of the following basic components of a criterion-referenced grading scheme:

1. It is based on clear, published criteria (e.g., many states publish a booklet telling both the kinds of questions to be asked, along with acceptable answers or ways of practicing).
2. Each separate component of the whole skill (in this case cognitive and motor skills) must be mastered; one cannot compensate for poor performance in one by a high score in another.
3. When novices pass all components at a minimally acceptable level—which, it should be noted, is much higher than required to pass subjects in most schools—they receive their certificate of mastery (in this case, a driver's license).
4. Until novices pass all components, they are considered "learners" and may continue to practice, again and again, until they finally earn the same license given to faster learners.

One difference between the driver's test and classroom tests is that the examiner in the former case is not the student's teacher. But that makes it all the more important in the classroom, where the expert is both teacher and examiner, that students have an opportunity, if needed, to fail gracefully before succeeding, without it affecting their grades. Morgan et al. (1979, p. 540) put it this way in distinguishing between *learning time* and *evaluation time*:

> . . . *often no clear distinction is made between learning and evaluation. Learning time is for the students; it is when they have the opportunity to ask questions, make mistakes, and practice new skills. Evaluation time is the instructor's; it includes gathering data and making decisions about the proficiency achieved by the students during the learning time. Without this distinction, faculty put students in a double-bind situation. While they often tell students that the practice setting is for learning, they may later use observations made during the learning time to determine students' grades. We believe that students must have a time to learn and make mistakes as distinct from a time to be evaluated.*

Viable Variations for Classroom Use

Despite the wide-spread acceptance of the driver's test as a model, most educators would balk at any recommendation for grading that was a simple Pass-Fail system. Tradition has established that such grades are usually associated with courses in which attendance is the primary requirement and the Pass is more-or-less automatic.[8] Such systems are not criterion-referenced; rather, PASS should be considered an acronym for *Person Attended Scheduled Sessions*.

It is well to be reminded that the more grading cutoffs, the more errors of judgment (because of the problem of nonsignificant differences between adjacent scores). Nevertheless, it is possible to expand on the basic Pass-Fail system and still keep such errors to a minimum. Three variations on a criterion-referenced system are provided in Table 14.1.

The first is particularly well-suited to grading skills or creative projects in science, language arts, fine arts, music, cooking, woodworking, etc. In such cases, there is no way to make judgments objective, as in multiple-choice tests. The instructor can demonstrate some of the required behaviors, can make a list of do's and don'ts, and give other good advice, but by the very nature of the clinical skill or creativity required, the instructor must observe the student's behavior and then evaluate it against professional standards. To take an example of a clinical skill, a nursing supervisor

Table 14.1 Alternative Criterion-Referenced Schemes for Within-Class Grading.

1. Honors (A) = Significantly exceeded the standard for each required skilll (or met the standard for each required skill and met the standard for optional skills).
   Satisfactory (B) = Met the standard for all required skills.
   Unsatisfactory (U) or Incomplete = Did not meet the standard for each required skill and must do remedial work until the skills are mastered.
2. A = Met the standard for all required work and satisfactorily completed two optional enrichment projects (or one advanced project).
   B = Met the standard for all required work and satisfactorily completed an optional enrichment project.
   C = Met the standard for all required work.
   D = Did not meet the standard for all required work and is required to make it up.
3. Scores above 80 are obtained by earning predetermined numbers of points for successful projects (one worth 3 points, one worth 5 points, etc.), which are added to the 80 earned for passing the test.
   80 = Scored 80 or above on the unit test
   50 = Scored below 80 percent on the unit test and is required to make it up.

Examples of Optional Projects for the Above Systems:
   a. book reports
   b. experiments
   c. creative projects in art, music, writing, poetry, dance
   d. term papers
   e. organizing and conducting a debate
   f. cooperative teams projects (see Chapter 13)
   g. tutoring someone else until he or she passes the unit test.

may well tolerate errors in drawing blood by beginners that she would not tolerate a few weeks or months later. During this learning time, the supervisor will provide appropriate feedback and have the student correct errors. Later, at evaluation time, the supervisor will have to certify that each nurse has mastered this skill, as well as a number of others. Mastery of each of these required skills, as judged by a qualified professional earns each student a Satisfactory or B grade.

The Honors or A grade, then, is reserved for the clinical student who goes beyond these techniques, either demonstrating the skills at a level that is truly expert, or having learned additional techniques or theory which allow the person to be classified as expert.

Similar logic prevails for a science or writing teacher judging a student's science report or essay, or for an artist or musician judging their protege's accomplishments. In each case, professional teachers may not be able to provide a priori lists of the components of a good science report, composition, painting, or musical performance, but assuredly they can evaluate and provide feedback on what students have just done. Recall that providing feedback implies (1) recognizing what was correct or good, (2) pointing out what was incorrect or inadequate, and (3) showing the student how to correct the inadequacies. Furthermore, for present grading purposes, the teacher must require the student to correct the inadequacies before the passing grade is awarded. If all of this seems to be a difficult job, indeed it is. On the other hand, supervisors and instructors are hired because they have the expertise to make such decisions. For some suggestions on how this can be done for evaluation objectives in Bloom's taxonomy, see anecdote 14.5.

For the subjects with the more normal, often state-mandated curricula, the Honors-Satisfactory-Unsatisfactory system may be used, but the second Alternative in table 14.1 will probably appear more appropriate. The grade of C could be interpreted as passing all mastery tests at the minimally acceptable level, e.g., 80% correct. In other words, a C stands for Competence on the important required objectives of the course (see the procedures for implementing mastery learning in the preceding chapter for more information on this). A grade of B, then, is used to encourage students to go beyond the basic minima, to do extra projects, to help other students (and thus overlearn the material), etc. The grade of A is further motivation to go beyond that to do extra enrichment work, and go further in depth on what has already been studied, or perhaps for cooperative team efforts (as described in the previous chapter).

Finally, alternative 3 in table 14.1 is provided for school districts in which student evaluations are reported on a numerical scale instead of by letter grades. In this alternative, 80% means that the student scored at or above 80% on the mastery test; there is no higher grade for a higher score. Then extra projects can have predetermined point values (e.g., 1–3 points for easy ones, 5–7 points for more difficult ones) which are added to the base score of 80.[9]

The numerical system seems to have a flaw in it—namely, how can you give two students, one who scored 87 and one who scored 80, the same score of 80? The answer is: just as we give students who receive 87 and 80 the same B. Numerical grades, in other words, are far less objective than they appear; rather they mean only what they are defined to mean.

This seeming arbitrariness can easily be defended by the teacher, preferably in writing as follows (adapted from my own course syllabus, for illustrative purposes):

Passing a multiple-choice test (written at the knowledge, comprehension, and application levels of thinking) attests to one kind of learning and, it is argued in this course, provides just the initial mastery of the material. That is why even a score of 100% correct earns the lowest passing grade, S. The purpose of mastering a skill or knowledge in life is not to be finished with it as an outcome (as this is commonly misinterpreted in schools), but to enable the student to begin to use and apply it in more advanced ways. To encourage you to go beyond the mastery objectives in this course, you can raise your grade to B by completing one Enrichment Objective on at least two of the three units, and to A by completing an Applications Paper showing how one or more of the concepts of the course applies to your life. Papers will be evaluated as OK or NOT OK. Papers judged NOT OK may be resubmitted, taking account of the instructor's feedback, until they are judged OK.

To conclude this section, let me emphasize a few points. First, I am not advocating a single best system of grading within a classroom. I am instead describing a family of variations designed (1) to assure that students master the fundamentals of a course; (2) to provide incentive for both the fastest and slowest learners to go beyond the fundamentals to practice and transfer the fundamentals; and (3) to do all of the above in as noncompetitive, and perhaps as cooperative, a manner as possible.

Second, to extend the last comment, it is worth considering the ways in which cooperative team methods can be incorporated into this system. One obvious way is to have the lowest passing grade (e.g., the grade of C in alternative 2 in table 14.1) remain as is. But then, for some units at least, all students in the class

Anecdote 14.5

Grading Evaluating Objectives in Art Education

One of the four disciplines in discipline-based art education (e.g., Eisner, 1987) is art criticism. It is a high level thinking skill (evaluation in Bloom's taxonomy) because it requires people to describe, analyze, and interpret their own or others' artwork according to specified criteria. Learning how to do this requires a carefully designed sequence of lessons which includes, among others, modeling the thinking processes by the teacher, practice giving verbal descriptions (i.e., giving feedback) according to specified criteria, and practice giving numerical ratings or rankings (optional).

To grade such complex performances is equally demanding. For this, the students may be required to present written or oral critiques of art, and teachers will have to practice what they preach in applying critical thinking criteria to these art criticism assignments. Gentile and Murnyack (1989) have suggested that a 0–10 point rating scale may be used for each of several criteria; for example, appropriately:

1. Uses criteria in judgments (0–10 points).
2. Uses technical vocabulary (0–10 points).
3. Provides feedback (0–10 points).
4. Presents the criticism (0–10 points).
5. Compares works (if rankings of several is part of the task according to criteria) (0–10 points).

For mastery learning purposes, it is possible to adopt a minimally acceptable standard—35 out of the 50 points, say. If students score below this level, they would be required to take the feedback into account and resubmit the criticism assignment.

This process—the same process used for evaluating art as for evaluating criticism of art—is highly personal and subjective and can lead to debates about what criteria should be used (which is why multiple judges are used for art shows and gymnastics meets). Gentile and Murnyack (1989, p. 3) argue that such judgments by a single teacher

> . . . are sufficient if (1) the objectives are at an appropriate level of difficulty for the students, (2) the criteria are appropriate to the task, (3) the students understand both the criteria and the grading/rating scheme the teacher plans to use, (4) the teacher gives appropriate feedback and encouragement, and (5) prerequisite component skills are mastered before they are to be used in more complex projects. When such criteria are met, the teacher becomes a mentor/coach instead of an adversary, and evaluative judgements are considered reasonable and informed.

or a team could raise their grade one letter by achieving a team project by one of the methods recommended in the last chapter. Or someone who passed a unit test could tutor someone who needs help; when the tutee passes, the tutor earns the enrichment credit. Among other possible benefits, this would encourage cooperation, would extend the learning beyond the basic objectives, and may allow people to use an entirely different style of learning than they used to demonstrate individual mastery.

Third, I stressed that the F grade is better conceived as I (Incomplete) or NYP (Not Yet Passed) than as Fail. This is because teachers are in the business of helping people succeed, not in making them fail. However, it is not unreasonable to have time limits, after which I turns to F. As long as the time limit follows school policy, or is made into a written contract among the interested parties, then an F grade is a logical consequence of inaction. It becomes equivalent to failing the driver's test.

Fourth, and related to the last point, one should never let students who do not do the minimum work pass with D grades. It gets them out of our hair (and we are thus negatively reinforced), but it also teaches them that they do not have to work to pass (they are likewise negatively reinforced). The proposed criterion-referenced grading scheme, contrary to what seems to some to be coddling students by giving them extra chances, in fact places the burden for success back on the student's efforts. It makes it clear that the student can succeed and will be helped to succeed, but that the next move is the student's. If the students, under these conditions do nothing, then they should not pass math or reading any more than they should get a driver's license.

Fifth, no mention has been made of final exams (or summative evaluations). They can serve some useful functions, such as to make

Cartoon 14.4.

students review a whole course and therefore possibly reorganize the material, relearn it, and remember it better. This same function can be served, however, by a spiral curriculum in which old concepts are reintroduced into new units, reviewing and reorganizing at more frequent intervals. Succeeding mastery tests (as was mentioned in the last chapter) can then be somewhat cumulative. In fact, if material is not mastered and organized into more comprehensive structures at each succeeding level, then it is likely to be forgotten, "Covering" material is not sufficient; as Hunter (1982, p. 102) put it, to cover the material " . . . use a shovel, cover it with dirt and lay it to rest, for that material will be dead as far as memory is concerned" (see cartoon 14.4). Where a spiral curriculum is not possible, times can be arranged for reviewing material (Madeline Hunter's "sponge activities, see Hunter, 1982). Thus, while I am not particularly in favor of final examinations, it is possible to integrate them into the basic criterion-referenced structure proposed here (1) by counting them some proportion of the grade (as Keller and Bloom do; see chapter 13), (2) by making them a requirement and allowing a certain passing level to raise the grade from C to B or B to A, or (3) by some other method.

Table 14.2 A Mastery Decision Table.

Level of Competence	Test Result	
	Pass	Fail
Truly Competent	A. Correct Positive	B. False Negative
Not Competent	C. False Positive	D. Correct Negative

Setting Passing Scores For Instructional vs. Licensing Purposes

As described earlier, there is a considerable amount of subjective judgment that goes into the decision of setting a passing score. The general argument I provided suggests that the passing cutoff should be high enough to exclude people from passing by guessing, but not higher than the test's reliability will support. Requiring 100% correct to pass, for example, assumes that the test is perfectly reliable. Continuing the logic of that position, there are few tests that could support a cutting score of much higher than 85 or 90%.

At the other extreme, to pass by guessing does not necessarily mean random guessing; rather, it means that the examinee's true knowledge is less than the passing score and guessing takes him or her over the top. Millman (1989, pp. 6–7) gives the following example:

> In our illustration of a 100-item test with a 70% passing score, a candidate who knew only 60 items and guessed randomly at the other 40 items could be expected to pass the test, if it is composed of four-option questions.

Clearly, passing by such a guessing strategy would be more serious on a competency test for a physician than for a French major. In other words, the cutting score for a surgeon (pun intended) needs to be higher than for a linguist.

Consider that the decisions to be made fall into the following four types:

a. That a truly competent individual passes the test (a correct positive decision).
b. That a truly competent individual fails the test (a false negative decision).
c. That a truly incompetent individual fails the test (a correct negative decision).
d. That a truly incompetent individual passes the test (a false positive decision).

If a cutting score is set low (e.g., 65%), then many people will pass, even some who are not really competent, and we will thus make very few false negative errors, but very many false positive errors. If the cutting score is set high (e.g. 85%), then we will likely make very few false positive errors, but a larger number of false negatives.

The severity of the types of errors made clearly depends upon whether the test is being used for formative purposes, such as to help students learn new concepts, or summative purposes, such as a licensing exam. In both cases, a false negative decision can be corrected by allowing the person to take the test again—that is, a parallel form of the test. A false positive decision, while not too serious for within-class grading, becomes extremely serious for such licensing uses as certification of physicians, lawyers and teachers. This is because the license is a societal protection mechanism designed to assure consumers that the licensee is competent to help people and is unlikely to do great harm.

Anecdote 14.6

> ### A Mastery Unit to Determine Readiness for Instruction
>
> The Army uses a mastery procedure for initial training in boot camp to teach basic drills, physical training, and how to dismantle and maintain a weapon. Recruits who achieve these goals satisfactorily in the first unit move on to more advanced training. Those who fail to master these fundamentals are recycled through the first unit. This is possible because there are parallel sections of basic training, beginning every two or three weeks.
>
> In comparison, high schools with four or five Math or English sections all start and end together, teaching the same content in parallel fashion. Instead, it would be possible to adapt the above idea from the military and establish a two-week course on prerequisites for course 2 by reviewing essential concepts and skills from course 1. Those whom the teachers judge are ready for the next course can go on to it. Those judged not ready can (1) be recycled through those concepts and get ready for a section staggered to begin perhaps a month hence, or (2) be placed in a more basic course.
>
> Such a procedure would need no additional resources, though it would require a new mentality about scheduling. It should help placement decisions, especially for students just transferring in to your school. Another advantage is that it reviews previous essential material, likely forgotten over the summer, in the context of the upcoming course, thus serving as a two-week anticipatory set. Finally, it should motivate students who want a chance to overcome any problems they had last year to take responsibility now for their learning if they want to move ahead.
>
>

But there is more. Licensing exams often fail to protect the consumer not only because of low passing scores, but also because their policy of multiple reexaminations increases the probability of passing by guessing. Consider, for example, a test with a 70% cutoff and a candidate with a true level of skill of 65%. Such people, according to calculations by Millman (1989), have only a 15% chance of passing the test on their first try, but have an 80% chance of passing the test if they take the test ten times, even if they learned nothing new in the interim.

If false positives are more serious errors than false negatives, as in licensing exams, then clearly a higher standard needs to be established. Alternatively or in addition, Millman (1989) argues that a higher requirement might be imposed on those who failed the test the first time. For example, if the original passing standard was 70%, then those who failed on the first try may have to score at least 75% correct to be considered competent. This reduces the probability of false positive decisions.

As I noted above, this problem is much less severe for within-class grading than for licensing exams. Nevertheless, it is not an unreasonable procedure for within-class grading since it (1) reduces the number of false positives and (2) may increase students' incentive to master material on the first try. Many teachers may like this feature of the procedure. To maintain consistency with the chapter's recommended grading schemes, passing the test on the first try or after repeated attempts would both earn the same grade (see table 14.1).

The above suggestions do not begin to exhaust the possibilities for instructional decisions. It is possible, for example, to use a whole mastery unit to make judgments about a student's readiness to go on to more advanced courses (see anecdote 14.6). Such uses constitute a kind of middle ground between high-stakes licensing decisions and low-stakes within-class instructional decisions.

A Final Observation on Grading

The comprehensive grading system just presented provides separate procedures for what Bloom (1976) calls the selecting talent vs. the developing talent assessment functions. Using statistically correct techniques for the norm-referenced function, we are able to obtain each student's rank in class (or, from appropriate sources, national ranking). Then within each class the teacher can use criterion-referenced measures to motivate students to master the course objectives and, hopefully, to go beyond those. Gentile and Stevens-Haslinger (1983, p. 54) put it this way:

Recognizing the importance of the instructor for setting the standards, along with the necessity of practice in order to become perfect, it can be seen that the mastery testing scheme is intimately connected with excellence: beginning with a student at his or her own level of competence on some set of objectives, the instructor must encourage, and reward with appropriate grades, repeated performance until a high standard is achieved. If the standard is too low, then some students will do the minimum and escape—perhaps with their D grade. That in no way is excellence. But the one-chance-only approach of most teaching-testing does not produce excellence either. Since excellence comes from repeated performances of successive approximations, then mastery procedures with high standards allow—indeed, require—excellence to develop.

Practice Exercises

A. **Practice Items.**

On the following items select the alternative which *best* answers the question. (Answers are in Note 10).

1. Which of the following is the best example of an *evaluation,* in contrast to a measurement?
   a. Chris was placed in the college preparatory track.
   b. Doug got 100's on each of his last three tests.
   c. Fred scored at the 38th percentile on the Graduate Record Exam.
   d. Jerry, at two meters tall, is the tallest person in his class.

2. A mastery standard of 90 means that
   a. a student who scores less than 90 gets a grade of C or lower.
   b. a score of 90 is at the 90th percentile for the class.
   c. a score of 90 or above has achieved the objectives.
   d. the class average is 90.

3. According to the text, creative projects in the arts or writings are best
   a. not graded.
   b. graded in norm-referenced fashion.
   c. graded OK or not-OK with corrections made for work judged not-OK.
   d. graded by giving everyone an A so that pressure does not interfere with creativity.

4. Which of the following is a criterion-referenced interpretation?
   a. Sidney was admitted to the Harvard Law School.
   b. Maxwell won a bronze medal for the 100-yard dash in the local track meet.
   c. Shirley did not pass the National Teacher Exam even on the second try.
   d. Philip moved from 50th to ninth on the computer tennis rankings in only one year.

5. According to the evidence in the text, for norm-referenced purposes
   a. you should convert your test scores to z-scores, then give A, B, C, etc. on the basis of z-scores.
   b. you may simply give percent correct (i.e., 90%, 80%, etc.) instead of grades (A, B, C, etc.).
   c. you may not add the results of two different tests unless you first standardize the scores (e.g., convert them to z-scores of percentile ranks).
   d. all of the above are accurate.

6. According to Gentile, grading within a class should be done as follows:
   a. If students do not pass a unit of the course, they must re-study and try again.
   b. If students pass most but not all units of the course, they pass the course only if their average for all units is above the mastery standard.
   c. If students score 100% on any mastery test, they obtain an A for that unit.
   d. Each of the above is recommended by Gentile.

7. Consider the following test results:

	Midterm	Final
Alice	60	80
Bert	70	70
Charlie	80	50
Mean	70	60
SD	5	10

   Assuming these test scores are weighted equally, are the only evidence for a final grade, and that students are graded competitively, then which of the following is true for the three students named?
   a. Charlie should receive the lowest grade.
   b. Alice and Bert should receive the same grade.
   c. Both 1 and 2 are true.
   d. Alice should receive the lowest grade.

8. On a standardized test, where the national average score is 75, your son scored 80. From this information we can infer
   a. that he mastered the material to a standard of 80%.
   b. that he is at the 80th percentile rank.
   c. that both 1 and 2 are true.
   d. none of the above.

9. Which of the following scores is the lowest relative to its group? (Note: x = score, $\bar{x}$ = mean, and SD = standard deviation)
   a. $x = 325$, where $\bar{x} = 500$ and SD = 100
   b. $x = 21$, where $\bar{x} = 30$ and SD = 3
   c. $x = 59$, where $\bar{x} = 64$ and SD = 2
   d. $x = 1000$, where $\bar{x} = 1500$ and SD = 250

B. For cooperative Study (in or out of class):

1. Have class members who are teaching describe the grading procedures used in their own schools for obtaining class ranks and for within-class grading (or survey some local teachers). Discuss those procedures in terms of the principles and procedures in this chapter. How can improvements be made in school practices?
2. For years in my own classes based on a mastery learning format, some students complained about having to take tests over if they did not score at or above 80% correct. Then I hit upon the idea of giving students a choice. In the course syllabus it now states that

on any test, students may choose to be graded on the mastery system or on a normal curve system (scores are converted to z-scores and the cutoffs for A's, B's etc. are described) and they may choose either before or after they receive their test score. Since giving this option a decade ago, no one as ever opted for the normal curve grading and students have stopped complaining to me. Is there a moral for other classes?
3. In small groups according to the level (elementary, secondary, or college) and/or subject (math, social studies, languages, etc.) you teach, plan a grading system that you and your colleagues could try to implement in your school (or when you have a class of your own).

C. **For More Information:**

1. Take the grading scheme you and your classmates developed in B.3 to local school administrators and obtain their reactions to it.
2. Quiz some local teachers and administrators on their knowledge of the material in this chapter (e.g., practice item #7 in A above). Write a report or present your findings to the class.
3. Read, and perhaps do a written or oral report on, authors on both sides of the criterion-referenced vs. norm-referenced assessment debate. Evaluate the arguments and draw your own conclusions.

CHAPTER

Study Questions

1. What is meant by each of the following terms? Give examples for both norm-referenced and criterion-referenced assessment purposes.
   a. validity
   b. construct-related evidence of validity
   c. content-related evidence of validity
   d. criterion-related evidence of validity

2. What is a Table of Specifications? How is it constructed and for what purpose?

3. What is meant by each of the following terms? Give examples for both norm-referenced and criterion-referenced assessment purposes.
   a. reliability
   b. test-retest reliability
   c. parallel or equivalent forms reliability
   d. internal consistency reliability

4. What is meant by each of the following?
   a. true score
   b. standard error of measurement
   c. confidence interval

   How is a confidence interval constructed, using the standard error, to estimate the boundaries of a person's true score? How is the width of the confidence interval related to the reliability of a test?

5. How is item discriminating power determined
   a. for norm-referenced tests?
   b. for criterion-referenced tests?

6. What is item difficulty? What is optimal difficulty of an item
   a. for norm-referenced purposes?
   b. for criterion-referenced purposes?

7. What does it mean to be an effective distractor in a test item?

8. Why might an item that has good item analysis statistics (i.e., good discriminating power, appropriate difficulty, and effective distractors) be contributing to the test's reliability, but not helping its validity?

9. Classify each of the following item types in terms of whether they require *selection* or *construction* of a response:
   a. Two-choice items
   b. Matching items
   c. Multiple-choice items
   d. Short-answer items
   e. Essay items
   f. Performance items
10. Concerning Two-choice (e.g., True-False) Items, answer the following questions. What are the
    a. advantages?
    b. disadvantages?
    c. rules for writing?
11. Concerning Matching Items, what are the
    a. advantages?
    b. disadvantages?
    c. rules for writing?
12. Concerning Multiple-choice Items, what are the
    a. advantages?
    b. disadvantages?
    c. rules for writing?
13. Concerning Short-answer Items, what are the
    a. advantages?
    b. disadvantages?
    c. rules for writing and scoring?
14. Concerning Restricted-response vs. Extended-response Essay Items, what are the
    a. advantages?
    b. disadvantages?
    c. rules for writing and scoring?
15. Concerning Performance Items, what are the
    a. advantages?
    b. disadvantages?
    c. rules for constructing and scoring?
16. What are the differences and similarities between a Written Report and an Essay?
17. Concerning Portfolios, what are the
    a. advantages?
    b. disadvantages?
    c. rules for constructing and scoring?
18. What is the relationship between testing and the purposes of education?

Principles of Measurement and Test Construction

Introduction

1. American school children are the most tested in the world and the least examined. (Resnick and Resnick, 1985, p. 17)
2. In testing, the temptation to relegate the human factor to minor significance is *a growing trend.* The trend is most visible in the administrative use of multiple-choice tests to make automatic policy decisions about such things as high school graduation, grade-to-grade promotion, teacher certification, and merit pay. Policymakers do not trust teachers' judgments about student achievement, or college professors' assessment of pre-service teachers, or administrators' evaluations of in-service teachers. Using tests this way is widely taken for granted by policymakers, the media, and the general public. Consequently, if a person falls below the magic cut-score, then he or she, ipso facto, is incompetent; the person—not the test—is automatically called into question. Performance on these tests becomes the operational definition of what is valued in education. (Madaus, 1986, pp. 87–88)

There is hardly anything in our schools as common, yet as important, as tests. From international tests that purport to tell us which nation has the best schools, to national tests that report which state has the best schools, to state tests which similarly rank the cities and districts, it is clear that we put great faith in tests and their resultant scores. When a survey reports that we Americans are illiterate vis-a-vis geography, we nod our heads in agreement. When the state norms portray our school district as below the median, we want changes. When our own children are reported to be learning disabled, we want special programs established or, at the least, we want the children sent for additional testing.

As important and ubiquitous as these phenomena are, one might think that we consumers would be quite knowledgeable about the adequacy, reliability, and methods of testing and reporting scores. More likely, however, tests are like automobiles: most of us use them, but few of us know how to make one, how to diagnose their malfunctions, or how to repair one. We take them for granted and accept them despite celebrated cases of (1) discrimination in hiring practices (e.g., whether teacher examinations discriminate against minorities), (2) misdiagnoses (e.g., children classified as retarded who were tested in their second language), or (3) errors in statistical reporting of scores.

The sad truth is that few of us, teachers and teacher educators included, are very knowledgeable about principles of measurement and test construction. (Many teacher preparation programs do not require a course in tests and measurements.) Thus we educators fall into the same trap as the citizenry when test results are touted in support of this or that. We do not question the tests. We may not even know the questions to ask.

This chapter has the goal of, first, enumerating the criteria for judging the adequacy of tests. Known generally as *principles of measurement,* they include such issues as *validity* (does the test measure what it was designed to measure?), *reliability* (does the test give consistent

Anecdote 15.1

Disabled Learners in a Gifted School

In one of the wealthy school districts with which I am familiar, teachers and administrators alike are proud of the fact that the average IQ of their students is close to 120 or about 1.3 standard deviations above the national average. One might think that this would free this district from worry about test scores, but if anything the worry is increased. Students are continually tested and a number of slow and otherwise disabled students have been found (which, incidentally, provides extra state funding to hire teachers to give these slow learners the extra help they need—a process I equated to "bounty hunting" earlier). Now students are often classified as slow to learning disabled if they are significantly below grade level in achievement. In this district being below grade level can still be above the national average. The sad fact is, however, that many of the students and parents who are learning to live with these learning disabilities in these schools would be acknowledged as above average students (with all the benefits thereunto pertaining) in other, poorer schools, within walking distance. What then, is the advantage of getting your child into a "better" school?

or repeatable measures?) and *item analyses* (is each item contributing to the test in a consistent, proper way?). Such questions are important to ask about any kind of test, commercially published or teacher-made.

The second goal of this chapter is to alert teachers to the advantages and disadvantages of various kinds of test items and the principles involved in writing them. Teachers who understand these principles can, with good practice and coaching, create not only better tests, but better curricula and learning environments.

Validity

Validity may be most simply defined as providing the answer to the question, "Does the test measure what it is supposed to measure?" or perhaps to the question, "Is the test being appropriately used, given what it measures?" For these reasons, validity is sometimes given the one-word definition, truthfulness (e.g., Green, 1975).

In the *Standards for Educational and Psychological Testing* (see AERA, 1985), the following introduction is given to this topic (p. 9):

Validity is the most important consideration in test evaluation. The concept refers to the appropriateness, meaningfulness, and usefulness of the specific inferences made from test scores. Test validation is the process of accumulating evidence to support such inferences. A variety of inferences may be made from scores produced by a given test, and there are many ways of accumulating evidence to support any particular inference. Validity, however, is a unitary concept. Although evidence may be accumulated in many ways, validity always refers to the degree to which that evidence supports the inferences that are made from the scores. The inferences regarding specific uses of a test are validated, not the test itself.

Perhaps the meaning of this definition becomes clearest with a few examples of invalid test interpretation. Suppose, for example, that you visited a classroom in which the students were solving 100 multiplication problems of the form $23 \times 57 = ?$ Suppose, further, that the teacher told you that with this test she was testing the students' mathematical reasoning ability. Would you say her test was valid for that purpose? Or, suppose a language teacher had students doing a written translation exercise for the midterm exam. Then, in a conversation about goals, she mentioned that her primary objective was conversational fluency. Would you think her test valid for that objective? Finally, suppose you studied the required textbook for a final exam and found that the exam covered mainly some obscure points out of recommended readings on reserve in the library. Would you be likely to pronounce your professor's test as valid? Most people would have no hesitation in crying foul on the basis of invalidity.

This is the commonplace—and quite correct—notion of validity. A few technical distinctions need to be added, however. First, note that it is not really the validity of the test itself to which we are referring; rather it is the *appropriateness of the interpretation of the test's results*. The multiplication test may be quite appropriate (i.e., valid) as a measure of mathematical calculations, while being quite inappropriately interpreted as a measure of reasoning. Likewise, the translation exercise may quite adequately assess various semantic and syntactic abilities, while being mostly misused to assess conversational fluency. This brings us to a second, related, point—namely, that a test is always *specific to some goal or purpose*. In other words, we never speak generally of validity, but we must go on to ask, "Valid for what?"[1]

A third point concerns the *relativity of validity*: there is neither a perfectly valid test, nor a perfectly invalid test; rather, validity is a matter of degree (high, moderate, or low).

Cartoon 15.1

Finally, though validity is currently conceived as a *unitary concept* there are three major ways to assess the validity of a test. Each of these emphasizes a different aspect of the design and use of a test, and each will be described in turn.

Construct-related Evidence for Validity

To what extent does the test measure a trait or state that is psychologically meaningful? This is the original and fundamental question about test interpretation, which came to be known as concern for a test's *construct validity* (Cronbach and Meehl, 1955). Or, as it often occurs in practice, the question can be rephrased to ask ". . . whether a test can be put to a certain use," or whether evidence exists ". . . to justify a particular interpretation of a test score" (Meier, 1994, p. 114).

Consider a test that is supposed to measure anxiety. Evidence that the test provides a valid measure of anxiety might be obtained by showing that a person's anxiety score is higher if the test is given during a period of great stress than if it is given under more relaxed conditions. Further evidence might be supplied by showing that high scores on the anxiety index are correlated with high blood pressure. In the personality domain of aggressiveness, high scores should be more related to starting fights than to "random acts of kindness." Such multiple ways of assessing a trait (e.g., aggressiveness) and contrasting it with other traits (e.g., peacemaking or submissiveness) help define the test's construct validity (e.g., Campbell & Fiske, 1959; Meier, 1994). The same argument applies to educational tests. For example, if a test is designed to measure mathematical reasoning ability, then scores on that test should be more highly correlated with scores on a test of word problems than a test of skill in using a simple calculation algorithm. And it should be less correlated still with the scores on a test of musical aptitude or knowledge of a foreign language.

As the above examples portray, people want to interpret results from assessments as measuring *something*—intelligence, honesty, anxiety, mathematical reasoning — not just predicting who will score highest on another test. That something is what psychologists call a "construct," and we feel more comfortable about assessment to the extent that we can point to such underlying constructs as explanations: Wendy scores high on that test because she is good at mathematical reasoning; Michael's anxiety shows up on the questionnaire.

Construct validity is of great concern to standardized test makers. It should also be the goal of teachers who are trying to assess a student's status in relation to a particular domain of behavior (criterion-referenced assessment). Popham (1978b, pp. 161–164) calls it *domain-selection validity* to emphasize this. In practice, teachers may be tempted to write items for the major objectives without considering the structure of knowledge that is implied. This may occur, for example, if elementary school students are tested on decoding individual letters and words to ascertain their reading skill. But reading skill is a construct or behavioral domain which surely includes more than the decoding of individual words and letters. Ideally, criterion-referenced assessment requires a clear specification of how the various component objectives of reading are related. Test items would then be written to reflect not only the individual objectives, but also the relationships among those, and perhaps the order in which they would optimally be mastered.

It is often the case, however, that a domain of knowledge can be well-defined without implying a hierarchical order of prerequisites (Nitko, 1980). Such domains as knowledge of particular periods in history, or classes of literature might be cases in point, since there is no reason why Robert Frost and Shakespeare have to be studied in any given order.

Teachers often use a single test to assess knowledge of a large number of different and more-or-less unrelated objectives (e.g., a few questions each on vocabulary, spelling, grammar, or pronunciation). This is not wrong. On the other hand, if assessments are to be meaningfully linked to the instructional program, then each of these separate sets of objectives should be systematically tested over the course of weeks or months. To the extent that our assessments systematically attempt to establish students' development (of schema) in relation to these well-defined domains, our testing program will be less fragmented and more valid.

Content-related Evidence of Validity

Validity related to content asks the question "How representative is the test to the material studied in class?" More specifically, then, *content validity* is concerned with obtaining, to the extent possible, a representative sample of the range of abilities, situations, and topics studied. If the test is to be a diagnostic test on only a few specific objectives (as in some mastery tests), then it may be possible to write at least one item for each objective (e.g., to test for ten spelling or vocabulary words). Usually, however, a test will be written to assess more content than can reasonably be assessed in one test (e.g., when the students have learned 200 spelling or vocabulary words). Then the only sensible plan is to write test items which sample from each of the domains of instructional objectives. This is where *representativeness* of the sample becomes a primary concern (and also avoids students' complaints that the test assessed only obscure points—a case of "mystery learning").

To assure a representative sample of items, most writers recommend that a *Table of Specifications* be established (e.g., Bloom, Hastings and Madaus, 1971; Gronlund, 1985). Such a table is a two-dimensional listing of the content area by specific objective, including level of objectives. In the body of the table are listed the number or percentage of items testing each objective. Table 15.1 provides a partial Table of Specifications for the content on behavior principles (chapter 6) of this text.

In this example, a twenty-item test is desired, with half the items testing basic knowledge and comprehension of the terms and the other half testing application and analysis (from Bloom's taxonomy). The questions below the table sample the range of content and level of complexity required to demonstrate mastery of the objective. The number of questions in each area should also be reflective of the emphases of the course, perhaps in time spent on the various topics in class and in the required readings. For example if the course coverage in lectures and reading assignments in a biology class was 50% of the objectives on physiology of the heart, 20% on the lungs, and 30% on the digestive tract, the test should reflect that emphasis by having about the same proportions of test questions on each area.

Obtaining an appropriate balance of test items for content validity is no trivial matter, especially if you also want to test for higher order skills like analysis or application of the material tested. It is easy to throw together a test at the appropriate time in the course schedule, but it is another matter to have the test be adequately representative of the topic

Photo 15.1. Is this going to be on the test?

or topics taught. By definition, a criterion-referenced test must specify in detail the *domain* of skills, knowledge, behaviors or attitudes the test items are supposed to sample. For this reason many have followed Hively's (1974a) suggestion to use the term "domain-referenced" in place of "criterion-referenced." Thus it is usually the case that specifications for criterion-referenced tests will need to be in greater detail than for norm-referenced tests. It is nevertheless true that a norm-referenced test is valid for a given classroom use only to the extent that it meets the above standards of representativeness.

Criterion-related (Predictive) Evidence of Validity

As mentioned, the fundamental question is "valid for what?" which implies that there must be an outcome criterion to be predicted by the test scores. As expressed in the Standards

Table 15.1 A Partial Table of Specifications for a 20-item multiple-choice test on behavior principles.

CONTENT	Level of Objectives			
	Knows Symbols and terms	Comprehends terms and sequences	Applies terms	Analyzes Interpersonal Situations into Components
Stimulus vs. Response	1a	1		
Behavior & Consequence	1	1		
Pos. Reinforcement		1	1	1
Neg. Reinforcement		1b	1	1d
Extinction		1	1	1
Punishment		1	1	1
Continuous Reinforcement		1	1	
Intermittent Reinforcement		1	1c	

Notes:
1. The following are potential test items for the entry in the above table.
    a. Which of the following symbols represents an undesirable situation?
        1. S^{RF}
        2. S^{AV}
        3. S^D
        4. All of the above
        5. None of the above
    b. Which of the following situations is likely to result in an increase in the behavior?
        1. $S^{\Delta} - R \rightarrow$ No S^{RF}
        2. $R \rightarrow S^{AV}$
        3. $S^{AV} - R \rightarrow$ No S^{AV}
        4. All of the above
        5. None of the above
    c. After giving her feedback on every tennis shot, Mary's tennis coach, Mr. McRacket, sends her off to practice hitting balls against the wall. McRacket wishes to give her intermittent reinforcement. Which of the following will provide the best intermittent reinforcement?
        1. McRacket comments to her after about every ten correct strokes, and ignores her incorrect strokes.
        2. McRacket comments to her after every correct stroke and ignores her incorrect strokes.
        3. McRacket comments to her after about every ten strokes, whether correct or not.
        4. McRacket comments to her after about every ten incorrect strokes and ignores her correct strokes.
    d. Burt Buzzard is continually disruptive in Al Gebra's math class because, he claims, he hates math almost as much as he hates Mr. Gebra. Mr. Gebra is just as upset by Burt's disruptive behavior and he has thus been throwing Burt out of class at the slightest hint of trouble. Which of the following best describes their interaction pattern?
        1. Burt's behavior is being punished; Mr. Gebra's is being positively reinforced.
        2. Burt's behavior is being extinguished; Mr. Gebra's is being punished.
        3. Both Burt and Mr. Gebra are receiving positive reinforcement.
        4. Both Burt and Mr. Gebra are receiving negative reinforcement.
2. The answers to the above questions follow: a (2); b. (3); c (1); d (4).

(AERA, 1985, p. 11), ". . . the fundamental question is always: "How accurately can criterion performance be predicted from scores on the test?"

Consider two examples, one criterion-referenced and one norm-referenced. If you were teaching a driver training course, you would expect your final exam or mastery test to predict who is likely to pass and who is likely to fail the state-licensing exam—that is, those who pass your test should obtain their licenses, while those who do not pass your test should fail to obtain their licenses (at least without further practice). To the extent that your test predicts these results, your test is a valid indicator of skill in driving (as defined by the state). If you developed a norm-referenced test to cover a year's worth of algebra, you might expect it to correlate highly with scores on the math section of the Scholastic-Aptitude Test—that is, those who ranked high on your test should also rank high on the SAT relative to those who rank low.

The above two examples point out that it is proper to speak of criterion-related or predictive validity for both norm-referenced and criterion-referenced testing purposes. Be careful not to confuse the terms criterion-referenced with criterion-related. *Criterion-referenced* tells us that an individual's score is to be interpreted in terms of a specific set of objectives. *Criterion-related* reminds us how the test is to be interpreted or validated—that is, do the scores on this test predict something important in real life? A loose synonym for criterion-related validity is, therefore, predictive validity.[2] Exactly what is meant by prediction differs, however, for norm-referenced and criterion-referenced assessment.

Norm-referenced Predictive Validity

Criterion-related validity in a norm-referenced sense implies predictability of rankings—that is, those whose scores rank near the top of the curve on the predictor test should also rank near the top on the criterion test, while those near the bottom on the predictor test should also score near the bottom on the criterion measure. In other words, there should be a high positive correlation between the ranks on the predictor and criterion measures. (The concept of correlation was presented somewhat intuitively in chapter 3, and an intuitive grasp is sufficient for following the logic of the present discussion. The reader who would like to understand the statistical calculations and logic underlying these concepts is referred to Appendix B, the section on "How To Calculate a Spearman Rank Order Correlation.")

Criterion-referenced Predictive Validity

Criterion-related or predictive validity in a criterion-referenced sense requires that a person's score be interpreted in relation to a domain of test objectives—e.g., how well the person has mastered those objectives. To assess the validity of the test items which are being used to assist that interpretation is to ask, "How accurately does the test classify people who are known to have mastered those objectives compared with those known not yet to have mastered them?" Known masters should pass the test, while known non-masters should not. Criterion-related validity for criterion-referenced tests, in other words, is a matter of the extent to which the tests accurately predict people's status in relation to the domain of objectives.

The immediate problem which arises from the above is how to define a "Known Master." Several possibilities suggest themselves. First, we could give our test to people who, by virtue of experience or attained status, are recognized to be competent in the field. For instance, if the test is on Spanish grammar, a native speaker or a teacher of Spanish should be able to pass the test, while people known to be just beginning Spanish instruction should not be able to pass the test. Similarly, an advanced educational psychology doctoral student or professor should be able to calculate the standard deviation of any set of scores, whereas a beginning graduate student may not. In these cases, the known masters are more-or-less recognized experts in the domain being tested.

Second, we could give our test to people who, though not yet recognized experts, have passed similar test items. For example, if the test is on grammar usually taught in Spanish I, then Spanish II or III students could be expected to be known masters. Likewise, students who have passed a statistics course should be known masters vis-a-vis calculating standard deviations. New enrollees in a first Spanish or statistics course should not be able to pass the tests and could reasonably be called known non-masters.

Of course, some known masters may have forgotten what they once mastered and, thus, a small minority of them may not pass the test. Likewise, some rank beginners may have learned some Spanish grammar or statistics incidentally through daily living and they may pass the test without instruction. But certainly, if more than a small minority of known masters fails the test, then the test is either too difficult or is an inappropriate sample of items to test that domain of skill or knowledge. Similarly, if more than a small minority of novices pass a test before instruction, then the test is either too easy or is an inappropriate sample of items. In either or both of these cases, the test would have to be judged not valid for measuring knowledge in the domain of expertise being tested.

This is the logic of criterion-related validity for criterion-referenced testing purposes (e.g., Martuza, 1977, pp. 289–292). The calculation of a criterion-referenced validity coefficient is based on the proportion of classifications (mastered or nonmastered) that are the same as that which is known by other evidence to be true (that is, the person is a known master of, or is known not to have mastered, the material being tested). Appendix B describes a procedure for calculating a criterion-referenced predictive validity coefficient based on Percent Agreement.

Reliability

Reliability is defined as the degree to which scores are free from errors of measurement (AERA, 1985). Depending on how you look at it, therefore, reliability also refers to the *consistency, repeatability* or *stability* of a score, rank or decision made about test results. If validity is the most important quality of a test for a certain purpose, then reliability is the second most important quality: it indicates how much *confidence* we can place in our results.

Unreliability implies a large component of luck or chance in the scores. If a person's scores are more due to luck or chance than to some acquired knowledge or stable trait, then those scores cannot be validly related to any other criterion scores. Thus *reliability of scores makes validity possible*. To put it another way, reliability is necessary but not sufficient for validity, from which the following points can be deduced:

1. *A test cannot be valid unless it is first reliable*, meaning that it yields consistent, stable scores or ranks. For example, if Mary and her classmates are given three parallel forms of a spelling test and she scores at the 90th, 50th and 20th percentile, respectively (with similar variability in her classmates), then the lack of repeatability of those scores does not make it possible to talk meaningfully about the construct of spelling ability. First, we have to get a repeatable measure before it will be correlated with a criterion score.

2. *A test which is reliable is not necessarily valid.* Even if Mary and her classmates received consistent scores on their teacher's spelling tests, they may score considerably differently on a vocabulary test, a math

test or even a nationally standardized spelling test (in which case, the teacher's test, while reliable, is not a valid predictor of those criterion scores).

3. *A test which is valid is, therefore, known to be reliable.* If Mary's teacher's test is known to yield scores that are highly correlated, say, with a nationally standardized test, then it must be true that the teacher has created a test on which students are likely to get consistent scores or ranks (e.g., if Mary is at the 90th percentile on both her own teacher's and the national test, then she is highly likely to score about the 90th percentile on the next spelling test her teacher creates).

As with validity, there are several ways of collecting evidence concerning the reliability of a test, which is the next order of business.

Types of Evidence for Reliability

There are basically three different methods of assembling evidence on the reliability of a test—namely, test-retest evidence, parallel (or equivalent) forms evidence, and internal consistency (split-half) evidence. A brief description of each of these procedures follows:

Test-retest reliability asks the question, "Will the same test items, given on two occasions, yield the same approximate scores or ranks of individuals on both occasions?" The interval between the two occasions might be anywhere from perhaps an hour to a year or more, as in estimating the stability of IQ scores, or in the consistency of a mastery decision.

Parallel or *equivalent forms reliability* asks the question, "Given a large population of items written to measure the same objectives, will one subset of those items yield the same approximate scores or ranks for individuals as some other subset of items from that same population?" Mastery testing, as we have seen, requires several parallel forms of tests so that students cannot simply memorize answers to specific questions. Many standardized tests likewise have alternative forms of the same generic questions. To accumulate evidence on equivalence of forms requires simply giving two forms of the test to the same individuals in succession (so that there is no opportunity for new learning in between).

Internal consistency reliability asks the question, "Do various ways of splitting the test into subtests yield the same approximate scores or rankings of individuals?" The most common way of doing this is to split the test into the odd numbered items (1,3,5,7, etc.) and even numbered items (2,4,6,8, etc.) and obtain the scores on each half as though they were parallel forms. Hence internal consistency reliability is often called *split-half* reliability. The odd and even scores for each individual can then be compared to see whether the same individuals scored or ranked in the same way on both halves.

As in the case of determining a test's criterion-related validity, how a numerical estimate of reliability is calculated depends upon whether the test is to be used for norm-referenced or criterion-referenced purposes (See Gronlund, 1985, and Appendix B for some recommended procedures).

Reliability as "True Score"

Hypothetically, it is possible to test a person over and over on the same domain of test items, just as it would be to have a person repeatedly hit golf balls. In both the distance the ball is hit and score on the test, there would be some variation in the results but, after 100 or more scores were obtained, they would form a normal distribution. The mean of this distribution of scores on the same person under the same conditions is known as that person's *true score*. The variability in the test results, then, is error of measurement. Recall that reliability was defined as absence of measurement error. Therefore, the amount of variability in test scores for our hypothetical person is inversely related to the reliability of the test. That is, a very reliable test will yield a distribution with a small spread of scores, while a less reliable test will have a larger spread of scores.

The spread of scores for an individual is estimated by a measure known as the *standard error of measurement*, by using the following formula:

Formula 15.1

$$\text{Standard Error (SE)} = SD\sqrt{1-r},$$

where SD = Standard Deviation of the test for all the test-takers, and r = the norm-referenced reliability coefficient.[3] Even though we cannot test a student repeatedly, this formula and knowledge of the normal curve allow us to estimate the person's true score within certain limits, known as a *confidence interval*.

For example, suppose John took an algebra test and scored 87% correct. Suppose further that the mean and standard deviation of the test, respectively, were 76 and 10. Furthermore, the internal consistency reliability of the test was calculated to be .75. Then, substituting in formula 15.1, we calculate the standard error (SE) as follows:

$$(SE) = SD\sqrt{1-r} = 10\sqrt{1-.75} =$$
$$10\sqrt{.25} = 10(.5) = 5$$

This means that 68% of John's scores can be expected to fall within one SE on either side of his obtained score—that is 87 ± 5, or between 82 and 92. Said another way, we can be 68% confident that John's true score lies between 82 and 92 (or 96% confident that his true score lies between 77 and 97, i.e., plus or minus 2 standard errors).

Note that this interpretation is based on the assumption that John's scores are normally distributed, with 34% of those scores falling between 0 and 1 SE on either side of the mean, just as they do for the larger test using SD units. Figure 15.1 shows this graphically.

It is common in standardized tests to express scores within a confidence band of 1 standard error, to estimate the reasonable limits within which the test-takers' true scores are likely to fall. Use of the confidence interval has several advantageous features over use of a single score, among which are the following two I should like to stress. First, as already mentioned, the confidence interval emphasizes that any test score is a probability estimate of ability within reasonable limits, not a fixed and immutable quantity. Second, the width of the confidence interval changes inversely with the reliability of the test. For example, had the reliability of the test in Figure 15.1 been .70, the standard error would have been 5.5 (SE = SD $\sqrt{1-r}$ = 10 $\sqrt{1-.7}$ = 10$\sqrt{.3}$ = 10(.55) = 5.5). If r had been .95, it would have been 2.2 (SE = SD $\sqrt{1-r}$ = 10 $\sqrt{1-.95}$ = 10 $\sqrt{.05}$ = 10(.22) = 2.2)[4]. As reliability increases, in other words, our confidence interval becomes narrower. With a reliability coefficient of .95, we are 68% confident that John's true score falls between 87 ± 2.2, or between 84.8 and 89.2. Unlike a single score, a confidence interval reminds you that a person's score must be interpreted in the context of the adequacy of the test, a point which is equally true of norm-referenced and criterion-referenced tests (e.g., Kane, 1986).

Item Analysis

Thus far in the discussion of validity and reliability of tests, attention has been focused on the whole test, or total score. To improve tests, however, it is necessary to focus on the individual test items to see whether each is functioning as intended. Like members of a team, each item should be contributing to the total score. To the extent that each item is discriminating, for example, those students who have mastered the material from those who have not, then that item is contributing to the

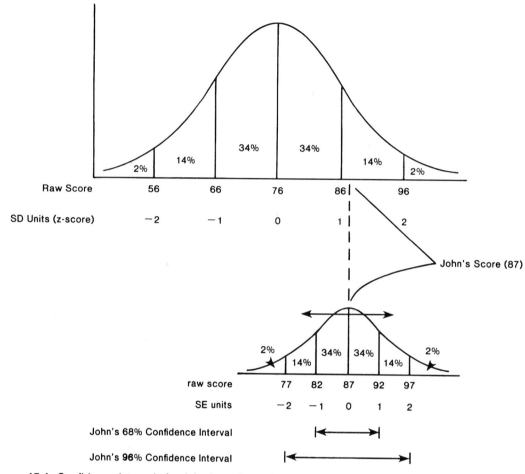

Figure 15.1 Confidence intervals for John based on a hypothetical distribution.

test's *internal consistency*. Item analysis helps us to identify items which are so contributing and which are not; the latter items can then be rejected or improved before being used in future tests.

There are three basic pieces of information which serve as indices for evaluating test items, and which need no complicated analyses to obtain. These are estimates of (1) item discriminating power, (2) item difficulty, and (3) distractor effectiveness. As usual, how each of these indices is interpreted depends upon whether the test is being used for norm-referenced or criterion-referenced purposes.

Item Discriminating Power

The *discriminating power* of an item is the degree to which it separates those who score high on the total test from those who score low. An item which is working properly, therefore, will have *positive discriminating power*: more students who scored high on the total test will get that item correct than those who scored low on the total test. An item which is not consistent with the total test will have *zero* or *negative discriminating power*: those who score low on the total test will do as well or better on that item than those who scored high on the total test. What is a high or low score, of course, depends upon the purpose for which the test is to be used, so we shall have to consider norm-referenced and criterion-referenced purposes separately.

Discriminating Power for Norm-Referenced Purposes

For norm-referenced purposes, high and low scores are defined in relative terms. Thus the steps for calculating discriminating power are the following:

1. Rank the test papers from highest to lowest on the basis of total test score.
2a. Divide the papers into the top and bottom halves on the basis of total score on the test. Any students scoring at the median may be ignored in Step 3.
2b. A variation on 2a for a class of 25 to 35 students is to select the top 10 students, or the top third of the class, on the total score to compare with the bottom 10 or bottom third students.
3. For each item, tabulate the number of students in the high and low scoring groups who selected each alternative choice. For example, Table 15.2 shows three four-choice multiple-choice items which were given to a class of 25 students. The teacher selected the top 10 and bottom 10 students (from step 2b) and tabulated how they distributed their choices among the alternatives. For Item 1, none of the top 10 chose alternative a, 2 chose b, 7 chose c (the correct answer), and 1 chose d. Of the bottom 10, only 2 chose c, while 5 chose b, 3 chose d, and none chose a.
4. Estimate the discriminating power of each item by observing whether the top students were more likely to get the item correct than the bottom students. In Item 1, the answer is yes: 7 of the top students, in contrast to only 2 of the bottom students, obtained the correct answer. Items two and three, however, have zero and negative discriminating power, respectively.

Items with negative discriminating power are suggesting that the worse students do on the total test, the better they do on this item (that is, there is a negative correlation between the item and the total test). Items with zero discriminating power indicate that the top and bottom students on the test do equally well on the item (that is, there is a zero correlation between this item and the total test). Since one of the criteria for adequacy of a test is internal consistency reliability, test items should have positive discriminating power (which implies a positive correlation between the item and the total test). Thus, test items with zero or negative discriminating power should be revised or discarded.

It is possible to quantify discriminating power by the following formula, which calculates the proportion of top students passing the item and subtracts the proportion of successful bottom students.

Formula 15.2

$$\text{Discriminating Power (DP)} = \frac{\text{Passing Top Students}}{\text{Total Top Students}} - \frac{\text{Passing Bottom Students}}{\text{Total Bottom Students}}$$

For Item 1 in Table 15.2, since we selected the ten top and bottom students, 10 goes in each denominator. The figures for the numerator are read out of the Table for Item 1 under the correct choice—namely, 7 top students and 2 bottom students. When plugged into the formula, the calculation is as follows:

$$\text{DP (Item 1)} = \frac{\text{Passing Top}}{\text{Total Top}} - \frac{\text{Passing Bottom}}{\text{Total Bottom}}$$

$$= \frac{7}{10} - \frac{2}{10} = \frac{5}{10} = .5$$

Table 15.2 Item Analyses For Norm-Referenced Purposes.

ITEM 1. An Item With Positive Discriminating Power. *Note c is CORRECT.*

Students	Choices					
	a	b	c	d	omits	Totals
Top 10	0	2	7	1	0	10
Bottom 10	0	5	2	3	0	10
Totals	0	7	9	4	0	20

ITEM 2. An Item With Zero Discriminating Power. *Note:* b is CORRECT.

Students	Choices					
	a	b	c	d	omits	Totals
Top 10	0	5	2	3	0	10
Bottom 10	1	5	1	2	1	10
Totals	1	10	3	5	1	20

ITEM 3. An Item With Negative Discriminating Power. *Note:* d is CORRECT.

Students	Choices					
	a	b	c	d	omits	Totals
Top 10	3	4	0	3	0	10
Bottom 10	2	3	0	5	0	10
Totals	5	7	0	8	0	20

The maximum positive discriminating power is 1.0, which would be obtained only in the event that all of the top students obtained the correct answer and none of the bottom students did, calculated as follows:

$$DP = \frac{10 - 0}{10} = 1.0$$

This will rarely, if ever, occur in real life and thus we are usually content with positive discriminating power, and quite pleased with any item which has a DP of .30 or greater.

You may wish to calculate the Discriminating Power of Items 2 and 3 in Table 15.2 to be sure you understand formula 15.2. The results should be 0 and –.2, respectively.

Discriminating Power for Criterion-Referenced Purposes

For criterion-referenced purposes, high and low scores are defined relative to the passing standard. Thus, instead of using the top vs. bottom students, we need to compare those

Table 15.3 Item Analyses For Criterion-Referenced Purposes.

ITEM 1. AN ITEM WITH POSITIVE DISCRIMINATING POWER BY MASTERS VS. NONMASTERS TECHNIQUE. *Note:* a is correct.

Students	Choices					Totals
	a	b	c	d	omit	
Masters	9	2	0	4	0	15
Nonmasters	4	1	0	5	0	10
Totals	13	3	0	9	0	25

ITEM 2. AN ITEM WITH POSITIVE DISCRIMINATING POWER BY THE POSTTEST MINUS PRETEST TECHNIQUE. *Note:* c is correct.

Students	Choices					Totals
	a	b	c	d	omits	
Posttest	0	3	20	2	0	25
Pretest	4	12	5	4	0	25
Totals	4	15	25	6	0	50

who have mastered the material, perhaps by virtue of having received instruction, with those who have not (e.g., Popham and Husek, 1969). This can be done in several ways, two of which are described below (see Berk, 1978; Crehan, 1974; and Popham, 1971, for other suggestions).

A. Procedure for Masters vs. Nonmasters

1. Obtain the number of masters and nonmasters on the basis of the total test score. For example, if there were 25 students taking the test, 15 of whom mastered it while 10 did not, then the masters will substitute for "Top 10" and nonmasters for "Bottom 10," as in the previous norm-referenced procedure.
2. For each item, tabulate the choices selected by students who mastered vs. those who did not master the total test, as shown in Table 15.3.
3. Calculate the discrimination power of each item using the following formula (which is a variation of formula 15.2).

Formula 15.3

$$\text{Discriminating Power (DP)} = \frac{\text{Passing Masters}}{\text{Total Masters}} - \frac{\text{Passing Nonmasters}}{\text{Total Nonmasters}}$$

Item 1 in Table 15.3 provides a comparison of 15 people who passed the whole test with 10 who did not achieve mastery. The calculation for this example is as follows:

$$\text{DP (Item 1)} = \frac{\text{Passing Masters}}{\text{Total Masters}} - \frac{\text{Passing Nonmasters}}{\text{Total Nonmasters}}$$

$$= \frac{9}{15} - \frac{4}{10} = .6 - .4 = .2$$

Since a higher proportion of masters than nonmasters passed Item 1, it can be said to have positive discriminating power, thus contributing to the total test's internal consistency.

B. Procedure for Posttest vs. Pretest Effects
 1. Give the same test to the students before they are given instruction (pretest) and then again after instruction (posttest).
 2. For each item, tabulate the choices selected by students on the pretest vs. those selected on the posttest, as in Item 2 in Table 15.3.
 3. Calculate the discriminating power of each item by the following formula:

Formula 15.4

$$DP = \frac{\text{No. Passing Posttest}}{\text{Total Taking Posttest}} - \frac{\text{No. Passing Pretest}}{\text{Total Taking Pretest}}$$

For Item 2 in Table 15.3 that would be as follows for a class of 25 students.

$$DP \text{ (Item 2)} = \frac{20}{25} - \frac{5}{25} = \frac{15}{25} = .60$$

The Posttest minus Pretest procedure is more properly called a measure of *Sensitivity To Instructional Effects* (Haladyna and Roid, 1981), since it shows whether students are more likely to pass the item following instruction than they were prior to instruction. I have included it here as an alternative way to estimate criterion-referenced discriminating power, on the logic that any item which is sensitive to instruction in this way will be contributing to the internal consistency of the test. In other words, after instruction students should demonstrate mastery on the whole test, as well as on each item, which they should not have been able to do prior to instruction.

Item Difficulty

Item difficulty is defined as the proportion of students taking the test who obtain the correct answer. Thus the formula for calculation is the following:

Formula 15.5

$$\text{Item Difficulty} = \frac{\text{Number of Students Answering Correctly}}{\text{Total Number of Students Responding to the Item}}$$

If there are 20 students taking each item and on one item 5 answered correctly, and on another 10 answered correctly, the first item has a difficulty of 5/20 = .25, while the second item has a difficulty of 10/20 = .50. In other words, 25% of the students answered the first item correctly, while 50% answered the second item correctly. The first item is more difficult than the second; and if the former were a four-choice multiple-choice item, students are answering it at the chance level.

Many people have noted that item difficulty should have been called item *ease*, since it is calculated as the proportion of students obtaining the correct answer. Unfortunately, tradition has prevailed to make us learn to use the term as defined above.

For norm-referenced purposes, the average item difficulty—which is also the total test difficulty—should approximate .5 to provide the maximum possible spread of students on the test. Only if item difficulty is .5 is it possible to have a discriminating power of 1.0, since all the top students must pass it while none of the bottom students do. Item difficulty of .5 is therefore optimal since it allows, but of course does not guarantee, the maximum possible discriminating power. This does not imply that all items in a test must have a discriminating power of .5. Sometimes very easy items (difficulty of about .9) are deliberately included in the beginning of a test to encourage test-anxious students. Very difficult items (difficulty of .35 or less) can also be useful provided they have positive discriminating power. But note that as difficulty approaches chance (.25 on a four-choice multiple-choice item), it is likely that discriminating power will approach zero, since nearly everyone will be guessing.

For criterion-referenced purposes, an optimal item difficulty is impossible to specify. Of course, the above point about guessing is true for very difficult items. But very easy items, even those with difficulty of 1.00 (where 100% of the people obtained the correct answer), are appropriate for mastery tests *provided that prior to instruction the students could not get the item correct*. In other words, if both nonmasters and masters get an item correct, then that item does not properly assess mastery of the objective.

Evaluating The Effectiveness Of Distractors

How does one decide how to revise an item? By evaluating the distractors—the alternative choices which are not correct answers. All evaluation can be done by looking at the same tables used for determining discriminating power. Two simple rules for evaluating distractors follow:

(1) *Each distractor should distract someone*. That is, a distractor is effective if some students select it as the best answer. According to this rule, all of the distractors were working in Item 2 in Table 15.2 (a, c and d), but a and c were not working in Items 1 and 3, respectively. Thus, as a start in revising the latter items, distractors a and c might be revised.

(2) Since an item with good discriminating power attracts more students from the top of the distribution than the bottom to the correct alternative choice, a *good distractor is one which attracts more students from the bottom than from the top*. A good distractor, in other words, acts to distract those students who do not really understand the concept—the low scoring or nonmastering students. By this criterion, distractors b and d in item 1 of table 15.2 are good distractors and so are distractors b and d in item 2 of table 15.3.

Some Final Comments On Item Analyses

An item which has positive discriminating power and which has most of its distractors working correctly is an item which is consistent with the total test. As a result, this item is improving the reliability of the test. Items which satisfy these requirements, however, need not be helping the test validity. Recall that validity of a test must be assessed in relation to some external criterion or some purpose for giving the test. In other words, finding an item about French grammar which satisfies the item analysis criteria does absolutely nothing to test whether the student knows German grammar. If the purpose of the test is to assess mastery of German grammar, then an item must do more than satisfy the item analysis requirements. The more that it must do can only be answered in terms of the purposes of the testing.

Similarly, items which do not discriminate but are very easy (difficulty approaching 1.0), should be examined for faulty wording of the distractors, but not necessarily discarded. If this item is measuring an important learning outcome that you want all students to know (and you do not necessarily want to discriminate among students), leave the item in the test. Again, this depends on the purposes of the test.

In summary, item analyses give useful but incomplete, and often tentative, information. The particular group of students, conditions of testing, and probably other factors all influence item analyses. Therefore, it is probably unnecessary to look for fine distinctions between items on discriminating power. If an item is discriminating positively, has most of its distractors functioning correctly, and there are no apparent difficulties, it is probably satisfactory in a technical sense. The real question for the teacher is: "Is it measuring an important learning outcome?"

Writing Tests

There is probably no professional activity that is as difficult and nonrewarding for most teachers as the activity of writing test items. Perhaps that is one reason it is put off until the last possible moment by most teachers. From all that has been said about instructional objectives, mastery of critical skills, teaching for transfer and higher level thinking, and content validity, however, it is clear that tests must be written according to an a priori plan.

For certain norm-referenced purposes, the plan would not have to be in great detail. For example, for a general math achievement test it would be sufficient to sample items from a wide range of topics covered by many math classes across the country. Since there is no nationally mandated curriculum for any given age group in the USA (as there is in other countries), a norm-referenced achievement test cannot be derived from a particular textbook or curriculum without being unfair to the hundreds of thousands of students who did not use that text. Thus the test questions must be general. To make this point even more strongly, recall two facts about norm-referenced tests you have already learned—namely, (1) that norm-referenced tests are more reliable and valid to the extent that they spread people out and (2) that items of about .5 difficulty are optimal for that purpose. Items of difficulty=.8 or .9 indicate that 80%–90% of the students know the material tested, probably because they received instruction on those points. Ironically, standardized achievement test developers will tend to drop such items from subsequent tests because they do not adequately discriminate the top from the bottom students. Popham (1978, p. 83) draws the following conclusion from these facts:

> *Test items on which pupils perform particularly well tend to be items covering the very concepts that teachers thought important enough to stress.*

> *The more important a topic is, the more likely a teacher is to emphasize it by devoting instructional time to its mastery. The more instructional time devoted to a topic, the more likely that the norm-referenced test items related to that topic will be answered correctly by many examinees. The more often a test item is answered correctly by many examinees, the more likely that item is to be removed from the test. In time, therefore, particularly with oft-revised norm-referenced achievement tests, items measuring the most important and most often taught things tend to be systematically eliminated from the tests. What we have left in norm-referenced achievement tests are items that measure unimportant things.*

Allowing for some hyperbole in Popham's argument, there is still a lot of truth to it, particularly when we are drawing implications for the development of classroom tests. The point is that a test must be derived from a list of behaviors, skills, knowledges, or attitudes that are well-specified in the teacher's instructional goals. This is what is meant by content validity, even for norm-referenced tests. For criterion-referenced purposes, a test must be linked to clearly specifiable objectives. And while it would be better that the specifiable objectives be related, so as to constitute a psychologically meaningful domain, this is a goal to be successively approximated for most teachers. But there can be no compromise on the first step—namely, writing test items for the instructional objectives at various levels of complexity according to a Table of Specifications.

Recognizing the importance of a Table of Specifications for planning a test, it is now time to turn to the task of item writing itself. While some kinds of tests are better or worse for certain purposes, each type has its strengths and weaknesses, as well as commonly accepted rules for writing. These are the topics of the next sections. Useful additional references on this topic are the following: Bloom, Hastings and Madaus (1971); Bloom, Madaus, and Hastings (1981); Green

(1975); Gronlund (1985; 1993); Miller, Williams and Haladyna (1978); and Popham (1978).

Strengths And Weaknesses Of Various Test Forms

One of the first distinctions that is often made in types of test items is whether examinees must *select* a response to the item, or *construct* or *supply* that response (e.g., Gronlund, 1993; Payne, 1992; Popham, 1978). Consider your own cognitive processes involved in the following two items.

Item 15.1

The psychologist whose name is most associated with the "magical number 7 ± 2" is_____.

Item 15.2

The psychologist who is most noted for the "magical number 7 ± 2" is

a. Harry Bahrick
b. George Miller
c. William James
d. Hermann Ebbinghaus

The first item requires *recall* of an item from memory—that is, the examinee must actively construct an answer. The second requires that the examinee *recognize* which of the given answers is correct and select that one. You may have had an easier time selecting "George Miller" than constructing his name, as was necessary in the first item. It is often easier to recognize a piece of information than to recall it, though that depends upon how the information was encoded and the specific cues available at testing (to refresh your memory on those issues or on the "Magical Number 7± 2" you may wish to return to chapter 10).

Though the process is somewhat different in the two cases, do not assume that recall items are more difficult than recognition items. Each of the above items can be changed in difficulty dramatically by the addition or deletion of a few cues in the stem of the item or, in the case of the multiple-choice item, by changes in the distractors. For example, let's rewrite item 15.1 to add a few more cues:

Item 15.1a

The American cognitive psychologist who, along with Galanter and Pribram, wrote *Plans and the Structure of Behavior* and who is most associated with the "magical number 7 ± 2" is _____.

This change should make the item much easier—that is, more people—possibly still not all—will get it correct.

Consider the following changes to item 15.2:

Item 15.2a

The American psychologist who is most associated with the "magical number 7 ± 2" is _____.

a. Ivan Pavlov
b. George Miller
c. Jean Piaget
d. Hermann Ebbinghaus

These changes are likely to be a virtual guarantee of a test-wise person getting the answer correct, since the only American among the choices is George Miller. These changes, in addition to making the item easier, would also make it incongruent with the objective—that is, a person can answer it correctly for the wrong reasons.

Consider how Item 15.2 can be made more difficult by the following changes in the distractors:

Item 15.2b

The American psychologist who is most associated with "the magical number 7 ± 2" is

a. Harry Bahrick
b. George Miller
c. Neil Miller
d. John Anderson

Now all the psychologists are Americans, three of whom have made a career of studying memory, and the fourth has the same surname but is famous for research in behavioral psychology.

The above examples, using content from a previous chapter in this text, were designed to demonstrate several points about item writing. First, note that what was required to answer the questions was factual knowledge and, moreover, knowledge which was not stressed in the text and for which there are no study questions, and which was probably not emphasized by your instructor. Such an item, however worded, is at best testing knowledge of an isolated historical fact, which may be mostly unrelated to the structure of knowledge that we really care about—namely, in this case, understanding how the magical number 7 ± 2 relates to the operation of memory.

Second, and related to the first, if such facts are to be learned by students, they need to know not only that they will be held accountable for them, but how they will be tested. Students need to study and practice recalling in a manner which is congruent with how they will be tested—namely, to construct or select answers. If you wish to try an experiment in riot control in your class, announce that they will have a multiple-choice test and then give an essay exam instead (or vice versa).

Third, note that wording of a question supplies the retrieval cues—or provides misleading cues—for students, while simultaneously affecting the difficulty of the item. We shall explore some rules for each item type next, but whatever item form is used, the item author should *never assume* that the item will be interpreted as intended. Thus it is a good rule to write a set of test items, set them aside for a few days, then look at them again to see whether they still seem as clear to you. (In addition to often making minor changes in the wording, I have sometimes given the wrong answer to my own question because the wording was so unclear!) Then ask trusted colleagues who are conversant with the topic to criticize the items both for wording and for the degree to which each item is congruent with the objective(s) the item presumes to assess. Popham (1978) calls this step obtaining *descriptive validity* for your test items. Whatever it is called, the process helps avoid major interpretation difficulties of items.

Two-Choice Items

True or False, Yes or No, Correct or Incorrect are the usual choices students are given, though many contrasts can qualify as a two-choice item (e.g., assimilation vs. accommodation, restitution vs. retribution, Republicans vs. Democrats). Such items are especially suited for testing ideas or statements that are unambiguously correct or incorrect or can clearly be placed into one category or another. When such conditions are met, two-choice items have the advantage that a large number of such test items can be given and objectively scored in a short period of time.

Unfortunately, there are also some major disadvantages. First of all, most examinees yearn for additional choices such as "usually true of most Democrats," "false, except when there is peer pressure," etc. The problem is that most things in the real world are *relatively* true or false and this item form requires more-or-less absolute judgments. Second, the apparent ease with which one can write such items is deceptive: since any misinterpretation or qualification of an absolute statement changes it, then the wording of such items has to be just about perfect to be a good item. Third, since the probability of obtaining the correct answer on any given item is .5, then a student will likely obtain 40-60% on a given test by guessing alone.

Finally, while two-choice item formats can test higher levels of cognitive processing, they are perhaps best suited and most-used for testing the knowledge level of Bloom's taxonomy. The following are two True-False items that test at higher cognitive levels:

Item 15.3

The mean of the following scores is the same as the median: 10,20,25,30,40

Item 15.4

The next term in the series 1,3,7,15, is 31.

Both of the above items are True. The first requires knowledge of two sets of procedures (mean=sum/N and median=midpoint) and a comparison of them. As long as the set of numbers was not used as an example in class, the item probably operates at the application level of Bloom's taxonomy. The second item requires analysis of the sequence to see that each successive number in the sequence is the sum of the previous number with the number which succeeds it in counting (i.e., 1+2=3, 3+4=7; 7+8=15; 15+16=31).

As these examples show, it is possible to write True-False items that test the higher levels of thinking, but the fact remains that 50% of them will be answered correctly by guessing and *teachers should be interested in the processes of thinking*. Thus such objectives are better tested by constructing answers to show their steps in solving the problems. Alternatively students can be instructed (1) to decide whether the item is true or false, and (2) if it is false, to change the relevant part of the statement to correct it. This is especially useful for practice tests, cooperative classroom exercises, or for quickly monitoring learning during large-group instruction.

Before offering specific suggestions for writing true-false items, consider the following items:

Item 15.5

A corelation has a range from −1.0 to +1.0.

Item 15.6

B. J. Skinner is widely recognized as the father of applied behavior analysis.

Item 15.7

According to Benjamin Bloom, who is also famous for the taxonomy of cognitive and affective objectives, ". . . our educational efforts can be assumed to be unsuccessful if achievement scores are normally distributed."

Item 15.8

No psychologist would disagree that a test should be shown to be both valid and reliable for a given purpose.

It is possible to score all of those items as false, but for trivial reasons. For example, items 15.5 and 15.6 have minuscule errors in them: Skinner's middle initial is F, not J; and correlation has two r's. If such picayune details are the purpose of the question, then the item should attack that directly:

Item 15.6a

The middle initial of B. J. Skinner is correct as written.

Item 15.5a

The word *correlation* is spelled correctly.

Of course, it is doubtful that either of these questions is worth asking (except perhaps 15.5a in a spelling class; but in that case, the student should have to correct any misspelled words). Since the obvious purpose of both these items was to assess knowledge of the *main idea*, then typographical or other minor errors should be ignored in scoring. Better yet, they should be corrected by the teacher. Furthermore, to avoid confusion on such issues, the instructions to the students should stress that *a statement is to be judged true or false on the basis of the main idea, not on perceived misspellings or other non-essential details.*

This brings us to Item 15.7, in which the main idea concerns the relationship between mastery learning and normal curves. As stated, that idea is basically what Bloom believes, but it is not his exact wording, though cited as though it were. Another picayune detail that is in error is in the other proposition: Bloom was the major author on the cognitive domain, but not on the affective domain. The major error in this item, however, is in its complexity. It is really assessing at least two (and maybe more) pieces of knowledge, which would be better done in separate items. An additional error is in using such a vague word as "famous for." It would be better to state that he wrote, edited, published, etc.

Item 15.8 errs in having a *specific determiner* and in having a double negative, which usually adds unnecessary confusion. Specific determiners like "all, always, never, no, none" almost always make a statement false. Thus you should always—that is, almost always—avoid their use.

Perhaps you can find other errors in these items, since it is difficult to write a perfect test item. To conclude this section, here are a few *rules for writing true-false test items:*

1. The statement should be unambiguously true or false, this or that.
2. Avoid making items false for trivial reasons (trick questions).
3. Avoid negatives when possible.
4. Never—that is, seldom—use specific determiners.
5. Test one proposition at a time; that is, avoid sentences with more than one basic idea.
6. Do not test recall of exact quotes (unless exact memory is the objective, as in theater arts).
7. To reduce the probability of getting the item right by guessing, or to stimulate discussion, instruct students to change incorrect items to make them correct.

Matching Items

Consider the following two matching items:

Item 15.9

Identify the person with his major contribution by placing the letter which appears before the name in the right hand column in the blank before the contribution. The person may have made one or more, or none of the contributions listed.

____ 1. The taxonomy of educational objectives
____ 2. Learned helplessness
____ 3. Learning for mastery
____ 4. Behavior modification

a. Skinner
b. Pavlov
c. Ebbinghaus
d. Seligman
e. Bloom

Item 15.10

Match the statement on the left with that on the right by placing the letter of the item on the right on the line.

____ 1. First studies of verbal learning
____ 2. First mastery learning publication
____ 3. Recent monumental study of 50 years of memory for Spanish

a. 1922
b. Harry Bahrick
c. 7 ± 2
d. 1968
e. Fred Keller

Both of these items are attempting to measure basic factual recall—the level of cognitive processing that is most easily assessed by matching tests. The second item, however, mixes up names, dates, and other information in a way that does not make it clear which is required at any time. That could be clarified by saying, for example, "Date of first mastery learning publication" for number 2 in item 15.10. However, that introduces yet another problem—namely, that the probability of making the correct match then becomes .5, given only two dates. The solution to this problem is to make both the premises (on the left) and the lettered options homogeneous, as in Item 15.9. That is, if you are testing knowledge of people and accomplishments, states and capitals, dates and places, do each of them in separate matching items, rather than in one long matching item.

The number of options is also of concern since too few (e.g., two or three) increases the probability of getting the correct answer by guessing. Too many options (e.g., 15–20) would make the reading and memory load for each premise onerous. Thus, it is best to keep the list between 4 or 5 and perhaps 10 or 12 options. There can be as many premises as you wish to test; again, to keep guessing to a minimum, you should not have a one-to-one correspondence between options and premises, including the stipulation that an option may be used once, more than once, or not at all.

As mentioned, matching items are admirably suited to measuring a lot of basic factual knowledge in a short time and space. Because they can be constructed in such a way as to make the probability of guessing essentially zero, they are much better than true-false or other two-choice items for measuring attainment of knowledge objectives.

Matching items are also capable of assessing higher levels of thinking. For example, consider the following item.

Item 15.11

Each of the following descriptions is best labeled by one of the procedures named in the list below. Place the letter of that procedure on the line.

    a. Positive Reinforcement
    b. Negative Reinforcement
    c. Extinction
    d. Punishment
    e. Discrimination Learning
    f. Generalization

_____ 1. Mike is so nervous and upset when he has math homework that he scribbles down any old answer and puts the book away with obvious relief.

_____ 2. George works hard in his special education class because he gets munchies for each assignment. In his regular class he gets no such payoff and he does more goofing off.

In items such as this, where the student is asked to classify statements on the basis of a set of rules, principles, or procedures, then students are operating at higher taxonomic levels than knowledge. In item 15.11, for example, students would be demonstrating comprehension or application, depending upon how close the examples were to those used in class.

In summary, here are some pieces of *advice for writing matching items*:

1. Make both the list of premises and the options homogeneous in form.
2. Write the directions as explicitly as possible to state the basis on which the matching is to be done.
3. Avoid one-to-one correspondence between premises and options, including the possibility that an option can be used once, more than once, or not at all.
4. Keep the list of options between four-or-five and ten-to-twelve.

Multiple-Choice Items

Experts agree that multiple-choice items are the most versatile because (1) they can test all levels of Bloom's taxonomy, except synthesis; (2) they can require judgments about the relative correctness of the choices provided; (3) they can test a large number of objectives in a relatively short period of time; (4) they are efficiently scored, including the possibility of machine-scoring; and (5) they can do all of the above while keeping the probability of arriving at the correct answer by guessing to a respectable .20 or .25. With proper wording and

Table 15.4 Multiple-choice items for five levels of Bloom's Taxonomy.

KNOWLEDGE: Which of the following is best defined as the mid-point of a distribution of scores?
- a. mean
- b. median
- c. mode
- d. all of the above

COMPREHENSION: In the curve to the right, the numbers 1–6 are labels for certain areas of the curve and 7–11 refer to specific points on the curve. Minus one-and-a-half standard deviations (z=–1.5) occurs
- a. to the left of 7
- b. at 7
- c. between 7 and 8
- d. between 8 and 9

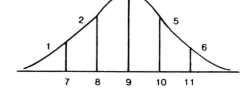

APPLICATION: Which of the following scores or ranks is *lowest* in norm-referenced terms?
- a. a score of 48, where the mean is 58 and the standard deviation is 10.
- b. a percentile rank of 16
- c. an IQ of 85
- d. a z-score of –1.5

ANALYSIS: The median of a distribution of scores is 20. Following are all the scores but one: 23, 21, 19, 17, and 15. Which of the following could be the missing score?
- a. 26
- b. 20
- c. 18
- d. 19.5

EVALUATION: Consider the following distribution of test scores and three of the students in a class of 30.

	Midterm Test	Final Test
Sally	80	80
Maria	90	60
Beth	60	100
Class Mean	80	60
Standard Deviation	10	20

Assuming that these test scores are to be weighted equally, are the only source of evidence for a final grade, and that students are to be graded in a norm-referenced fashion, then which of the following should be done?
- a. Sally and Beth should receive the same grade, which should be higher than Maria's.
- b. Sally and Maria should receive the same grade, which should be higher than Beth's.
- c. Beth should receive a higher grade than Sally, who should receive a higher grade than Maria.
- d. Sally, Maria and Beth should all receive the same grade.

The answers to the above items are b,c,d,a, and b respectively.

distractors, they can also be made to vary sufficiently in difficulty to be used for both novices and budding experts. To measure thinking objectives, and avoid the label "multiple-guess," however, requires a certain sophistication of writing.

Table 15.4 provides an example of a multiple-choice item written for each level of Bloom's taxonomy, except synthesis. Although many text authors insist that synthesis items can be written at this level, I find it extremely difficult to write anything but the most trivial kinds, which emphasize unscrambling words to make a meaningful whole (e.g., good, news, no, is, news; from Green, 1975, p. 70) or to ask what step in an operation or hypothesis-testing procedure comes next. Even Bloom, Madaus and Hastings (1981, p. 271), give examples in which the students are asked:

> . . . only to judge particular details of a proposed set of operations. The value of this test form is that it can sample a variety of details in a brief amount of time. However, these would be clearer illustrations of synthesis if the student were asked to propose the hypothesis and state how he or she would test them.

In other words, although they attempt sample multiple-choice items to assess synthesis, they prefer that synthesis be assessed by construction (essay or performance items) rather than by selection. I concur.

The other levels of the taxonomy can be adequately and efficiently assessed by multiple-choice items. Of course, you have to be clear that the *stem*, or premise, of the item states the problem clearly, that each alternative choice follows logically and grammatically, but that there is a clearly correct or best answer. Consider the following item:

Item 15.12

Spread of scores in a distribution is

a. measured by correlations.
b. standard deviation.
c. mean, median or mode.
d. known as the variance.

This item has a number of faults. Among them are the fact that conceptually either the variance or the standard deviation could be correct answers, since the latter is the square root of the former. But one suspects d was supposed to be the correct answer because that choice grammatically completes the stem. In addition, the wording of b implies that only the standard deviation is a measure of spread of scores, which is not true. Choice c can also be dismissed on grounds other than comprehension of the concepts, since it does not grammatically complete the stem. Here's another negative exemplar:

Item 15.13

A person who is interested in the transfer of operant principles to real life is known as an

a. cognitive psychologist.
b. analytic psychologist.
c. applied behavior analyst.
d. all of the above.

Whatever your view of the conceptual basis of this item (c is correct), the fact that the stem ends in "an" immediately eliminates choice a. All of the above is also eliminated on grammatical grounds, and thus the number of viable choices has been reduced to only two. Such minor details as these reduce the effectiveness of multiple-choice items.

To organize the above points, consider the following *suggestions regarding multiple-choice items:*

1. The stem should establish the problem clearly.
2. If possible, avoid negatively worded items.

3. Write items with four or five alternative choices (three is probably too few).
4. Avoid very long choices. It is better to place words that would be repeated in each choice in the item stem, along with any other information that would shorten the choices.
5. Alternative choices should be plausibly and grammatically related to the stem.
6. Alternative choices should be of approximately the same length or, if of differing lengths, no pattern should occur across items (such as the longest choice is usually keyed correct).
7. Try not to have any consistent pattern in frequency or keying of correct answers—that is, whether the correct choice appears more frequently in "e" than in any other position.
8. Use "all of the above" or "none of the above" sparingly. If you use one of them, be sure to include it as a foil more frequently than as the correct answer to keep students from simply guessing that choice.
9. Write distractors so that each is related to the stem in plausible, but different ways. Writing plausible distractors is the most sophisticated part of multiple-choice item writing, but it is a skill which develops with practice. Some useful advice for beginners was given by Miller, Williams and Haladyna (1978). They suggest the following techniques (pp. 45–77):
    a. Write nonsense in technical jargon that fits the stem.
    b. Use a correct answer to a different question.
    c. Write a sensible but trivial answer.
    d. Write a straight recall answer to attract the student who has simply memorized isolated facts.
    e. Write answers that are partially correct, but leave out an important component.

As an example of the last suggestions, consider the following item:

Item 15.14

Mastery testing has the main purpose of:

a. comparing students' relative standing on a specific domain of knowledge.
b. providing a non-normal distribution of scores.
c. evaluating the effects of various teaching methods on student achievement.
d. applying educational psychology principles to classroom instruction.
e. motivating students to achieve certain objectives to a high standard.

In this item, where e is correct, the distractors are built on the Miller-Williams-Haladyna suggestions. Choice a mixes up the jargon of norm-referenced and criterion-referenced assessment to produce something that could be true, but hardly ever is, and is certainly not the purpose of mastery testing. Choice b is a frequent result of mastery, but it is not a purpose. Choice c is more evaluation jargon, but it is at best the answer to a different question. Choice d is sensible, but trivial, since this is probably the goal of all instructional and evaluation techniques. How well each of these foils distracts people would depend on the quality of instruction and relative sophistication of the students vis-a-vis this objective. Thus empirical data, subjected to an item analysis, are required to be sure which distractors worked. Nevertheless the item shows a strategy for writing distractors.

Short-Answer Items

A question which requires students to produce rather than select a response of one or two words, a phrase, or a short sentence is called _____ item. The short-answer item as in the above incomplete sentence form, may require the answer to a question, or may require the identification of some part of a diagram or map. Following are a few examples:

Item 15.15

Define the mean: _____
_____
_____

Item 15.16

The level of Bloom's taxonomy of objectives that includes translation or paraphrasing is know as _____.

Item 15.17

Identify the part of speech of each of the words italicized in the paragraph below.

1. _____ Once upon a time there was a *beautiful* princess, who lived
2. _____ in a mountainous *kingdom* at the top of one of the mountains. On a *neighboring* mountain top lived a handsome prince. . .
3. _____

Item 15.18

On the map before you, identify the type of terrain and elevation that is labeled number 7. _____

The short-answer, or fill-in-the-blanks, form of item is most uniquely suited to test factual recall, but it is not limited to that level of thinking. For example, Items 15.17 and 15.18 are probably testing at the comprehension level, and Items 15.3 and 15.4 could easily be converted to short answer to test at the application and analysis levels, as follows:

Item 15.3a

What number can fit into the sequence 10, 20, ___, 30, 40 to be both the mean and the median?

Item 15.4a

The next item in the series 1, 3, 7, 15, is _____.

Provided there is only one correct response, or perhaps two or three acceptable synonyms, the short-answer form can maintain objective scoring and still require production of a response. Furthermore, it can test a large number of objectives in a short space and time.

The short-answer form shares with all other item types the requirement that much care go into proper wording, and has some unique requirements concerning the selection of words to be filled in. Consider the following item:

Item 15.19

In calculating the standard deviation by the definitional formula, you first calculate the _____, then subtract each _____ from the _____, then _____ the difference, _____ the _____.

This item has too many blanks and many of them are not testing important steps. The teacher who writes such an item is trying not to give anything away; but the result is likely to confuse students who know the procedure, but not in the rigid form in which it is expressed above. Better, would be to test just one step in the process, as follows:

Item 15.19a

In calculating the standard deviation by the definitional formula, you first calculate the mean, then subtract each score from the mean, and then _____.

Alternatively, if you wish to check the whole procedure, you could give them a problem and have them solve it.

There are times, however, when you may want to test recall of two terms, particularly when they are contrastive technical terms, such as accommodation vs. assimilation or operant vs. respondent. Consider the following item:

Item 15.20

When a fact is known to be stored in memory, but the cues present are not sufficient to retrieve the fact, cognitive psychologists say the material is _____ but not _____.

Such an item tests recall of the technical terms "available vs. accessible" in a straightforward manner.

What, then, are the *rules for writing good short-answer items*?

1. Omit only one or two significant words in the incomplete sentence variety.
2. Make sure there is only one correct answer, or at most an acceptable synonym. If such precision is not possible, use a different item type to test the concept.
3. Test only recall of important information or terms, not trivial points or recall of exact quotes.
4. Avoid grammatical cues: for example, a or an can be written a(an).
5. Make all blank spaces of equal length so that the student is not cued as to length or number of words required.

Essay Items and Written Reports

One of the most commonly used item types, the essay item is also commonly abused. Like the short-answer form, it requires a constructed response; unlike the short-answer form, its primary uses are in testing the ability to synthesize, organize, evaluate, and create, which raise significant problems for judging and scoring the responses.

Essay questions fall into two main categories: *restricted-response* items, which limit the scope and length of the response, and *extended-response* items, in which the examinee is given wide latitude in content, style and length of the response. The latter have two great disadvantages—namely, (1) they test

Photo 15.2. An essay exam in a Nigerian school. (Photo Courtesy of Doug A. Gentile)

only a few objectives (sometimes only one) in a given time period and (2) scoring is extremely subjective and usually unreliable.

For some purposes, such as the measurement of ability to organize a large body of information, the extended-response format may be the only viable option. However, these purposes are usually better served by a *written report* or term paper, which has such components as (1) requiring research and analysis of the findings, (2) inventing an organizational structure for comparing approaches or presenting an argument, and (3) synthesizing or evaluating the findings. These are higher levels of thinking indeed and, when done in the real world by professionals, are accomplished in stages over days or weeks, not in a one- or two-hour essay test.

To teach novices how to do such complex work, it is initially useful to break the assignment into a hierarchy of components, establishing deadlines so that students can receive feedback on prerequisite skills before tackling more complex, inclusive skills. This, in fact, has been the traditional procedure for teaching elementary school students how to do a written report: first, they go to the library to learn to look up articles and reference material, then they take notes on the articles and submit them to the teacher, then they submit an outline, etc.

For more conventional testing purposes, therefore, the restricted-response variety of essay testing is much superior to the extended, both because it can test more academic objectives in a given period of time and because the scoring can be made more reliable by focusing narrowly on the content being tested. Contrast the following two essay items:

Item 15.21

Discuss the differences between Bloom's Learning for Mastery and more traditional instructional approaches.

Item 15.21a

In three short paragraphs, describe the differences between Bloom's Learning for Mastery and more traditional instructional approaches in regard to the following: (1) philosophy in relation to the normal curve; (2) establishment of objectives and standards for passing grades; and (3) provisions for students who have not met the passing standard.

The latter item is a restricted-response type of the former. It states the parameters for scoring and establishes the ground rules for organization and length of the required response. The former item is so open-ended that it encourages a student who does not know the critical attributes of mastery learning to bluff in as many words as possible. Thus for assessing a student's higher levels of cognitive processing of certain bodies of information, restricted-response items are much preferable to extended-response items.

As implied above, another common difficulty with essay testing concerns what specifically is being assessed, content or style. Consider the following four exercises:

Item 15.22

Write a brief report on the similarities and differences between Erikson's and Piaget's stage theories of human development.

Item 15.23

In one paragraph each, summarize at least three points central to Bloom's argument in his original article on mastery learning. Then in another 2 or 3 paragraphs, express whether you think you could apply those points to your own classroom or, if not, why not.

Item 15.24

Write a letter to your congressman requesting his/her position on Medicare. Use appropriate business letter form.

Item 15.25

Write an original poem or rap song on a topic of interest to you.

The first two of these items have an explicit academic content being tested—namely, how well the student comprehends the various theorists, can analyze components of their theories, or can apply or evaluate their ideas. Scoring keys for assessing these objectives should therefore emphasize accuracy of what is said about the theorists' positions, ability to find similarities and differences or weaknesses in the theories, inventiveness in applying what is known to one's own setting, etc.

Items 15.24 and 15.25, on the other hand, have the main purpose of testing skill in writing—that is, they are testing *writing performance* as opposed to academic content.

This does not imply that there is no academic content required, since one needs to know business letter form to write a good business letter. Scoring, nevertheless, would emphasize organization and adequacy of the writing instead of the content of what was written.

This distinction between scoring for content or style is the essence of the difference between an essay test and a performance test of the art of writing (often called an "authentic test" of writing). Scoring essays like Items 15.22 and 15.23 for grammar, spelling and style as well as for academic content runs the risk of students obtaining equivalent scores, say 80, for different reasons: for example, E. Z. Riter just muddles through on content but writes well, while Ed Syke can't write but learns his psychology. This issue is particularly cogent for teachers with ethnically and linguistically diverse students.

Two solutions to the above dilemma appear most satisfactory. First, keep essays and writing performances as entirely separate tasks, the former to assess higher levels of thinking of academic content and the latter to assess grammar, spelling and writing style. Writing errors in the essay can still be noted without points being deducted, (as can content errors in writing), given appropriate feedback, and even corrected before the assignment is accepted as complete.

Alternatively, two grades can be given for the essay: one for content and one for points of style. If this route is taken, it still seems necessary to give feedback and have errors corrected.

To reiterate and conclude this section, please note that essay questions are uniquely suited for measuring synthesis and evaluation objectives, and they should not be wasted on testing recall of facts or writing performances, which are better measured by other item types. Some *suggestions for writing essay items are the following:*

1. Focus the question as much as possible, specifying clearly the issues you wish the students to address and any limits on scope, length, or time.
2. Prepare a scoring key ahead of time: what will you be looking for and how many points will each component be worth? For example, in Item 15.21a., one point might be awarded for each of the three areas specified if the response captured the essence of the distinction.
3. Provide explicit directions for the test, perhaps including the number of points each part of each question is worth, whether and how separate grades will be awarded for content and style, etc.
4. Do not allow students to choose from among several items which they will answer. The purpose of essay items is to assess learning of certain key higher-level academic objectives, and students should no more be able to opt to be tested on these any more than they would be allowed to choose which multiple-choice items they would answer.

Performance Items and "Authentic" Testing

When the "proof of the pudding is in the eating," there is no point in developing a multiple-choice test; rather, have the students make pudding. Home economics has traditionally been a class in which performance tests have played a major role. So have the vocational arts, secretarial studies, languages, fine arts, music, laboratory sciences, and physical education. Perhaps not as obvious as these are the skills involved in writing (as contrasted to essays; see previous section), inventing computer programs, or demonstrating a new teaching technique. While other kinds of tests can assess knowledge in such areas, the essence of competence is the ability to *do* something, usually under actual or simulated conditions. Piano recitals, gymnastics meets, practice teaching, and driving tests are all examples of performance tests conducted under close-to-real-life conditions—hence the name

Anecdote 15.2

The Standardized Patient

Standardized patients are average people or actors trained and paid to simulate an actual patient with a specific illness or set of symptoms and to present these symptoms in a standardized, unvarying way to physicians who interview them. Thus anyone, from beginning medical students to experienced physicians, can practice interviewing and diagnostic skills under life-like conditions, where a series of treatment rooms hold different patients complaining of different problems. Like authentic science laboratory work stations, each standardized patient assesses ability within a limited domain of objectives, but a series of these can provide a fairly representative sample of work-related skills. This allows standardized patients to be useful for practicing interviewing skills and diagnostic reasoning for in-class mastery testing, and even for high-stakes licensing exams. For more information about their uses, as well as evaluations of the evidence on standardized patients, see Barrows (1993); Colliver & Williams (1993); Stillman (1993); and Swanson, Norman & Linn (1995).

Do you see any applications for this idea for teaching or evaluating teachers? Counselors? School Psychologists? Principals?

authentic testing is often reserved for these kinds of demonstrations (see anecdote 15.2 for an example from medical education).

The word "authentic" must be carefully used, however, or it may imply that other kinds of testing are "inauthentic." Drivers tests provide a perfect example of the problem: most states require passing both a driving skills test and a multiple-choice test on the rules of the road. Few of us would argue that, "Driving skill is authentic, but knowing the rules of the road is inauthentic." Thus it is not the type of test that determines authenticity; rather it is how closely the test assesses the knowledge and skills required in real life (which is a variation on the validity problem; e.g., Messick, 1994; Shavelson, Baxter & Pine, 1992).

That said, the essence of what is meant by authentic testing is performance, and I shall use the terms interchangeably here. Consider some of the phrases used to capture the flavor by authentic testing's proponents: the "performance of exemplary tasks" (Wiggins, 1989a), the "exhibition of mastery" (Sizer, 1984), "Just Do It" (Nike commercial), and "Don't talk of love; show me!" (Eliza Doolittle in My Fair Lady).

As the above examples imply, performance testing provides the greatest breadth of topical coverage of all the kinds of assessment. Some of these performances can be more easily objectively scored, even machine scored, than so-called "objective" tests: speed of running, weight lifted, height jumped, whether blood pressure is within a certain range, etc. Often, however, the scoring of performances is just as subjective as the scoring of essays, since directions, rules of the game, difficulty of the task, and criteria on which the performance is to be scored must be understood in the same way by evaluators and performers.

For high stakes exams, such as auditions or Olympic competitions, the various components and how they will be scored must be

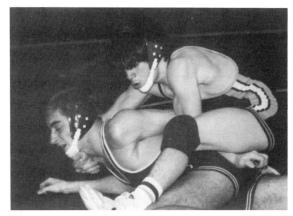

Photo 15.3. An authentic test?

stated in advance. In the case of gymnastics, experts have rated the difficulty of various moves and gymnasts know what each is worth before working on their routines. They also know that certain mandatory components of the skills receive more scrutiny than others from judges. Despite great effort at removing bias from the scoring, there are sometimes vast differences among judges on the same performance, and various procedures are used to remove such bias (e.g., the highest and lowest judges' ratings are discarded and the rest are averaged to obtain a final score).

Teachers do not have the luxury of having 4–6 judges available to score their students' performances. The problems remain, nevertheless. To reduce bias, as well as to increase the value of their feedback to the students, teachers need to have the criteria clearly identified. Indeed, if teachers are assessing whether learning has occurred—that is, if the purpose is criterion-referenced assessment—then it is literally true that "Whether you win or lose is less important than how you played the game." For example, in a performance test of spontaneous conversation in a second language, the teacher should let students know that (or whether) they will be judged on their pronunciation, their accent (or lack thereof), their fluency, their comprehension of the teacher's statements (as shown by appropriateness of their responses), their choice of vocabulary and grammar. The teacher may then rate the students on each of these dimensions (on a 10-point scale perhaps) and go over each of these components with the students later.

This must be done individually and is therefore a lot of work, but the result will be more reliability in measurement and greater perceived fairness than if the criteria are not specified.

By these criteria, Item 15.24 is vague as a writing performance unless what is meant by appropriate business form is well-defined. Same for Item 15.25 which, without some limits of length or style, seems to have the same scoring problems as extended essays. Consider the following improvements to item 15.24:

Item 15.24a

Write a letter to your congressman requesting his/her positions on Medicare. Use appropriate business form, (including heading, greeting, body, signature [and whatever else is required]), and print the letter on the word processor to be ready to send.

A scoring key would still need to be developed, but the rubric is at least partially created in the instructions. The following item also attempts to be clear on the limits:

Item 15.26

Your task is to check the five objects at the lab station to see whether each of them conducts electricity (e.g., a penny, a popsicle stick). Then write a general conclusion about what kinds of materials conduct electricity and which do not.

This item, paraphrased from the New York State Elementary Science Program Evaluation Test (see Doran and Zinnerstrom, 1995), has separate scores for conductivity of each object (maximum = 3) and for the quality of generalization (maximum = 2). Since these items are part of a science manipulative skills assessment, a number of experienced science teachers are brought in as scorers. Still, similar projects could be invented for individual classrooms.

Useful, additional information on issues involved in the specification of performance objectives and the variety of ways of scoring them can be found in Airasian (1994); Gentile and Murnyack (1989); Gronlund (1993); and Wiggins (1989a & b). See also Anecdote 15.3. To summarize, here are a few *rules for constructing performance tests:*

1. Specify clearly the limits of the performance:
   a. How much time may be taken.
   b. How many tries may be taken.
   c. What space may be used.
   d. What materials or equipment may be used.
   e. Etc.
2. Be clear on the rules of the game or dialogue and the importance of the final product (or result) vs. the process.
3. Prepare a scoring key ahead of time: what you will be looking for and how many points each will be worth (e.g., each component might be worth 1 point, some might be worth more points than others on the basis of difficulty, or each will be judged on a rating scale where 10=perfect and 1=totally incompetent). Make this available to the participants.
4. If the test is to be used for facilitating learning, take sufficient notes on the performance to be able to give feedback on what was done well, what went poorly, and how to improve it. If it is for a competition or some credential, this is not as necessary (though validity and reliability of scoring are then more important).

Portfolios

Portfolios have certainly become popular "alternative assessments" in public schools in recent years, though they have a long history of use in fields like art, architecture, music, journalism, and the professoriate. In applying for a job, achieving a promotion or tenure, or winning prizes, candidates in such fields often submit a portfolio of their best paintings, design ideas, compositions or recordings, articles or books. Note that the candidates must *reflect* on their past work and *select* the best to include in the portfolio, since no one would wish to present evaluators with his or her worst, or even average, work.

The above account has much to teach us about some basics of portfolios. They are certainly alternatives to objective tests in that, first, there are creative products that accrue and, second, the reflection-selection process engages the analysis, synthesis and evaluation levels of thinking. On the other hand, just requiring portfolios in the way many teachers require homework will neither guarantee good products nor reflective processes. Even requiring students to justify why a piece was selected for a portfolio may not be sufficient. As Lambdin and Walker (1994) complained about their students' initial portfolios in math,

Then I was extremely disappointed when many portfolios consisted primary of computational work with comments such as "I chose this because it is neat" or "I chose this because I got all the right answers." (p. 319)

Not surprisingly, they had to teach their students how to be reflective, to categorize, to edit and critique, and to select items for inclusion because (1) of what was learned while doing it, or (2) to show how this work connects with other activities in school or life.

Because of these complexities, portfolios have much in common with Written Reports, described earlier: they have multiple components, some of which may be prerequisite to others. All of these components require practice and good feedback from the teacher to set these reflective thinking processes in motion. To paraphrase Schön's (1987) description of the process, the learner does x, the teacher

Anecdote 15.3

> ### Scoring a Performance While Also Teaching
>
> Wiggins (1989a) points to British APU (Assessment of Performance Unit) test protocols as a model for how assessors can ". . . probe, prompt, and even teach, if necessary, to be sure of the student's actual ability and to enable the learner to learn from the assessment" (p. 709). The following are some of the steps involving the concept of perimeter:
>
> 1. Ask: "What is the perimeter of a rectangle? [Write the student's answer.]
> 2. Present sheet with rectangle ABCD. Ask: "Could you show me the perimeter of this rectangle? *If necessary, teach.*
> 3. Ask: "How would you measure the perimeter of the rectangle?" *If necessary, prompt for full procedure. If necessary, teach. . .*
>
> The steps go on to test circumference and area of circles with questions designed to elicit the use of string (which is on the table) to estimate the accuracy of answers and to show concrete understanding of the formulas.
>
> Scoring is divided into categories of successful or nonsuccessful, with the former being subdivided into unaided or aided success. Wiggins (1989a) describes the scoring as follows (p. 709):
>
> > *1) unaided success; 2) success following one prompt from the tester; 3) success following a series of prompts; 4) teaching by the tester, prompts unsuccessful; . . . 6) an unsuccessful response despite prompting and teaching; . . .*
>
> A point that should not go unnoticed is how closely this procedure reflects Vygotsky's ideas for measuring the zone of proximal development (see Chapter 2).

provides feedback and gets the learner to reflect on doing x, and the teacher gives further feedback to get the learner to reflect on the reflections. Used in portfolio production, students may need to keep a *working portfolio* and a more *permanent portfolio* (e.g., Lambdin & Walker, 1994) for works in process and more-or-less finished products, respectively.

Items usually recommended for inclusion in portfolios, e.g., as shown in anecdote 15.4, represent breadth as well as depth or excellence, (see also Abruscato, 1993). While a professional artist or musician can display a specialized portfolio, an important instructional purpose is to broaden the student's thinking. Thus proponents also recommend that each portfolio also include some organizing features: a table of contents, a summary letter explaining the contents, and the criteria and/or categories for selecting the pieces for inclusion.

Regarding grading, if the purpose of a portfolio is reflection and self-evaluation, then a teacher grade seems to be an interference while student self-grading (i.e., A,B,C or 80, 90, 100) is too simplistic. Individual pieces could be graded, of course, according to criteria set

Anecdote 15.4

Suggestions for Inclusion in a Portfolio

For a writing portfolio (e.g., Maeroff, 1991, p. 279):

1) a favorite piece of writing of any genre, 2) a set of revisions showing the evolution of the writing process, 3) a creative and/or informative piece that responds to literature that the student has read, 4) a piece illustrating the student's understanding in a particular content area, and 5) a wild card that the student wants to include for whatever reason.

For a math portfolio (e.g. Lambdin & Walker, 1994, p. 320):

1. a *Writing Sample* including journal entries, autobiographies of mathematicians, explanations, etc.
2. *Investigation Discoveries*, including data, ways of gathering data, simulations.
3. *Applications*, including uses of concepts and formulas in the real world.
4. *Interdisciplinary*, including uses of concepts and formulas in other courses or fields.
5. *Nonroutine Problems*, for which solutions are not apparent.
6. *Projects*, including reports, computer programs, research, etc.

for them, but the entire portfolio would be better used as an enrichment paper, in my view, and graded as suggested in chapter 14 as a way of going beyond mastery of basics. In that case, the teacher gives feedback designed (1) for self-reflection and (2) for ensuring that the portfolio is complete. Then when it is complete, the student's grade is raised from C to B, 85 to 92, etc. according to the within-class criterion-referenced grading scheme adopted. Alternatively, if all the components have been graded, then the portfolio becomes the display cabinet and needs no grade at all.

In contrast to the above argument, you may wish to follow Lambdin and Walker's (1994) advice and assign grades not on the quality of each piece (which has presumably already been graded at another time), but on how well the criteria for the portfolio have been met: that is, is there a work of each kind, is there evidence of reflection, and is the portfolio well organized? That is, a grading rubric is needed, much like for grading essays or performances.

Suggestions for constructing portfolios include the following:

1. Specify clearly the number and kinds of pieces to be included.
2. Require that students organize the material, provide a rationale for each piece included, and/or show evidence of reflection.
3. Provide rules on when and how the student will upgrade the portfolio, discarding, revising or adding to it.
4. Plan how you will give feedback to the students and how they should use it.
5. Teach the thinking and reflecting skills you wish the students to use in assembling the various parts of the portfolio.

Testing, Alternative Assessment, and the Purposes of Education

Bodies of knowledge are important of course, but they often become outdated. Thinking skills never become outdated. To the contrary, they enable us to acquire knowledge and to reason with it, regardless of the time or place or the kinds of knowledge to which they're applied. So, in my opinion, teaching thinking skills is not only a tall order but the first order of business for a school. (Robert Sternberg, interviewed by Quinby, 1986, p. 53)

The back-to-basics debate has raised an interesting question: "Which is more basic—knowledge or reasoning ability?" One might have assumed that you must first acquire facts before you can reason about them, but the cognitive theory presented earlier suggests that we may be able to recall and use facts only to the extent that they were organized as they were first acquired. Thus, thinking and the acquisition of knowledge are currently viewed as interdependent components of a continually developing intelligence.

How does testing fit into this? The tests we write are our operational definition for students of what the goals of instruction really were. Students subsequently study for the tests and thus is set in motion a cycle which can be beneficial or pernicious, depending upon the tests.

Recent critics of objective tests would argue for alternative assessments—authentic tests, portfolios, simulations (e.g., Fredericksen, 1984), and variations on these—for many of the above reasons. As Reynolds (1994) reminds us, however, it is wise to recall our history:

About sixty years ago in this country an "alternative assessment" appeared on the scene.

Cartoon 15.2

It was called the "multiple-choice" test. This was based on an effort to avoid the subjectiveness of the rater than often creeps into the rating of free response tests. Today, many educators use the term "alternative assessment" to mean all testing styles other than objective tests. . . . (pp. 4–5)

"Education isn't what it used to be; but then it never was," Mark Twain reportedly quipped. He could have been talking about testing. If we jump from one alternative scheme to another, how long will it take until the pendulum swings back and multiple-choice tests once again become the "alternative assessment"? How long until our concern with Higher Order Thinking Skills (or HOTS, as Fremer and Daniel, 1985, call them) will be replaced again by another back-to-basics movement?

Perhaps the only possible way to stop the pendulum is to provide a proper balance of testing. A table of specifications is a systematic attempt to keep a proper balance. In addition, it is often useful to test the same concept in several ways: for example, in a series of objective items testing at different levels of the taxonomy, at another time in a restricted-response essay item, and at still another time in a simulation exercise. Many of these test items can be embedded in the curriculum (e.g., Kearney et al., 1985) as criterion-referenced formative or diagnostic tests, as well as used for summative purposes. In any case, classroom testing must never be an afterthought or externally imposed obligation ("It's a dirty job, but somebody's got to do it"). It must be a preplanned part of the curriculum because, intended or not, it will be a significant determiner of what and how students learn and think.

Practice Exercises

A. Practice Items

For the following items select the alternative choice which *best* answers the question. (Answers are in Note 5.)

1. "Will the same test items, given on 2 occasions to the same individuals, yield the same approximate scores or rank orderings of individuals on both occasions?" This question is the concern of:
   a. parallel forms reliability.
   b. test-retest reliability.
   c. internal consistency reliability.
   d. predictive validity.

2. A correlation coefficient (such as the rank order correlation r_s) can be used to estimate all but which one of the following?
   a. parallel-forms reliability.
   b. content validity.
   c. test-retest reliability.
   d. predictive validity.

3. One state devised a new driver's test. Before the test could be used to certify new drivers, however, a state court ruled that the test would have to be shown to be valid. Which of the following procedures would be best to demonstrate the test's validity for that purpose? To show that
   a. known skilled drivers could pass and known novices could not.
   b. there was a high positive correlation between rank on that test and rank in driver-training class.
   c. the test had a difficulty of about .5 and had a normal distribution.
   d. the test had norm- and criterion-referenced reliabilities of greater than .80.

4. Which of the following is the most accurate statement with regard to tests used for norm-referenced purposes?
   a. A test which is not reliable cannot be valid.
   b. A test which is not valid cannot be reliable.
   c. A test which is reliable is, therefore, also valid.
   d. A valid test is more difficult than a non-valid test.

5. Paula took a test, the results of which were reported as follows:
   Paula's score=75
   Test mean=70
   Test reliability=.75
   Standard Deviation=5
   The 68% confidence interval (that is ±1 Standard Error) would calculate her true score to be between ____ and ____.
   a. 67.5 and 72.5
   b. 70 and 80
   c. 72.5 and 77.5
   d. 65 and 75

6. The IQ (Intelligence Quotient) score for most people does not change very much (that is, it stays within a range of 10–20 points) from testing to testing. This indicates that IQ scores are
   a. both valid and reliable.
   b. neither valid nor reliable.
   c. valid, but not necessarily reliable.
   d. reliable, but not necessarily valid.

7. Consider the following statistics on a test item:

	Alternative Choice			
	a	b	c	d
Top Half	0	30	20	0
Bottom Half	40	10	0	0

   Which alternative choice must be correct in this item for both the difficulty and the discrimination power to be .40?
   a. Choice b
   b. Choices b or c
   c. Choice a
   d. None of the above

8. Which of the following types of tests can measure the widest variety of educational objectives?
   a. matching
   b. multiple-choice
   c. short-answer
   d. true-false

9. Which of the following is the best true-false item?
   a. All statements should be either entirely true or entirely false in true-false tests.
   b. Specific determiners should be avoided in true-false tests.
   c. "It is good practice to quote exact statements from the text," according to the author.
   d. It will rarely be the case that students will score less than 50% on a true-false test unless the rules of good testing are not followed.

10. Which of the following is the best short-answer test question?
    a. The formula for Z– _____ is $\dfrac{X - \bar{X}}{SD}$
    b. The _____ for a Z–score is $\dfrac{X - \bar{X}}{SD}$
    c. The formula for _____ is $\dfrac{X - \bar{X}}{SD}$
    d. The formula for a Z–score is $\dfrac{\overline{} - }{}$

11. Which of the following does not belong with the rest?
    a. essay items
    b. restricted-response items
    c. extended-response items
    d. short-answer items

12. Which of the following types of tests is best for measuring recall (in contrast to recognition)?
    a. short-answer
    b. multiple-choice
    c. matching
    d. true-false

13. Which of the following is an example of a performance test?
    a. The student must sing the melody from notes on a musical score.
    b. The student must identify the major parts of an automobile engine.
    c. The student must draw blood from a patient in a hospital.
    d. All of the above are performance tests.

B. For Cooperative Study (in or out of class):

1. The author states (p. 532): "The tests we write are our operational definition for students of what the goals of instruction really were." What does he mean by this? What implication does this have for the level of thinking (by Bloom's taxonomy) required by the tests or curriculum?
2. For homework, write one or more test items of various types on the content in this book. Write them on 3 × 5 cards so that the authors are anonymous. Then distribute the items to small groups to analyze according to the principles for that item type. (Don't forget to mention the good features of an item, as well as the bad.)
3. Find a news item on current debates about testing issues (e.g., national standards, comparisons of students among school districts, declines or inclines of SAT scores). Analyze the debate in terms of the principles in this chapter.

C. For More Information:

1. Obtain a curriculum guide or textbook for a class that you teach and establish a Table of Specifications and write test items according to it. You may wish to refer to other sources recommended in the chapter for further ideas.
2. Write test items of various types for given objectives and try them out on your classmates. Discuss the items in terms of their adequacy in fulfilling the "rules of item writing" for that item type. You may also want to analyze the practice items in this textbook from the same standpoint.

UNIT SEVEN

EPILOGUE

As the preceding chapters have attempted to show, we know quite a lot about human emotion, behavior, social processes, and cognition and how to engage those processes in productive, fulfilling instructional experiences. Why, then, is there so much criticism directed at our schools? This unit—one short chapter—does not attempt an answer, but does suggest that reform requires a broader context.

CHAPTER

Epilogue: School Reform and Society

Introduction

Consider the following criticisms of education:

1. Our nation is at risk. Our once unchallenged preeminence in commerce, industry, science and technological innovation is being overtaken by competitors throughout the world. . . . If an unfriendly foreign power had attempted to impose on America the mediocre educational performance that exists today, we might well have viewed it as an act of war. As it stands, we have allowed this to happen to ourselves.
2. Many 17-year-olds do not possess the "higher order" intellectual skills we should expect of them. Nearly 40 percent cannot draw inferences from written material; only one-fifth can write a persuasive essay; and only one-third can solve a mathematics problem requiring several steps.
3. . . . what is mostly wrong with the public schools is due not to venality or indifference or stupidity, but to mindlessness . . . it simply never occurs to more than a handful [of educators] to ask *why* they are doing what they are doing—to think seriously or deeply about the purposes or consequences of education.
4. . . . the vast mass of American . . . schools show no trace of the influence of advanced educational theory or practice. They are practically what they have been for the last fifty years; worse, one is tempted to say, but that perhaps is an exaggeration.

Cartoon 16.1

5. To find out what is the matter with the schools, we have to make an examination of teachers; to find out what is the matter with teachers, we have to examine ourselves.
. . . First, are we willing to pay, to give, to sacrifice, to get and keep in our . . . schools the kind of men and women teachers who alone can make our schools be what they should be? And, secondly, apart from money for salaries and equipment of schools for educational work, what are we willing to do in the way of esteem, respect, social prestige, hearty backing? For neither question is the answer very encouraging. . . .

The first criticism was one of the most quoted statements in the education literature of the 1980's, from *A Nation at Risk* by The National Commission on Excellence in Education (1983, p. 5). This distinguished committee report to the U.S. Department of Education went on to detail a long list of the specific failings of our schools, including

SIXTEEN

continual declines in the Scholastic Aptitude Test scores, poor student achievement in comparison to students from other industrialized nations, unacceptable performance in science on national assessments, and the points made in quotation #2 above (from p. 9).

The remaining three criticisms also sound contemporary, though they arose in different eras. The "mindlessness" of education was the major theme of Silberman's book, *Crisis in the Classroom* (1970, pp. 10–11), the education potboiler of its own decade. The remaining two quotes were taken from a 1925 essay by John Dewey, called "What Is the Matter with Teaching?" (see Dewey, 1984, pp. 116–117).[1]

I juxtaposed these quotes to make two points. First, criticism of the schools is not a new phenomenon, so that those who long for the "good old days" may find that nostalgia for education, like nostalgia for everything else, isn't what it used to be. Second, there seems to be a deja vu about the problems—and proposed solutions—in education. The problems do not seem to be solved; they just get recycled. Speaking of teacher education, for example, Cornbleth (1986) spoke of the "ritual language" and "technical rationality" which appears in the proposed solutions to problems as presented by the reformers. These serve, she says (p. 6) ". . . to maintain rather than reform existing institutions and social conditions." Substantive and long lasting reforms, she goes on to say, will require structural changes in the conditions of schooling, as well as in the competencies of school personnel.

Have we invented a perpetual motion machine? New reformers suggest reforms, while critics point out that the same suggestions were made decades earlier by equally fervent reformers. Other critics could point to the rituality and redundancy of the critics' criticisms, since their points were likewise made decades earlier. The more things change, the more they remain the same.

But to solve a problem we must first diagnose it correctly. As Benjamin Barber (1992) asked,

> *. . . what are we to make of a society that deploys rigorous standards of culture and learning in its schools which are nowhere to be found in the practices and behavior of the society itself? (pp. 215–216)*

In other words, he asks, are our 17-year-olds any less literate than our 47-year-olds? (See Anecdote 16.1 for his answer).

Seymour Papert (1980) gives another example of our hypocrisy:

> *When a teacher tells a student that the reason for those many hours of arithmetic is to be able to check the change at the supermarket, the teacher is simply not believed. Children see such "reasons" as one more example of adult double talk. The same effect is produced when children are told school math is "fun" when they are pretty sure that teachers who say so spend their leisure hours on anything except this allegedly fun-filled activity. (p. 50)*

Perhaps, in the words of the old comic strip character, Pogo, "We have met the enemy and he is us." Education isn't failing; it is succeeding all too well in inducing the students "to forget all you learned in school." Ironically, when they *do* forget it—the math, the history, the nonviolent conflict resolution strategies—then we the public want the schools to solve the problem even while we hate and fear math, do not understand history, and won't tolerate any Wyatt Earp who wants us to check our guns when we come into town.

On the other side of the coin, teachers are all too willing to take on additional roles—guard; sex, AIDS, and drug instructor; special educator—even when they are unqualified to do so. (Where are the churches, for

Anecdote 16.1

What Do Our 47-Year-Olds Know?

Barber (1992) devised his own test of cultural literacy to parody those popularized by Ravitch & Finn (1987), among others, for 17-year-olds. His bonus question asks:

> Name the ten living poets who most influenced your life, and recite a favorite stanza. Well, then, never mind the stanza, just name the poets. Okay, not ten, just five. Two? So, who's your favorite running back? (p. 220)

Barber concludes that the critics of our 17-year-olds

> . . . want our kids to know things the country at large doesn't give a hoot about. But the illiteracy of the young is our own, reflected back at us with embarrassing force. We honor ambition, we reward greed, we celebrate materialism, we worship acquisitiveness, we commercialize art, we cherish success, and then we bark at the young about the gentle arts of the spirit. The kids know that if we really valued learning, we would pay teachers what we pay lawyers and stockbrokers; if we valued art, we would not measure it by its capacity to produce profits or to produce intolerance in prudish government funders; . . . If literacy were truly an issue, we would start addressing the one in five American adults who are completely illiterate—and perhaps pay some attention to the additional 34 percent who are functionally illiterate. (pp. 220–221)

example, and why aren't they enlisted in, say, the sex education effort?) By agreeing to take on those additional roles, teachers are frequently too exhausted to expand their own teaching repertoire and content knowledge.

It is all too clear that knowledge is not static and thus, as in the caucus race in *Alice in Wonderland*, you have to run as fast as you can just to say in the same place. A mentality of continual growth, study and practice is needed just to maintain skills and keep up with the research, even if the educator is a master teacher. To take an example from medicine, orthopedic specialists who did not learn the newest diagnostic and surgery procedures (e.g., arthroscopic surgery) would soon find the field had left them behind. And how would a colleague react to the physician's complaint, "I tried that once, but it didn't work." If other physicians are successfully using a technique, you can bet that most physicians will find ways of learning that technique (even at their own expense). And it would be faint praise indeed to say of such physicians that they have been successfully setting bones the same way for the last thirty years. But such phrases by educators are common.

This assumes that there is something new in educational research that is worth keeping up with. Dissenters may wish to argue that the analogy between medicine and education breaks down precisely on this point. (Of course, they would have to keep up at least a little just to make sure they didn't miss the educational equivalent of the arthroscopic surgery breakthrough). The point of this book has been to make the case that there are important new educationally-relevant developments in research (along with some old ones we never properly understood or implemented). From emotions to cognitions, from cooperative learning to instruction in thinking, from memory to principles of measurement, there have been many new discoveries and practical applications that were largely unheard of twenty or, in some cases, even ten years ago. In addition, developments occur within each specialty discipline, both in terms of its structure of knowledge and how best to teach it.

Many teachers do keep up and do model critical thinking and excitement about their field and, as we know, it rubs off on students. They are the reason one can still be an optimist and remain in education. But make no mistake about it: when a society which is a gun or sex merchant asks its teachers to teach non-violence and abstinence, (1) the students will see through the sham, (2) the teachers will have been conned, and (3) no amount of school reform will help. In the long run it is society itself which will suffer.

A Wish List

The topic of criticism and reform of the schools has only begun to be approached in the above description. I have to leave you to explore the history of educational reforms and even other current suggestions on your own. Most of us have our pet ideas on what would make the schools better in one way or another. If I found Aladdin's lamp, for example, I would wish for the following:

1. That we build elementary schools as the ground floor of senior citizen complexes so that the seniors could be free teacher aides and the children could adopt a grandparent for whom to do chores for part of the day.
2. That we truly professionalize the life of a teacher, from teacher organizations controlling who is admitted to the profession (e.g., Shanker, 1986) to the enhancement of the environment in the places we call Schools (Goodlad, 1983a,b).
3. That we provide released time from school one-half day a week, at every grade level, for students to receive moral, religious, and sex education according to the preferences of their families, which will generally be at a church or synagogue. Note that, in addition to freeing teachers from trying to satisfy the diverse ethical viewpoints in this society, it frees them for an afternoon a week for planning and/or staff development (see anecdote 16.2 for a more complete proposal).
4. That we adopt some of Sizer's (1985) suggestions that secondary students be required to earn their "diploma by exhibition" of central skills and knowledge, and by credits earned. With these central requirements established, students would no longer have mandatory attendance (nor would schools' budgets be based on student attendance), but would enroll in courses because (a) they need help in meeting these graduation requirements, (b) they need certain optional courses for college entrance or to increase their job marketability, or (c) they wish to try something new. This would reduce the schools' need to act as policemen, as well as to allow teachers to stop being evaluators of students, but instead to be learning resources.

Anecdote 16.2

An Alternative to School Prayer

As usual, the public schools have been caught in the middle of an emotional, political and irrelevant (to their mission) issue—namely, whether and what kind of prayer should be part of the school day. I am not going to take either side in the debate; rather I wish to sidestep the issue with a proposal that both sides might find reasonable and will solve the larger goals of both the debaters and the public at large.

The motivation for voluntary prayer in schools is certainly broader than just to allow people to pray in schools, which is already possible. The point seems to be to proclaim in schools that we are a nation under God, and that we have been and will continue to be a better people if we actively pursue our religious heritages. (I use the plural to emphasize our melting-pot history).

But prayer in public schools hardly begins to address this intent and, as the intensity of the debate has shown, it may in the long run prove counterproductive by polarizing the population. A much more productive approach is to achieve directly the broader goal—that of making a highly visible place for religious education, in its broadest meaning, in the educational process. When the problem is stated that way, the solution is to provide released time for religious education.

Many who are my age or older probably recall getting a couple of hours free once a week during which we students went to the church of our choice for religious education. I'm not sure why that was eliminated, but I propose that we do something similar now.

However, we can expand the concept and suggest that the hours spent during that time include not only the learning of religious doctrine, but also the application of that doctrine to practical problems like sex education, abortion, AIDS education, and other value-laden issues. This will guarantee time in the curriculum for such education according to the moral dictates of the parents and church of which each family is a member. It also will remove the schools from responsibility for instruction which, I think we have adequately learned, they are incapable of doing to the satisfaction of all but a small minority of people.

A fringe benefit of the released time is that it will give teachers a welcome respite from teaching for a couple of hours per week, time they desperately need for planning, curriculum development, meetings, in-service workshops, and mental health.

Parents who wish not to send their students to church should probably be charged with taking responsibility for their children during this released time period, although other options may be explored, such as the students be placed in a study hall supervised by someone other than teachers.

I cannot but imagine that churches would be pleased to have this opportunity to provide such education and, as an educator myself, I cannot imagine other than that teachers would welcome this time. Is it an idea whose *time has come (again)*?

First published in slightly altered form by J. Ronald Gentile in *The Buffalo News*, Viewpoints, Sunday, March 25, 1984.

Practice Exercises

A. For Cooperative Study (in or out of class):

1. Benjamin Barber and Seymour Papert were quoted as arguing that if students do not learn the formal curriculum well, it is because they learn that society—including many teachers—doesn't believe in the curriculum. Can you think of examples? Counter-examples? What is your opinion?
2. Discuss the author's "wish list." What would you add or change? Why?
3. "Schools aren't what they used to be," the saying goes. But just what did they used to be? Interview people of different ages about the same topics—how they were graded, what they remember learning, what proportion of their peers graduated, etc.—and discuss any differences.

B. For Further Information:

1. Read some of the criticisms of education:
   a. from various historical periods (e.g., the Dewey, Silberman, and *A Nation at Risk* citations at the beginning of the chapter).
   b. from the last decade (e.g., A. Bloom 1987; D. Ravitch & C. Finn, 1987). Critically analyze what they think is wrong and what should be done.
2. Survey local school districts to see how they view current criticisms and what plans they have to respond to those criticisms (e.g., staff development programs, smaller classes).

Notes

Chapter One

1. This first-person account is a true confession of the author. He is now overcoming his fear of dentists through ``transcend-dental'' meditation.
2. Most physicians and veterinarians are indeed kind. In fact, one toddler was so impressed with a veterinarian's kindness toward his dog that he asked his parents if they were going to send the vet a card on Veteran's Day. (Yes, Doug, you said it, but I published first!)
3. With thanks to Dr. Gene Brockopp who may be held responsible for the true story (which is in there somewhere), but not necessarily for my embellishments of it.
4. We shall confront the heredity vs. environment issue more directly on the topic of intelligence in chapter 3.
5. Note that an arrow → implies ``produces'' or ``elicits'' (e.g., pain produces fear) while a dash — implies ``occurs in the presence of'' (e.g., dentist is present when pain occurs).
6. As we shall see in Chapter 5, however, this statement will have to be qualified slightly to take into account species-specific behaviors.
7. Note that R = Response, which is the traditional symbol for Operant Behavior, and S = Stimulus, sometimes with superscripts (e.g., S^{RF} = Reinforcing Stimulus or S^{AV} = Aversive Stimulus) to indicate operant conditioning, while CS, US, CR and UR were used as symbols in respondent conditioning. This distinction of symbols for the two levels of behavior will be maintained throughout the book.
8. The quote is actually from an interpretation of an animal experiment on avoidance learning in which the environment provided shock depending upon the organism's behavior.
9. Answers to Practice Items in A: 1-b, 2-b, 3-c, 4-a, 5-c, 6-b, 7-a, 8-c, 9-b, 10-a, 11-c, 12-b, 13-b, 14-a, 15-c.

Chapter Two

1. The sources for these views of the Ages of Man follow:
   1. William Shakespeare's *As You Like It*, Act II. Scene VII.
   2. Richard J. Needham, from *Reader's Digest*, 1981 (Dec.), p. 134.
   3. J. Ronald Gentile's attempt at wit and wisdom.
   4. Ronald Goldman's wit and wisdom (personal communication).
2. John R. Dilendik has been a chairman and professor of Education at Moravian College, Bethlehem, PA, where since 1973, he has been teaching teachers to apply psychological concepts to their work.
3. As described here the term schema is being used much as other psychologists have used it (e.g., as described in chapter 11). Piaget himself used the word *scheme,* which has usually been translated into English as *schema,* or in the plural, *schemata* (Ginsburg and Opper, 1988, p. 20). A problem arises here, however, in that Piaget uses the French word schema for another purpose. In any case, to be consistent with the rest of this book and most translations of Piaget, I shall use the term schema as a synonym for a mental structure, as defined in this section.

4. From a classroom experience observed by John R. Dilendik.
5. Piaget and Inhelder here have a footnote explaining that ages indicated are "always average and approximate."
6. This explanation is consistent with the social learning view expressed throughout this book that different things are simultaneously being acquired in each of the three levels of behavior: respondent, operant, and cognitive.
7. The problem is from Gardner (1978). The steps in the solution follow:

$$x = 20 + 1/2x$$
$$x - 1/2x = 20 + 1/2x - 1/2x$$
$$1/2x = 20$$
$$2(1/2x) = 2(20)$$
$$x = 40$$

8. Vygotsky (1962, pp. 73-105) critiques Piaget, Thorndike, the Gestaltists and others in this section, drawing a reciprocally deterministic view of development and learning.
9. With thanks to Timothy Karda for suggesting this portrayal.
10. To illustrate some of these points, Erikson analyzed psycho-histories of famous people, among them Adolf Hitler, Maxim Gorky, George Bernard Shaw, and William James. He also wrote separate psychohistories of Martin Luther (1958) and Mahatma Gandhi: (Gandhi's Truth,1969).
11. Erikson's second stage corresponds to the anal stage in psychoanalytic theory. While the control issues of holding on vs. letting go dominate this period, Erikson (1968, p. 107-108) points out the cultural relativity of the crises:

As far as anality proper is concerned, everything depends on whether the cultural environment wants to make something of it. There are primitive and agrarian cultures where the parents ignore anal behavior and leave it to the older children to lead the toddler out to the bushes so that his compliance in this matter may coincide with his wish to imitate the bigger ones.

12. The "Oedipal Conflict" was named by Freud after King Oedipus of Greek mythology (as described in the play *Oedipus Rex* by Sophocles). Through a series of fateful events Oedipus, who was separated at birth from his parents, unknowingly engaged in battle with his father and killed him. Later he married his mother. When he discovered what he had done, his shame and guilt was so great that he blinded himself. Freud took this legend as an analogy of a basic crisis children of four or five have to resolve—namely, how to deal with love for the parent of the opposite sex and the resultant rivalry with the same gender parent. This is occurring, of course, at the stage of development when children are exploring the anatomical differences between the genders.
13. Answers to Exercises in A: 1-d, 2-k, 3-g, 4-i, 5-a, 6-i, 7-j, 8-a, 9-c, 10-d, 11-b, 12-c, 13-g, 14-e, 15-e, 16-a, 17-h, 18-a, 19-a, 20-c, 21-b, 22-c, 23-c, 24-b, 25-d, 26-b, 27-c.

Chapter Three

1. Much of this history is indebted to the following sources: Boring (1957), Hunt (1961), Minton and Schneider (1980), and Tuddenham (1962).
2. A Belgian, A. Quetelet, had recently demonstrated how the laws of probability (i.e. the "law of frequency of error") could be applied to humans. As we shall see, the histories of intelligence testing and educational and psychological statistics have been inextricably intertwined.
3. In retrospect, it is clear from Binet's work that Galton and Cattell had chosen mental tests which were too narrow and elemental. In addition, statistical techniques (e.g., factor analysis and multiple correlation) had not yet progressed far enough to suggest how these tests, tapping individual

psychological abilities, could nevertheless be reasonable predictors. Finally, Cattell chose an unreliable criterion (college grades, as strange as it may seem, sometimes bordered on the whimsical) and a restricted sample to study (250 college students, who around 1900, were mostly representative of only the upper levels of the distribution of intelligence and economic advantage), thus making prediction extra difficult.

4. This was partly on the basis of a new statistical development, called factor analysis, in which Charles Spearman (1904) showed that a group of mental tests had two basic factors, a "g" factor which could be interpreted as the *general* intelligence which is common to all mental tests, and a group of "s" factors which were specific to each of the separate tests. Goddard assumed that Binet's overall intelligence score provided an adequate measure of this general intelligence factor and assumed, furthermore, that it was genetically determined.

5. This view of mental testing was also used by immigration officials to keep mental defectives out of the USA (Gould, 1981). Though the intent was laudable, the linguistic and cultural barriers of such a test for immigrants, who did not know the culture and language, probably invalidated the test for such uses. Unfortunately, as Cummins (1984) points out (e.g., in quote #3 in the Introduction) similar inappropriate ("unethical?") uses of intelligence testing occur today for ethnically different children.

6. The committee was chaired by R. M. Yerkes (who had developed a point scale scoring system later adopted in the Wechsler intelligence tests, among others) and included, among others, such luminaries of the mental testing movement as Terman, E. G. Boring (who in 1923 provided a famous defense of the now infamous argument that "intelligence is what intelligence tests measure"), and A. S. Otis (who also developed an intelligence test). The development of the Army Alpha and Beta tests is documented in Yoakum and Yerkes (1920).

7. Relevant references are Terman and Merrill (1937, 1960) and McNemar (1942).

8. They were speaking of intelligence tests for brain damaged children, but the same point has been made for other populations as well (e.g., Gentile, 1966; Tuddenham, 1962).

9. This estimate was taken from Jensen (1969, table 2, p. 124). Jensen's table was based on data collected by Cyril Burt, who has since been accused of fabricating his data to make them fit his theories (Kamin, 1974). However, the general trend of the correlations is of interest here, and those seem to be approximately similar over a wide variety of studies. Most of the data in this section have been based on Table 1 in Hendersen (1986). Minton and Schneider (1982) and Herrnstein and Murray (1994) provide similar estimates.

10. For those who prefer to think of this advantage the American white majority appears to show over various minorities as evidence of the genetic superiority of whites, it may be humbling to recall that the Japanese consistently outscore white populations on western-made IQ tests (Lynn, 1977).

11. Ironically, two years previously Jensen had argued almost the opposite, especially with regard to racial differences in IQ. The fact that Blacks and Mexicans are disproportionately represented in the lower classes cannot be taken as evidence of lower genetic potential. Rather it ". . . seems a reasonable hypothesis that their low-average IQ is due to environmental rather than genetic factors" (Jensen, 1967, p. 10). Whether his reversal was a true reversal from "environmentalist" to

hereditarian, or was a matter of journalistic attention and hype is open to some speculation. (Cronbach, 1975, puts this issue in historical perspective). Nevertheless, Jensen remained optimistic about boosting academic achievement, if not IQ, even at his most "jensenistic" (i.e., in the 1969 article).
12. You may recall that the WISC-R is the Wechsler Intelligence Scale for Children-Revised edition, which uses some nonverbal stimuli as test items to obtain a performance IQ (e.g., picture arrangement to tell a story in the proper sequence; block design to match pictures), and verbal stimuli to obtain a verbal IQ (e.g., basic information, similarities, vocabulary, arithmetic).
13. Answers to Practice Items in A: 1-c, 2-a, 3-d, 4-b, 5-d, 6-d, 7-d, 8-b, 9-c, 10-b 11-b, 12-a, 13-c.

Chapter Four

1. Although Sternberg was not the father of componential analysis of intelligence—that distinction probably belongs to Charles Spearman (1923)—he was certainly the reinventor and popularizer of the modern cognitive theoretical approaches. Beginning with his 1977 publication, he has been a prolific contributor to the data base and to the theoretical accounts of intelligence, as well as to the idea that intelligence can and should be taught (1985, 1986, 1987).
2. Answers to problems in Table 4.1:
    A. 1. 24
    A. 2. The solution is in chapter 9.
    B. Fallacies are 1. representativeness, 2. irrelevant conclusion, 8, appeal to authority, 13. invalid disjunction, 19. argumentum ad hominem (personal characteristics).
    C. 1. a. Nadir in this case means low point (from astronomy, the closest point to earth of a satellite).
       b. Archipelago is a cluster of islands.
       c. Ecchymosis is a bruise, contusion, or black-and-blue mark.
       d. Hazanga is a common four-letter word often hyphenated with bull-_____.
    2. three
3. There is a large and growing literature on the effects of teacher expectations on students' attainments. The interested reader is referred to Brophy & Good (1986), Good (1987), and Jussim (1989) as a beginning. Interestingly, much of the recent research is showing that teachers' expectations are more likely to arise from accurately perceiving their students' current ability or achievement rather than from biased preconceptions. Nevertheless, if current perceptions—accurate or biased—put limits on what or how something is taught, then the argument in this section holds.
4. Elkind's paper was a commentary from the Piagetian perspective on Jensen's (1969a) notorious paper on the heritability of intelligence (discussed in chapter 3). The reader may wish to compare this quote with what is said in the last paragraph of the section entitled Heredity and Environment in chapter 3.
5. Muuss (1982) is here reviewing James Marcia's (1967) extensions of Erikson's theory, which include the substages of *foreclosure* (in which individuals commit to a vocation or set of beliefs without experiencing a crisis, by adopting somebody else's values) and *moratorium*.
6. Answers to Exercises in A: 1-f, 2-a, 3-e, 4-g, 5-b, 6-a, 7-c, 8-d, 9-a, 10-b.

Chapter Five

1. This true story was related by Kay Johnson-Gentile, who worked with children and their parents while she was Director of a Music Therapy Project at Roswell Park Memorial Hospital in Buffalo, NY from 1977–1979.
2. See Gormezano and Moore, 1969, if you wish to follow the history of the search.
3. This case of the US preceding the CS is technically called backward conditioning. For the reasons described, conditioning cannot easily be attained by this procedure, if at all. In fact, there is now evidence (e.g., Hulse et al., 1980) that organisms actively learn to suppress making an association between US and CS when presented in this order. This is because the CS signals the end of a trial, and thus a long wait until the beginning of the next trial when the US will be presented.
4. Differential definitions of fears and phobias have not been conclusively stated to the agreement of all in the field. However, it is generally agreed that ". . . fear is a normal response to threatening stimuli, whereas phobia is an unreasonable response, often to usually benign or ill-defined stimuli" (Graziano et al., 1979, p. 805). Furthermore, it is common to regard phobias as fears which (1) are out of proportion to the situation, (2) cannot be reduced by reasoning, (3) are beyond voluntary control, and (4) lead to avoiding the feared object or setting (e.g., Marks, 1969; Morris and Kratochwill, 1983).
5. The reader interested in the measures taken and the control groups established by Rescorla and his colleagues is encouraged to consult Rescorla's very readable monograph entitled, *Pavlovian Second-Order Conditioning* (1980).
6. Death may not be directly associated with pain or immediate personal loss for some people, particularly children. It can nevertheless become a CS by being paired with the sorrow or pain felt by a parent or significant other. Technically, this parent's reaction might not be a US, but another CS, which would make Stage 1 of Figure 5.2 another case of higher-order conditioning. When emotions are conditioned via the emotional reactions of others (e.g., when a child learns to fear snakes through a parent's fear of snakes), the process is called *vicarious emotional conditioning*. We shall discover more about this kind of higher-order conditioning in Chapter 7.
7. See also Early (1968) and Roden and Hapkiewicz (1973).
8. There was a serious design problem that inadvertently led Brady and his collaborators to the wrong conclusion. More carefully controlled research was done by Weiss (1968; 1970, 1971) who, in studies on rats, isolated the operative factors to be predictability and control—or rather, their absence—in producing ulcers and emotionality. An excellent discussion of the "executive monkey" and related research is found in Seligman's book Helplessness (1975, particularly pp. 116–121), which provided the impetus for this section in the book.
9. The reader interested in attribution theory and its relevance to learned helplessness is encouraged to pursue the following sources as a beginning: Abramson, Seligman and Teasdale (1978); Diener and Dweck (1978); Dweck (1975); Dweck and Repucci (1973); Garber and Seligman (1980); Hiroto (1974); Heusmann (1978); Miller and Norman (1979).
10. The interested reader is encouraged to consider their arguments by going directly to Lazarus (1982, 1984) and Zajonc (1980, 1984).

11. Some of these kinds of problems may be what Sidman (1960) had in mind when he spoke of "Normal Sources of Pathological Behavior"—that is, abnormal behaviors which arise from lawful, normal interactions between organism and environment.
12. Psychophysiologist David Lykken (1978, p. 173) pointed out the following about polygraphs:

    . . . the same physiological response can have very different meanings, can be associated with different psychological responses, in different individuals. Thus, for example, if two subjects both give the same large GSR [galvanic skin response] in response to a certain question, it may be that one of them is lying— and fearful of being found out—while the other is telling the truth—and fearful or even indignant about being wrongly accused.

    He went on to provide a reasoned argument about the uses and abuses to which the polygraph can be put, pointing out, among other things, how its use as a screening device for employees is biased against honest, truthful people. This well-written well-reasoned paper should perhaps be required reading for all people concerned with civil rights. In particular, it is difficult to ignore his concluding comment (p. 190):

    I once believed that the single application in which the lie detector might do more good than harm would be in official criminal investigation. I now withdraw that opinion. In every arena in which the lie test is used, it is apparently abused. It is time for the lie detector to be retired to those same museums where we keep examples of the rack and the Iron Maiden.

13. Answers to Practice Items in A: 1-d, 2-c, 3-c, 4-b, 5-a, 6-b, 7-a.

Chapter Six

1. A Phrase coined in a song by Kay Johnson-Gentile (1978).
2. It is sometimes said that this definition is circular, to wit: a reinforcer is something that increases the frequency of a behavior; thus if a behavior is followed by something that increases the frequency of a behavior, then that behavior will increase in frequency. This statement of the "law of effect" or the principle of reinforcement does indeed sound like a vacuous tautology. But more is implied than that.
   For one thing, as implied in our definition, any reinforcer is trans-situational (as first demonstrated by Meehl, 1950). This means, for example, if money reinforces the study behavior of an individual, it will also reinforce another behavior. More generally, it is always possible to demonstrate the effectiveness or noneffectiveness of a reinforcer in a given situation by the proper experimental design, in which a targeted behavior is monitored to prove that only that behavior is affected by the treatment. The interested reader is referred to Kazdin (1973) for some of the issues involved.
3. This incident was reported by Margaret L. Zabranskey and first published in Gentile, Frazier and Morris, 1973, pp. 1–2.
4. In contrast to this most typical of American experiences, I like to consider the time I spent with a Japanese father, and his son (aged 13) and daughter (aged 12) on a long drive in their car one evening. He and I were talking in the front seat. After a while it dawned on me that the children in the back seat were totally quiet, just sitting. They weren't hitting each other, insulting each other, etc.—just sitting quietly. Finally, I questioned my host why the children were so quiet. His matter-of-fact answer was that they were quiet because adults were talking.

5. To be technically complete, I should call attention to the fact that some investigators define two types of punishment analogous to the two types of reinforcement—namely, *positive punishment* and *negative punishment* (Boe, 1969). Positive punishment is the case we have described in which a behavior has the consequence of receiving an aversive stimulus ($R \rightarrow S^{AV}$). Negative punishment is the withdrawal of an available attractive stimulus contingent on the behavior ($S^{RF} \rightarrow NoS^{RF}$, which is similar, but not identical, to extinction. This usage is not widespread and I have chosen not to adopt it.
6. To be more technically accurate, this is a definition of *stimulus generalization* and should be labeled as such to distinguish it from *response generalization*. The latter is the performance of different responses to the same stimulus, such as shutting a certain door with varying degrees of force. For our purposes, we are not very concerned with these slight differences in responses, and we shall therefore describe only stimulus generalization.
7. The Premack studies demonstrating this punishment effect were all done on animals. Klara Papp (1980) was able to demonstrate this effect on children, aged ten to fourteen.
8. Hulse (1958) was the first to demonstrate this phenomenon experimentally, though others have replicated it. The frustration explanation builds on Amsel's theory (Amsel, 1958; 1962), though the results can be explained in other ways. The reader who wishes to pursue the topic further would be advised to begin with Hulse, Egeth & Deese, 1980, Chap. 5.
9. I shall go into more detail on feedback and its similarities and differences from reinforcement in Chapter 12.
10. See also Balsam and Bondy (1983) and Lepper and Greene (1978) for cases of how inappropriately used tangible rewards can prove troublesome.
11. Because of the difficulties—and ethical issues—involved in doing research on punishment, most research has been conducted on animals. Thus this section will have few classroom examples. It is my belief, however, that this research is important for teachers to know and has implications for discipline (see chapter 6), among other things.
12. For example, Sandler and Quagliano (1964).
13. At home, as in Church (if you'll excuse the pun), it is good advice not to say to your child, "Wait till your Daddy gets here—you're going to get a spanking."
14. There is also a smaller amount of evidence on humans using noise as the aversive stimulus (Johnston, 1972).
15. Answers to Practice Items in A: 1-a, 2-d, 3-d, 4-b, 5-a, 6-a, 8-c, 9-e, 10-b, 11-a, 12-b.

Chapter Seven

1. I am adopting the terms imitation and modeling as synonyms because of the relative simplicity they provide in describing common situations. Other terms have also been used as labels for the imitation process, the most common among them being "identification" which usually implies that O is strongly attracted to M for various reasons. In the example of the big brother-little sister given above, that was probably operating. But in other situations such strong attraction may not be obvious. Thus we shall use the more neutral terms modeling and imitation. For further discussion of definitional issues, see Bandura (1969) and Flanders (1968).

2. The famous experiments on "latent learning" were some of the first strong evidence on that (e.g., Tolman, 1932, 1959).
3. Brim (1958) gives evidence that boys with a sister as their only sibling manifest more feminine traits than those whose only sibling is also male.
4. Huston-Stein (1978) provides a very readable review and bibliography of both the anti-social and pro-social effects of television.
5. She is speaking here primarily of the following publications of Bandura and Berkowitz: Bandura (1965b); Bandura and Huston (1961); Bandura, Ross and Ross (1963a, 1963c); Berkowitz, (1962, 1964, 1970); Parke, Berkowitz, Leyens, West and Sebastion(1975).
6. Edwin Newman was narrating a 1992 program called "On Television: Teach the Children" (PTV Publications, P.O. Box 701, Kent OH 44140) which summarized many studies, and illustrated many of the issues with examples of TV programs and commercials.
7. This was a performance in January 1996 by the Greater Buffalo Opera Company with the Buffalo Philharmonic Orchestra, sponsored by the Arts in Education Institute of Western New York of The Genteels' creation, "The Great Horse and the Greater Horses: A Kids' Opera."
8. As I pointed out earlier, the only two kinds of people I recognize are those who divide the world into two kinds of people and those who don't.
9. This is not to say that group pressure is the only determiner of such behavior—there are also, as we have seen, developmental histories and other situational factors that contribute to conformity behaviors.
10. Ali Mazrui's book, *The Trial of Christopher Okigbo*, begins with the untimely death of the Igbo poet Okigbo and follows him to heaven, where he is put on trial for betraying his art by becoming involved in the politics of the Nigerian civil war. Along the way Mazrui expressed some utopian views. I highly recommend it. The passage cited here is intended to show that our conceptions of competition are culture-bound; there are alternatives to what we usually take for granted.
11. Answers to Practice Items in A: 1-d, 2-c, 3-a, 4-a, 5-b, 6-norms, 7-cooperative goal structure, 8-cognitive dissonance, 9-sociometric wealth or the sociodynamic law, 10-vicarious emotional conditioning, 11-habituation.

Chapter Eight

1. The author had the good fortune to spend sabbatical leaves in Japan (from January to April of 1976) and China (from April to June 1983) observing classrooms, among other things. Whenever possible he visited a school for as much as a week and stayed with a class from a full day to three days. This allowed him to see their entire schedule as well as to have the students and teachers become accustomed to him. The observations in this section are based on these experiences.
2. Sensei (pronounced sen-say) is the Japanese word for teacher, which is used with great respect. For example, to show honor to a physician, you call him or her "Sensei."
3. Based on the psychiatric techniques of Milton Erickson (see Haley, 1973).
4. Unfortunately, Glasser's Control Theory is, in my view, a misguided attempt to provide a broader theory for his very practical suggestions. This is partly because he spends too much time trying to distance his approach from other social and behavioral principles into which, as this whole unit demonstrates, his practical suggestions fit. Thus I recommend that teachers consider his advice and ignore his theorizing.

5. Berkowitz (1962) and Feshbach (1964) also stress the importance of intent in inciting aggression. The latter gives the following example (p. 265): "A student may be annoyed and disappointed at receiving a failing grade. But if he should discover that the instructor is pleased by his failure, he is likely to become furious."
6. Ginott also pointed out that people who refused his advice would often insist, "Haim ginott gonna do it!"
7. There is a good deal of research and theorizing on this topic, sometimes known as the Ainslie-Rachlin Theory; for a good description, see Mazur (1986, pp. 331 337).
8. Dr. Kay Johnson-Gentile is Associate Professor of Elementary Education at Buffalo State College where, among other things, she teaches pre-service teachers how to incorporate conflict resolution procedures into their classroom management plans.
9. Answers to Practice Items in A: 1-a, 2-b, 3-b, 4-a, 5-d, 6-a, 7-a, 8-b, 9-c, 10-c, 11a—any action taken where it is not wanted, 11b—any behavior which disrupts instruction or any student's learning.

Chapter Nine

1. Colleen McNeil is a Ph.D. candidate in Educational Psychology at the State University of New York at Buffalo.
2. Answer to Problems 9.12 and 9.13. The principle involved is that occupations are not gender-specific. For example, females as well as males can be surgeons, as the women's movement pointed out.
3. Anderson, Reder and Simon (1996) give a similar example of police academy graduates who, upon reporting to the job, are commonly told to forget all they learned at the academy.
4. But see Bruner's (1960) interpretation of general transfer described later in this chapter.
5. Current cognitive researchers such as Sternberg (1986) have redefined insight by breaking it into its component parts. Such reanalysis of the insight concept may ultimately make it a more useful tool.
6. Answers to Practice Items in A: 1-d, 2-d, 3-e, 4-b, 5-c, 6-d, 7-a, 8-c, 9-a, 10-a
7. Answers to Problems in Exercise C3: a - in a pyramid (by hanging one or placing it in a ditch); b - in the shape of a star; c - Oslo, which is in the middle of the word Czechoslovakia; d - a half dollar and a nickel (one is not a nickel, but the other one is).

Chapter Ten

1. The automatic-controlled distinction described here, now widely accepted in cognitive psychology, is based on the following papers: Hasher and Zacks (1979); Posner and Snyder (1975); Schneider and Shiffrin (1977); and Shiffrin and Schneider (1977). However, there is reason to doubt the simplicity of the dichotomy. G.D.Logan (1985) argued, for example, that automaticity is in itself a learnable skill, and while automatic processes are components of skills, a skill is more than the sum of its automatic components.
2. The four or five items perceived under conditions such as these have been classically referred to as the "span of apprehension."
3. Classically, short-term memory has been known as primary memory (e.g., James, 1890), a term that is still used. But current researchers seem to prefer the more theoretically neutral labels, short-term store (STS) or short-term memory (STM), or working memory.
4. Classically known as secondary memory (James, 1890).

5. McGeoch (1932) was one of the first to demonstrate that forgetting was less due to disuse or trace decay than to such factors as interference. The evidence, which is beyond the scope of this treatment, can be found in such general learning texts as Hall (1982) or Hulse, Egeth and Deese (1980).
6. The example assumes the professor is intentionally trying to learn the names. I have heard that there are some professors who make no such attempt, but even the proverbial "absent-minded professor" is capable of learning and remembering names.
7. See also Cofer et al. (1969) and Tulving and Thomson (1971, 1973).
8. An alternative theoretical account of many of these findings is provided by Craik and Lockhart's (1972) depth of processing theory, though I believe it is not as succinct or comprehensive as dual coding theory in accounting for the results described here.
9. The achievements of Ebbinghaus were indeed epoch-making for psychology because there were many firsts involved in this research. Primary among them was the fact that he showed that an experimental science of learning and memory was possible. The epigraph for his book was the phrase, "From the most ancient subject we shall produce the newest science." Other incredible achievements were (1) the invention of the nonsense syllable from, as historian E. G. Boring (1957, p. 388) put it, "it would seem, out of nothing at all in the way of ancestry;" (2) the development of the "savings" method of measuring retention; (3) the description and analysis of what has come to be known as the forgetting curve; (4) the presentation of the first replicated experimental test of learning and retention as a function of such variables as number of practice trials, conditions of practice, and time; and (5) the mathematical and statistical ways in which he analyzed his data. He later turned to other research, including a theory of color vision, but he is mainly recognized today for opening up to science the study of higher mental processes.
10. The actual number of seconds was 1270, or a little over 21 minutes for the 96 syllables (6 lists × 16 syllables each). Rather than the specific numbers, what is important here is the technique and the shape of the findings. The interested reader is referred to Ebbinghaus (1885, Chap. 4, Section 23).
11. Some of the early experiments on the comparative retention of "fast" and "slow" learners did not bother to equate them in original learning. As Underwood (1954; 1964) pointed out, this was a major methodological flaw. In simplest of terms, since speed of learning is the criterion being used to discriminate among the learners, then in any given amount of time, "fast" learners will learn more than "slow" learners. Of course, those who originally learn more have a decided advantage on a subsequent retention test.
12. A quick answer might appear to be "intelligence," since IQ is known to be highly correlated with learning rate. This answer satisfies few psychologists, however, since it prompts a successive question—namely, what accounts for the differences in intelligence? Even if you regress to the next step and answer "heredity" few are satisfied, since genetic potentials are known to interact with environments to produce structural (e.g., height and weight) or functional (e.g., skillful or intelligent behavior) manifestations of those potentials. For educators, "intelligence" is also less an answer than a prompt for further questions, since they can do nothing about students' genes, but they can do much about the learning environments with which genetic potentials interact.

13. Neisser (1982) has compiled a very interesting collection of real-life memory experiences and analyses from flash-bulb memories to cases of total recall.
14. Answers to Problems in Exercise A: 1-e, 2-c, 3-f, 4-a, 5-h, 6-d, 7-b, 8-a, 9-a, 10-a, 11-b, 12-c, 13-savings, 14-encoding or organizing, 15-overlearning.
15. Doing the laundry.

Chapter Eleven

1. It should be noted that other investigators have adopted Premack's communication system to teach children with language problems. One noteworthy study was that of Hughes (1975) who used "Premackese" to teach aphasic children (children without language despite adequate intelligence and learning) several different language functions.
2. Halpern and Bower (1982) also included a third variety of melody, comprised of randomly produced notes. On this melody, nonmusicians did slightly worse than they did on the other melodies; musicians did much worse than they did on "bad" melodies, but still better than the nonmusicians.
3. Adelson's (1984) study tested computer programming experts and beginners. The experts tended to look at a program and deduce its purpose and utility (abstract), while beginners studied its detail statements (concrete). When the questions concerned specific details, novices did better than experts.
4. This particular hierarchy was stimulated by Collins and Quillian (1969). Many other similar models of the structure of memory and, more broadly, knowledge have been proposed, but discussion of them here would take us too far afield. The interested reader is encouraged to consult Anderson (1983), Anderson and Bower (1973), Kintsch (1974), or any recent cognitive psychology text for fuller details on a few such theories.
5. The distinction between reproductive and reconstructive memory is usually related to Tulving's (1972; 1983) distinction between "semantic" and "episodic" memory. There is currently a debate on how separate these types of memory are, however, (e.g., Ellis & Hunt, 1993, pp. 189–190), and since it is not directly relevant here, I have ignored this distinction.
6. These problems, as well as the tennis tournament problem, are based on those in Chapter 2 of Bransford and Stein (1984). Problem 11.6 was in turn borrowed by them from Whimbey and Lochhead (1980).
7. The solution to Problem 11.6 is 33 boxes.
8. The solution is to take one of the 3-link mini-chains and open all three of the links, at a cost of 6 cents (3 × .02). Then use each of these to join the other three mini-chains together, at a cost of 9 cents (3 × .03).
9. The solution to the 4-player tournament is not directly proportional to the 100-player tournament. Since it takes 3-matches for a 4-player tournament, it would take 75 matches for a 100-player tournament, if it were proportional. But it is not.
10. Thus the correct solution is to multiply 8 × 2/3, which gives 5 and 1/3 pints needed.
11. deBono (1986) has also produced an extensive training program, called the CoRT Thinking Program, which includes student exercises and teachers' notes.
12. See Bransford et al. (1985) for a more extended analysis of Whimbey and Lochhead's (1980) program.
13. Problem 11.11 is adapted from Sternberg (1987, p. 108). The correct answer is (b) affection.
14. The example is adapted from Bransford and Stein (1984). Readable explanations of the theory can be found in Barnett (1948) and Gardner (1962).

15. The answer is it will appear to go backward, perhaps best expressed in the following limerick (from Gardner, 1962, p. 119):
    There was a young lady named Bright,
    Who traveled much faster than light.
    She started one day
    In the relative way
    And returned on the previous night.
16. Answers to Exercise in A: 1-e, 2-a, 3-f, 4-b, 5-c, 6-c, 7-c, 8-a, 9-d, 10-d, 11-c.

Chapter Twelve

1. I have chosen Madeline Hunter's model to introduce this chapter, despite the fact that most reviewers of instructional models tend to ignore it, probably because of Hunter's own resistance to citing empirical research; instead her early writings usually cited only her own texts (e.g., Hunter, 1967 a, b & c; 1971a). But as Ron Brandt, editor of Educational Leadership, volunteered in 1985, Hunter ". . . probably had more influence on U.S. teachers in the last ten years than any other person" (p. 61). Since most of the teachers in this country have been "Hunterized," critics (Profs. of Ed, as the second cartoon puts it)

    > . . . could advise teachers to ignore or resist Hunter. Alternatively, we could accept Hunter's essential elements as a start in the right direction—an initial scaffold — and build from there. (Gentile, 1993, p. 58)

    Much of the material in this chapter has been incorporated into a more detailed analysis published separately by the National Staff Development Council, Oxford, Ohio (1993, Second Edition) under the title *Instructional Improvement: A Summary and Analysis of Madeline Hunter's Essential Elements of Instruction and Supervision.*

2. These suggestions have their roots in a long line of fruitful work at the intersection of learning research and curriculum development, much of it beginning with B. F. Skinner's work on programmed instruction (e.g., Skinner, 1954; 1968) and with Robert Gagné's conception of *learning hierarchies* (e.g., Gagné, 1962; 1968; Gagné and Briggs, 1974; Gagné et al., 1962). The interested reader will find good research and practical examples, particularly on mathematical and science concepts, in the above citations, as well as in the revised editions of Gagné's *Conditions of Learning* (1985) and Gagné and Briggs' *Principles of Instructional Design* (1979) and in Dick and Carey (1985). Other influential work in this area has been reported by researchers at Pittsburgh's Learning Research and Development Center (e.g., Glaser, 1977; Resnick, 1973; Resnick Wang, and Kaplan, 1973).
3. Hunter (1982, p. 83) describes Evaluation as ". . . the making of judgments when there is no one answer which is right for everyone. . . ." Later, she says, "Note that in evaluation, any judgment that can be supported is valid." She gives examples such as writing your reasons for the poet you enjoy most and for ranking three opening paragraphs you write from best to worst. While such "personal value judgments" do seem to be a part of Bloom's (1956) conception of Evaluation, Hunter neglects the more important judgments that may not be personal, but are rather made according to other criteria. For example, a cost-benefit analysis of one or more courses of action would be an evaluation. So would a comparison of the potential benefits weighed against the side effects of various drugs or nuclear vs. synthetic fuels. This broader view of Evaluation is described in this section.

4. Other taxonomies of thinking skills exist, notably a very comprehensive one by Ennis (1987). Critics of Bloom notwithstanding (e.g., see Brown, 1994, and Gentile's, 1996, response), any taxonomy is useful only to the extent it stimulates teachers to broaden their own and their students' thinking. That was the purpose of the Bloom taxonomy. Furthermore, it has two advantages: (1) it has only six major categories of thinking, and (2) with the exception of evaluation, these categories are widely and easily understood by educators already.

5. Marilyn Bates, along with Ernest Stachowski, were two of the excellent leaders of workshops for teachers on the Hunter model that I had the privilege of observing.

6. Cognitive studies since the 1980's have tended to take a very broad view of skill learning. For example, in a special issue of the *Canadian Journal of Psychology* (Charness, 1985), skills in such areas as the following were considered: memory, reading, piano playing, sports, and multiplication. In that same issue, MacKenzie and Marteniuk (1985) show how the importance of feedback is taken as a given in motor skills research, with the new frontiers being how feedback is encoded, organized, and used to improve performance.

   Another portion of the history of knowledge of results in cognitive tasks traces back to the earliest teaching machines (e.g., Pressey, 1960; Skinner, 1958). One of the touted virtues of programmed instruction was the immediate feedback students received. Interestingly, Hunter herself must have been influenced by the programmed instruction movement, since her earlier books are partially programmed (e.g., 1967a, b, c, d; 1971a). The current incarnation of programmed instruction, is of course, computer-assisted learning, and a review of feedback in that field has recently been provided by Lalley (1996).

7. Answers to Exercises In A:
   1. motivation or attention
   2. feedback
   3. anticipatory set, activating prior knowledge, or the like
   4. encoding
   5. 40 minutes spent/160 minutes needed = 25%
   6. opportunity or time allowed
   7. subject matter pedagogical
   8. learning hierarchy or task analysis
   9. monitoring progress (or checking for understanding or providing guided practice).
   10. a. what to teach (content)
       b. what activities the students will do to learn and demonstrate their learning.
       c. what the teacher will do to have the students learn the content.
   11. –d
   12. –a
   13. –b
   14. –c
   15. –a
   16. –F
   17. –F
   18. –F
   19. –F
   20. –F

Chapter Thirteen

1. Joyce and Weil (1980) refer here in a footnote, to a book by Shulman and Keislar (1966) entitled *Learning By Discovery: A Critical Appraisal,* which points out the limits as well as the uses of discovery learning. It is ironic that Piaget, on whose theories much of the learning-by-discovery

approach was based, did not expect discovery to replace all other techniques. For example, he even defended Skinner and the use of teaching machines for certain purposes as a complement to his discovery/reconstruction of knowledge approach (Piaget, 1970, pp. 75–80).

2. It is always possible to argue about the research designs used in those studies, a topic that can keep academics publishing (and not perishing!) for years. To be honest, I have been one of the critics of the designs most frequently used in such studies, and have published alternative approaches which I believe more likely to demonstrate real differences among methods, if any exist (Gentile, 1982), and to more adequately evaluate programs in an absolute sense (Reynolds and Gentile, 1978). Nevertheless, I fully concur with Joyce and Weil.

3. Further elaborations of these ideas, along with such things as model newsletters, can be found in Slavin (1980, 1983).

4. A voluminous and growing literature exists on the various methods of cooperative learning teams and their effects. This presentation is based primarily on the reviews provided by Slavin (1983, 1986) and Slavin, Sharan, Kagan, Hertz-Lazarowitz, Webb and Schmuck (1985). Readers interested in accessing this interesting body of research are referred to these sources.

5. It should be noted that what is here called cooperative methods really include two somewhat different approaches—namely, purely cooperative groups and cooperative groups with intergroup competition. Johnson et al. (1981, p. 57) tentatively advanced the hypothesis that "Cooperation without intergroup competition promotes higher achievement and productivity than cooperation with intergroup competition." They wished not to draw firm conclusions on this score, however, because of the limited number of studies which directly compared the two methods. Cooperation with intergroup competition may produce somewhat different affective outcomes than cooperation alone (Johnson et al., 1983). Further research may delineate such different effects and the conditions under which they occur. The general conclusion—that learning is enhanced by cooperative incentives and task structures—is nevertheless supported by a vast array of methodologically sound research.

6. The technical, semantic, and effectiveness problems raised by Gentile (1967) were concerned, respectively, with computer hardware (equipment), computer languages (e.g., Fortran, Basic, Pascal, etc.), and educational programs (the material which teaches).

7. It would take us too far afield to continue the history of Bloom's "Learning for Mastery" (LFM) in this section. Instead, I shall attempt to summarize the essentials of LFM as it has evolved, as well as to review some of the evidence on its efficacy, and some of the controversial issues. Some of the best sources for obtaining the flavor of the LFM proponents are the writings of Anderson, Block and Bloom, listed in the References, and the Nov. 1979 issue of *Educational Leadership*.

8. It was even used on the cover of Block's (1971a) book.

9. But see Slavin (1987) for a more negative conclusion.

10. Keller noted that PSI could stand for either Personalized, Proctorial, or Programmed System of Instruction (Keller and Sherman, 1974, p. 15).

11. For more on the history and background of Keller's PSI system, see Chance (1984), Keller (1968), Keller and Sherman (1974), and Sherman (1974). For reviews of the research studies on PSI, sometimes compared with Bloom's CFM, see Block (1974b), Block and Burns (1977), Dunkin (1986), Kulik et al. (1970), Robin (1976), and Ryan (1974).

In general, these studies show PSI to be quite effective compared to regular control groups, to have an average of 13% better recall of the material anywhere from 2 to 26 months after the course, and to be preferred by students. The research also points to the following components as most important to the success of the method: frequent testing, immediate feedback, review of material not mastered, and the unit-mastery requirement. Self-pacing seems not to matter. One definite negative is that there is a high dropout rate: Keller (1968, p. 82) even encourages students to withdraw if they do not pass at least one of the first tests in the first two weeks. Presumably, if that happens, the student has not mastered the prerequisites for the course, has poor reading skills, or is not ready to do the self-pacing and self-initiated study required. In any case, Keller comments (in Chance, 1984, p. 46); "It's better to find out early if you're in over your head." That comment may suffice for college level courses, but in public schools it requires that the proper courses be found for such students, since they are not allowed just to withdraw.

12. Recall that we have already studied some exercises (in chapter 11) which were recommended for stimulating creativity, among them lateral thinking and brainstorming.
13. I took a brief course on this idea, using Edwards' (1979) book, taught by my good friend Forrest (Woody) Hawley. I improved my drawing skill only slightly—I stopped practicing—but the course indeed opened my eyes to many other ways of seeing.
14. A fourth type of analogy, *fantasy analogy*, was described in Gordon's earlier work as an exercise in wish-fulfillment. "If you could have something work exactly as you wanted it to, what would it do? Subsequent publications (Gordon, 1970; Stein, 1975) described this as often occurring as part of the other three analogies, and thus no longer needed as a separate exercise.
15. From Gordon (1970).
16. Torrance (1986) is a good place to start for the central arguments and references; Isaksen (1987) also provides a good history of the research and reprints of many historically important articles.
17. It is an additional irony that some of the best research on Lipman's program for teaching philosophical thinking through novels has been done on "creative and gifted learners" (reviewed in Torrance, 1986), though Lipman and associates wanted their philosophy available to all learners.
18. Answers to Exercises in A: 1-c; 2-a,b, and c; 3-b; 4-c; 5-a,b, and c; 6-d; 7-a; 8-a; 9-c; 10-b; 11-d; 12-b; 13-c.

Chapter Fourteen

1. If you wish to sing along, the music to this verse is in Appendix A.
2. This quote comes from an essay entitled, "Who Ever Cheats to Learn?" which has several fine moments, including the following introductory statement (Simon, 1976, p. 20):

The big thing about cheating that we all should remember is that no one—man, woman, or child—ever cheats to learn. Cheating gains us neither information, nor knowledge, nor least of all, wisdom.

Unfortunately, from my point of view, Simon then goes on to overstate the case, implying that cheating would disappear if grading were abolished. How I wish. Children learn to cheat long before they come to school, and they may continue to do so as long as they perceive that there is an advantage to be gained by cheating. To prevent or reduce the frequency of cheating, therefore, requires a system that can detect when it occurs, that provides restitution, and that therefore convinces the cheater that honesty is the best—and easiest—policy.

3. The distinction between assessment for the purposes of selection vs. facilitating instruction probably owes its popularity, if not its origin, to a paper by Glaser (1963), and a further elaboration of those ideas by Glaser and Nitko (1971). The distinction between these purposes and their corresponding measurement theories—namely, norm-referenced and criterion-referenced assessment—is now widely acknowledged in measurement textbooks, with different procedures for calculating reliability, validity, and item statistics for each purpose (e.g., Gronlund, 1985; Hambleton et al., 1978; Popham, 1978). More will be said on these issues later in this chapter.
I shall make no distinction among the terms criterion-referenced, domain-referenced, and objectives-referenced. As Hambleton et al. (1978, p. 3) noted, both criterion-referenced and domain-referenced imply that test items are ". . . a representative set of items from a clearly defined domain of behaviors measuring an objective, whereas with an objectives-referenced test no domain of behaviors is specified. . . ." Objectives-referenced, by this reasoning implies that individual items were written to measure the attainment of specific objectives, without specification of the how the objectives interrelate or any attempt to define the population of which the given item is presumably a sample. In practice (as both Hambleton et al., 1978, and Popham, 1978, recognized), most teachers will only be able to write objectives-referenced tests since domain-referencing is too technically demanding. For purposes of this text, however, objectives-referencing is a good place to start.

4. It is beyond the scope of this treatment to explain the procedures used to determine such high predictability, but Astin and Panos (1971) and Cooley and Lohnes (1976) have presented the relevant data and statistical analyses.

5. Another long-raging statistical issue in educational measurement concerns the reliability of student growth scores (e.g., Cronbach and Furby, 1970). But a solution to that problem also arises from the distinction of the purposes of prediction/selection vs. facilitating learning. The reader interested in such issues is referred to Reynolds and Gentile (1978).

6. On rare occasions there are discontinuous distributions—that is, with large gaps separating clusters of scores—in which there are possibly significant differences between those groups. For those cases the argument in this section would not be valid. To give A, B, C, D, and F grades under this assumption, however, requires four large gaps in the distribution—a rare situation indeed.

7. The proposal suggested here is designed to be comprehensive and adoptable by a whole school or district. However, the system does not depend upon complete adoption. Some teachers, for example, could resist the criterion-referenced suggestions I have made for their own classes, while others may adopt them. While not optimal from my point of view, this would not affect the operation of the entire system, as long as the other improvements were made. Likewise, a single teacher can profitably adopt the within-class grading suggestions made here even if the rest of the school does not.

8. My wife discovered this when, as a one-semester substitute elementary music teacher, she attempted to teach musical literacy, among other things, and grade in a manner commensurate with her objectives. Her program was not received well.

In this school, at least, tradition had it that music class was not for learning music; rather, it was a time for both students and regular teachers to have a break from learning.

9. An option on alternative 3 is to give a higher grade for higher test scores and allow people multiple opportunities to achieve the higher score. An example of such a system follows:

> 90 = Scored 90 percent or more on the unit test.
> 75 = Scored between 75 and 89 on the unit test.
> 50 = Scored below 75 percent on the unit test and is required to make it up.

This example is predicated on the logic that those students who pass, but who opt to study to score higher, will overlearn the material and thus remember it better. One disadvantage of this system is that the entire grading emphasis is placed on objective tests (which is likely to keep cognitive activity at the lower levels of Bloom's taxonomy). A second disadvantage is that a 90% cutoff implies that the test is sufficiently reliable to make such judgments. This is a difficult burden for teachers who are not expert item writers and furthermore is very difficult in some fields (e.g., social studies). Finally, it will encourage students to quibble over additional points.

10. Answers to exercises in A: 1-a, 2-c, 3-c, 4-c, 5-c, 6-a, 7-d, 8-d, 9-b.

Chapter Fifteen

1. You may recall the discussion of misuses of intelligence testing in chapter 3 (e.g., Cummins, 1984), which were problems of validity, in the sense of inappropriateness of the tests for the purposes for which they were used.

2. It is customary to describe two basic designs for criterion-related validity, of which predictive validity is the first (e.g., AERA, 1985). Thus it is not strictly appropriate to a purist to use predictive validity as a synonym for criterion-related validity. The second kind of design is known as concurrent validity, in which the criterion to be predicted is measured concurrently with the test being validated. Although this is not a prediction of a future event, it is nevertheless a prediction. Thus for present purposes, it seems reasonable to use the terms criterion-related and predictive as synonyms.

3. Appendix B presents step-by-step procedures for calculating both the standard deviation (SD) and correlation using ranks (r_s).

4. Other properties of the Standard Error, along with a table showing the inverse relationship between reliability and standard error for various standard deviations, can be found in Gronlund (1985, pp. 96–100).

5. Answers to Exercises in A: 1-b, 2-b, 3-a, 4-a, 5-c, 6-d, 7-a, 8-b, 9-b, 10-c, 11-d, 12-a, 13-d.

Chapter Sixteen

1. Dewey was specifically lamenting the problems in elementary schools, but I deleted references to elementary to keep the focus on the general issue. I do not believe he would object because he made the same points about secondary schools, but thought . . . "that all conditions are at the worst in elementary schools" because, he believed, it was at those years that ". . . all the underlying emotional habits and unconscious attitudes are being formed." (p. 119)

References

Abbot, E. A. *Flatland: A Romance of Many Dimensions*. New York: Dover, 1952.

Abramson, L. Y., Seligman, M. E. P. and Teasdale, J. D. "Learned Helplessness in Humans: Critique and Reformulation," *Journal of Abnormal Psychology*, 1978, 87, 49–74.

Abruscato, J. "Early Results and Tentative Implications from the Vermont Portfolio Project." *Phi Delta Kappan*, 1993, 74 (6), 474–477.

Adelson, B. "When Novices Surpass Experts: The Difficulty of a Task May Increase With Expertise." *Journal of Experimental Psychology: Human Learning and Memory*. 1984, 10, 483–495.

AERA, *Standards for Educational and Psychological Testing* (by a joint committee of the American Educational Research Association, the American Psychological Association, and the National Council on Measurement in Education). Washington, D.C.: American Psychological Association, 1985.

Ahukanna, J. G. W., Lund, N. J. and Gentile, J. R. "Inter- and Intra-Lingual Interference Effects in Learning a Third Language," *Modern Language Journal*, 1981, 65(Fall), 281–287.

Airasian, P. W. "The Role of Evaluation in Mastery Learning" in J. H. Block (Ed.) *Mastery Learning: Theory and Practice*. New York: Holt, Rinehart and Winston, 1971, pp. 77–88.

Airasian, P. W. *Classroom Assessment (2nd)*. New York: McGraw-Hill, 1994.

Alexander, R. N. and Apfel, C. H. "Altering Schedules of Reinforcement for Improved Classroom Behavior," *Exceptional Children*, 1976, 43, No. 10, 97–99.

Amsel, A. "The Role of Frustrative Nonreward in Noncontinuous Reward Situations." *Psychological Bulletin*, 1958, 55, 102–119.

Amsel, A. "Frustrative Nonreward in Partial Reinforcement and Discrimination Learning: Some Recent History and a Theoretical Extension." *Psychological Review*, 1962, 69, 306–328.

Amsel, A. "Positive Induction, Behavioral Contrast, and Generalization of Inhibition in Discrimination Learning," in H. H. Kendler and J. T. Spence (Eds.) *Essays in Neo-Behaviorism: A Memorial Volume to Kenneth W. Spence*, New York: Appleton-Century-Crofts, 1971.

Anderson, J. R. *Cognitive Psychology and Its Implications*, San Francisco: Freeman, 1980.

Anderson, J. R. *The architecture of Cognition*, Cambridge, MA: Harvard University Press, 1983.

Anderson, J. R. and Bower, G. H. *Human Associative Memory*, Washington, D.C.: Winston, 1973.

Anderson, J. R., Reder, L. M., and Simon, H. A. "Situated Learning and Education." *Educational Researcher*, 1996, 25 (4), 5–11.

Anderson, L. "A Retrospective and Prospective View of Bloom's 'Learning for Mastery'." in M. C. Wang and H. J. Walberg (Eds.) *Adapting Instruction to Individual Differences*, Berkley, CA: McCutchan, 1985, pp. 254–268.

Anderson, L. W., and Burns, R. B. "Values, Evidence, and Mastery Learning." *Review of Educational Research*, 1987, 57 (2), 215–223.

Anrig. G. R. "Introduction" in *The Redesign of Testing for the 21st Century*. Proceedings of the 1985 ETS Invitational Conference. Princeton, NJ: Educational Testing Service, 1986, pp. v–vi.

Appel, L. F., Cooper, R. G., McCarrell, N., Sims-Knight, J., Yussan, S. R. and Flavell, J. H. "The Development of the Distinction Between Perceiving and Memorizing." *Child Development*, 1972, 43, 1365–1381.

Arlin, M. "Teacher Responses To Student Time Differences in Mastery Learning." *American Journal of Education*, 1982, 90, 334–352.

Arlin, M. "Time, Equality, and Mastery Learning." *Review of Educational Research*, 1984, 54, 65–86.

Armstrong, T. *Multiple Intelligences in the Classroom*. Alexandria, VA: Association for Supervision and Curriculum Development, 1994.

Arnedt, C. S. and Gentile, J. R. "A Test of Dual-Coding Theory for Bilingual Memory," *Canadian Journal of Psychology*, 1986, *40*, 290–299.

Arnoult, M. D. "Stimulus Predifferentiation: Some Generalizations and Hypotheses," *Psychological Bulletin*, 1957, *54*, 339–350.

Asch, S. E. "Studies of Independence and Conformity: A Minority of One Against a Unanimous Majority," *Psychological Monographs*, 1956, *70* (No. 9), Whole No. 416.

Astin, A. W. and Panos, R. J. "The Evaluation of Educational Programs". In R. L. Thorndike (Ed). *Educational Measurement*. Washington, D.C.: American Council on Education, 1971 (2nd Ed.), pp. 733–751.

Atkinson, R. C. "Mnemotechnics in Second Language Learning." *American Psychologist*, 1975, *30*, 821–828.

Ausubel, D. P. "Use of Advance Organizers in the Learning and Retention of Meaningful Verbal Material." *Journal of Educational Psychology*. 1960, *51*, 267–272.

Ausubel, D. P. *The Psychology of Meaningful Verbal Learning*, New York: Grune & Stratton, 1963.

Azrin, N. H. and Holz, W. C. "Punishment" in W. K. Honig (Ed.) *Operant Behavior: Areas of Research and Application*. New York: Appleton-Century-Crofts, 1966, pp. 380–447.

Baehre, M. R. & Gentile, J. R. "Cumulative Effects of the Keyword Mnemonic and Distributed Practice in Learning Social Studies Facts: A Classroom Evaluation." *Journal of Research in Education*,k 1991, *1* (1), 70–78.

Bahrick, H. P. "Maintenance of Knowledge: Questions About Memory We Forgot to Ask," *Journal of Experimental Psychology: General*, 1979, *108*, 296–308.

Bahrick, H. P. "The cognitive Map of a City—50 Years of Learning and Memory," in G. Bower (Ed.) *The Psychology of Learning and Motivation: Advances in Research and Theory*, New York: Academic Press, 1983, Vol. 17, pp. 125–163.

Bahrick, H. P. "Semantic Memory Content in Permastore: Fifty Years of Memory for Spanish Learned in School." *Journal of Experimental Psychology: General*, 1984, *113*, 1–29. (a)

Bahrick, H. P. "Associations and Organization in Cognitive Psychology: A Reply to Neisser," *Journal of Experimental Psychology: General*, 1984, *113*, 36–37. (b)

Bahrick, H. P., Bahrick, P. O. and Wittlinger, R. P. "Fifty Years of Memory for Names and Faces: A Cross-Sectional Approach," *Journal of Experimental Psychology: General*, 1975, *104*, 54–75.

Balsam, P. D. and Bondy, A. S. "The Negative Side Effects of Reward," *Journal of Applied Behavior Analysis*, 1983, *16*, 283–296.

Bandura, A. "Social Learning Through Imitation," in M. R. Jones (Ed.) *Nebraska Symposium on Motivation*, Lincoln: University of Nebraska Press, 1962, pp. 211–269.

Bandura, A. "Vicarious Processes: A Case of No-Trial Learning," in L. Berkowitz (Ed.) *Advances in Experimental Social Psychology*, Vol. II, New York: Academic Press, 1965, pp. 1–55. (a)

Bandura, A. "Influence of Models' Reinforcement Contingencies on the Acquisition of Imitative Responses," *Journal of Personality and Social Psychology*, 1965, *1*, 589–595. (b)

Bandura, A. *Principles of Behavior Modification*, New York: Holt, Rinehart and Winston, 1969.

Bandura, A. "Vicarious and Self-Reinforcement Processes," in R. Glaser (Ed.) *The Nature of Reinforcement*, New York: Academic Press, 1971.

Bandura, A. *Social Learning Theory*. Englewood Cliffs, NJ: Prentice-Hall, 1977. (a)

Bandura, A. "Self-efficacy: Toward a Unifying Theory of Behavior Change." *Psychological Review*, 1977, *84*, 191–215. (b)

Bandura, A. *Social Foundations of Thought and Action: A Social Cognitive Theory*. Englewood Cliffs, NJ: Prentice-Hall, 1986.

Bandura, A. and Huston, A. C. "Identification as a Process of Incidental Learning," *Journal of Abnormal and Social Psychology*, 1961, 63, 311–318.

Bandura, A., Ross, D. and Ross, S. A. "Imitation of Film-Mediated Aggressive Models," *Journal of Abnormal and Social Psychology*, 1963, 66, 3–11. (a)

Bandura, A., Ross, D. and Ross, S. A. "A Comparative Test of the Status Envy, Social Power, and the Secondary Reinforcement Theories of Identificatory Learning," *Journal of Abnormal and Social Psychology*, 1963, 67, 527–534. (b)

Bandura, A., Ross, D. and Ross, S. A. "Vicarious Reinforcement and Imitative Learning," *Journal of Abnormal and Social Psychology*, 1963, 67, 601–607. (c)

Bandura, A. and Walters, R. H. *Social Learning and Personality Development*, New York: Holt, Rinehart and Winston, 1963.

Barber, B. R. *An Aristocracy of Everyone*. Ballantine Books, 1992.

Barnett, L. *The Universe and Dr. Einstein*, New York: Mentor, 1948.

Baron, J. B. & Sternberg, R. J. (Eds.) *Teaching Thinking Skills: Theory and Practice*. New York: W. H. Freeman, 1987.

Barrows, H. S. "An Overview of the Uses of Standardized Patients for Teaching and Evaluating Clinical Skills." *Academic Medicine*, 1993, 68 (6), 443–453.

Bartlett, F. C. *Remembering: A Study in Experimental and Social Psychology*, Cambridge: Cambridge University Press, 1932.

Bauer, R. H. "Memory Processes in Children with Learning Disabilities: Evidence for Deficient Rehearsal," *Journal of Experimental Child Psychology*, 1977, 24, 415–430.

Bauer, R. H. "Memory Acquisition, and Category Clustering in Learning Disabled Children," *Journal of Experimental Child Psychology*, 1979, 27, 365–383. (a)

Bauer, R. H. "Recall After a Short Delay and Acquisition in Learning Disabled and Nondisabled Children," *Journal of Learning Disabilities*, 1979, 19(9), 596–607. (b)

Bayley, N. "On the Growth of Intelligence," *American Psychologist*, 1955, 10, 805–818.

Bayley, N. "Development of Mental Abilities." In P. Mussen (Ed.) *Carmichael's Manual of Child Psychology*, New York: Wiley, 1970, Vol. I, pp. 1163–1209.

Becker, W. C., Madsen, C. H., Arnold, C. R. and Thomas, D. R. "The Contingent Use of Teacher Attention and Praise in Reducing Classroom Behavior Problems," *Journal of Special Education*, 1967, 1, 287–307.

Belmont, J. M. "Individual Differences in Memory: The Case of Normal and Retarded Development," in M. M. Gruneberg and P. Morris (Ed.) *Aspects of Memory*, London: Methuen, 1978, pp. 153–185.

Belmont, J. M., Butterfield, E. C. and Borkowski, J. G. "Training Retarded People to Generalize Memorization Methods Across Memory Tasks," in M. M. Gruneberg, P. E. Morris and R. N. Sykes (Eds.) *Practical Aspects of Memory*, London: Academic Press, 1978, pp. 418–425.

Bem, D. J. *Beliefs, Attitudes and Human Affairs*, Belmont, CA: Brooks/Cole, 1970.

Berk, R. A. "A Consumers' Guide to Criterion-Referenced Test Item Statistics". *Measurement in Education*, 1978, 9 (No. 1), 1–8.

Berkowitz, L. *Aggression: A Social Psychological Analysis*. New York: McGraw-Hill, 1962.

Berkowitz, L. "The Effects of Observing Violence," *Scientific American*, 1964, 210, 2–8.

Berkowitz, L. "The Contagion of Violence: An S-R Mediational Analysis of Some Effects of Observed Aggression," in W. J. Arnold and M. M. Page (Eds.) *Nebraska Symposium on Motivation*, Lincoln: University of Nebraska Press, 1970, 18, 95–136.

Berliner, D. C. "The Half-Full Glass: A Review of Research on Teaching." In P. L. Hosford (Ed.), *Using What We Know About Teaching*, Alexandria, VA: Association for Supervision and Curriculum Development, 1984, pp. 51–77.

Berliner, D. C. "In Pursuit of the Expert Pedagogue," *Educational Researcher*, 1986, 15(7), 5–13.

Berliner, D. C. & Casanova, U. *Putting Research to Work in Your School*. New York: Scholastic, 1993.

Biehler, R. F. *Child Development: An Introduction*. Boston: Houghton-Mifflin, 1976.

Bilodeau, E. A., & Bilodeau, I. McD. "Variation of Temporal Intervals Among Critical Events in Five Studies of Knowledge of Results." *Journal of Experimental Psychology*, 1958, 55, 603–612.

Bilodeau, E. A., & Bilodeau, I. McD. "Motor Skills Learning." In P. R. Farnsworth, O. McNemar, & Q. McNemar (Eds.), *Annual Review of Psychology*, 1961, 12, 243–280.

Binet, A., & Simon, T. "The Child Is An X." (from *A Method of Measuring the Intelligence of Young Children*, translated by C. H. Town). Chicago, IL: Chicago Medical Book Co., 1915. Part II.

Binet, A., & Simon T. *The Development of Intelligence in Children* (translated by E. S. Kite). Baltimore, MD: Williams and Wilkins, 1916.

Bloch, A. *Murphy's Law and Other Reasons Why Things Go Wrong*. Los Angeles: Price/Stern/Sloan, 1980.

Block, J. H. (Ed.) *Mastery Learning: Theory and Practice*. New York: Holt, Rinehart and Winston, 1971. (a)

Block, J. H. "Criterion-referenced Measurements: Potential". *School Review*, 1971, 79 (Feb.), 289–297. (b)

Block, J. H. (Ed.) *Schools, Society and Mastery Learning*. New York: Holt, Rinehart and Winston, 1974. (a)

Block, J. H. "A Description and Comparison of Bloom's Learning for Mastery Strategy and Keller's Personalized System of Instruction" in J. H. Block (Ed.) *Schools, Society and Mastery Learning*. New York: Holt, Rinehart and Winston, 1974, pp. 16–26. (b)

Block, J. H. and Anderson, L. W. *Mastery Learning in Classroom Instruction*. New York: Macmillan, 1975.

Block, J. H. and Burns, R. B. "Mastery Learning," in L. S. Shulman (Ed.), *Review of Research in Education*. Itasca, IL: F. E. Peacock, 1977, 4, 3–49.

Block, J. H., Efthim, H. E., and Burns, R. B. *Building Effective Mastery Learning Schools*. New York: Longman, 1989.

Bloom, B. S. (Ed.) *Taxonomy of Educational Objectives: The Classification of Educational Goals. Handbook 1. Cognitive Domain*, New York: McKay, 1956.

Bloom, B. S. *Stability and Change in Human Characteristics*, New York: Wiley, 1964.

Bloom, B. S. "Mastery Learning" in J. H. Block (Ed.) *Mastery Learning: Theory and Practice*. New York: Holt, Rinehart and Winston, 1971, pp. 47–63. (Reprinted from "Learning for Mastery", UCLA-CSEIP *Evaluation Comment*, 1968, 1 (No. 2), 1–16.)

Bloom, B. S. *Human Characteristics and School Learning*, New York: McGraw-Hill, 1976.

Bloom, B. S. *All Our Children Learning*, New York: McGraw-Hill, 1981.

Bloom, B. S. "Automaticity: The Hands and Feet of Genius." *Educational Leadership*, 1986, 43(5), 70–77.

Bloom, B. S. and Broder, L. J. *Problem-Solving Processes of College Students*, Chicago, IL: University of Chicago Press, 1950.

Bloom, B. S., Hastings, J. T., & Madaus, G. F. (Eds.). *Handbook on Formative and Summative Evaluation of Student Learning*. New York: McGraw-Hill, 1971.

Bloom, B. S., Madaus, G. F. and Hastings, J. T. *Evaluation To Improve Learning*. New York: McGraw-Hill, 1981.

Bloom, K. C. and Shuell, T. J. "Effects of Massed and Distributed Practice on the Learning and Retention of Second-Language Vocabulary," *Journal of Educational Research*, 1981, 74(No. 4), 245–248.

Boe, E. E. "Bibliography on Punishment," in B. A. Campbell and R. M. Church (Eds.) *Punishment and Aversive Behavior*, New York: Appleton-Century-Crofts, 1969, pp. 531–587.

Bonwell, C. C. and Eison, J. A. *Active Learning: Creating Excitement in the Classroom.* ASHE-ERIC Higher Education Report No. 1, Washington, DC: George Washington University Press, 1991.

Boring, E. G. "Intelligence as the Tests Test It." *New Republic,* 1923 (June 6), *35,* 35–37.

Boring, E. G. *A History of Experimental Psychology* (2nd), New York: Appleton-Century-Crofts, 1957.

Borkowski, J. G. and Büchel, F. P. "Learning and Memory Strategies in the Mentally Retarded," in M. Pressley and J. R. Levin (Eds.) *Cognitive Strategy Research: Psychological Foundations*, New York: Springer-Verlag, 1983, pp. 103–128.

Boulle, P. *Planet of the Apes*, (translation by X. Fielding), New York: Vanguard Press, 1963.

Bower, G. H. "A Contrast Effect in Differential Conditioning," *Journal of Experimental Psychology,* 1961, *62,* 196–199.

Bower, G. H. and Hilgard, E. R. *Theories of Learning* (Fifth Edition), Englewood Cliffs, NJ: Prentice-Hall, 1981.

Brady, J. V. "Ulcers in 'Executive' Monkeys," *Scientific American,* 1958, *199,* 95–100.

Brady, J. V., Porter, R. W., Conrad, D. G. and Mason, J. W. "Avoidance Behavior and the Development of Gastroduodenal Ulcers," *Journal of the Experimental Analysis of Behavior,* 1958, *1,* 69–72.

Brainerd, C. J. *Piaget's Theory of Intelligence,* Englewood Cliffs, NJ: Prentice-Hall, 1978.

Brandt, R. "On Teaching and Supervising: A Conversation with Madeline Hunter." *Educational Leadership,* 1985, *42*(5), 61–66.

Bransford, J. D. and Johnson, M. K. "Contextual Prerequisites for Understanding: Some Investigations of Comprehension and Recall," *Journal of Verbal Learning and Verbal Behavior,* 1972, *11,* 717–726.

Bransford, J. D., Sherwood, R. D. and Sturdevant, T. "Teaching Thinking and Problem-Solving," in J. B. Baron and R. J. Sternberg (Eds.) *Teaching Thinking Skills: Theory and Practice.* New York: Freeman, 1987, pp. 162–181.

Bransford, J. D. and Stein, B. S. *The IDEAL Problem Solver.* New York: Freeman, 1984.

Bransford J. D., Stein, B. S., Arbitman-Smith, R. and Vye, N. J. "Improving Thinking and Learning Skills: An Analysis of Three Approaches," in J. W. Segal, S. F. Chipman, and R. Glaser (Eds.) *Thinking and Learning Skills, Vol. 1. Relating Instruction to Research*, Hillsdale, NJ: Erlbaum, 1985, pp. 133–206.

Bräten, I. (1991). "Vygotsky as precursor to metacognitive theory: II. Vygotsky as Metacognivist." *Scandinavian Journal of Educational Research*, 1991, 35, (4), 305–320.

Bregman, E. "An Attempt to Modify the Emotional Attitude of Infants by the Conditioned Response Technique," *Journal of Genetic Psychology,* 1934, *45,* 169–198.

Brim, O. G. "Family Structure and Sex Role Learning by Children: A Further Analysis of Helen Koch's Data," *Sociometry,* 1958, *21,* 1–16.

Brophy, J. and Good, T. L. "Teacher Behavior and Student Achievement." In M. C. Wittrock (Ed.) *Handbook of Research on Teaching* (Third Ed.), New York: Macmillan, 1986, pp. 328–375.

Brown, A. L. "Metacognitive Development and Reading." in R. J. Spiro, B. C. Bruce, & W. F. Brewer (Eds.) *Theoretical Issues in Reading Comprehension.* Hillsdale, NJ: Lawrence Erlbaum, 1980, pp. 453–481.

Brown, A. L. "The Advancement of Learning." *Educational Researcher,* 1994, *23,* (8), 4–12.

Brown, G. D. and Tyler, V. O., Jr. "The Use of Swift, Brief Isolation as a Group Control Device for Institutionalized Delinquents," *Behavior Research and Therapy,* 1967, *5,* 1–9.

Brown, J. S., Collins, A. & Duguid, P. "Situated Cognition and the Culture of Learning." *Educational Researcher*, 1989, *18* (1), 32–42.

Brown, J. S., and Duguid, P. "Stolen Knowledge." *Educational Technology*, 1993, *33* (3), 10–15.

Brown, R. *Social Psychology*, New York: Free Press, 1965.

Brown, R. and McNeill, D. "The Tip of the Tongue Phenomenon," *Journal of Verbal Learning and Verbal Behavior*, 1966, *5*, 325–337.

Brown, S. I. and Walter, M. I. *The Art of Problem Posing*. Philadelphia, PA: The Franklin Institute Press, 1983.

Bruner, J. S. *The Process of Education*. New York: Vintage, 1960.

Bruner, J.S. "The Act of Discovery," *Harvard Educational Review*, 1961, *31*, 21–32.

Bruner, J. S., Goodnow, J. J., and Austin, G. A. *A Study of Thinking*. New York: Science Editions, 1965.

Bruner, J. E. and Minturn, A. L. "Perceptual Identification and Perceptual Organization," *Journal of General Psychology*, 1955, *53*, 21–28.

Bruner, J. S., Olver, R. R., Greenfield, P. M., et al. *Studies in Cognitive Growth*, New York: John Wiley & Sons, 1966.

Bugelski, B. R. "Images as Mediators in One-Trial Paired-Associate Learning. II. Self-Timing in Successive Lists," *Journal of Experimental Psychology*, 1968, *77*, 328–334.

Bugelski, B. R. *Principles of Learning and Memory*, New York: Praeger, 1979.

Bugelski, B. R., Kidd, E. and Segmen, J. "Images as a Mediator in One-Trial Paired-Associate Learning," *Journal of Experimental Psychology*, 1968, *76*, 69–73.

Burden, P. R. *Classroom Management and Discipline*. White Plains, NY: Longman, 1995.

Burgess, A. *A Clockwork Orange*, New York: W. W. Norton, 1963.

Burns, R. B. "Mastery Learning: Does It Work?" *Educational Leadership*, 1979, *37* (Nov.), 110–113.

Butkowski, I. S. and Willows, P. M. "Cognitive-Motivational Characteristics of Children Varying in Reading Ability: Evidence for Learned Helplessness in Poor Readers," *Journal of Educational Psychology*, 1980, *72*, 408–422.

Cain, L. F. and Willey, R. DeV. "The Effect of Spaced Learning on the Curve of Retention," *Journal of Experimental Psychology*, 1939, *25*, 209–214.

Cairns, R. B. "The Emergence of Developmental Psychology." In P. E. Mussen (Ed.) *Handbook of Child Psychology*. Vol. I. (Fourth Edition). New York: Wiley, 1983, pp. 41–102.

Cameron, J. and Pierce, W. D. "Reinforcement, Reward, and Intrinsic Motivation: A Meta-Analysis." *Review of Educational Research*, 1994, *64*, 363–423.

Cameron, J. and Pierce, W. D. "The Debate About Rewards and Intrinsic-Motivation: Protests and Accusations Do Not Alter the Results." *Review of Educational Research*, 1996, *66* (1), 39–51.

Campbell, D. T. and Fiske, D. W. "Convergent and Discriminant Validity By the Multitrait-Multimethod Matrix." *Psychological Bulletin*, 1959, *56*, 81–105.

Campione, J. C. and Brown, A. L. "Toward a Theory of Intelligence: Contributions from Research with Retarded Children," *Intelligence*, 1978, *2*, 279–304. (a)

Campione, J. C. and Brown, A. L. "Training General Metacognitive Skills in Retarded Children," in M. M. Gruneberg, P. E. Morris and R. N. Sykes (Eds.) *Practical Aspects of Memory*, London: Academic Press, 1978, pp. 410–417. (b)

Canter, L. and Canter, M. *Assertive Discipline: A Take-Charge Approach for Today's Educator*. Seal Beach, CA: Canter and Associates, 1976.

Carey, S. *Conceptual Change in Childhood*. Cambridge, MA: MIT Press, 1985.

Carey, S. "Cognitive Science and Science Education," *American Psychologist*, 1986, *41*, 1123–1130.

Carroll, J. B. "A Model of School Learning". *Teachers College Record*, 1963, *64*, 723–733.

Carroll, J. B. "Problems of Measurement Related to the Concept of Learning for Mastery". *Educational Horizons*, 1970, *48*(3), 71–80. Reprinted in J. H. Block (Ed.) *Mastery Learning: Theory and Practice,* New York: Holt, Rinehart and Winston, 1971, pp. 29–46.

Carroll, J. B. "The Model of School Learning: Progress of an Idea." In L. Anderson (Ed.) *Perspectives in School Learning: Selected Writings of John B. Carroll.* Hillsdale, NJ: Lawrence Erlbaum, 1985, *8* (1), 26–31.

Carroll, J. B. "The Carroll Model: A 25-Year Retrospective and Prospective View." *Educational Researcher*, 1989, *8* (1), 26–31.

Carroll, J. B. *Human Cognitive Abilities.* Cambridge: The University of Cambridge Press, 1993.

Cattell, J. McK. "Mental Tests and Measurements." *Mind*, 1890, *15*, 373–380.

Ceci, S. J. and Hembrooke, H. "The Contextual Nature of Earliest Memories." in J. M. Puckett & H. W. Reese (Eds.) *Mechanisms of Everyday Cognition.* Hillsdale, NJ: Lawrence Erlbaum, 1993, pp. 117–136.

Ceci, S. J., Ross, D. F. and Toglia, M. P. "Suggestibility of Children's Memory: Psycholegal Implications." *Journal of Experimental Psychology: General*, 1987, *116*, 38–49.

Chaffee, S. H. "Television and Adolescent Aggressiveness (an Overview)," in G. A. Comstock and E. A. Rubinstein (Eds.) *Television and Social Behavior.* Technical Report (Vol. III) To The Surgeon General's Scientific Advisory Committee on Television and Social Behavior, Washington, D.C., U.S. Government Printing Office, 1972.

Chance, P. "Fred Keller: The Revolutionary Gentleman", *Psychology Today*, 1984, *18* (No. 9), 42–48.

Charles, C. M. *Building Classroom Discipline: From Models to Practice,* New York: Longman, 1981.

Charness, N. "Memory for Chess Positions: Resistance To Interference," *Journal of Experimental Psychology: Human Learning and Memory*, 1976, *2*, 641–653.

Charness, N. (Ed.) "Special Issue on Skill." *Canadian Journal of Psychology*, 1985, *39*(2), 181–386.

Chase, W. G. and Ericsson, K. A. "Skilled Memory," in J. R. Anderson (Ed.), *Cognitive Skills and Their Acquisition*, Hillsdale, NJ: Erlbaum, 1981, pp. 141–189.

Chase, W. G. and Simon, H. A. "Perception in Chess," *Cognitive Psychology*, 1973, *4*, 55–81.

Cherry, E. C. "Some Experiments on the Recognition of Speech with One and Two Ears," *Journal of the Acoustical Society of America*, 1953, *25*, 975–979.

Chi, M. T. H., Glaser, R. and Rees, E. "Expertise in Problem Solving" in R. J. Sternberg (Ed.) *Advances in the Psychology of Human Intelligence. Vol. I.* Hillsdale, NJ: Erlbaum, 1982, pp. 7–75.

Child, I. L. "Socialization," in G. Lindzey (Ed.) *Handbook of Social Psychology,* (Vol 2), Cambridge, MA: Addison-Wesley, 1954, pp. 655–692.

Church, R. M. "The Varied Effects of Punishment on Behavior." *Psychological Review*, 1963, *70*, 369–402.

Church, R. M. "Response Suppression," in B. A. Campbell and R. M. Church, (Eds.) *Punishment and Aversive Behavior*, New York: Appleton-Century-Crofts, 1969.

Churchill, W. "My Early Life," in F. W. Heath (Ed.) *Great Destiny*, New York: Putnam, 1965.

Clarizio, H. F. "Intellectual Assessment of Hispanic Children." *Psychology in the Schools*, 1982, *19*, 61–71.

Cleary, T. A., Humphreys, L. G., Kendrick, S. A., & Wesman, A. "Educational Uses of Tests with Disadvantaged Students." *American Psychologist*, 1975, *30*, 15–41.

Cofer, C. N., Segal, E., Stein, J. and Walker, H. "Studies in Free Recall of Nouns Following Presentation Under Adjectival Modification," *Journal of Experimental Psychology*, 1969, *79*, 254–264.

Cohen, P. A., Kulik, J. A. and Kulik, C. C. "Educational Outcomes of Tutoring: A Meta-analysis of Findings", *American Educational Research Journal*, 1982, *19*, 237–248.

Colby, A. and Kohlberg, L. *The Measurement of Moral Judgment, Vol. I. Theoretical Foundations and Research Validation.* Cambridge: Cambridge University Press, 1987a.

Colby, A. and Kohlberg, L. *The Measurement of Moral Judgment, Vol. II. Standard Issue Scoring Manual.* Cambridge: Cambridge University Press, 1987b.

Cole, M., Gay, J., Glick, J. and Sharp, D. W. *The Cultural Context of Learning and Thinking.* New York: Basic Books, 1971.

Collins, A. M. and Quillian, M. R. "Retrieval Time from Semantic Memory," *Journal of Verbal Learning and Verbal Behavior*, 1969, *8*, 240–247.

Colliver, J. A. and Williams, R. G. "Technical Issues: Test Application [of Standardized Patients]." *Academic Medicine*, 1993, *68* (6), 454–463.

Combs, A. W. "A Contract Method of Evaluation". In S. B. Simon and J. A. Bellanca (Eds.), *Degrading the Grading Myths: A Primer of Alternatives To Grades and Marks.* Washington, D.C.: Association for Supervision and Curriculum Development, 1976, pp. 70–73.

Cooley, W. W. and Lohnes, P. R. *Evaluation Research in Education.* New York: Irvington, 1976.

Cornbleth, C. "Ritual and Rationality in Teacher Education Reform". *Educational Researcher*, 1986, *15*(4), 5–14.

Costa, A. L. *Developing Minds: A Resource Book for Teaching Thinking.* Alexandria, VA: Association for Supervision and Curriculum Development, 1985.

Craik, F. I. M., and Lockhart, R. S. "Levels of Processing: A Framework for Memory Research," *Journal of Verbal Learning & Verbal Behavior*, 1972, *11*, 671–684.

Crehan, K. D. "Item Analysis for Teacher-Made Mastery Tests". *Journal of Educational Measurement*, 1974, *11*, 255–262.

Crespi, L. "Quantitative Variation of Incentive and Performance in the White Rat," *American Journal of Psychology*, 1942, *15*, 467–517.

Cronbach, L. J. "Course Improvement Through Evaluation", *Teachers College Record*, 1963, *64*, 672–683.

Cronbach, L. J. "The Logic of Experiments on Discovery" in L. S. Shulman and E. R. Keislar (Eds.) *Learning By Discovery: A Critical Appraisal.* Chicago, IL: Rand McNally, 1966, pp. 76–92.

Cronbach, L. J. "Five Decades of Public Controversy Over Mental Testing." *American Psychologist*, 1975, *30*, 1–14.

Cronbach, L. J. and Furby, L. "How Do We Measure Change—or Should We?" *Psychological Bulletin*, 1970, *74*, 68–80.

Cronbach, L. J. and Meehl, P. E. "Construct Validity in Psychological Tests". *Psychological Bulletin*, 1955, *52*, 281–302.

Cummins, J. *Bilingualism and Special Education: Issues in Assessment and Pedagogy,* Avon, England: Multilingual Matters, 1984.

Cureton, L. W. "The History of Grading Practices". NCME Measurement in Education Special Report, 1971, Vol. 2, No. 4.

Damarin, S. K. "Schooling and Situated Knowledge: Travel or Tourism?" *Educational Technology*, 1993, *33* (3), 27–32.

Davenport, J. W. "Higher-order Conditioning of Fear," *Psychonomic Science*, 1966, *4*, 27–28.

Davis, M., Eshelman, E. R. and McKay, M. *The Relaxation and Stress Reduction Workbook,* Richmond, CA: New Harbinger Publications, 1980.

Davison, G. C. "Systematic Desensitization as a Counter-Conditioning Process," *Journal of Abnormal Psychology*, 1968, *73*, 91–99.

de Bono, E. *Lateral Thinking: Creativity Step by Step.* New York: Harper and Row, 1970.

de Bono, E. *The CoRT Thinking Program* (Second Ed.), Elmsford, NY: Pergamon Press, 1986.

DeCecco, J. P. *The Psychology of Learning and Instruction: Educational Psychology.* Englewood Cliffs, NJ: Prentice-Hall, 1968.

DeCecco, J. P. and Richards, A. K. "Civil War in the High Schools," *Psychology Today*, 1975, 9 (November), 51–56; 120.

Deese, J., and Hulse, S. H. *The Psychology of Learning.* New York: McGraw-Hill, 1967.

de Groot, A. D. *Thought and Choice in Chess,* The Hague: Mouton, 1965.

de Groot, A. D. "Perception and Memory versus Thought: Some Old Ideas and Recent Findings," in B. Kleinmuntz (Ed.) *Problem Solving: Research, Method and Theory.* New York: Wiley, 1966, pp. 19–50.

Derry, S. J. and Murphy, D. A. "Designing Systems That Train Learning Ability: From Theory to Practice," *Review of Educational Research*, 1986, 56, 1–39.

de Saint Exupery, A. *The Little Prince,* New York: Harbrace Paperbound Library, 1971.

Detterman, D. K. & Sternberg, R. J. (Eds.), *Transfer on Trial: Intelligence, Cognition and Instruction.* Norwood, New Jersey: Ablex Publishing Corporation, 1993.

Deutsch, M. *The Resolution of Conflict.* New Haven, CT: Yale University Press, 1973.

Deutsch, M. "Constructive Conflict Resolution: Principles, Training, and Research," *Journal of Social Issues*, 1994, 50, 13–32.

Devin-Sheehan, L., Feldman, R. S., and Allen, V. L. "Research on Children Tutoring Children: A Critical Review", *Review of Educational Research*, 1976, 46, 355–385.

Dewey, J. *How We Think.* Boston: Health, 1933.

Dewey, J. "What Is The Matter With Teaching?" In J. A. Boydston (Ed.) *John Dewey: The Later Works, 1925–1953* (first published in *Delineator*, 1925, 107, 5–6, 78). Carbondale, IL: Southern Illinois University Press, 1984, pp. 116–123.

Dick, W., & Carey, L. *The Systematic Design of Instruction* (2nd ed.). Glenview, IL: Scott, Foresman, 1985.

Diener, C. I. and Dweck, C. S. "An Analysis of Learned Helplessness: Continuous Changes in Performance, Strategy, and Achievement Cognitions Following Failure," *Journal of Personality and Social Psychology*, 1978, 36, 451–462.

Dilendik, J. R. "A Sociometric Analysis of Two Sixth Grade Integrated Classrooms," State University of New York at Buffalo, unpublished manuscript, 1972.

Dobzhansky, T. *Genetic Diversity and Human Equality.* New York: Basic Books, 1973.

Dollard, J., Miller, N. E., Doob, L. W., Mowrer, O. H. and Sears, R. R. *Frustration and Aggression.* New Haven: Yale University Press, 1939.

Dooling, J. L. and Lachman, R. "Effects of Comprehension on Retention of Prose," *Journal of Experimental Psychology*, 1971, 88, 216–222.

Doran, R. L. and Zinnerstrom, K. "Analysis of the ESPET Manipulative Skills Test. *Science Teachers Bulletin*, 1995, 58 (2), 3–8.

Dowling, M. "Mary Ann—A Lesson in Determination," *Educational Leadership*, 1985, 43(1), 72–74.

Doyle, W. "Are Students Behaving Worse Than They Used To Behave?" *Journal of Research and Development in Education*, 1978, 11, 3–16.

Dreikurs, R. *Psychology in the Classroom,* New York: Harper & Row, 1968.

Dreikurs, R., Grunwald, B. and Pepper, F. *Maintaining Sanity in the Classroom,* New York: Harper and Row, 1971.

Driscoll, M. P. *Psychology of Learning for Instruction.* Boston: Allyn & Bacon, 1994.

Duncan, C. P. "Description of Learning to Learn in Human Subjects," *American Journal of Psychology*, 1960, 73, 108–114.

Dunkin, M. J. "Research on Teaching in Higher Education" in M. C. Wittrock (Ed.) *Handbook of Research on Teaching*, Third Edition, New York: Macmillan, 1986, pp. 754–777.

Dweck, C. S. "The Role of Expectations and Attributions in the Alleviation of Learned Helplessness," *Journal of Personality and Social Psychology*, 1975, 31, 674–685.

Dweck, C. S. "Motivational Processes Affecting Learning." *American Psychologist*, 1986, 41, 1040–1048.

Dweck, C. S. and Leggett, E. L. "A Social-Cognitive Approach To Motivation and Personality." *Psychological Review*, 1988, 95, 256–272.

Dweck, C. S. and Licht, B. G. "Learned Helplessness and Intellectual Achievement," in J. Garber and M. E. P. Seligman (Eds.) *Human Helplessness: Theory and Applications*, New York: Academic Press, 1980.

Dweck, C. S. and Reppucci, N. D. "Learned Helplessness and Reinforcement Responsibility in Children." *Journal of Personality and Social Psychology*, 1973, 25, 109–116.

Early, C. J. "Attitude Learning in Children," *Journal of Educational Psychology*, 1968, 59, 176–180.

Ebbinghaus, H. *Memory: A Contribution to Experimental Psychology* (translated by H. A. Ruger and C. E. Bussenius). New York Dover, 1964 (first published 1885).

Ebel, R. L. "Criterion-referenced Measurements: Limitations". *School Review*, 1971, 79 (Feb.), 282–288.

Ebel, R. L. "The Case for Norm-Referenced Measurements". *Educational Researcher*, 1978, 7 (Dec.), 3–5.

Edwards, B. *Drawing on the Right Side of the Brain*. Los Angeles, CA: Tarcher, 1979.

Eisner, E. *The Role of Discipline-Based Art Education in America's Schools*. Los Angeles: The Getty Center for Education in the Arts, 1987.

Elkind, D. "Piagetian and Psychometric Conceptions of Intelligence". *Harvard Educational Review*, 1969, 39, 319–337.

Elkind, D. *A Sympathetic Understanding of the Child Six to Sixteen*. Boston: Allyn and Bacon, 1971.

Elliott, J. L. and Gentile, J. R. "The Efficacy of a Mnemonic Device for Learning Disabled and Nondisabled Adolescents," *Journal of Learning Disabilities*, 1986, 19(4), 237–241.

Ellis, H. C. *Transfer of Learning*. New York: Macmillan, 1965.

Ellis, H. C. "Transfer and Retention," in M. H. Marx (Ed.) *Learning: Processes*, New York: Macmillan, 1969, pp. 379–478.

Ellis, H. C. and Hunt, R. R. *Fundamentals of Cognitive Psychology* (5th). Madison, WI: Brown & Benchmark, 1993.

English, H. B. "Three Cases of the 'Conditioned Fear Response'," *Journal of Abnormal and Social Psychology*, 1929, 24, 221–225.

Ennis, R. H. "A Taxonomy of Critical Thinking Dispositions and Abilities." In J. B. Baron & R. J. Sternberg (Eds.) *Teaching Thinking Skills: Theory and Practice*. New York: W. H. Freeman, 1987, pp. 9–26.

Ericsson, K. A., Chase, W. G. and Faloon, S. "Acquisition of a Memory Skill," *Science*, 1980, 208, 1181–1182.

Erikson, E. H. *Childhood and Society* (2nd ed.). New York: W. W. Norton, 1963.

Erikson, E. H. *Identity: Youth and Crisis*. New York: W. W. Norton, 1968.

Erikson, E. H. *Identity and the Life Cycle*. New York: W. W. Norton, 1980.

Evans, F. B. "What Research Says About Grading". In S. B. Simon and J. A. Bellanca (Eds.), *Degrading the Grading Myths: A Primer of Alternatives to Grades and Marks*. Washington, D.C.: Association for Supervision and Curriculum Development, 1976, pp. 30–50.

Farnham-Diggory, S. *Cognitive Processes in Education: A Psychological Preparation for Teaching and Curriculum Development*, New York, Harper and Row, 1972.

Feldhusen, J. F. "Behavior Problems in Secondary Schools," *Journal of Research and Development in Education*, 1978, 11, 17–28.

Feldmesser, R.A. "The Positive Function of Grades," in M.D. Gall and B.A. Ward (Eds.). *Critical Issues in Educational Psychology*. Boston: Little, Brown, pp. 579–587.

Ferguson, G. A. "On Transfer and the Abilities of Man," *Canadian Journal of Psychology*, 1956, 10, 121–131.

Ferritor, D. E., Buckholdt, D., Hamblin, R. L. and Smith, L. "The Noneffects of Contingent Reinforcement for Attending Behavior on Work Accomplished," *Journal of Applied Behavior Analysis*, 1972, *5*, 7–17.

Ferster, C. B. "Individualized Instruction in a Large Introductory Psychology College Course", *The Psychological Record*, 1968, *18*, 521–532.

Ferster, C. B. and Appel, J. B. "Punishment of S Responding in Matched-To-Sample By Timeout from Positive Reinforcement," *Journal of the Experimental Analysis of Behavior*, 1961, *4*, 45–56.

Ferster, C. B. and Perrott, M. C. *Behavior Principles.* New York: Appleton-Century-Crofts, 1968.

Feshbach, S. "The Drive-Reducing Function of Fantasy Behavior." *Journal of Abnormal and Social Psychology*, 1955, *50*, 3–11.

Feshbach, S. "The Function of Aggression and the Regulation of Aggressive Drive," *Psychological Review*, 1964, *71*, 257–272.

Feshbach, S. "Aggression," in P. H. Mussen (Ed.) *Carmichael's Manual of Child Psychology* (3rd. Ed.), Vol. 2, New York: Wiley, 1970, pp. 159–260.

Festinger, L. *A Theory of Cognitive Dissonance.* Evanston, IL: Row, Peterson, 1957.

Festinger, L., Riecken, H. W., Jr., & Schachter, S. *When Prophecy Fails*, Minneapolis: University of Minnesota Press, 1956.

Feurerstein, R. *The Dynamic Assessment of Retarded Performers: The Learning Potential Assessment Device, Theory, Instruments and Techniques.* Baltimore: University Park Press, 1979.

Feurerstein, R., Rand, Y., Hoffman, M. B. and Miller, R. *Instrumental Enrichment: An Intervention Program for Cognitive Modifiability*, Baltimore: University Park Press, 1980.

Flanders, J. P. "A Review of Research on Imitative Behavior," *Psychological Bulletin*, 1968, *69*, 316–337.

Flavell, J. H. *The Developmental Psychology of Jean Piaget*, Princeton, NJ: D. Van Nostrand, 1963.

Flavell, J. H. "Metacognition and Cognitive Monitoring: A New Area of Cognitive-Developmental Inquiry," *American Psychologist*, 1979, *34*, 906–911.

Flavell, J. H., Friedrich, A. G. and Hoyt, J. D. "Developmental Changes in Memorization Processes," *Cognitive Psychology*, 1970, *1*, 324–340.

Flavell, J. H., Green, F. L. & Flavell, E. R. "Young Children's Knowledge About Thinking." *Monographs of the Society for Research in Child Development.* Serial No. 243, 1995, *60*, (1).

Forgan, H. W. "Teachers Don't Want To Be Labeled." *Phi Delta Kappan*, 1973, *55*(1), Back Cover.

Foster, H. L. *Ribbin', Jivin', and Playin' the Dozens: The Persistent Dilemma in Our Schools* (2nd Ed.), Cambridge, MA: Ballinger, 1986.

Fowler, S. and Baer, D. M. " 'Do I Have To Be Good All Day?' The Timing of Delayed Reinforcement as a Factor in Generalization," *Journal of Applied Behavior Analysis*, 1981, *14*, 13–24.

Franklin, B. In B. F. Skinner, "Operant reinforcement of prayer." *Journal of Applied Behavior Analysis*, 1969, *2*, 247.

Frederiksen, N. "The Real Test Bias," *American Psychologist*, 1984, *39*, 1–10.

Fremer, J. and Daniel, M. "The Assessment of Higher Order Thinking Skills: Recent Development". In C. P. Kearney, M. H. Kean, E. D. Roeber, B. L. Stevens, J. B. Baron, J. Fremer, and M. Daniel, *Assessing Higher Order Thinking Skills*, ERIC/TME Report 90, Princeton, NJ: Educational Testing Service, 1985, pp. 48–61.

Friedenberg, E. *The Vanishing Adolescent*, New York: Dell, 1959.

Friedrich, L. K. and Stein, A. H. "Aggressive and Prosocial Television Programs and the Natural Behavior of Preschool Children," *Monographs of the Society for Research in Child Development*, 1973, *38*, 94, Serial No. 151).

Friedrich, L. K. and Stein. A. H. "Prosocial Television and Young Children: The Effects of Verbal Labeling and Role Playing on Learning and Behavior," *Child Development,* 1975, *46,* 27–38.

Gage, N. L. *Hard Gains in the Soft Sciences: The Case of Pedagogy.* Bloomington, IN: Phi Delta Kappa, 1985.

Gagné, R. M. "The Acquisition of Knowledge." *Psychological Review,* 1962, *69,* 355–365.

Gagné, R. M. "Learning Hierarchies." *Educational Psychologist,* 1968, *6,* 1–9.

Gagné, R. M. *The Conditions of Learning* (2nd ed.). New York: Holt, Rinehart, and Winston, 1970.

Gagné, R. M. *The Conditions of Learning* (4th ed.). New York: Holt, Rinehart, and Winston, 1985.

Gagné, R. M., & Briggs, L. J. *Principles of Instructional Design.* New York: Holt, Rinehart, and Winston, 1974.

Gagné, R. M., & Briggs, L. J. *Principles of Instructional Design* (2nd ed.). New York: Holt, Rinehart, and Winston, 1979.

Gagné, R. M. and Driscoll, M.P. *Essentials of Learning for Instruction.* Englewood Cliffs, NJ: Prentice-Hall, 1988.

Gagné, R. M., Mayor, J. R., Garstens, H. L., & Paradise, N. E. "Factors in Acquiring Knowledge of a Mathematics Task." *Psychological Monographs,* 1962, *76*(7). (Whole No. 526).

Gagné, R. M. and Paradise, N. E. "Abilities and Learning Sets in Knowledge Acquisition," *Psychological Monographs,* 1961, *75,* No. 14, (Whole No. 518).

Gallagher, J. J., Benoit, E. P., & Boyd, H. F. "Measures of Intelligence in Brain Damaged Children." *Journal of Clinical Psychology,* 1956, *12,* 69–72.

Galton, F. *Hereditary Genius: An Inquiry into Its Laws and Consequences.* London: Macmillan, 1869.

Galton, F. *Inquiries into Human Faculty and Its Development.* London: Macmillan, 1883.

Garber, J. and Seligman, M. E. P. *Human Helplessness: Theory and Applications.* New York: Academic Press, 1980.

Garcia, J. and Koelling, R. "Relation of Cue to Consequence in Avoidance Learning," *Psychonomic Science,* 1966, *4,* 123–124.

Gardner, H. *Frames of Mind: The Theory of Multiple Intelligences.* New York: Basic Books, 1983.

Gardner, H. *Multiple Intelligences: The Theory in Practice.* New York: Basic books, 1993.

Gardner, H. and Hatch, T. "Multiple Intelligences Go to School: Educational Implications of the Theory of Multiple Intelligences." *Educational Researcher,* 1989, *18,* (8), 4–10.

Gardner, H., Krechevsky, M., Sternberg, R. J, and Okagaki, L. in K. McGilly (Ed.). *Classroom Lessons: Integrating Cognitive Theory and Classroom Practice.* Cambridge, MA: MIT Press, 1996, pp. 105–127.

Gardner, M. *Relativity for the Million,* New York: Macmillan, 1962.

Gardner, M. *Aha! Insight Box* (Filmstrip/Cassette Kit). New York: W. F. Freeman, 1978.

Gardner, R. A. and Gardner, B. T. "Teaching Sign Language to a Chimpanzee," *Science,* 1969, *165,* 664–672.

Garner, R. & Alexander, P. A. "Metacognition: Answered and Unanswered Questions." *Educational Psychologist,* 1989, *24,* (2), 143–158.

Gebhart, R. H. (Ed.) *A Standard Guide to Cat Breeds,* New York: McGraw-Hill, 1979.

Gentile, J. R. "In Search of Research: Four Children's Tests." *Journal of School Psychology,* 1966, *5*(1), 1–13.

Gentile, J. R. "The First Generation of Computer-Assisted Instructional Systems: An Evaluative Review", *AV Communication Review,* 1967, *15* (1), 23–53.

Gentile, J. R. "Pigeons, Pecking Orders and Public Education," *The Worm-Runner's Digest,* 1972, *14,* 105–108.

Gentile, J. R. "Universal Primary Education for Pigeons", *Nigerian Journal of Education,* 1976, *1,* 28–33.

Gentile, J. R. "Rapanoia: A New Psychiatric Syndrome," *The Worm-Runner's Digest*, 1974, *16.*, 140–142; Also recorded on the double-album set *Randy and Ron*, Clarence, NY: Mark Records, 1977.

Gentile, J. R. "Help Me Find the Rest I Need," a song on the double-album set *Randy and Ron*, Clarence, NY: Mark Records, 1977.

Gentile, J. R. "Education and Other Social Diseases: Rapanoia Revisited," *Newsletter for Educational Psychologists*, 1981, *5*(1), 11.

Gentile, J. R. "Significance of Single-Subject Studies (and Repeated-Measures Designs)". *Educational Psychologist*, 1982, *17*, 54–60.

Gentile, J. R. "Education and Other Social Diseases: The Miracle Method." *Newsletter for Educational Psychologists*, 1983, *6*(2), 12.

Gentile, J. R. "Recent Retention Research: What Educators Should Know". *The High School Journal*, 1987, *70* (2), 77–86.

Gentile, J. R. *Instructional Improvement: A Summary and Analysis of Madeline Hunter's Essential Elements of Instruction and Supervision* (2nd ed.). Oxford, OH: National Staff Development Council, 1993.

Gentile, J. R. (1996). "Setbacks in 'The Advancement of Learning'?" *Educational Researcher*, 1996, *25*, (7), 37–39..

Gentile, J. R., Frazier, T. W. and Morris, M. C. *Instructional Applications of Behavior Principles*, Monterey, CA: Brooks/Cole, 1973.

Gentile, J. R. and Monaco, N. M. "Learned Helplessness in Mathematics: What Educators Should Know," *Journal of Mathematical Behavior*, 1986, *5*, 159–178.

Gentile, J. R. and Monaco, N. M. "A Learned Helplessness Analysis of Perceived Failure in Mathematics," *Focus on Learning Problems in Mathematics*, 1988, *10*, 15–28.

Gentile, J. R., Monaco, N., Iheozor-Ejiofor, I. E., Ndu, A. N. and Ogbonaya, P. K. "Retention By 'Fast' and 'Slow' Learners," *Intelligence*, 1982, *6*, 125–138.

Gentile, J. R. and Murnyack, N. C. "How Shall Students Be Graded in Discipline-based Art Education?" *Art Education*, 1989.

Gentile, J. R. and Stevens-Haslinger, C. "A Comprehensive Grading Scheme," *Nursing Outlook*, 1983, *31*(No. 1), 49–54.

Gentile, J. R., Voelkl, K. E., Mt. Pleasant, J. and Monaco, N. M. "Recall After Relearning By Fast and Slow Learners." *Journal of Experimental Education*, 1995, *63*, 185–197.

Gentile, J. R. and Wainwright, L. C. "The Case for Criterion-Referenced Grading in College-Level Courses for Students with Disabilities." *Research & Teaching in Developmental Education*, 1994, *11* (1), 63–74.

Gibboney, R. A. "A Critique of Madeline Hunter's Teaching Model from Dewey's Perspective." *Educational Leadership*, 1987, *44* (Feb.), 46–50. (a)

Gibboney, R. A. "The Vagaries of Turtle Research: Gibboney Replies." *Educational Leadership*, 1987, *44* (Feb.), 54. (b)

Gibson, E. J. *Principles of Perceptual Learning and Development*, New York: Appleton-Century-Crofts, 1967.

Gibson, E. J. "Perceptual Learning in Educational Situations," in R. M. Gagné and W. J. Gephart (Eds.) *Learning Research and School Subjects*, Itasca, IL: F. E. Peacock, 1968, pp. 61–86.

Gilligan, C. *In a Different Voice.* Cambridge, MA: Harvard University Press, 1982.

Ginott, H. *Teacher and Child*, New York: Macmillan, 1972.

Ginsburg, H. P. and Opper, S. *Piaget's Theory of Intellectual Development.* Englewood Cliffs, NJ: Prentice-Hall, 1988.

Glaser, R. "Psychology and Instructional Technology." In R. Glaser (Ed.), *Training Research and Education*. Pittsburgh: U. of Pittsburgh Press, 1962, pp. 1–30.

Glaser, R. "Instructional Technology and the Measurement of Learning Outcomes: Some Questions". *American Psychologist*, 1963, *18*, 519–521.

Glaser, R. *Adaptive Education: Individual Diversity and Learning.* New York: Holt, Rinehart, and Winston, 1977.

Glaser, R. "Education and Thinking: The Role of Knowledge," *American Psychologist*, 1984, 39, 93–104.

Glaser, R. and Bassock, M. "Learning Theory and the Study of Instruction." *Annual Review of Psychology*, 1989, 40, 631–666.

Glaser, R. and Nitko, A. J. "Measurement in Learning and Instruction." In Thorndike, R. L. (Ed.), *Educational Measurement*. Washington, D.C.: American Council on Education, 1971 (2nd Ed.), pp. 625–670.

Glasser, W. *Reality Therapy*. New York: Harper and Row, 1965.

Glasser, W. *Schools Without Failure*, New York: Harper and Row, 1968.

Glasser, W. "10 Steps to Good Discipline," *Today's Education*, 1977, 66(4), 61–63.

Glasser, W. *Control Theory in the Classroom*. New York: Harper and Row, 1986.

Glasser, W. *The Quality School: Managing Students Without Coercion*. New York: Harper Perennial, 1992.

Glucksberg, S. "The Influence of Strength of Drive on Functional Fixedness and Perceptual Recognition," *Journal of Experimental Psychology*, 1962, 63, 36–41.

Glucksberg, S. "Problem-Solving: Response Competition and the Influence of Drive," *Psychological Reports*, 1964, 15, 939–942.

Gnagey, W. J. *The Psychology of Discipline in the Classroom*, Toronto: Macmillan, 1968.

Goddard, H. H. *Human Efficiency and Levels of Intelligence*, Princeton, NJ: Princeton University Press, 1920.

Good, T. "Research on Classroom Teaching." In L. S. Shulman and G. Sykes (Eds.), *Handbook on Teaching and Policy*. New York: Longman, 1983, pp. 42–80.

Good, T. L. "Teacher Expectations," In D. C. Berliner and B. V. Rosenshine (Eds.), *Talks to Teachers. A Festschrift for N. L. Gage*. New York: Random House, 1987, pp. 159–200.

Good, T. L. "Two Decades of Research on Teacher Expectations: Findings and Future Direction." *Journal of Teacher Education*, 1987, 38 (4), 32–47.

Good, T. L. and Brophy, J. E. *Looking in Classrooms*, New York: Harper and Row, 1978.

Good, T. L. and Brophy, J. E. *Educational Psychology: A Realistic Approach* (4th). New York: Longman, 1990.

Goodlad, J. I. *A Place Called School*. New York: McGraw-Hill, 1983. (a)

Goodlad, J. I. "The School as Workplace". In G. A. Griffin (Ed.) *Staff Development: Eighty-Second Yearbook of the National Society for the Study of Education, Part II*. Chicago: University of Chicago Press, 1983, pp. 36–61. (b)

Gordon, T. *T.E.T.: Teacher Effectiveness Training*, New York: David McKay, 1974.

Gordon, W. J. J. *Synectics*, New York: Harper and Row, 1961.

Gordon, W. J. J. *The Metaphorical Way of Learning and Knowing*, Cambridge, MA: Synectics Education Systems, 1970.

Gormezano, I. and Moore, J. W. "Classical Conditioning," in M. H. Marx (Ed.) *Learning: Processes*, London: Macmillan, 1969, pp. 119–203.

Gould, S. J. *The Mismeasurement of Man*, New York: Norton, 1981.

Gray, J. A. and Wedderburn, A. A. I. "Grouping Strategies with Simultaneous Stimuli," *Quarterly Journal of Experimental Psychology*, 1960, 12, 180 184.

Graziano, A. M., De Giovanni, I. S. and Garcia, K. A. "Behavioral Treatment of Children's Fears: A Review," *Psychological Bulletin*, 1979, 86, 804–830.

Green, J. A. *Teacher-Made Tests* (2nd Ed.). New York: Harper and Row, 1975.

Greeno, J. *Situativity of Learning: Prospectus for a synthesis of theory and practice* (Cassette Recording No. 94-83). Washington, DC: American Psychological Association, 1994.

Gregory, S. C., Jr. and Bunch, M. E. "The Relative Retentive Abilities of Fast and Slow Learners," *Journal of General Psychology*, 1959, 60, 173–181.

Gronlund, N. E. *Measurement and Evaluation in Teaching* (5th Ed.). New York: Macmillan, 1985.

Gronlund, N. E. *How to Make Achievement Tests and Assessments* (5th ed.) Boston: Allyn & Bacon, 1993.

Gross, A. M. and Drabman, R. S. "Teaching Self-Recording, Self-Evaluation, and Self-Reward to Nonclinic Children and Adolescents," in P. Karoly and F. H. Kanfer (Eds.) *Self-Management and Behavior Change: From Theory to Practice,* New York: Pergamon, 1982, pp. 285–314.

Gruber, H. E. "Giftedness and Moral Responsibility: Creative Thinking and Human Survival," in F. D. Horowitz and M. O'Brien (Eds.), *The Gifted and Talented: Developmental Perspectives,* Washington, D.C.: American Psychological Association, 1985, pp. 301–330.

Guilford, J. P. "Creativity," *American Psychologist,* 1950, 5, 444–454.

Guilford, J. P. "The Structure of Intellect." *Psychological Bulletin,* 1956, 53, 267–293.

Guilford, J. P. "Three Faces of Intellect." *American Psychologist,* 1959, 14, 469–479.

Guilford, J. P. *The Nature of Human Intelligence,* New York: McGraw-Hill, 1967.

Guskey, T. R. "Staff Development and the Process of Teacher Change." *Educational Researcher,* 1986, 15(5), 5–12.

Guskey, T. R. and Gates, S. L. "Synthesis of Research on the Effects of Mastery Learning in Elementary and Secondary Classrooms." *Educational Leadership,* 1986, 33 (8), 73–80.

Guskey, T. R. and Pigott, T. D. "Research on Group-Based Mastery Learning Programs: A Meta-Analysis." *Journal of Educational Research,* 1988, 81, 197–216.

Guthrie, E. R. *The Psychology of Learning,* New York: Harper, 1935.

Guttman, N. and Kalish, H. I. "Discriminability and Stimulus Generalization," *Journal of Experimental Psychology,* 1956, 51, 79–88.

Haladyna, T. M. and Roid, G. "The Role of Instructional Sensitivity in the Empirical Review of Criterion-Referenced Test Items". *Journal of Educational Measurement,* 1981, 18, 39–53.

Haley, J. *Uncommon Therapy. The Psychiatric Technique of Milton H. Erickson, M.D.,* New York: W. W. Norton, 1973.

Hall, R. V., & Hall, M. C. *How To Use Planned Ignoring (Extinction).* Lawrence, KS: H & H Enterprises, 1980. (a)

Hall, R. V. and Hall M. C. *How to Use Time Out,* Lawrence, KS: H & H Enterprises, 1980. (b)

Hall, R. V. and Hall, M. C. *How to Negotiate a Behavioral Contract.* Lawrence, KS: H & H Enterprises, 1982.

Hall, R. V., Lund, D., and Jackson, D. "The Effects of Teacher Attention on Study Behavior," *Journal of Applied Behavior Analysis,* 1968, 1, 1–12.

Halpern, A. R. and Bower, G. H. "Musical Expertise and Melodic Structure in Memory for Musical Notation," *American Journal of Psychology,* 1982, 95, 31–50.

Hambleton, R. K., Swaminathan, H., Algina, J. and Coulson, D. B. "Criterion-Referenced Testing and Measurement: A Review of Technical Issues and Developments". *Review of Educational Research,* 1978, 48, 1–47.

Haney, C. and Zimbardo, P. G. "The Socialization into Criminality: On Becoming a Prisoner and a Guard," In J. L. Tapp and F. L. Levine (Eds.) *Law, Justice and the Individual in Society: Psychological and Legal Issues,* New York: Holt, Rinehart & Winston, 1977, pp. 198–223.

Harlow, H. "The Formation of Learning Sets". *Psychological Review,* 1949, 56, 51–65.

Harlow, H. F. "The Development of Learning in the Rhesus Monkey". *American Scientist,* 1959, 47, 459–479.

Harter, S. "Discrimination Learning Set in Children as a Function of IQ and MA," *Journal of Experimental Child Psychology,* 1965, 2, 31–43.

Harter, S. "A Developmental Perspective on Some Parameters of Self-Regulation in Children." In P. Karoly and F. H. Kanfer (Eds.) *Self-Management and Behavior Change: From Theory to Practice,* New York: Pergamon, 1982, pp. 165–204.

Hasher, L. and Griffin, M. "Reconstructive and Reproductive Processes in Memory," *Journal of Experimental Psychology: Human Learning and Memory*, 1978, *4*, 318–330.

Hasher, L. and Zacks, R. T. "Automatic and Effortful Processes in Memory," *Journal of Experimental Psychology: General*, 1979, *108*, 356–388.

Hayes-Roth, B. "Evaluation of Cognitive Structure and Processes," *Psychological Review*, 1977, *84*, 260–278.

Haywood, H. C., Brooks, P. & Burns, S. "Stimulating Cognitive Development at Developmental Level: A Tested Non-remedial Preschool Curriculum for Preschoolers and Older Retarded Children." In M. Schwebel & C. A. Maher (Eds.). *Facilitating Cognitive Development: International Perspectives, Programs, and Practices.* New York: Haworth, 1986, pp. 127–147.

Heider, F. *The Psychology of Interpersonal Relations,* New York: Wiley, 1958.

Henderson, N. D. "Human Behavior Genetics," in M. R. Rosenzweig and L. W. Porter (Eds.) *Annual Review of Psychology,* 1982, *33*, 403–440.

Hendrickson, G. and Schroeder, W. H. "Transfer of Training in Learning to Hit a Submerged Target," *Journal of Educational Psychology,* 1941, *32*, 205–213.

Herrnstein, R. and Murray, C. *The Bell Curve.* New York: The Free Press, 1994.

Hilgard, E.R. and Bower, G.H. *Theories of Learning* (3rd and 4th Ed.). New York: Appleton-Century-Crofts, 1966, 1975.

Hiroto, D. S. "Locus of Control and Learned Helplessness," *Journal of Experimental Psychology,* 1974, *102*, 187–193.

Hively, W. "Introduction to Domain-Referenced Testing". In W. Hively (Ed.) *Domain-Referenced Testing,* Englewood Cliffs, NJ: Educational Technology Publications, 1974, pp. 5–15. (a)

Hoffman, B. *The Tyranny of Testing*, New York: Crowell-Collier, 1962.

Hoffman, K. *Graduate Students' Experiences with Initial Exposure to Mastery Learning: A Case Study Approach.* State University of New York at Buffalo: unpublished Ed.M. Project, 1994.

Holt, J. *How Children Fail.* New York: Dell, 1964.

Holt, J. "Marking and Grading". In M. D. Gall and B. A. Ward (Eds.), *Critical Issues in Educational Psychology.* Boston: Little, Brown, 1974, pp. 571–579. (Adapted from *What Do I Do Monday?*, New York: Dutton, 1970).

Hosie, T. W., Gentile, J. R. and Carroll, J. D. "Pupil Preferences and the Premack Principle," *American Educational Research Journal,* 1974, *11*, 241–247.

Hovland, C. I. "The Generalization of Conditioned Responses: I. The Sensory Generalization of Conditioned Responses with Varying Frequencies of Tone," *Journal of General Psychology,* 1937, *17*, 125–148.

Hovland, C. I. "Human Learning and Retention," in S. S. Stevens (Ed.) *Handbook of Experimental Psychology,* New York: Wiley, 1951, pp. 613–689.

Huesmann, L. R. (Ed.) "Special Issue: Learned Helplessness as a Model of Depression," *Journal of Abnormal Psychology,* 1978, *87* (Whole No. 1), 1–198.

Hughes, J. "Acquisition of a Nonvocal 'Language' by Aphasic Children." *Cognition,* 1975, *3*, 41–55.

Hulse, S. H. "Amount of Percentage of Reinforcement and Duration of Goal Confinement in Conditioning and Extinction," *Journal of Experimental Psychology,* 1958, *56*, 48–57.

Hulse, S. H., Egeth, H., and Deese, J. *The Psychology of Learning,* New York: McGraw-Hill, 1980.

Hunt, E., Lunneborg, C., & Lewis, J. "What Does It Mean To Be High Verbal?" *Cognitive Psychology,* 1975, *7*, 194–227.

Hunt, J. McV. *Intelligence and Experience.* New York: Ronald, 1961.

Hunter, I. M. L. "The Role of Memory in Expert Mental Calculations," in M. M. Gruneberg, P. E. Morris, and R. N. Sykes (Eds.) *Practical Aspects of Memory*, London: Academic Press, 1978, pp. 339–345.

Hunter, M. "When the Teacher Diagnoses Learning." *Educational Leadership*, 1966, 23(7), 545–549.

Hunter, M. *Motivation Theory for Teachers*. El Segundo, CA: TIP Publications, 1967a.

Hunter, M. *Reinforcement Theory for Teachers*. El Segundo, CA: TIP Publications, 1967b.

Hunter, M. *Retention Theory for Teachers*. El Segundo, CA: TIP Publications, 1967c.

Hunter, M. *Teacher More—Faster*. El Segundo, CA: TIP Publications, 1967d.

Hunter, M. "You—As a Diagnostician." *Instructor*, 1967, 76(6), pp. 31, 126. (e)

Hunter, M. *Teacher for Transfer*. El Segundo, CA: TIP Publications, 1971. (a)

Hunter, M. "The Teaching Process." In D. W. Allen and E. Seifman (Eds.) *The Teacher's Handbook*, Glenview, IL: Scott, Foresman, 1971, pp. 146–157. (b)

Hunter, M. "The Learning Process." In D. W. Allen and E. Seifman (Eds.) *The Teacher's Handbook*, Glenview, IL: Scott, Foresman, 1971, pp. 158–166.

Hunter, M. "Teaching Is Decision Making." *Educational Leadership*, 1979, 37(1); 62 64, 67. (a)

Hunter, M. "Diagnostic Teaching." *The Elementary School Journal*, 1979, 80, 41–46. (b)

Hunter, M. *Mastery Teaching*. El Segundo, CA: TIP Publications, 1982.

Hunter, M. "Comments on the Napa County, California, Follow-Through Project," *Elementary School Journal*, 1986, 87, 173–179.

Hunter, M. *Discipline That Develops Self-Discipline*. El Segundo, CA: TIP Publications, 1990.

Hunter, M. *Enhancing Teaching*. New York: Macmillan, 1994.

Hunter, M. and Brown, M. "Individualization of Foreign Language Learning." In J. D. Arendt, D. L. Lange, P. J. Meyers (Eds.) *Foreign Language Learning, Today and Tomorrow,* New York: Pergamon, 1979, pp. 41–65.

Huston-Stein, A. "Televised Aggression and Prosocial Behavior," in H. L. Pick, Jr., H. W. Liebowitz, J. E. Singer, A. Steinschneider, and H. W. Stevenson (Eds.) *Psychology From Research To Practice*, New York: Plenum, 1978, pp. 75–94.

Huyghe, P. "Voices, Glances, Flashbacks: Our First Memories." *Psychology Today,* 1985, (19, Sept.), 48–52.

Hyman, J. S. and Cohen, S. A. "Learning for Mastery: Ten Conclusions After 15 Years and 3000 Schools." *Educational Leadership*, 1979, 37(Nov.), 104–109.

Isaksen, S. (Ed.). *Frontiers of Creativity Research*. Buffalo, NY: Bearly Limited, 1987.

Jackson, P. W. *Life in Classrooms,* New York: Holt, Rinehart and Winston, 1968.

Jacobsen, E. *Progressive Relaxation*, Chicago: University of Chicago Press, 1938.

James, W. *Talks to Teachers*, New York: W. W. Norton, 1958 (first published, 1904).

James, W. *The Principles of Psychology*, Vol 1, Cambridge, MA: Harvard University Press, 1981 (first published 1890).

Jenkins, H. M. and Harrison, R. H. "Effect of Discrimination Training on Auditory Generalizations," *Journal of Experimental Psychology*, 1960, 59, 246–253.

Jensen, A. R. "The Culturally Disadvantaged: Psychological and Educational Aspects." *Educational Research*, 1967, 10, 4–20.

Jensen, A. R. "How Much Can We Boost IQ and Scholastic Achievement?" *Harvard Educational Review*, 1969, 39, 1–123. Reprinted in A. R. Jensen (Ed.) *Genetics and Education*. London: Methuen, 1972, pp. 69–203. (a)

Jensen, A. R. *Bias in Mental Testing*. New York: Free Press, 1980.

Jensen, A. R. "The Chronometry of Intelligence." in R. J. Sternberg (Ed.), *Advances in the Psychology of Human Intelligence, Vol. I.* Hillsdale, NJ: Erlbaum, 1982, 255–310.

Jensen, A. R. and Rohwer, W. D., Jr., "The Effect of Verbal Mediation on the Learning and Retention of Paired-Associates By Retarded Adults," *American Journal of Mental Deficiency*, 1963, *68*, 80–84. (a)

Jensen, A. R. and Rohwer, W. D., Jr., "Verbal Mediation in Paired-Associate and Serial Learning," *Journal of Verbal Learning and Verbal Behavior*, 1963, *1*, 346–352. (b)

Jenson, W. R. "Behavior Modification in Secondary School: A Review," *Journal of Research and Development in Education*, 1978, *11*(4), 53–63.

Johnson, D. W. *The Social Psychology of Education*, New York: Holt, Rinehart & Winston, 1970.

Johnson, D. W. and Johnson, R. "Conflict in the Classroom: Controversy and Learning." *Review of Educational Research*, 1979, *49*, 51–61.

Johnson, D. W. and Johnson, R. T. *Learning Together and Alone: Cooperation, Competition, and Individualization*, Englewood Cliffs, NJ: Prentice-Hall, 1975.

Johnson, D. W. and Johnson, R. T. "Cooperative Learning and Adaptive Education" in M. C. Wang and H. J. Walberg (Eds.) *Adapting Instruction To Individual Differences*. Berkeley, CA: McCutchan, 1985, pp. 105–134.

Johnson, D. W. and Johnson, R. T. "What Goes On Inside the Groups?" *American Educator*, 1986, *10*(2), p. 12.

Johnson, D. W. and Johnson, R. *Cooperation and Competition: Theory and Research*. Edina, MN: Interaction Book Company, 1989.

Johnson, D. W. and Johnson, R. *Teaching Students to Be Peacemakers*. Edina, MN: Interaction Book Company, 1991.

Johnson, D. W. and Johnson, R. T. *Reducing School Violence Through Conflict Resolution*. Alexandria, VA: Association for Supervision and Curriculum Development, 1995.

Johnson, D. W., Johnson, R. T., Holubec, E. J. and Roy, P. *Circles of Learning: Cooperation in the Classroom*, Alexandria, VA: Association for Supervision and Curriculum Development, 1984.

Johnson, D. W., Johnson, R., and Holubec, E. *Cooperation in the Classroom*, 6th ed. Edina, MN: Interaction Book Company, 1993.

Johnson, D. W., Johnson, R. T. and Maruyama, G. "Interdependence and Interpersonal Attraction Among Heterogeneous and Homogeneous Individuals: A Theoretical Formulation and a Meta-Analysis of the Research", *Review of Educational Research*, 1983, *53*, 5–54.

Johnson, J. & Immerwahr, J. "First Things First: What Americans Expect From the Public Schools." *American Educator*, 1994/95, *18* (4), 4–6, 8–13, 44–45.

Johnson, D. W., Maruyama, G., Johnson, R., Nelson, D., and Skon, L. "Effects of Cooperative, Competitive and Individualistic Goal Structures on Achievement: A Meta-Analysis", *Psychological Bulletin*, 1981, *89*, 47–62.

Johnson-Gentile, K. & Gentile, J. R. "Integrating Music Into the Elementary Classroom Curriculum." *Kappa Delta Pi Record*, 1996, *32* (2), 66–69.

Johnston, J. M. "Punishment of Human Behavior," *American Psychologist*, 1972, *27*, 1033–1054.

Jones, H. E. "The Retention of Conditioned Emotional Reactions in Infancy," *Journal of Genetic Psychology*, 1930, *37*, 485–498.

Jones, H. E. "The Conditioning of Overt Emotional Responses," *Journal of Educational Psychology*, 1931, *22*, 127–130.

Jones, H. E. and Jones, M. C. "Genetic Studies of Emotions," *Psychological Bulletin*, 1930, *27*, 40–64.

Jones, M. C. "The Elimination of Children's Fears," *Journal of Experimental Psychology*, 1924, *7*, 382–390.

Joyce, B. and Showers, B. "Improving Inservice Training: The Messages of Research," *Educational Leadership*, 1980, *37*(5), 379–382, 384–385.

Joyce, B. R. and Showers, B. "The Coaching of Teaching." *Educational Leadership*, 1982, *40*, 4–10.

Joyce, B. and Weil, M. *Models of Teaching* (Second Edition). Englewood Cliffs, NJ: Prentice-Hall, 1980.

Joyce, B., Weil, M. and Showers, B. *Models of Teaching* (4th ed.). Englewood Cliffs, NJ: Prentice Hall, 1992.

Joyce, B. R., Hersh, R. H. and McKibbin, M. *The Structure of School Improvement.* New York: Longman, 1983.

Judd, C. H. "The Relation of Special Training to General Intelligence," *Educational Review,* 1908, *36,* 28–42.

Jung, J. "Transfer of Training as a Function of Degree of First-List Learning," *Journal of Verbal Learning and Verbal Behavior,* 1962, *1,* 197–199.

Jussim, L. "Teacher Expectations: Self-fulfilling in Prophecies, Perceptual Biases, and Accuracy." *Journal of Personality and Social Psychology,* 1989, *57* (2), 469–480.

Kagan, S. "Co-op Co-op: A Flexible Cooperative Learning Technique" in R. Slavin, S. Sharan, S. Kagan, R. Hertz-Lazarowitz, C. Webb and R. Schmuck (Eds.) *Learning To Cooperate, Cooperating To Learn,* New York: Plenum, 1985, pp. 437–462.

Kalish, H. I. "Stimulus Generalization," in M. H. Marx (Ed.) *Learning: Processes,* London: Macmillan, 1969, pp. 205–297.

Kamin, L. F. *The Science and Politics of IQ.* New York: Halsted, 1974.

Kane, M. T. "The Role of Reliability in Criterion-Referenced Tests". *Journal of Educational Measurement,* 1986, *23,* 221–224.

Kanfer, F. H. "Self-Regulation: Research, Issues and Speculations," in C. Neuringer and J. L. Michael (Eds.) *Behavior Modification in Clinical Psychology,* New York: Appleton, 1970, pp. 178–220.

Karier, C. J. "Testing for Order and Control in the Corporate Liberal State," *Educational Theory,* 1972, *22,* 154–180.

Kaufman, B. *Up the Down Staircase,* New York: Avon Books, 1964.

Kazdin, A. E. "Methodological and Assessment Considerations in Evaluating Reinforcement Programs in Applied Settings," *Journal of Applied Behavior Analysis,* Monograph No. 3, 1973, *6,* 1–23.

Kazdin, A. E. "The Token Economy: A Decade Later," *Journal of Applied Behavior Analysis,* 1982, *15,* 431–445.

Kazdin, A. E. and Bootzin, R. R. "The Token Economy: An Evaluative Review." *Journal of Applied Behavior Analysis,* 1972, *5*(Whole Monograph #1), 1–30.

Kazdin, A. E. and Mascitelli, S. "The Opportunity to Earn Oneself Off a Token System as a Reinforcer for Attentive Behavior." *Behavior Therapy,* 1980, *11,* 68–78.

Kearney, C. P., Kean, M. H., Roeber, E. D., Stevens, B. L., Baron, J. B., Fremer, J. and Daniel, M. *Assessing Higher Order Thinking Skills,* ERIC/TME Report 90, Princeton, NJ: Educational Testing Service, 1985.

Keeney, T. J., Cannizzo, S. R. and Flavell, J. H. "Spontaneous and Induced Verbal Rehearsal in a Recall Task," *Child Development,* 1967, *38,* 953–966.

Keller, F. S. "Good-bye Teacher . . ." *Journal of Applied Behavior Analysis,* 1968, *1,* 79–89.

Keller, F. S. and Sherman, J. G. *The Keller Plan Handbook.* Menlo Park, CA: W. A. Benjamin, Inc., 1974.

Kelley, M. L. and Stokes, T. F. "Contingency Contracting with Disadvantaged Youths: Improving Classroom Performance," *Journal of Applied Behavior Analysis,* 1982, *15,* 447–454.

Kelly, E. W. "School Phobia: A Review of Theory and Treatment," *Psychology in the Schools,* 1973, *10,* 33–42.

Keppel, G. "Facilitation in Short- and Long-Term Retention of Paired Associates Following Distributed Practice in Learning." *Journal of Verbal Learning and Verbal Behavior,* 1964, *3,* 91–111.

Kibler, R. J., Barker, L. L., & Miles, D. T. *Behavioral Objectives and Instruction.* Boston: Allyn & Bacon, 1970.

Kimble, G. A. *Hilgard and Marquis' Conditioning and Learning.* New York: Appleton-Century-Crofts, 1961.

Kintsch, W. *The Representation of Meaning in Memory,* New York: Wiley, 1974.

Kirschenbaum, H., Simon, S. B., and Napier, R. W. WAD-JA-GET? *The Grading Game in American Education.* New York: Hart, 1971.

Kohlberg, L. "The Development of Children's Orientations Toward Moral Order: 1. Sequence in the Development of Moral Thought." *Vita Humana.* 1963, *6,* 11–33.

Köhler, W. *The Mentality of Apes,* (translated by E. Winter), New York: Harcourt-Brace, 1925.

Kohn, A. *Punished By Rewards.* Boston: Houghton Mifflin, 1993.

Kohn, A. "By All Available Means: Cameron and Pierce's Defense of Extrinsic Motivators." *Review of Educational Research, 1996, 66,* 1–4.

Kopfer, P. M. "Metacognitive and Attributional Processes and Memory Task Performance in Individual's with Mental Retardation." *Mental Retardation,* in press.

Kounin, J. S. and Gump, P. V. "The Ripple Effect on Discipline," *Elementary School Journal,* 1958, *59,* 158–162.

Kozol, J. *Death at an Early Age,* Boston: Houghton-Mifflin, 1967.

Krasner, L. "Behavior Therapy." in P. H. Mussen and M. R. Rosenzweig (Eds.), *Annual Review of Psychology,* 1971, *22,* 483–532.

Krech, D., Crutchfield, R. S. and Ballachey, E. L. *Individual in Society,* New York: McGraw-Hill, 1962.

Kreidler, W. *Creative Conflict Resolution,* Glenwood, IL: Scott, Foresman, 1984.

Kreidler, W. *Elementary Perspectives: Teaching Concepts of Peace and Conflict.* Cambridge, MA: Educators for Social Responsibility, 1990.

Kreschevsky, I. "Hypotheses' in Rats," *Psychological Review,* 1932, *38,* 516–532.

Krueger, W. C. F. "The Effect of Overlearning on Retention," *Journal of Experimental Psychology,* 1929, *12,* 71–78.

Krumboltz, J. D. and Krumboltz, H. B. *Changing Children's Behavior,* Englewood Cliffs, NJ: Prentice-Hall, 1972.

Kulik, J. A. and Kulik, C. C. *Developmental Instruction: An Analysis of the Research.* (Report No. 1). National Center for Developmental Education and the Exxon Education Foundation, 1991.

Kulik, C. C., Kulik, J. A. and Bangert-Drowns, R. L. "Effectiveness of Mastery Learning Programs: A Meta-Analysis." Review of Educational Research, 1990, *60* (2), 265–299.

Kulik, J., Kulik, C. and Cohen, P. "A Meta-analysis of Outcome Studies of Keller's Personalized System of Instruction", *American Psychologist,* 1979, *34,* 307–318.

Kuypers, D. S., Becker, W. C. and O'Leary, K. D. "How to Make a Token System Fail," *Exceptional Education,* 1968, *35,* 101–109.

LaBerge, D. and Samuels, S. J. "Toward a Theory of Automatic Information Processing in Reading," *Cognitive Psychology,* 174, *6,* 293–323.

Lalley, J. P. "Feedback and Computer Assisted Learning" SUNY at Buffalo: unpublished manuscript, 1995.

Lambdin, D. W. and Walker, V. L. "Planning for Classroom Portfolio Assessment." *Arithmetic Teacher,* 1994, *41* (6), 318-324.

Larkin, J.H. "Enriching Formal Knowledge: A Model for Learning to Solve Textbook Problems." In J.R. Anderson (Ed.), *Cognition Skills and Their Acquisition.* Hillsdale, NJ: Erlbaum, 1981.

Lazarus, R. S. "Thoughts on the Relations Between Emotion and Cognition," *American Psychologist,* 1982, *37,* 1019–1024.

Lazarus, R. S. "On the Primacy of Cognition," *American Psychologist,* 1984, *39,* 124–129.

Leeper, R. W. "Cognitive Learning Theory," in M. H. Marx (Ed.) *Learning: Theories,* New York: Macmillan, 1970, 235–331.

Leinhardt, G. "Expertise in Mathematics Teaching." *Educational Leadership,* 1986, 43(7), 28–33.

Leith, G. O., Biran, L. A. and Opollot, J. A. "The Place of Review in Meaningful Verbal Learning." *Canadian Journal of the Behavioural Science,* 1969, 1, 113–118.

Lepper, M. R. and Greene, D. *The Hidden Costs of Reward: New Perspectives on the Psychology of Human Motivation,* Hillsdale, NJ: Lawrence Erlbaum, 1978.

Lepper, M. R., Kearney, M. and Drake, M. "Intrinsic Motivation and Extrinsic Rewards: A Commentary on Cameron and Pierce's Meta-Analysis." *Review of Educational Research,* 1996, 66, 5–32.

Levin, J. R. "The Mnemonic '80s: Keywords in the Classroom," *Educational Psychologist,* 1981, 16, 65–82.

Lewis, C. "Skill in Algebra," in J. R. Anderson (Ed.) *Cognitive Skills and Their Acquisition,* Hillsdale, NJ: Erlbaum, 1981, pp. 85–110.

Lewis, M. "On the Nature of Intelligence: Science or Bias?" In M. Lewis (Ed.) *Origins of Intelligence: Infancy and Early Childhood,* New York: Plenum, 1983, pp. 1–24.

Lewis, R. and St. John, N. "Contribution of Cross-Racial Friendship To Minority Group Achievement in Desegregated Classrooms," *Sociometry,* 1974, 37, 79–91.

Light, L. L. and Carter-Sobell, L. "Effects of Changes Semantic Context on Recognition Memory," *Journal of Verbal Learning and Verbal Behavior,* 1970, 9, 1–11.

Lipman, M. *Harry Stottlemeier's Discovery.* Upper Montclair, NJ: Institute for the Advancement of Philosophy for Children, 1974.

Lipman, M. *Mark.* Upper Montclair, NJ: Institute for the ADvancement of Philosophy for Children, 1980.

Lipman, M. "Some Thoughts on the Foundations of Reflective Education," in J. B. Baron and R. J. Sternberg (Eds.) *Teaching Thinking Skills: Theory and Practice,* New York: Freeman, 1987, pp. 151–161.

Lipman, M. and Sharp, A. M. *Social Inquiry: Instructional Manual to Accompany "Mark".* Upper Montclair, NJ: Institute for the Advancement of Philosophy for Children, 1980.

Lipman, M., Sharp, A. M., and Oscanyan, F. S. *Philosophy in the Classroom,* Philadelphia: Temple University Press, 1980.

Livingston, J. A. and Gentle, J. R. "Mastery Learning and the Decreasing Variability Hypothesis," *Journal of Educational Research,* 1996, (in press).

Logan, F. A. "Micromolar Behavior Theory and Performance Speed in Education," *Harvard Educational Review,* 1963, 33, 178–185.

Logan, F. A. "Experimental Psychology of Animal Learning and Now." *American Psychologist,* 1972, 27, 1055–1062.

Logan, G.D. "Skill and Automaticity: Relations, Implications and Future Directions." *Canadian Journal of Psychology* 1985, 39 (2), 367–386.

Loftus, E. F. "When a Lie Becomes Memory's Truth: Memory Distortion After Exposure to Misinformation." *Current Directions in Psychological Science,* 1992, 4 (1), 121–123.

Loftus, E. F. and Hoffman, H. G. "Misinformation and Memory: The Creation of New Memories." *Journal of Experimental Psychology: General,* 1989, 118, 100–104.

Loftus, E. F. and Ketcham, K. *Witness for the Defense: The Accused, the Eyewitness, and the Expert Who Puts Memory on Trial.* New York: St. Martin's Press, 1991.

Luchins, A. S. "Mechanization in Problem-Solving: The Effect of Einstellung," *Psychological Monographs,* 1942, 54, Whole Number 248.

Lykken, D. T. "Uses and Abuses of the Polygraph." in H. L. Pick, Jr., H. W. Liebowitz, J. E. Singer, A. Steinschneider, and H. W. Stevenson (Eds.), *Psychology from Research to Practice,* New York: Plenum, 1978, pp. 171–191.

Lynn, R. "The Intelligence of the Japanese." *Bulletion of British Psychological Science,* 1977, 30, 69–72.

MacKenzie, C. L., & Marteniuk, R. G. "Motor Skill: Feedback, Knowledge, and Structure Issues." *Canadian Journal of Psychology*, 1985, *39*(2), 313–337.

Madaus, G. F. "The Perils and Promises of New Tests and New Technologies: Dick and Jane and the Great Analytical Engine?" in *The Redesign of Testing for the 21st Century*. Proceedings of the 1985 ETS Invitational Conference. Princeton, NJ: Educational Testing Service, 1986, pp. 87–101.

Madsen, C. H., Becker, W. C. and Thomas, D. R. "Rules, Praise and Ignoring: Elements of Elementary Classroom Control," *Journal of Applied Behavior Analysis*, 1968, *1*, 139–150.

Madsen, C. H., Jr. and Madsen, C. K. *Teaching/Discipline: A Positive Approach for Educational Development*, Boston: Allyn and Bacon, 1981.

Maeroff, G. I. "Assessing Alternative Assessment." *Phi Delta Kappan*, 1991, 72 (Dec.), 273–281.

Mager, R. F. *Preparing Instructional Objectives*. Palo Alto, CA: Fearon Publishers, 1962.

Maltzman, I. "On the Training of Originality," *Psychological Review*, 1960, *67*, 229–242.

Marcia, J. E. "Ego Identity Status: Relationship to Change in Self-Esteem, 'General Maladjustment' and Authoritarianism". *Journal of Personality*, 1967, *35*, 118–133.

Marks, I. M. *Fears and Phobias*, New York: Academic Press, 1969.

Martinez, J. G. R. and Martinez, N. C. "Re-examining Repeated Testing and Teaching Effects in a Remedial Mathematics Course. *British Journal of Educational Psychology*, 1992, *62*, 356–363.

Martuza, V. R. *Applying Norm-Referenced and Criterion-Referenced Measurement in Education*, Boston: Allyn and Bacon, 1977.

Maslow, A. H. *Motivation and Personality*, New York: Harper, 1954. (and 2nd Ed., 1970).

Mazur, J. E. *Learning and Behavior*, Englewood Cliffs, NJ: Prentice-Hall, 1986.

Mazrui, A. A. *The Trial of Christopher Okigbo*, London: Heinemann, 1971.

McGeoch, J. A. "Forgetting and the Law of Disuse," *Psychological Review*, 1932, *39*, 352–370.

McGeoch, J. A., and Irion, A. L. *The Psychology of Human Learning*, New York: Longmans, Green, 1952.

McIntire, R. W. *For Love of Children: Behavioral Psychology for Parents*, Del Mar, CA: CRM Publishers, 1970.

McKibbin, M. and Joyce, B. "Psychological States and Staff Development." *Theory into Practice*, 1980, *19*, 248–256.

McNamara, J. R. "Teacher and Students as Sources for Behavior Modification in the Classroom." *Behavior Therapy*, 1971, *2*, 205–213.

McNemar, Q. *The Revision of the Stanford-Binet Scale*. Boston, MA: Houghton-Mifflin, 1942.

Meadows, A. and Parnes, S. J. "Evaluation of Training in Creative Problem Solving," *Journal of Applied Psychology*, 1959, *43*, 189–194.

Mearig, J. S. "Assessing the Learning Potential of Kindergarden and Primary-Age Children." In C. S. Lidz (Ed.). *Dynamic Assessment*. New York: Guilford, 1987, pp. 237–267.

Meehl, P. E. "On the Circularity of the Law of Effect," *Psychological Bulletin*, 1950, *47*, 52–75.

Meier, S. T. *The Chronic Crisis in Psychological Measurement and Assessment*. San Diego, CA: Academic Press, 1994.

Meier, S. T. and Davis, S. R. *The Elements of Counseling* (3rd Ed.). Pacific Grove, CA: Brooks/Cole, 1996.

Messick, S. "The Interplay of Evidence and Consequences in the Validation of Performance Assessments." *Educational Researcher*, 1994, *23* (2), 13–23.

Milgram, S. "Behavioral Study of Obedience," *Journal of Abnormal and Social Psychology*, 1963, *67*, 371–378.

Miller, G. A. "The Magical Number Seven, Plus or Minus Two: Some Limits on Our Capacity for Processing Information," *Psychological Review*, 1956, *63*, 81–97.

Miller, G. A., Galanter, E. & Pribam, K. H. *Plans and the Structure of Behavior.* New York: Holt, Rinehart & Winston, 1960.

Miller, H. G., Williams, R. G. and Haladyna, T. M. *Beyond Facts: Objective Ways to Measure Thinking.* Englewood Cliffs, NJ: Educational Technology Publications, 1978.

Miller, I. W. and Norman, W. H. "Learned Helplessness in Humans: A Review and Attribution Theory Model," *Psychological Bulletin,* 1979, *86,* 93–118.

Millman, J. "Reporting Student Progress: A Case for a Criterion-Referenced Marking System". *Phi Delta Kappan,* 1970, *52* (Dec.), 226–230.

Millman, J. If at first you don't succeed: Setting passing scores when more than one attempt is permitted. *Educational Researcher.* 1989, *18*(6), 5–9.

Minton, H. L. and Schneider, F. W. *Differential Psychology.* Belmont, CA: Brooks/Cole, 1980.

Moely, B. E., Olson, F., Halwes, T. G. and Flavell, J. H. "Production Deficiency in Young Children's Clustered Recall," *Developmental Psychology,* 1969, *1,* 26–34.

Monaco, N. M. and Gentile, J. R. "Cognitive Developmental Level, Gender and the Development of Learned Helplessness on Mathematical Calculation and Reasoning Tasks," *Contemporary Education Psychology,* 1987, *12,* 62–76.

Moreno, J. L. *Who Shall Survive? Foundations of Sociometry, Group Psychotherapy and Sociodrama,* Beacon, NY: Beacon House, 1953.

Morgan, B., Luke, C., and Herbert J. "Evaluating Clinical Proficiency". *Nursing Outlook,* 1979, *27* (Aug.) 540–544.

Morris, R. J. and Kratochwill, T. R. *Treating Children's Fears and Phobias: A Behavioral Approach,* New York: Pergamon Press, 1983.

Mowrer, O. H. "The Psychologist Looks at Language," *American Psychologist,* 1954, *9,* 660–694.

Mowrer, O. H. *Learning Theory and Behavior,* New York: John Wiley & Sons, 1960.

Mowrer, O. H. and Viek, P. "An Experimental Analogue of Fear from a Sense of Helplessness," *Journal of Abnormal and Social Psychology,* 1948, *43,* 193–200.

Moynihan, D. P. "Defining Deviancy Down." *American Educator,* 1993/94, *17* (4), 10–18.

Murdock, B. B., Jr. "Transfer Designs and Formulas," *Psychological Bulletin,* 1957, *54,* 313–326.

Murdock, B. B., Jr. "The Retention of Individual Items," *Journal of Experimental Psychology,* 1961, *62,* 618–625.

Murphy, G. and Murphy, L. B. *Asian Psychology,* New York: Basic Books, 1968.

Muuss, R. E. *Theories of Adolescence* (4th ed.). New York: Random House, 1982.

National Commission on Excellence in Education (D. P. Gardner, Chair). *A Nation at Risk: The Imperative for Educational Reform,* Washington, D.C.: U.S. Office of Education, 1983.

National Council of Teachers of Mathematics. *Curriculum and Evaluation Standards for School Mathematics.* Reston, VA: NCTM, 1989.

Neimark, E., Slotnick, N. S. and Ulrich, T. "Development of Memorization Strategies," *Developmental Psychology,* 1971, *5,* 427–432.

Neisser, U. *Cognitive Psychology,* New York: Appleton-Century-Crofts, 1967.

Neisser, U. (Ed.) *Memory Observed,* San Francisco: Freeman, 1982.

Neisser, U. "Interpreting Harry Bahrick's Discovery: What Confers Immunity Against Forgetting?" *Journal of Experimental Psychology: General, 1984, 113,* 32–35.

Nelson, D. S. *An Evaluation Study of the Implementation of "The Cognitive Curriculum for Young Children" in a Rural Special Education Preschool Classroom.* State University of New York at Buffalo; unpublished Ed.D. Dissertation, 1993.

Nichols, R. C. "Racial Differences in Intelligence." In S. Modgil and C. Modgil (Eds.) *Arthur Jensen: Consensus and Controversy.* London: Palmer Press, 1986, pp. 213–220.

Nitko, A. J. "Distinguishing the Many Varieties of Criterion-Referenced Tests". *Review of Educational Research*, 1980, *50*, 461–485.

Noble, C. E. "The Analysis of Meaning," *Psychological Review*, 1952, *59*, 421–430.

O'Leary, K. D. and Drabman, R. "Token Reinforcement Programs in the Classroom: A Review," *Psychological Bulletin*, 1971, *75*, 79–398.

O'Leary, K. D. and O'Leary, S. G. (Eds.) *Classroom Management: The Successful Use of Behavior Modification*, New York: Pergamon Press, 1972.

Osborn, A. *Applied Imagination*. New York: Scribner's, 1957.

Osborne, J. G. "Free-time as a Reinforcer in the Management of Classroom Behavior," *Journal of Applied Behavior Analysis*, 1969, *2*, 113–118.

Osgood, C. E. "The Similarity Paradox in Human Learning: A Resolution" *Psychological Review*, 1949, *56*, 132–143.

Paivio, A. *Imagery and Verbal Processes*, New York: Holt, Rinehart & Winston, 1971.

Paivio, A. "Coding Distinctions and Repetition Effects in Memory," in G. H. Bower (Ed.) *The Psychology of Learning and Motivation*. New York: Academic Press, 1975.

Paivio, A., and Begg, I. *Psychology of Language*, Englewood Cliffs, NJ: Prentice-Hall, 1981.

Paivio, A., and Csapo, K. "Picture Superiority in Free Recall: Imagery or Dual Coding?" *Cognitive Psychology*, 1973, *5*, 1976–206.

Paivio, A. and Desrochers, A. "A Dual-Coding Approach to Bilingual Memory," *Canadian Journal of Psychology*, 1980, *34*, 388–399.

Paivio, A., and Lambert, W. E. "Dual-Coding and Bilingual Memory," *Journal of Verbal Learning & Verbal Behavior*, 1981, *20*, 532–539.

Palincsar, A. S. and Brown, A. L. "Reciprocal Teaching of Comprehension-Fostering and Comprehension-Monitoring Activities," *Cognition and Instruction*, 1984, *1*(2), 117–175.

Papert, S. *Mindstorms: Children, Computers, and Powerful Ideas*. New York: Basic Books, 1980.

Papp, K. K. *A Test of Premack's Relational Theory*. State University of New York at Buffalo, unpublished Ph.D. dissertation, 1980.

Parke, R. D., Berkowitz, L., Leyens, J. P., West, S. G. and Sebastian, R. J. "Some Effects of Violent and Nonviolent Movies on the Behavior of Juvenile Delinquents." in L. Berkowitz (Ed.) *Advances in Experimental Social Psychology*, New York: Academic Press, 1977, *10*, pp. 136–172.

Paul, R. W. "Dialogical Thinking: Critical Thought Essential to the Acquisition of Rational Knowledge and Passions," in J. B. Baron and R. J. Sternberg (Eds.) *Teaching Thinking Skills: Theory and Practice*, New York: Freeman, 1987, pp. 127–148.

Pavlov, I. P. *Conditioned Reflexes*, (Trans. G. V. Anrep), London: Oxford, 1927.

Payne, D. A. *Measuring and Evaluating Educational Outcomes*. New York: Merrill, 1992.

Pea, R. *Distributed Intelligence in Learning and Reasoning Processes*. Paper presented at the meeting of the Cognitive Science Society, Montreal, 1989.

Perkins, D. N. and Salomon, G. "Are Cognitive Skills Context Bound?" *Educational Researcher*, 1989, *18* (1), 16–25.

Peters, A. S. *How Does Cooperation Affect Learning? An Observational Study of Group Process Variables*. State University of New York at Buffalo: Ph.D. Dissertation, 1986.

Peterson, C. and Seligman, M. E. P. "Causal Explanations as a Risk Factor for Depression: Theory and Evidence," *Psychological Review*, 1984, *91*, 347–374.

Peterson, E., Maier, S. F. and Seligman, M. E. P. *Learned Helplessness: A Theory for the Age of Personal Control*. New York: Oxford University Press, 1993.

Peterson, L. R. and Peterson, M. J. "Short-Term Retention of Individual Items," *Journal of Experimental Psychology*, 1959, *58*, 193–198.

Piaget, J. *The Child's Conception of Number*. London: Routledge and Kegan Paul, 1964.

Piaget, J. *Science of Education and the Psychology of the Child* (Trans. Coltman, D.). New York: Orion, 1970. (a)

Piaget, J. "Piaget's Theory" (Trans. Gellerier, G., and Langer, J.). In P. H. Mussen (Ed.), *Carmichael's Manual of Child Psychology (3rd ed.)*. New York: Wiley, 1970, pp. 703–732. (b)

Piaget, J. "Piaget Takes a Teacher's Look." *Learning*, 1973 (Oct.), 22–27.

Piaget, J. and Inhelder, B. *Le developpement des quantites chez l'enfant*. Neuchatel: Delachaux et Niestle, 1941.

Piaget, J. and Inhelder, B. *The Psychology of the Child* (Trans. Weaver, H.). New York: Basic Books, 1969.

Popham, W. J. *Criterion-Referenced Measurement: An Introduction*. Englewood Cliffs, NJ: Educational Technology Publications, 1971.

Popham, W. J. "The Case for Criterion-Referenced Measurements." *Educational Researcher*, 1978, 7 (Dec.), 6–10. (a)

Popham, W. J. *Criterion-Referenced Measurement*, Englewood Cliffs, NJ: Prentice-Hall, 1978. (b)

Popham, W. J. and Husek, T. R. "Implications of Criterion-Referenced Measurement". *Journal of Educational Measurement*, 1969, 6, 1–9.

Porter, R. W., Brady, J. V., Conrad, D., Mason, J. W., Galambos, R. and Rioch, D. McK. "Some Experimental Observations on Gastrointestinal Lesions in Behaviorally Conditioned Monkeys," *Psychosomatic Medicine*, 1958, 20, 379–394.

Posner, M.I. and Synder, C. R. R. "Attention and Cognitive Control." In R. L. Solso (Ed.) Information Processing and Cognition: The Loyola Symposium, Hillsdale, NJ: Erlbaum, 1975, pp. 55–85.

Postman, L. "Retention as a Degree of Overlearning," *Science*, 1962, 135, 666–667. (a)

Postman, L. "Transfer of Training as a Function of Experimental Paradigm and Degree of First-List Learning," *Journal of Verbal Learning and Verbal Behavior*, 1962, 1, 109–118. (b)

Premack, D. "Toward Empirical Behavior Laws: 1. Positive Reinforcement," *Psychological Review*, 1959, 66, 219–233.

Premack, D. "Reversibility of the Reinforcement Relation," *Science*, 1962, 136, 255–257.

Premack, D. "Reinforcement Theory." in D. Levin (Ed.) *Nebraska Symposium on Motivation (Vol. 13)*, Lincoln: University of Nebraska Press, 1965.

Premack, D. "Catching Up With Common Sense or Two Sides of a Generalization: Reinforcement and Punishment," in R. Glaser (Ed.) *The Nature of Reinforcement*, New York: Academic Press, 1971, pp. 121–150. (a)

Premack, D. "Language in Chimpanzee?" *Science*, 1971, 172, 808–822. (b)

Premack, D. "Language and Intelligence in Ape and Man," *American Scientist*, 1976, 64, 674–683. (a)

Premack, D. *Intelligence in Ape and Man*, Hillsdale, NJ: Erlbaum, 1976. (b)

Premack, D. and Woodruff, G. "Chimpanzee Problem Solving: A Test for Comprehension," *Science*, 1978, 202, 532–535.

Pressey, S. L. "A Simple Apparatus Which Gives Tests and Scores—and Teaches" in A. A. Lumsdaine and R. Glaser (Eds.) *Teaching Machines and Programmed Learning: A Source Book*. Washington, D.C.: National Educational Association, 1960, pp. 33–41 (reprinted from *School and Society*, 1926).

Pressey, S. L. "A Machine for Automatic Teaching of Drill Material" in A. A. Lumsdaine and R. Glaser (Eds.) *Teaching Machines and Programmed Learning: A Source Book*. Washington, D.C.: National Education Association, 1960, pp. 42–46 (reprinted from *School and Society*, 1927).

Pressey, S. L. "A Third and Fourth Contribution Toward the Coming 'Industrial Revolution' in Education" in A. A. Lumsdaine and R. Glaser (Eds.) *Teaching Machines and Programmed Learning: A Source Book*. Washington, D.C.: National Education Association, 1960, pp. 47–51 (reprinted from *School and Society*, 1932).

Pressley, M., Borkowski, J. G., and O'Sullivan, J. T. "Memory Strategy Instruction is Made of This: Metamemory and Durable Strategy Use," *Educational Psychologist*, 1984, 19, 94–107.

Pressley, M. and Dennis-Rounds, J. "Transfer of a Mnemonic Strategy at Two Age Levels." *Journal of Educational Psychology*, 1980, 72, 575–582.

Pressley, M. and Levin, J. R. (Eds.) *Cognitive Strategy Research: Educational Applications*, New York: Springer-Verlag, 1983. (a)

Pressley, M. and Levin, J. R. (Eds.) *Cognitive Strategy Research: Psychological Foundations*, New York: Springer-Verlag, 1983. (b)

Pressley, M., Levin, J. R. and Delaney, H. D. "The Mnemonic Keyword Method." *Review of Educational Research*, 1982, 52, 66–91.

Pressley, M. and Yokoi, L. "Motion for a New Trial on Transfer." *Educational Researcher*, (1994). 25 (5), 36–38.

Pruitt, D. G. and Rubin, J. Z. *Social Conflict: Escalation, Stalemate, and Settlement.* New York: Random House, 1986.

Pryor, K. "The Porpoise Caper". *Psychology Today*, 1969, 3(7), 47–48, 64.

Quinby, N. "On Testing and Teaching Intelligence: A Conversation with Robert Sternberg". *Educational Leadership*, 1986, 43 (No. 2), 50–53.

Ravitch, D. and Finn, C. E., Jr. *What Do Our 17-Year-Olds Know? A Report on the First National Assessment of History and Literature.* New York: Harper & Row, 1987.

Redfield, D. L., & Rousseau, E. W. "A Meta-Analysis of Experimental Research on Teacher Questioning Behavior." *Review of Educational Research*, 1981, 51, 237–245.

Reese, E. P., *The Analysis of Human Operant Behavior*, Dubuque, Iowa: William C. Brown, 1966.

Renner, K. E. "Delay of Reinforcement: A Historical Review," *Psychological Bulletin*, 1964, 61, 341–361.

Rescorla, R. A. *Pavlovian Second-Order Conditioning: Studies in Associative Learning*, Hillsdale, NJ: Lawrence Erlbaum, 1980.

Rescorla, R. A. and Holland, P. C. "Behavioral Studies of Associative Learning in Animals," in M. R. Rosenzweig and L. W. Porter (Eds.) *Annual Review of Psychology*, 1982, 33, 265–308.

Resnick, D. P. and Resnick, L. B. "Standards, Curriculum, and Performance: A Historical and Comparative Perspective." *Educational Researcher*, 1985, 14(4), 5–20.

Resnick, L. B. "Applying Applied Reinforcement," in R. Glaser (Ed.) *The Nature of Reinforcement*, New York: Academic Press, 1971, pp. 326–333.

Resnick, L. B. (Ed.) "Hierarchies in Children's Learning: A Symposium." *Instructional Science*, 1973, 2, 311–362.

Resnick, L. B., Wang, M. C., & Kaplan, J. "Task Analysis in Curriculum Design: A Hierarchically Sequenced Introductory Mathematics Curriculum." *Journal of Applied Behavior Analysis*, 1973, 6, 679–710.

Reynolds, C. and Gentile, J. R. "Measuring Growth in Education". *Psychology in the Schools*, 1978, 15(1), 62–65.

Reynolds, D. S. "Multifaceted Assessment in Science." *Science Teachers Bulletin*, 1994, 58 (1), 3–8.

Reynolds, G. S. "Behavioral Contrast," *Journal of the Experimental Analysis of Behavior*, 1961, 4, 57–71.

Reynolds, J. H. and Glaser, R. "Effects of Repetition and Spaced Review Upon Retention of a Complex Learning Task." *Journal of Educational Psychology*, 1964, 55, 297–308.

Rieber, R. W. & Carton, A. S. *The Collected Works of L. S. Vygotsky. Vol 2I. The Fundamentals of Defectology.* New York: Plenum, 1993.

Robin, A. L. "Behavioral Instruction in the College Classroom". *Review of Educational Research*, 1976, 46, 313–354.

Roden, A. H. and Hapkiewicz, W. G. "Respondent Learning and Classroom Practice," in R. D. Klein, W. G. Hapkiewicz, and A. H. Roden (Eds.) *Behavior Modification in Educational Settings*, Springfield, IL: Thomas, 1973, pp. 421–437.

Rogers, C. *Freedom to Learn*, Columbus, OH: Merrill, 1969.

Rogers, C. "Forget You Are A Teacher". *Instructor*, 1971, 81(1), 65–66.

Rohwer, W. D., Jr. "Prime Time for Education: Early Childhood or Adolescence?" *Harvard Educational Review*, 1971, *41*, 316–341.

Rohwer, W. D., Jr. "Elaboration and Learning in Childhood and Adolescence." in H. W. Reese (Ed.). *Advances in Child Development and Behavior.* (vol. 8). New York: Academic Press, 1973.

Rosenshine, B. & Meister, C. "Reciprocal Teaching: A Review of the Research." *Review of Educational Research*, 1994, *64* (4), 479–530.

Rosenshine, B. and Stevens, R. "Teaching Functions." In M. C. Wittrock (Ed.) *Handbook of Research on Teaching* (Third Edition), New York: Macmillan, 1986, pp. 376–391.

Rosenshine, B. V. "Synthesis of Research on Explicit Teaching," *Educational Leadership*, 1986, *43*(7), 60–69.

Rosenthal, G. *Conflict Resolution in the Schools.* State University of New York at Buffalo: M.A. Thesis, 1995.

Rotter, J. B. "Generalized Expectancies for Internal versus External Control of Reinforcement," *Psychological Monographs: General and Applied*, 1966, *80*, 1–28.

Rounds, J. B., Jr. and Hendel, D. D. "Measurement and Dimensionality of Mathematics Anxiety," *Journal of Counseling Psychology*, 1980, *27*, 138–149.

Rozin, P., Poritsky, S. and Sotsky, R. "American Children with Reading Problems Can Easily Learn to Read English Represented by Chinese Characters." *Science*, 1971, *171*, 1264–1267.

Rumelhart, D. E. and Norman, D. A. "Analogical Processes in Learning," in J. R. Anderson (Ed.) *Cognitive Skills and Their Acquisition*, Hillsdale, NJ: Erlbaum, 1981, pp. 335–359.

Ryan, B. A. *PSI: Keller's Personalized System of Instruction: An Appraisal.* Washington, D.C.: American Psychological Association, 1974.

Ryan, B. A. "A Case Against Behavior Modification in the 'Ordinary' Classroom," *Journal of School Psychology*, 1979, *17*, 131–136.

Ryan, R. M. and Deci, E. L. "When Paradigms Clash: Comments on Cameron and Pierce's Claim that Rewards Do Not Undermine Intrinsic Motivation." *Review of Educational Research*, 1996, *66*, 33–38.

Sandler, J. and Quagliano, J. "Punishment in a Signal Avoidance Situation," Southeastern Psychological Association Meetings, Gatlinburg, TN, 1964. In A. Bandura *Principles of Behavior Modification*, New York: Holt, Rinehart & Winston, 1969, p. 297.

Savell, J. M., Twohig, P. T. and Rachford, D. L. "Empirical Status of Feuerstein's 'Instrumental Enrichment' (FIE) Technique as a Method of Teaching Thinking Skills," *Review of Educational Research*, 1986, *56*, 381–409.

Scarr, S., & Weinberg, R. A. "IQ Test Performance of Black Children Adopted by While Families." *American Psychologist*, 1976, *31*, 726–739.

Scarr, S., & Weinberg, R. A. "Nature and Nurture Strike (Out) Again." *Intelligence*, 1979, *3*, 31–39.

Schmuck, R. A. and Schmuck, P. A. *Group Processes in the Classroom*, Dubuque, Iowa: William C. Brown, 1983.

Schneider, W. and Shiffrin, R. M. "Controlled and Automatic Human Information Processing: I. Detection, Search and Attention," *Psychological Review*, 1977, *84*, 1–66.

Schoer, L. "Effect of List Length and Interpolated Learning on the Learning and Recall of Fast and Slow Learners," *Journal of Educational Psychology*, 1962, *53*, 193–197.

Schön, D. A. *The Reflective Practitioner.* New York: Basic Books, 1983.

Schön, D. A. *Educating the Reflective Practitioner.* San Francisco: Jossey-Bass, 1987.

Schulz, R. W. "Problem Solving Behavior and Transfer," *Harvard Educational Review*, 1960, *30*, 61–77.

Schunk, D. H. "Self-efficacy and Cognitive Learning Skill." In C. Ames & R. Ames (Eds.) *Research on Motivation in Education Vol. 3: Goals and Cognitions.* San Diego: Academic Press, 1989, pp. 13–44.

Seligman, M. E. P. "Phobias and Preparedness," *Behavior Therapy*, 1971, *2*, 307–320.

Seligman, M. E. P. *Helplessness: On Depression, Development, and Death.* San Francisco: Freeman, 1975.

Seligman, M. E. P. *Learned Optimism.* New York: Knopf, 1990.

Selinker, L., Swain, M. and Dumas, G. "The Interlanguage Hypothesis Extended To Children," *Language Learning,* 1975, 25(No. 1), 139–154.

Semb, G. G. and Ellis, J. A. "Knowledge Taught in School: What is Remembered?" *Review of Educational Research,* 1994, 64(2), 253–286.

Shanker, A. "Our Profession, Our Schools: The Case for Fundamental Reform". *American Educator,* 1986, 10(3), 10–17, 44–45.

Shanker, A. "Privileging Violence." *American Educator,* 1994/95, 18 (4), 7.

Shanker, A. "Classrooms Held Hostage." *American Educator,* 1995, 19, (1), 8–13, 47–48.

Sharan, S., Kussel, P., Hertz-Lazarowitz, R., Bejarano, Y., Raviv, S. and Sharan, Y. "Cooperative Learning Effects on Ethnic Relations and Achievement in Israeli Junior-High-School Classrooms" in R. Slavin, S. Sharan, S. Kagan, R. Hertz-Lazarowitz, C. Webb and R. Schmuck (Eds.) *Learning To Cooperate, Cooperating To Learn,* New York: Plenum, 1985, pp. 313–344.

Shavelson, R. J. "Teacher's Decision Making." In N. L. Gage (Ed.), *The Psychology of Teaching Methods,* Seventy-fifth Yearbook of the National Society for the Study of Education. Part I. Chicago: University of Chicago Press, 1976, 372–414.

Shavelson, R. J., Baxter, G. P. & Pine, J. "Performance Assessments: Political Rhetoric and Measurement Reality." *Educational Researcher,* 1992, 21 (4), 22–27.

Sherif, M. "Group Influences Upon the Formation of Norms and Attitudes," In T. M. Newcomb and E. L. Hartley (Eds.) *Readings in Social Psychology,* New York: Holt, 1947.

Sherman, J. G. (Ed.) *Personalized System of Instruction.* Menlo Park, CA: W. A. Benjamin, 1974.

Shiffrin, R. M. and Schneider, W. "Controlled and Automatic Human Information Processing: II. Perceptual Learning, Automatic Attending, and a General Theory," *Psychological Review,* 1977, 84, 127–190.

Shirley, K. W. The Prosocial Effects of Publicly Broadcast Children's Television. Unpublished Doctoral Dissertation. University of Kansas, 1974.

Shuell, T. J. "Clustering and Organization in Free Recall," *Psychological Bulletin,* 1969, 72, 353–374.

Shuell, T. J. "The Effect of Instructions to Organize for Good and Poor Learners," *Intelligence,* 1983, 7, 271–286.

Shuell, T. J. "Cognitive Conceptions of Learning," *Review of Educational Research,* 1986, 56, 411–436.

Shuell, T. J. "The Role of the Student in Learning from Instruction." *Contemporary Educational Psychology,* 1988, 13, 276–295.

Shuell, T. J. "Designing Instructional Computing Systems for Meaningful Learning." In M. Jones and P. H. Winne (Eds.) *Adaptive Learning Environments: Foundations and Frontiers.* New York: Springer-Verlag, 1992, pp. 19–54.

Shuell, T. J. "Toward an Integrated Theory of Teaching and Learning." *Educational Psychologist,* 1993, 28, 291–311.

Shuell, T. J. "Teaching and Learning in a Classroom Context." In D. C. Berliner and R. Calfe (Eds.) *Handbook of Educational Psychology,* New York: Simon & Schuster Macmillan, 1996, pp. 726–764..

Shuell, T. J. and Keppel, G. "Learning Ability and Retention," *Journal of Educational Psychology,* 1970, 61, 59–65.

Shuell, T. J., and Lee, C. Z. *Learning and Instruction,* Monterey, CA: Brooks/Cole, 1976.

Shulman, L. S. "Those Who Understand: Knowledge Growth in Teaching." *Educational Researcher,* 1986, 15(2), 4–14.

Shulman, L. S. and Keislar, E. R. (Eds.) *Learning By Discovery: A Critical Appraisal,* Chicago: Rand McNally, 1966.

Sidman, M. "Two Temporal parameters of the Maintenance of Avoidance Behavior By the White Rat." *Journal of Comparative and Physiological Psychology*, 1953, *46*, 253–261.

Sidman, M. "Normal Sources of Pathological Behavior," *Science*, 1960, *132*, 61–68.

Siegler, R. S. *Children's Thinking.* Englewood Cliffs, NJ: Prentice-Hall, 1986.

Silberman, C. E. *Crisis in the Classroom.* New York: Random House, 1970.

Simon, S. B. "Grades Must Go . . .". *School Review*, 1970, *78*, 397–402.

Simon, S. B. "Who Ever Cheats To Learn?". In S. B. Simon and J. A. Bellanca (Eds.), *Degrading the Grading Myths: A Primer of Alternatives To Grades and Marks.* Washington, D.C.: Association for Supervision and Curriculum Development, 1976, pp. 20–22.

Simon, S. B. and Bellanca, J. A. (Eds.). *Degrading the Grading Myths: A Primer of Alternatives To Grades and Marks.* Washington, D.C.: Association for Supervision and Curriculum Development, 1976.

Simon, S. B. and Hart, L. B. "Grades and Marks: Some Commonly Asked Questions". *The Science Teacher*, 1973, *40* (Sept.), 46–48.

Sizer, T. S. *Horace's Compromise: The Dilemma of Our American High School.* Boston: Houghton Mifflin, 1985.

Skinner, B. F. *The Behavior of Organisms,* New York: Appleton-Century-Crofts, 1938.

Skinner, B. F. "Superstition in the Pigeon," *Journal of Experimental Psychology*, 1948, *38*, 168–172.

Skinner, B. F. *Science and Human Behavior,* New York: Free Press, 1953.

Skinner, B. F. "The Science of Learning and the Art of Teaching." *Harvard Educational Review*, 1954, *24*(2), 86–97.

Skinner, B. F. *Verbal Behavior,* New York: Appleton, 1957.

Skinner, B. F. "Teaching Machines". *Science,* 1958, *128*, 969–977.

Skinner, B. F. *The Technology of Teaching.* New York: Appleton-Century-Crofts, 1968.

Skinner, B. F. *Beyond Freedom and Dignity,* New York: Alfred A. Knopf, 1971.

Skinner, B. F. *About Behaviorism,* New York: Knopf, 1974.

Skinner, B. F. "The Shame of American Education." *American Psychologist*, 1984, *39*, 947–954.

Slavin, R. E. "Cooperative Learning," *Review of Educational Research*, 1980, *50*, 315–342. (a)

Slavin, R. E. *Using Student Team Learning: Revised Edition,* Baltimore, MD: Center for Social Organization of Schools, The Johns Hopkins University, 1980. (b)

Slavin, R. E. "Mastery Learning Reconsidered." *Review of Educational Research*, 1982, *57* (2), 175–213.

Slavin, R. E. *Cooperative Learning.* New York: Longman, 1983.

Slavin, R. E. "Learning Together." *American Educator*, 1986, *10*(2), 6–13. (a)

Slavin, R. E. "The Napa Evaluation of Madeline Hunter's ITIP: Lessons Learned." *Elementary School Journal*, 1986, *87*, 165–171. (b)

Slavin, R. E. "The Hunterization of America's Schools." *Instructor*, 1987, *96* (April), 56–59.

Slavin, R. E. "PET and the Pendulum: Faddism in Education and How To Stop It." *Phi Delta Kappa*, 1989, *70*(10), 752–758.

Slavin, R., Sharan, S., Kagan, S., Hertz-Lazarowitz, R., Webb, C. and Schmuck, R. (Eds.) *Learning To Cooperate, Cooperating To Learn,* New York: Plenum, 1985.

Smith, E. E., Adams, N. and Schorr, D. "Fact Retrieval and the Paradox of Interference," *Cognitive Psychology*, 1978, *10*, 438–464.

Smith, K., Johnson, D. W., and Johnson, R. "Can Conflict Be Constructive? Controversy Versus Concurrence Seeking in Learning Groups." *Journal of Educational Psychology*, 1981, *73*, 651-663.

Spearman, C. "General Intelligence' Objectively Determined and Measured." *American Journal of Psychology*, 1904, *15*, 72–101.

Spearman, C. *The Nature of "Intelligence" and the Principles of Cognition.* London: Macmillan, 1923.

Spence, K. W. "The Differential Response in Animals to Stimuli Varying within a Single Dimension." *Psychological Review,* 1937, 44, 430–444.

Spence, K. W. "Continuous vs. Non-continuous Interpretations of Discrimination Learning," *Psychological Review* 1940, 47, 271–288.

Spence, K. W. "A Theory of Emotionally Based Drive (D) and Its Relation to Performance in Simple Learning Situations," *American Psychologist,* 1958, 13, 131–141.

Sperling, G. A. "The Information Available in Brief Visual Presentations," *Psychological Monographs,* 1960, 74, Whole Number 498.

Spiro, R. J. "Accommodative Reconstruction in Prose Recall," *Journal of Verbal Learning and Verbal Behavior,* 1980, 19, 84–95.

Staats, A. W. and Staats, C. K. "Attitudes Established by Classical Conditioning," *Journal of Abnormal and Social Psychology,* 1958, 57, 37–40.

Stainback, W. C., Payne, J. S., Stainback, S. B., and Payne, R. A. *Establishing a Token Economy in the Classroom,* Columbus, Ohio: Merrill, 1973.

Stallings, J. "A Study of Implementation of Madeline Hunter's Model and Its Effects on Students." *Journal of Educational Research,* 1985, 78, 325–337.

Stallings, J. and Krasavage, E. M. "Program Implementation and Student Achievement in a Four-Year Madeline Hunter Follow-Through Project." *Elementary School Journal,* 1986, 87, 117–138.

Stallings, J., Robbins, P., Presbrey, L. and Scott, J. "Effects of Instruction Based on the Madeline Hunter Model on Students' Achievement: Findings From a Follow-Through Project." *Elementary School Journal,* 1986, 86, 571–587.

Stallings, J. and Stipek, D. "Research on Early Childhood and Elementary School Teaching Programs" in M. C. Wittrock (Ed.) *Handbook of Research on Teaching* (Third Edition), New York: Macmillan, 1986, pp. 727–753.

Starch, D. and Elliott, E. "Reliability of the Grading of High School Work in English". *School Review,* 1912, 20, 442–457.

Starch, D. and Elliott, E. "Reliability of Grading Work in Mathematics". *School Review,* 1913, 21, 254–295. (a)

Starch, D. and Elliott, E. "Reliability of Grading Work in History". *School Review,* 1913, 21, 678–681. (b)

Stein, A. H. and Friedrich, L. K. "Television Content and Young Children's Behavior." In J. P. Murray, E. A. Rubenstein, and G. A. Comstock (Eds.) *Television and Social Behavior, Vol. 2. Television and Social Learning.* Washington, D.C.: U.S. Government Printing Office: 1972, pp. 202–317.

Stein, M. I. *Stimulating Creativity, Vol. 2, Group Procedures,* New York: Academic Press, 1975.

Sternberg, R. J. *Intelligence, Information Processing, and Analogical Reasoning: The Componential Analysis of Human Abilities,* Hillsdale, NJ: Erlbaum, 1977.

Sternberg, R. J. *Beyond IQ: A Triarchic Theory of Human Intelligence.* Cambridge: Cambridge University Press, 1985.

Sternberg, R. J. *Intelligence Applied.* San Diego: Harcourt Brace Jovanovich, 1986. (a)

Sternberg, R. J. (Ed.) *Advances in the Psychology of Human Intelligence,* Hillsdale, NJ: Erlbaum, 1982, Vol. 1; 1984, Vol. 2; 1986b, Vol. 3.

Sternberg, R. J. "Teaching Intelligence: The Application of Cognitive Psychology to the Improvement of Intellectual Skills," in J. B. Baron and R. J. Sternberg (Eds.) *Teaching Thinking Skills: Theory and Practice,* New York: Freeman, 1987, pp. 182–218.

Sternberg, R. J. *The Triarchic Mind.* New York: Viking, 1988.

Sternberg, R. J. "Myths, Countermyths, and Truths About Intelligence." *Educational Researcher,* 1996, 25 (2), 11–16.

Stillman, P. A. "Technical Issues: Logistics [of Standardized Patients]." *Academic Medicine*, 1993, *68* (6), 464–470.

Stokes, T. F. and Baer, D. M. "An Implicit Technology of Generalization," *Journal of Applied Behavior Analysis,* 1977, *10,* 349–367.

Stroud, J. B. and Carter, L. J. "Inhibition Phenomena in Fast and Slow Learners," *Journal of Educational psychology,* 1961, *52,* 30–34.

Stroud, J. B. and Schoer, L. "Individual Differences in Memory," *Journal of Educational Psychology,* 1959, *50,* 285–292.

Suchman, J. R. "Inquiry Training in the Elementary School." *Science Teacher,*k 1960, *27*(7), 42–47.

Suchman, J. R. "Inquiry Training: Building Skills for Autonomous Discovery." *Merrill-Palmer Quarterly Behavior Development,* 1961, *7,* 147–169.

Sulzer-Azaroff, B. and Reese, E. P. *Applying Behavioral Analysis: A Program for Developing Professional Competence,* New York: CBS College Publishing Co., 1982.

Swanson D. B., Norman, G. R., & Linn, R. L. "Performance-Based Assessment: Lessons from the Health Professions." *Educational Researcher,* 1995, *24,* (3), 5–11, 35.

Taffel, S. J. and O'Leary, K. D. "Reinforcing Math with More Math: Choosing Special Activities as a Reward for Academic Performance." *Journal of Educational Psychology,* 1976, *68,* 579–587.

Taylor, J. A. "A Personality Scale of Manifest Anxiety," *Journal of Abnormal and Social Psychology,* 1953, *48,* 285–290.

Terhune, J. and Premack, D. "On the Proportionality Between the Probability of Not-Running and the Punishment Effect of Being Forced to Run," *Learning and Motivation,* 1970, *1,* 141–147.

Terman, L. M. *The Stanford Revision and Extension of the Binet-Simon Scale for Measuring Intelligence,* Baltimore, MD: Warwick and York, 1917.

Terman, L. M. *The Measurement of Intelligence.* London: Harrap Co., 1919.

Terman, L. M., & Merrill, M. A. *Measuring Intelligence.* Boston, MA: Houghton Mifflin, 1937.

Terman, L.M. and Merill, M.A. *The Stanford-Binet Intelligence Scale.* Boston: Houghton-Mifflin, 1960.

Thoresen, C. E. and Mahoney, M. J. *Behavioral Self-Control,* New York: Holt, Rinehart & Winston, 1974.

Thorndike, E. L. *Animal Intelligence,* New York: Macmillan, 1911.

Thorndike, E. L. *Educational Psychology, Volume II: The Psychology of Learning,* New York: Teachers College, 1913.

Thorndike, E. L. "The Influence of First-Year Latin Upon the Ability to Read English," *School and Society,* 1923, *17,* 165–168.

Thorndike, E. L., Bregman, E. O., Tilton, J. W. and Woodyard, E. *Adult Learning.* New York: Macmillan, 1928.

Thorndike, E. L. and Woodworth, R. S. "The Influence of Improvement in One Mental Function Upon the Efficiency of Other Functions," *Psychological Review,* 1901, *8,* 247–267, 384–395, 553–564.

Thorndike, R. L. *Intelligence as Information Processing: The Mind and the Computer,* CEDR Monograph, Bloomington, IA: Phi Delta Kappa, 1984.

Thurstone, L. L. *The Vectors of the Mind.* Chicago: University of Chicago Press, 1935.

Thurstone, L. L., & Thurstone, T. G. *Factorial Studies of Intelligence.* Chicago: University of Chicago Press, 1941.

Tobias, S. "Computer-Assisted Instruction" in M. C. Wang and H. J. Walberg (Eds.) *Adapting Instruction To Individual Differences.* Berkeley, CA: McCutchan, 1985, pp. 135–159.

Tobias, Shiela, *Overcoming Math Anxiety,* Boston: Houghton-Mifflin, 1978.

Tobin, K. "The Role of Wait Time in Higher Cognitive Level Learning." *Review of Educational Research,* 1987, *57,* 69–95.

Toby, J. "Everyday School Violence: How Disorder Fuels It." *American Educator,* 1993/94 *17* (4), 409, 44–48.

Tolman, E. C. *Purposive Behavior in Animals and Men*, New York: Appleton-Century-Crofts, 1932.

Tolman, E. C. "Principles of Purposive Behavior," In S. Koch (Ed.) *Psychology: A Study of a Science* (Vol. 2), New York: McGraw-Hill, 1959, pp. 92–157.

Torgesen, J. K. "Memorization Processes in Reading-Disabled Children," *Journal of Educational Psychology*, 1977, 69, 571–578.

Torgesen, J. K. "Conceptual and Educational Implications of the Use of Efficient Task Strategies by learning Disabled Children," *Journal of Learning Disabilities*, 1980, 13, 364–371.

Torgesen, J. K. and Goldman, T. "Verbal Rehearsal and Short-Term Memory in Reading-Disabled Children," *Children Development*, 1977, 48, 56–60.

Torrance, E. P. *Encouraging Creativity in the Classroom*, Dubuque, IA: Brown, 1970.

Torrance, E. P. "Teaching Creative and Gifted Learners" in M. C. Wittrock (Ed.) *Handbook of Research on Teaching* (Third Edition). New York: Macmillan, 1986, pp. 630–647.

Travers, R. M. W. *Essentials of Learning* (Fourth Edition), New York: Macmillan, 1977.

Triesman, A. M. "Contextual Cues in Selective Listening," *Quarterly Journal of Experimental Psychology*, 1960, 12, 242–248.

Tuddenham, R. D. "The Nature and Measurement of Intelligence." In L. Postman (Ed.) *Psychology in the Making: Histories of Selected Research Problems*, New York: Knopf, 1962, pp. 469–525.

Tulving, E. "Subjective Organization in Free Recall of 'Unrelated Words,' " *Psychological Review*, 1962, 69, 344–354.

Tulving, E. "Episodic and Semantic Memory." In E. Tulving & W. Donaldson (Eds.). *Organization of Memory*. New York: Academic Press, 1972.

Tulving, E. *Elements of Episodic Memory*. New York: Oxford University Press, 1983.

Tulving, E. and Psotka, J. "Retroactive Inhibition in Free Recall: Inaccessibility of Information Available in the Memory Store," *Journal of Experimental Psychology*, 1971, 87, 1–8.

Tulving, E. and Thomson, D. M. "Retrieval Processes in Recognition Memory: Effects of Associative Context," *Journal of Experimental Psychology*, 1971, 87, 116–124.

Tulving, E. and Thomson, D. M. "Encoding Specificity and Retrieval Processes in Episodic Memory," *Psychological Review*, 1973, 80, 352–373.

Turnure, J., Buium, N. and Thurlow, M. "The Effectiveness of Interrogatives for Promoting Verbal Elaboration Productivity in Young Children," *Child Development*, 1976, 47, 851–855.

Tyler, L. E. "The Intelligence We Test—An Evolving Concept." In L. B. Resnick (Ed.) *The Nature of Intelligence*. Hillsdale, NJ: Erlbaum, 1976, pp. 13–26.

Underwood, B. J. "Speed of Learning and Amount Retained: A Consideration of Methodology," *Psychological Bulletin*, 1954, 51, 276–282.

Underwood, B. J. "Interference and Forgetting," *Psychological Review*, 1957, 64, 49–60.

Underwood, B. J. "Degree of Learning and the Measurement of Forgetting," *Journal of Verbal Learning and Verbal Behavior*, 1964, 3, 112–129.

Varela, J. A. "Attitude Change," in H. L. Pick, Jr., H. W. Liebowitz, J. E. Singer, A. Steinschneider, and H. W. Stevenson (Eds.) *Psychology From Research To Practice*, New York: Plenum, 1978, pp. 121–144.

Vygotsky, L. S. *Thought and Language*. Cambridge, MA: The M.I.T. Press, 1962.

Vygotsky, K. S. *Mind in Society: The Development of Higher Psychological Processes*. Cambridge, MA: Harvard University Press, 1978.

Walker, L. J. "The Sequentiality of Kohlberg's Stages of Moral Development." *Child Development*, 1982, 53, 1330–1336.

Warren, R. M. and Warren, R. P. "Auditory Illusions and Confusions," *Scientific American*, 1970, 223(No. 6), 30–36.

Washburne, C. W. "Educational Measurement as a Key to Individual Instruction and Promotions." *Journal of Educational Research*, 1922, 5, 195–206.

Watson, D. L. and Tharp, R. G. *Self-Directed Behavior: Self-Modification for Personal Adjustment* (4th Ed.), Monterey, CA: Brooks/Cole, 1985.

Watson, J. B. "Psychology as the Behaviorist Views It," *Psychological Review*, 1913, 20, 158–177.

Watson, J. B. *Psychology from the Standpoint of a Behaviorist*, Philadelphia: J. B. Lippincott, 1919.

Watson, J. B. *Behaviorism.* New York: W.W. Norton, 1930.

Watson, J. B. and Rayner, R. "Conditioned Emotional Reactions," *Journal of Experimental Psychology*, 1920, 3, 1–14.

Webb, N. M., Ender, P. and Lewis, S. "Problem-Solving Strategies and Group Processes in Small Groups Learning Computer Programming." *American Educational Research Journal*, 1986, 23, 243–261.

Wechsler, D. *The Measurement and Appraisal of Adult Intelligence* (4th). Baltimore, MD: Williams and Wilkins, 1958.

Weiner, B. *Achievement Motivation and Attribution Theory*, Morristown, NJ: General Learning Press, 1974.

Weiner, B. and Litman-Adizes, T. "An Attributional Expectancy-Value Analysis of Learned Helplessness and Depression," in J. Garber and M. E. P. Seligman (Eds.) *Human Helplessness: Theory and Applications*, 1980.

Weiss, J. M. "Effects of Coping Response on Stress," *Journal of Comparative and Physiological Psychology*, 1968, 65, 251–260.

Weiss, J. M. "Somatic Effects of Predictable and Unpredictable Shock," *Psychosomatic Medicine*, 1970, 32, 397–409.

Weiss, J. M. "Effects of Coping Behavior in Different Warning Signal Conditions on Stress Pathology in Rats," *Journal of Comparative and Physiological Psychology*, 1971, 77, 1–13.

Whimbey, A. and Lochhead, J. *Problem Solving and Comprehension: A Short Course in Analytical Reasoning.* Philadelphia: The Franklin Institute Press, 1980.

Whimbey, A. and Lochhead, J. *Problem Solving and Comprehension* (4th ed.). Hillsdale, NJ: Erlbaum, 1986.

White, R. W. "Motivation Reconsidered: The Concept of Competence," *Psychological Review*, 1959, 66, 297–333.

Wiggins, G. "A True Test: Toward More Authentic and Equitable Assessment." *Phi Delta Kappan*, 1989, 72 (May), 703–713. (a)

Wiggins, G. "Teaching to the (Authentic) Test." *Educational Leadership*. 1989, 46 (7), 42–47. (b)

Winograd, E. "Memory in the Laboratory and Everyday Memory: The Case for Both:" In J. M. Puckett & H. W. Reese (Eds.) *Mechanisms of Everyday Cognition.* Hillsdale, NJ: Lawrence Erlbaum, 1993, pp. 55–70.

Wissler, C. "The Correlation of Mental and Physical Tests." *Psychological Review*, 1901, 8, 539–540 (summarized from Monograph Supplement No. 16).

Wittrock, M. C. "Three Conceptual Approaches to Research on Transfer of Training," in R. M. Gagné and W. J. Gephart (Eds.) *Learning Research and School Subjects*, Itasca, IL: F. E. Peacock, 1968, pp. 150–184.

Wolf, M. M., Hanley, E. L., King, L. A., Lachowicz, J. and Giles, K. "The Timer-Game: A Variable Interval Contingency for the Management of Out-of-Seat Behavior," *Exceptional Children*, 1970, 37(No. 2), 113–117.

Wolpe, J. *The Practice of Behavior Therapy*, New York: Pergamon Press, 1969.

Worden, P. E. "Memory Strategy Instruction with the Learning Disabled," in M. Pressley and J. R. Levin (Eds.) *Cognitive Strategy Research: Psychological Foundations*, New York: Springer-Verlag, 1983, pp. 129–153.

Yoakum, C. S., & Yerkes, R. M. *Army Mental Tests*, New York: Holt, 1920.

Young, J. C. "What Is Creativity?" *Journal of Creative Behavior*, 1985, *19*, 77–87.

Young, M. "Instructional Design for Situated Learning." *Educational Technology Research and Development*, 1993, *41* (1), 43–58.

Yussen, S. R., Gagné, E., Garguilo, R. and Kunen, S. "The Distinction Between Perceiving and Memorizing in Elementary-School Children," *Child Development*, 1974, 45, 547–551.

Zajonc, R. B. "Feeling and Thinking: Preferences Need No Inferences," *American Psychologist*, 1980, *35*, 151–175.

Zajonc, R. B. "On the Primacy of Affect," *American Psychologist*, 1984, *39*, 117–123.

Zeaman, D. and House, B. J. "The Relation of IQ and Learning," in R. M. Gagne (Ed.) *Learning and Individual Differences*, Columbus, Ohio: Merrill, 1967, pp. 192–212.

Zimmerman, E. H. and Zimmerman, J. "The Alteration of Behavior in a Special Classroom Situation," *Journal of the Experimental Analysis of Behavior*, 1962, *5*, 59–60.

GLOSSARY

Ability to understand instruction. In Carroll's model, the verbal and general reasoning abilities of students allowing them to profit from instruction (as well as compensate for poor instruction).

Accessibility. The capacity to retrieve material once stored in long-term memory. Usually accessibility depends upon whether the cues that were associated with the information when it was encoded are also present when it is to be retrieved.

Accommodation. One of the two opposing forces of Equilibration in Piaget's theory, it is the process of modifying current schemata to allow new or conflicting knowledge to be incorporated. (See also Assimilation.)

Active participation. The continual involvement of all students with what is being learned in the lesson. It must be immediate, not eventual. (See also Participation, Overt and Covert.)

Algorithm. An application of a rule or formula in a step-by-step method to solve a problem. (Usually contrasted with Heuristic.)

Amount of learning. In Carroll's model, the amount learned is a ratio of Time Spent to Time Needed, in which Time Spent is a combination of Opportunity and Perseverance and Time Needed is a combination of Quality of Instruction, Aptitude, and Ability to Understand Instruction.

Analysis by synthesis. Understanding something by actively constructing or reconstructing its meaning from what is already known.

Anticipatory set. See Set, Anticipatory.

Aptitude. In Carroll's model, time needed to master a particular learning task.

Assessment. The process of reviewing or judging a performance (through tests or activities). In educational use, such assessment has either or both of the following purposes: (1) prediction or selection (a norm-referenced purpose) or (2) diagnosis and facilitation of learning (a criterion-referenced purpose).

Assimilation. One of the two opposing forces of Equilibration in Piaget's theory, it is the process of incorporating new information into an already existing knowledge structure. (See also Accommodation.)

Associability. The capacity of words or concepts to evoke other words or concepts which are related to or otherwise associated with them.

Attention. The active process of seeking or ignoring (discriminating among) sensations.

Attribution. A causal explanation, or belief about what behavior and its consequences can be attributed to. In attribution theory, attributions are said to occur on continua in three dimensions:

1. **Internal-External Dimension.** The extent to which events are attributed to internal, personal factors or external, environmental factors.
2. **Stable-Unstable Dimension.** The extent to which events are attributed to long-term, stable factors or short-lived, transient factors.
3. **Global-Specific Dimension.** The extent to which events are attributed to a wide variety of generalizable factors or to a single isolated factor.

Authentic Test. See Performance items.

Automatic attentional processing. Performance of tasks which are so well practiced that they take little effort or attention, do not interfere with nor are they disrupted by whatever else is going on, and are usually operating outside of conscious awareness. (See Controlled attentional process for the opposite end of the continuum.)

Availability. A term used to describe the condition that once material is adequately learned or encoded in some way, it is maintained in long-term memory. Even though some material may not be recalled under all conditions, such material is said to be available (it is in storage), **but not accessible.**

Aversive stimulus. An unpleasant stimulus, such as a slap, blow, loud noise, or electric shock.

Avoidance. Removing an aversive situation before the noxious event begins as a result of learning to respond to a cue which predicts the onset of the aversive stimulus; avoidance is therefore discriminated escape learning and is based on negative reinforcement.

Belongingness. The relationship between US and CS that exists along a natural dimension—e.g., between taste and food or between a sudden loud noise and a startle behavior.

Between-class grading. Norm-referenced procedures, using standardized test scores (e.g., z-scores), to combine grades from various subjects and teachers to provide statistically sound class ranks.

Biofeedback. A process whereby physiological functions not ordinarily under voluntary control are mirrored back to us, usually by instrumentation, to allow these functions to be brought under voluntary control.

Bodily-Kinesthetic Intelligence: See Multiple Intelligences.

Chunking. The process of combining separate pieces of information into meaningful units.

Classroom goal structures. The types of interactions occurring among students striving to fulfill educational objectives. (See Competitive, Cooperative, and Individualistic Goal Structures.)

Cognitions. A general term which includes any behavioral process not included under respondents or operants; examples follow: verbal communication; the learning, retention and transfer of facts, concepts and principles; thinking; creativity; analysis and synthesis.

Cognitive conflicts. Information or attitudes which are beyond, or contradictory to, what is now known creates a disequilibrium which may motivate individuals to modify their current knowledge structures to accommodate this intellectual challenge, and thus to grow. This is a means of providing developmentally appropriate instruction according to Piaget. (See also Cognitive dissonance).

Cognitive Constructivism. The theory which suggests that mental processing, as in academic and other knowledge acquisition, is an attempt to find meaning through processes that are active rather than passive, constructive rather than reproductive, purposeful rather than incidental or reactive, cumulative rather than isolated, metacognitive rather than mindless, and usually socially mediated rather than individual. (See also Learning and Cognitive Learning.)

Cognitive dissonance. The situation that exists in a person when two contradictory beliefs are held concurrently or when facts are not consistent with the beliefs.

Cognitive Learning. A change in knowledge or competence in a learner who is actively and purposefully seeking meaning from the experience. (See also Learning and Cognitive Constructivism.)

Competence. The capability to control one's own environment and, therefore, the consequences of one's own behavior; mastery over the situation.

Competitive goal structures. The situation that exists when individual students succeed at the expense of others in achieving educational objectives.

Componential Analysis of Intelligence. The study of solution processes of people on parts of a cognitive task in order to understand how the parts combine to create the whole.

Computer-assisted instruction (CAI). A form of programmed instruction taught by computer.

Concrete operations stage. Generally considered the third stage of Piaget's theory, corresponding to late childhood (age 8–11 or 12); the child learns to reason about objects and problems presented in manipulable fashion, to solve problems involving Conservation of relations, seriation, and classification, as well as interpersonal skills.

Conditioned reinforcer. Same as **Secondary reinforcer.**

Conditioned response (conditioned reflex; CR). A reflex that has been transferred from an unconditioned stimulus to a neutral stimulus, now called the conditioned stimulus.

Conditioned stimulus (CS). A stimulus that was neutral before conditioning began, but became capable of eliciting the response after being paired with an unconditioned stimulus.

Conditioning. A procedure in which an increase in the frequency of response occurs because a stimulus is paired with the response.

Confidence interval. An estimate of the range of scores a person is likely to have on a given test, based on the test's standard error and that person's obtained score. It is usually expressed as follows: we can be 68% confident that a person's score falls between X and Y, or at X plus or minus one Standard Error.

Conflict Resolution. Systematic programs designed to teach alternatives to violence by practicing such communication skills as comprehending the other's point of view, finding a way that each party can be successful (a win-win situation), and monitoring the solution to be sure it is working. (See also Peer Mediation.)

Conformity. Behavior that is in agreement with a reference group.

Consequence. The event that follows a behavior; e.g., a reinforcing or punishing stimulus.

Conservation. A Piagetian concept in which a child learns that substance or amount can be conserved despite changes in shape or appearance (e.g., the amount of clay remains the same despite its being rolled into the shape of a ball or a sausage, where length and width change). Conservation is acquired during the Concrete Operations stage.

Contingent reinforcement. The presentation of a reinforcing stimulus only if the correct response has been made.

Continuous reinforcement. The procedure of reinforcing every correct response.

Contracts. Written agreements (e.g., between teachers and students) specifying acceptable behavior and the consequences of fulfilling or not fulfilling the agreement.

Contrast (or Context) effect. Comparing the magnitude of a reinforcer with previous reinforcements; it usually produces larger effects than if no previous experience occurred with such reinforcers.

Controlled attentional processing. Performance, usually at a novice stage, of a task which is fully conscious, requires much effort and attention, and is easily disrupted by external stimuli. As practice continues, the attentional demands become less. (See automatic attentional processing.)

Cooperative goal structures. The situation that exists when individual students' efforts are coordinated in order to achieve instructional objectives.

Cooperative teams. A systematic approach for organizing classrooms into groups to provide incentive for the individuals (1) to learn academic objectives and (2) to cooperate in doing so.

Correlation. The extent to which scores on two measures are related. If a higher score on one variable tends to go with a higher score on the other, then we say the variables are **positively correlated** (e.g., height and weight). If a higher score on one variable tends to go with a lower score on the other, then they are **negatively correlated** (e.g., wind speed and perceived temperature). If a higher score on one variable has no consistent relationship with score on the other variable, then the variables are said to have about a **zero correlation** (e.g., height and IQ).

Counter conditioning. The process of replacing an emotional response (e.g., fear and tension) with an opposite emotional response (e.g., relaxation).

Creativity. Any behavior, idea or invention that is novel but repeatable for a given individual.

Criterion (pl. Criteria). The domain or population of objectives expected to be mastered in criterion-referenced assessment. In measurement theory, the domain of test items or activities expected to be predicted by some other test or activity.

Criterion-referenced assessment. The interpretation of a person's score (e.g., test score) compared with an established and more-or-less absolute standard of performance on a given set of objectives.

Cue-dependent recall. The explanation often given for the capacity to retrieve material from long-term memory—namely, that retrieval depends upon the presence of cues similar to those present when the information was encoded. (See also Accessibility).

Curriculum. A course of study, including the ultimate goals, the more immediate objectives which are the stepping stones toward the goals, and the sequencing of those objectives in such a way as to maximize the transfer of prior learnings to subsequent situations. Although we usually think of curriculum in terms of particular subject areas (math, social studies, tennis, etc.), a more comprehensive view concerns the affect, knowledge, skills, and cognitive strategies which are to be learned via the curriculum, many of which transcend particular subject areas, and all of which require mastery at developmentally increasing levels of expertise. Thus the concept of an ever-widening spiral curriculum, with ideas and procedures being revisited in different subjects or contexts and at different skill levels as the student progresses from novice to relative expert, is the most comprehensive view of curriculum.

Declarative knowledge (Knowledge that): Information about things, facts, anecdotes, attitudes, and the like.

Detached teaching strategies. See Domain-General Strategies.

Development. A process of mental growth that is due to the interaction of learning and maturation (what Piaget calls learning in the broad sense).

Developmental stage. A level of conceptual ability or skill attained which is presumed to involve a qualitative difference in functioning from the previous level and which is presumed to be prerequisite to the next level.

Deviancy. See Misbehavior.

Diagnostic test. A kind of formative evaluation.

Dialogical thinking. A procedure for giving students experience with alternative points of view by having them defend positions different from those they prefer.

Difficulty of a test item. See Item difficulty.

Discriminating power. In test item analysis, the degree to which an item contributes to the internal consistency of the total test, as measured by the proportion of high vs. low scorers (or masters vs. nonmasters) on the total test who correctly answered the item.

Discrimination training. The procedure of increasing the rate of responding in the presence of one stimulus and decreasing it in the presence of another.

Discriminative stimulus (S^D or S^+). The particular stimulus in the presence of which a correct response is likely to be reinforced.

Distractor effectiveness. An item analysis procedure, particularly for multiple choice questions, which assesses whether the non-correct alternative choices (distractors) are working correctly by, first, attracting some individuals and, second, attracting proportionally more individuals who score low on the total test.

Domain-general strategies. Teaching thinking skills and learning strategies which are detached from any given curriculum, and which are applicable to some extent to many curriculum areas. Usually contrasted with Domain-specific strategies.

Domain-specific strategies. Teaching thinking skills and learning strategies that are embedded in and specific to a given curriculum (e.g., history). Usually contrasted with Domain-general strategies.

Dual coding theory. A theory of memory which postulates the existence of two separate but interacting systems for encoding, storing, and retrieving information. The one system is verbal, the other is imaginal.

Egocentric Speech. A transitional stage of speech (between social and inner speech in Vygotsky's theory) in which thought is beginning to control behavior.

Elaboration. The process of expanding on the context of items to be learned in order to facilitate their learning and retention. There are two basic types:
1. **Verbal elaboration** can be done by placing the items into a sentence or episode, or
2. **Imagery elaboration** can be done by visualizing a setting or relationship for the items.

Embedded teaching strategies. See Domain-specific strategies.

Encoding. The process of categorizing, labeling, or finding meaning in incoming information or other stimuli. This allows the information to pass from working memory into long-term storage.

Entering behavior. The specific behaviors the student can perform in relation to the hierarchy of skills required by the task. Knowing the student's entering behavior allows the teacher to start the student at the point in the curriculum at which the material will be neither too easy nor too difficult.

Equilibration. In Piaget's theory, a regulatory mechanism (analogous to homeostasis) which attempts to maintain a proper intellectual balance. For example, when a lack of information is sensed, the organism seeks to **assimilate** new knowledge; when current knowledge is challenged, the knowledge structures are changed to **accommodate** that information.

Escape. Removing an aversive situation (e.g., leaving a smoky room), the consequence of which is favorable and, therefore, likely to be repeated. Escape is based on negative reinforcement.

Essay items. Test questions which require construction of an answer to a question in which academic content is the primary concern. Two major types of essay items are **Extended Response,** in which the examinee is given wide latitude in style, content and length of essay, and **Restricted Response,** in which certain criteria for scope and length of response are specified. Essay items are best suited for measuring the ability to organize, analyze and synthesize the content. The major difficulty with such items is the subjectivity and unreliability of their scoring. Compare with Written Reports and Writing Performances.

Essential elements of effective instruction. In Madeline Hunter's model of teaching as decision making, the components of effective instruction. These fall into four broad categories—namely, (1) selecting objectives at the correct level of difficulty, (2) teaching to those objectives, (3) monitoring progress and adjusting teaching, and (4) correctly using principles of learning.

Evaluation. The process of making qualitative or value judgments about a performance or trait. Though quantitative measures often serve as the basis for an evaluative judgment, Evaluation goes beyond such Measurement to make a value-laden statement (e.g., "good or poor," "retarded or normal," "pass or fail").

Evaluation time. Time allotted after Learning time has been completed to make final assessments of the adequacy of the instructional achievements. (See also Summative evaluation.)

Events of Instruction: An analysis, due to Gagné, of the learning processes (e.g., attention, encoding) which form the basis for effective instructional techniques (e.g., getting the lesson started, guiding the learning). (See also Teaching-Learning Functions.)

Extinction. In operant conditioning, the process of withholding reinforcement following performance of an operant; in respondent conditioning, the process of withholding the unconditioned stimulus following the presentation of the conditioned stimulus. Its usual effect is to reduce the strength or frequency of the response.

Facilitation: the helpful effect of experience on one task on the learning or retention of another task. There are two basic types:

1. **Proactive:** positive transfer from one task to a subsequent task.
2. **Retroactive:** material which comes later assists in the organization and recall of material learned earlier. (See also Interference and Transfer.)

Far transfer. The ability to apply past learnings to situations or problems which are quite different from the original tasks. (See Near transfer for the opposite end of the continuum.)

Feedback. Specific knowledge of results on what parts of a student's behavior are correct and what are incorrect (and how they can be corrected).

Fixed-interval (FI) schedule. An interval schedule in which reinforcement is given for the next correct response after a fixed amount of time since the last reinforcement.

Fixed-ratio (FR) schedule. A ratio schedule in which a fixed number of responses must be emitted before reinforcement is given.

Formal operations stage. The most advanced stage of Piaget's theory, beginning with adolescence and continuing into adulthood, in which formal, abstract, propositional, logic is possible (though not universally attained or practiced).

Formative evaluation. Testing which is conducted during learning to diagnose what has been well-learned and what needs further work. Formative evaluation has the purpose of facilitating instruction and should therefore be criterion-referenced.

Frustration effect. In extinction, an increase in the rate of a behavior shortly after non-reinforcement has begun.

Generalization. See Stimulus generalization.

Generalization gradient. The curve of response frequencies which shows that the more similar a stimulus is to the original S^D, the more likely the response will be performed in its presence.

General transfer. The learning of techniques which, though not specific to the particular task at hand, may facilitate performance on that task. Examples are warm-up or stretching exercises in music or athletics and general problem solving strategies in academics.

Grading. The evaluative process of providing value judgments ("good-poor," "pass-fail"), letters ("A, B, C, D, F;" "S-U"), or numbers ("78, 83, 95") as a summary of student performances.

Habituation. The process by which one gradually adjusts to higher and higher levels of stimulation (noise, shock, TV violence, etc.).

Helplessness. See Learned helplessness.

Heritability (h^2). A measure of the extent to which a trait or ability is determined by genetics or by environment. If $h^2=1$, then the variation among the population on that trait would be totally determined by genetic factors. If $h^2=0$, then the variation among the population would be totally determined by environmental factors (e..g., learning, nutrition). While some traits might be mostly attributable to heredity, and others mostly to environment, all apparently require both genes and environments in order to exist.

Heuristic. A general strategy for solving problems and checking whether the result is sensible; an intelligent guess; a selective search. (Usually contrasted with Algorithm.)

Higher-order conditioning. The process of attaching a CR (e.g., fear) learned to one stimulus (CS_1) to another neutral stimulus (CS_2) by following CS_2 by CS_1. In this case CS_1 acts as a US to transfer the CR to the new stimulus (CS_2).

Higher-order thinking skills (HOTS). Cognitive processes involving application (transfer) of ideas, analysis, synthesis, evaluation, creativity, dialogical thinking, synectics, critical thinking, etc.

IDEAL problem solver. An acronym for Identify the problem, Define and represent the problem, Explore alternating strategies, Act on the strategies, and Look at the effects; A heuristic strategy for improving problem solving due to Bransford and Stein.

Identical or Similar Elements. One of the variables of transfer, this refers to the extent to which the components (knowledge, skills, associations) of one task are identical to those required to perform another task. The more similar or identical the elements, the higher the probability of transfer.

Identity. The central concept of Erikson's theory, in which a sense of continuity, uniqueness, competence and self-worth are strived for through resolution of various normal developmental and psycho-social crises or challenges. (See Psychosocial Development Theory.)

Imagery. The capacity of words and concepts to evoke images; in general the greater the imagery, the faster the learning or better the retention.

Imitation. The procedure whereby an observer performs the behavior performed by some other person (the model).

Imitative behavior. The behavior performed by an observer as a result of witnessing the behavior of some other person (a model).

Incentive structure. The manner in which students of varying ability levels are handicapped so as to give each an opportunity to contribute to a cooperative group and to have incentive to do so.

Incompatible behavior. Behavior that is opposed to the behavior of interest. Examples of incompatible behaviors are competing and cooperating, hoarding and sharing, paying attention and being inattentive.

Indiscipline. See Misbehavior.

Individualistic goal structures. The situation that exists when students achieve instructional objectives without interaction with other students.

Inhibition. See Interference.

Inhibitory or disinhibitory effect of modeling. The suppression or facilitation of a performance as a result of witnessing the consequences of a model's similar behavior.

Inner Speech. Thought. In Vygotsky's theory, the final stage of language and thought (from social speech through egocentric speech to inner speech) which is self-controlling and therefore a precursor of metacognition.

Instructional objectives. Specific performances stated in terms of observable behaviors that students are expected to acquire through instructional procedures.

Instructional Events. See Events of Instruction.

Instrumental enrichment. A strategy for restructuring the knowledge, learning strategies, and cognitive and metacognitive processes of people, particularly retarded individuals (associated with Feuerstein).

Intelligence. The sum total of an individual's declarative (factual) and procedural knowledge, as well as general strategies for obtaining information, solving problems, and monitoring one's own cognitive processes. As such, intelligence cannot properly be assessed outside of its cultural context.

Intelligence Quotient. Originally, the IQ was a person's Mental Age (as determined by score on various test items) divided by that person's Chronological Age. Currently, IQ is determined by comparing the person's score to the mean and standard deviation of the test.

Item analysis. A collection of procedures to assess whether individual test items are contributing to the internal consistency of the test as a whole and are at the proper level of difficulty to achieve the test's purposes. The three most common procedures are the following: Discriminating Power, Difficulty, and Distractor Effectiveness.

Item difficulty. The proportion of test-takers who correctly answer a test question: the fewer people who answer correctly, the greater the item's difficulty.

Interference. The debilitating effect of experience on one task on the learning or retention of another task. There are two basic types of interference:

1. **Proactive:** The debilitating effect of learning one task on the learning or retention of a subsequent task.
2. **Retroactive:** The debilitating effect of learning one task on the retention of previously learned material. (See also Transfer and Facilitation.)

Intermittent reinforcement. A reinforcement schedule in which reinforcement is provided after some, not all, of the correct responses. Two basic types of intermittent schedules are Interval and Ratio schedules.

Interpersonal Intelligence: See Multiple Intelligences.

Interval schedule. A reinforcement schedule in which reinforcement is contingent on a correct response following a specified amount of time that has passed since the last reinforcement.

Intrapersonal Intelligence: See Multiple Intelligences.

Involuntary behaviors. Environmentally controlled behaviors; reflexes; respondents.

Keyword method. A mnemonic technique for paired-associates in which a concrete keyword is identified for each member of the pair and then the two are visualized interacting (e.g., Harrisburg-Pennsylvania becomes "hairy" and "pencil," or a "hairy pencil").

Knowledge-acquisition components. Aspects of intelligence that obtain and discriminate information, such as obtaining meaning from context and selective encoding (one of Sternberg's Components of Intelligence).

Knowledge of results. See Feedback.

Knowledge structures. The organization of knowledge in some, usually hierarchical, manner. As such structures become habitual, we speak of them as schemata (as in experts).

Lateral thinking. A method of generating alternative approaches to solving a problem, such as asking "why," trying to create component parts of a problem, or reversing the process to begin at the end and go backwards (due to de Bono).

Learned helplessness. An emotional, motivational and cognitive disability that results from exposure to noncontingent, unavoidable punishing consequences.

Learned optimism. In Seligman's theory, a positive, constructive attributional style based on realistic chances for success; a mastery orientation.

Learning. A relatively permanent change in behavior due to experience (and not due to maturation or temporary factors such as fatigue or drugs). Often distinguished from **performance,** from which learning is inferred. Something can be learned and not performed (because conditions or reinforcers are not conducive to performing the behavior), but something that is performed can be assumed to be learned if it is not attributable to the factors mentioned above. (See also Cognitive Constructivism and Cognitive Learning.)

Learning effect of modeling. New behaviors that are acquired as a result of observing a model perform them.

Learning for mastery (LFM). A mostly group-based mastery learning system made popular by Bloom.

Learning hierarchy. An ordered set of intellectual or motor skills such that each step in the sequence is prerequisite to, and therefore provides positive transfer for, the next.

Learning time. Time allotted for students to practice what they do not know, to make errors, and to begin to develop competence in a grade-free environment (see also Formative evaluation).

Learning-to-learn (Learning set). The improvement that occurs in speed and efficiency of acquisition or problem-solving when a person continues to be faced with tasks of the same type (i.e., with many similar elements).

Linguistic Intelligence. See Multiple Intelligences.

Locus of control. In attribution theory, the extent to which people attribute their successes or failures to their own efforts (internal locus of control) or to outside forces (external locus of control).

Logical consequences. Outcomes of a behavior which naturally or logically follow from the behavior and, in the optimal case, correct for any misbehavior—that is, logical consequences provide restitution for misbehavior or accidents.

Logicomathematical experience. In Piaget's theory, discoveries by a child of logical relations that allow reasoning to develop.

Logical-Mathematical Intelligence. See Multiple Intelligences.

Long-term memory. The processes involved in maintaining knowledge or skills for hours, days, or years, even when that material is not being actively used. Long-term memory processes interact with short-term processes, so that new information may call up stored information, both then are reconsidered in working memory, and then restored in long-term memory.

Magic number 7 ± 2. The number of unrelated items of information that can be learned or attended to at a time (in short-term memory) without being encoded or chunked in some way.

Mastery learning. An instructional system based on mastery testing.

Mastery testing. Requiring that a student achieve above a minimum standard of performance on a specified set of educational objectives (criterion-referenced assessment), even if several attempts must be made to achieve that standard.

Matching items. Test items in which two lists of randomly ordered names, concepts or premises are to be paired or matched with each other. When properly constructed, they reduce the probability of guessing associated with two-choice items and are, therefore, admirably suited for measuring knowledge objectives, though they can also measure comprehension or application.

Matching law. The generalized finding that behavioral choices occur in proportion to the frequency, magnitude or delay of reinforcement obtained by the various behaviors. That is, the frequency of or effort put into a particular behavior will tend to match the reinforcement available; e.g., we spend twice as much time on behaviors that reap twice the reward.

Maturation. A process of physical and mental growth that is primarily, if not solely, due to a genetic unfolding with age.

Mean. The arithmetic average of a set of scores (as well as the fulcrum or balance point of those scores if they were placed on a balance beam); calculated by summing the scores and dividing by the number of scores.

Meaningfulness of material. A measure of the learnability or memorability of material. High meaningfulness implies that the material can be related to a person's previous experience.

Measurement. The process of numerically quantifying performances or traits by scoring or ranking.

Median. The midpoint of a set of scores, so that there are an equal number of scores above that point as below it.

Metacognitive processes. Processes of monitoring one's own cognitive processes; for example, knowing when you have adequately memorized a list, planning how to allocate time to solve a problem, etc.

Metacomponents. Aspects of intelligence that deal with controlling and monitoring solution processes—e.g., defining the problem, ordering the steps to proceed, deciding whether to represent a problem verbally or visually, allocating time and energy, and checking your solution to be sure it makes sense (one of Sternberg's Components of Intelligence).

Misbehavior. Any action taken where it is not wanted.

Mnemonics. Memory aids; specifically a class of techniques using imagery or other elaborative techniques to memorize lists of isolated material or otherwise difficult-to-associate items.

Mode. The most frequent score in a distribution of scores.

Model. In imitation, the person whose behavior is imitated.

Modeling. The process of demonstrating a behavior and thus increasing the probability that it will be learned and remembered.

Monitor progress and adjust teaching. The essential element of instruction that implies that a teacher must assess, formally or informally, whether students are assimilating the material in the lesson. Student behavior must be checked so that the teacher knows whether to reteach, have a practice session, or move on to a new objective.

Motivation. An active participation in, attention to, or focus on a task. (See Motivation: Intrinsic and Extrinsic.)

Motivation, extrinsic. Active participation in a task which is maintained by the consequences of the behavior (e.g., attention, praise, remuneration). Please note that this does not necessarily destroy internal motivation, but can enhance it.

Motivation, intrinsic. Active participation in a task which is maintained by satisfaction in the task or performance itself.

Multiple-choice items. Test items, usually with a stem (premise) and four or five options from which to select. Properly constructed, they can measure the attainment of instructional objectives from basic knowledge to analysis and evaluation.

Multiple Intelligences. Gardner's theory that intelligence is the capacity to solve problems or create valuable products in one or more of seven domains:

1. **Linguistic:** sensitivity to language and its meanings, as in writers or poets.

2. **Logical-Mathematical:** skill in logic, abstract reasoning, and data analysis, as in scientists and mathematicians.
3. **Spatial:** capability of visualizing and perceiving space from various perspectives, as in architects and artists.
4. **Musical:** creativity in playing or writing music, as in composers and musicians.
5. **Bodily Kinesthetic:** expressiveness through controlling body movements, as in dancers or surgeons.
6. **Interpersonal:** capacity to understand and empathize with other people, as in therapists and teachers.
7. **Intrapersonal:** capacity to self-reflect and access one's own emotions, behaviors, and beliefs, as in therapists.

Musical Intelligence: See Multiple Intelligences.

Near transfer. Performance on a target task which is quite similar to the original, or previous, learning task. (See Far transfer for the opposite end of the continuum.)

Negative reinforcement. The removal of an aversive stimulus as a consequence of the performance of an operant response (e.g., escape). Its effect is to increase or maintain the rate of the response.

Negative reinforcer. A consequence of a person's behavior that removes an aversive situation or a threat and therefore increases the probability that the behavior will be repeated.

Noncontingent reinforcement. The presentation of a reinforcing stimulus whether or not the correct response has been made.

Norm-referenced assessment. The interpretation of a person's score (e.g., test score) compared with the distribution of others' scores (the norm) on the same exercise.

Norms. Shared expectations or attitudes about what are appropriate and inappropriate behaviors. In statistics, averages.

Objective. A description of the student's behavior at the end of the lesson. It specifies the specific **content** to be learned, the **behavior** the student will be able to perform, the **standard** of performance, and often the **conditions** under which the behavior will be able to be performed.

Objectives, selecting at the correct level. Defining the goals of the lesson to match the entering level of skill and/or knowledge of each student.

Objectives, taxonomy of. See Taxonomy.

Objectives, teaching to. Congruency between the teacher's actions, the students' behaviors (See Teacher Actions), and the lesson's objectives.

Observer. In imitation, the person who witnesses the behavior of a model.

Operant. A response for which no eliciting stimulus can be found, but whose rate is determined by its consequences (the stimuli that follow). Such a response is usually called "purposeful," or "voluntary."

Opportunity (Time allowed): In Carroll's model, the time allotted for learning to occur.

Original learning, degree of. The extent to which students master material when first exposed to it. The degree of original learning is critical for retention.

Overlearning. Practice beyond first mastery of material or skills. Overlearning greatly enhances retention.

Partial reinforcement. Same as Intermittent reinforcement.

Participation, covert. The student's mental involvement in the lesson.

Participation, overt. Involvement of the student in the lesson in active, behaviorally observable ways.

Peer coaching. In Staff Development, any of several methods of teachers observing and providing Feedback for other teachers while they are both in the process of attaining competence in using a new instructional skill.

Peer mediation. An approach to conflict resolution in which a cadre of students are trained in communication and negotiation skills to assist their peers in solving disputes. Also see Conflict Resolution.

Peer tutoring. A procedure in which more advanced students help less advanced students achieve instructional objectives.

Percent agreement. A criterion-referenced measure of predictive validity or reliability in which such test decisions as "pass" or "fail" are made on the predictor and criterion tests (or test and retest, etc.). Decisions which are the same for both tests are then divided by the total number of decisions to give the proportion of same decisions.

Percentile rank. A standardized score to describe a person's position in a distribution of scores; the percentile tells the percentage of people who scored below that person (e.g., the 84th percentile means the person scored higher than 84% of the people taking the test).

Perception. The active process of interpreting or giving meaning to stimuli; making sense of sensations.

Performance. An observable behavior. (See also Learning.)

Performance components. Aspects of intelligence which involve the final step in solving problems, such as selecting among alternatives, doing calculations and drawing inferences (one of Sternberg's Components of Intelligence).

Performance items. Test situations in which the examinee is expected to demonstrate a skill or knowledge through actual performances. To avoid unreliability of scoring, it is necessary to establish criteria to be judged for the various important components of the skill tested.

Permastore. Bahrick's term for material once learned that survives five years: it will then likely be permanently stored for the next 25 years as well.

Perseverance. In Carroll's model, the time the learner is willing to spend.

Persistence. The ability to continue to respond despite non-reinforcement; frustration tolerance; resistance to extinction.

Personalized System of Instruction (PSI). A mostly individualized method of mastery learning popularized by Keller.

Phobia. An extreme fear which is out of proportion to the situation, cannot be reduced by reasoning, is usually beyond voluntary control, leads to avoidance of the feared object, and for which we may have some biological preparation.

Physical restraint. "Holding back" a person from aggressive behavior until the person calms down and assumes self-control (an alternative to punishment).

Portfolios. Systematic collections of student work, in which students (1) select work that is representative of their best efforts, (2) reflect on their work and development, (3) revise and update the pieces to be included, and (4) organize the material and provide a rationale for what is included.

Positive reinforcement. The use of a (reinforcing) stimulus to increase or maintain the rate or frequency of an operant response.

Positive reinforcer. A consequence of a person's behavior that increases the probability that the behavior will be repeated.

Practice. Repeated active involvement with material or a skill in order to learn and remember it better.

Practice, distributed. Repeated active involvement with material or a skill, but with breaks between practice sessions. It is very important for good retention.

Practice, guided. Repeated active involvement with material or a skill by a student in the presence of and with active coaching by the teacher.

Practice, independent. Repeated active involvement with material or a skill undertaken by a student without the teacher present (for example, homework). The teacher should make certain that the student can do the task correctly before assigning independent practice.

Practice, massed. Repeated active involvement during one continuous time period. It is often helpful for new learning, but not for retention.

Preferred activity. A type of secondary or conditioned reinforcer that consists of activities or behaviors people engage in frequently (given no external constraints).

Premack principle. A behavioral principle which states that of two activities, if the more preferred (more probable) behavior is a consequence of the less preferred, it will act to reinforce the latter (and therefore increase its probability).

Preoperational stage. The second stage of Piaget's theory, corresponding to early childhood (age 2–7), in which the child, though still primarily egocentric, learns social communication through language and action and learns some of the rudiments of mentally representing objects and ideas.

Primary reinforcement. (a) A reinforcer that satisfies a biological need (e.g., food); (b) The process of rewarding an operant response with a primary reinforcer.

Primary reinforcer. A stimulus that is rewarding because it fulfills some basic biological need (for example, food, water, or sleep).

Procedural knowledge (Knowledge how). Information and skills on how to perform things, combine information, solve problems.

Proctor. In Keller's Personalized System of Instruction, a peer tutor who also administers and scores tests and generally helps a portion of the class master the objectives.

Production deficiency. A transfer problem or lack of metacognitive processing in which people do not adequately use a learning or memory strategy spontaneously at appropriate times, even though they have used it appropriately in the past.

Programmed instruction. The generic term for a variety of self-instructional materials in which learners progress through the material at their own rate, often in small steps, until they master the instructional objectives. This has often been accomplished in book form, through specially designed teaching machines, and more recently via computers.

Progressive relaxation. A systematic procedure for relaxing the whole body by tensing and then relaxing each major muscle group in turn.

Pro-social behavior. Behaviors such as cooperation, sharing and showing empathy; opposite of aggressive or hostile behavior.

Proximal Development. See Zone of Proximal Development.

Psychosocial development theory. Erikson's theory of a person's development of identity and competence through the resolution of a series of developmental challenges or crises in eight more-or-less distinct stages. Resolution of these crises allows a healthy progression and identity development; failure to resolve a crisis results in arrested psychosocial development or various pathological stages. The stages and to-be-resolved crises follow:

1. **Infancy (0–12 months).** Learning to trust or mistrust one's environment and significant others.
2. **Early Childhood (2–3 years).** Learning autonomy vs. shame and doubt through expressions of controlling and being controlled by others, as in potty training.
3. **Childhood (3–5 years).** Learning initiative vs. guilt by extending the previous stage to intruding upon the world through curiosity, by voice and behavior, by sexual imaginations (i.e., the Oedipal conflict).

4. **School Age (6–11 years).** Learning to deal with the industry vs. inferiority crises, in which mastery of societally prescribed skills and knowledges, often in competition with others, are fundamental.
5. **Puberty and Adolescence.** Learning to synthesize an identity vs. having identity confusion, through the roles that are assumed, the cliques or lifestyles joined, and the experiments with dating and love.
6. **Young Adulthood.** Learning intimacy (to become "we" instead of "me") with a partner vs. continued isolation and perhaps promiscuity; also achieving in a world of work.
7. **Middle Age.** Resolving the crisis of generativity vs. stagnation, in which the adult becomes a helper or teacher and continues to grow in his/her profession and love relationship or becomes bored and unfulfilled.
8. **Old Age.** If the previous crises are resolved, the adult will have achieved an ego integrity in which contentment and acceptance of the life that was lived allow even death to be faced fearlessly; failure to resolve these crises leads to despair, regrets and the belief that existence is meaningless.

Punishment. The procedure of applying an aversive stimulus to the subject as a consequence of his behavior. Its usual effect is to decrease temporarily the rate of responding.

Quality of instruction. In Carroll's model, the extent to which material is properly sequenced and mastered at each stage of learning.

Rapanoia. The (pathological?) non-fear of real threats that should be feared.

Rate of response. Same as **Response frequency**.

Ratio schedule. A reinforcement schedule in which reinforcement is contingent on the number of responses performed, no matter how long it takes to emit the response.

Reality therapy. An approach to learning self-discipline that makes people accept the logical consequences of their own behavior, accepts no excuses for inappropriate behavior, and requires people to recommit to new, more appropriate behavior if their behavior is unsuccessful.

Reciprocal determinism. The interdependence of organism with organism or organism with environment in which each affects, causes or in some way controls the other.

Reconstructive memory. Recall of prose material along with, or perhaps replaced by, embellishments that are purely the invention of the reader (or listener). Such reconstructive processes are not necessarily errors; rather they result from the natural "analysis by synthesis" processes of learning and retention.

Reinforcement. A consequence of a behavior that has the effect of increasing or maintaining the frequency of that behavior; the procedure of regulating behavior in the above way.

Reinforcement contingency. The operative rule governing which responses are to be reinforced.

Reinforcement schedule. A statement or rule that specifies how many or what proportion of the correct responses will be reinforced.

Reinforcer. A reinforcing stimulus.

Reinforcing stimulus. (a) A stimulus that comes after a response has been made and that increases the rate or frequency of that response; (b) A reward.

Reliability. In testing, the extent to which we can place confidence in the consistency, repeatability or stability of scores, ranks or decisions derived from a test. There are several ways of collecting evidence on reliability, as follows:

1. **Test-retest reliability.** The extent to which the same test items, administered on two separate occasions, will provide the same scores ranks, or decisions on the individuals tested.

2. **Parallel or equivalent forms reliability.** The extent to which two subsets of items sampled from the same domain or population of test items will provide the same scores, ranks or decisions on the individuals tested.
3. **Internal consistency reliability.** The extent to which various subsets of a particular test (e.g., the odd items vs. the even items) will provide the same scores, ranks or decisions on the individuals tested.

Reproductive memory. Recall of material much as it was presented, without embellishments; particularly used to describe factual recall of prose material.

Resistance to extinction. The ability of a response to be maintained at its previous frequency when it is no longer reinforced; persistence; frustration tolerance.

Respondent. A response that follows a stimulus and is elicited by it as a reflex; involuntary behavior.

Response. An act that can be described as a single operation. The act can be as simple as a reflex or as complicated as the operation of walking or talking.

Response facilitation effect of modeling. A behavior of an observer that occurs because a model's behavior serves as a cue (e.g., applauding when others do).

Response frequency. A description of how often a response occurs in some period of time.

Restitution. Correcting for misbehavior, making right what went wrong; using logical consequences of a misbehavior to correct the behavior (an alternative to punishment).

Retention. The amount of material remaining some time after it was originally learned.

Retribution. Punishment based on retaliation or revenge: "an eye for an eye."

Retrieval. The processes by which material once encoded and stored in long-term memory is able to be recalled. (See Availability and Accessibility.)

Satiation. The process of making a stimulus excessively available so that it is no longer reinforcing.

Savings. A measure of retention which tells the amount of time saved relearning. It is calculated as time needed for original learning minus time needed for relearning the same material.

Scaffolding. Teaching which begins with the current structure of students' knowledge, erects a temporary scaffold to build a more complex structure, and then rebuilds as needed to complete the students' knowledge structure. (See also Curriculum.)

Schema (pl. Schemata). Structures of organized knowledge (e.g., hierarchies of knowledge) which are active, well-practiced and often therefore automatic, allowing people to interpret new information or solve problems in terms of this prior store of knowledge.

S-delta (S^Δ or S^-). The particular stimulus that represents an occasion on which a response is not reinforced, in contrast to S^D, which represents the occasion on which the response will likely be reinforced.

Second-order conditioning. See Higher-order conditioning.

Secondary reinforcer. A stimulus, such as money or praise, that is reinforcing because it has been paired with (or is exchangeable for) a primary reinforcer.

Self-control. Behavior that occurs in the relative absence of external constraints that is less likely than some alternative available behavior (e.g., not eating instead of eating when at a buffet).

Self-efficacy. Belief in one's competence.

Self-evaluation. Comparing one's own behavior to some standard of acceptable performance; part of the self-control process.

Self-monitoring. Observing and recording one's own behavior (usually for the purpose of developing self-control).

Self-reward. Reinforcing oneself with praise or a favorite activity as a result of a favorable self-evaluation; part of the self-control process.

Sensation. Stimulation that is registered by a sense organ, such as light to the eye or pressure to the touch.

Sensori-motor stage. The first stage of Piaget's theory, corresponding to infancy (birth to 18–24 months), in which the child through actions transforms simple reflexes into structured, coordinated patterns (schemata), learns object permanence (that things do not cease to exist when out of sight), and learns the rudiments of language, thought and imagination.

Sensory memory. The "after-image" or "echo" that extends sensations in time to allow us to encode, interpret or rehearse them. Under the best of conditions, sensory memory may last only up to perhaps 10 seconds, and is usually only a second or two.

Set, anticipatory. The initial parts of a lesson (verbal or visual stimuli) which engage the students' prior knowledge and past experiences, bringing them through active participation into contact with the current lesson's objectives. If the set is congruent with the objectives, it facilitates understanding of the lesson. If it is not congruent, it can interfere with understanding the lesson.

Set, mental or (perceptual). A tendency to perceive or respond to problems or situations in a fixed manner because of previous experience; mental rigidity.

Shaping. The procedure of reinforcing successively closer approximations of the desired behavior in order to teach a new response.

Short-answer items. A test question which requires the examinee to recall and a word or short definition to complete a sentence or identify what has been described. Such items are best suited for measuring recall of factual knowledge.

Short-term memory. The active processes that keep small amounts of information in our attention while we rehearse or otherwise encode them to place them in long-term memory. The material in this **working memory,** usually lasts only for a few seconds, or perhaps up to a minute or two, before decaying rapidly. Material which is adequately rehearsed or otherwise encoded is stored for future use in long-term memory.

Significant difference. A difference between two scores or means of distributions which is statistically reliable.

Situated cognition: A constructivist theory of cognitive processes and knowledge acquisition which states (1) that what is learned is determined by how it is learned, (2) that learning is dependent on the context or situation in which it occurs, and (3) that knowledge is specific to the culture in which it has been developed and used.

Social cognitive theory. A theory (due to Bandura) explaining behavior as multi-determined by three sets of interacting variables—namely, (1) environmental events, (2) the behavior itself and its intrinsic and external consequences; and (3) cognitive or other personal thoughts or beliefs.

Social reinforcer. A type of secondary or conditioned reinforcer that is provided by interaction with another person. Examples are smiles, praise, and attention.

Social speech. The first stage of speech development (in Vygotsky's theory of language and thought), characterized by the need to communicate and have one's needs met. See also Egocentric and Inner Speech.

Socialization. The developmental process whereby children adopt the behavioral patterns within the range of what is acceptable to the culture in which they grow up.

Sociodynamic law. In any group of people a few will have many friends and admirers and the majority will have few friends and admirers.

Sociometric wealth. See the Sociodynamic law.

Sociometry. A procedure for assessing the friendship patterns (liking and disliking) within a group.

Spatial Intelligence: See Multiple Intelligences.

Spearman Rank Order Correlation r_s). A measure of the correlation (relationship between two sets of scores) which is calculated by ranking each set of scores from first to last and then calculating the degree to which individuals maintain approximately the same rank order on both measures. It is calculated by (1) obtaining two scores on the same individuals, (2) ranking the scores for all individuals on each of the measures, (3) finding the difference (d) between ranks for each individual, (4) squaring those differences, (5) summing those squared differences (to obtain sum d^2), and (6) calculating r_s by the following formula:

$$r_s = 1 - [6\,(\text{sum } d^2)]/[N^3-N]$$

Specific determiner. A word (such as all, always, none, never) which almost always makes a test item or alternative choice false and, therefore, makes the item easier to solve by a test-wise examinee no matter what the content. Such words should always—that is, usually—be avoided in item writing.

Specific transfer. Facilitation of one learning task as a result of previous experience with another task that had many similar elements (also see Identical elements); usually contrasted with General transfer.)

Spiral curriculum. See Curriculum.

Spontaneous recovery. In extinction, an increase in the rate of behavior after the rate of behavior has been reduced to nearly zero; the cause is seldom known, but it is a well-known effect during long sequences of non-reinforced behavior.

Staff development. A systematic program for teachers, administrators and other relevant personnel for maintaining continual growth (and motivation for growth) and expansion of the repertoire of instructional skills and knowledge.

Standard. A pre-established minimum level of achievement for instructional objectives, necessarily adopted for criterion-referenced assessment and mastery learning programs.

Standard deviation. A measure of the amount of variation or average spread of the scores around the mean. It is calculated by (1) subtracting the mean from each score, (2) squaring each difference score obtained, (3) summing the squares, (4) dividing by the number of scores, and (5) taking the square root of the average obtained in 4.

Standard error (SE) of measurement. An estimate of the spread of scores an individual might be expected to have on a test as a result of the test's own unreliability and variability in scores. Where r=Reliability, and SD=Standard Deviation, $SE = SD\,\sqrt{1-r}$.

Stimulus. An environmental event to which an animal or person is sensitive.

Stimulus generalization. The finding that a response originally reinforced in the presence of one stimulus will also occur in the presence of other similar stimuli.

Storage. The long-term processes which maintain material in memory (See Availability and Accessibility.)

Subjective organization. The self-imposed, idiosyncratic ways people have of structuring or organizing information to be learned or stored in memory.

Successively closer approximations. Responses that are getting closer and closer to the desired behavior. These responses are reinforced in order to shape more complex responses out of simple responses.

Summative evaluation. Testing which is conducted after the time for learning has expired and serves, like a final exam, to assess the final outcome of learning. It can be criterion-referenced or norm-referenced.

Synectics. A form of creativity training (devised by Gordon) which attempts to bring together diverse and apparently irrelevant elements by techniques which "make the strange familiar" and "make the familiar strange."

Systematic desensitization and counter conditioning. A procedure for establishing a hierarchy of anxiety-producing stimuli or events and learning to relax instead of feel tense in their presence; used to reduce fears and phobias.

Task analysis. A list of the essential objectives, and the hierarchy and sequence in which they must be learned, in order best to achieve a higher order objective (or an objective to be revisited in a spiral curriculum).

Taxonomy of educational objectives in the cognitive domain. (By Bloom, 1956): A classification of objectives according to a hierarchical level of complexity of cognitive processes involved. The six levels follow:

1. **Knowledge.** Recall of specific information (e.g., definitions).
2. **Comprehension.** Understanding, organizing or extrapolating information (e.g., paraphrasing or translating an idea).
3. **Application.** The ability to transfer an idea or principle learned in one setting to another setting (e.g., to use a mathematical formula in solving a real problem).
4. **Analysis.** The ability to find the component parts of a whole and show how they are related (e.g., to divide a discipline situation into its component behaviors and consequences).
5. **Synthesis.** To assemble parts into a whole (e.g., to be able to take various components of a discipline situation and construct a plausible sequence of events in terms of reinforcements).
6. **Evaluation.** The ability to make judgments about the relative usefulness of various materials or ideas according to certain criteria (e.g., to judge when positive reinforcement would be more effective than punishment with what side effects in solving a discipline problem).

Teacher actions. The behaviors of the teacher designed to have the students learn the objectives. They are of four types: (1) Asking Questions, (2) Providing Information, (3) Designing Activities, and (4) Responding to Students.

Teaching-learning functions: An analysis, due to Shuell, of such learning processes as motivation, feedback and encoding, and how they are likely enacted when initiated by the teacher and by the student. See also Events of Instruction.

Time out (from reinforcement). A technique for reducing the frequency of undesirable behaviors by removing the person from the situation in which reinforcements are available to a situation in which they are not available.

Token. A type of secondary or conditioned reinforcer that is a physical or countable item, such as money or course grades.

Token economy. A small social system in which reinforcement in the form of some kind of token is provided immediately following the performance of desired responses by its members.

Transfer. A change in performance on one task as a result of experience on another task. There are therefore three possible types of transfer:

1. **Negative.** The inability to use previously learned knowledge or skills—or the misapplication of such knowledge or skills—in a novel situation; the interference of components of two or more learning tasks, such that skill in one task makes learning the second task more difficult.

2. **Positive.** The ability to use relevant knowledge or skills learned in one situation in another, novel situation; the similarity of components of two or more learning tasks, such that skill in one task makes learning the second task easier.
3. **Zero.** The independence of components of two or more learning tasks, such that skill in one task neither helps nor hinders learning the other task.

Triarchic Theory of Intelligence. Sternberg's theory which suggests that intelligence has three parts: (1) the internal, cognitive mechanisms (knowledge acquisition, metacognitive, and performance components) which produce intelligent behavior; (2) the interaction of those mental processes with experience that, with practice, leads to automatization and expertise; and (3) the cultural environment in which those mental processes occur.

True score. The mean score a person would have on a particular test if he or she took a test, say, 100 times. This is estimated on the basis of the person's obtained score by the Standard Error of Measurement of the test, and by calculating a Confidence Interval.

Two-choice items. Test items which require selection from among two alternatives; e.g., true-false or yes-no. They are most suited to measuring knowledge objectives, though they are particularly susceptible to guessing.

Unconditioned response (UR). A response that is automatically elicited by a stimulus; a reflex. Also called a Respondent.

Unconditioned stimulus (US). A stimulus that comes before and elicits or causes a reflexive response (the response is called a respondent or unconditioned response).

Validity. In testing, the extent to which a test—or more precisely, the use and interpretation of a test—is measuring what it was designed to measure. There are several ways of collecting evidence on validity, as follows:
1. **Construct-Related Evidence for Validity.** The extent to which the test measures a meaningful trait or domain of behavior.
2. **Content-Related Evidence for Validity.** The extent to which the test provides a representative sample of the range of abilities, situations and/or topics being tested.
3. **Criterion-Related (Predictive) Evidence for Validity.** The extent to which a test accurately predicts performance on a criterion test or in the real-life situation of interest.

Variable-interval (VI) schedule. An interval schedule in which reinforcement is contingent on performance of the next correct response following passage of the average of some predetermined amount of time.

Variable-ratio (VR) schedule. A ratio schedule in which reinforcement is contingent on performance of the average of some predetermined number of responses.

Vicarious consequences. Witnessing the consequences of a model's behavior (e.g., reinforcement or punishment) which has a parallel effect on the observer's behavior.

Vicarious emotional learning. The situation that exists when an observer imitates the emotional response of a model, despite not directly being influenced by the cause of the model's behavior (e.g., fearing a spider because a model fears spiders).

Vicarious reinforcement. In imitation, the procedure of an observer witnessing a model's behavior reinforced, with the usual result that the probability of that behavior by the observer is increased.

Voluntary behavior. Purposeful behavior; operants.

Winnetka Plan. Possibly the first system of mastery learning (in the 1920s) which required minimum standards to be met on necessary instructional objectives; on other nice-to-know objectives, called "social work," simple exposure to the material replaced mastery requirements.

Within-class grading. Criterion-referenced grading for use in a mastery learning program designed (1) to motivate each student to master the minimum objectives at a high level and (2) to go beyond those to achieve enrichment objectives and strive toward expertise in the area of study.

Working memory. See Short-term memory.

Writing performances. Authentic tests of the student's ability to write. The academic content is not being tested; style, organization, grammar and other aspects of skill as a writer are.

Written report. An extended essay or term paper requiring days or weeks to complete, which may include such components as (1) requiring research and data analysis, (2) inventing an organizing structure for comparing findings, and (3) synthesizing and evaluating results.

Z-score. A standardized score interpreted in terms of the normal curve, with a mean of zero and standard deviation of one. It is calculated for any individual by subtracting the mean from the person's score and dividing by the standard deviation.

Zone of proximal development. In Vygotsky's theory, a measure of the mental activity of children who may not be successful on their own but, with stimulation from an adult or more advanced peer, can be successful. The less assistance needed, the more ready the child is for independent success.

APPENDIX A

RAPANOIA: WORSE THAN PARANOIA

APPENDIX B

SOME USEFUL STATISTICS AND HOW TO CALCULATE THEM

I. Calculating the Mean and Standard Deviation

The standard deviation is a measure of the variability or spread of scores in a distribution. It is defined in relation to the mean of those scores, since the mean is the balance point (or fulcrum, to use an analogy to a plank and weights placed at various distances from the mean) of the distribution of scores.

For example, suppose we have the following scores on a 10-point test for five individuals:

Student	Test Score	Plank and Weight Analogy
John	10	
Mary	8	
Susan	8	
Joseph	6	
Walter	3	
Total	35	

The total score of 35 is obtained by summing all five scores (represented by X). The mean ($\overline{X}$) is the sum of the scores (Sum X) divided by the number of scores (N):

$$\text{Mean } (\overline{X}) = \frac{\text{Sum of Scores}}{\text{Number of Scores}} = \frac{\text{Sum X}}{N} = \frac{35}{5} = 7$$

Now, if the fulcrum is placed at 7, and at no other place, the plank will be balanced, which is why the mean can be called the balance point of the distribution of scores.

The standard deviation, then, is a measure of the spread of scores around the mean. The closer the scores are clustered around the mean, the smaller the standard deviation. The extreme case is that in which all scores are the same (e.g., 7, 7, 7, 7, and 7), in which case the standard deviation would be zero, since there is no variability of scores. The further the scores are spread out, the larger the standard deviation.

To calculate the standard deviation, we first calculate the mean. Then we subtract the mean from each person's score to obtain a deviation or difference score, as follows (using the above example):

Student	Test Score (X)	Mean ($\bar{X}$)	Score minus Mean $X-\bar{X}$	Squared (Score minus Mean) $(X-\bar{X})^2$
John	10	7	10−7=3	9
Mary	8	7	8−7=1	1
Susan	8	7	8−7=1	1
Joseph	6	7	6−7=−1	1
Walter	3	7	3−7=−4	16
				Sum $(X-\bar{X})^2 = 28$

John's score of 10 minus the mean of 7=3. Mary's 8−7= 1, and so on.

Next, we square those difference scores. John's difference score of 3, when squared is 9. Mary's $1^2 = 1$, and so on.

Next, we sum the squares: 9+1+1+1+16 = 28.

Next, we divide by the number of scores (to obtain the mean squared differences). This result is technically called the *variance*.

$$\text{Variance} = \frac{\text{Sum}(X-\bar{X})^2}{N} = \frac{28}{5} = 5.6$$

Finally, the standard deviation is the (positive) square root of the variance. That is, we take the square root of the result just obtained:

$$\text{Standard Deviation} = \sqrt{\text{Variance}} = \sqrt{\frac{\text{Sum}(X-\bar{X})^2}{N}} = \sqrt{5.6} = 2.366$$

In summary, the steps in calculating a standard deviation are as follows:

1. Calculate the mean ($\bar{X}$), by summing the scores (Sum X) and dividing by the number of scores (N): $\bar{X} = \frac{\text{Sum } X}{N}$
2. For each individual tested, subtract the mean from each score $(X-\bar{X})$, to obtain the deviation or difference score.
3. For each individual, square that deviation score: $(X-\bar{X})^2$.
4. Sum all of the squared deviations (differences) from the mean: $\left[\text{Sum}(X-\bar{X})^2\right]$

5. Obtain the mean of those squared differences by dividing the sum of the difference scores by the number of scores: $\frac{\text{Sum }(X-\overline{X})^2}{N}$. This is called the variance.

6. Take the square root of the variance $\sqrt{\frac{\text{Sum }(X-\overline{X})^2}{N}}$. This is called the standard deviation, which is a measure of the average amount of deviation from the mean.

II. Calculating a Correlation Coefficient Using Ranks

A correlation coefficient is a measure of the degree of relationship between two sets of scores. The most common method for calculating correlation coefficients (Pearson's r) determines the relationship between two *scores* on the same individuals (or things). An alternative method developed by Charles Spearman (r_s) uses two *ranks* for the same individuals. For our present didactical purposes, the ranking method has two advantages: (1) it is intuitively relatively obvious and (2) it is able to be calculated rather simply by hand. Consider the following sets of scores (and resultant ranks) on five individuals:

Person	Score 1	Rank	Score 2	Rank	d	d2
Alfred	20	1	65	3.5	2.5	6.25
Bertha	18	2	70	2	0	0.
Charles	16	3	40	5	2	4.
Darlene	14	4	75	1	3	9.
Edward	12	5	65	3.5	1.5	2.25
						Sum d² = 21.50

The steps involved in calculating a Spearman rank order correlation are the following:

Step 1. Obtain two sets of scores on each individual. (For the example provided, the scores might be two different tests, one test and the students' weights, etc.)

Step 2. Rank each set of scores from 1 to N, where N is the number of individuals for whom you have scores (in this case N = 5). Where ties occur, the average of the ranks is given to each person tied (i.e., since Alfred and Edward are tied for third place on Measure 2, they get the average of the third and fourth ranks they occupy, or 3.5. (If there had been three people tied for third, they would occupy ranks 3, 4 and 5, the average of which would be 4). Note that the next-ranked person, Charles receives a rank of 5, not 4. NOTE: The sum of the ranks with ties must be equal to the sum of the ranks without ties (i.e., 1 + 2 + 3 + 4 + 5 = 15 and 1 + 2 + 3.5 + 3.5 + 5 = 15).

Step 3. For each individual calculate the absolute difference (d) between the two sets of ranks. (Absolute difference means without regard to whether the difference is positive or negative). For Alfred d = 1 − 3.5 = 2.5; for Bertha, d = 2 − 2 = 0; etc.

Step 4. For each individual, square the absolute differences (d) obtained in Step 3 to obtain d². For Alfred (2.5)² = 2.5 × 2.5 = 6.25.

Step 5. Total the d²s to obtain the Sum d², in this case 21.5.

Step 6. Insert the values for N and Sum d² into the following formula and solve the equation (where N3 = N × N × N):

$$r_s = \left[1 - \frac{6(\text{Sum } d^2)}{N^3 - N}\right]$$

$$= \left[1 - \frac{6(21.5)}{(5)^3 - 5}\right]$$

$$= \left[1 - \frac{129.0}{125 - 5}\right]$$

$$= 1 - 1.075$$

$$= -.075$$

Step 7. Interpret the correlation in terms of the extent of relationship. Correlations distribute themselves on a normal curve with the most likely correlations being about zero, but with possible extreme values of + 1.0 and – 1.0.

The present correlations of –.075 is slightly negative, but very close to zero and is thus considered to show essentially *no relationship* between the two measures (as would probably occur if the measure were test performance and weight of elementary school students).

Exercise: Interested readers may want to demonstrate to themselves that the rank order correlations between scores 1 and 2 and between 1 and 3 are +1 and –1, respectively. (Note that N = 6).

Score 1	Score 2	Score 3
120	10	20
110	9	30
100	8	40
90	7	50
80	6	60
70	5	70

III. Calculating the Percent Agreement (as a Measure of Criterion-Referenced Predictive Validity or Reliability)

A Validity Example

Continuing with the argument for assessing the validity of criterion-referenced testing (from Chapter 15), suppose a teacher wrote a 25-item mastery test for a unit in Spanish II. One way of finding the predictive validity of the test—that is, whether the test accurately predicts the competence level of the students—is to see whether it accurately classifies students about which we already have independent evidence. Thus students who are now in Spanish III, having already passed Spanish II, can be said to be "Known Masters." Students who have not yet been exposed to this material, such as a Spanish I class, could constitute a comparison group since they would be "Known Nonmasters."

Following this logic, one can calculate a percent agreement between the two measures, previous accomplishments, and current test (based on such procedures as those in Martuza, 1977, pp. 289–292). Consider the following table for five Spanish III students and five Spanish I students who took the 25-item test, where 80% was considered passing:

Student	Prediction Based on Known Accomplishments	Test Result	Agreement (A) or Disagreement (D)
1. Sp. III	Pass	21	A
2. Sp. III	Pass	18	D
3. Sp. III	Pass	19	D
4. Sp. III	Pass	25	A
5. Sp. III	Pass	25	A
6. Sp. I	Fail	16	A
7. Sp. I	Fail	17	A
8. Sp. I	Fail	12	A
9. Sp. I	Fail	13	A
10. Sp. I	Fail	20	D

First, note that in column 2 students are predicted to pass or fail the test based on their current level of accomplishment—that is, whether they are in Spanish I or Spanish III.

Second, since this is a mastery test, their actual test scores in column 3 have to be converted to a pass or fail decision, based on the 80% passing standard for the test (80% of 25 = passing score of 20). Thus student #1, who is known to have mastered the material actually did pass, as did students #4 and 5. These can be considered correct positive decisions (see also table 14. 2) and thus counted as Agreements in column 4. Students #2 and 3, however, did not pass and thus there was a Disagreement (column 4) regarding the prediction and the outcome. These students may have forgotten some of this Spanish II material over time or, perhaps, the test is making a false negative decision—a kind of invalidity.

Regarding the Spanish I predictions, students #6–9 all failed the test as predicted and thus they are counted as Agreements. Since they are known to be nonmasters, they should not be able to pass a valid test—that is, these are correct negative decisions. Regarding student #10, who was predicted to fail but passed, this is a false positive decision or Disagreement from the standpoint of the test's validity.

The calculation of the percent agreement, then, is straightforward, as follows:

$$\text{Percent Agreement} = \frac{\text{Number of Agreements}}{\text{Number of Agreements + Disagreements}}$$

In this case,

$$\text{Percent Agreement} = \frac{7}{10} = .7 \text{ or } 70\%$$

The higher the % agreement, of course, the more valid the test. Each Disagreement constitutes evidence that either the test or our validating information is incorrect. In either case, it shows the fallibility of our test. Thus we should strive for agreement scores of 80% or above.

A Reliability Example

As noted in Chapter 15, there are three standard ways of collecting classroom data on test reliability: test-retest, parallel forms, and split-half reliability. If mastery testing is the plan for the Spanish II unit described above, the teacher should have invented at least two 25-item parallel forms of the unit test. To check parallel-forms reliability, she could give both forms at the same time to her actual Spanish II class and ask if both forms make the same decision. Consider the following example for a class of 12 Spanish II students:

Student	Score on Form 1	Score on Form 2	Agreement (A) or Disagreement (D)
1	25	25	A
2	25	23	A
3	23	21	A
4	22	22	A
5	22	19	D
6	22	20	A
7	20	18	D
8	19	20	D
9	19	23	D
10	18	19	A
11	15	14	A
12	13	12	A

In this case (based on Pass = 20 or above, Failing = 19 or less), the calculation is as follows):

$$\% \text{ Agreement} = \frac{\text{Agreements}}{\text{Agreements} + \text{Disagreements}} = \frac{8}{12} = .67 = 67\%$$

This would be marginally adequate reliability: OK for classroom use in which students who failed would have another opportunity to demonstrate mastery, but insufficient for a higher-stakes exam for licensing or certification.

It should be noted that the above procedure is exactly the same as would be done if two raters were judging performances as passing or failing; that is, the percent agreement score is analogous to and calculated the same way as *inter-rater agreements..*

Finally, consider the following alternate way of tabulating the above data (for either validity or reliability):

		Form 2		
		Pass	Fail	Totals
Form 1	Pass	A 卌	B ‖	7
	Fail	C ‖	D ‖‖	5
	Totals	7	5	12

In this case, student #1, who passed both forms of the test is counted as a stroke in Box A, as are #2,3,4, and 6. Students #5 and 7, who passed Form 1, but failed Form 2 are counted in Box B. Students #8 and 9 failed form 1 and passed form 2 and thus there are two strokes in Box C. And Students #10-12 all failed both forms and are counted in Box D.

Now since Boxes A and D constitute Agreements between the two tests and B and C Disagreements, then a percent agreement can be calculated by the following formula:

$$\% \text{ Agreement} = \frac{\text{Agreements}}{\text{Agreements} + \text{Disagreements}} = \frac{A + D}{A + B + C + D}$$

$$= \frac{5 + 3}{5 + 2 + 2 + 3} = \frac{8}{12} = .67 \text{ or } 67\%$$

The same procedure can be used for Odd vs. Even halves of a test or test-retests. Finally, it can also be used for Known Masters vs. Known Nonmasters and a test, as in the Validity example above, as follows:

	Spanish II Test		
	Pass	Fail	Totals
Known Masters	A III	B II	5
Known Nonmasters	C I	D IIII	5
Totals	4	6	10

AUTHOR INDEX

Abbott, E., 52–54, 563
Abramson, L. Y., 140, 549, 563
Abruscato, J., 530, 563
Adams, N., 363, 593
Adelson, B., 359, 555, 563
Ahukanna, J. G. W., 294, 563
Airasian, P. W., 529, 563
Aitkin, A. C., 354, 355
Aldrich, C., 256
Alexander, P. A., 36, 115–116, 575
Alexander, R. N., 181, 563
Allen, V. L., 434, 571
Amsel, A., 183, 551, 563
Anderson, J. R., 290, 291, 295, 310, 313, 317, 322, 325, 553, 555, 563
Anderson, L., 445–446, 449, 473, 558, 563, 566
Anrig, G. R., 441, 563
Apfel, C. H., 181, 563
Appel, J. B., 255, 573
Appel, L. F., 337, 563
Arbitman-Smith, R., 111, 567
Arlin, M., 447, 449, 563, 564
Armstrong, T., 103, 564
Arnedt, C. S., 328, 564
Arnold, C. R., 565
Arnoult, M. D., 294, 564
Asch, S. E., 218–220, 229, 564
Astin, A. W., 560, 564
Austin, G. A., 54, 568
Atkinson, R. C., 326, 564
Ausubel, D. P., 288, 291, 300, 302, 408, 564
Awooner-Williams, G., 334
Azrin, N. H., 253, 564

Baehre, M. R., 333, 564
Baer, D. M., 181, 184, 191, 340, 574, 594
Bahrick, H. P., 332, 343–345, 564
Bahrick, P. O., 343, 564
Ballachey, E. L., 219, 583
Balsam, P. D., 264, 551, 564
Bandura, A., xiv, 13–16, 35, 140, 152, 162, 206–212, 217, 551, 552, 564, 565
Bangert-Drowns, R. L., 451, 583
Barber, B. R., 539–540
Barker, G., 565
Barker, L. L., 396, 582
Barnett, L., 555, 565
Baron, J. B., 399, 565, 582
Barrows, H. S., 527, 565

Bartlett, F.C., 341, 343, 565
Bassock, M., 412, 576
Bates, M., 408, 557
Bauer, R. N., 336, 565
Baxter, G. P., 527, 591
Bayley, N., 76, 565
Becker, W. C., 178, 565, 583, 585
Begg, I., 328, 587
Bejarano, Y., 591
Bellanca, J., 472, 592
Belmont, J. M., 338, 340, 565
Bem, D. J., 149, 565
Benoit, E. P., 68, 594
Berk, R. A., 511, 565
Berkowitz, L., 212, 231, 552, 553, 565, 566, 587
Berliner, D. C., 364, 410, 417, 566
Biehler, R. F., 36, 566
Bilodeau, E. A., 409, 566
Bilodeau, I. McD., 409, 566
Binet, A., 62–65, 88, 90, 111, 546, 547, 566
Biran, L. A., 332, 584
Bloch, A., xiii, 566
Block, J. H., 446–447, 449, 451, 473, 482, 558, 566
Block, K. E., 190
Bloom, B. S., 77, 298, 376, 380, 394, 398–401, 410, 412, 417, 426, 444–449, 462, 473, 488, 489, 492, 502, 514, 517–521, 556, 557, 558, 566, 567
Bloom, K. C., 331–332, 567
Boe, E. E., 551
Bondy, A. S., 264, 551, 564
Bonwell, C. C., 410, 567
Bootzin, R. R., 184, 187, 189, 582
Boring, E. G., 546, 547, 554, 567
Borkowski, J. G., 336, 340, 565, 567, 589
Boulle, P., 272, 567
Bower, G. H., 131, 183, 282, 297, 299, 358, 555, 563, 567, 578, 579
Boyd, H. F., 68, 574
Brady, J. W., 139, 549, 567, 588
Brainerd, C. J., 33, 54, 567
Brandt, R., 556, 567
Bransford, J. D., 111, 341, 343, 367, 370–372, 378–379, 408, 459, 555, 567
Bråten, I., 36, 567
Bregman, E., 130, 567, 595
Briggs, L. J., 300, 412, 556, 574
Brim, O. G., 552, 567

Brockopp, G., 545
Broder, L. J., 380, 567
Brooks, P., 111, 579
Brophy, J. E., 36, 89, 227, 231, 404, 548, 568, 577
Brown, A. L., 36, 113, 115, 292, 301, 324, 335, 338, 340, 379, 557, 568, 569, 587
Brown, G. D., 255, 568
Brown, J. S., 288–290, 294, 568
Brown, M., 394, 402, 580
Brown, R., 205, 214, 337, 568
Brown, S. I., 463, 568
Bruner, J. S., 24, 54, 288, 291, 292, 300, 311, 398, 457, 461, 553, 568
Büchel, F. P., 336, 340, 567
Buckholdt, D., 573
Bugelski, B. R., 280, 282, 283, 326–327, 568
Buium, N., 596
Bunch, M. E., 334, 577
Burden, P. R., 238, 568
Burgess, A., 128, 568
Burns, R. B., 449, 451, 558, 563, 566, 568
Burns, S., 111, 579
Buros, O.K., 68
Burt, C., 547
Butkowski, I. S., 144, 568
Butterfield, E. C., 565

Cain, L. F., 332, 568
Cairns, R. B., 64, 568
Cameron, J., 265, 568
Campbell, B. A., 587, 589
Campbell, D. T., 501, 568
Campione, J. C., 335, 338, 340, 379, 569
Cannizzo, S. R., 337, 582
Canter, L., 251, 257, 569
Canter, M., 251, 257, 569
Carey, L., 556, 571
Carey, S., 368, 383, 569
Carroll, J. B., 69, 96–97, 415–417, 444, 449, 452, 569
Carroll, J. D., 179, 579
Carter, L. J., 334, 594
Carter-Sobell, L., 320, 584
Carton, A. S., 33, 34, 590
Casanova, U., 417, 566
Cattell, J. McK., 63–64, 546–547, 569
Ceci, S. J., 342, 569
Chaffee, S. H., 214, 569

Chance, P., 558–559, 569
Charles, C. M., 251, 569
Charness, N., 357, 557, 569
Chase, W. G., 323, 356–357, 365, 561
Cherry, E. C., 312, 569
Chi, M. T. H., 362, 383, 569
Child, I. L., 5, 569
Church, R. M., 194–196, 551, 570
Churchill, W., 383–384, 570
Clarizio, H. F., 88, 570
Clarke, D. E., 255
Cleary, T. A., 83, 87–88, 570
Cofer, C. N., 554, 570
Cohen, P. A., 434, 570, 583
Cohen, S. A., 449, 580
Colby, A., 45, 48, 118, 570
Cole, M., 570
Collins, A., 288, 568
Collins, A. M., 555, 570
Colliver, J. A., 527, 570
Combs, A. W., 473, 570
Conrad, D. G., 567, 588
Cooley, W. W., 560, 570
Cooper, R. G., 563
Cornbleth, C., 539, 570
Costa, A. L., 399, 570
Craik, F. I. M., 554, 570
Crehan, K. D., 511, 570
Crespi, L., 183, 570
Cronbach, L. J., 83, 404, 428, 461, 463, 500, 548, 560, 570
Crutchfield, R. S., 219, 583
Csapo, K., 328, 587
Cummins, J., 62, 84, 87, 561, 571
Cureton, L. W., 471–472, 571

Damarin, S. K., 289, 571
Daniel, M., 532, 574, 582
Davenport, J. W., 135, 571
Davis, M., 152, 571
Davis, S. R., 262, 586
Davison, G. C., 152, 571
deBono, E., 370, 372, 379, 380, 382, 459, 461, 555, 571
DeCecco, J. P., 245, 285, 571
Deci, E. L., 265, 590
Deese, J., 282–283, 298, 551, 571, 579
deGiovanni, I. S., 577
deGroot, A. D., 356, 571
Delaney, H. D., 326, 589
Dennis-Rounds, J., 326, 589
Derry, S. J., 378, 571
deSaint Exupery, A., 237, 571
Desrochers, A., 328, 587

Detterman, D. K., 290, 571
Devin-Sheehan, L., 434, 571
Deutsch, M., 260, 571
Dewey, J., 287, 392–393, 539, 561, 571
Dick, W., 556, 571
Diener, C. I., 549, 571
Dilendik, J. R., 21, 36, 226, 545, 571
Dobzhansky, T., 78, 571
Dollard, J., 212, 571
Doob, L. W., 571
Dooling, J. L., 343, 408, 572
Doran, R. L., 528, 571
Dowling, M., 354, 380, 572
Doyle, W., 245–246, 572
Drabman, R. S., 189–190, 192, 577, 587
Drake, M., 265, 584
Dreikurs, R., 127, 240, 247, 252, 256, 572
Driscoll, M. P., 413, 572, 574
Duguid, P., 288–290, 568
Dumas, G., 294, 591
Duncan, C. P., 294, 299, 572
Dunkin, M. J., 450, 558, 572
Dweck, C. S., 142, 146, 147, 549, 571, 572
Dyer, G., 87

Early, C. J., 549, 572
Ebbinghaus, H., 328–329, 332, 343, 345, 554, 572
Ebel, R. L., 482, 572
Edwards, B., 458, 559, 572
Efthim, H. E., 449, 451, 566
Egeth, H., 298, 551, 579
Eisenhauer, M., 197
Eisner, E., 488, 572
Eison, J. A., 410, 567
Elkind, D., 30, 119, 548, 572
Elliott, E., 471, 594
Elliott, J. L., 327, 572
Ellis, H. C., 280, 282, 283, 285, 297, 408, 555, 572
Ellis, J. A., 345, 591
Ender, P., 434, 596
English, H. B., 130–131, 572
Ennis, R. H., 557, 573
Erickson, M., 552
Ericsson, K. A., 323, 365, 569, 573
Erikson, E., 34, 36–44, 50, 112, 119–120, 144, 248, 546, 548, 573
Eshelman, E. R., 152, 571
Evans, F. B., 472, 573

Farnham-Diggory, S., 274, 573
Farnsworth, P. R., 587
Feldhusen, J. F., 245, 573
Feldman, R. S., 434, 571
Feldmesser, R. A., 482, 573
Ferguson, G. A., 280, 283, 573
Ferritor, D. E., 189, 573
Ferster, C. B., 255, 451, 573
Feshbach, S., 212, 553, 573
Festinger, L., 216, 573
Feuerstein, R., 96–97, 106–111, 112, 372, 399, 573
Finn, C. E., Jr., 540, 589
Fiske, D. W., 501, 568
Flanders, J. P., 551, 573
Flavell, E. R., 574
Flavell, J. H., 36, 44, 115, 336–337, 563, 573, 574, 582, 586
Forgan, H. W., 90, 574
Foster, H. L., 253, 574
Fowler, S., 184, 574
Franklin, B., 186, 574
Frazier, T. W., 264, 550, 575
Frederiksen, N., 532, 574
Fremer, J., 532, 574, 582
Freidenberg, E. Z., 264, 574
Friedrich, L. K., 213, 573, 574, 594
Friedrichs, A. G., 115
Freud, S., xii, 36, 40, 42, 43, 546
Furby, L., 560, 570

Gage, N. L., 420, 574
Gagné, E., 597
Gagné, R. M., 285, 292, 300, 412–414, 556, 574
Galambos, R., 588
Galanter, E., 326, 586
Gallagher, J. J., 68, 574
Galton, F., 63–64, 546, 574
Garber, J., 549, 574
Garcia, J., 133, 574
Garcia, K. A., 577
Gardner, B. T., 198, 354, 575
Gardner, H., 68, 96–97, 101–106, 111, 112, 151, 372, 379, 574, 575
Gardner, M., 546, 555–556, 575
Gardner, R. A., 198, 354, 575
Garner, R., 36, 115–116, 575
Garguilo, R., 597
Garstons, H. L., 574
Gates, S. L., 578
Gay, J., 570
Gebhart, R. H., 131, 575
Gentile, J. R., xi, 85, 105, 113, 141, 143, 144, 147, 179, 259, 264, 278,

291, 294, 326, 327, 328, 333–336, 396, 404, 443, 448, 450, 482, 488, 492, 529, 542, 545, 547, 550, 556–557, 558, 560, 563, 564, 572, 575, 576, 579, 581, 584, 586, 590, 620–621
Gerstle, G., 339
Gibboney, R. A., 393, 576
Gibson, E. J., 294, 576
Giles, K., 597
Gilligan, C., 48–49, 576
Ginott, H., 252, 257, 553, 576
Ginsburg, H. P., 23, 114, 545, 576
Girton, K., 373
Glaser, R., 72, 292, 332, 362, 366–367, 383, 402, 412, 414, 556, 560, 569, 576, 590
Glasser, W., 51, 248–251, 253, 255, 257, 552, 576
Glick, J., 98, 570
Glucksberg, S., 274, 576
Gnagey, W. J., 237, 253, 596
Goddard, H. H., 62, 65–67, 547, 577
Goldman, R., 545
Goldman, T., 336, 595
Good, T. L., 36, 89, 227, 231, 404, 405, 548, 568, 577
Goodlad, J. I., 541, 577
Goodnow, J. J., 54, 568
Gordon, T., 252, 577
Gordon, W. J. J., 457–458, 461, 559, 577
Gormezano, I., 132, 549, 577
Gould, S. J., 97, 547, 577
Gravelle, R., 374
Gray, J. A., 312, 577
Graziano, A. M., 549, 577
Green, A., 230
Green, F. L., 576
Green, J. A., 499, 514, 521, 577
Greene, D., 264–265, 551, 584
Greenfield, P. M., 568
Greeno, J., 288, 577
Gregory, S. C., Jr., 334, 577
Griffin, M., 373, 578
Gronlund, N. E., 502, 506, 515, 529, 560, 561, 577
Gross, A. M., 192, 577
Gruber, H. E., 55, 577
Grunwald, B., 572
Guilford, J. P., 68, 381, 461, 578
Gump, P. V., 253, 583
Guskey, T. R., 149, 420, 451, 578
Guthrie, E. R., 196, 578
Guttman, N., 174, 578

Haladyna, T. M., 512, 515, 522, 578, 586
Haley, J., 552, 578
Hall, M. C., 256, 258, 578
Hall, R. V., 178, 256, 258, 578
Halpern, A. R., 358, 555, 578
Halwes, T. G., 586
Hambleton, R. K., 560, 578
Hamblin, R. L., 573
Hamilton, J., 136
Haney, C., 221–222, 224, 226, 245, 578
Hanley, E. L., 597
Hapkiewicz, W. G., 549, 590
Harlow, H. F., 118, 293, 578
Harrison, R. H., 174, 580
Hart, L. B., 472, 592
Harter, S., 192–193, 298–299, 578
Hasher, L., 314, 343, 553, 578
Hastings, J. T., 445–446, 473, 502, 514, 521, 567
Hatch, J., 101, 103–104, 106, 575
Hays-Roth, B., 365, 578
Haywood, H. C., 111, 579
Heider, F., 226, 579
Hembrooke, H., 342, 569
Hendel, D. D., 149, 590
Henderson, L. D., 79, 547, 579
Hendrickson, G., 282, 295, 579
Henri, V., 64
Herbert, J., 586
Herrnstein, R., 7, 62, 63, 77, 79–80, 97, 547, 579
Hersh, R. H., 293, 420, 582
Hertz-Lazarowitz, R., 558, 591, 593
Hilgard, E. R., 131, 282, 292, 299, 567, 579
Hiroto, D. S., 140, 549, 579
Hively, W., 502, 579
Hoffman, B., 86, 579
Hoffman, H. G., 342, 584
Hoffman, K., 454, 579
Hoffman, M. B., 96, 573
Holdsworth, N. A., 241
Holland, P. C., 137, 589
Holt, J., 146, 231, 302–304, 471, 472, 482, 579
Holubec, E. J., 435, 438, 581
Holz, W. C., 253, 564
Hosie, T. W., 179, 579
House, B. J., 299, 335, 597
Hovland, C. I., 132, 135, 294, 295, 579
Hoyt, J. D., 115, 573
Huesmann, L. R., 549, 579

Hughes, J., 555, 579
Hulse, S. H., 183, 185, 282–283, 298, 551, 571, 579
Humphreys, L. G., 570
Hunt, E., 376, 579
Hunt, J. McV., 77, 96–97, 111, 546, 579
Hunt, R. R., 555, 572
Hunter, I. M. L., 355, 358, 579
Hunter, M., 279, 285, 291, 302, 393–410, 411, 413–414, 471, 489, 556–557, 579, 580
Husek, T. R., 511, 588
Huston, A. C., 552, 565
Huston-Stein, A., 212, 552, 580
Huyghe, P., 342, 580
Hyman, J. S., 449, 580

Iheozor-Ejiofor, I. E., 334, 576
Immerwahr, J., 246, 581
Inhelder, B., 21, 26, 30, 546, 588
Irion, A. L., 284, 585
Isaksen, S., 559, 580

Jackson, D., 578
Jackson, P. W., xi, 580
Jacobsen, E., 152, 580
James, W., 148, 150, 205, 209, 303, 311, 313, 553, 580
Jenkins, H. M., 174, 580
Jensen, A. R., 7, 78–80, 83–84, 86–88, 338, 340, 376, 547, 548, 580, 581
Jenson, W. R., 257, 581
Johnson, D. W., 228–229, 259–260, 262, 430, 435–436, 438, 558, 581, 593
Johnson, J., 246, 581
Johnson, M. K., 341, 343, 408, 567
Johnson, R. T., 228–229, 259–260, 262, 430, 435–436, 438, 581, 593
Johnson-Gentile, K., 105, 259, 549, 550, 553, 581
Johnston, J. M., 256, 551, 581
Jones, H. E., 130, 581
Jones, M. C., 130, 581
Joyce, B., 120, 293, 404, 418, 420, 428, 459–460, 463, 557, 558, 581, 582, 585
Judd, C. D., 282, 295, 582
Jung, J., 294, 582
Jussim, L., 548, 582

Kagan, S., 433, 558, 582, 593
Kalish, H. I., 135, 174, 578, 582
Kamin, L. F., 547, 582

Kane, M. T., 507, 582
Kanfer, F. H., 192, 582
Kaplan, J., 556, 590
Karda, T., 546
Karier, C. J., 86, 582
Kaufman, B., 224–225, 582
Kazdin, A. E., 184, 187, 189, 191, 550, 582
Kean, M. H., 582
Kearney, C. P., 533, 582
Kearney, M., 584
Keeney, T. J., 115, 336–337, 473, 582
Keller, F. S., 444, 450, 489, 558–559, 582
Keller, H., 96, 103
Kelley, M. L., 178, 582
Kelly, E. W., 153–154, 582
Kenefic, L., 152
Kendrick, S. A., 570
Keppel, G., 332, 334, 582, 592
Ketcham, K., 342, 584
Kibler, R. J., 396, 582
Kidd, E., 326–327, 568
Kieslar, E. R., 461, 557, 592
Kimble, G. A., 131, 583
King, L. A., 597
Kintsch, W., 555, 583
Kirschenbaum, H., 471, 472, 583
Koelling, R., 133, 574
Kohlberg, L., 44–49, 55, 112, 114, 117, 118, 207, 570, 583
Köhler, W., 272, 583
Kohn, A., 265, 583
Kopfer, P. M., 336, 583
Kounin, J. S., 253, 583
Kozol, J., 227, 583
Krasavage, E. M., 393, 593
Krasner, L., 152, 583
Kratochwill, T. R., 152, 549, 586
Krech, D., 218–219, 583
Krechevsky, M., 105, 575
Kreidler, W., 260, 262, 263, 583
Kreschevsky, I., 198, 583
Krueger, W. C. F., 329, 583
Krumboltz, H. B., 178, 583
Krumboltz, J. D., 178, 583
Kulik, C. C., 434, 449, 451, 558, 570, 583
Kulik, J. A., 434, 449, 451, 570, 583
Kunen, S., 597
Kussel, P., 591
Kuypers, D. S., 188, 583

LaBerge, D., 314, 583
Lachman, R., 343, 408, 572

Lachowitz, J., 597
Lalley, J. P., 557, 583
Lambert, W. E., 587
Lambdin, P. W., 521–531, 583
Larkin, J. H., 359, 584
Lave, J., 289
Lazarus, R. S., 127, 149, 549, 584
Lee, C. Z., 285, 302, 592
Leeper, R. W., 185, 584
Leggett, E. L., 146, 572
Leinhardt, G., 419, 584
Leith, G. O., 332, 584
Lepper, M. R., 264–265, 551, 584
Levin, J. R., 326, 584, 589
Lewis, C., 359, 584
Lewis, J., 376, 579
Lewis, M., 73, 76, 584
Lewis, R., 230, 584
Lewis, S., 434, 596
Leyens, J. P., 552, 587
Licata, L., 164
Licht, B. G., 142, 146, 572
Light, L. L. 320, 584
Linn, R. L., 527, 594
Lipman, M., 376–379, 559, 584
Litman-Adizes, T., 140. 596
Livingston, J. A., 448, 584
Lochhead, J., 380, 555, 597
Lockhart, R. S., 554, 570
Loftus, E. F., 342–343, 584
Logan, F. A., 149, 296, 584
Logan, G. D., 553, 584
Lohnes, P. R., 560, 570
Luchins, A. S., 274, 408, 584
Luke, C., 586
Lund, D., 578
Lund, N. J., 294, 563
Lunneborg, C., 376, 579
Lykken, D. T., 550, 584
Lynn, R., 547, 585

MacKenzie, C. L., 557, 585
Madaus, G. F., 445–446, 473, 498, 502, 514, 521, 567, 585
Madsen, C. H., 178, 565, 585
Madsen, C. K., 178, 585
Maeroff, G. I., 531, 585
Mager, R. F., 396, 585
Mahoney, M. J., 192, 595
Maier, S. F., 588
Maltzman, I., 381, 585
Marcia, J. E., 548, 585
Marks, I. M., 549, 585
Marteniuk, R. G., 557, 585
Martinez, J. G. R., 451, 585

Martinez, N. C., 451, 585
Martuza, V. R., 505, 585
Maruyama, G., 436, 581
Marx, M. H., 591, 594, 597, 598
Mascitelli, S., 191, 582
Maslow, A. H., xii, 49–52, 112, 120, 163, 246, 248, 585
Mason, J. W., 567, 588
Mayor, J. R., 574
Mazrui, A. A., 228, 552, 585
Mazur, J. E., 259, 553, 585
McCarrell, N., 563
McDivitt, H.,184
McGeoch, J. A., 284, 554, 585
McIntire, R. W., 178, 585
McKay, M., 152, 571
McKibbin, M., 120, 293, 420, 582, 585
McNamara, J. R., 189, 585
McNeil, C., 278, 553
McNeil, D., 337
McNemar, Q., 547, 585
Meadows, A., 370, 585
Mearig, J. S., 111, 586
Meehl, P. E., 500, 550, 570, 586
Meier, S. T., 262, 500–501, 586
Meister, C., 292, 590
Merrill, M. A., 547, 595
Messick, S., 527, 586
Miles, D. T., 396, 582
Milgram, S., 218, 222–223, 225, 586
Miller, G. A., 317, 326, 586
Miller, H. G., 515, 582, 586
Miller, I. W., 549, 586
Miller, N. E., 571
Miller, R., 96, 573
Milliken, S., 373
Millman, J., 482, 490–491, 586
Milne, A. A., 334
Minton, H. L., 77, 81, 83, 546, 547, 586
Minturn, A. L., 311, 568
Moely, B. E., 115, 336–337, 586
Monaco, N. M., 141, 143–144, 147, 334–335, 576, 586
Moore, J. W., 132, 549, 577
Moreno, J. L., 225–226, 586
Morgan, B., 485, 586
Morris, M. C., 264, 550, 575
Morris, R. J., 152, 549, 586
Mowrer, O. H., 127, 138, 139, 194, 571, 586
Moynihan, D. P., 218, 231, 246, 586
Mt. Pleasant, J., 335, 576

Murdock, B. B., Jr., 281, 316–317, 586
Murnyack, N. C., 482, 488, 529, 576
Murphy, D. A., 378, 571
Murphy, G., 205, 586
Murphy, L. B., 205, 586
Murray, C., 7, 62, 63, 77, 79–80, 97, 547, 579
Muuss, R. E., 119, 548, 587

Napier, R. W., 472, 583
Ndu, A. N., 334, 576
Neal, M., 11
Needham, R. J., 545
Neimark, E., 337, 587
Neisser, U., 288, 310–311, 313, 315, 343, 345, 555, 587
Nelson, D., 581
Nelson, D. S., 111, 587
Newman, E., 215, 218
Nichols, R. C., 82, 84, 587
Nitco, A. J., 72, 501, 560, 576, 587
Noble, C. E., 325, 587
Norman, D. A., 361–362, 590
Norman, G. R., 527, 594
Norman, W. H., 549, 586

Ogbonaya, P. K., 334, 576
Okagaki, L., 105, 575
O'Leary, K. D., 178, 179, 189–190, 583, 587, 594
O'Leary, S. G., 178, 587
Olson, F., 586
Olver, R. R., 568
Opollot, J. A., 332, 584
Opper, S., 23, 114, 545, 576
Osborn, A., 370, 587
Osborne, J. G., 179, 587
Oscanyan, F. S., 376, 584
Osgood, C. E., 281, 587
O'Sullivan, J. T., 589

Paivio, A., 328, 587
Palincsar, A. S., 292, 301, 379, 587
Panos, R. J., 560, 564
Papert, S., 112, 117, 281, 539, 587
Papp, K. K., 177, 551, 587
Paradise, N. E., 300, 574
Parke, R. D., 552, 587
Parnes, S. J., 370, 585
Paul, R. W., 114, 379, 588
Pavlov, I P., 7, 8, 12, 129–131, 135, 588
Payne, D. A., 515, 588
Payne, J. S., 593

Payne, R. A., 593
Pea, R., 289, 588
Pepper, F., 572
Perkins, D. N., 282, 290–292, 588
Perrott, M. C., 451, 573
Peters, A. S., 434, 588
Peterson, C., 140, 142, 145, 588
Peterson, L. R., 316–317, 588
Peterson, M. J., 316–317, 588
Piaget, J., xii, 21–32, 36, 44, 112–113, 118, 296, 322, 328, 342, 366, 409, 426–427, 545, 546, 548, 557–558, 588
Pierce, W. D., 265, 568
Pigott, T. D., 451, 578
Pine, J., 527, 591
Popham, W. J., 476, 482, 501, 511, 514, 515, 516, 560, 588
Porter, R. W., 139, 567, 588
Posner, M. I., 553, 588
Postman, L., 294, 329, 588
Premack, D., 176–179, 198, 354–355, 351, 555, 588, 589, 594
Presbrey, L., 593
Pressey, S. L., 442–443, 557, 589
Pressley, M., 290, 326, 337–338, 589
Pribram, K. H., 326, 586
Pruitt, D. G., 260, 589
Pryor, K., 456, 589
Psotka, J., 321, 596

Quagliano, J., 551, 591
Quetelet, A., 546
Quillian, M. L., 555, 570
Quinby, N., 532, 589

Rachford, D. L., 111, 591
Rand, Y., 96, 573
Ravitch, D., 540, 589
Raviv, S., 591
Rayner, R., 8, 130, 135–137, 596
Reder, L. M., 290, 553, 563
Redfield, D. L., 410, 589
Rees, E., 569
Reese, E. P., 174, 257, 589
Renner, K. E., 184, 589
Reppucci, N. D., 147, 549, 572
Rescorla, R. A., 133, 135, 549, 589
Resnick, D. P., 498, 589
Resnick, L. B., 191, 498, 556, 589, 590
Reynolds, C., 558, 560, 590
Reynolds, D. S., 532, 590
Reynolds, G. S., 183, 590
Reynolds, J. H., 332, 590

Richards, A. K., 245, 571
Rieber, R. W., 33, 34, 590
Riecken, H. W., Jr., 216, 573
Rioch, D. McK., 588
Robin, A. L., 558, 590
Robbins, P., 593
Roden, A. H., 549, 590
Roeber, B. L., 582
Rogers, C., xii, 427, 590
Rohwer, W. D., Jr., 325, 338, 340, 580, 581, 590
Roid, G., 512, 578
Rosenshine, B. V., 292, 404, 405, 413–414, 590
Rosenthal, G., 260, 261, 590
Ross, D. F., 342, 569
Ross, D. M., 207, 209, 212, 552, 565
Ross, S. A., 207, 209, 212, 552, 565
Rotter, J. B., 140, 590
Rounds, J. B., Jr., 149, 590
Rousseau, E. W., 410, 589
Roy, P., 438, 581
Rozin, P., 147
Rubin, J. Z., 260, 589
Rummelhart, D. E., 361–363, 590
Russell, D., 449, 596
Ryan, B. A., 191, 558, 590
Ryan, R. M., 265, 590

St. John, N., 230, 584
Salomon, G., 282, 290–292, 588
Samuels, S. J., 314, 583
Sandler, J., 551, 591
Savell, J. M., 111, 591
Scarr, S., 79, 83, 591
Schachner, J., 437
Schachter, S., 216, 573
Schmuck, P. A., 224, 591
Schmuck, R. A., 224, 558, 591, 593
Schneider, F. W., 77, 81, 83, 546, 547, 553, 586, 591, 592
Schneider, W., 313
Schoer, L., 334, 448, 591, 594
Schön, D. A., 278, 286, 289, 418, 529, 591
Schorr, D., 363, 593
Schroeder, W. H., 282, 295, 579
Schulz, C., 470
Schulz, R. W., 284, 591
Schunk, D. H., 146, 591
Scott, J., 593
Sears, R. R., 571
Sebastian, R. J., 552, 587
Segal, E., 570
Segmen, J., 326–327, 568

Selfridge, O. G., 311
Seligman, M. E. P., 127, 134, 139–146, 193, 195, 296, 549, 563, 574, 588, 591
Selinker, L., 294, 591
Semb, G. B., 345, 591
Shakespeare, W., 545
Shanker, A., 246, 541, 591
Sharan, S. 433, 436, 558, 591, 593
Sharan, Y., 591
Sharp, A. M., 376–377, 584
Sharp, D. W., 570
Shavelson, R. J., 393, 527, 591
Shaw, G. B., 420
Sherif, M., 218, 591
Sherman, J. G., 558, 582, 591
Sherwood, R. D., 567
Shiffrin, R. M., 313, 553, 591, 592
Shirley, K. W., 213, 591
Showers, B., 404, 418, 420, 581, 582
Shuell, T. J., 113, 279, 285, 302, 322, 324, 325, 331–332, 334, 336, 414–415, 567, 592
Shulman, L. S., 393, 418, 420, 461, 557, 592
Sidman, M., 165, 550, 592
Siegler, R. S., 118, 592
Sievenpiper, T., 214
Silberman, C. E., 539, 592
Simon, H. A., 290, 356–357, 553, 563, 569
Simon, S. B., 471–472, 559, 583, 592
Simon, T., 64–65, 88, 90, 566
Sims-Knight, J., 563
Sizer, T. S., 456, 527, 541, 592
Skinner, B. F., xii, 7, 9, 13, 151, 160, 163, 185, 296, 409, 426–427, 443, 556, 557, 558, 592, 593
Skon, L., 581
Slavin, R. E., 393, 427, 431–436, 473, 558, 593
Slotnick, N. S., 587
Smith, E. E., 363, 593
Smith, K., 259, 593
Smith, L., 573
Snyder, C.R.R., 553, 588
Sophocles, 546
Spearman, C., 68, 288, 504, 547, 548, 624, 593
Spence, K. W., 198, 274, 593
Sperling, G. A., 314–315, 593
Spiro, R. J., 317, 343, 593
Staats, A. W., 137, 593
Staats, C. K., 137, 593
Stachowski, E., 557

Stainback, S. B., 593
Stainback, W. C., 188, 593
Stallings, J., 393, 436, 449, 451–452, 593, 594
Starch, D., 471, 594
Stein, A. H., 213, 574, 594
Stein, B. S., 111, 367, 370–372, 378–379, 459, 555, 567
Stein, J., 570
Stein, M. I., 461, 559, 594
Stern, W. L., 66
Sternberg, R. J., 96–101, 105, 112, 115, 290, 372, 374–376, 379, 382, 399, 532, 548, 553, 555, 565, 571, 575, 594
Stevens, B. L., 582
Stevens, R., 404, 405, 413, 590
Stevens-Haslinger, C., 482, 492, 576
Stillman, P. A., 527, 594
Stipek, D., 436, 449, 451–452, 594
Stokes, T. F., 178, 181, 184, 191, 340, 582, 594
Stroud, J. B., 334, 448, 594
Sturdevant, T., 567
Suchman, J. R., 461, 463, 594
Sulzer-Azaroff, B., 257, 594
Swain, M., 294, 591
Swaminathan, H., 578
Swanson, D. B., 527, 594

Taffel, S. J., 179, 594
Taki, Y., 243
Taylor, J. A., 274, 594
Teasdale, J. D., 140, 549, 563
Terhune, J., 177, 594
Terman, L. M., 65–67, 547, 595
Tharp, R. G., 257, 596
Thomas, D. R., 178, 565, 585
Thomson, D. M., 321, 554, 596
Thoresen, C. E., 192, 595
Thorndike, E. L., 9, 280–281, 286–287, 288, 540, 595
Thorndike, R. L., 360, 376, 595
Thurlow, M., 596
Thurstone, L. L., 68, 595
Thurstone, T. G., 595
Tilton, J. W., 595
Tobias, S., 443, 595
Tobias, Shiela, 287, 595
Tobin, K., 410, 595
Toby, J., 246, 595
Toglia, M. P., 342, 569
Tolman, E. C., 160, 552, 595
Torgesen, J. K., 336, 595
Torrance, E. P., 461, 559, 595

Travers, R. M. W., 282, 285, 295, 298, 595
Triesman, A. M., 312, 595
Tuddenham, R. D., 62, 67, 546, 547, 595
Tulving, E., 321–322, 554, 555, 595, 596
Turnure, J., 338, 596
Twain, M., 211, 265, 532
Twohig, P. T., 111, 591
Tyler, L. E., 63, 596
Tyler, V. O., Jr., 255, 568

Ulrich, T., 587
Underwood, B. J., 284, 334, 408, 554, 596

Varela, J. A., 216, 596
Viek, P., 139, 586
Voelkl, K. E., 335, 576
Vye, N. J., 111, 567
Vygotsky, L. S., 33–36, 44, 54, 107, 112, 115, 119, 530, 546, 596

Wainwright, L. C., 482, 576
Walker, H., 570
Walker, L. J., 114, 596
Walker, V. L., 529–531, 583
Walter, J., 285
Walter, M. I., 463, 568
Walters, R. H., 13, 207, 565
Wang, M. C., 556, 590
Warren, R. M., 311, 596
Warren, R. P., 311, 596
Washburne, C. W., 441–443, 596
Watson, D. L., 257, 596
Watson, J. B., xii, 5–8, 130–131, 134, 596
Webb, C., 558, 593
Webb, N. M., 434, 596
Wechsler, D., 67–69, 596
Wedderburn, A. A. I., 312, 577
Weil, M., 404, 428, 459–460, 463, 552, 558, 582
Weinberg, R. A., 79, 83, 591
Weiner, B., 140, 596
Weiss, J. M., 549, 597
Wesman, A., 570
West, S. G., 552, 587
Whimbey, A., 380, 555, 597
White, R. W., 145, 597
Wiggins, G., 527, 529, 530, 597
Willey, R. DeV., 332, 568
Williams, R. G., 515, 522, 570, 586
Willows, P.M., 144, 568

Winograd, E., 345–346, 597
Wissler, C., 64, 597
Wittlinger, R. P., 343, 564
Wittrock, M. C., 294, 597
Wolf, M. M., 181, 597
Wolpe, J., 152, 597
Woodruff, G., 354, 589
Woodworth, R. S., 280, 595
Woodyard, E., 286, 595
Worden, P. E., 336, 597

Yerkes, R. M., 547, 597
Yoakum, C. S., 547, 597
Yokoi, L., 290, 589
Young, J. C., 457, 597
Young, M., 289, 597
Yussen, S. R., 337, 563, 597

Zabranskey, M. L., 550
Zacks, R. T., 314, 553, 578
Zajonc, R. B., 127, 149, 549, 597
Zeaman, D., 299, 335, 597
Zampogna, J., 439
Zimbardo, P. G., 221–222, 224, 226, 245, 578
Zimmerman, E. H., 177, 597
Zimmerman, J., 177, 597
Zinnerstrom, K., 528, 571

SUBJECT INDEX

Ability to understand instruction, 415, 599
Abusive behavior, 193–194, 195–196
Accessibility (in memory), 319–321, 332, 347, 599
Accommodation, 25–26, 599
Active learning (see also Participation, active), 24, 105, 160, 288–290, 364, 366, 378, 409, 426, 433–434, 599
Activities as reinforcers (see also Preferred activities), 176–179
Advance organizers (see also Set, anticipatory), 291, 302, 341, 408
Affective domain, 154
Aggression, 15, 128–129, 194, 205, 209–214, 231, 245–246, 255
Algorithm, 359–361, 599
Amount of learning (see also Original learning), 415–417, 599
Analysis by synthesis, 310–312, 599
Antecedent (see Discriminative stimulus),
Anticipatory set (see Set, Anticipatory),
Aptitude, 415–417, 444, 446–449, 599
Assessment, purposes of, 470–471, 599
Assimilation, 25–36, 599
Associability (see also Identical elements), 599
"At promise" individuals, 103
"At risk" (deprived) individuals, 103, 106, 111, 330–331
Attention
 as a reinforcer, 160, 163–165, 167–170, 173, 177–178, 180–182, 186–193, 196, 239, 256–257
 to stimulation, 262, 299, 311–314, 347, 413–415, 599
Attitude change, 149
Attributions, 140–146, 296, 549, 599
Authentic activities or tests (see also Performance tests), 288–289, 483–485, 526–529
Automatic attentional processing (Automaticity), 108, 291, 312–313, 347, 599

Availability (in memory), 319–321, 599
Aversive stimulus, 9, 162, 165–167, 169–172, 238–248, 545, 600
Avoidance, 165–167, 172, 193–194, 241–242, 600

Behavior (see also Response), 1, 9–10, 11–15, 140, 160–199, 206–207, 210–217, 237–265, 396
Beliefs, 10, 14, 15, 48, 140–151, 215–217, 218–219, 260, 379
Belongingness, 132–133, 600
Between-class grading, 481–483, 600
Bias in testing, 84–90, 528, 547
Biofeedback, 9, 145, 600
Bodily-kinesthetic intelligence, 102–103, 105, 609
Brainstorming, 220

Checking for understanding (see Instruction: Monitoring progress),
Chronological age (CA in IQ measures), 64, 66–68
Chunking, 317, 356–359, 600
Classroom goal structures (see also Incentive structures), 228–229, 430, 438, 600
 Competitive goal structures, 228–229, 600
 Cooperative goal structures, 228–229, 429–441, 602
 Individualistic goal structures, 228–229, 434, 606
Cognitions (cognitive processes), 1, 10–11, 84, 115–116, 140, 142–144, 198–199, 230, 287–293, 310–348, 353–384, 394, 398–401, 408–409, 515, 600
Cognitive conflicts, 22, 25, 113–114, 116, 600
Cognitive constructivism, 36, 112–113, 287–290, 345, 600
Cognitive dissonance, 216, 600
Cognitive domain (see Taxonomy),
Cognitive learning, 113, 324, 412, 600
Cognitive structure (see also Knowledge structure; Schema), 106, 300–302, 347

Compensation of relations, 22
Competence (see also Mastery), 14, 41, 51, 104, 144–148, 151, 264, 504–505, 526–529, 600
Competition, 228–230, 432, 436–438, 558
Competitive goal structures (see Classroom goal structures),
Componential analysis (of intelligence), 98–101, 461, 548, 600
Computer-assisted instruction (CAI), 117, 442–444, 601
Concrete operations stage (see Piagetian),
Conditioned reinforcer (see Secondary reinforcer)
Conditioned response (CR), 7–8, 128–138, 194, 601
Conditioned stimulus (CS), 7–8, 128–138, 217, 601
Conditioning, 127–199, 601
 Operant (Instrumental or Skinnerian), 9–10, 160–199, 238–242, 456
 Respondent (Classical or Pavlovian), 7–9, 127–154, 242, 549
Confidence interval, 507–508, 601
Conflict resolution, 48–49, 214, 259–262, 601
Conformity, 218–225, 601
Consequences (see also Vicarious and Logical consequences), 9–10, 160–172, 176–179, 193, 207–208, 247–250, 601
Conservation, 21–28, 601
 of amount (substance), 21–22, 30, 54
 of number, 29
 of volume, 30–31
 of weight, 30–31
Constructed responses (in testing), 515–516
Constructive processes (see also Reconstructive), 36, 112–113, 287–290, 311–312, 324, 402, 557–558
Contiguity, 8, 132
Contingent reinforcement, 14, 184–188, 255–258, 601
Continuous reinforcement, 179–182, 601

Contracts, 250–251, 477, 601
Contrast (or context) effect, 183, 601
Controlled attentional processing, 312–313, 601
Cooperation, 228–230, 231, 473
Cooperative goal structures (see Classroom goal structures),
Cooperative teams, 405, 426, 429–441, 486–488, 558, 602
Correlation, 73–80, 504, 507, 602, 624–625
Counter conditioning, 134, 154, 602
Creativity, 220, 302, 370–372, 451–452, 455–463, 485–486, 529, 559, 602
Criterion (Criteria), 68, 447, 485, 504–506, 526, 527–528, 602
Criterion-referenced assessment, 72–75, 88–89, 111–112, 444–455, 470–471, 475–476, 483–492, 501–502, 504, 510–513, 514, 533, 560, 602, 625–629
Critical attributes (see Distinctive features),
Cue-dependent recall, 319–323, 327, 347, 516, 602
Cues (see also Discriminative stimuli), 165, 294–295
Culture/context (see also Environment), 98–99, 106, 183, 242–245, 287–290, 302, 418
Curriculum (see also Spiral curriculum), 262–263, 286–287, 299–302, 376–379, 395–401, 443, 452, 453, 456, 533, 602

Declarative knowledge (see Knowledge)
Delay of reinforcement, 183–184, 258–259
Deprivation-satiation history, 183
Desensitization (see Systematic desensitization)
Detached teaching strategies (see Domain-general)
Development, 23–25, 96–97, 142–145, 173, 336–340, 602
Developmental crisis (see also Identity crisis), 34–35, 119
Developmental stage, 26, 52–55, 602
  Cognitive, 26–33, 35–36, 96–119
  Psychosocial, 36–44
  Moral, 44–49

Deviancy (see Discipline and Misbehavior)
Dialogical thinking, 114, 379, 603
Difficulty of a test (see Item difficulty)
Discipline, 196–198, 223–225, 237–265
Discovery learning (see Creativity and Teacher actions)
Discriminating power, 508–512, 603
Discrimination, 135–165, 170–175
Discrimination training, 135, 170–175, 294–295, 603
Discriminative stimulus, 165, 170–175, 195–196, 208, 238, 456, 603
Distinctive features, 294–295
Distractor effectiveness (see also Item analysis), 513, 522, 603
Domain-general strategies, 378–379, 603
Domain-specific strategies, 378–379, 603
Domains (of test items or objectives), 501–502
Dual coding theory, 326–328, 603

Egocentric speech, 36, 54, 603
Elaboration, 96, 107, 325–328, 335, 341–343, 347, 603
  Imagery elaboration, 325–328, 337, 347, 603
  Verbal elaboration, 325–328, 337, 603
Embedded teaching strategies (see Domain-specific)
Emotional intelligence (EQ), 151
Emotions (and Conditioned emotions), 1, 3–4, 7–9, 11–12, 127–154, 194, 198, 216–218, 242, 252–253, 296–297, 314, 458, 549
Encoding, 318–325, 347, 410, 414, 603
Enrichment activities, 451, 453, 455, 486–487
Entering behavior (or knowledge), 262, 299–302, 412, 491, 603
Equilibration, 23, 25–26, 603
Escape, 165–167, 172, 195, 238–2424, 296, 603
Essay items, 524–526, 528, 603
Essential elements of instruction (see Instruction, Essential elements)

Evaluation (see also Grading)
  vs. Measurement, 470, 473–475, 488, 604
Evaluation time, 485
Events of instruction, 413, 604
Expectations, 36, 89, 140, 149, 190, 224–225, 227, 452, 548
Experts vs. Novices, 313–314, 355–365, 382–383, 417–420, 555
Extinction, 128–130, 134, 164, 167–170, 172, 180, 184, 241, 604
Extrinsic reinforcement (see Motivation, extrinsic)

Facilitation (see also Transfer positive),
  Proactive, 284, 286–287, 604
  Retroactive, 284, 286–287, 604
Failure, 248–249
Far transfer, 297–298, 604
Fast vs. Slow learners, 298–299, 332–340, 347, 446–449, 554
Feedback, 147, 187, 292, 408–409, 413–414, 444–446, 470–471, 473, 486, 488, 528, 531, 557, 604
Forgetting (see Retention)
Formal operations stage (see Piagetian)
Formative evaluation, 445–446, 490, 604
Frustration-aggression, 212
Frustration effect (of extinction), 169, 551, 604
Frustration tolerance (see also Persistence), 151, 180–182

Gender (see Sex differences)
General factor ("g") (see Intelligence)
Generalizability (see Transfer)
Generalization (see also Stimulus generalization), 134–135, 173–175, 551, 616
Generalization gradient, 135, 173–175, 605
General transfer, 291, 298, 605
Goal structures (see Classroom goal structures)
Grades, 176, 178, 187, 469–492
Grading, 231, 404, 431, 440, 444–446, 449, 451–453, 455, 469–492, 525–526, 530–531, 560–561, 605
Grandma's law (see Premack principle)

Groups (see also Conformity, Cooperative groups), 206, 218–227, 457–458

Habituation, 193, 218, 231–232, 605
Handicapping (for Cooperative teams; see also Incentive structures), 430–432
Hierarchy of needs (Maslow's), 49–52, 246
  Physiological, 49–50
  Safety, 49–50, 246
  Belongingness and love, 49–50, 52
  Esteem, 49, 51
  Self-actualization, 49, 51–52
Helplessness (see Learned helplessness)
Heredity vs. Environment (see also Intelligence, Inheritance), xiii, 5–7, 78–82
Heritability, 78–82, 605
Heuristic, 359–361, 605
Higher-order conditioning, 135–138, 216–218, 549, 605
Higher-order thinking skills (HOTS), 462–463, 488, 524–526, 529–532, 538, 605
High road to transfer, 291–292, 294, 295, 302

IDEAL problem solver, 367, 369–374, 378–379, 459, 463, 605
Identical (or similar) elements, 281–283, 287, 293–294, 302, 320, 605
Identity
  Argument (in Piaget's theory), 22
  Crises, 34, 36–44, 605
  Psycho-social (see also Psychosocial development), 36–44, 248, 605
Imagery, 152, 297, 605
Imitation, 205–217, 551, 605
Incentive structure, 428–432, 434, 435–436, 440, 605
Individualistic goal structures (see Classroom goal structures)
Individualized instruction, 229, 443–444, 450
Inhibition (see Interference)
Inhibitory (or disinhibitory) effect of modeling, 208, 606

Inner speech, 35–36, 54, 606
In-service training (see Staff development)
Insight, 299, 302, 553
Instruction, Essential elements of, 393–410, 556, 604
  Selecting objectives, 394–401, 609
  Teaching to objectives, 395, 401–404, 455, 609
  Monitoring progress and adjusting teaching, 395, 404–406, 608
  Using principles of learning, 395, 407–410
Instructional objectives, 395–401, 412, 413, 416, 444–446, 606
Instructional outcomes, 412, 415–417, 420, 435–436, 444–452, 512, 558–559
Instrumental enrichment, 96–111, 461, 606
Intelligence, 7, 62–90, 354–355, 461, 476, 546–547, 606
  Components of (see also Componential analysis), 98–101
  "g" (General factor), 64, 68–69, 76, 96–97, 101, 106, 111, 547
  Growth of, 65, 96–120
  Inheritance of, 7, 23, 66–67, 78–82, 547–548, 554
  Stability of, 76–77
Intelligence Quotient (IQ), 62, 66–77, 83–89, 96, 101, 105, 298–299, 376, 499, 606
Interdependence of cognition, emotion, and misbehavior, 11–15, 140, 142–144, 148–153, 198–199, 237, 242, 296–297, 345, 392, 470
Interference, 281, 283–285, 294, 319, 363, 554, 606
  Proactive, 140, 284–285, 311, 319, 606
  Retroactive, 284, 319, 321–322, 606
Intermittent reinforcement, 164, 179–182, 186–187, 606
Interpersonal intelligence, 102–103, 105, 151, 609
Interval schedule, 181, 606
Intrapersonal intelligence, 102–103, 105, 151, 609

Intrinsic reinforcement (see Motivation, intrinsic)
Involuntary behaviors, 7–9, 127–154, 606
Item analysis, 499, 507–513, 522, 606
Item difficulty, 508, 512–513, 514, 603
Item discriminating power (see Discriminating power)
Item writing, 514–531

James-Lange theory, 148

Keyword mnemonic, 326, 333, 338, 606
Knowledge (types of; see also Teaching Knowledge), 287–290
  Declarative (knowing that), 322, 358, 362, 602
  Procedural (knowing how), 322, 359, 362, 611
Knowledge-acquisition components, 99–101, 372, 375–376, 607
Knowledge of results (see Feedback)
Knowledge structures (see also cognitive structures and Schema), 355–358, 362–367, 382–383, 402, 607
  Remodeling of, 363–367
Known masters vs. Known non-masters, 504–505, 626–629

Labeling
  categories, 84–90, 223, 224, 382, 498–499, 552
  as disabling, xi, xiii, 89, 137–138, 227, 499
Lateral thinking, 370, 459, 563, 607
Learned helplessness, 139–148, 193, 195, 221, 252, 607
Learned optimism, 146, 607
Learning, 10, 173, 182, 288, 415–417
  definition of, 278, 324, 607
  in the broad sense (see also Development), 23
  in the narrow sense, 23
  (see also Mediated learning and Meaningful learning)
Learning effect of modeling, 208, 607

Learning for Mastery (LFM), 444–449, 607
Learning hierarchy, 292, 300–302, 412–413, 556, 607
Learning time, 415–417, 444, 485, 607
Learning vs. Performance, 11, 208, 607
Learning vs. Persistence, 179–182, 182–184
Learning-to-learn (Learning set), 116, 293–294, 298–299, 607
Linguistic intelligence 102–103, 609
Locus of control (see Attributions)
Logical consequences, 247–251, 254, 607
Logical-mathematical intelligence, 102–103, 105, 609
Logicomathematical experience (Propositional logic), 24, 31–33, 607
Long-term memory, 317–324, 340–347, 607
Low road to transfer, 291–292, 294, 296

Magic number 7±2, 317, 608
Masochistic behavior, 193–194
Masters (see Known masters)
Mastery (see also Competence), 117–118, 144–148, 193, 263–264, 285, 291, 299, 302, 329, 457, 479
Mastery learning, 416–417, 426, 441–455, 456, 473, 608
Mastery testing, 441–442, 444–445, 483–492, 527, 608
Matching items, 518–519, 608
Matching law, 259, 608
Maturation, 23–24, 28, 76, 118–119, 608
Mean, 70–72, 476–478, 608, 622
Meaningful learning, 113, 287–290, 324, 414–415
Meaningfulness (of material), 310, 325–326, 347, 608
Measurement, 473–474, 498–513, 608
Median, 71, 608
Mediated learning, 33–35, 106–111, 192–193
Memory (see also Recall and Retention), 213–214, 278, 283–284, 314–348, 356–359, 366, 407–408, 489
Mental age (MA), 64–67, 298

Mental flexibility (see Creativity, Lateral thinking, Higher-order thinking)
Mental rigidity (see Set, mental)
Metacognitive processes, 33, 36, 100, 115–117, 151, 292, 301, 336–340, 372, 375–376, 608
Metacomponents, 99–101, 372–376, 608
Metamemory (see also Metacognitive processes), 338
Misbehavior, 164–170, 180–181, 187–191, 214, 218, 237–259, 608
Mnemonics, 325–328, 338, 347, 608
Mode, 71, 608
Model, 207–218, 230–231, 252, 608
Modeling (see also Learning effect, Inhibitory effect and Response facilitation effect), 196, 205–218, 230–232, 608
Monitor progress (see Instruction, Essential elements)
Moral development (behavior and reasoning), 45–49, 114, 218, 222–223
Moral dilemmas, 45–49, 114
Motivation, (see also Hierarchy of needs), 13–15, 49–52, 109, 120, 127–128, 140–148, 228–229, 248–249, 414, 416–417, 470, 483, 491, 608
  Extrinsic, 14, 189–191, 609
  Intrinsic, 14, 191, 426, 609
Multiple intelligences, 96, 101–106, 609
Multiple-choice items, 483, 487, 519–522, 527, 609
Musical intelligence, 102–103, 105, 609
Music and conditioning, 135–137, 150, 151–153

Nature-nature issue (see also Intelligence, Inheritance of), 5–7
Near transfer, 297–298, 609
Needs (see Hierarchy of needs)
Negative reinforcement, 165–167, 172, 195, 238–242, 253, 489, 551, 609
Noncontingent reinforcement, 178, 185, 609
Non-masters (see Known non-masters)
Nonreinforcement (see Extinction)

Normal curve, 69–72, 75–77, 446–449, 475–483
Norm-referenced assessment, 64–65, 72–75, 88, 111, 470–471, 474–483, 492, 502, 509–510, 512, 514, 560, 609
Norms
  Cultural, 223–226, 609
  Statistical, 54–55, 64, 69–72, 474, 476–478, 483, 609

Object permanence, 27–28
Objectives (see also Instruction, Selecting objectives), 257–258, 394–401, 412, 433, 438, 440, 452–453, 462, 473, 483, 487, 501, 514, 529, 609
Objective tests (see also Matching, Multiple-choice, Short-answer, and Two-choice items), 515–524, 529
Objectives, taxonomy of (see Taxonomy)
Observer, 207–218, 609
Operant (see also conditioning), 9–10, 17, 140, 142–144, 160–199, 324, 545, 609
Opportunity (Time allowed), 416–417, 444, 449, 610
Original learning, degree of, 294–295, 329–332, 334–335, 345, 347, 610
Originality (see also Creativity, Lateral thinking), 353–354, 370, 380–382, 457
Organization in memory, 318–323, 329–330, 332, 336–340, 345, 347, 410, 414, 532
Overlearning, 329–331, 347, 413, 433–434, 610

Partial reinforcement (see Intermittent reinforcement)
Participation, active, 394, 404–405, 409–410
  Continual, 410
  Eventual, 410
  Covert, 407, 409–410, 610
  Overt, 407, 409–410, 610
Peer coaching, 420, 610
Peer mediation, 259–262, 610
Peer pressure, 167, 206, 218–227, 259
Peer tutoring, 427, 433–435, 486–488, 610

Subject Index

Percent agreement, 505, 610, 626-629
Percentile rank, 70, 477, 610
Percent of transfer, 280-281
Perception, 52-53, 183, 185, 260, 274-278, 302, 311-312, 347, 458-459, 610
Perceptual set (see Set)
Performance (see also Learning vs.), 208, 458, 610
Performance components, 99-100, 372, 375-376, 610
Performance items, 526-530, 610
Permastore, 343-346, 348, 610
Perseverance, 416-417, 444, 610
Persistence, 180-182, 183-184, 187, 194, 610
Personalized system of instruction (PSI), 449-451, 558-559, 610
Phobia, 133-134, 549, 610
Physical restraint, 253, 610
Piagetian developmental stages
  Sensori-motor, 26-27, 614
  Preoperational, 27, 611
  Concrete operational, 27, 30-32, 328, 601
  Formal operational, 27, 32-33, 328, 604
Portfolios, 529-531, 532, 610
Positive reinforcement (see also Attention), 162-165, 174, 176, 187-190, 611
Practice, 285-286, 294-296, 328-333, 359, 362-363, 442, 611
  Distributed, 285-286, 295, 330-333, 347, 611
  Massed, 330-333, 611
  Guided, 413, 443, 611
  Independent, 405-406, 414, 611
Praise (see Attention as a reinforcer)
Predictor, 68, 77, 504-507
Preferred activity, 176-179, 611
Premack principle, 176-179, 611
Preoperational stage (see Piagetian)
Prepared behaviors (see also Belongingness), 133-134
Primary reinforcement (primary reinforcer), 174, 176, 611
Principles, 281-283, 286-287, 291-292, 295-296, 300-303
Proactive design (see also Interference and Facilitation), 280, 284

Problem solving, 198, 231, 272-278, 286-287, 289, 296-297, 361-362, 367-372, 538, 539
Procedural knowledge (see Knowledge)
Production deficiency, 337, 611
Production of a response (see Constructed responses)
Pro-social behavior, 213-215, 246, 259-262, 552, 611
Proximal development. (see Zone of proximal development)
Psychosocial development theory, 36-34, 548, 612
  Infancy, 38, 612
  Early childhood, 38-39, 612
  Childhood, 38-40, 612
  School age, 38, 40-41, 612
  Puberty and adolescence, 38, 41-42, 612
  Young adulthood, 38, 42-43, 612
  Middle age, 38, 43, 612
  Old age, 38, 44, 612
Punishment, 165, 169-172, 177, 193-198, 205-208, 238-239, 252-253, 551, 612
  Alternatives to, 196-197
  As a cue for reinforcement, 195-196
  Contingent vs. noncontingent, 195
  Purposeful behavior (see also Operant, Voluntary behavior), 160-161

Quality of instruction, 415-417, 444, 612
Quantity of reinforcement, 182-184
Questioning, Art of (see Teacher actions)

Rank order correlation (see Correlations)
Ranks, 64, 73-75, 78-80, 473, 475-483, 504, 624
Rapanoia, xi, xii, 3, 144, 152, 303, 470, 612, 619-622
Rate of learning (see fast vs. slow)
Rate of response (see Response frequency)
Ratio schedule, 180, 612
Readiness (see Entering behavior)
Reality therapy, 247-252, 612

Reasoning (see Higher-order thinking and Intelligence: components)
Recall (see also Retention), 213-214, 331-346, 408, 515, 523
Reciprocal determinism, 13-15, 163, 166-170, 238-242, 612
Reciprocal teaching; 292, 301
Recognition (see also Retention), 345, 515
Reconstructive memory, 340-343, 347-348, 366, 555
Reflective teaching (the Reflective practitioner), 292-293, 418-420
Reflex (see Respondent)
Reinforcement, 149, 207-208, 215-216, 395, 409, 550, 613
  of operants, 161-199, 208
  of respondents, 132, 183
Reinforcement contingency, 184-187, 189-191, 206, 436, 613
Reinforcement schedule, 179-182, 183-184, 186-187, 613
Reinforcer (Reinforcing stimulus), 9-10, 161-163, 545, 613
Relaxation (see also Systematic desensitization), 148, 152-154, 242, 303
Relearning (see also Practice, Overlearning), 329-336, 448
Reliability, 73, 76, 471, 476, 490, 498, 505-507, 513, 528, 613, 627-628
  Test-retest, 506, 613
  Parallel (Equivalent forms), 506, 613
  Internal consistency, 506, 508, 509, 613
Reproductive memory, 340-343, 555, 613
Resistance to extinction, 180-182, 613
Respondent (see also Conditioning), 3-4, 7-9, 12, 128-138, 198, 242, 545, 613
Response (see also Operant and Respondent), 3-4, 7-10, 545, 613
Response facilitation effect of modeling, 208, 613
Response frequency, 161-163, 172, 182-184, 613
Response strength (see Response frequency)
Restitution, 197, 252-255, 613

Retention, 316–317, 324–336, 343–345, 395, 447, 455, 554, 613
Retribution, 196, 252–256
Retrieval (see also Accessibility and Availability), 318–323, 613
Retroactive design (see also Interference and Facilitation), 283–284
Reversibility, 22, 29–30
Reward, 162–163, 264–265, 551
Roles, 220–225, 232, 245, 539–540
Rules, 237–238, 250–258

Savings, 329–331, 335–336, 613
Scaffolding, 366–367, 402, 451, 613
Schema, 22–23, 300, 362–367, 382–383, 545, 614
S-delta (S^Δ), 171–174, 614
Second-order conditioning (see Higher-order conditioning)
Secondary reinforcer, 174, 176, 187–190, 614
Selecting a response (see also Recognition), 515–516
Self-control, 151, 191–193, 258–259, 614
Self-discipline (see Self-control)
Self-efficacy (or Perceived self-efficacy), 14, 35, 140, 614
Self-esteem, 35, 49–52, 119, 127–128, 163, 264–265
Self-evaluation, 192–193, 614
Self-monitoring (see also Metacognition), 192–193
Self-reward, 192–193, 614
Sensation, 311–312, 614
Sensori-motor stage (see Piagetian)
Sensory memory, 314–315, 318, 347, 614
Set, anticipatory, 291, 302, 407–408, 414, 614
Set, mental (or perceptual), 274–275, 277, 294, 408, 614
Sex differences, 48, 142, 212, 552
Shaping, 179–181, 206, 614
Short-answer items, 522–524, 614
Short-term memory, 315–318, 347, 553, 614
Significant difference, 474, 478–479, 614
Similarity (see Identical elements)
Situated cognition, 287–290, 294–295, 615
Social class, 77, 81–83

Social cognitive theory, xiv, 2, 13–15, 615
Social learning (see also Reciprocal determinism), 13–15, 36, 199, 230–232, 237–242
Social reinforcer, 163, 176, 191, 615
Social speech, 35–36, 615
Social transmission (Piaget's educative factor), 24–25
Socialization, 222–223, 242–245, 615
Sociodynamic law, 225, 615
sociometric wealth (see Sociodynamic law)
Sociometry, 225–227, 231, 615
Spatial intelligence, 102–103, 609
Spearman rank order correlation (see also Correlation), 615
Species-specific behavior, 133–134, 185, 194
Specific determiner, 518, 615
Specific transfer, 298, 615
Spiral curriculum (see also Curriculum), 292, 295, 322, 398
Spontaneous recovery, 130, 169, 615
Staff development, 292–293, 401, 418–420, 540, 615
Standard, 54–55, 231–232, 396, 445, 449, 452–453, 485–492, 615
Standard deviation, 70–72, 448, 476–478, 507–508, 615, 622–624
Standard error of measurement, 507–508, 616
Stimulus, 3–4, 7–10, 161–172, 311–314, 545, 616
Stimulus generalization, 135, 616
Stimulus substitution, 129
Storage, 318–323, 616
Strategies
  Learning, Memory or Problem solving, 33, 36, 100, 115–117, 151, 292, 310, 325–328, 336–340, 359–361, 413–415
  Teaching, 34, 100, 104–119, 147–148, 152, 167–169, 231, 262, 285–287, 302–303, 345–348, 364, 366–367, 392–420, 426–463, 529–533, 555
Stress, 135, 138–139, 274, 314
Subjective organization (see also Organization), 322–323, 336–344, 616

Success, 35, 41, 145–148, 248–249, 263, 395
Successively closer approximations, 179, 184, 206, 492, 616
Summative evaluation, 445–446, 489, 490–492, 616
Superstitious behavior, 185
Synectics, 457–460, 616
Systematic desensitization and counter conditioning, 134, 148, 154, 616

Table of specifications, 446, 502–503
Tangible rewards (see Motivation, Extrinsic)
Task analysis, 396–398, 449, 616
Taxonomy of educational objectives, cognitive domain, 298, 394, 398–401, 410, 446, 451, 462, 487–488, 502–503, 557, 616
  Knowledge, 398–401, 487, 517, 519, 520, 616
  Comprehension, 398–401, 487, 519, 520, 523, 616
  Application, 398–401, 487, 517, 519, 520, 523, 616
  Analysis, 398–401, 488, 517, 520, 523, 529, 616
  Synthesis, 398, 400–401, 521, 524, 526, 529, 616
  Evaluation, 398–401, 488, 520, 526, 529, 556, 616
Teacher actions (see also Strategies), 617
  Asking questions, 378–379, 383–384, 394, 403, 404–406, 410, 461–463
  Designing activities, 367–382, 394, 403, 404–406
  Providing information, 494, 401–404
  Responding to students (see also Feedback), 166–170, 379, 394, 403
Teacher knowledge (Types of), 393, 418–420
  Pedagogical (generic), 393, 418
  Subject-matter content, 418
  Subject-matter pedagogical, 418
  Curricular, 418
Teaching (see also Instruction),
  Accountability, 392, 426
  as Decision making, 393–396, 402, 404–406, 413–415

Intellectual skills, 99–101, 104–106, 107–111, 112–120, 366–384
 The one-best-method mentality, 402, 404, 427–428
 Strategies (see Strategies, Teaching)
Teaching-learning functions, 414–415, 617
Tension (see also Stress), 150–154, 166, 242
Test anxiety, 136
Testing (see also Evaluation, Grading), 498–533
Thinking aloud, 231, 380
Time out, 250, 255–257, 617
Token, 176, 178, 187–190, 617
Token economy, 187–191, 617
Transfer (see also High road and Low road), 272–304, 320, 336–340, 372, 395, 397, 617
 Negative, 280–281, 302, 408, 617
 Positive, 280–281, 302, 408, 617
 Zero, 280–281, 617

Triarchic theory of intelligence, 98–101, 617
True-false items (see Two-choice items)
True score, 77, 506–507, 617
Two-choice items, 516–518, 617

Unconditioned response (UR), 4, 7–8, 128–138, 617
Unconditioned stimulus (US), 7–8, 128–138, 617

Validity, 490–492, 498–506, 516, 560, 617, 626–627, 629
 Construct-related evidence for, 500–501, 617
 Content-related evidence for, 501–502, 618
 Criterion-related (Predictive) evidence for, 502, 504–505, 618, 626–627, 629
Values, 44–49, 218, 260–261, 548
Vicarious consequences, 207, 208, 618

Vicarious emotional learning, 217–218, 549, 618
Vicarious punishment, 208
Vicarious reinforcement, 207–208, 216, 618
Violence (see Aggression, Misbehavior)
Voluntary behavior, 9–10, 148, 154, 160–199, 618

Wait time, 410
Warm-up, 298
Winnetka plan, 441–443, 445, 618
Within-class grading, 481, 483–489, 491, 618
Working memory (see Short-term memory)
Writing performances, 525–526, 618
Written reports, 524–525, 529, 618

Z-score, 70, 72, 473, 476–478, 483, 508, 618
Zone of proximal development, 33–35, 107, 530, 618